St. Alcmundsbuffe, RHVD 4 am. 20 ...... March 1948.

hy dear Matthew, ... to send this to you because ... ... mum (my wife) because ... ... me to know you are a good boy, and I like lots of things I hear about you, but I'm very tired of trains. I prefer balloons and ships. I want to draw you some pictures of ships but unfortunately theres a prying gentleman called Peeping Carson and he HATES pictures of anything, but particularly ships or anything to do with the wall. — I cant draw like mummy can, I'm afraid. Well, this is what I've been doing.

(1) I used to live in a ship, and it didn't look like this one, because ... ... to tell you what would be making Peeping Carson angry.

(2) Then the sea got very rough So I decided to live

(3) in a house.

(4) But I work on an island, on which stands a castle.

(5) I usually walk to my island — very fast

(6) But if I'm very late I take a horse ...

world, so I dont expect ... Be kind to mummy and Christopher, with love from Daddy.

blue pork sausages and there are blue fishes on my ... and bonny Beatrice sits by me while I write to you ... and refuses, but REFUSES to give off any heat, because, she says, I can stuff her as I like (if you get my meaning) with paraffin, but what good's that if her wick is low." Well, Beatrice I say sometimes, it appears to me you want a wick a week!" "That I do, sir," she invariably

P. T. O

alec guinness

THE AUTHORISED BIOGRAPHY

PIERS PAUL READ

SIMON & SCHUSTER

NEW YORK   LONDON   TORONTO   SYDNEY

B
GuinA

SIMON & SCHUSTER
Rockefeller Center
1230 Avenue of the Americas
New York, NY 10020

First published in Great Britain in 2003 by Simon & Schuster UK Ltd

Published by arrangement with Simon & Schuster UK Ltd

SIMON & SCHUSTER and colophon are registered trademarks
of Simon & Schuster, Inc.

For information about special discounts for bulk purchases,
please contact Simon & Schuster Special Sales at
1-800-456-6798 or business@simonandschuster.com

Manufactured in the United States of America

1 3 5 7 9 10 8 6 4 2

Library of Congress Cataloging-in-Publication Data
Alec Guinness : the authorized biography / Piers Paul Read.
p.   cm
Originally published: London ; New York : Simon & Schuster, 2003.
1. Guinness, Alec, 1914– 2. Actors—Great Britain—Biography. I. Title.
PN2598.G8R43 2005
792.02'8'092—dc22   2004062601
[B]
ISBN-13: 978-0-7432-4498-5
ISBN-10:   0-7432-4498-2

PICTURE CREDITS
Line drawings and sketches by Alec Guinness, courtesy of the Alec Guinness Estate.
All photographs are courtesy of the Alec Guinness Estate, except for:

Mary Ann Cuff by permission of Jane de Courcy Cato; Michel Salaman by
permission of Toby Salaman; the d'Ascoyne family by permission of Rex; Alec with
Joan Greenwood by permission of Rex; Alec with Noel Willman by permission of
Mander & Mitchenson/ArenaPAL; Alec with Grace Kelly by permission of
Photo fest/Retna UK; Alec as Colonel Nicholson by permission of Photofest/Retna
UK; Alec as Major Jock Sinclair by permission of Photofest/Retna UK; Alec as Hitler
by permission of Photofest/Retna UK; Alec as George Smiley by permission of
Photofest/Retna UK; John Gielgud by permission of Photofest/Retna UK; Tyrone
Guthrie by permission of Mander & Mitchenson/ArenaPAL; Leueen MacGrath and
Anne Kaufman-Schneider by permission of Anne Kaufman-Schneider; Alec with
Merula, Natasha and Otis by permission of Sally Guinness; Alec with Walter by
permission of Camera Press on behalf of Lord Snowdon.

ACKNOWLEDGEMENTS

I wish to express my gratitude first and foremost to Matthew Guinness who has helped not only with his own recollections of his father and mother, but also by persuading their friends to give me the benefit of theirs. The only stipulation made by Matthew Guinness in respect of my use of Alec's letters and diaries was that he could ask to remove from the final typescript any sentiment expressed by Alec that might be deemed offensive to a living person. To this I agreed. In all other respects, I have been given a free hand and all the judgements are my own.

My thanks are also due to those friends who have let me see the letters they received from Alec, particularly Anne Kaufman-Schneider, whose letters drew out one side of Alec's character, and Dame Felicitas Corrigan, OSB, who drew out another – and to the Prioress of Stanbrook Abbey, Dame Ethelreda Hession, OSB, who took the trouble to photocopy the 832 letters that Alec wrote to Dame Felicitas over forty years, and to the archivist, Dame Margaret Truran, OSB. I thank, too, Janet Moat of the British Film Institute for making available letters in the Institute's archive.

I am very grateful to those who talked to me about Alec and Merula, volunteered information and responded to my queries: Joss Ackland, Mark Amory, James Astor, Dame Eileen Atkins, Jill Balcon, Frith Banbury, Annabel Bartlett, Keith Baxter, Sam Beazley, Alan Bennett, Frieda Berkeley, Michael Billington, Kitty Black, Nicholas Blatchley, Lord Boyd of Merton, James Cairncross, John Coldstream, David Cornwell (John le Carré), Jane Cornwell, Dame Felicitas Corrigan, OSB, Jane de Courcy Cato, Sir Tom Courtenay, the Marchioness of Dufferin and Ava, Patrick Garland, Simon Gray, Andrée Guinness, Sally Guinness, Natasha Harwood, Ronald Harwood, Dame Drue Heinz, Edward Herrmann, John Irvin, Gareth Johnson, Lord Kelvedon, Marigold Kingston, Mark Kingston, Marguerite Littmann, Richard Mangan, Bridget, Lady McEwen, Sheridan Morley, Sir John Mortimer, Monsignor Cyril Murtagh, Ivor Powell, Corin Redgrave, James Roose-Evans, Mary Salaman, Toby Salaman, Christopher Sinclair-Stevenson, Helen Spurdle, Quentin Stevenson (the actor John Quentin), David Stewart, Alan Strachan, Roger Tabraham, Geoffrey Toone and Jehane West.

I should like to thank Alexandra Campbell who helped me sift through much of the correspondence; and my wife Emily who typed out Alec's diaries. Both became quite as knowledgeable as I did about the lives of Alec and Merula Guinness and I have benefited greatly from their insights and advice. Thanks also to Robyn Karney for her thoughtful copy-editing of the manuscript; and I am particularly grateful to my editor at Simon & Schuster, Amanda Harris.

CONTENTS

INTRODUCTION

In the late summer of 1988, when he was about to make his last stage appearance in Lee Blessing's *A Walk in the Woods* at the Comedy Theatre in London, Sir Alec Guinness agreed to be interviewed for the *Independent Magazine*. I was given this assignment – one of a series – by the then editor, Alexander Chancellor. I telephoned Sir Alec's agent to ask his distinguished client to lunch but was told firmly that I would be Sir Alec's guest at the Connaught Grill.

The lunch on 9 September passed pleasantly. It turned out that Sir Alec had read one or two of my novels, and before I could express my admiration for his work he managed to compliment me on mine. It was immediately apparent that my subject would say only what he wanted to say and could not be drawn into any indiscretion. As a result my profile was based as much on what I had gleaned from his autobiography, *Blessings in Disguise*, as on our conversation.

I had only seen Sir Alec once on stage – as King Berenger in Ionesco's *Exit the King* in 1963 – and so my judgements on his acting came largely from what I recalled of his performances in films. 'The other theatrical knights,' I wrote, 'may have outdone him in playing classical roles on stage; but none of them combines that mixture of kindliness, impudence and pathos which Sir Alec can put into a single smile . . . His talent was to be convincing not as men as we imagine them to be but as men as they are – shy, uncertain and ambiguous.'

I repeated Aldous Huxley's maxim, quoted in *Blessings in Disguise*, that 'no actor can be good because no actor can develop his own personality and know reality' and speculated that:

> . . . if Sir Alec does at times appear to conceal his true feelings, it is not so much to hide himself from others as to spare them the sting of his sharp tongue. By his own admission he can be bitchy and irascible; and, given his dreadful childhood, he has every reason to be thoroughly unpleasant. If he is not – if, in fact, there is real kindness behind that kindly smile, and a check on his caustic wit, it is perhaps because of an early determination to prove Aldous Huxley wrong.[1]

On 1 October, after the article had been published, Sir Alec wrote to me to say: 'The piece you did on me for the *Independent* gave me great pleasure.'[2]; but, even before it was published – just a week after our lunch at the Connaught – I was invited to bring my wife to dine with Sir Alec at Cecconi's.

This was the first of more than two dozen such invitations issued irregularly over the next twelve years and the start of a friendship based on a shared interest in politics, literature and the Catholic Church. On rare occasions, Alec's wife Merula would join us, and we also met her at the opening of two exhibitions of her paintings and embroidered works of art. I would occasionally correspond with Alec (always writing to thank him, of course, after a lavish dinner; he was punctilious about good manners), but there were also exchanges on political, religious and literary questions. We were both against NATO's bombing of Serbia, and in May of 1999 he posted me the draft of a letter he had written to the *Daily Telegraph* but had decided not to send: 'It seemed to me too long and clumsy, and apart from the chore of trying to get it right, I suddenly realised I didn't want to step into Vanessa Redgrave's shoes . . . I have always resented actors airing their views in the press and here I was about to do just that.'[3]

Alec sometimes wrote to me on religious questions. For example, he had been disappointed by a young priest at the Jesuit church on Farm Street whom he had asked for advice on the question of forgiveness:

> I had said that I had learned to forgive (eventually) someone who had more or less slandered me but I found it virtually impossible to forgive him for the hurt, through me so to speak, done to those whom I love and are close to me. I was asking him for advice on this – but he said he didn't know any answer . . . Perhaps *you* would have advice. I find it a tricky area. I suppose forgiveness should be *total* and in all directions but – but – but. One day it will all have blown over and been forgotten – I hope.[4]

In June of 1999, Alec suggested that 'perhaps one warm day we can entice you down to Steep Marsh for a night – then you will see how really tatty open-plan (of a sort) life can be. If the weather is decent we could eat out and avoid the dog hairs in which we live and have our being.'[5] In December of 1999 he repeated his suggestion that we should come and stay, and added:

> Early in the new year, when I can get hold of my solicitor, I am going to make an addition to my Will. (Merula knows of this and approves.) I have in my possession a sweet letter from St François de Sales to a Madame de la Fléchère, written in – I think, 1605. It is prettily framed with glass at front and back so you can see both sides. It was given to me by a charming priest who was my confessor at St Germain-des-Prés. He spoke perfect English and I was fond of him. He died, very young, of appendicitis, about twenty years ago. He had been given the letter for work done for the Sisters of the Visitation at Annecy. Anyway, it is to be yours when I die. I can't have it sold, of course, and if given to a

church would be lost in all their clobber. And, as I said, I have very few Catholic friends so who better than you? Besides, as you are going to be living on and off in Burgundy, I like to think of it going back to France, if that was also your will.[6]

On 22 February 2000, I dined alone with Alec at Odette's on the Regent's Park Road. There he told me that he had been diagnosed with prostate cancer. Two days later, in answer to my letter of thanks and commiseration, he reassured me that:

> My sentence of death (of 6 to 10 months or possibly a year) was *only* if I did *nothing* about treatment. Surgery was ruled out. Anyway it is now, I assume, under control and I start the injections of diamonds, emeralds and sapphires next week . . .
>   Lourdes crossed my mind (Merula and I went once, about 35 years ago) – *not* for a cure but just to pray and learn acceptance. But now I think the journey could bump me off. I may settle for a couple of days at Quarr Abbey. Or even Lisieux, among the scattered marble roses.[7]

On 3 May 2000, at dinner at the Connaught, it was arranged that we would pay our long-postponed visit to Petersfield. 'So glad you and Emily can come down. You must be prepared for the worst – scruffiness, hit-or-miss food, dog hairs all over you and general untidiness. We *wear* any old thing that comes to hand, so don't put us to shame. Your barn-dancing clogs would be fine.'[8] He enclosed a hand-drawn map with directions to Kettlebrook Meadows, '54 miles from Hyde Park Corner'. Soon afterwards, however, he telephoned to say that he had developed phlebitis and so our visit would have to be postponed. In July we left for our house in France and there, in August, learned that Alec had died.

In answer to a letter of condolence, Merula asked me to come down to Kettlebrook Meadows to pick up the framed letter of St Francis of Sales. She had had cancer for some time, had been expected to die before Alec, and now awaited death with a serene certainty that she would soon be reunited with him in paradise. Sitting by her bedside with my wife, and with Matthew, Merula's son, there was some talk of whether or not she should authorise a biography of Alec. Merula's anxiety was that, if she did *not* authorise a biography, Alec's reputation would fall into the hands of an established 'theatrical' biographer who would fail to understand, or under-play, the other aspects of his life.

It did not occur to me at that time to suggest myself for the task. However, after returning to France I received a letter from Christopher Sinclair-Stevenson, once Alec's publisher and later his literary agent, passing on a request from Merula that I should write Alec's biography. Not wishing to disappoint a dying friend; assured that Matthew concurred with her choice, and reflecting on the ample evidence that Alec was an exceptional man, I accepted Merula's offer. I immediately arranged to return to England to see her but her condition had deteriorated rapidly and she died before it could be done.

Did Alec Guinness want a biography? He said nothing on the subject to either Merula or Matthew but, after his death, two of his closest friends, Anne Kaufman and Mark Kingston, recalled Alec saying to them that *if* a biography was ever to be written he would like it to be written by me. During his lifetime, as will be seen from the ensuing narrative, he was unhappy, even angry, that he was the subject of biographies – John Russell Taylor's *Alec Guinness. A Celebration* published in 1984 and Garry O'Connor's *Alec Guinness: Master of Disguise* published ten years later. All offers from would-be biographers were politely declined. However, he took no exception to Robert Tanitch's illustrated compendium *Guinness* published in 1989 and kept a copy in his study; it remains the definitive source for information on Alec's career in cinema and on the stage.

In his autobiography, *Blessings in Disguise*, Alec wrote that he had left instructions for his diaries to be destroyed, but there were no such instructions in either the letter he wrote to Merula shortly before his death or in his complex and detailed Will; and his reason for wanting them destroyed was probably not, as we shall see, because they contained any sensational revelations but because he felt he may have spoken unkindly of others, and that they were dull.

There is also evidence that, in anticipation of a biography, he had made some selection of the letters in his files. Some had been marked with an x. An arbitrary judgement seems to have been made as to whether to keep letters from his friends. He wrote over 800 letters to Dame Felicitas Corrigan, but only a fraction of those she wrote to him survive. Clearly many, including the sacks of fan mail that he received after *Star Wars*, had been thrown away. Untouched were the 580 or so letters that Alec had written to Merula during World War II, and some of the letters that Merula wrote to him, that were tied in dusty bundles and stored in a drawer.

It should also be borne in mind that Alec loved chatting on the telephone. He spoke with his friend Mark Kingston every Sunday morning, and so it is only to be expected that there would be few letters from some of his closest friends such as Kingston, Alan Bennett, Jill Balcon, Peter Glenville or Peter Bull. But it is also possible that he destroyed letters from some of these friends because they revealed aspects of his life that Alec preferred to conceal from posterity. Coral Browne wrote to him in July, 1990, saying: 'I will be sending an envelope to you within the next week – it will contain your letters to me – which have given me so much pleasure – thought you might like to have them before someone went thru my panties & gave them to Alan Bennett to read on the BBC.'[9] These letters were not found in Kettlebrook and must have been destroyed.

Here again, the presumption is that he regretted some of the uncharitable things he had said. 'I can't help feeling,' he wrote to Dame Felicitas Corrigan in 1972, that 'all letters should be kept absolutely private or returned to the writer if she or he is living. I'd hate people to have access to certain of my letters as I suppose they *could* cause trouble.'[10] But he may also have felt that there were some things that should not be aired; and, as if to fire a shot across the bows of a future biographer, there appears in Alec's posthumously published

Commonplace Book this quotation from Cardinal Newman: 'And so, as to the judgement of society, a just indignation would be felt against a writer who brought forward, wantonly, the weaknesses of a great man, though the whole world knew that they existed.'

It has been my intention in what follows neither to dwell on Alec's weaknesses nor to overlook them where they seem pertinent to an understanding of his character.

Alec kept two sets of diaries – one in canvas notebooks, the first of which, written during World War II, was 'destroyed at Barletta 11th February, 1945'[11], the eve of his return to England from wartime service in the Mediterranean. These were not continuous: the first of the surviving notebook runs from 1945–1946; the second 1952; the third 1954–1955. The fourth, of only a few pages, was written in 1967, and the last three notebooks ran from 1973–1994. From 1961 onwards, Alec also made daily entries in small leather-bound diaries, often recording simply what the weather had been like that morning, or what he had done that day. He did so, he wrote, because he liked to remind himself what he had been up to in preceding years; but there are also brief passages that are more revealing of what was passing through his mind than the more composed and self-conscious narrative of the journals. I have referred to these as the Small Diaries. The last entry was made only two weeks before he died.

part one

the seeds of genius

one

'My mother was a whore,' Alec told the author John le Carré and his wife Jane, standing in the kitchen of le Carré's house, Tregiffian, on the cliff top of the south coast of Cornwall. 'She slept with the entire crew on Lord Moyne's yacht at the Cowes Regatta and when she gave birth she called the bastard Guinness but my father was probably the bloody cook.'[12] This wild conjecture about his paternity reveals more about Alec's feelings for his mother, or of the competitive spirit that sought to outdo le Carré who had earlier been telling Alec of the misery of his own childhood as the son of a convicted con man, than it does of the reality of Alec's conception.

The refusal of his mother to divulge the identity of Alec's father was one of the sources of the bitterness he felt towards her. When Matthew, towards the end of her life, asked his grandmother about his grandfather, a dreamy look came over her face and she said, 'Ah, he was a lovely man, so kind' – which hardly suggests a brief liaison with a customer by a woman of the streets. Matthew then asked, 'What was his name?' Agnes looked cross, called him a 'cheeky monkey' and the subject was closed.

Agnes Cuff, who later embellished her name to Agnes de Cuffe, was the youngest daughter of Edward Cuff and Mary Ann Cuff, née Benfield. Edward Cuff, originally from Lambeth in South London, was a coastguard in Bournemouth on the south coast of England. In the 1891 census he and his wife were registered at 2 Coastguard Station in Bournemouth and at that time had seven children. The Benfields were a family local to that part of England, mostly stonemasons working from the quarries in Swanage, where Mary Ann's grandfather, Thomas Benfield, had a pub. Agnes, who was also called Ann, Agatha and even Agony by her siblings, was born on 8 December 1890, the seventh of twelve children. It is difficult to place the Cuffs in the complex hierarchy of class to which the English were then prone. The family tree, which could be traced back to the seventeenth century, included a number of seamen. Many of the family were privately educated and a cousin of Alec's mother was an officer in the Royal Navy who returned home after four years' service in China with enough money to buy a pub – the Horns Inn at Coalhill in Essex.

There might have been gypsy blood in the family: Mary Ann Cuff, Alec's grandmother, had black eyes, black hair and smoked a pipe. Agnes and her sisters had dark auburn hair and hazel eyes. Mary Ann, at this stage in her life, was religious and never let alcohol pass her lips. Agnes may have rebelled against this strict upbringing: she took snuff, as did her sisters, and had already taken to tippling in her late twenties when Alec was a child.

It is clear that Edward Cuff found it hard to provide for his children on a coastguard's wage, and after his death the family's predicament was still worse. Some of the sons were classified as orphans and sent to work as indentured labourers in Canada. Agnes must therefore have had to earn her living as soon as she left school, thereby gaining a certain independence and escaping from the confines of her home. Her older sister Louisa was apprenticed as a seamstress and worked on clothes for the royal family.[13] It seems possible that Agnes joined the large numbers who, before World War I, worked as domestic servants though Alec, in later life, took the trouble to take an early biographer, John Russell Taylor, to lunch at the Mirabelle in 1984 to persuade him to alter one or two inaccuracies in the book, 'particularly his speculation about my mother having been "in service" – which she never was in my life-time and unlikely before I was born'.[14] He would rather his mother had been a whore than a housemaid.

In whatever capacity, it would seem that the pretty, auburn-haired, hazel-eyed Agnes Cuff found herself, at the age of twenty-three, in the town of Cowes on the Isle of Wight at the time of the Regatta. One theory has it that she had a summer job working behind the bar of the Royal Yacht Squadron clubhouse and there met members of the Guinness family whose fortune, based on breweries in Dublin, was and remains so vast that even the youngest sons and daughters of the cadet branches are substantial millionaires.

The head of the family in 1913, the first Earl of Iveagh, had both a house on the Isle of Wight and a yacht at Cowes for the Regatta and, according to his granddaughter Honor, was there that year with his sons Ernest and Walter, and perhaps a banking cousin, Benjamin Guinness. Different Guinnesses later claimed to see a distinct resemblance between Alec and one or other of the Guinnesses at Cowes in 1913. Honor Guinness, who made Alec's acquaintance on board the *Queen Mary* in 1950 by sending him a note asking him to take tea with 'his cousin', thought Alec's father was either her uncle, Ernest Guinness, or his brother Walter, a well-known seducer of women who was ennobled as Baron Moyne in 1932 and assassinated by Zionist terrorists in Cairo in 1944. She brought diaries and photograph albums down to Kettlebrook Meadows to point out the resemblances between Lord Moyne and Alec, and even the teenage Matthew. The nanny employed by the Elwes family, neighbours of Alec's parents-in-law, the Salamans, who had seen the Guinnesses pass through the nursery of her previous employers, was convinced that Alec was the son of Lord Moyne. She said both Alec's voice and the way he walked were the same. The supporters of the Lord Moyne theory of Alec's paternity also point out that he was not only a celebrated seducer but was estranged from his wife, Lady Evelyn Erskine, in 1913.

However, Belinda Guinness, later the Marchioness of Dufferin and Ava, who also became a friend of Alec's, said that his distinctive, slightly pudgy hands were identical to those of her father Loel, the son of the banker, Benjamin Guinness: and it is quite possible, as Alec's son Matthew later speculated, that Agnes Cuff's reluctance to disclose the identity of Alec's father might have been because she had slept with a Guinness, and a friend of the Guinnesses as well.

It was certainly a friend, or perhaps only a business acquaintance of the Guinnesses, who *believed himself* to be Alec's father. The Scottish banker Andrew Geddes was considerably older than the glamorous Guinnesses and his background more modest. He had been born in 1861, the son of a tenant farmer on the estates of the Dukes of Buccleuch in Dumfriesshire in Scotland. His eldest brother, Dick, was a blacksmith; his second brother, William, took over the family farm when Andrew went to London to work in the City.

By 1913, when he is presumed to have been a guest of the Guinnesses for the Cowes Regatta, Geddes was a director of the Anglo-South American Bank and a rich man with an older wife and six children. He lived in a large house in Barnet, just north of London, but took holidays in the resorts of the south coast such as Bournemouth and Eastbourne. Photographs show him with a round face and sticking-out ears, which makes him credible as Alec's father. That face wears a benign expression which fits with Agnes' testimony that he was a kindly man.

It was Geddes who, through a solicitor, provided an allowance for Agnes Cuff and paid for Alec's education. Alec even claimed in a letter to a cousin written at the end of his life that the sum of £25,000 had been settled on his mother,[15] though presumably she only received the income from this fund. It was suggested by Eric Warne, one of Alec's Cuff cousins, that Agnes later took holidays with Geddes in the South of France.[16] After the premature death of the eldest of his two sons, John, and the decline of his second son, Stuart, shell-shocked in World

War I, Geddes seems to have shown as much interest in Alec as he dared. His youngest daughter, Katie Weldon, later told Alec how her father, after he had moved to a house near Lewes, would watch out for him when the school was on a walk, or going to church, and, if he had seen Alec, always returned home in a very disturbed state of mind.[17]

Geddes would occasionally visit Alec and his mother, posing as an uncle. The last such encounter was at Bournemouth station in the summer of 1922:

I was eight then and it was summer-time. He was white-haired, top-hatted, frock-coated, grave and Scots. He kept an open carriage at the door while he paid a brief, unhappy visit to my mother. I remember her saying, 'Get ready to go with Uncle to the station,' and me saying I didn't want to. Then I quickly recalled that he always used to give me a sovereign when he said good-bye; so I got ready quickly and went with him. We trotted slowly and silently to the station – he, my mother and I. When he got into his railway compartment he still hadn't handed over the expected sovereign. Just before the train started he fished in his waistcoat pocket and with cold disapproving eyes handed me half-a-crown. Exit a father. Or possibly an uncle, but the former is more likely.[18]

Andrew Geddes died in 1928. There is no mention of Alec in his will; however, there must have been some kind of bequest because in 1935, when he was twenty-one, Alec was told by Geddes's solicitor that he had come into some shares invested in a ranch in Tierra del Fuego. Their sale realised £700.[19]

two

Before World War I – indeed until well into the second half of the twentieth century – conceiving a child out of wedlock gave rise to scandal and led to ostracism by polite society. It was considered irresponsible to bring a child into the world with no father to provide for it, and the word 'bastard' was not simply a term of abuse but also defined the legal status of an 'illegitimate' child.

Members of Agnes's family did not exempt her from the stigma attached to her misdeed. Her sisters, with the exception of Louisa May, living precariously on the margins of gentility, ostracised her to avoid being contaminated by the scandal. Her mother stood by her but, no doubt to minimise any embarrassment she might cause to her family, Agnes moved to London where, in a flat in Lauderdale Mansions, Paddington, she gave birth to a son on 2 April 1914. The name given on his birth certificate was Alec Guinness de Cuffe, while the box provided for the father's name remained empty – 'an intriguing, speculative blank'.[20]

Little is known about the first five years of Alec's life but a charming photograph of him as a baby suggests that he was loved and cosseted as babies tend to be. He and his mother probably lived close to home on the south coast of England; and Agnes seems to have revisited Cowes, perhaps for the Regatta. 'My mother used to try and impress me with the story that Prince Louis of Battenberg once poked me in the stomach with his finger in a Post Office on the Isle of Wight when I was 2½ years old.'[21]

For his fourth birthday, which he spent in Bournemouth, Alec was given 'a blue and gold bucket (very handsome) and a spade – but I behaved filthily because I couldn't have it on the breakfast table with me – and I ruined my day'.[22] He later remembered being rowed out to the minesweepers 'working up and down the bay . . . to hand over packets of cigarettes to the seamen' who either had the 'full-set beards as in the picture on a packet of Players, gazing through a life-belt', or he simply imagined that they had because 'at the age of four or five I felt they should have such beards'.[23]

Alec's mother may have had gentlemen friends but for four of his first five years, Britain was at war with Germany and there can have been few men around to court his pretty mother. In 1919, however, she married a demobbed army officer, Lieutenant David Stiven. Stiven was a Scot, the son of a gas engineer, divorced and, though aged thirty-eight, merely a lieutenant after four years of war. His rank, and the address on his marriage certificate – the Ordnance Depot, Didcot – do not suggest a distinguished military career. He was possibly an acting captain when demobilised – Alec calls him 'the Captain' in his memoirs; or he may have exaggerated his rank in the same way as Agnes did her father's: on the marriage certificate Edward Cuff is described as 'Captain RN'.

As a divorcé, Stiven too would have been subject to a certain measure of stigma, which may have made him more open to the idea of marrying a woman with an illegitimate child. It seems likely that he had served not in the trenches in France but in Ireland: 'He always has his gun with him, in case the Sinn Fein come after him,' Alec overheard his mother tell their landlady in their flat in St John's Wood; and from the time of her marriage to Stiven his mother would drag Alec quickly 'past London pillar-boxes in case they contained revolutionary Irish bombs'.[24]

The Stiven portrayed by Alec in his autobiography is a violent eccentric who, for three years, made his life 'a terrifying hell' by, for example, holding his revolver to Alec's head and, on another occasion, dangling him from a bridge and 'threatening to kill me and himself' to get what he wanted from Agnes. Alec did, however, concede that his mother may well have goaded Stiven into this extreme behaviour; and it is also common, even for a boy of six, to resent the advent of a competitor for his mother's love.

At the time of her marriage, Agnes and Alec were living in Bloomsbury at 31, Upper Bedford Place. Later the Stivens took a flat in St John's Wood. When, at the age of six, Alec was sent to board at Normandale, a prep school at Bexhill-on-Sea, they were living in an airless residential hotel on the Cromwell Road, one of up to 'thirty different hotels, lodgings and flats, each of which was hailed as "home" until such a time as my mother and I flitted, leaving behind, like a paper-chase, a wake of unpaid bills'.[25] Here Alec fell ill and remained sick for more than a year. He never returned to Normandale but spent several weeks recuperating in Brighton in a small hotel in Regency Square:

I am almost positive, that I spent several weeks when I was seven, recovering from nearly a year of colitis. I can remember a dismal 'tweeny' maid who scared the wits out of me by being creepy about noises in a water tank. And I can remember having a tiny tin kitchen range which was heated by a candle and on which I fried minute pieces of meat. It was at that time, too, on a blustery day, that my straw boater blew into the sea and I dashed in after it and was knocked down by a wave, or at any rate made to stumble in the foam. That was near the small stone jetty between the piers. I recall my mother screaming at some youths, dangling their legs over the jetty, to rescue me, at which they rightly laughed. No rescue was necessary but my mother remained in a furious panic, calling them 'louts' and 'good-for-nothings'. The straw hat was lost though.[26]

When Alec was seven or eight, the Stivens moved to digs in Southbourne in Dorset, a village on the east side of Poole Bay. Agnes's older sister, Louisa May, lived a few miles away, in Poole.

> She was rather nice, Aunty May, and always kind to me when I was a small boy, and really the only one of my mother's family I could tolerate. She had terrible teeth but a charming smile. I used to have tea with her in an untidy dark house in Poole and she would lash on the butter and jam on great slices of new bread for me. She was, I assume, very poor.[27]

Alec's grandmother, now widowed, lived on the other side of Poole in Swanage, was 'a great black bombazine figure, drunk I suspect, and although she looked ninety perhaps she wasn't much more than in her late seventies – if that'.[28] She lived in a cottage with an earth floor, had 'black fingernails, black eyes, black hair and was dressed in black from head to foot' and smoked a clay pipe.[29]

Alec would later recall his days in Southbourne as 'the unhappiest period of my life' with 'endless rows, bullyings and general horrors'.

> It was at Southbourne that David Stiven held his loaded revolver to my head, threatening to kill me and then himself. And it was at Southbourne I saw the last of him, when he emigrated to New Zealand on the understanding that my mother would follow.[30]

There were some happy moments. In a letter dated 9 February 1943, while Alec was in New York, he told Merula how reading Jane Austen's *Mansfield Park* had filled him with nostalgia for the English summer, and had taken him back:

. . . strangely enough, to the long time I spent as a child in Southbourne, when Crusaders were my heroes and my greatest pleasure picking thick wet river flowers along the banks of the Avon or Stour, or exploring Hengistbury Head, or going on my cheap red scooter up and down the hot dull pavements or being asked *not* to scoot outside the red brick house at the corner, where the blinds were down and black horses and carriages were waiting at the door. We lived in a house (v. small) with a woman called Miss Garrett, who had a chicken's plucked throat and a big fat niece at the Bournemouth High School. Miss Garrett's back yard had a pear tree, a few rows of potatoes, a few chickens, a glossy black Indian or Persian cock, and an empty rabbit hutch. Once I took into the kitchen a piece of white, sun-dried wholesome dog shit and pretended it was a new potato. My mother thought that quite funny but not Miss Garrett.

Once Miss Garrett and my mother took me to Evensong at Christchurch Priory and halfway through the psalms my mother said, 'For God's sake let's get a drink. You stay here, Alec.' And I was left, way on into the night, until pale men in black were closing the big barred doors and asked me where I belonged. It was a very dark night and Miss G and my mamma didn't come to collect me until the pubs were closing and they were in a pretty high giggly state by then.

This incident clearly left its mark: almost forty years after this letter to Merula, Alec again recalled in his diary how his mother had left him in the church at Christchurch 'while she and her cronies set off on a pub-crawl and failed to collect me until after the church was shut up'.[31] It was added to the inventory of grudges he held against his mother.

As a result of the chaos and instability of his home life, Alec welcomed the order and discipline of school life. At the age of seven he was sent to a private fee-paying school in Southbourne called Pembroke Lodge.

The headmaster, Mr Meakin, 'was a kindly man . . . but he was horribly impatient, except with handsome boys who were good

cricketers'. For the first time we now come across the tinge of homo-
eroticism that was to be found in so many of the all-male institutions
at the time. Alec and a friend called McCloughlin were 'tanned by
Meakin on our bare behinds for fooling around with torches and
playing cards in the dormitory after lights out'.[32] Meakin's occasional
visits to the boys in the dormitory were 'usually to tickle the Captain
of the First XI'.[33] His successor, 'Punch' Hill, was 'a devious character,
given to holy words and unholy glints of the eye'. Here Alec learned,
'like most children, an acute awareness of the hypocrisy of grown-
ups'. But he much preferred the company of the other boys to that of
his mother and stepfather, David Stiven.

Alec longed to conform: 'I can remember when I was seven so
well wondering what I'd be like at thirty. Broad, blond, v. frank and
heroic and the possessor of a smashing push bike with 3 speed;'[34] and
'school life . . . provided a dimension of security, a stable routine, and
a happy freedom from the domestic dramas of holiday-time, with
their financial and emotional upsets . . .'[35] The other pupils came
from stable homes and better backgrounds than did Alec. A retired
colonel, whom Alec came across in 1973, he remembered as 'a
friendly, genial boy at his happiest in the cricket nets . . . very very
charming and civilised' and known as 'Dolly' Dickens.

Among the extra-curricular activities at Pembroke Lodge was
ballroom dancing:

On Friday nights we used to put on black striped trousers, clean Eton
collars, white ties, white gloves and pinchy shiny pumps and slide and
gawk about the French-chalked gym with an angular lady in a green
tea gown. But I had to give it up after a term, like my awful piano
playing, because my solicitor told the Head I had to economise. It
was always cold in the gym, I remember, and the only nice thing
about the dancing lessons were the Swiss buns – those long things
with icing – which we used to get afterwards. Buns still mean quite
a lot to me . . .[36]

Now, at the age of eight or nine, Alec found that he 'liked to dress up and pretend to be other people or animals' and was 'consciously acting, giving imitations of other people like teachers and matrons'; and there were amateur dramatics with end-of-term plays that 'were always farces and often quite funny', but when Alec asked to play a part he was turned down by the headmaster with the words: 'You'll never make an actor.' This may have been because Alec had difficulty in pronouncing his 'th's, frequently substituting an 'f'; but, rather than smothering the secret ambition to go on the stage that he already had at that age, it 'put in my soul a little grain of iron determination'.[37]

Agnes Cuff's marriage to David Stiven ended around 1927 when Stiven emigrated to New Zealand. Now aged thirteen, Alec graduated from Pembroke Lodge and went to Roborough School in Eastbourne – not as Alec Stiven or even Alec de Cuffe but, he was told by his mother 'almost casually', as Alec Guinness. There had been a plan to send him to the prestigious Scottish public school, Fettes, possibly the choice of the Scot Andrew Geddes; but it was abandoned either because Agnes decided it was too inconvenient or, more likely in Alec's view, from 'lack of funds'.

Roborough, though a very minor public school, gave Alec a sound education. The clarity and elegance of the style found in his earliest letters and the extreme rarity of a misspelled word suggest a good grounding in English. He failed to master Latin, though he was taught it for eight or nine years, and later blamed the poor teaching 'without interest . . . like mathematics';[38] but he liked History and won a 'distinction' in the Cambridge School Certificate.

At school at Roborough, theatrical make-believe became both a private and public passion. In the dormitory after lights-out he would enact imaginary dramas under the blankets. In free-time, during winter evenings, while some of the boys indulged in 'ragging and sitting around on radiators', Alec joined those who pursued their hobbies, building 'a very collapsible cardboard theatre'. He constructed a shadow theatre using a sheet and a strong light, and directed plays and operettas, among them *The Pirates of Penzance*, recited a musical monologue called 'Dangerous Dan McGrew' wearing a slouch hat belonging to one of the masters and with a thin black moustache painted on his upper lip; and he played in *Macbeth*, running round the school yard so that he could appear breathless as the King's messenger – the first intimation of the professional dedication that was to be such a significant feature of his career.

Alec's first experience of the theatre had come when he was around six years old from an old lady living below the Stivens in St John's Wood. The former dancer had tried to teach the boy deportment: 'Why do you always run? A young gentleman should *walk*, not run.'[39] Later, Alec had been taken to the musical *Chu-Chin-Chow* which he loved; and to the pantomime, *Puss in Boots*, which he hated. 'All the chorus girls came on dressed as cats and I was sitting in the front row and it terrified me . . . I think it put me off women for years.'[40] He was taken backstage at the Theatre Royal, Drury Lane, 'when v. small to see a quite mythical "aunty" whom I liked. I remember being shocked at greasepaint and shouting "Take it off!"'[41] During his long stay in the Turkey-carpeted hotel on the Cromwell Road, a Russian lady, also a resident, took him to a matinée at the Coliseum to see jugglers, clowns, maidens in flimsy frocks and, Top of the Bill, the saucy *comedienne*, Nellie Wallace, for whose sake Alec turned down the offer of an ice-cream soda made by the Russian lady after the show, asking that the money be spent on a bunch of flowers instead – the first of many bouquets he was to send to those he admired in the course of his lifetime.

In one of the residential hotels where he stayed with his mother during the holidays, he recruited two girls to act in 'playlets I devised which we performed, with storms of giggles, to anyone in the hotel who could be persuaded to sit still for twenty minutes'; while alone in his room he climbed inside a pillowcase to try and emulate the escape artist he had seen at the London Coliseum.

When staying in Bournemouth he would take any chance he could to go to the theatre and, aged sixteen, he had the audacity to write to the celebrated actress Sybil Thorndike, whom he had seen with her husband Lewis Casson in Ibsen's *Ghosts* and a melodrama called *The Squall*, to ask her to show him how the effect of thunder and lightning was achieved on stage. 'It is important for me to know as I want to be an actor.' He was duly invited backstage and given a demonstration. By now he had discovered that one could actually earn a living as an actor, 'earning as much as sixteen pounds a week'.[42]

To the other boys at Roborough, Alec's family life remained mysterious: he was known to have a mother but a father was never mentioned. Agnes, when she appeared at the school, was a source of intense embarrassment, on one occasion borrowing five pounds from the Maths master to pay for her taxi. During the holidays Alec would either stay in a residential hotel or, between the ages of fifteen and seventeen, in digs in Ealing, London, where the landlady was a Mrs Gosse. 'Almost every week she would take me to the Walpole Cinema in Ealing and a couple of times to a musical in London. I must often have been a pain in the neck to her, with adolescent tantrums, but she seemed to retain an affection.' Mrs Gosse was a good cook and great fun with 'a sharp/sour wit'. She was an unostentatious Catholic, 'a regular Mass goer rather than a deeply devout woman'. She later told Alec that she had considered herself a second mother to him. 'My life would have been happier,' he noted in his diary, 'if she had been the first'.[43]

Alec's years at Roborough had two lasting effects on the development of his character. The first was the importance he came to attach to the code and mannerisms of what would then have been called a 'gentleman'. It is perhaps an exaggeration to say that Alec was educated 'above his station'. His cousins Clifford and Walter, the sons of his Aunt May, were also privately educated. But his illegitimacy, his tipsy, scrounging mother, and the grandmother who smoked a clay pipe and lived in a hovel with a packed-earth floor were terrible secrets that Alec had to conceal from himself through fantasy and from others by a closed countenance – a dissimulation even greater than that common to boys in public schools.

For the same reasons, Alec came to distance himself from his mother's family – either because he felt he might be drawn back into the chaos and vulgarity that he associated with his mother and her drinking companions; or because they were privy to the dark secrets that he wanted to keep from the world; or simply because they were 'common'. 'Clifford and Walter knew Alec very well,' a great-niece of Agnes' recalled, 'but even as a child Alec was aloof. I think he felt rather grand.'[44]

The second effect on his character came from the influence of the headmaster, D.G. Gilbert:

He was headmaster at Roborough and was particularly good to me, and was one of the first people in my life to give me a measure of self-confidence. Although he was very extrovert, with a rich hearty laugh, and nearly always good-humoured, he reacted with sympathy to the (very few) boys, such as myself, to whom the cricketing-nets and soccer were anathema. The off-beat individualist no doubt puzzled him, but he was never sarcastic. He encouraged us in reading books unlikely to interest many other boys, seemed to be rather impressed by my art work and didn't, in any way, stand up against my theatre enthusiasms. His passions were small boats and fishing. He took me, once, to a classical concert at Devonshire Park and easily talked me into 'producing' Gilbert and Sullivan for the school shows. On the day I left Roborough, he came to town with the London-bound boys, bought me a grey trilby hat, gave me lunch and took me to see the Coliseum. I suspect that, during the financial difficulties which always worried my last years of schooling, he either waived or greatly reduced the fees that were paid for me.[45]

Though there were a number of women who had felt sorry for Alec as a child, and had been kind to him, Gilbert was the only man. Given the hatred that Alec felt for his stepfather, David Stiven, Gilbert would seem to have been the only role model during Alec's adolescence.

The Gilberts had a daughter called Beryl who was 'warm-hearted, laughed easily, was sympathetic, and a superb listener when the subject was serious'.[46] She was seven years older than Alec but, together with several other boys, Alec was in love with her in his last year at school. Beryl, too, seems to have been touched by the poignancy of this thin young man with his sticking-out ears, who had no father, a dreadful mother and almost no money going out to make his way in the world: when he left Roborough for London she found him a job.

three

Arks Publicity, at 63 Lincoln's Inn Fields, where Alec went to work in the autumn of 1932, was an advertising agency owned by C.O. Stanley, later chairman of Pye Electronics. The chief copywriter was William Connor, later a celebrated columnist on the *Daily Mirror* under the name 'Cassandra'; the chief designer was Donald Zec who also went to the *Mirror* and became a high-profile show business columnist. Among Arks' clients were the Dutch electronics conglomerate Pye and Mullards, the manufacturer of radio valves.

Alec was employed as a copywriter at thirty shillings a week but, aged only eighteen, he also acted as office boy and general dogsbody – for example, pasting copies of the Arks' advertisements into a book. The office was run in a haphazard way but the atmosphere was friendly, and C.O. Stanley was something of a philanthropist who liked to give work to the young. Initially Alec felt 'lost, nervous and acutely self-conscious' and in his leisure time he was lonely: later, looking back, he remembered 'suicidal tendencies'. 'I would lie on my bed reading, perhaps, nearly all day, or walking the deserted London streets half the night out of a melancholy search of I didn't know what;'[47] but he made friends with some of his young colleagues – Boog Barries, Adolf Deys and David Stewart. The young men would come to work wearing suits and bowler hats, eat lunch in a snack bar near Lincoln's Inn Fields, and then return to their lodgings in rented rooms or boarding houses known as 'private' hotels.

After initially living in digs, Alec joined one of his new friends, David Stewart, in his private hotel in Kensington Gardens Square. It was a large Victorian house with small rooms created from larger ones with flimsy partitions. However, it represented good value for money at thirty-five shillings a week for breakfast and dinner on weekdays and full board at the weekend. Alec could afford this because his wages were supplemented by an allowance of twenty-seven shillings a week paid to him through Geddes' solicitor.

David Stewart came from a more privileged background than Alec but was also poor and had been raised by his mother: his father, after a series of business failures in Scotland, had left to make his fortune in Canada, on the understanding that his wife and son would follow. Like Agnes and Alec, they never did. David, then aged nine and an only child, grew up, 'a poor, lonely boy'.[48]

Alec spent some of his leisure time with David Stewart. In summer they would go swimming at the Roehampton Club or a pool called the Ace of Spades. They talked about girls: Stewart was to recall in his eighties that Alec confessed he was in love with a girl called Sybil and hoped to sleep with her. Stewart was not sure that Sybil was her name and this was possibly Beryl, the headmaster's daughter. Stewart had a girlfriend called Josephine who, like many 'decent' girls at the time, thought that a couple should only kiss if they were engaged.

On one occasion, Alec took Stewart to visit his mother in 'some seedy hotel in South London'. She struck him as being 'rather beaten down', in marked contrast to Stewart's own mother who came from a distinguished family of Scots lawyers and, despite her poverty, had rich friends. One of these, Alice Coates, lived in Castle Toward opposite the Island of Bute on the Firth of Clyde, and in the summer of 1933, David took Alec to stay at Castle Toward. They travelled from London to Glasgow on an overnight bus, then took a train to Greenock and crossed on the ferry to Dunoon where they were met by a car that took them to the castle.

It was Alec's first taste of the grand life but he appeared to David to be unintimidated by a country house with thirty bedrooms, and changing every evening into a dinner jacket that had been rustled up by his friend. They walked and swam, took the ferry across to the resort of Rothesay on the Island of Bute and there spent five shillings on a tour in a flying boat. And Alec proved popular with the older ladies. He was not obviously handsome, with his 'meaty' hands and prominent ears; he was also shy and bumbling; but he stimulated the motherly instincts of both Mrs Stewart and Mrs Coates.

The only thing at that time that drew Alec out of his shell of reserve was reciting poetry or playing roles in front of his friends. After dinner at the hotel in Kensington Gardens Square, Alec would go to Stewart's room or Stewart to his and he would recite speeches from Shakespeare's plays; and once, following one of these readings, said to his friend, 'I feel I have the seeds of genius in me,' which struck Stewart as a remarkably self-confident statement for one so young.

Certainly, Alec's mind was not on his work at Arks Publicity. After his stint cutting out advertisements and sticking them into a scrapbook, he was given the more responsible job of ordering photographic blocks. For an advertisement for Mullards, Arks' best customer, he inadvertently wrote feet for inches – a mistake that was not noticed until two men arrived carrying a huge block. The space reserved in the *Daily Mail* appeared without an illustration but, thanks to the easy-going regime under C.O. Stanley, Alec received only a mild rebuke.

In the office there was a predictable amount of smutty talk, and a copy of the banned novel, *Lady Chatterley's Lover*, that had been smuggled in from France by one of the staff, went the rounds. After a month it reached Alec's desk with some of the pages 'greasy and dog-eared'.[49] Thereafter his friend Boog Barries called him 'Phallic Alec' but the nickname 'didn't last long – and I suspect I was rather flattered by it. It was, in any case, quite meaningless and only used for euphony'.[50]

More serious-minded was his friend Adolf Deys, who lived with his wife Daisy in a small flat on the Gray's Inn Road. Alec would often spend the weekend with them where 'I was not only fed but permitted to read aloud to them nearly all Shakespeare's plays and a good deal of Shaw'.[51] He also saw his ex-headmaster's daughter, Beryl Gilbert, and her brother Roger who was studying medicine at Barts Hospital, and they persuaded him to join a discussion group that they had started with Ernest Race and his sister Sally. It was called the Thirty-Nine Club because the first meeting was held in a basement flat at 39 Nevern Square in Earl's Court. Thereafter, the members would gather in one another's houses or flats to read aloud and discuss art and politics. They were mostly professionals of one kind or another, older than Alec and university graduates, and it was there, Alec judged later, 'that my tardy education really began'.

One member, John Rotton, was to become one of Alec's closest friends – 'a handsome, wild-natured young boy, a couple of years older than me, taciturn and sometimes given to smashing lampposts', with a sister called Monica who 'was placid and sweet natured'.[52] Another, Rupert Woodhouse, Alec thought 'a bit suspect and pretentious' but 'he was very good to me, taking me to the occasional play or opening my eyes to a variety of books etc in the days of the Thirty-Nine Club when I was about nineteen. I suppose he may have had secret designs on me but he never laid a finger on me, which would have appalled me at that age'.[53]

What were Alec's contributions to these discussions? He had been raised as a member of the Church of England and Roborough had had a sound Anglican ethos, with prayers at night and hymns sung in the chapel. At the age of sixteen, Alec had been confirmed into the

Church of England in Eastbourne's Holy Trinity Church at the hands of the Bishop of Lewes, but had come away from the ceremony 'a confirmed atheist'.[54] 'I think I must have expected to see a Dove come down and sit on me,' he later wrote to Merula, 'or anyway to feel different afterwards, but to my horror I was left with as many perplexities as ever and quickly & foolishly decided it was all rubbish and bishops just buttoned-up nonsenses.'[55]

By the time Alec came to live in London, it was not just the bishops that had earned his contempt but 'FILTHY CAPITALISTS and HYPOCRITICAL BISHOPS and MAJORS and the majority of worldly successful people'.[56] He was not the only revolutionary working for Arks Publicity: as well as *Lady Chatterley's Lover* copies of *U.S.S.R. Today* were passed surreptitiously from desk to desk. Alec was enrolled by a Communist friend to hand out Marxist-Leninist leaflets under cover of darkness and got a frisson from feeling that he 'was doing something clandestine and illegal'. But he was put off Communism by the show trials in Moscow in the early 1930s and moved towards the more moderate views of his friends in the Thirty-Nine Club who were mostly liberal in politics and agnostic in religion. He had sufficient curiosity in other systems of belief to attend a Quaker meeting 'but I soon got the impression that the Spirit usually "moved" the most garrulous and boring person present . . .';[57] and, with other members of the Club, he went to a meeting of Buchmanite Moral Rearmers, but here too he was unimpressed; and thereafter, his curiosity about the meaning of life receded before his all-absorbing passion for the theatre.

four

Every penny that Alec could save from his wages was spent on tickets for the cinema or the gallery of London's theatres. From the movies came a lifelong admiration of Buster Keaton, and also Stan Laurel whom he to some extent resembled. However, his chief passion was the stage. In October 1932, on the night of the fiasco over the block for the Mullards advertisement in the *Daily Mail*, Alec, embarrassed and ashamed, did not return to the residential hotel in Kensington Gardens Square but went to see Cathleen Nesbitt play Fräulein von Nordeck in *Children in Uniform* at the Duchess Theatre.[58] He saw Ernest Milton give what he later regarded as 'the most thrilling performance' of *Hamlet* he had ever seen at Sadler's Wells; and, when *Richard of Bordeaux* was staged at the New Theatre in February 1933, with John Gielgud in the starring role, Alec went to see it a dozen times.

Besides the commercial theatres in the West End, there was also the Old Vic, a former music hall called the Royal Victoria which had been bought by high-minded philanthropists to provide sober and wholesome entertainment for London's working classes. By 1914, it had come under the direction of 'a rather short, stout person with glasses', Lilian Baylis. Baylis, a devout Christian, after 'a divine command', had launched the Old Vic Shakespeare Company, and by the 1930s the Old Vic had become the power-house of classical theatre in Britain. The prices of the tickets were low – at five shillings for the stalls or dress circle, half the price of the West End theatres – and a mere sixpence for a seat in the gallery.

It was these sixpenny tickets that drew Alec time and again to go south of the river to the Waterloo Road. His arrival in London coincided with the engagement for the 1933–4 season of a dynamic young director from Ireland, Tyrone Guthrie. Guthrie was the first of the university-educated, non-actor directors to take charge at the Old Vic. He had started directing as an undergraduate at Oxford, then worked in repertory and, later, for the BBC where he had pioneered the broadcasting of radio drama. His reputation as an avant-garde director had been established with Pirandello's *Six Characters in Search of an Author* in 1932. He arrived at the Old Vic determined to do away with the old-fashioned actor-manager type of Shakespearean production that dated from the Victorian era. He also overcame – temporarily – Lillian Baylis's legendary parsimony to meet the conditions demanded by the best actors: Charles Laughton agreed to join Flora Robson in the new company only if the costumes were not cobbled together but made by professionals.

Alec greatly admired Laughton, and a number of other actors, but nothing compared to his adulation of John Gielgud. 'It is impossible to convey to a younger generation,' he wrote at the time of Gielgud's ninetieth birthday, 'the glamour and theatrical innovations he represented . . . He was hero-worshipped by many young actors like myself who copied, in the cheapest form possible, his outward trappings without being able to emulate the inner man'.[59]

Not only young actors hero-worshipped Gielgud: he had become the pre-eminent star and heart-throb of the public. Particularly after the success of *Richard of Bordeaux*, Gielgud could look out of the window of his flat in St Martin's Lane to see queues 'coiled like serpents' down the street, waiting to buy tickets: he was photographed, painted, caricatured and interviewed in every newspaper. He received gifts and fan letters by every post and was asked for his autograph 'a dozen times a day'.[60]

'Gielgud is the only real star of the British theatre, under thirty,' wrote the drama critic of the London *Evening News*, defining stardom as 'a quality above and beyond sheer acting ability; it is a personal, even an emotional quality, and it has undeniably a great deal to do with sex appeal, which in turn has very little to do with good looks'. It was this sex appeal that drew crowds of besotted women to his plays. They did not know – indeed no one outside the closed circle of the theatre was to know for another twenty years – that Gielgud was homosexual.

For a man to have sexual relations with a member of his own sex was, at the time, a criminal offence. The moral prohibition that formed part of Christian teaching, combined with the sense of revulsion felt by the public at large, gave force to the law. But, with what Alec had noticed as 'the hypocrisy of grown-ups', facultative homosexuality was quite common in the all-male institutions that formed the sinews of the British state – the Army, the Navy, the universities, the public schools and the Church.

The theatre at this time was almost certainly the profession where the homosexual condition was most common, and where it was therefore safe to be homosexual so long as liaisons were kept discreet. Ivor Novello, Noël Coward and the immensely powerful impresario, 'Binkie' Beaumont, were all 'queer': indeed Binkie Beaumont was to pinch Gielgud's lover, John Perry, a handsome, languid actor who also wrote plays with Molly Keane. Both Gielgud and Binkie Beaumont were to exert so powerful an influence over the London theatre both before and after World War II that they came to be accused of prejudice against heterosexual actors such as Donald Wolfit: but, though the high incidence of homosexuality among actors at the time might seem to support this contention, there were wholly heterosexual actors such as Jack Hawkins and Anthony Quayle who were employed by Gielgud and Beaumont and flourished within the profession. And there were others who were either 'bisexual', or married homosexuals, such as Ernest Milton, Michael Redgrave and Robert Flemyng, all of whom were to play a significant part in Alec's later life.

Some came to regard their homosexuality as an affliction, others as the mark of a higher sensibility. At Cambridge University, for example, John Maynard Keynes 'and his friend Lytton Strachey had half-seriously tried to rationalise and theorise their situation, calling it "the higher sodomy". The idea was that homosexuality might be a way of life superior to heterosexual life.'[61] Being 'queer' was a gesture of revolt against the stifling conventions and paralysing inhibitions of the British bourgeoisie, and an *entrée* into a Masonic brotherhood identifiable not by a secret handshake but a glint in the eye.

Realising that the only way he could afford to train as an actor was to win a scholarship to one of London's acting schools, Alec applied in October 1933 for the Leverhulme Scholarship at the Royal Academy of Dramatic Art, which provided the winner with two years' free tuition and a living allowance of five pounds a week. He paid the fee of one pound to register and was given short pieces he would have to recite at the audition. He had four months in which to prepare them but, feeling that he needed some coaching, got hold of the telephone number of John Gielgud's apartment on St Martin's Lane and, with the audacity he had shown when writing to Sybil Thorndike at the age of sixteen, now made a cold call to Gielgud.

Gielgud was clearly impressed by the name Guinness and, though he declined the post as Alec's theatrical coach for himself, suggested the actress Martita Hunt: 'She'll love the money.' Alec duly rang Martita Hunt who was also impressed by the name and invited Alec to visit her in her flat.

The sight of an ill-fed young man with sticking-out ears, wearing a shabby suit immediately brought home to her that this was not one of *the* Guinnesses but she had the grace to ask Alec to mix her a Martini.

Tall, slim and elegant with the voice and demeanour of a dowager
duchess, Martita Hunt had been born in Argentina and had befriended
Gielgud when she had played Elsa Mardon and he Gerald Marlowe in
Holding Out the Apple at the Globe Theatre in 1928. It is possible that
she was 'resting' at the time and did indeed need the money: by the
time Alec left she had agreed to give him ten one-hour weekly lessons
at a pound a session.

After the first five lessons, which Alec could only attend after office
hours or at weekends, Martita told him to take back his money and
forget about the theatre. Alec refused, she relented, and gave him the
agreed ten lessons and a further twelve at no cost. She told him always
to put the emphasis on the *verb* when speaking, then the noun, and let
the adjectives and adverbs take care of themselves – a lesson evident
in the way Alec spoke both on- and off-stage for the rest of his life.

Martita also broadened his cultural horizons, expanding the ad hoc
education he had received from his friends in the Thirty-Nine Club.
She was a cultivated woman who aroused in Alec a curiosity about art
and 'a more sophisticated world than I had encountered among
schoolmasters and advertising agents'.[62] She continued to give Alec
lessons right up until the time of his audition at the Royal Academy of
Dramatic Art.

To get the day off for the audition, Alec had to tell both his boss and
his sceptical friends of his plans to become an actor. When he reached
RADA, however, he was told that the Leverhulme Scholarship had
been cancelled for that year. Profoundly dejected, and dreading the
ridicule of his friends and colleagues at Arks Publicity, Alec walked
away down Gower Street where he bumped into one of the girls who
had acted in the playlets he had staged in the residential hotel in
Eastbourne when he was a child. He told her of his disappointment,
whereupon she suggested that he go at once to the Fay Compton
Studio of Dramatic Art who were holding auditions that afternoon.
There, he delivered the pieces he had prepared for RADA before the
five judges, together with twenty other would-be young actors, and
won a scholarship that provided free tuition for a two-year course.

five

Alec went to work at Arks Publicity the next day, triumphantly announced his scholarship, and gave in his notice. However, his position was precarious because, though the scholarship paid for tuition, no living allowance was attached. He still received, at this stage, an allowance from Geddes, and he borrowed a further sum from a former housemaster at Roborough. But he had to cut his living expenses to the bone and so moved from the residential hotel in Kensington Gardens Square to a rented attic in deepest Notting Hill for ten shillings a week.

For six months he went each day to the Fay Compton Studio, usually walking to save the cost of the bus fare, sometimes barefoot to save wear on his shoes. There he learned voice production, tap-dancing and fencing, and rehearsed scenes from Greek tragedy and the plays of Shakespeare. He lived frugally off jam sandwiches and baked beans out of a tin. Martita Hunt, whom he had kept informed of his progress, sometimes gave him 'a chic little meal'; and two of his

friends from Arks, one of them Boog Barries, would take him once
a week to Lyons Corner House on the Strand where a shilling bought
a bumper breakfast which included bacon, sausages, tomatoes and
fried bread.

At the end of the first term in the summer of 1934, Alec won the
end of term award – a miniature volume of Shakespeare's collected
works. One of the three judges who awarded it was John Gielgud. At
the same time, as he started his summer holiday, he was informed by
Mr Martin, the Geddeses solicitor, that the trust fund that had hitherto
paid his allowance had run out. Now penniless, Alec had to get a job
and was determined to find work as an actor.

Remembering Gielgud's civility when he had telephoned him the
year before, and hoping that he might recall awarding him the prize,
Alec went backstage after a mid-week matinée at Wyndham's Theatre
where Gielgud was appearing in *The Maitlands*. Gielgud received him
in his dressing-room and, 'though he wasn't exactly welcoming',
suggested he apply for a job he knew was available understudying
Douglas Fairbanks Jr.

Since Alec's appearance was now that of an emaciated waif, this
may have been intended as a practical joke; but when Alec returned
the next day, having predictably failed to get the role, Gielgud sent him
out again – this time to the Old Vic, where they were auditioning for
Antony and Cleopatra. 'You're no actor,' the director shouted at him
from the stalls after Alec had delivered a couple of lines. 'Get off the
fucking stage.'

By the end of the week Gielgud gave up. 'I believe in you,' he said.
'Next time I do a play, I'll get on to you. But you're too thin. You're not
eating enough.' He told Alec to take a twenty-pound note off the top
of a pile that lay on his make-up table but Alec, though he had only
fourpence left in his pocket, and had survived for the past two days on
two buns, two apples and a couple of glasses of milk, declined his offer,
reassuring Gielgud that money was not a problem.

After taking leave of Gielgud at Wyndham's, Alec started on his
long walk back to Notting Hill. Passing the Piccadilly Theatre he saw

that the management were auditioning for parts in a play called *Queer Cargo*. Alec went to the box office where he met the stage manager who, after hearing him read some of the lines, gave him the job of understudying all the male roles, and playing walk-on parts as a Chinese coolie, a French pirate and a British sailor at a wage of three pounds a week.

This was not Alec's first appearance on the professional stage: he had, earlier in the year, been given a non-speaking role as a barrister in Edward Wooll's play *Libel* at the Playhouse Theatre. His latest job did not give him a chance to show off his talents either. However, *Queer Cargo* did at least earn him a living in his chosen profession. He did not pester Gielgud again but, later that summer, saw him in the Old Vic audience at a matinée of *Richard II* and, in the interval, hovered close to the actor in the coffee bar. Gielgud spotted him and called him over. 'Where have you been? I've made enquiries for you all over London. I want you to play Osric in *Hamlet*. Rehearsals start on Monday week at the New Theatre.' Alec's salary would be seven pounds a week.

Why did Gielgud, who at that time could have taken his pick of the acting profession to fill any role in one of his productions, choose the waif-like, moon-faced youth with receding hair and sticking-out ears whom he had seen act only once in the end of term production at his drama school? The suggestion that there was some homosexual attraction seems unlikely, if only because Alec was so unattractive at the time. Gielgud may have been touched by his poignancy or impressed by his determination; or, though this does not appear to have occurred to Alec, he may have been doing a favour for Martita Hunt who had so clearly become fond of Alec.

Of course, there is a more obvious explanation – that Gielgud recognised Alec's potential. However, the fledgeling actor did not have an easy time when, having been released from the cast of *Queer Cargo*, he turned up for rehearsals at the New Theatre. 'The theatre was so different in those days. It was *Mr* Gielgud and *Miss* Cowie [Laura

Cowie]. You arrived at rehearsals in a tweed jacket and grey flannel trousers . . .'[63] Rather like a new boy at a public school going through rites of initiation at the hands of a head boy, Alec was bullied and humiliated by Gielgud – even being told, at one point during rehearsals, to leave: 'Oh, go away! I don't want to see you again.' Alec walked the streets for a week and found, when he returned to the theatre, that he was 'teacher's pet'.

John Gielgud's production of *Hamlet* opened in November 1934, and played to packed houses for the next ten months. This was largely due to what was regarded as a definitive performance by Gielgud himself, but enhanced by the costumes designed by two sisters, Sophie and Margaret ('Percy') Harris, and Elisabeth Montgomery, whom Gielgud had discovered when producing plays for the Oxford Playhouse in the 1920s – they called themselves 'The Motleys' from Jacques' line in *As You Like It*: 'Motley's the only wear' – and fine performances from his chosen cast: Frank Vosper as Claudius, Glen Byam Shaw as Laertes, Jack Hawkins as Horatio, Laura Cowie as Gertrude, Anthony Quayle as Guildenstern and George Devine, the husband of Sophie Harris, as Bernardo. But among the many satisfactions felt by Gielgud at the success of his production was the evidence that his gamble on Alec had paid off.

The role of Osric, the courtier sent by Claudius to welcome Hamlet back to Denmark and umpire his duel with Laertes, is small, and Osric appears only towards the end of the long play, but it is far more than a walk-on part, and gave Alec the chance to show what he could do. He impressed both the audience and his fellow actors with his ability to transform himself from a balding, half-starved pauper with 'banana bunch hands', wide eyes and protruding ears into a suave and elegant courtier, and demonstrated with the panache of his performance that here was an exceptional actor. He became admired and liked by the company: 'Everybody could see that he was very promising,' fellow-actor Sam Beazley, recalled, 'and he was very nice and very funny. Quite wickedly funny. And very ambitious.' Gielgud, too, was delighted with his protégé: for Christmas he gave Alec a beautifully bound edition of Ellen Terry's letters inscribed, 'To Alec, who grows apace', and then Hamlet's reflection on death which Alec adopted as his lifelong motto: 'The readiness is all.'

Alec's success as Osric greatly increased his confidence in himself. Sam Beazley, who had shared a dressing-room with Alec, noted how he had grown less shy as the run proceeded:

> We had dressers, one to each dressing-room. Their job was to sit in the corridor and when we required their services we would call 'Dresser!' They'd come in and help you on with your clothes. We had a horrible old dresser called Frank, a horrible old man [hawking and coughing], who didn't wait in the corridor but sat in our dressing-room; and Alec said, 'Frank, your place is in the corridor, and we'll call you when we want you.'[64]

Yet it was also remarked upon that Alec had a reserved and brittle personality and could quickly take offence. Frith Banbury, a contemporary of Alec's who played a small role and who, like Sam Beazley and another young actor in the company, Geoffrey Toone, was homosexual, felt in the early stages of the production that Alec lacked confidence in himself and so wrote a note saying how fond he was of him and how much he admired his acting. The next day Alec cut him dead. 'I think he thought I was making a pass at him which, being gay, I might have been but in fact was not.'[65]

Beazley, who acted one of the Players, was intrigued by Alec. 'He was very, very good. I could see that. Very camp and flowery and amusing. But he was pathetic; starving, almost. No money at all. Nowhere to live . . . There was all this mystery about him being illegitimate but he was gentlemanly. He wasn't a low-class boy at all. But that awful mother . . .'[66]

Agnes de Cuffe was by now aware that Alec was in work, and the worst humiliation that her son had to endure was the appearance of his mother at the stage door of the New Theatre on pay day, quite evidently drunk, to ask Alec for money. It seems likely that her allowance from Geddes' settlement had been stopped at the same time as Alec's, or at any rate, greatly reduced. Alec now had to worry not only about her debts but also about her 'financial fiddles and kleptomania'. He himself became one of her victims when she gained access to his bed-sitter in Notting Hill Gate and removed all his possessions, leaving behind 'a little stack of pawnbroker tickets which I suppose was not unwitty of her but very inconvenient for me'.[67]

At around this time, however, Alec left his digs in Notting Hill and moved into the centre of London. When *Hamlet*'s long run finally came to an end in May 1935, he wrote from 5 Tiverton Mansions, 140 Gray's Inn Road, to the man who had done so much for him – no longer as 'Mr Gielgud' but as 'John'.

> Dear John,
> I could write you such a long letter thanking you not only for giving me a part but also for your countless little kindnesses which have made working with you so delightful, but I'll spare you that. It was very courageous of you to give an inexperienced person a part like 'Osric' and knowing how badly I was playing at the end of the run and how much I had improved I shudder to think what I must have been like at the beginning. But thank you a thousand times! I suppose one never forgets one's first part – I certainly shall never forget how happy I have been during the past six months.
>
> You asked me to let you know about the Vic *Hamlet*. Well I went last night but I got so bored after an hour that I came out. Bits and pieces of it were very good indeed – the atmosphere they got into the ghost scenes when the ghost wasn't there (directly he was of course it was laughable) – but on the whole it was dull. Maurice Evans was very fine but his soliloquies are appalling I thought and he could never have been a scholar or a poet – certainly not a prince. The [illegible] were unbelievably awful, there was no pageantry about the play, I hated the groupings and most of the small parts were stupidly played. Anyway, I went almost unbiased and I came away bored. The friend I went with

stopped to the end and came away believing Osric had been played by a woman. So I can't even be jealous for myself.

I do hope I shall see you again soon John and once more – my gratitude for all you have done for me and ever my very best wishes.

Sincerely, Alec G.[68]

six

Every night, during the long run of *Hamlet*, Alec had stood in the wings watching and learning from Gielgud's performance. There were, however, three other men who were perhaps of more significance in drawing out of Alec a talent that would distinguish itself from Gielgud's and prove to be unique – one French – Michel St Denis; one Russian – Theodore Komisarjevsky; and one Irish – Tyrone Guthrie.

Michel St Denis was the nephew and disciple of the enormously influential French theatre director and theorist of stagecraft, Jacques Copeau.* Together with André Gide, Copeau had been one of the founders of *La Nouvelle Revue Française* which he edited until 1911 when he left to stage an adaptation of Fyodor Dostoevsky's novel, *The Brothers Karamazov*. In 1913 he founded a theatre in Paris called *le Théâtre du Vieux-Colombier* to put his radical ideas into practice.

---

* 'In the history of French theatre,' wrote Albert Camus, 'there are only two periods: before and after Copeau.'

Breaking down the traditional barrier between the stage ('a box of illusions') and the audience, he brought the acting area out into the auditorium, abandoning the proscenium arch and using only a simple backdrop to set the scene. No attempt was made to conceal the grey plaster walls or cement floor with stage sets or concealed lighting.

Copeau's views on acting were as radical as those on the *mise-en-scène*. He held that the essence of theatre was not literary but ritualistic as in Ancient Greece. His staging of plays by Molière or Shakespeare were stylised in the manner of the Italian *commedia dell'arte*; while modern plays were acted realistically but with the words of the author's text of secondary importance to the acting. He taught his actors to empty themselves of their own personalities and become the characters they were playing on-stage. He insisted that movement was quite as important as articulation: like Stanislavsky at the Moscow Art Theatre, Copeau sought to strike a balance between his actors' subjective introspection, their objective study of the character and their technique in movement and speech.

Copeau's ideas did not appeal to the Parisian theatregoers in the years following World War I; and so in 1924 he took his company back to Pernand Verglesse, a small village near Beaune in Burgundy. If the urban bourgeoisie would not appreciate his work, then perhaps the peasants would. Calling themselves 'Les Copiaux', Copeau's troupe performed in a converted barn in Pernand Verglesse and toured the neighbouring villages where the productions, often improvised and designed to be seen rather than heard, proved popular and attracted substantial audiences.

'Les Copeaux' even had their in-house playwright, André Obey, who would write his plays as part of an integrated process of casting, staging, and planning the sets and costumes. Obey continued the experiments already conducted by Copeau whereby different scenes could be acted simultaneously on the same stage. He supplemented the mime which was fundamental to Copeau's acting technique with a form of mime language which they called 'grummelotage' or 'the music of meaning'.

In 1929 Jacques Copeau returned to the *Théâtre du Vieux-Colombier* in Paris and 'Les Copeaux' became *La Compagnie des Quinze*. In 1930 he handed over the direction to his nephew and principal disciple, Michel St Denis. St Denis, the son of Copeau's sister, had, because of his father's early death, been raised by Copeau and had worked with him since 1920, taking on part of the stage management and the company's administration. In 1931 the *Compagnie des Quinze* under St Denis' direction, staged two plays by André Obey at the *Théâtre du Vieux-Colombier* – *Le Viol de Lucrèce* and *Noé* – both to great acclaim, and later that same year St Denis brought *Noé* to the Arts Theatre in London.

Noé, a play that embodied all the ideas that had been developed by Copeau over the decades, was a revelation to English audiences and became the talking point of the season. 'The public's reaction,' St Denis later recalled:

> . . . the tone of the press, the daily visits we received from leading members of the acting profession made us feel that the impact of our performances was something more than just an ordinary theatrical success . . . George Bernard Shaw and G.K. Chesterton came to see us perform. The great classical actors John Gielgud, Sybil Thorndike, Laurence Olivier and Edith Evans visited our dressing-rooms, as did Michael Redgrave, Peggy Ashcroft, Alec Guinness, Charles Laughton.[69]

Gielgud was so impressed that he at once asked Michel St Denis to stage an English-language production of *Noé*, or *Noah*, with himself in the title role. He proposed Alec for the role of the Wolf.

Alec's polite expression of hope in his thank-you letter to Gielgud that he 'might see him again soon' had proved superfluous because, after the friendships he had formed during the long run of *Hamlet*, Alec had entered Gielgud's circle. Frank Vosper, hearing that Alec had no plans to celebrate his twenty-first birthday, gave a party for him with his sister Margery, inviting other members of the cast, among them Jack Hawkins, Martita Hunt, Laura Cowie, George Devine and Jessica

Tandy. Alec was also welcomed by the group that dropped in and out of the Motleys' studio workshop off St Martin's Lane. 'The "Motleys",' wrote Anthony Quayle in his autobiography *A Time to Speak*:

> . . . became an unofficial and unique club – a sort of eighteenth-century 'coffee house'. It was the most haphazard coffee house in London; the people who dropped in from time to time – Peggy Ashcroft, Edith Evans, Gwen Ffrangcon-Davies, Jack Hawkins and Jessica Tandy, Robert Donat, the Redgraves, the Byam Shaws, Michel St Denis; younger actors like Alec Guinness, Stephen Haggard – were all friends who enjoyed each other's company, shared each other's aims, and were to a greater or lesser extent under Gielgud's patronage. At its centre was John himself, lord of the London stage – but never lording over it, always generous to young actors, and always blithely tactless.[70]

Gielgud would also drop in to the digs Alec now shared in Hasker Street, off Walton Street in Knightsbridge, with Sam Beazley and Harry Andrews – Andrews at the time being an object of Gielgud's affections. A third lodger, Philip Clowes, was the brother of their landlord, Dickie Clowes, who worked as a reader for the all-powerful production company run by Binkie Beaumont, H.M. Tennent. The 'sexual relations with men' that Alec mentioned to the actor Simon Callow much later in his life – 'but then one married and gave up all that sort of thing'[71] – may belong to this period of his life.

Alec's friendship with Sam Beazley, like that with David Stewart when he worked at Arks Publicity, led to a free summer holiday – this time at Portmeirion in North Wales where Beazley's mother, Nelto, estranged from her husband, had a country house provided by her cousin Clough Williams-Ellis, the owner of Portmeirion, and the Portmeirion Hotel. It was a ramshackle old castle that had belonged to Nelto's grandfather, where Alec would sit in the lotus position on a broad oak shelf under a stained-glass window doing yoga. 'He wasn't a bit shy,' Beazley recalled:

He fitted in. It was a very social life. My mother was queen of local society and London when she came. She loved entertaining. It was a country house in North Wales. It wasn't very grand. We had very little money but a lovely house and all this dizzy life going on down the road at the hotel. Casual life, and we swam a lot. So I don't think he was all that shy, especially if he knew people were fond of him. And my mother was very fond of him.[72]

seven

Michel St Denis's production of André Obey's *Noah* started rehearsals in the unusually hot summer of 1935. Alec, playing the Wolf, already knew a number of the cast from *Hamlet*: George Devine played the Bear, Harry Andrews the Lion and Sam Beazley the Monkey for the first few weeks, after which he was sacked and replaced by Ewynn Owen. But there were some newcomers, among them Marius Goring as Japhet, and two girls called Salaman – Susy, Goring's girlfriend, a choreographer from the Ballet Rambert who had worked with St Denis in Paris; and Merula, her younger sister, a student at the Old Vic School who, though Alec no doubt had failed to notice her, had had a walk-on part as a lady-in-waiting in the Old Vic production of *Hamlet* that Alec had described in his letter to Gielgud.

John Gielgud, as we have seen, could be a bully as a director but there had been a certain charm in his inconsistency and lack of tact. St Denis was equally domineering and single-minded but more radical and ruthless in his technique: he was 'a perfectionist, a martinet, cruel and charming' who hypnotised the actors 'like a rabbit in front of a stoat', believing that they had to be 'stripped mentally and, more or less physically, so that he could build us up into actors and actresses to his own moulding'.[73]

As part of this method, not because of the heat, St Denis told the actors and actresses at the read-through of *Noah* to wear bathing suits for the first rehearsal. There were murmurs of dissent and the threat of a strike so St Denis restricted this instruction to those actors and actresses playing the roles of the beasts. As a result, on the first day of rehearsals, Alec would have enjoyed the spectacle of young Merula Salaman in her bathing suit, crawling on her hands and knees up to John Gielgud, who was dressed immaculately in a dark suit and trilby hat, place a paw on his shoulder and then roar into his face.

The costumes and animal masks for *Noah*, designed by the Motleys, were unusually heavy: in the heat, the dressing-rooms began to smell like a zoo. George Devine came out in boils and Alec became fed up with his role as the Wolf. Still aged only twenty-two and low in the hierarchy of players, he befriended the younger of the two Salaman sisters, Merula, who was the same age and of similar standing. He was touched by her air of innocence and reassured, perhaps, when during one performance, to pass the time as the animals waited beneath the stage with their masks off, the actress Eve Roberts pranced around the group, tapping one actress after another on the shoulder and singing quietly: 'You're not a virgin, you're not a virgin,' until she came to Merula Salaman when she stopped, pointed to her, and said: 'You *are* a virgin' – at which everyone laughed.[74]

The English staging of *Noah,* partly because of an unsatisfactory American translation of Obey's text, was less successful than the original production by the *Compagnie des Quinze*. However, it was followed at the New Theatre in the autumn of 1935 by a second Gielgud production of a Shakespeare play – *Romeo and Juliet* – with the radical contrivance that Gielgud and another up-and-coming actor,

Laurence Olivier, should alternate in the roles of Romeo and Mercutio. Peggy Ashcroft and Edith Evans, both of whom Gielgud had directed in the same play at Oxford, played Juliet and the Nurse respectively, and Alec was cast in the small but significant role of the Apothecary – an old man and therefore a new challenge for an actor of twenty-two.

With the scrupulous courtesy he was to show throughout his life, Alec had again written to Gielgud from 62 Pembridge Villas in Notting Hill Gate on 8 August 1935:

> Just a brief formal note to thank you immensely for having me in 'Noah'. It was a lovely production to be connected with and I am most grateful for the work.
>
> And you will swear at me as much as you want in 'Romeo' rehearsals, won't you? I'm an awful fool and take ages to do anything anyone wants! I'm not a very gay or happy person by nature but I find the confidence you have in me a great source of happiness. I felt I'd like to write that – it's one of those things which mean a lot to me but are hard to speak.[75]

Despite poor notices after the first night for Olivier as Romeo, which put Olivier into a rage, Gielgud's *Romeo and Juliet* was a great success, running at the New Theatre for 189 performances and then going on a triumphal tour.

Alec, watching Laurence Olivier from the wings, formed a mixed opinion of his personality and performance:

> We all thought he looked and behaved like the leader of a dance band. But his Romeo was as arresting and beautiful as his Mercutio was vulgar and gimmicky. Perhaps many of us were prissy and too adoring of John to value Larry's qualities fully. I remember the sniggers that went round when he said, during a rehearsal I think, of the procession at George V's jubilee, 'Jill (Esmond) and I had a wonderful view of the whole corsage.'
>
> Looking through a Shakespeare play he must have deliberately sought

out one particular, and often obscure line and given it extraordinary emphasis . . . His 'I defy you, stars' in Romeo was memorable.[76]

Alec's own performance did not go unnoticed: 'There was a goodly drawing by Mr Alec Guinness of the Apothecary,' wrote Alan Dent in the *Manchester Guardian*.

After directing *Noah* for Gielgud, Michel St Denis remained in England to found the London Theatre School with George Devine and Glen Byam Shaw. Alec enrolled and, at the same time as playing in *Romeo and Juliet*, attended classes. With its first premises at 14 Beak Street, the school offered training not just to drama students, but also to young actors already at work in the profession. Alec was in this latter category and paid fees of £1 a week. Both Devine and Byam Shaw, who normally smoked cigarettes, began to puff at a pipe like Michel St Denis, 'and I maintained that for a time they all spoke with French accents'.[77]

Though Alec would quietly mock the St Denis obsession with mime, and sometimes resented his domineering technique – 'a rape of unformed talent' – he later recognised the defining moment in his understanding of acting came when St Denis demonstrated to Marius Goring, during a rehearsal of Chekhov's *The Cherry Orchard*, that his noiseless gym shoes were actually squeaking as demanded by the stage directions. 'From then on I was in love with the idea of trying to exercise a touch of magic on an audience, of persuading people to see and hear what wasn't there.'

Alec's chance to show that he had mastered this technique came in May 1936, when he was given a very small role in another prestigious production with John Gielgud, *The Seagull*, also by Anton Chekhov. Alec understudied Stephen Haggard who played Constantin and had a walk-on part as a workman. One of the tasks of the workman was to draw the curtains of the outdoor stage in Act I. This became the object of a wager over lunch between Peggy Ashcroft and her then husband, the director, Theodore Komisarjevsky. Komisarjevsky insisted that Alec had pulled a rope to open the curtains; Ashcroft that he had merely mimed it. Ashcroft won her bet: there was no rope. Alec had worked his magic, persuading Komisarjevsky to see something that was not there.

Theodore Komisarjevsky was, after Gielgud and St Denis, the third important influence on Alec as a young actor. He was Russian, the son of a princess and an opera singer; his sister, Vera Komisarjevskaya, had been one of the most celebrated actresses and producers in Russia prior to the 1917 Revolution. Komis, as he came to be called, had directed both the Imperial and State theatres in Moscow, bridging the Russian Revolution, but emigrated to London in 1919. There, in a small theatre in Barnes, he pioneered English-language productions of Chekhov, recruiting John Gielgud to play Tusenbach in *Three Sisters* in 1926. He had radical ideas about the theatre comparable to Copeau's: the sets of the *Macbeth* he staged in 1933 were made of aluminium.

Komis was a notoriously difficult man – moody, violent, depressive, dynamic, ruthless – and a compulsive seducer of women. Like St Denis, he believed in puncturing the vanity of actors and exploited what he regarded as their perverse exhibitionism, 'the desire to exhibit themselves bodily and a neurotic desire to put *le coeur a nu*'; and the actors, it seems, loved him for it. 'He made me realise that to be an actor is to be a perfectionist,' Peggy Ashcroft said of him later in her life; and Gielgud claimed, rather unconvincingly, that it was Komis who made him feel that 'I need no longer worry whether I was moving gracefully or looking handsome . . . Instead, I must try to create a character utterly different from myself, and then behave as I imagined the creature would behave, whose odd appearance I suddenly saw in the looking glass.'[78]

Like Copeau, Komisarjevsky had only contempt for the 'plasterboard and paint' of the conventional theatre and, despite making his name on the back of Chekhov, regarded playwrights as mere adjuncts to the art of theatre. 'The art of the Theatre is essentially an art of actors and *régisseurs*, and not of writers. Perhaps, from the point of view of *les hommes de lettres* the "unliterary" Theatre is an inferior art, nevertheless, it is the only genuine form of theatrical art.'[79]

Komisarjevsky's political views were as provocative as those on the theatre. 'The political doctrines of Mussolini, Lenin, Stalin and Hitler,' he wrote, 'are the only ones in our time that have genuine idealistic foundations, a definiteness of aim and a constancy of purpose, all of which were so utterly lacking under the so-called democratic regimes.'[80] Then as now, the public was prepared to indulge the extreme views of thespians and Komis, while married to Peggy Ashcroft, was welcomed into the homes of English friends, including that of the Jewish Michel Salaman, father to Susy, the established choreographer, and Merula the aspiring young actress.

eight

The Salamans were an unusual family. Chattie Salaman, the mother of Susy and Merula, was a Wake, claiming direct descent from the Saxon nobleman, Hereward the Wake – the hero of Charles Kingsley's novel of that name. Michel Salaman, their father, came from a family of Ashkenazi Jews called Solomon which had moved from Spain to Holland in the sixteenth century, and from Holland to England in 1870. Meyer Solomon, who made this move, changed his name to Salaman and made a fortune importing ostrich feathers from South Africa – ostrich feathers then being an expensive accoutrement for the well-dressed woman. The family flourished in their adopted country. Michel's mother had had fourteen children and, fed up with thinking of names for them, called them after the addresses where she was living when they were born: thus one son was called Redcliffe after Redcliffe Square; another Elgin after Elgin Crescent; a third Euston after Euston Square.

The family wealth was large enough to provide for all: in 1910 each

son inherited around half a million pounds – a substantial fortune at
the time which enabled the children to do as they pleased. Redcliffe
Salaman became a botanist and wrote the definitive book on the
potato while Michel, Merula's father, decided to become a painter. He
went to the Slade School where he became friends with the young
Augustus John, to whom he lent twenty pounds; stayed with him at
Victoria House, Tenby; sold him the caravan in which he had spent his
honeymoon for thirty pounds; went on holiday with him in France but
was shocked by his womanising; and cooled off the young genius
when he made a pass at his wife.[81]

This wife, Chattie Wake, a little older than Michel, had also been
a student at the Slade. Her father's family, with its impressive lineage,
had a large estate in Northamptonshire, Corteen Hall. They were,
according to one Wake cousin, Lois Lang-Sims, 'a county family of
monumental social complacency'[82] whose initial opposition to their
daughter's marriage to a Jew was overcome only when they learned
the size of his fortune. Moreover, as a young man Michel Salaman did
his best to prove wrong the poet, Humbert Wolfe, who once told
Alec that, 'You can't be an artist, a country gentleman *and* a Jew.'[83]
Michel was the Master of the Exmoor Hunt, and had his portrait
painted in full hunting kit by Augustus John, but he soon gave up his
calling as a painter because his talent was so paltry beside that of his
friend.

Michel persuaded Chattie Wake, when they married, to do the
same. As Merula wrote in her memoir of her childhood and early
life:

> He managed to stop her painting. Augustus John was the hero of his
> life, and no one should paint who wasn't a genius. He gave up himself
> when he left the Slade, and he couldn't bear to see Mummy continuing
> her work. He says he was jealous, because she was more talented than
> he, but I think he really couldn't stand her being content with her own
> modest gift with no ambition to be a great artist. It was a very
> destructive attitude.[84]

Instead of devoting their lives to painting, Michel and Chattie invested their creativity in their family life. They bought a large house in Surrey called Ruckmans with a farm, horses, dogs, housemaids, a cook and, of course, children. Lois Lang-Sims, Merula's cousin who often stayed at Ruckmans as a child, had fond memories of her Uncle Michel:

> . . . whose strong and enormously attractive personality had dominated the circle of family and friends in the kindly old house, smelling in summer of a multitude of flowers and always of a particular kind of beeswax, where as a child I had spent six months sharing a governess with my cousins Merula and Little Chat. The rest of my mother's family had invariably referred to Ruckmans with an odd mingling of envy, affection, slight disapproval – and a certain awe. Ruckmans was an alien world, bohemian, Jewish, continuously being invaded by artists, actors and others of a type not generally to be associated with the name of Wake . . .[85]

Michel and Chattie Salaman had six children. The eldest was Susy, then came Euston or Eusty, named after Michel's childless brother who had led Michel to believe that he would leave his fortune to his namesake but did not; the third, Michael or Mikey; then three daughters – Jill, Merula and Chattie, known as 'Little Chattie'. Little Chattie was the best looking and, together with Virginia and Vanessa Bell, was the model for a mural painted by Duncan Grant on a church near Lewes. All the children had frizzy red hair. The Salamans had mostly married into other Jewish families such as the Cohens and Seligmans; but Michel and Chattie were emphatically secular and raised their children as atheists. No prayers were allowed in the nursery.

Michel Salaman, like his sons, was short and broad-shouldered but very fit – it was said that he could keep up with the horses on foot. Every weekday he would go up to an office near the British Museum in London to administer his properties and portfolio of investments; it had a comfortable leather sofa and the family would use it as a depot for their shopping. He lunched every day at the Athenaeum.

Big Chattie, his wife, remained at Ruckmans. She was, in the words of Eusty's future wife, Mary Alexander, 'a wonderful, awful woman – a tigress in defending her children'. When Alec first met her, he thought she was the most beautiful woman he had ever seen. She was unpredictable with her children – sometimes affectionate, sometimes remote. Her great interest, once Michel had persuaded her to give up painting, was the garden: 'Her scent,' wrote Merula, 'was midge repellant.' Big Chattie showed an aristocratic disdain for convention: 'One suffered agonies,' Merula remembered, 'having to hold her horse out hunting while she squatted behind a tuft of grass, the whole field galloping by; and Mummy with her eyes shut, convinced that no one could see her . . . She drove a car as if she was riding in the Grand National, every other car was a rival to be passed at all costs. She would urge it on, rocking backwards and forwards and shouting at it as if it were a horse; if she had had a whip she would have beaten it'.[86]

Merula was left to run wild in her early childhood, playing in the fields and barns with 'Kitten' Wake, a cousin who lived in the Bailiff's cottage and Betty, Billy and Nutty Elwes who lived two miles away at Oakdale Farm. She became something of a tomboy. 'I never thought of myself as a girl, I was a sort of nothing. I certainly didn't want to be a girl, or a boy either, I was just me.' Her human affections took second place to her love for her dog Sally and her pony Chloe. Among her siblings, she was fondest of Eusty 'because he was glamorous and gay'. The most influential member of the family was Susy, the Salamans' eldest child. 'She was head girl at school and organised us and cultivated a Family Mystique. She thought we were all geniuses. She produced us in plays and ballets, and made all the costumes and scenery.'

At the age of four, when Michel had returned from the trenches at the end of World War I, Merula had taken against him, stubbornly refusing to obey him until 'he picked me up . . . and carried me upstairs to his dressing-room and beat me with a hunting crop. I don't think he hurt me but after that there was no more trouble between us.

He went right up to the top of the list and stayed there.' Merula in turn became her father's favourite: she was 'Daddy's pet'.

Merula's education began with a governess that she and Little Chattie shared with the Elwes girls, and included dancing classes at neighbours', the Piggott Browns of Ockley Court. When she was fourteen, she went to a boarding school, Heron's Gill, where she did well in her School Certificate exams but her particular talent was in the handling of horses. On leaving school, she went to work at a riding school run by a Major Faudel Phillips. The work was so hard and the pay so poor that her mind turned to the stage. 'To earn a living as an actress, it seemed to me, you didn't have to be all that good at it.' Her sister Susy's fiancé, Marius Goring, gave her an introduction to Michael MacOwan, the director of the Old Vic School, who gave her a place. To the irritation of the other students who had been there before her, Merula was chosen for a walk-on part as a lady-in-waiting to Queen Gertrude in Henry Cass's production of *Hamlet*, and in the summer of 1934 she was offered the part of the Tiger in *Noah*.

While in *Noah*, Merula came under the spell of Michel St Denis and left the Old Vic to enrol in his London Theatre School. After its first year at 14 Beak Street, the school moved to premises in Islington where there were proper rehearsal rooms, dressing-rooms and a small theatre. The Motleys designed uniforms for the pupils – short shorts for the young men that 'exposed their knobbly knees' and thick, grey sleeveless tunics for the girls with divided skirts that Merula found 'exceptionally unbecoming'. Marius Goring taught them Shakespeare, George Devine, comedy, while Michel St Denis reserved Chekhov and the Greek tragedies for himself. The author Antonia White lectured on Greek myths and the historian Richard Southern on the history of theatre. The ethos of the school was puritanical: St Denis talked about his training as 'the work' as if it were some quasi-religious mission, despised the commercial theatre, and held the cult of theatrical 'stars' in contempt – though Merula was to discover, 'when turned out into the hard cold world of reality that Michel was as enamoured of stars as anyone else'.[87]

At the London Theatre School Merula formed a circle of new friends from very varied backgrounds. There was Marriott Longman, a member of the publishing family whose father co-founded Darton, Longman and Todd; Pierre Lefèvre, the son of a French engineer posted to London by a French cable company; John Blatchley, whose parents were music-hall performers from South London; and Mary Alexander who began going out with Merula's brother Eusty, then studying architecture at the RIBA. Merula's younger sister, 'Little' Chattie, also enrolled in the school; and, of course, Alec was part of this gang.

nine

In the autumn of 1936, Alec broke the link with John Gielgud for the first time in his professional career. He was summoned by Lilian Baylis to work at the Old Vic at the request of the dynamic young Irish theatre director, Tyrone Guthrie – the fourth and last of the significant influences on Alec's early career. Guthrie, sacked by Baylis in 1934 for his extravagance in spurning the old costumes stored away in the Old Vic greenroom and his insistence on casting stars, now returned to the Old Vic. He cast Alec as Boyet in *Love's Labour Lost*, Le Beau in *As You Like It*, and Old Thorney in *The Witch of Edmonton* by John Ford. Alec resumed the role of Osric, but also played Reynaldo, in *Hamlet*, Sir Andrew Aguecheek in *Twelfth Night* and the Duke of Exeter in *Henry V*. When the company went to Denmark to stage *Hamlet* at Elsinore, he was Reynaldo, the Player Queen, and Osric yet again.

Alec was paid seven pounds a week and, as well as playing so many minor roles, he understudied Laurence Olivier's Hamlet. He was now able to study the techniques of major actors other than Gielgud and

Olivier – among them Ernest Milton and Michael Redgrave; and to learn from the direction of the forceful Tyrone Guthrie. But it was also here that he suffered his first setback.

Alec had been cast as Mr Sparkish in a lavish production of *The Country Wife* and was rehearsing with the star, Ruth Gordon, playing Mrs Pinchwife, when she laid aside her script and said to Guthrie, 'I can't act with this young man. Would you get another actor for the part, please?' Alec was laid off for the next six weeks and, instead of receiving the forty-two pounds due under his contract, was fobbed off by Lilian Baylis with three 'dirty, crumpled one pound notes'.

More valuable compensation came, however, from Edith Evans who, upon hearing of what had happened, took him aside to say that, while he was perhaps not quite right for the part, Gielgud believed in him, Guthrie believed in him and *she* believed in him, and that in ten years' time he would have his name in lights.

In the autumn of 1937, Alec returned to work in Gielgud's company for a season of plays at the Queen's Theatre. He was cast as Aumerle and the Groom in *Richard II*, directed by Gielgud himself; Snake in Sheridan's *The School for Scandal* directed by Guthrie; Fedotik in Chekhov's *Three Sisters* directed by Michel St Denis in January 1938, and as Lorenzo in *The Merchant of Venice*. Here he saw more of Merula who, having graduated from the London Theatre School, had been engaged by Gielgud as an understudy and to play minor roles. In *The School for Scandal* she played Mrs Sneerwell's maid, and every evening before the curtain went up she and Alec would dance to the music of the overture.

Merula had come out from the shadow of her sister Susy and was gradually gaining a reputation as an exceptional actress: though it was a non-speaking role, her performance as Mrs Sneerwell's maid drew a compliment from the theatre critic of the *News Chronicle*, Alan Dent. Off-stage, she retained an air of invulnerable innocence: she would walk back to her lodgings in Islington alone after the performance, and sit in pubs and rough bars where she was the only woman, to read a novel when she had time off. But her feelings of affection for Alec had grown beyond friendship and she welcomed his attentions. Alec began taking her to supper on Friday nights after the show and always presented her with a gardenia bought from a gypsy lady outside the theatre.

Though now living in a milieu where those around him slipped in and out of sexual liaisons – heterosexual and homosexual – with ease, Alec was clearly apprehensive about a love affair with this innocent young woman. 'Before I married Merry,' he was to write to his future sister-in-law, Chattie, 'sex . . . took up and stole a lot of my imagination. Supposing one's sexual life was a fiasco and on on.'[88] Faced with doubts about his own competence as a lover, and Merula's innocence, their relationship had hitherto remained chaste or, as Merula termed it, 'platonic'. They were assumed by Merula's parents to be no more than close friends. Big Chattie withdrew her objection to Merula going alone with Alec to Iceland when Michel assured her that Alec was no more of a threat to Merula's virtue than Billy Chappell, a 'pansy' young ballet dancer who was a friend of the Salamans.[89]

The holiday in Iceland was cancelled but they took a brief trip to Bruges in the winter of 1937–38. The course of true love did not run smoothly. Alec was exceptionally touchy, and fiendishly jealous of a young man called Alastair Bannerman who had taken a fancy to Merula; but from the very first it would seem that Merula was able to deal with his moods. Writing to Alec during the war, she recalled:

> . . . our first days – and all the exalted love I had for the Kings Cross Rd
> and the coal cart men on my walks to and from the Queen's. And your
> back view walking off from Percy Circus in a huff one evening and as
> I watched you go then I knew and knew that you loved me and I could
> have died for joy – though I didn't know why as I never dreamed that
> you would ever think of marrying me.[90]

Eventually Alec's attentions to Merula went beyond the gift of a gardenia. 'At a dress rehearsal of *The Merchant of Venice*,' wrote Merula in *Family Matters*, 'which went on till about three in the morning, after a lot of black-and-tan in the dressing-room, we found ourselves locked in one another's arms at the back of the stalls with smudged make-up and crumpled costumes'.[91]

Alec was now in love, and on the first night of *The Merchant of Venice* he invested the passion for Merula in his performance. 'Lorenzo . . .' wrote John Russell Taylor, 'is not a role anyone can make very much of – or so one would have thought. But it does contain in the last act some of Shakespeare's most exquisite poetry, introducing at last into this rather nasty tale of unpleasant people a touch of true romantic passion . . .'[92] Merula would like to have played Jessica, and thought that her Jewish blood would have made her especially credible as the daughter of Shylock, but the role went to Genevieve Jessell. But it was unquestionably Merula who, in her role as a lady-in-waiting, inspired Alec to give a performance which, in the view of the theatre critic of *The Times*, 'lifts the final scene to an unspectacular, meditative, star-struck beauty that takes the breath away'.[93]

Now Alec became a regular guest at Ruckmans, and also at Selsey on the Sussex coast where Big Chattie had commissioned Eusty to build his first house on the site of a beach hut belonging to the Salamans. Alec's attitude towards Merula's family was, and was to remain, ambivalent. He had had some experience of life in the country houses of the upper classes staying with his friends David Stewart and Sam Beazley, but the atmosphere at Ruckmans was something new. The talk was free and uninhibited, and the Salamans of both generations behaved as if they were unquestionably part of a social and cultural elite. Uneasy about his own standing in English society, and acutely embarrassed by his own lack of a background, Alec envied in Merula and her family the confidence that he himself lacked.

Alec also experienced for the first time at Ruckmans the rough and tumble of family life. David Stewart and Sam Beazley had both been without fathers or siblings, cosseted by their adoring mamas. Merula and her brothers and sisters were quite untamed, and the whole family not only relished violent quarrels about the most trivial things but were also quite pitiless in teasing both one another and their guests. The household was heavy with tensions. Merula's mother, Big Chattie, exasperated her rentier husband by professing to be a Communist and subscribing to the New Left Book Club. She also suspected Michel of having an affair with a ballet dancer, Varda, a frequent guest at the house. There was some rivalry between the siblings until, at Christmas 1935, the whole family was hit by a tragedy: Susy Salaman fell ill.

It was thought initially that she had suffered from jaundice: there had been an epidemic at Ruckmans caused, it was thought, by a dead rat found in the water tank. At first Susy seemed to recover, and returned to London where she was both choreographing and designing the scenery and costumes for a major ballet. However, when she came home for Christmas she complained about her erratic driving. She suffered from terrible headaches and kept dropping things and, finally, on New Year's Eve while Eusty and Chattie were at the Chelsea Arts Ball in London, she fell to the ground and could not move.

The next morning, Susy was taken to hospital in London. She was thought at first to have a brain tumour but after a hole had been bored into her head none was found. Instead, the diagnosis was of acute encephalitis – a virus that attacks and causes irreparable damage to the brain. Susy was taken back to Ruckmans and two nurses were engaged to take care of her. Marius Goring, who was engaged to marry her, wanted to go ahead with the wedding but Michel would not allow it: she was to remain an invalid in the care of her family for the next fifty-four years.

Given this catastrophe, Michel Salaman might have been upset at the thought that he might lose another daughter – his favourite – in a different way, but reassured that Alec was 'not the marrying kind', he raised no objection to the weekend in Bruges or, when in the summer of 1938 Alec and Merula, to earn extra money, went to teach drama classes at Hays Court, the exclusive girls' school that had so peremptorily rejected Merula as a pupil. Michel was always hospitable to talented artists, and Alec's reputation as an up and coming actor made up for his lack of an identifiable background. The only doubt that Michel expressed about Alec was about his age: he could not believe that the already balding young man was only twenty-four. He told Merula that Alec must have lied to her about his age.

However, nothing said by her father or anyone else could affect Merula's feeling for Alec: she was utterly in love with him but never dreamed that he might want to marry someone who 'still felt like a frumpy red-faced schoolgirl'; and so, when he proposed over supper at the Criterion one Friday night, she was struck dumb. 'I could only gape like a fish on dry land,' she later recalled:

> . . . and clutch your hand and say, 'Oh Alec,' and you were so worried and puzzled and looked so unlike ever being a husband – O my darling angel – it gives me a pain in the pit of my stomach to think of it – it was all a myrical [sic] – how did we manage it, what have I ever had that you should have thought of marrying or loving me – only my love for you, and you didn't even know I had it then. I did love you and do and ever will with all my soul. I was head over heals [sic] in love with you in a moment from then on. Oh yes and we kissed in the taxi and my new hat went all askew, and I told Chattie as soon as I got home . . .[94]

Wholly given over to her happiness, Merula lay on the carpeted floor kicking, and shouting, 'He's asked me to marry him, he's asked me to marry him!'

An unpleasant shock awaited her the next day: a note from Alec to say that he had changed his mind. Alec had lost his nerve – not because he doubted his love for Merula, but because he lacked confidence in his ability to make her happy. 'If anyone has been less fit to marry than I was,' he wrote to Chattie three years later:

> . . . or more unworthy, or took a greater risk with his wife's happiness than I took, I'll eat my hat . . . That seems to me the *point*, from the man's

view. The awful vision and misgiving about his wife's happiness. I never faced up to it, personally. I *saw* it and tried to get out of my love for Merry – tried to break it up – and eventually quite callously married her because I loved her. We both, I believe, were as frightened as hell . . .[95]

Whatever delicate qualms of conscience may have accounted for this jilting, they were not appreciated by Merula who wrote him a scathing letter ('whatever sort of letter did I write you? How shaming it is, it makes me blush'), and when she got to the Queen's Theatre she and Alec passed one another in a cold silence on the stairs.

Merula's fury was compounded when she got to her dressing-room and found, on her make-up table, a box of face paints as a gift from Alec – 'That bloody box of paints!' She fell on the floor and had a fit of hysterics. Her dresser, alarmed, summoned Alec. He came and calmed her, reassured her and threw his misgivings to the wind. He loved her. He wanted to marry her. The wedding would go ahead.

When they announced their engagement to the company and their friends, they gave 'a lovely party where Richard Ainley gave me the silk handkerchief'. Afterwards, Merula recalled, 'we spent the night at your room and you slept on the floor and I saw you shave for the first time – and we crept out in the early morning and had breakfast in a Lyons and then went on the Serpentine'.[96]

Among their theatrical friends, George Devine was at first taken aback – 'Think! Nonsense!' – but then came round to the idea. Edith Evans told Alec that he was making a mistake: 'You're an artist! You shouldn't marry!' And Michel St Denis made the same objection to Merula: she had the potential to be a great actress and marrying Alec would blight her career. Among the Salamans, the only recorded reaction was that of Merula's mother, Chattie, who, when told of the engagement, exclaimed, 'And the cook's given notice!' before falling on the floor in a faint.

On 19 June 1938, the night before Alec and Merula were to be married, Michel and Chattie Salaman gave a lavish party at Ruckmans. The gardens were decorated with fairy lights and students from the London Theatre School performed a masque on the terrace. The celebrated Carl Dolmetsch gave a recital on his recorder; George Devine and Marius Goring fooled about in masks while Merula's brother Mikey who was studying painting in Paris, suddenly appeared with the French actor, Auguste Bovério, in the costumes of characters from the *commedia dell'arte*.

Upstairs, her sister Chattie examined Merula's trousseau and said that the pink spots on the nightdress that she had bought for her wedding night would make Alec think that she had measles. Big Chattie took Merula aside to prepare her: 'You know, this sex business isn't all it's cracked up to be.'

Below, Alec felt ill-at-ease. His mother had not been invited, nor were there any of his friends from Arks Publicity. It was a Salaman affair. 'I hardly knew a soul there and I felt I was disapproved of.' He also felt 'humiliated and hurt' because his wedding present to Merula had been upstaged by the gift from a rich cousin:

> I gave Merula a dreary fibre suitcase. I was very put-out to find Dennis Cohen had given her a smart white leather hatbox and matching case. Susy gave us a pretty ivory clock, which never worked decently; Chattie (mère) ivory brushes in a tray; Michel the Augustus John pastel of an Irish peasant woman in a red dress. Edith Evans provided some fiddly soup cups and the Redgraves a handsome eiderdown. And Michel St Denis *The Oxford Book of 17th Century Verse*. Merula gave me a Leica camera, which got dropped over the side of a rowing-boat on Lake Como the following year.[97]

The next morning, 20 June, Alec and the Salamans drove from Ruckmans to the Register Office in Redhill. Alec was nervous and self-conscious.

On the wedding morning I kept dropping my hat. Just as we were leaving, Bovario (who had come over from France with Mikey, whom

I'd never met before) shook hands vigorously with me over a rose bush and thorns pierced both the palms of our hands. I remember I wore a grey suit with a white chalk stripe.[98]

He had also forgotten to bring any money and had to borrow two shillings and sixpence from the taxi driver to pay for the marriage licence.

Merula wore an outfit designed by the Motleys – a dark grey two-piece suit with an embroidered design on one shoulder of their two initials, and a round straw hat. The ceremony was delayed because Big Chattie had gone off in search of a lavatory. She returned and Alec and Merula were married: Michel Salaman and Juliet O'Rorke, a friend of the Salamans, were their witnesses. When the moment came to sign the register, Merula was so nervous that her signature became a mere squiggle.

The same fleet of cars drove the party back to Ruckmans where, after lunch, they cut the wedding cake on the lawn flanked by 'Spenny and the maids'. The bride and bridegroom then left for Croydon airport and flew to Dublin for a honeymoon in Ireland.

part two

the sweet prince

ten

The first two nights of Alec and Merula's married life were spent at the Gresham Hotel in Dublin at a cost of ten pounds. With only twelve pounds left to pay for the planned hiking holiday in Donegal, the young couple took up an offer from Tyrone and Judy Guthrie to stay in Anna-ma-kerrig, their estate in County Monaghan.

They were met at the station by the Guthries: the immensely tall Tony – the diminutive used for Tyrone – with his close-cropped hair and moustache, and Judy, also tall with her long black hair tied up in a bun and so like Tony that it seemed to Alec that they might have been twin brother and sister. Alec and Merula were driven by their hosts to their large Victorian mansion 'with a red turret and no electricity' where they felt themselves to be in a Chekhov play. 'At any moment one expected to encounter the Irish equivalents of Madame Ranevsky, Trofimov, Constantin, the Three Sisters or Uncle Vanya.'[99]

While Merula was left to wonder at the eccentricity of the Guthrie household, Alec and Tony retired to the nursery to prepare for a project that Guthrie had proposed and Alec had accepted before they had left London. This was that Alec should return to the Old Vic that autumn and play the title role in a modern-dress production of *Hamlet*.

This was an extraordinary gamble for Guthrie to take on a twenty-four-year-old actor who until then had played only minor roles. It was not just Alec's youth and inexperience, but the comparisons that would inevitably be made between this skinny young man, prematurely bald and with prominent ears, and those matinée idols who had so recently played Hamlet – John Gielgud and Laurence Olivier. However, Guthrie felt that he could do it, and Alec had no intention of letting this opportunity pass him by: what he lacked in confidence he made up for with ambition.

Also, with the intuition of an inspired director, Guthrie sensed that there was something in Alec's psyche that would animate his performance. Like Komisarjevsky, Guthrie's work with actors had persuaded him that their very talent came from a psychological flaw. 'I've had plenty of time to wonder why people take up the theatre as a profession,' he was to write some years later:

> Some, it is perfectly true, want to show off, but it is my belief that these are a minority. Far more people go on the stage as a hiding-place, as an escape from the real world, which they find unsatisfactory and feel powerless to change, into a world of make-believe where they can be someone else, an assumed character over whose nature and environment they have some control.[100]

Guthrie knew enough about Alec and his upbringing to recognise a potential Hamlet. He was, at the time, impressed by the ideas of the Freudian psychoanalyst Ernest Jones and, when he asked Alec to say in one word what *Hamlet* was about, had provided the answer himself: 'Mummy'. By and large, Guthrie was more interested in the staging of a play than in the acting. Jehane West, who had worked with him, felt that 'he wasn't good with actors. He had wonderful ideas for the play but he couldn't help you if you couldn't help yourself'.[101] Now, in the nursery at Anna-ma-kerrig, when they discussed how Alec should play the prince, he grabbed at anything the actor suggested. Alec would later claim that he made only two significant contributions to the production – the tapping of his fingers on an upturned drum at the opening of the third act, and – which would seem to vindicate Guthrie's perception – the explosion of misogyny when he turns on Ophelia, subjecting her to the fury provoked by the treachery of his mother, beginning 'Get thee to a nunnery. Why wouldst thou be a breeder of sinners?'[102]

Merula was shaken, she later told Matthew, by the vitriol in Alec's performance when Hamlet remonstrates with his mother, Gertrude. She was not altogether comfortable staying with the Guthries: her attempt to return their hospitality by digging out the 'refuse about four inches deep' on the kitchen floor had only annoyed Judy Guthrie, who called her 'Little interfering Miss Bourgeois Missy'.

To start off the next phase of their honeymoon, Alec and Merula were driven by the Guthries to Dunnow in Donegal from where they set off hiking across the peat bogs with packs on their backs. It was very wet and Alec, fastidious and urban, was not happy. They spent the night in cheap hotels or bed-and-breakfasts and sleeping in '. . . peculiar beds. Those that threw one apart and those that threw one on top of one another'. The last straw came when they were shown to a room 'where there was a large, iron bedstead with a straw mattress and sheets that were greasy and grey. We peered under the bed: there was a china pot; on examination it was full to the brim.' They crept downstairs, hoping to slip out without being noticed but 'the villainous-looking characters' who were seated around the peat fire all rose up and followed them out onto the moor.

They bolted, and ran until they found a railway line where a train stopped when they hailed it and took them to Belfast, 'entertained all the way with songs and a mouth-organ and a lot of merry chatter'. From Belfast they returned to England and spent the rest of their honeymoon 'in luxury in John Gielgud's cottage in Essex which he lent us, plus cook and his sweet Schnauzer bitch'.[103]

Back in London, Alec and Merula went to live in a maisonette in Warwick Gardens belonging to Helen and Jimmy Beaumont, neighbours of the Salamans. They furnished it with rugs, china, cutlery, and battered antiques bought at the Caledonian market for forty pounds. Alec began rehearsing *Hamlet* at the Old Vic: Merula missed Ruckmans. When she had first come to London to study drama, she had carried a small clod of earth from the garden at Ruckmans in her pocket. Now she brought her dog Sally to town; but Sally hated the crowds and the traffic. She had diarrhoea, first on a traffic island then in Woolworths and was sent back to Ruckmans. To console her, Alec bought Merula a dormouse which they called Trotwood – the first of their many pets. Trotwood was no happier than Sally and so followed her to Ruckmans 'where he was put on the radiator for the winter and was cooked'.[104]

Before opening in London, the Old Vic company went on tour and staged the plays for the new season at a drama festival in the small spa town of Buxton in Derbyshire.

Now, for the first time, we have letters that express Alec's feelings for his young bride:

> Oh my love. I wish I was a poet who could write to you in the way you should be written to. I keep seeing you about the place here – peopling Buxton with hundreds of Merulas and then I give praise to God that there is only one – just one – and that I love her as much as my poor old heart can ever love – oh! I shall burst. What a good thing we didn't have to go through a long separation before we married. I couldn't have done it. I love you even more now but the parting is more exquisite and sweetly painful because there are no doubts as to when you'll be back with me and not the least doubt of the wisdom of it all. Good morning my bride – look after yourself . . .[105]

The fears that his conjugal life might turn out to be a fiasco had proved chimerical: as he was to write to Chattie, 'a short time, and faith, and love – and sex takes its rightful and simple place in the natural order of things'.[106] And though Alec would later say that, at the start of his married life, 'I was acutely self-conscious and I think probably ill at ease for several months, not used to sharing my life with anyone,' his reply to a letter from Merula suggests an intimacy equal to the happiest of young married couples.

> I liked what you said about Bach. I know very little of him. You must teach me and make me hear more. I can't wait for the home, when we can sit down on our Caledonian carpets and sprawl and listen to the gramophone and read books aloud and gaze at our model ships – and me look at you and touch you my love. And the hours of love making we can have my poppet – just you and me – oh its too exciting and heavenly.

Alec's expression of hope that they might soon have a baby – 'I . . . long for the day, don't you my darling, when we can have a horrid little cross between us' – was accompanied by an ink sketch of what he had in mind, one of many witty illustrations to his letters to his wife.

Alec was apprehensive as he embarked on such a major *professional* challenge, and his confidence that he could master the role of Hamlet was hardly bolstered when, bumping into John Gielgud in Piccadilly before the start of the tour, his former mentor had said, 'I can't think why you want to play big parts. Why don't you stick to those funny little men you do so well instead of trying to be important?'[107] Echoing Gielgud in a letter to Merula, he ridiculed his own ambition. 'Don't talk such rubbish about the possibility of me becoming a great man! I was pulling your leg the other evening about being a big actor – you mustn't *let* yourself think things like that even *half* seriously. I'm dreary No 1. my sweet and know myself only too well – I think I'm even lower than mediocre – no, perhaps I'm just about mediocre – and when a person's like that there's no hope. I shan't even be a "tinselly star".'

The fear of failure pushed him to promote Merula's prospects as an actress. 'I know I'm not going to make a success of this place. What the hell! You can do lots and lots of BBC jobs and take tiny tots riding and I'll do the domestic work and give a few bogus lessons in voice production.' There seemed no question but that her career was as important as his:

> You must work and work dear and not centre your life too much in me – because I have such faith in you. My faith in you as my wife is boundless and I *know* – know that you have a little something that none of my contemporaries have – a *little* bit of balance or unbalance that may easily make you a great woman of the theatre. You have such bigness in life as my sweet Merry – but don't neglect Miss Salaman sweetest – because she must be fostered and your funny aunt's letter about Ellen Terry may not be so funny as it should. Its* going to be a little humiliating for me to be known as Salaman's husband but believe me my darling I'm not joking when I say that. Your personality comes with a bang through everything you do – and I believe someone like you may be able to teach in your acting. People like me just act sillily and aren't artists at all but you have got to let what's in you grow – because its something infinitely exquisite and more difficult to control than my talents . . .[108]

Though a mood of pessimism about the future was now widespread in Britain – Hitler had annexed Austria that spring and was threatening to seize the Sudetenland from Czechoslovakia – Alec refused to accept that his hopes for their future might be thwarted by a war:

> We *must* go to beautiful places together my darling – and we must make and save money so we can – and of course there won't be any war – it's too stupid. People are stupid but they can't be as foolish as

---

*Alec tended to ignore the apostrophe in his letters and diaries.

that – we *must* rise and change the leaders of the country if they do –
I warn you I shall be an awful little nuisance to you if the silly buggers
do decide to fight. But they wont my darling so don't listen to those
dreary Londoners who get into a scare about everything. We have each
other and oh my love I love you. There's nothing else to say.

Alec was clearly unsettled by the prospect of war which, with his love
for Merula and the prospect of fathering a child, seems to have led to
some philosophical introspection. He was no longer quite as confident
in the atheism he had professed after being confirmed by the Bishop
of Lewes. 'God bless you Miss Fuzzy Hair and drop his good dew on
you and preserve you from bombs (they won't come anyway) – oh! I
should go mad – but madly mad within three seconds – no god
wouldn't do a thing like that. In all this instability I'm beginning to
believe in him again – aren't we humans weak.[109]

From these early letters we see emerge some of the qualities of Alec's
relationship with Merula that were to persist throughout their married
life: bossiness, combined with mild exasperation at her impracticality,
combined with an almost paternal solicitude for her welfare:

Have just sent you wire to get rid of carpenter. I've never heard of such
an absurd fraud . . . Really I never thought that a Jew like you could be
so weak! And the same goes for the gas people. They must stick to their
original estimate.

. . . you have to do the following with my *love*. 1. Eat! 2. Cross the roads
carefully!! 3. Enjoy yourself!!! 4. And write to me when you can and
when its not a bore to do so.

Alec also reveals an intolerance of those he felt did not come up to
his own high standards, among them the inhabitants of the
Derbyshire spa: 'I hate this place almost as much as I adore you,' he
wrote to Merula. 'The people are too tedious – their brain cavities

are the size of walnuts.' He was particularly irked by a young woman who composed sonnets about his performance and left them with gifts at the stage door. However, he had the company of the other players – Hermione Hannen, who played Ophelia, and her husband Anthony Quayle; Veronica Turleigh, whom he decided was 'one of the greatest, but *greatest* mathematicians in the country!' and, of course, Tony and Judy Guthrie. Merula paid a visit from London; so too did his old friend from Arks Publicity, Adolf Deys. John Gielgud's mother, the niece of the great Ellen Terry, was staying at the Palace Hotel. She stood him up for lunch but he took tea with her when she opened the swimming pool at the Palace Hotel: 'I found her first rate company and shall treasure the note she sent me excusing herself from lunch as the most perfect and delicious piece of Edwardian manners.' Alec also heard from John, her son, then performing in 'a low brow play' at the Theatre Royal in Newcastle: 'I suppose you are well in the throes. I shall come over one day and collect you for lunch while we are in Manchester. I hope you're happy and excited.'[110]

Before the first night of *Hamlet*, Alec received numerous telegrams wishing him luck – 'a sweet one from John "The readiness is all!" and some fifteen others'. Alec's performances as Hamlet, and as Bob Acres in Sheridan's *The Rivals*, were acclaimed by the audiences, but he was not won round to the bourgeois Buxtonians. 'People came round and raved to me – but Christ – the bulk of them might have been at a funeral. Oh! I hate the Buxtonians with a great hate & hate them, loathe and detest them.'[111]

The Old Vic's 1938–39 season opened in London with Pinero's sentimental comedy, *Trelawny of the 'Wells'* in which Alec appeared in the undemanding part of Arthur Gower. Then, in October, came the official first night of the long-awaited Tyrone Guthrie production of *Hamlet* in modern dress. Alec came on-stage dressed not in the somewhat threadbare pin-striped suit in which he had been married, and which he had been wearing when he had originally called on

Guthrie at the Old Vic to discuss the project earlier that year – his *only* suit, which Guthrie had thought fine for the role; but, for certain scenes, in a suit tailor-made in Savile Row at his own expense – the first but not the last of his sartorial extravagances. In the graveyard scene he wore a seaman's sweater and boots, and in the palace of Elsinore he wore the World War I dress uniform of his father-in-law, Michel Salaman.

The production was, by and large, a success. Guthrie's staging – particularly the carrying of open umbrellas by the mourners at Ophelia's funeral – was thought to work. Alec's playing of Hamlet divided the critics. Harold Hobson in the *Observer* wrote that he had 'never seen a better young Hamlet than this'. James Agate in the *Sunday Times* was more measured: in a prophetic appreciation of what was to become the salient feature of Alec's particular style, he called his interpretation 'non-acting'. 'This young actor is obviously not trying any of the things in Hamlet which are the ABC of the part. He attempts neither play of feature nor gesture. He rejects mordancy.'

Guthrie himself was later to write that, though he felt that Alec's 'youth, combined with rare intelligence, humour and pathos, realised a great deal of the part', he had lacked the authority 'to support a whole evening' (the play, uncut, ran for four hours) or 'give the tragedy its full stature'. Alec himself felt that he had failed to escape the influence of Gielgud's interpretation of Hamlet which he had observed from the wings night after night at the New: but it was a performance the memory of which lingered in the minds of those who saw it. Many years later, Joan Wyndham wrote to Alec:

I found this description of your modern-dress Hamlet in a 60 year old diary. I was then a stage mad teenager, at RADA . . . Extract: 'Little Alec Guinness played Hamlet and a lovely job he made of it. He was terribly thin and wasted away, with the queerest face, a lovely smile and ears like a young bat . . . He was very young, and unaffected. Not ranting and roaring, but moving, quiet realism – with touches of elfin humour, and at times, an unbearable pathos, as of something lost and bewildered. He had the quality of being able to stand still and yet arrest the attention. Slow unhurried moves, and then stillness. Nothing fussy or unnecessary.'[112]

Nor did the spleen he directed at Ophelia go unnoticed or un-remembered. Another friend, also a drama student at the time, wrote to Alec from retirement in Switzerland in 1991. He said that Alec had been:

> . . . the first famous actor I watched working on a great classical role and I can't forget the goose pimples that crawled up my arms and neck as I watched you – for the first time in a semblance of costume – playing the Ophelia scene. The full blast of your misogynistic rage astonished me. You were unrecognisable as the kind, gentle and reserved man I had so recently met. You were Hamlet and, of course, for me you have always remained the only Hamlet.[113]

More significant for Alec than the opinion of drama students was the praise from the masters of his profession. Charles Laughton, one of the actors Alec most admired, came to visit him backstage with his wife, Elsa Lanchester, and invited him back 'for a scrappy meal' in their Golden Square flat. Gielgud, too, even some years afterwards, would praise the achievement of his young protégé: 'I read some Keats on the air the other night for Eddie Sackville-West,' he later wrote to Alec, 'and we talked at some length about your Hamlet. I hope your ears burnt.'[114]

One backstage visitor – a small white-haired man dressed as an ordinary theatregoer – was to have a significant influence on Alec's later life. He introduced himself as the Rev. Cyril Tomkinson, the Vicar of All Saints in Margaret Street, which was the centre of High Church Anglicanism in the West End of London. He had come to point out that, when Alec crossed himself on-stage, he passed his hand horizontally from right to left to right when it should be from left to right. Subsequently, Alec accepted an invitation from the Rev. Tomkinson to lunch at the Oxford and Cambridge Club and found him 'witty, eccentric, rather old-maidish in a naughty way, and with an absorbing passion for Jane Austen and Dr Johnson'.[115]

eleven

In September 1938, while Alec was playing Hamlet at the Old Vic, the British Prime Minister, Neville Chamberlain had, with his French counterpart Daladier, reached an accommodation with Hitler and Mussolini in Munich whereby, in exchange for the ceding of the Sudetenland to Germany by Czechoslovakia, there would be 'peace for our time'.

Encouraged by this new mood of optimism, the British Council decided to send the Old Vic on a tour of Mediterranean countries – Portugal, Italy, Egypt, Greece and Malta. The company sailed on the SS *Alcantara* from Southampton on 20 January 1939, and crossed to Cherbourg. Merula went along with Alec. It was almost a second honeymoon: Alec would later recall standing on the deck that first night in Cherbourg 'with ALL those stars and the ship turning round in that black water and the mast making the stars tip over our heads and all the noises and the strangeness of it all . . .'[116]

The *Alcantara* arrived in Lisbon on 23 January where, as it was unloading, some of the Old Vic's scenery was lowered into the River Tagus. The company was booked into the Victoria Hotel but Alec and Merula took against it because it was 'horrid and chromium plated' so moved to the hotel next door. Both were excited by the sights and sounds of Lisbon – 'gay washing hanging out of windows, dirty dives, women and children with fishes on their heads screaming, birds singing in cages in every house'. But even Merula, less fastidious than Alec, was horrified by the squalor: 'we had to walk carefully – shit everywhere . . .' They took a train to Sintra: 'the station is disgusting, great lumps of gob all over the floor, and stinks. The train filthy and we were 1st Class.'

On 26 January the company performed *The Rivals* with Alec playing the country bumpkin Bob Acres. The auditorium, to Merula, was 'a glorious sight, everybody grandly dressed, everybody bowing to one another from the boxes, glittering diamonds, feather plumes, deliciously pretty theatre'. The performance was a success but the evening was spoiled for the liberal-minded Guinnesses by the celebrations going on in the city streets at the news of the fall of Barcelona to Franco's troops – 'cars hooting, wind blowing ladies skirts over their heads, crowds swelling . . . and swastikas flying on their car bonnets'.[117] 'We were in Lisbon when Barcelona fell,' Alec recalled over thirty years later, 'and the fascist goings on – burnings of effigies etc. – sickened us.'[118]

There were a number of official engagements, among them an 'awful, embarrassing' tea with the British Ambassador, and a reception at the Portuguese Ministry of Propaganda at which Merula felt 'embarrassed and uncomfortable' and returned to the hotel 'very drunk'. 'We don't like Lisbon, we don't like the Portuguese and we don't like the British in Lisbon,' Merula wrote in her diary. The latter she thought snobs.

The company sailed at the end of January for Marseilles, where they disembarked from the *Alcantara* and travelled by train to Italy to play in Milan, Florence and Rome. Guthrie's *Hamlet* in modern dress was a triumph. 'They are so struck with the production of *Hamlet,*' wrote Merula. 'They know nothing of modern methods and a co-ordinating company. Guthrie is becoming quite a God: they are terribly disappointed he didn't come and are amazed he is so young. They are amazed at the youthfulness of the company altogether.' In the absence of Tony Guthrie, Alec became the object of adulation. Anthony Quayle, one of the company, recalled, in his autobiography, how 'all over Italy the production of *Hamlet* and Alec's performance were acclaimed. People stood up and clapped when he walked into a restaurant; everywhere we were feted and entertained.'[119]

Such was Alec's success in the role that Mussolini himself, *Il Duce*, had issued an invitation for Alec to take tea in his box when he came to see the play in Rome; but his attendance was cancelled because of the death of the Pope.

Perhaps the most touching tribute to Alec's performance comes from a letter he received more than forty years later from a Contessa Marcella Pavolini, then living in Cortona. His Hamlet, she remembered, had been:

> . . . a marvellous experience, a revelation of the real, human, intelligent, and immensely unhappy Prince. You were so young, so helpless, so lost, among those worldly, stupid and selfish people, it made my heart ache to see you and to listen to you; I couldn't even get up from my seat, during the intervals, I trembled so much – and I was not a sensitive, emotional girl, but a woman forty years old.[120]

In mid-February the company sailed from Genoa to Alexandria. Alec and Merula took turns with a copy of *Gulliver's Travels* and Merula began to tire of their Old Vic companions. 'I know I am a half wit but I do think mental level of this co. is bottom – Alec seems a genius in comparison.' They were met in Alexandria by a Salaman cousin, Betty Grieves, and in Cairo by a Salaman uncle who 'crushed a £10 note into my hand, said "You'll need this" and then whisked us into a grand car and took us to our hotel.'

On the first night of *Hamlet* Alec felt that he was losing his voice. In Act IV Scene V, Tony Quayle, playing Laertes, ran on stage shouting,

'Where is the king?' then fell through the floor of the rostrum, rotten after its dip in the Tagus, which greatly amused the audience and the other actors – all, that is, except Alec who, Quayle wrote in his memoirs, 'was not best pleased to have his opening in Cairo so ruined, but he was generous and had forgiven me by the next day'.[121]

As always in a small expatriate community, the presence of interesting visitors from the home country led to a large number of social engagements. The Guinnesses were invited to lunch by the brother of Robert Graves. Afterwards, Alec complained that Merula had not behaved *comme il faut*. 'I didn't think I had spoken but A says I said something very stupid and I threw my food about quite a bit.' Alec went to lunch at the British Embassy without Merula where he 'ate off golden plates'. And a lifelong friendship sprang from a tea party to which they were taken by an expatriate English couple called Barnard.

Their host was the multi-millionaire, Chester Beatty, who had a blue and white tiled palace by the Pyramids with armed guards at the gate, and a great library with a notable collection of Arabic manuscripts although he only read Edgar Wallace. Staying with Chester Beatty, Merula wrote in her diary, was:

> . . . a nice old highbrow gentleman called Sydney Cockerell who tries to reform Mr C.B.'s reading by scattering Shakespeare in his way. He frightened the Barnards who thought him a very cross old thing . . . Mrs C.B., thin legs and dark glasses, fell heavily for Alec, thinks he is going to be a big actor and says she is going to dedicate a seat to him in the National Theatre which would cost her £100: much better give it to Alec. A. did his stuff and talked about the poverty of the Old Vic very eloquently, while Mrs C.B. talked to me about mosquitoes. Before we left Mr Cockerell gave Alec a paperback of *Twelfth Night*.[122]

Sydney Cockerell, formerly the curator of the Fitzwilliam Museum in Cambridge, was an omnivorous scholar, bibliophile and collector of famous friends.[123] Alec, though he was never unduly impressed by the famous in later life, was to pick up a number of Cockerell's traits: he was to ply his friends with books, flowers and fruit; he modelled his handwriting on Cockerell's italic script; when he came to keep a daily diary, he always recorded the weather, as did Cockerell (and Queen Victoria); and there is an echo of Cockerell's school-masterly tone in his letters to his wife in some of Alec's letters to Merula.[124] Clearly, Cockerell was impressed by Alec and hoped to add him to the list of his famous friends.[125]

The diary kept by Merula on the Old Vic tour reveals a hatred for the arrogance and snobbery of the British upper class. She was not a Communist fellow-traveller like her mother, and would always remain immensely proud of being a Salaman, but there remained enclaves in British society where a long lineage and cultural distinction did not make up for the misfortune of being born a Jew. Still smarting, perhaps, from being turned down flat for the exclusive girls' school, Hays Court, and feeling uncomfortable that she was not tall and blonde but short with fuzzy red hair, Merula suffered now in Cairo – as she was to suffer throughout her married life – at having to appear with Alec as his consort at those official functions that were a reward for his success. The Wolf from *Noah* had now become a lion, while the Tiger had not turned into a lioness but, rather, bristled like a hedgehog. 'Had my hair done and a manicure so as to be able to face the snobs at the Ambassador's garden party with a brazen front,' she records in her diary; but inevitably she found the party 'deathly': 'We were introduced to some young ladies who were so well bred their fingers melted in one's hand. One of them was too grand to speak at all and nearly too grand to stand. Left as soon as possible and fell into another big hate.'[126]

In mid-March 1939, Alec went to lunch with the Egyptian Prime Minister and afterwards met Merula at the swimming pool at Gezira. Merula thought she would show off her skill by doing a back dive off a high springboard. Alec 'could see she was crookedly aligned and called out to her not to do it. But she did and crashed her legs on the side of the pool. She was on crutches for weeks and I found it hard to forgive her.'[127]

Alec's reaction to Merula's accident shows the complexity of his feelings. On the surface, he behaved as one might expect of a husband: 'Poor Alec like a ghost hopping up and down saying "You're quite all right, cheer up, it's all right" and looking so frightened.' But, as he later described it to Merula, his principal emotion was 'a terrible anger that burned in me when you had your accident in Cairo. It made me sick. It was then that I knew exactly how deeply I loved and valued you.'[128] He hated Merula at that moment because she had exposed the one weak point in the otherwise impregnable defences that he had raised to protect himself from the suffering that he had endured as a child.

From Egypt, the Old Vic Company went to Greece, docking at Piraeus on 26 March. They played in Athens, then sailed for Malta. It was Good Friday and Alec and Merula tried to go to a service in a Catholic church there but found they were too late. They had attended an Orthodox service on Palm Sunday in Athens: whether or not this church-going was from folkloric curiosity, or a sign of that 'weakness' that Alec had confessed to Merula when writing from Buxton – the erosion of his atheistic certainties – is not clear. At midnight on the Saturday, while Merula remained in their hotel, Alec and Tony Quayle went to midnight Mass in Valetta, 'all charming and happy and very poor'.

Because Malta was then a British colony and a major naval base, much of the Old Vic's audience was composed of Navy personnel. In the middle of a performance of *Henry V* the word came that all leave was cancelled and half the audience left to return to their ships. One of the warships was HMS *Cossack*, whose captain, Daniel de Pass, was another cousin of Merula's. A small man with great charm, he invited Alec and Merula to lunch in the wardroom of the *Cossack* which they found decorated with paintings, including one by Matthew Smith and another by Matisse. Both Alec and Merula fell for the Navy. 'They all have lovely open honest faces and kind twinkly eyes,' Merula wrote in her diary. 'I think the Navy is WONDERFUL.' So, too, did Alec. 'Alec

has fallen for Dan, I knew he would, and we have both fallen for
Commander Brewer . . . They are real people and adore their work
and are generous and frank about one another – so different from the
Cairo Cocktail round.'[129]

twelve

The Old Vic tour of the Mediterranean, seen largely through Merula's eyes because it was Merula who kept a diary, was to affect Alec's still malleable character in a number of ways. It was already clear from the letters he wrote from Buxton that the young man, whose apparent vulnerability melted the hearts of the ladies in his audience, was not just ambitious but contemptuous of those, such as the Buxtonians, whom he thought fell short of the mark.

Merula, too, seethed with a hatred of those she felt condescended to her: and though Alec does not seem to have shared his wife's dislike of the British upper classes *per se*, his chief aspirations outside the theatre were not social but intellectual, which accounts for his immediate liking for Sydney Cockerell. Alec had great intellectual curiosity and did what he could to make up for the lack of a university education through voracious reading, not just of the great classic novels but of history and the history of ideas. 'PS V. important!' he bossily wrote to Merula in a letter from Buxton. 'Would you go to

Millers & Gill or Zwemmers in Shaftesbury Av and buy a copy of "Civilisation and its Discontents" by Trend (8/6d) [eight shillings and sixpence] and send it to me immediately.'[130]

Alec was less impressed by lunch with British Ambassadors than the lunch at his flat in Whitehall Mansions with George Bernard Shaw in the summer of 1939, to which Sydney Cockerell took him and Merula after their return to England; and at meeting the poet, Siegfried Sassoon, in the house of Glen Byam Shaw. But Alec was also drawn to men of action such as Daniel de Pass, and his brief experience of life in the Navy no doubt turned his mind towards service at sea in the war that seemed increasingly likely as Hitler annexed Bohemia and Moravia and began to prepare for an attack on Poland.

Alec was later to say that he was drawn to the role he played on his return to Britain and the Old Vic, Michael Ransom in *The Ascent of F6* by Christopher Isherwood and W.H. Auden because the character of Ransom, the leader of a mountaineering expedition in Tibet, had been based by the authors on T.E. Lawrence, 'Lawrence of Arabia', a man of action who was also an intellectual and whom Alec particularly admired. It was a tricky part, its lines written in a mixture of verse and prose; and Alec would later describe his portrayal of Ransom as 'priggish'; but the critics were impressed. 'In Mr Guinness's hands Ransom becomes not merely a great acting part, but one of the finest achievements of contemporary drama,' wrote Anthony Squire in the *News Chronicle*. W.A. Darlington told the readers of the *Daily Telegraph* that 'Alec Guinness brings to the playing of Michael Ransom a sense of concentration and integrity which belong to genius.' Audrey Williamson, in her *Theatre of Two Decades*, judged it 'undoubtedly Guinness's most forceful achievement before the war'.

In July 1939, Alec went to Scotland as a guest artist to play Romeo in *Romeo and Juliet* at the newly founded Perth Theatre Festival. Encouraged, no doubt, by the success of his Hamlet and knowing the play well, having acted the Apothecary to John Gielgud's Romeo,

Alec hoped that he could master another major Shakespearean role: but the psychological conditioning that had made him such fertile soil for the disturbed Hamlet made him wholly unsuited to the role of the uncomplicated Romeo. It was, judged John Russell Taylor, 'one of his few major professional errors . . . Romeo was not and never would be his role . . . it was just outside his range'.[131] Alec himself concurred. 'The worst Romeo ever to disgrace our boards was given by none other than me, *moi-meme*. It was to be seen, a bird of ill omen, in Perth during the summer of 1939.'[132] Yet even as Romeo he had his admirers. The Scottish actor, James Cairncross, who, though two years younger than Alec, played his father, greatly admired his performance: '. . . his rendering of the speech beginning "How oft when men are at the point of death have they been merry" still rings in my memory over the long years since I first heard him utter the words.'[133]

On 1 September 1939, Germany invaded Poland and Neville Chamberlain issued an ultimatum to the German government. Alec was then rehearsing Chekhov's *The Cherry Orchard* under the direction of Michel St Denis, playing the student Trofimov with a cast that included Edith Evans, Peggy Ashcroft, and Cyril Cusack as Firs.

On 2 September, the day after Chamberlain's ultimatum, Binkie Beaumont came to the rehearsal and told them that, since war was imminent and London would be bombed, the theatres would have to close and the production must be cancelled. He cited the *force majeure* clause in their contracts, which meant no compensation – a hard blow for Alec since he was being paid more than he had ever earned before – twenty-eight pounds a week. [In the event, London theatres remained open for most of the war but for a few that were bombed.]

The next day Alec and Merula went down to a crowded Ruckmans, filled as usual with 'displaced persons, London Theatre School students, refugees, evacuees, drifting family'. It was here that they heard the declaration of war. 'I can remember,' Alec wrote five years later, 'going out cutting thistles in the field by the Wakes*. And I can remember the rather hysterical lunch very well.'[134] The advent of war had added to the chaos endemic to Ruckmans. Merula wrote:

> The staff seem to have melted away and Chattie is in command and manning the kitchen and allocating jobs. I am given laundry, the boys dig up the tennis court to grow potatoes, the conscientious objectors play Ouija Board and talk Art and Philosophy. Papa doles out drinks and commutes and grumbles about the conscientious objectors, especially the refugee ones, the one whose underpants I object to: why can't he wash his own dirty underwear.[135]

A number of Alec's actor friends were to become conscientious objectors, among them Frith Banbury and the young Michael Gough whom Alec had first met staying with Edith Evans; Frith Banbury, having held to a consistent position since 1935 when he had joined the Peace Pledge Union, was registered as a conscientious objector on condition that he remained an actor; Michael Gough was obliged to serve in the Non-Combatant Corps and was given 'very disagreeable and tough physical work'.[136] John Gielgud received his call-up papers but the summons was rescinded twenty-four hours later after an intervention by Binkie Beaumont. Like Edith Evans, Gielgud saw the war subjectively. When the British Army in France was thrown back on Dunkirk, Gielgud, playing Lear, almost despaired. 'Terrible,' he said to Alec. 'Don't know what we shall do – dropped £120 last night.'[137]

Despite his protestations to Merula in his letters from Buxton that 'we *must* rise and change the leaders of the country if they do' (decide to go to war), Alec seemed to have come to accept not just the inevitability but the righteousness of the conflict with Nazi Germany. But the outbreak of war only made both Alec and Merula more

---

* cousins who lived in the lodge.

determined to have a child: 'We thought the only creative thing we could do was to make a baby.'[138]

Finding himself unemployed for the first time since he had appeared in *Queer Cargo* five years before, Alec made use of his leisure to adapt a novel by Charles Dickens for the stage. This was *Great Expectations*, whose story of an orphaned boy from a socially ambiguous background unquestionably resonated in Alec's mind. Like Alec, the hero, Pip, has a miserable home life but rises to gentility thanks to the money of an unknown benefactor. 'Why,' says the haughty young Estella when asked to play cards with the young Pip by *her* benefactor, Miss Havisham, 'he is a common labouring-boy!' – the kind of remark Alec must have dreaded being made about him. Pip, like Alec, attaches enormous importance to wearing the right kind of clothes, and his embarrassment at the humble origins of his sister's husband, the good Joe Gargery, was matched by Alec's disdain for his Cuff cousins. 'It is a most miserable thing,' says Pip, 'to feel ashamed of home.'

Alec was assisted by Merula in writing his stage adaptation. 'Do you remember how you had to be tortured sitting up in bed listening to each new page of *Expectations*? And you were so helpful.'[139] Quite apart from the emotional support she provided, he came to rely on Merula's critical judgement. When she had passed his dramatisation, Alec showed it to a group of his friends whom he had joined in forming an actors' cooperative, the Actors' Company.

The leaders of this enterprise were George Devine and his wife Sophie Harris, one of the Motleys, and included his old friends Martita Hunt and Marius Goring. They were all sufficiently impressed by Alec's adaptation of *Great Expectations* to choose it for their first production. The only obstacle was a lack of funds. Alec and Merula could only afford to invest five pounds; Marius Goring put up fifty. Mr John Lewis, the founder of the department store, who had earlier taken Alec to lunch at Prunier in a fruitless effort to persuade him to run three theatres that his company had bought on Shaftesbury

Avenue, contributed ten pounds; while Edith Evans, to their astonishment, gave them the same sum she had spent on a fur coat she had bought the week before – seven hundred pounds. 'Can't have actors out of work for the sake of seven hundred pounds when I buy a coat for the same amount.'[140]

The play was staged in the Rudolph Steiner Hall off Baker Street with the price of tickets ranging from one-and-sixpence to six shillings. 'At last a Theatre in the middle of London everyone can afford', read the poster advertising 'an entirely original adaptation by Alec Guinness of Charles Dickens' "Great Expectations"'. George Devine directed the play; the Motleys designed the costumes and sets. Marius Goring played Pip, Martita Hunt Miss Havisham, Yvonne Mitchell the young Estella, Roy Emerton was Magwitch and Vera Poliakoff the adult Estella. Alec and Merula, sitting opposite one another on the stage, were the narrators, with Merula also playing Biddy 'getting rather bulgy round the middle' and Alec Pip's delightful friend, Herbert Pocket.

The play was well received and Alec's Herbert Pocket particularly admired. Among those who came backstage to congratulate him were the eminent authors, Osbert and Edith Sitwell who, it turned out, were remote cousins of Merula's through the Wakes. However, of more relevance to Alec's subsequent career than the backstage visit of the Sitwells, was that of an actress friend of Martita's, Kay Walsh, whom Martita had persuaded to come to the play, and who in turn had persuaded her reluctant husband to accompany her. Kay Walsh came to see Martita at the end of the performance to congratulate her and introduced her companions – two film producers, Anatole de Grunwald and Carl Mayer, and her husband, a thirty-one-year-old film editor, David Lean.[141]

Great Expectations received favourable reviews, particularly from the influential *Sunday Times* critic James Agate, and did 'fair but modest business'; but the war scotched any prospect of it transferring to a larger theatre and it made a loss. Edith Evans and Mr John Lewis saw no return on their investment and after this, its sole production, the Actors' Company went bust.

Towards the end of 1939, Merula suspected that she was pregnant and consulted Roger Gilbert, the son of Alec's headmaster at Roborough and a student at Barts at the time of The Thirty-Nine Club, who was now a qualified doctor. He confirmed her suspicions and refused payment for the consultation.

The prospect of a child delighted them both; they had been hoping for one for some time. Their new friend, Edith Sitwell, wrote to Alec to congratulate him:

> *How* excited I am to hear the grand news about Merula. My dear, I feel so happy for you both. Which do you want it to be, a boy or a girl? Veronica is a lovely name. My greatest living woman friend is called that – she is a first cousin and is married to one of the nicest men in the world. – I shall love to think of your and Merula's daughter being called that, if it *is* a daughter. I shall start making woollies which is the only way I can help.[142]

Alec and Merula needed more than woollies from Edith Sitwell: they had very little money and no home of their own. They were forced to move out of the Beaumonts' house on New Year's Day, 1940, when a thaw after a freeze led to a burst pipe and water cascading through the house. 'Jimmy and Helen's house was a wreck, their belongings, including a grand piano, a write off. We were homeless and penniless.'

They found temporary refuge in Peggy Ashcroft's house on Campden Hill in Kensington, and later spent 'a few comfortable weeks' with Merula's parents at Ruckmans – or so Alec described them in *Blessings in Disguise*. In reality, while they may have stayed in some physical comfort, the atmosphere for Alec was poisoned by his mother-in-law's reaction to their news: 'How can you bring a child into such a dreadful world! Oh well, I suppose it's no use crying over spilt milk.' 'I am *very* fond *indeed* of your mum,' Alec wrote to Merula's sister Chattie a year or so later, 'but she made one *terrific* blunder, so far as I am concerned, when we told her Merry was going to have a child, and now and then something crops up which has a sort of bearing on that and makes me feel I never want to see her again . . .'[143]

Alec felt equally ill at ease with his father-in-law, sensing that Michel Salaman felt a 'perfectly natural antipathy to having a son-in-law . . . At least I hope its only that'.[144] Indeed, all the Salamans seemed to irritate Alec. 'I think I could listen to Michel more readily if he expressed himself better. You all express yourselves abominably. You splutter and mumble and dilly dally.' However, there was no spluttering and mumbling and dilly-dallying among the younger male Salamans when it came to the war. Both Merula's brothers were now married – Eusty, the architect, to Merula's fellow student at the London Theatre School, Mary Alexander; and Mikey, the painter, to a White Russian émigrée he had met in Paris, Natasha Borisova. Both now joined up and gained commissions – Mikey in the Army, Eusty in the Navy.

Alec, too, intended to volunteer: he would, in any case and in due course, be subject to the 'call-up' of all men between the ages of eighteen and forty-one, but he hoped to delay his induction until after the birth of his child. As temporary war work he thought he might read stories to hospital patients. Sydney Cockerell sent him ten pounds towards his expenses but Alec only read once, to a dying man in Dorking cottage hospital. He was also undecided as to which branch of the armed forces he should choose. He first considered the Army and Peggy Ashcroft put Alec in touch with her uncle, a colonel in the Army, whose advice after meeting Alec was that he should apply to the Navy. A fellow actor, Dennis Price, who Alec bumped into in Piccadilly, sent him to see a Major Cazalet, commanding an anti-aircraft battery near Sevenoaks in Kent: but finding that it was a safe billet for theatrical 'pansies', Alec made a quick retreat.[145]

In March of 1940, deciding that London's theatres were no longer at risk from German bombs, Binkie Beaumont staged Clemence Dane's *Cousin Muriel* at the Globe Theatre with Edith Evans in the title role, Peggy Ashcroft as Dinah Sylvester and Alec, at thirty pounds a week, as Cousin Muriel's son.

Cousin Muriel is a liar, a thief and a cheat: and there is a scene when her son rebukes his mother for her thieving. Edith Evans, who was unquestionably fond of Alec – no mention was made of the money she lost in the Actors' Company – was so taken aback by the venom with which he delivered the lines that she flung her arms in the air, screamed, 'Alec doesn't love me any more! He doesn't love me! He *hates* me!' then fell onto the stage, kicked her feet and began to chew the corner of a Persian rug.

Many years later, Alec wrote that it had never occurred to him to blame himself for this incident, 'and it still doesn't', but he acknowledged that it had something to do with his mother's 'financial fiddles and kleptomania'. For, though there is almost no mention of Agnes Cuff in the letters of this period, there is no doubt that she remained a dread presence in Alec's life. It would seem that he continued to give her an allowance out of his scant resources: 'So far as money is concerned,' he wrote to Merula during the war, 'she ought to be more or less all right for I've been letting her have thirty shillings a week for some time and she has been earning as well.'[146] But, despite this allowance, Agnes Cuff attempted to supplement her income through petty theft. 'At the age of eighteen I managed to save her from jail by pleading with the very kind couple from whom she had stolen money,' he wrote to a cousin towards the end of his life. 'Again, during the war, friends of mine went to her rescue when she was had up before a magistrate. These pathetic things were, as you can imagine, hurtful, embarrassing and distressing.'[147]

Edith Evans had recovered her composure the next morning: 'We were all very quiet, polite, formal and perhaps a touch cool.' However, the incident did not bode well for the play. Alec had his first week's pay picked from his pocket during the blackout, the reviews were poor and *Cousin Muriel* closed after a short run. However, in May 1940 Alec was back at the Old Vic as Ferdinand in *The Tempest* with his old friend and mentor John Gielgud playing Prospero, Jessica Tandy playing Miranda and the production staged by his companions from the

Actors' Company, George Devine and Marius Goring. Now he was back on form. 'Mr Alec Guinness, one of the best actors in England, was inevitably good as the tranced Ferdinand,' wrote the theatre critic of the *New Statesman and Nation*.

Alec was also happy at the prospect of becoming a father: 'And what happy times we had when I was pregnant,' Merula would later write to Alec, 'and we had all those picnikcs [sic] in St James Park. Heeps [sic] and heeps and heeps of happy times.'[148] They were now living in 'a rather gloomy flat, institutional green' near Victoria station which had been lent to them for a month by the actress Marjorie Fielding who, soon after they were married, had let them stay in a nicer flat in Victoria Square. It was from the gloomy flat that Merula went to King's College Hospital on Denmark Hill where, on 6 June, she gave birth to a son. 'A far from easy birth,' Alec recalled in his diary forty years later. 'M very indignant and hysterically said she would have no more children. Difficulty in breast feeding. His head squashed a little on delivery.'[149]

Merula's account is more graphic:

When I came round and the nurse brought him to show me, I nearly had a fit. They hadn't warned me beforehand that he looked odd but would be fine in a day or two. The top of his head was all skew whiff and he had red stripes all down his face and I thought I had given birth to a freak. I must have behaved badly because the gynecologist gave me a rocket.[150]

When Alec was not visiting Merula or at the Old Vic, where he shared a dressing-room with Jack Hawkins, he 'spent most of the time sitting lonelyly [sic] in St James's Park, where M had sat so often in the last days of her pregnancy. The name of Matthew had come swiftly and easily and was her decision. The trips to Denmark Hill were a bit grim and worrying. What with the war and shortage of cash I remember it all being rather fraught.'[151]

Merula seems to have had little support from her own family. 'You are probably thinking me a most neglectful sister,' Chattie wrote to her, 'but NOBODY NEVER TOLD ME! Can you believe it? However it is rather exciting really isn't it – a teeny tiny boy too – you are a clever old thing – I'm dying to see it, at least I'm not really because I expect it looks horrid, but it seems so funny that there really is a little something brought into the world by you & Alec . . .'

Merula was eventually discharged from hospital, and she and Alec took their baby son down to Ruckmans. Feeding Matthew remained a nightmare. In the hospital:

> . . . in those days, one wasn't allowed to have one's baby with one; they were kept somewhere miles away at the end of a corridor and one could hear them crying and one worried and fretted. The baby was brought to one at meal times and screwed onto one's tits and weighed and if it hadn't eaten enough, the nurse thumped it and screwed it on again and I got an abscess which was torture.

At Ruckmans, the daily weighing of Matthew on scales became a nightmare; Matthew 'bawled night and day and got smaller' until Daniel de Pass, the glamorous naval officer who they had asked to be Matthew's godfather, told Merula to throw away the scales, after which: 'Matthew stopped bawling, grew fat and bonny and we were able to sleep again.'

The unwanted guests had mostly left Ruckmans and the household 'was almost normal again'; but the Battle of Britain was being fought in the skies above them. Each night, the German bombers could be heard making for London and 'the sky over London was lit up red with the fires'. Occasionally, a rogue bomb would fall in the country near Ruckmans, one close enough to make them all dive under the table during dinner. At the time of the evacuation of the British Army from Dunkirk, Alec was bicycling into the local town of Ockley when he was fired on by a hedge-hopping Messerschmitt and had to take cover in the ditch.

They both found living with Merula's parents difficult but did not want to take the baby back to London and looked for somewhere to live near Ruckmans. They were offered an empty keeper's lodge on the estate of their neighbours, Tommy and Dulcie Deuchar, at a rent of seven shillings a week.

When Merula told her mother that they wanted to live on their own, she was furious. '"What do you want to go and live in a horrid hovel for when you can live here?" she said in tears. I said, "But surely, when you married, you wouldn't have wanted to live with your mother?" That was a mistake. "I HATED my mother," she sobbed. "You must HATE me".'

Soon after this, however, Michel and Big Chattie moved out of Ruckmans into a smaller but still substantial house called Wadlington at Lickfold near Midhurst in Sussex. It already belonged to Michel Salaman and had remained empty since they had lived there during World War I. Alec and Merula helped with the move which left them 'like wet rags'. Ruckmans was subsequently sold.

Alec described their new home, Middle Lodge, as a 'primitive but pretty' cottage on the edge of a wood. Merula's Wake cousins lived at the lodge at the other end of the lane. There was no furniture, no electricity and no bath: at night they lit candles and kept warm with an oil 'Beatrix' stove that smoked. 'Dear me it's cold,' Alec wrote to Chattie:

And my fingers are blue pork sausages and there are blue icicles on my pen and bonny Beatrice sits by me while I write to you and REFUSES to *give off* any heat, *because*, she says, I can stuff her as I like (if you get my meaning) with *paraffin*, but what good's that if her *wick* is low. 'Well, Beatrice,' I say sometimes, 'it appears to me you want a wick a week.' 'That I do, sir,' she *invariably* replies, 'it's only *proper* for a girl to be *given* what she wants!' 'But there are *no* wicks to be got, Beatrice.' And she just snorts and *goes out*.'[152]

The wood-burning oven, too, was erratic and only worked if the wind was in the right direction. They mostly had to cater just for themselves: their only house guest was Martita Hunt, who came for the weekend and drifted around the primitive cottage 'in a long pink peignoir, edged with Ostrich feathers and in high-heeled mules and her hair in curlers. She was very gallant, didn't complain about not having a bath or the smoking Aladdin and offered to make a Béchamel Sauce. It took her nearly all day. The wind was in the wrong direction.'

Despite these privations, however, Alec and Merula were happier than they had ever been before and, to crown this happiness, it was now that Alec came into his Geddes inheritance – the shares in a ranch in Tierra del Fuego which, when they were sold and taxes paid, enabled him to buy a gramophone, a dressing-gown for Merula, a pair of slippers for himself, a bottle of Apricot Brandy, a whole Cheshire cheese and a slap-up dinner for the two of them at the Savoy.[153]

thirteen

In September of 1940 Alec went on tour with Robert Ardrey's play *Thunder Rock*, replacing Michael Redgrave in the role of Charleston. The company played in Glasgow, Leeds, Sheffield, Blackpool, Birmingham, Stratford on Avon and Bristol. Passing through London, Alec stayed the night with the play's promoter, Binkie Beaumont. 'The night in London was very noisy,' he wrote to Merula:

> . . . and once or twice I thought a bomb was coming in the next room. But I felt very safe – even when the ceiling came down in Binkie's bedroom. And even when their Irish maid woke me up in the passage at 2.0 a.m. saying 'Theresh two shommen schreaming their heads off in a takxi outshide. Never mind – they'll be dead in two tics,' and went out again.[154]

Glasgow, when Alec got there, was 'crowded beyond belief. The streets are so packed it takes about ten minutes to wend one's way for about a hundred yards. They all seem to think Hitler is going to launch an attack on the city this week end.' Alec took against Glasgow, as he took against all the northern industrial cities:

> Nothing elegant, nothing remotely clean, not a building which we could bear to live in. Great black bleak tenements. The children are so pale and ill looking. They are carried about by flat-footed bedroom slippered mothers who strap them to their bosoms in great greasy white shawls. And the babies are dirtier and paler than the wool. Each time I've seen them I've felt how lucky we are and Matthew is with his lovely woolies and clean nappies. Women get on the busses and they stink. Frankly, they smell of unwiped arse-hole poor dears and one has to shift one's seat. It's a great sordid city this, quite frightening and, on as dull a day as today, depressing beyond words.[155]

'I've started saying my prayers,' he wrote on 2 October:

> When it was a habit, I can't remember – so long ago. I don't know who I pray to. Not the old gentleman, certainly. The Spirit of Life behind Buddha & Christ – I don't know Who – anyway God. There is a pattern to life I'm sure even if we don't live by it. In any case I feel we need it.

And then, in case Merula should think that he was getting too solemn 'I've just made a BIG POOF in the lounge – its such a BIG POOF that its wearing a tartan and I think I must go out and leave the Scots commercial travellers to pass out.'

By now Merula had forgotten the dreadful time she had giving birth to Matthew and was thinking of a second child. Alec begged her to wait:

> Darling, darling don't have the baby just yet. You want a servant to be able to do that sort of thing. You haven't been constructed as a drudge. You like a little time each day for walking, knitting, reading, writing and a hundred other things. Do you realise you've got to feed yourself and

Matthew. Wait, wait, wait. It's lovely of you to want to have the child
but for God's sake be practical. It's not fair on any of us if you kill
yourself. There are plenty of bombs about.

When the play moved to Edinburgh, Alec tried to persuade Merula to
join him:

Its *lovely* digs here . . . Oh darling, darling – couldn't you come. If only
it wasn't for that bloody London, and the expensive journey! I do so
want to be with you . . . And now that trains are getting machine
gunned its frightening to think of you on a train. Dear heart, I love you
so and hate HATE being apart from you. I wish I was making more
money. Then I could phone you every day. My 'phone calls to you last
week, I was horrified to find out yesterday, cost me 23 shillings!! And
I thought I was spending just two or three bob a time. Still, it was worth
it to hear your voice . . .

Alec longed for more than the sound of Merula's voice:

I think on your face and hair and your lovely chin and neck and those
beautiful straight shoulders and your voice, and your nose and your
sweet hands and your lovely look and you and your tummy and your
funny ladies knees and your silly feet and your sweet smell and your
smoothness and warmth which makes my John Thomas want to stand
up, down wanton, down, and even your funny little sweet little –
goodness where are their eyes. God, I love and want you. I feel near you
darling. God bless you and baby, Alec.

The separation was too painful for them both so it was agreed that
Merula would risk the journey through London and join him in
Edinburgh. Carrying Matthew in a cot, she arrived in London during
an air raid and had difficulty in persuading a taxi to take her across
London to Euston station. The train from Euston was packed with
sailors who helped her with her luggage:

. . . the worst bit of clobber was Matthew's gas mask which looked like a small zeppelin. In the event of a gas raid, one was supposed to put the baby inside and zip it up, and then pump air into it, having first put on one's own gas mask. I saw very little hope of either of us surviving but the beastly thing was obligatory and I used it to pack nappies in.[156]

The sailors were helpful and friendly and 'even took Matthew's nappies to wash in the lavatory' and, when they arrived at Edinburgh's Waverly station, helped her with her luggage and found her a taxi.

Alec and Merula were reunited, and they remained together when *Thunder Rock* moved south to Yorkshire. During the run in Sheffield, they were invited by Edith Sitwell to stay with her and her brother Osbert at Renishaw, their ancestral home outside the city.

The Sitwell siblings – Edith had a second brother, Sacheverell – were not to everyone's taste. 'I think they are very tiresome,' Cyril Connolly told his friend Noel Blakiston. 'Edith is tedious, humourless and combative, Osbert advertises, Sachie is the most remote, but none is really our style.' Osbert was homosexual. 'Edith adorned herself in a fantastic fashion with huge bracelets, necklaces, and rings of jet and ivory' and 'woollen dresses with the narrow bodice, long, flowing skirts, and wide sleeves reminiscent of the gown of an abbess.'[157]

Renishaw was a vast house with no electricity: huge wood fires burned at each end of the dining room. Evelyn Waugh liked to stay there while on leave during the war because there were 'no evacuees or billeted soldiers; no dust sheets except in the ballroom. Banks of potted plants & bowls of roses; piles of new and old books and delicious cooking . . .'[158]

The feudal grandeur of Renishaw intimidated the young Guinnesses. Edith had warned them that her brother loathed babies and so Matthew had been smuggled in and remained hidden until the butler, Robins, came to tell Merula, in the middle of dinner, that he was crying. 'I expect the baboon has got him,' Edith Sitwell said 'in a sepulchral voice'. 'I leapt up,' wrote Merula, 'knocking over my chair and raced up miles of dark stairs and along dark corridors to our bedroom where I found the baboon was only a rather ugly maid making up the fire.'

Osbert was magnanimous about Matthew: he said he did not mind him being at Renishaw as long as he did not have to see him. On the Saturday:

> Edith said she would take us for a drive to see the moors. We set off in an old fashioned limousine with an old fashioned chauffeur and Edith made Alec sit in the front and carried on a conversation with him through a speaking tube. We didn't see the moors as there was a thick mist. As we approached the house, Edith turned to me and said 'The house looks so gloomy from this side, don't you think? Or perhaps you don't think.'

In the evening, Edith sat by the fire in a high-backed armchair knitting seamen's socks with the longest needles Merula had ever seen, her fingers so weighed down with jade, she could hardly wield them.

The tour continued in some confusion. *Thunder Rock* was playing to very thin audiences and Alec estimated that his earnings for the first week in Leeds were two shillings and fourpence. In Nottingham they did no better. 'I'm scribbling this during a matinée,' he wrote to Chattie:

> . . . playing to *12* people and the Germans over-head. Outside the rain is pouring so heavily it drowns the gun fire. Inside the wind is screeching through the empty stalls choking the twelve theatre disciples. There are literally only 2 in the dress circle. And the town is crowded. But they are all in a fearful funk. When a bomb fell close last night I thought they were going to stampede. In all the other towns, which have had it much worse, the audiences have never paid any attention. Its a sod of a place this. Its supposed to be very gay. There is more vice than any other Midland town. Its not unattractive to look at

but *very* dreary to be in. I've started writing a book. Can think of nothing to say – feel too dreary.

The dreariness of Nottingham was forgotten when *Thunder Rock* played at the Arts Theatre in Cambridge. The journey from Stratford, where Alec had left Merula and Matthew in the cottage he had rented for three weeks, was '*horrid* – standing all the way'; but Alec took to the university town. 'It's such a beautiful place,' he wrote to Merula. 'It reminds me a bit of Bruges – a rather modern, cleaner Bruges bursting with life . . . One day we must come and stay here. I wouldn't mind living here if we have to live in a town.' His spirits also lifted because of the success of the play. 'It's been a wonderful evening. A *packed* house of mostly young people who were as quick as knives and most enthusiastic. I suppose I gave my best performance as everyone says so. I have a delicious *minute* flat at the theatre – a dressing room, a bathroom and a lav. I had a bath in my bathroom and *my* was I black!'[159]

As the stay continued, his enthusiasm for Cambridge increased. 'Darling darling you would so love this city . . . Hundreds of lovely little bridges. And its so quiet but alive and clean and beautiful . . . Sir Sydney's museum is *lovely* outside but haven't been in yet. It's a very polite town. Oh, let's live here some time.' Alec particularly loved the bookshops and stocked up to indulge his passion for reading that was to continue throughout his life:

And the *book* shops – oh! The *book shops!* – beautiful ones . . . I've got you Journal to Stella. Its jolly decent of me to send it and not read it myself. But I've got myself Barnaby Rudge. I *must* be careful of the book shops here. I've found a leather bound Gibbon in 12 vols published in 1788 and the whole 12 only costs 7 shillings and 6 pence . . .

Alec bought Matthew *Struwelpeter* and looked for a book on St Francis of Assisi for Merula but resisted the Gibbon until he heard from Tennent's that *Thunder Rock* had made seven pounds, ten shillings in Blackpool, two pounds, ten shillings in Nottingham and five pounds so far in Cambridge, whereupon he went back to the bookshop and 'bought the seven-and-sixpenny Gibbon. Its very sweet in its twelve pale brown worn leather jackets. I also want to buy a Montaigne. Like your father's green edition (the big one in 5 vols) only white. Very good condition and only 25 shillings.'

Cambridge was not immune from the war, however, and Alec became enraged when the audience laughed as the all-clear was sounded during Act II of *Thunder Rock* – 'about the best performance I've given':

> The house lights were turned up at the climax and the audience laughed. The Stinkers! The Shits. Fuck them fuck them bugger them . . . Shit. They don't deserve to have an actor like me. O sweet I can feel the power come over me nowadays – during this past week – the confidence of decent houses (which I haven't acted for years) unleashed my experience and emotions and I know I can act anything – Falstaff – anything. Or almost. And I was on top form when those bloody Germans WENT AWAY! Bugger them . . .

While in Cambridge Alec received letters from, among others, Tony Guthrie suggesting parts in future Shakespeare plays, and he began to consider which plays he and Merula could act in together:

> I've been thinking of you as an actress a lot, my sweet dove. I think you'd better start learning Lady Macbeth. I think you essentially right for *me* in the part. We'll work on it together. You can play Ophelia on your head and that can wait. When I get back we'll get down to *Macbeth* and see if *someone* can't be persuaded to let us do it. – Yes, I adore Antony & Cleopatra, though not so familiar with it as the others. I like to read it as a poem. I despair of ever seeing a Cleopatra on the stage and I know and realise only too too well how right out of my frame is Antony. And when there is nothing to play in a Shakespeare play one is inclined to treat it as literature. As a matter of fact I would love to play the Soothsayer.

Yet all these plans, he knew, were mere dreams because of the war. 'DAMN the WAR its SENSELESS, BRUTAL and MONEY RUN. Why don't we WIN it!' And there was still his preoccupation with the second child. It would seem that Merula, at Stratford, had complained of stomach pains and thought she might be pregnant. Alec wrote:

> I've talked to *Selma*, and she says it's impossible to conceive a child *while* your breasts are working. Also she says that she's never heard of a woman having periods when feeding. An odd bloody day, she said, now and then, representing a period but *never* regular and usually not occurring *at all*. Well, she should know. I haven't had a chance to talk to Rob about it. I will, though. It *is* possible to force a period without harm by going to a chemist and getting a bottle of Hydrochloroid Quinine pills, taking five pills and 1 oz of Castor Oil. But strictly unadvisable while feeding Matthew. But your pains must be other things. Go to a doctor *anyway* and ask him about weaning Matthew, which seems to me sensible to start doing, and if by some almost immaculate conception there is a Sarah or Sebastian inside you, then its high time you finished with Master M. But Sarah or Sebastian aren't in you, either together or with Mildred or Gwenny or Hyacinth or James, John, Zebedee or alone. So there! And if they are, well – what a GREAT BIG NUISANCE they are, but very *very sweet* I'm sure! But they aren't, can't be, impossible, go to a doctor and find out what your pains are. Rheumatism I expect.

Alec advised on the smallest detail of his son's wellbeing – 'If Matthew's bog's still bad give him charcoal biscuits' – but there were compensations for his absence from home. 'It's touching, but a trifle embarrassing. I'm seized at by students who are would-be actors who pour out their life's ambitions and say they will give up *everything* for the stage – anything – but – "oh! I *love* the theatre sir!" – with earnest faces. But none of them have actors faces and they are all too gentlemanly.' He was visited backstage by the eminent economist

John Maynard Keynes. 'Mr Keynes called on me last night – the Economics man who wants to take away my income. I liked him very much and am dining with him & Lopokova* on Friday.' And, two days later: 'Mr Keynes is in the box again to-night like a great big pale-eyed swan.'[160]

Alec returned to the holiday cottage at Shottery near Stratford but the week's holiday idyll was brought to an end when, as Merula recalled:

> We woke to hear splashing sounds and peered through the floorboards which had big gaps between and could see a light moving about and our landlady, who lived next door, wading about with a candle and water up to her knickers and cups and saucers bobbing by like little boats.[161]

Forced to leave the cottage because of the flood, Merula and Matthew went off to stay with an aunt of hers near Pewsey in Wiltshire while Alec travelled to Bristol for the final week of the tour.

Alec reached the city during a heavy air raid on Monday 25 November. 'I arrived here on Monday,' he wrote to Chattie two days later:

> . . . to find the theatre I was billed at a rubble. But just a *rubble*. My make-up etc has I believe, fried and disappeared in the ash. I've loitered round the ruins but never bumped into or contacted any of the company or my manager. Whether alive or dead I dont know. Can't get in touch with Tennent's – can't phone Merry – and am having difficulty in getting out of Bristol. Do I sound depressed? I'm not a bit but enjoying myself hugely at the Vicarage. The priest being Anglo-Catholic is quite jolly and keeps good wines and wears fancy clothes. I shall be a Christian by the time I leave!

---

* Lydia Lopokova, the ballerina and Keynes's wife.

After the bombing raid, Bristol had been a conflagration – 'fires climbing everywhere, water-mains broken, streets cordoned off'. Alec had walked from the station dragging his suitcase, taking cover in doorways to avoid shrapnel, looking for somewhere to stay. A policeman told him that all the hotels and guest houses were full, and that his best bet was to ask for a bed for the night at the vicarage up the road. Alec knocked on the door of the large, redbrick house and the door was opened by the Reverend Cyril Tomkinson – the clergyman who had twice come backstage at the Old Vic to show Alec how Hamlet would have made the sign of the cross.

Alec stayed in the vicarage for four days. The water had been cut off by the bombing but 'the Rev. Tomkinson kept a good cellar'. He found in his host a man with a brilliant mind – 'very perceptive, very snobbish, delighting in the famous, the rich, the beautiful or the talented' – a Sydney Cockerell in a cassock. He showed Alec his church, sprinkled him with holy water, told him 'with mock horror' of the lesbian tendencies of many of his female parishioners, and taught him to genuflect towards the altar as a sign of respect to the bread lodged in the tabernacle that had been turned into the body of Christ. 'I do believe in The Real Presence, you see,' he told Alec. Alec had no idea what he meant.

The Rev. Tomkinson also offered to hear Alec's confession. 'Just kneel at my feet and tell me everything that is on your conscience. You are unlikely to surprise me. I assure you I will have heard it all before.' Alec declined politely and received a blessing instead.

Many years later, in an interview in the *Sunday Times* with the author and playwright John Mortimer, later published as 'The Rope Trick' in a volume of Mortimer's collected journalism, Alec gave an account of his stay in Bristol with the Rev. Tomkinson which differed from that in his autobiography in one significant particular. He describes his arrival in bombed-out Bristol and how he found shelter in the vicarage with his acquaintance, Cyril Tomkinson. 'I stayed with him for four days,' he goes on. 'He had a very good cellar. He made a pass at me, of course, but I found I could cope with that and he talked and amused me.'[162]

This disclosure, thrown away so casually, suggests that Alec, aged twenty-six at the time of his visit to Bristol, was sufficiently familiar with the uninvited approaches of homosexuals for it to have no adverse effect on his feelings for the Anglican vicar. He makes no mention of the vicar's advances in *Blessings in Disguise* but, as so often in his autobiography, knowing readers were perhaps invited to read between the lines. Had the vicar's talk of his lady parishioners' lesbian tendencies – 'with mock horror' – and his promise that Alec, if he were to confess, could tell him 'nothing that he had not heard before' been intended to prepare him for the pass, or persuade him that, were Alec to respond, the consequent sin would be a mere *peccadillo*? Or was the invitation to confess mistaken by Alec as an invitation to sin?

What seems clear is that the priest's pass did not shock Alec, or lead him to dismiss him as a hypocrite and fraud. Quite to the contrary, Alec's four-day stay at the vicarage in Bristol was a turning point in his life. He not only lost the feeling that he had carried since, as a boy, he had wandered into a High Anglican church in Bournemouth, that he was 'on spooky Roman property': he was also introduced to the works of Christian writers that answered both his spiritual and intellectual yearning. He was always to remain grateful to Cyril Tomkinson, because 'he opened me up to a new world – the world of Hooker, William Law, Bishop Gore, Archbishop Temple; and the wide world of St Augustine and Newman.'

Four days later, when the trains were running again, Alec returned to Middle Lodge with a number of books lent to him by Cyril Tomkinson, among them the works of very *Roman* Catholic saints, St Teresa of Avila and St Francis of Sales. The search for some meaning in life, the inchoate prayers to a vague deity, now had a focus: Alec devoured the books and rediscovered his childhood faith in Christ. He was transported by an almost mystical elation. 'Suddenly,' he later wrote to Merula, 'if I can say "sudden" of something so still – a feeling of forgiveness and renewal swept over me and a vibrancy in the air . . .

All and every sound was wiped out in a noticeable way. My watch stopped. I could hear it stop . . . I was left so joyful.'[163]

Both Alec and Merula believed that Middle Lodge was haunted by a poltergeist or fairies: both were woken in the middle of the night by a thin spray of water on their faces, and Merula found a handful of pebbles between the sheets of their bed. Every night Alec would go out and bless Middle Lodge with the sign of the cross, and then the rooms where Matthew and Merula were sleeping; he did not tell Merula because 'I had a silly feeling that you would think it superstitious.'

Merula was baffled. 'Alec got religion,' she wrote in her memoir:

> . . . and bicycled off to Oakwood hill church on Sunday mornings. It was a puzzle to me, having been brought up a strict atheist. Everything to do with Christianity had either been abhorrent or a joke in the family . . . Then he announced that he wanted Matthew to be baptised. I thought: those two are going to leave me and I will be left out in the cold.

But Merula raised no objections and Matthew was duly christened in the High Anglican Church in Roffey with Merula's cousin Dan de Pass and the actress Ros Atkinson as his godparents.

On 18 December Alec went up to London to visit another High Anglican priest, Fr Hutchinson, at the church near the Old Vic on the Waterloo Road. Fr Hutch, as he was always called, was quite different from Cyril Tomkinson – jovial and outgoing. He had been 'an informal chaplain to the Old Vic' and Lillian Baylis' confessor: now he became Alec's. He went down on his knees and unburdened himself of his sins and was given absolution in the name of Christ.

Alec's newfound serenity did not save him from all vexations. A new production of *Great Expectations* fell through because he declined to take part. 'It's a long story,' he wrote to Chattie, 'and I'm not sure I can be bothered to tell it. G. Expectaggers is not being done. It was all but cast, the scenery was half out, the publicity was under way and because I said I couldn't possibly be in it they gave up.'[164]

Many of Alec's friends were upset. Merula wrote to him:

> By the way, did you know that you had offended every one mortally by not doing G. Expectations – Marty told me and told me not to tell you, but I don't see any sense in not telling you – otherwise you would be so surprised at being cold-eyed when you meet people again – and its all these misunderstandings that are so maddening. It seems darling that you don't state yourself very plainly to people and they misinterpret what you are trying to say.[165]

There was also an incident which exacerbated Alec's irritation with his father-in-law. On Christmas Eve, while Alec was in London doing a broadcast for the BBC, Michel Salaman dropped by to see his daughter. Lying on the kitchen table at Middle Lodge was a duck that Alec had obtained with great difficulty for their Christmas dinner. 'Just what I want for the Bakers*,' said Michel, exchanging Alec's prized duck for a huge unplucked turkey. Alec disliked turkey and it would not fit into the oven.

These vexations, however, did not significantly detract from the serenity of Alec and Merula's life at Middle Lodge. 'We lived such a quiet, peaceful life, Alec reading aloud in the evenings while I fed the baby: it was all so full of love and, discovering our inner lives, such a valuable interlude to sustain us through the difficult times ahead.'[166] 'I have been dreaming of Middle Lodge all the evening,' she wrote to Alec later in the war, 'of supper in our dressing gowns and beautiful St Teresa† in front of the stove and candles and the dresser twinkling lights and colours. How lovely it was . . .'[167] And later still, towards the end of the war, she told her brother Eusty 'that our month together in Middle Lodge was worth the whole of the rest of my life – almost –

---

* a couple who worked for the Salamans.
† It is not clear whether this is St Teresa of Avila or St Teresa of Lisieux.

and one or two days or weeks have been as important as whole years: length of time doesn't really count.'[168]

Then, at the end of January 1941, the idyll came to an end. Alec received his call-up papers 'and walked off down the lane to become a sailor'.

part three

lieutenant a. guinness cuffe, RNVR

fourteen

Alec had been summoned by the British Admiralty to HMS *Raleigh*, a shore-based training camp at Torpoint in Cornwall, facing the naval base at Plymouth across the Tamar estuary. He spent the night before his induction at the Duke of Cornwall Hotel in Plymouth and dashed off the first of his many wartime letters to Merula: 'Not miserable I hope . . . you know how I love you and will never cease to love you. Let's make that a happiness in our temporary separation – not a misery sweet.' He also reported that, dutiful to the last, he had taken leave of his mother. 'I saw my mamma. If I was feeling a little jollier I'd write the whole of her chit chat – never stopped "So I said well if they don't like bacon as I said to her and her [sic] replied no they don't not sausages either well I said" etc etc. AND etc. Pretty grim.'[169]

The following day, 12 February, he wrote from the naval barracks as Ordinary Seaman Alec Guinness Cuffe – Cuffe was still his legal family name.

The men seem very nice and all sympathetic and say it's the best place in England. I'm here for 10 weeks and then go to Chatham or Plymouth. I can't understand what anyone says – they have the thickest Scots, Irish, Yorks, Lancs, Stepney accents. Haven't had to do anything yet except pull 17 pillow slips on 17 pillows. There are 300 new boys! Its an enormous camp. There's a sailor telling a story as I write this. 'Fuckin'' has occurred 3 times every word of story . . . I think of you all the time.

For the first couple of weeks in HMS *Raleigh* Alec was wretched, confessing to Chattie that he had been unable to stop weeping during the first two days, and to Merula that he had never felt 'so tearful so many times in so short a period' – not because of his incarceration 'which so far hasn't proved unpleasant but the constant thought that I have the most adorable wife and baby and I can't watch them all day'. Instead, he was just one among many anonymous recruits:

This camp is enormous. There are 3000 training here and about 300 come in and go out every week. Apparently, after 10 weeks here I get a week or ten days leave and then go to sea for 2 or 3 months . . . We are a very odd collection. There are 30 of us in Class 54 – mostly factory hands, lorry drivers, navvies, half-wits, nondescripts (the majority) and a Glasgow university man, and a young school master (a pleasant young man but with that *indelible* stamp). He and I are the only two who speak B.B.C. English. Most of them *snatch* their food and won't pass down the table. However I persisted in passing at lunch (dinner) time (to my cost) and at supper to-night everyone passed. But I suspect it's only for one meal . . . It's hell, hell, hell being cook as its called, which I was yesterday. 4 of you have to get and dish out and clear up for the other impatient 30. (And there are about 600 in the dining mess.) I have far too many clothes. They issued us with vests, long pants, socks and two suits of everything. And a suitcase, towels, soap, over-coat, oilskin, two hats, two pairs boots etc. etc. and we are expected to keep it all in a small locker. We've spent most of the last 36 hours in marking with paint our bedding and odds and ends . . . We get up at 6.30. And lights out at 10.0 p.m. Breakfast 7.0 a.m. Dinner at 12.0 and tea at 4.0 and Supper at 6.0. And all of them whacking great meals. None of us have sized each other up yet . . . Isn't it wonderful – none of those awful soccers, ruggers etc are compulsory. And neither is boxing. But indoor games are and gym is. Oh, well, I'll survive though I've never been known to vault a horse clearly yet . . .

Despite his initial misery, Alec was relieved to be in uniform at last, and even regretted that he had not joined up sooner, recalling 'how swiftly and gallantly Eusty & Mikey and dozens of others didn't hesitate to take up some duty – and how uselessly I fretted & puzzled & let myself be guided by events . . .' He also made a friend, learning within a week of his arrival that among the new recruits there was actually another *actor*, Peter Bull.

Peter Bull was the son of the Member of Parliament for Hammersmith, Sir William James Bull, Bart. He had been educated at Winchester, then studied at the University of Tours in France and had worked for a time as a journalist before becoming an actor. Two years older than Alec, he was a heavily built man with a deep voice and the face of a pugnacious frog, and was an unabashed homosexual. Alec had met him once before: in 1933 Bull had summoned him to his parents' house in Chelsea and offered Alec a job acting at the Perrenporth summer theatre festival – an offer which Alec, 'for financial reasons', had declined.

Coming across 'Bully' at HMS *Raleigh* dispelled the wretchedness that Alec had felt at exchanging the cosiness of Middle Lodge for the bleak life of a naval recruit. Bull was not just exceptionally companionable and amusing but exuded the kind of social *savoir faire* that Alec had always craved:

You'll be delighted to hear that I'm almost enjoying myself now. Not on account of anything doing but the future isn't quite so blank as it was two days ago. And I've chatted with Peter Bull, whom I rather like in spite of his looks, and we laughed a lot and are both pretending to be FEARFUL SNOBS. He's given me an invaluable tip which is, if ticked off by an officer, not to say 'Sorry Sir' but 'Sir, I couldn't be sorrier!' It's class you see. I'm rushing up to anyone with gold braid to ask the silliest question, merely to let them know I don't drop my Haitches (as my steeple jack friend insists on calling them).[170]

When given shore leave, Alec would 'slip away on the 4.30 "Liberty Boat" and have supper in a café run by old ladies' where a cup of tea cost a penny and 'enormous hot Cornish pasties' were tuppence. His sailor's pay was low – thirty shillings a week – so money was short. Merula sent him food parcels containing luxuries bought with an invaluable allowance from her father of four pounds a week. And Alec himself, when he could afford it, indulged his more sophisticated tastes. 'Peter Bull and I had arranged to visit Plymouth to see if I could buy some Balkan Sobranie or Egyptian cigs. as I was longing for some – just a taste.'

Bully's sense of humour tempered even the vilest aspects of their basic training:

> This morning . . . I went out to defend Cornwall against Invasion . . .
> I'm not good at jumping barbed wire entanglements at the best of
> times, but when armed with rifle, pick-axe, bayonet, gas-mask,
> haversack, helmet, oil skin, water bottle, ammunition etc and etc . . .
> I found it more or less impossible . . . And the mud. Thank heaven for
> Peter Bull. We had terrible giggles and actually played Red Indians on
> our own. He's rather less good at barbed wire than I am, which is a
> sort of comfort. And he sinks rather deeper in the mud.

Within a week of his arrival at HMS *Raleigh*, Alec had been persuaded by Bully that he must try to become an officer. 'I feel somehow a commission must be strived for. The competition is terrific and I can think of *no* qualification that I have . . .' It was to convey that they were officer material that Alec and Bully drawled to their superiors, and after being told that 'we may have something better for you' by an officer, 'followed by a brilliant Naval smile and twinkling blue eyes', Alec concluded that he might have 'drawled to effect'.

To gain a commission in the Royal Navy's Volunteer Reserve would not only ensure a more comfortable war in more congenial company, it would also establish Alec as a member of the upper class – an 'officer and a gentleman'; yet it was precisely his doubts about his provenance that eroded Alec's confidence that he could succeed. He was afraid that his illegitimacy and lack of a background would exclude him. 'I shall never make an officer I fear,' he wrote to Chattie. 'At the first opportunity I'm going to say "my aunt Lady Wake" or my sister-in-law "La Chattie". But never "Prisoner 24622 – my mother".'

'I get my big interview . . . on Monday,' he wrote to Merula in April, 'when I have a chat with the Commodore. (Are you related to Lord Harmsworth? How many country houses have you? Do you play BRIDGE?)'; and after the interview he wrote again to say that he had been asked the inevitable question: 'What was my father?' But four days later, on 14 April, a cause for rejoicing. 'This little piece of paper is to tell you I've got my white paper and am recommended for a commission!!!!!!!!!!!!!! Of course that doesn't mean I get a commission, as I explained. But its the first step . . . Tell Matthew he ought to be jolly proud.'[171]

Alec had moral support from high places. 'I do *hope* you get this commission,' wrote Edith Sitwell. 'It is so monstrous to think of your being taken away from your own work, anyhow. But it adds to the horror to think of the kind of manual work you are doing.'[172] She wrote regularly to Alec, trying to raise his morale: 'I have seen several great admirers of yours in the last month or so. Did I tell you, in my last letter, that Charles Morgan had been here, and had expressed a most powerful admiration for you? He said "He is the only really beautiful romantic actor we have". I was knitting a suit for Matthew while he (C.M.) was here, and he was so interested in hearing about Merula & Matthew.'[173]

As the day of his appearance before the Admiralty Board grew closer, Alec protected himself from disappointment by pretending to Merula that it was only for the pay. 'Personally I don't mind but I do want you to have more than 30 shillings a week for yourself and Matthew . . . and Mary has clever Eusty earning pounds for her.' Bully, too, had misgivings. 'I don't much want to be an officer,' he wrote to Alec when on leave, '& there is little chance of it.' But whatever reservations the Navy might have had in peacetime, the need for officers was now acute and both Alec and Bully were recommended for officer training.

Although Alec's leave was mostly too short for him to journey any distance from Plymouth, he discovered that his former headmaster at Roborough, D.G. Gilbert, had retired with his wife to a cottage at Newton Ferrers, about six miles away. The Gilberts offered to have Merula and Matthew to stay. 'You *would* like to come near here for a bit wouldn't you?' Alec wrote to Merula on 17 February:

> Plymouth is vastly unsafe (most of the country round is risky) and there's nothing my side of the water. The Gilberts place (a newly built rather suburban little house) is in a heavenly position and they would like to have you and Matthew until the Uncle (P.G. Gilbert) comes. Well, I wouldn't be able to see you much, dear love, but it would be *two* weekends, skipping the week-end between . . .

Merula took the train from London to Plymouth, laden with Matthew, her luggage, and the bundles of food that Alec had told her to bring 'whether to sustain us on the train or sweeten the Gilberts, I don't know'. Leaving Matthew in the care of Mrs Gilbert at Newton Ferrers, Merula took the bus into Plymouth to have dinner with Alec 'in a gloomy hotel full of brown leather furniture'. On her way through London, Merula had stayed with her friend Marriott Longman in her house on Ladbroke Grove and had picked up news about Michel St Denis, who had gone to fight in France at the outbreak of war, and

Pierre Lefèvre, their fellow student at the Actors' School who had
been called up into the French army. Michel had been evacuated
from Dunkirk and was now broadcasting for the Free French at the
BBC, and Pierre, who also escaped from Dunkirk, was working with
him.

Merula's most important news, however, was that after Alec had left
Middle Lodge she had read the New Testament for the first time and
'had been bowled over, knocked sideways, turned upside down. I read
St Luke straight through at a sitting and it seemed to me that no one
could have invented such an extraordinary story, it just had to be
true'.[174] Her fear of estrangement from Alec, which she'd felt
following his rediscovery of religion and Matthew's baptism, was now
allayed.

‹ After dinner, Alec returned to his barracks while Merula boarded
the bus that would take her back to Newton Ferrers. Although
stationary, the vehicle began to sway and shudder: Plymouth was
being bombed. She left the bus and went to an air raid shelter and sat
in silence: 'It was like being in a church.' Then, 'At the height of the
racket going on outside, the curtain was pulled aside. One saw a blaze
of light and a white-faced, wild-eyed young woman thrust a bundle
into the warden's hands and shouted: "I've got to go back. They're all
dead in there," and vanished.' The bundle contained a baby which was
passed around the women in the shelter until 'one woman had the
courage to say "The baby's dead".' When the 'all clear' sounded, they
went out into the street, brightly lit by the burning buildings. Merula
returned to the bus station: her bus was now 'just a tangle of metal'.
She found shelter for the rest of the night and, the next morning, got
a lift to Newton Ferrers.

That night she wanted to return to Plymouth to spend the night
with Alec as they had arranged; but the Gilberts refused to look after
Matthew. Merula 'fretted and fumed' until suddenly Alec appeared. He
had been given compassionate leave to discover if Merula was alive. At
HMS *Raleigh*, the air raid shelter had received a direct hit and everyone
in it had been killed.

Merula's discovery of Christianity through reading the New Testament enabled Alec to open his mind as well as his heart in his letters. 'That night when you cried in bed and said you thought a wedge had been driven between us by my conversion was one of the most startling unhappy moments I've ever experienced. It was so intense and burned me up and seemed to send me hurtling away into loneliness. But you retrieved it and made me happier than man can ever have been made happy.'[175]

Alec's newfound Christian zeal was not blunted by life in the barracks. 'You would be amazed at the number of men who admit to belief in Christ (even if their language is filthy). At least ¾ I should say. There are an enormous number of R.C.s too. About ¼ of our mess.' He had received a letter from Cyril Tomkinson in Bristol, thanking Alec for returning the books he had borrowed, giving the news that their friend, Father Hutch, had been made a Canon of Southwark Cathedral – 'a mark of honour that's well deserved' – and saying that, at Cyril's request, some nuns at Malling Abbey in Herefordshire were praying for Alec and his family. 'They pray much and some are praying before the Blessed sacrament always all thro the 24 hrs.'[176]

Alec shared his mentor's High Church convictions. 'The C. of E. priests here,' he wrote to Merula, 'have, I'm delighted to find, fairly marked Catholic tendencies.' After receiving a letter from the Abbess at Malling Abbey, saying that he and Merula and Matthew were the beneficiaries of the prayers of the community, Alec started to mark his letters, as she had done, with a cross and the word 'Pax' – peace. 'I like the Xtian sign on the Abbess's letter – I've repeated it,' he told Merula.

Alec did not want Merula to follow him into the Church for his sake, nor did he claim any credit for her conversion:

One thing I must say. You did not find Xtianity through me, my loved one. I find the word 'grace' the most gentle and powerful in the language and I believe all spiritual blessings are the workings of the Grace of God. It was the Grace of God working in you. The fact that I found the formula, so to speak, before you has practically nothing to do with it. We both owe our greater happiness and mutual greater happiness elsewhere. I pray continually (when I pray properly) that God will help my unbelief. And I pray for His Grace. And that He will pour his Grace on you and Matthew. And that I may understand His mysteries – which I can only feel to be spiritually true – and that I may trust His Church . . .[177]

Alec could understand, he wrote, that Merula, because of her upbringing, was 'naturally still very suspicious of the Church'. But he could not resist infecting her with his enthusiasm. 'I do so want to read more about the Saints. St Teresa was a terrific find, thanks to Cyril Tomkinson. And apparently St Francis de Sales is. And now, reading the Jesuit book, I'm crazy about St Francis Xavier. St Ignatius is terrific but not so lovable really . . .'

He also read a biography of Charles de Foucauld, the French soldier who became a hermit in the Sahara Desert, which had been mentioned in a broadcast by T.S. Eliot, a poet Alec particularly admired.*

It reminds me, in a remote way, of our pony ride round the Pyramids. Or perhaps I'm thinking of sand and wind because of the De Foucauld book. Its terrific! Couldn't be more pleased about it. What ignorant, isolated beasts we are not to know about a man like that. It's beautifully written, reasonably translated, and reads rather like a Western. Robbers and camels and buried gold and sand and midnight meetings and the philosopher's stone and continuous disguises. Very exciting – I can't believe it keeps it up. How right of Mr Eliot to talk about it. Incidentally, I'm enclosing his broadcast talk, which was published in the *Listener*. It is good.[178]

---

* In a broadcast talk which he gave in the spring of 1941, 'Towards a Christian Britain', Eliot talked about the sacrifices which would be necessary to bring about such a national conversion, and the need for Christian 'prophets' who would alter the social consciousness of the people. In this context, he described the life of Charles de Foucauld . . . Peter Ackroyd, *T.S. Eliot*, p. 257.

Alec also wrote a fan letter to T.S. Eliot to which the eminent poet replied on 9 April from his office at Faber and Faber:

> A broadcast talk takes me so many weeks' work to prepare and is so soon over that but for such letters of encouragement as yours one would doubt whether it was all worth while . . . I remember you very well though we have never met. What I remember is not merely your asking permission to read some of my verse, but the most satisfying performance of Hamlet that I have ever seen.[179]

Alec did not hide from Merula his own spiritual travails:

> I'm a huge hypocrite and never stop doubting in the most horrible way . . . My constant prayer is for the grace to be able to believe. I *say* believe, go to Mass in faith – all that I can muster, and if asked *exactly* what I believe I would be stumped. We've been brought up darling in a world which hasn't required *faith* of us. And faith is the foundation of Xtianity and has always been about the biggest pillar in the Jewish religion . . . I'll tell you three or four things I *like* about the Church. I like the very practical opportunity it gives me for trying to practise humility . . . T.S. Eliot pointed out to my dull ears the nature of humility and it seems to me the most startling, charming virtue . . . Then the Church is a constant, hard reminder that the universe wasn't built for me and my sins and problems aren't all important – other people go through similar experiences. And the Church is a community, to-day we no longer live in any sort of community . . . Then – on religious grounds I support it more definitely. The C. of E. service *is* capable of being very beautiful . . . Then I believe Christ's commands are worth obeying . . . Then I also believe that priests, bona fide ones, are in direct line of laying on of hands from the apostles . . . each week, each day, even if with a certain hesitant embarrassment, I can accept Christ more readily and simply. Look what has come into our lives, darling. That's not an illusory, acceptive [sic] piece of wishful thinking. Its real and more sweetly real than you know or I can tell you. Since my

first confession and the formal forgiveness of my past sins my life has changed from top to bottom. That is a *real* thing and is the work of God's grace, not of a disillusioned mind. If it is *delusion* then for God's sake let's be deluded . . . You are a much better Xtian than I am . . . Dearest don't be depressed by it all and *don't think about it too much* . . .[180]

One difficulty Merula faced in following Alec into the Church of England was her knowledge of the distress it would cause her atheist parents. Alec coaxed her on with a certain caution. 'I wish you were b'tised and c'med so that on Sunday you were going to take your First Communion. But there's plenty of time.' But he also recognised that temperamentally she was less disposed to a spiritual quest – 'a contented person,' as he told Chattie, 'so of the earth'.[181] But the question of a shared faith became urgent when, on 20 April 1941, Alec wrote to Merula to say that he had been called by God to become a priest:

Darling – half a dozen words written at night to post first thing in the morning. I am happy! Very, very happy, but apprehensive. Pray for me, I beg you. I know you do. And let this make you happy dearest heart, fondest wife my dear dear lover, – God has spoken to me quite firmly, quite gently and quite decisively. Not a guess on my part. He has handed me his gift on a plate. I am called to the priesthood! Have courage, bear with me and strengthen me. I can write no more now, nor explain. So sudden too – there was no saying No, let me think. All love, forgive this mysteriousness – due to briefness. All love, dear dear one, in the Love of our Lord.

Alec's absolute certainty of the authenticity of this call from God was tempered the very next day. 'I came across these lines in the Foucauld book,' he wrote to Merula. '"Does this come from God, the devil, or my imagination?"' But the question was not enough to change his mind. He went to the Chaplain at HMS *Raleigh*, the Rev. G. Gater, who made an enquiry on his behalf to the Diocese of Lincoln, receiving a reply from the Warden of the Bishop's Hostel on 24 April, 1941:

Thank you very much indeed for your letter concerning Alec Guiness [sic] Cuffe. I will await a letter from him unless you think that it is better for me to write to him direct. I imagine that as the war proceeds, quite a number of men will begin to consider the question of reading for Holy Orders, and it is this situation which we have had in mind and are trying to meet. So far, I have only heard of four or five such men, but they are a beginning.[182]

Alec's vocation to the priesthood threw Merula into confusion: how could she rise to the challenge of being a vicar's wife? Alec sought to reassure her. 'But darling, darling how can you think you could be a hindrance to me? How can you? When I owe you all? . . . My confidence is rested in your love. Without your love I could do nothing. Act, sail, motoring! . . . You must and can help me . . . You'll be a wonderful "priest's wife".'[183]

The decision, however, made Merula decide that 'it was high time I got baptised'. Early in May, Alec had a few days' leave and met Merula in London. There was a Salaman family reunion over lunch at the Ivy Restaurant off St Martin's Lane, after which Alec and Merula went down 'into the grubbiness of the Waterloo Road' to have tea with Father Hutch 'in his crowded shitty little room'.[184] 'He was very merry and easygoing,' Merula recalled in her memoir, *Family Matters*, 'and, after a little chat, he took us along the New Cut, where he was greeted by all the stall holders, to a big gloomy church where he baptised me in the name of the Father and the Son and the Holy Ghost and Alec and the cleaning lady were my godparents.' It was all 'sweet and pleasant and simple and unfussing,' Alec wrote to Chattie, 'and it all appeared so much more real than the Ivy and our day in town took a new and happier turn . . .'[185]

Merula's conversion delighted her Aunt Mab, Big Chattie's sister, who wrote to congratulate her. 'I think God has been specially good to you in giving you such a depth of insight into the unfathomable treasures of the Faith.'[186] However, it came as an unpleasant surprise to her brother Eusty serving in the Navy. 'When I first heard . . . that you had been baptised,' he wrote to Merula, 'it was a terrible shock, almost like hearing about someone you love having died, as I thought I had lost you completely and that I could never write to you or speak to you again without a stone wall between us'; but he had come to accept her Christianity when he realised that 'worship was another name for love'.[187]

More difficult to reconcile were Merula's atheist parents, particularly her father, Michel. 'If only Daddy, Daddy in particular, had faith,' Merula wrote to Alec:

> . . . it would be alright – he seems so unhappy it is dreadful, he is unhappy right in the centre and it is just there he won't look it seems – I am sure his scorn of Dostoevsky is because he is afraid of delving into the heart of himself, because of the void . . . The religious question has never come up again – not since Middle Lodge – I am so afraid of it because it would estrange Daddy and me more than ever, and I feel he is very lonely and feels the estrangement very much. He is so cut off from all his children now – how odd it must feel for him after years of laying down laws and saying sayings which have been listened to and implicitly believed in and repeated by all his children to find them drifting away and leading lives and thinking things differently.[188]

Merula was unable to avoid religious disputes with her father altogether. On 12 October she told Alec that:

> . . . there has been a stupid argument about religion – bother – Oh Dear – if only I wasn't a graceless ignorant cow! Oh dear Daddy – his creed is simply suicidal, the logical conclusion is that a man should kill himself to prove himself master over his own destiny – there is a man in *The Possessed* who does that. But it is lucky such people are not usually either logical or brave enough to carry their view of life to such an end.[189]

Alec did what he could to console her – now very much in vicar mode:

Darling I'm sorry – deeply – to hear of your estrangement from your
mamma and difficulty with poppa. Try to break it down. Be gentle and
forgiving – if there is anything to forgive – and don't give offence. Rest
yourself in the Spirit in your prayers. Miss no opportunity of . . . giving
thanks to God for all things – all the things that you love and mean so
much to you. Do not rush into talk or gossip but keep your still centre
and your wisdom and love, and with praying you may find the situation
eased, because God will deny you no good thing . . . Don't be fretted
by any of it. Give thanks for being able to serve in the silliest things –
washing, scrubbing, cleaning silver, milking the goat – nearly
everything that is work can be turned to the glory of God. Because
God is so easily pleased . . . There is no laziness with God in his
service.[190]

Alec had sufficient self-knowledge to admit to Merula that 'the
temptation to *preach* is gross in me'; but if he was going to be a vicar,
that was as it should be, and Merula put a brave face on her future as
a priest's wife. She wrote to Alec, using a typewriter:

I thought it would be a good idea to learn, so as I can be a useful
vicaress . . . I am typing my story for practice, so you won't get it for
ages as it takes me a *long* time . . .

   Dear how I look forward to typeing [sic] out lists of ladies to mow
the church lawn and arrainge [sic] the flowers. Maybe there will be the
parish mag to tip-tappit on my typer, and obscure poems composed by
the vicar for the Sunday School children . . . Ummmmm there are all
sorts of possibilities for the future. O BUT how I wish this war was over
and done with. O Lord let there be a letter tomorrow, there was
nothing this morning I am sure those horrible sensor [sic] people have
been sitting on them. I am sorry this is ANOTHER dull letter, it's only
merit is the *beatifull* [sic] typeing [sic] . . . Yes I must go to boring bed.
If only you were there in it. I would squease [sic] you to pieces with
hugs.

Alec returned this letter to Merula with circles drawn around the spelling mistakes and a note at the end: 'I don't know *what* you want to do to me but I hope it's only *SQUEEZE.*'[191]

By this stage in his naval training, Alec had been posted to Chatham:

> . . . the nadir of my lower-deck experiences where thousands of men slept, snored or vomited – their hammocks slung three-deep in a cavernous tunnel which served as dormitory, bomb-shelter and lavatory; Chatham, where to get a meal you had to fight your way to the food – which sometimes I refused to do. If it hadn't been for kind, tough messmates who took pity on me, I think I might have starved.[192]

The memory was still painful more than fifty years later. 'At all times you had to listen carefully to the Tannoy system in case your number was called out, summoning you to a ship. That was something we partly dreaded, as it would mean leaving England and family and really facing up to the war.'[193]

Alec seems to have persuaded himself that his number would be called, and that he would see action as an Ordinary Seaman. 'I must write this calmly and quietly and not upset you,' he wrote to Merula:

> It does look as if I shall be given my ship within the next few days . . . Dear love I am not afraid – though afraid of making a fool of myself – and you are never once to doubt of my existence or health or anything. If I should be killed – well, poppet – I shall pray for you and be with you in spirit and always love you and seek God's help more so. Marry again if you want to. Because its good to be married as we have known and know. But marry a better man than me and one who'll work for you and love you truly. Not Bannerman. How gloomy oh how gloomy that reads. But of course I shan't be killed. If I am, cry dear love and get rid of it – don't stifle your unhappiness. Then in a short time you will be happy again and I shall pray for your happiness. And bring Matthew [up] strictly, so he may know we love him properly, and oh I'm sure

he'll be wonderful to you and care for you. I commend you to his care
and love.

How silly, silly to write like this and I wish I could stop crying . . .
Pray for me, Love me. God keep you and Baba. Don't dig too much.
Rest in the afternoons. Don't get lonely. A kiss on your sweet warm
lips.[194]

In fact, instead of being sent on active service, Alec was asked to act
in a propaganda film for the Navy and, a few days later, wrote to
Merula from the set 'wearing make-up and Pleydel and wig and
monocle and carnation and camping umbrella and gloves'. His only
previous experience of cinema had been as an extra in a film called
Evensong eleven years before, and now he rediscovered the tedium
involved. 'I did ten solid hours in front of the camera today,' he wrote
to Merula, 'which will take *eight minutes* to show.'

fifteen

In June 1941, Alec was transferred first to HMS *Northney*, an officers' training establishment on Hayling Island in Hampshire, and then, on 18 June, to Inveraray on Loch Fyne in Scotland. Here he graduated from learning how to tie knots to the more sophisticated skills of command and navigation that would be required of a naval officer.

Alec's main consolation for his exile in Scotland was coming across his old friend from the Thirty-Nine Club, John Rotton, now married but also serving in the Navy, and who accompanied him on a tour of duty on HMS *Quebec* in August: the first time that Alec had put out to sea. 'How wonderful God is,' he wrote to Merula:

> . . . and how *extraordinarily* and surprisingly he works. Ah, I feel it all surging back and roots being refreshed. Soon, perhaps, growth will begin again. John Rotton and I decided we would like to walk about the deck and talk . . . I liked him and admired him before. The fact that he was a master at Borstal interested me. But I'd got him wrong, a bit. I

found that he, too, is a recently converted Christian and wants, he
thinks, to enter the Church. I don't think I've ever agreed with anyone
so much as I found myself in agreement with him. Our feelings on the
subject seem to be identical. Except that he is an intellectual and can
think. But we both have been influenced vastly by T.S. Eliot being
Xtian! We have both been reading the saints – though he knows
nothing of blessed Teresa. St Francis de Sales is his favourite, and we
each have the Devout Life with us. Our fears, prejudices are the same.
We have each been in the deepest gloom, it appears, for the past three
weeks. And now – how glorious it is to find another Christian and
somehow, when one is flagging and falling off, one *does*![195]

Alec could not get over his good fortune in finding such a kindred
spirit in his old friend: it was almost as if he had fallen in love. 'He's an
enchanting, good – really good – person. And his intelligence is
shaming . . . John . . . is rapidly taking the place that Adolf* occupied
when he was alive . . . I have nothing in common with John – except
Christ – and oh, everything. I couldn't admire him more. His vitality,
manliness, intellect, sensitivity and sweet naturedness. I do so want you
to meet him.' And later on the voyage: 'John and I walked silently up
and down the deck for ages last night, and then he produced Eliot's
"Burnt Norton" out of his duffel coat and asked me if I would read it
to him. So we climbed into the enormous grey funnel on this ship –
and I read Mr Eliot . . . Anyway, we have discovered the funnel which
is lovely and warm . . .'

In the autumn of 1941, Alec's training intensified: he returned to
England, changed ship three times in three days in mid-September, but
by Christmas of 1941 was back at Inveraray, and went to a New Year's
Eve party with 'streamers and seventy WRENS'. 'It was a dull dance,'
he told Merula, 'and I left before midnight. Besides, there is a dreadful
little Wren from Bradford who wants me as a *friend*.' In February 1942,

---

*   Adolf Deys, AG's friend from Arks Publicity, was killed by a bomb.

Alec was sent south again to the Officers' Training establishment in Hove on the south coast. He went before the Selection Board on 10 February and by 3 May 1942, was commissioned as a Sub-Lieutenant in the Royal Navy Volunteer Reserve.

For a man bearing the stigma of bastardy, with no university degree, and a demeanour that had led his father-in-law to think he was a pansy, securing a commission was a triumph on many different levels. Alec was both delighted and overawed. 'As quick as lightning I got measured by Messrs. Gieves for my midnight-blue Sub-Lieutenant uniform, with its thin, squiggly, gold-braid stripe,' he recalled in *Blessings in Disguise*[196] and he was delighted with the result. 'I look terrifically dandy in my uniform,' he wrote to Chattie, 'and nearly faint with amazement and pride when saluted in the streets . . .' But then added: 'It's a pity I don't know anything about the sea . . .'

His first posting as an officer was back in Scotland, serving in Combined Operations in the small port of Troon on the Firth of Clyde in Ayrshire. 'It's a bleakish life here and the people are dullish,' he wrote to Merula. 'My life is a routine one. I live it quietly on my own and don't have much to do with the majority of my brother officers . . .' For Merula and Matthew to join him would be pointless. 'Apparently there is nowhere to get rooms and even if one is lucky enough it's a four-guinea rent at lowest; and on top of that I'm not allowed to sleep ashore and I work until 6.00 p.m. and later each day. And up early!'

His best chance of escape from Troon came from Peter Bull. After the first months at HMS *Raleigh* their ways had parted, but Bully had written to him in September 1941 to say that 'one of my firmest resolves in this war is never to lose touch with you . . .' Now, also commissioned and given a command, he wrote to Alec to say that he had requested him as his next 'numéro un'. The request was turned down. 'It was most depressing not getting the job with Peter,' Alec wrote to Merula.

The lack of confidence in his ability as an officer that Alec had expressed to Chattie was not feigned: at the end of July he was offered a command 'but I asked for it to be postponed for I don't quite feel ready yet'.[197] He remained in a limbo in Troon – 'not yet on the high seas but I'm not allowed to go home'. Despite the smart uniform that he had had made in London, he felt uncomfortable playing the role of a naval officer yet could find no other. The feeling that he had been called to the Anglican priesthood had faded; and his future as an actor seemed remote. He wrote to Chattie in an undated letter:

> The theatre – Well, I suppose the theatre has meant more to me than most people. It has meant breaking with a stifling past (the dullness of a lonely schoolboy life, the drabness of uncongenial office work), it has meant self-realisation, the achievement of a few odd ambitions, it has even meant a certain amount of success, it has meant money and a home, Merry, Matthew, 90% of my friends, it has been a liberation of or escape from a very bad suicidal tendency and above all it has meant the *theatre* – the thing I've dreamed about and longed for since the age of seven. Such a theatre doesn't slip easily out of the blood nor is it likely to, nor at the moment, am I encouraging it to. It is true that for the time being I can work up no interest in anything I go to see and that I'm not even anxious to see things which not long ago I would have fought to see. Partly jealousy I know, partly because I think the war has left the decadents where they've always longed to be and worse than the decadents the weaklings, and partly a hangover from my first flush of religious conviction when I thought perhaps I ought to be an Anglican priest.

Alec was now suffering – not from religious doubts so much as religious confusion – a dissatisfaction with the Church of England and a measure of disappointment that he had not retained the serenity that came with his conversion. The letter continued:

> I still have my religious convictions but they have undergone deep sea changes one way and another and I have not lived by the Church, or

prayer in the way I genuinely tried to eighteen months ago. I stand in no man's land. No, that's not true. I'm quite definitely in enemy territory and through my own silly lazy inquisitive wandering. I want to get back to where I was and start again but although I *know* the way I'm a bit apprehensive about taking it. Besides, although I know I'm in the wrong camp (unwillingly now, though there is a certain vicarious excitement) I'm not sure to which Regiment I belong. The *crack* one – the Roman one – has expensive uniforms which I can't afford – but which I think I *ought* to belong to but can't quite manage – the other one, which I have loved, seems to have lost its colonel or something and although full of wise and good nice and friendly men – well, it's a bit of a rabble, and it's so easy to get lost (as in my present plight) when you are semi free to make your own attacks – cutting your own barbed wire and throwing your own rather damp bombs. More fun, but not such good sense. Of course the corruption and goings on in the crack regiment is terrific – but so it is in the streets, air raid shelters and town halls throughout the land. I apologise for writing in this sort of metaphorical way, but it comes nearer the truth or is at any rate less misleading. You always seem to come in for a nasty dose of my religious scruples but it appears to interest you and it helps me quite a bit to write them down.

Alec's confusing metaphor is significant because it reveals that at this early stage in his life he considered joining the Roman Catholic Church. Hitherto he seemed to have accepted the claims of High Anglicans that their priests and bishops were the successors of Christ's Apostles – that there had been a laying on of hands down the centuries since the time of Christ, a claim rejected by the Roman Catholic Church.* Now, although it is not the question of the validity of Anglican Orders that seemed to concern him, there is the sense that

---

* On 13 September 1896, in the Bull *Apostolicae Curae*, Pope Leo XIII declared Anglican Orders to be 'absolutely null and utterly void' on the ground of defect of form in the rite, and defect of intention in the minister.

the very tolerance and absence of authority among the Anglican clergy had failed to deal with Alec's own remorse and sense of sin. 'I don't write often to Merry in this way,' Alec tells Chattie in this same letter, 'for a great many reasons. Partly because – oh, ever so many reasons. I do not wish to give her offence nor do I wish to influence her until I know which way I'm *bound* to go.' He goes on:

> If I crawl and wriggle on my stomach through all the barbed wire and find myself in the lines of the crack regiment – well it's too easy for words. The priesthood is then right out of the question* (I'm not sure that it's not anyway) and I can plunge back into the theatre. I want to pour out all the snakes from my mind in Macbeth and rid myself of tears and wit in Hamlet. I want to gain such an economy over myself that only a pure stream of movement and voice and thought flows. I want to acquire and beget the TEMPERANCE, and the MODESTY that isn't *tame*.[198]

Alec liked to confide in Chattie, his 'pretty sister-in-law', and also to receive her confidences and offer advice: while playing in the Perth Theatre Festival in the summer of 1941 she had fallen in love with a Roman Catholic actor whom Alec, having met him briefly the year before, considered unsuitable. He also thought Chattie and her lover should stop acting and either join the armed forces or do war work. 'It must be dreadful to be a young unmarried woman, with the prospect of be[ing] hauled into a factory,' he wrote to Merula, 'but I think she should do something useful. Even if she was a better actress, or established as one at all, I would still think that. There is so much to be done if we are not to lose this war.'[199]

Alec's contempt for wartime shirkers did not extend to his old friends and patrons, John Gielgud and Martita Hunt. Hearing that they were

---

* Roman Catholic priests are obliged to be celibate.

appearing together in Sheffield, Alec wrote to Edith Sitwell to suggest that she and Osbert invite them to Renishaw. Gielgud had had news of Alec and written to him at Troon to commiserate about his isolated posting – 'your lonely watch, and no Horatio to your Bernardo!' and asked about the rumours of his religious vocation. 'Why did somebody tell me yesterday you were going to become a monk? Surely a façon de parler, pis aller, or permis de séjour.'[200]

The reference to the taking of Holy Orders as a 'permis de séjour' – viz. a way of escaping active duty in the armed forces – cannot have pleased Alec who felt only contempt for 'the decadents' and 'weaklings' who had been left to run the theatre in London.

Alec's confession to Chattie that he could not write to Merula in the same way casts light on one aspect of his relationship with his wife. Merula was older than Chattie, and more or less the same age as Alec, yet her innocence and lack of sophistication made her seem younger. Alec frequently treated her as a slightly backward child. He was maddened by her failure to date her letters correctly: 'A long letter from you at lunchtime today. The postmark was Aug 20th which I should think, from the letter, is correct, but you've dated it the 12th. Poppet!!! How hopeless you are at anything like that.'[201] And he continued to be exasperated by her incorrect spelling. 'Did the window panes squeak in the Logia or Loggia – not the Lodger dearest, unless you've taken in a P.G. without telling me . . .'[202] Orderly and methodical by nature, Alec was irritated by Merula's incompetence in practical matters. 'Please send me Lickfold p.o. address for *my* business goings on up here – this is the 60th time of asking.' And, in another letter: 'I nearly blew up with vexation at the registered letter – I so expressly said a pound note – not a two pound cheque. But thank you, my sweet, all the same. The cheque is no direct use to me at all, as you must know, not having a bank or friends in the district.'[203]

Merula's response to Alec's badgering was simultaneously to crave his forgiveness and ignore his commands. Rarely, throughout her life,

did she write more than the day of the week at the top of her letters;
nor, despite Alec's mockery, did her spelling improve. Yet she seemed
terrified of his rages and abject in her attempts to placate him. One
revealing quarrel by correspondence in September of 1941 was caused
by Merula's telling Alec how her mother had come to drop her
objection to her travelling abroad alone with Alec.

> I have been awfully reminiscing this evening – do you remember we
> were going to Iceland together, in our platonic days, and when I told
> them at home that I might be going Mummy said 'But Merry can't go
> with a young man' – and Daddy said 'that's all right, it's just as if she
> was going with Billy Chappell – isn't it?' and I said 'Oh yes.' That was
> a godsend – they never had to bother about us till we told them we
> were getting married.[204]

This touched a raw nerve and provoked an icy response from Alec. 'I
was enchanted with both letters but mortally offended at your
reminiscing – did Michel ever say you could go to Iceland with me
because I was Billy Chappell No. 2? It takes a lot of forgiving. And you
said Oh, yes. I wonder if all this reminiscence is good.'[205] Which in
turn led to a grovelling apology from Merula:

> How can I have offended you, Oh you know I am stupid and say stupid
> things – but I thought you had got over being offended – my love Please
> forgive – I am miserable that I have offended you and you haven't
> forgiven me – when Daddy said you were Billy Chappell he didn't
> know you, and Mummy would have been horrified at me going on a
> holiday alone with a 'young man' and darling our friendship was so
> innocent – it had never struck me that any one could think things of
> our going away together – and it seemed quite a good idea to let them
> have that impression as they had invented it out of nothing.[206]

The war, now in its second year, had led to severe privations for the
civilian population and Merula, quite apart from the emotional

anguish caused by such long-distance spats with her touchy husband, suffered at home. The Deuchars, the owners of Middle Lodge, who had led the young Guinnesses to understand that they could live there for as long as they liked, had changed their mind and decided to live in the cottage themselves. Merula was obliged to move with Matthew and their furniture to Wadlington, the home of her parents now that Ruckmans had been sold. The sale of Ruckmans in itself had been traumatic: the surplus furniture had been auctioned off at Midhurst for knock-down prices – 'the great mahogany dining table and chairs, all our nursery furniture, etc. and when the two little four-poster beds came up, I begged Papa to withdraw them. Poor Papa, he was in tears when we left'.[207]

Wadlington was overcrowded and the atmosphere was tense. Besides Michel and Big Chattie, there was Eusty's wife Mary with their son Christopher; Mikey's adopted daughter Annie and daughter Pauline; the brain-damaged Susy; Big Chattie's favourite sister, Dolly; her cousin, and Ramon, 'the little Jewish refugee boy, lonely and lost'. The household was held together by the cook, Mrs Gooding, who:

> . . . was always cheerful and unruffled, coped with the continual muddle over everybody's Ration Books, kept the accounts, coped with everybody's food grumbles . . . teased Papa, collected food from all the shady sources and secret agents in the countryside, redid our washing and ironing if she thought we hadn't done it well enough, adored her boring husband and was wise, witty and good, a real dyed-in-the-wool cockney.

The Salamans themselves were less serene:

> Susy stumped around in her calipers, ate too much and was sick and was nagged by Papa. Susy swore at Mummy, Mummy swore at Papa, Papa tore his hair and moaned that he was ruined. So many mouths to feed and nobody contributed a penny and he went on doling out the

drinks and spending a fortune on black market foods provided by the cook's husband who was a butcher in London and came down every weekend, laden with joints of pork, etc.*

Big Chattie, as perceived by Merula, was tormented with jealousy, first of Mrs Gooding the cook, but, more acutely, of her daughter-in-law, Mary. 'When Mary received a letter from Eusty, Mummy's eyes would burn through the envelope and Mary would clutch it to her bosom and run upstairs to devour it in secret.' Mary, the former fellow student of the Salaman sisters at Michel St Denis' London Acting School, was utterly miserable because Eusty was posted abroad. Their separation; the steady sequence of disasters broadcast over the radio at Wadlington that 'was on full blast for every news bulletin so that by the end of the day one thought four ships had been sunk instead of one'; a sense that the Wake aunts preferred Matthew to her son Christopher; and a certain irritation, perhaps, at Merula's newfound religious serenity beside her lapsed-Catholic confusion – all might have been tolerable had not Eusty's letters been so full of unmitigated misery and gloom.

Merula was able to pay occasional visits to Alec. During his first stint of duty at Inveraray, they arranged to meet halfway, staying with the Guthries who, with the remaining staff and actors of the Old Vic, had been evacuated to Burnley in Lancashire. Merula arrived two days

---

* 'On one occasion I remember being asked by my father-in-law to receive a parcel, at Victoria station, from a butcher whose wife worked for him in the country. The war was still on and the parcel, well wrapped up, was a joint of beef. "He's a nice man, Mr Salaman," said the butcher, "even if he is a Jew." My instinct was to throw the beef on the platform but I knew my father-in-law was desperate for food to feed a large, fluctuating household, some of whom were likely to be without ration cards, so I knuckled under the flagrant anti-Semitism.' *A Positively Final Appearance*, p. 79 But cf. *Family Matters*, p. 156. 'Mrs Gooding . . . had two boys of her own, about the same age as Ramon and she took that poor, neglected child to her bosom, saw that he had clothes and washed and treated him just the same as her own boys and at last he had a family to cling to.'

before Alec and found conditions in their terrace house similar to those at Anna-ma-kerrig in Ireland:

> It was bitterly cold. The wind poured through the window frames. Judy was writing a play, crouched on the floor, on little scraps of paper which she would fling over her shoulder and they lay scattered over the grubby carpet. Every now and then, she would mutter about the draughts and gather up the bits of paper and stuff them into the gaps in the window frames.

The house was so filthy that 'in no time, Matthew was black and sharing the cat's food on the floor'. Alec came for a long weekend. Merula stayed on after he had returned to Scotland but made the same mistake that she had made at Anna-ma-kerrig. Judy Guthrie complained that the milk came out of the spout of a jug in a trickle. Merula saw that this was because it had never been washed and the spout had become clogged with the caked residue. She cleaned it and boasted to the Guthries of what she had done. Again, it was a case of 'interfering little bourgeois miss'. 'I was out of favour and returned to Wadlington.'

There were other, happier encounters. When Alec was attending a course on Hayling Island near Portsmouth, they rented a room in a semi-detached cottage 'with a bed that took up most of the space and a Beatrix stove. Once a week, I pushed the broken-down borrowed pram to Havant and bought a sack of Semolina and a wadge of dried dates and Matthew's allowance of two oranges. Matthew and I lived on Semolina and dates, about the only thing I could cook on the Beatrix, except when Alec had shore leave and brought sardines and spam from the NAAFI.'[208]

Merula was able to join Alec during his officer training at Hove; and at Lancing, where they rented a room in a bungalow where the 'really nasty little pasty-faced landlady' would not let Merula hang Matthew's nappies to dry in her garden. There were a number of trips to join Alec in Scotland. On her first stay at Troon the only lodging she could find was 'a cupboard with a mattress in it' and 'a pump in the yard to wash

at, for ten shillings a week.' On a later visit to Troon, she and Alec
stayed with John and Polly Rotton at the digs they rented off a lady
doctor on Temple Road.

The journeys were an ordeal. On one occasion, Merula and
Matthew were turned off a train that came to a halt at a station in the
Midlands in the middle of the night. The woman serving tea in the
buffet would not sell any milk for Matthew: she said that it was against
regulations to sell milk without tea. Finally, after much haggling, she
agreed to sell Merula the milk from twelve cups of tea.

Merula's last stay in Scotland was at Inveraray where she found a
loft with two brass beds in the stables of Inveraray Castle, the home
of the Duke of Argyll. It was here, in early September 1942, that Alec
received a telegram to say that he was to be posted abroad. He had a
week's leave before his departure, which they spent first in a guest
house on Loch Lomond, then staying a night with Martita Hunt in her
flat in London. 'In the morning, we saw Alec off at Euston station. He
got out of the taxi and walked away without looking back. We didn't
see one another for two and a half years.'[209]

sixteen

The train from Euston station took Alec to Glasgow where he boarded the Cunard liner, the *Queen Mary*, berthed on the Clyde. He was put in a two-bed cabin with seven out of fifty young RNVR officers travelling, like Alec, to the United States. Alec's orders were to take delivery of a landing craft being built in dockyards on Quincy Bay near Boston and sail it back across the Atlantic.

When Alec disembarked in New York, he was billeted on the fourteenth floor of the Barbizon-Plaza Hotel. Writing to Merula on 14 September, he could not contain his excitement. 'My darling – I want you to be with me *so* badly, so very badly – it's all so exhilarating and alive and in its way very beautiful.' He was particularly pleased that his reputation as an actor had preceded him and that the letters of introduction he had obtained from John Gielgud had proved superfluous. A number of his theatrical friends from London were in New York – among them Percy Harris and Elisabeth Montgomery of the Motleys; Margaret ('Peggy') Webster; Rosamond Gilder, then

editing *Theatre Arts*, and Laurence Olivier's then wife, the actress Jill
Esmond. They all pounced on the brilliant young actor now playing a
heroic real-life role. Within a day of his arrival, Peggy Webster had
given Alec fifty dollars and Jill Esmond had asked the celebrated
theatrical actor, producer, director and performer, Guthrie McClintic,
if she could bring 'a naval officer who used to be an actor' to a select
party, and gave his name, Alec Guinness. McClintic had exploded, Alec
reported to Merula:

> 'My *God*! *No*! Why, he has the reputation here of being the finest
> Hamlet since Barrymore. Ruth Gordon came back from London saying
> we didn't know what acting in Shakespeare *meant* until we'd seen him.'
> And along he came and made a terrific fuss of me and I've never
> stopped being fêted since which is funny and exciting and jolly for the
> old ego . . .[210]

Alec was exhilarated by life in New York. 'How I'd love Matthew to be
here to whizz up and down in the lifts! How he'd adore leaving his
pretty tummy at the top of a sky-scraper and *dropping* 50 floors and his
tummy coming down afterwards!' He clearly felt a little guilty that he
could so enjoy himself without Merula. 'I feel I'm cheating you by
having such an experience. But when the war is over we must come
and visit. I'm sure I'm laying foundations for getting a job here – to do
one play, anyway.' He was taken to a striptease which he thought was
'horrible' and decided that 'a great streak of evil' ran through the city.
But he did not want to leave this Sodom and Gomorrah and was 'a bit
depressed' when, only a few days after his arrival in New York, he was
sent to Asbury Park in New Jersey – 'a sort of luxurious Blackpool' –
to prepare quarters for naval ratings in the Monterey Hotel.

Alec was back in New York by 26 September with time on his hands
because the landing craft had not been completed. Thinking that he
might be able to take advantage of the delay to act on Broadway, Alec
ordered a wig at the cost of seventy dollars, despite the fact that 'there
is no really reliable wigmaker in New York – they all go to Hollywood'.

Percy Harris and Elisabeth Montgomery were designing the sets for a production by Guthrie McClintic of Chekhov's *Three Sisters* and McClintic offered Alec the role of Tusenbach 'at a salary equivalent to about £150 a week'. Alec explained that his superior officer, 'a nice conservative old gentleman, had told me, very sweetly, that I oughtn't to even attempt to get permission to perform but McClintic, who is obviously having difficulties casting, wasn't prepared to drop the matter so lightly, and, if you please, is pushing off a deputation to Lord Halifax about me.'[211] Lord Halifax was the British Ambassador in Washington.

Merula was not forgotten: Alec sent her a parcel containing two volumes of Marcel Proust's *Remembrance of Things Past*, chocolate, face powder, stockings, lipstick and a refill – 'you twirl the bottom of it to make it come again – sounds rude'. Nor was Chattie neglected: he enclosed a Max Factor make-up pack that she had asked for. Nor was his soul. 'When I have been to confession I shall take communion . . . but until I have, I daren't. My soul feels very grubby and unhygienic.'

On 6 October, Alec was ordered by the Navy to take a fortnight's 'refresher course' in New York 'which will give me a few hours navigational work during the day and leave my evenings free . . . I'm back at the Barbizon Plaza – I've got a sort of little flat to myself here which is cosy . . .' He had breakfast in the local diner. 'You don't ask for fried eggs in this country – you must clap yourself down on a stool and shout "coffee, toast, marmalade, bacon and two sunny-side up".' When not being wined and dined and lionised, or taken to the theatre or the ballet, Alec sniffed around the bookshops and the New York Public Library: 'I think I shall become a Public Library addict here. It's like the B. Museum, but more convenient. You phone up and say: will you get out for me by tomorrow all your books on Chekhov, or whatever . . .' And, energised by the bracing air of Manhattan, and affected by a book he had read on the stigmata of St Francis of Assisi, he started to write a play about a young man who pretends to be a saint and develops the stigmata. 'People accuse him of fraud with regard to his stigmata and such is his shame he says that it *is* a fraud. But it isn't – and – oh, I don't know. Do you think there can possibly be anything there?'[212]

While he was awaiting a response to McClintic's request to Lord Halifax, Alec in fact met the British Ambassador himself in bizarre circumstances. He was strolling along the street in New York wearing his elegant naval uniform when, as he passed the Greek Orthodox Cathedral, he was taken firmly by the arm and led in to a seat next to Lord Halifax and the British Consul:

> Finally I tumbled – and I was right – it was a re-hash funeral for the Duke of Kent and I was representing the British *Navy*!!!!!!!!!!!!! It's absolutely true!!! I've never been so gittered . . . Finally we all shook hands with the archbishop and picking up our top hats, canes, gloves etc (or just *cap* as in my case) away we trooped down the aisle where flunkeys and guards conducted everyone . . . to his TERRIFIC CAR. But my TERRIFIC CAR wasn't there, so with a sweet smile and a salute which bewildered them all I turned on my heel and sauntered back to lunch.[213]

Alec found that life in New York was expensive, and his Sub-Lieutenant's pay, even with an additional living allowance of four dollars a day, was barely sufficient to cover his costs when a haircut and shampoo cost a dollar fifty and dinner at Victor's a dollar twenty-five. He was tantalised by the high rates of pay for actors appearing on Broadway. 'If only there wasn't a war on and the three of us were over here,' he wrote to Merula, 'there'd be a FORTUNE to be made. I know you *dread* a FORTUNE but it *would* be *rather* nice – because then we could day dream and have a cottage again.'[214] Terence Rattigan, the English playwright, whom Alec met at a party given by Elisabeth Montgomery, told him that he had sold the rights to his play, *Flare Path*, for eighty thousand dollars.

Flare Path was to be staged on Broadway and Rattigan asked Alec if he would like to direct it. 'I was so taken aback,' Alec told Merula, 'that unfortunately I indicated he must be insane'; but Rattigan had clearly taken to Alec. He took him to the ballet and introduced him to a fashionable nightclub, the 21 Club, where they *'just* missed seeing

Alec Guinness de Cuffe, aged 8 months.

Agnes Cuff, who styled herself Agnes de Cuffe, aged 21 years, two years before she became pregnant at the Cowes Regatta.

The photograph of Andrew Geddes, given to Alec by Geddes's legitimate daughter, Katie Weldon.

Mary Ann Cuff, born Benfield, Alec's maternal grandmother, who had black hair, black eyes and smoked a clay pipe. Alec would visit her in her earth-floored cottage in Swanage.

Michel Salaman, Alec's father-in-law, Master of the Exmoor Hunt, posing in front of his portrait by his friend Augustus John.

Alec de Cuffe, aged 14 years old, when he went to board at Roborough School under the name of Alec Guinness.

Merula Salaman, the fifth of Michel and Charlotte Salaman's six children. Born Wake, Charlotte Salaman was a descendant of the Saxon nobleman, Hereward the Wake.

Sketch of Alec, aged eighteen, by a colleague at Arks Publicity, Donald Zec, later a cartoonist on the *Daily Mirror*.

Both Alec and Merula were heavy smokers; Alec would often rehearse with a cigarette dangling from his mouth. After repeated attempts, Alec succeeded in giving it up but Merula remained a chain-smoker throughout her life.

From his youth when he contemplated suicide, Alec suffered from bouts of depression that were exacerbated by his success. In 1956, his search for a religious or philosophical system that would counteract them ended with his conversion to the Roman Catholic Church.

Ordinary Seaman Alec Guinness
Cuffe, with his son Matthew, on
leave from the naval induction
centre HMS Raleigh at Torpoint in
Cornwall.

Lieutenant Alec Guinness Cuffe,
RNVR. 'I look terrifically dandy in
my uniform and nearly faint with
amazement and pride when saluted in
the streets . . .'

Alec with the crew of the LCI (L) 124 in North Africa. 'I'm devoted to my
crew. There are about three of them who bore me or whom I *can't* take much
notice of – but the others I find enchanting.'

Garbo'; and in mid-November, after the idea of Alec directing *Flare Path* had been abandoned, offered him the part of the juvenile lead, Flight Lieutenant Graham.

Alec missed Merula's counsel, and was frustrated that her letters seemed to take a month to cross the Atlantic. 'I'm in a flat spin and agitated and want you right here at my side to advise me,' he wrote to Merula:

Actually if you *were* right here I would only be spinning very slowly and wouldn't be worried . . . Last night Terry offered me the lead in his RAF play *Flare Path* – very unsuited, hearty juvenile pilot, full of 'fun', beer and back slapping, and a good part but very un me. I read the play last night and liked it and returned it to Terry saying 'unsuitable'. He said it could be rewritten in places to overcome that and asked me to go with him & see Peggy Webster, who is producing*, and Gilbert Miller, who's putting it on. I *knew* I oughtn't to go, but thought it'd be nice to see Peggy. Well, they are all clamouring for me and all *certain* they can pull strings etc. etc. for permission. Oh, my darling, I'd love to do it, but I'm sure I'd be bad, and I'd love to have the *lots* of money to buy you and Ba lovely things with, but anything that delays my homecoming to you gives me the horrors. Do you think it would be *awful* if I said (permission granted of course) that I'd do it for just six weeks? It'd be so foolish to turn it down for the sake of six weeks and then not be seeing you in any case in that time. God, God, *God* you don't know what a sweat I'm in . . . Sweetheart, I have to make up my mind this afternoon. You will of course *know* by the time you get this, because I'd cable. But if I *do* do it – forgive me. I promise I'll only do it for the *minimum* of time because I *ache* for you.[215]

Because *Flare Path* had a patriotic message – the unfaithful actress married to the young Flight Lieutenant gives up her lover and her

---

* i.e. directing.

career to bolster her husband's morale – and because Alec's landing craft was still being built, permission was given by the Admiralty for Alec to take the role. Alec had mixed emotions: he still seems to have thought that he would be returning to Britain from New York, and went out of his way to reassure Merula that he was eager to get home. 'I wouldn't have you think that I'd postpone seeing you for the sake of Broadway.' On the other hand he was delighted that he was to be paid five hundred dollars a week. 'That's about £125!!!! By the time income tax here and in England and Equity have all poked a finger in my pie, it will leave me about £25!!! Or £30!!! A week – isn't it *extraordinary*!!' And to prove to Merula that he was doing it for her as much as for himself, he bought her a pig-skin handbag from his first week's pay.

Terence Rattigan was homosexual and suffered at the time from 'an acute *coup de foudre* for a tough young dancer'[216] from the New York Ballet. Alec's yearning was only for his wife. 'I miss your sweet warm body in bed,' he wrote to Merula, 'your throat and your shoulders and all of you – how badly I want to feel my tummy pressing against yours. Darling, I *will* be back quite soon, really. If we've done this much with equanimity we can bear another three months, I suppose. But not longer':

> And when I see you, my heart, it will be as if we were only parted yesterday. And when we go to bed that night we will lie naked and still by each other's side and all will seem complete again and we will make love. Funny phrase – make love. Make *more* love, love out of love, I suppose it means. And we will make love and I know I dont want any other love in the world but yours, and I dont know any other anyway. And dammit all this probably reads like something for a Ladies Magazine and thats not what I mean at all.[217]

Though such protestations were undoubtedly sincere, Alec was clearly in no hurry to return to the austerity of wartime Britain. He was vaguely aware that his letters to Merula, detailing the parties, art galleries ('I saw exhibition of paintings by a Russian called Marc Chagall, who seems to be causing a stir . . .') plays and movies ('I went to see a picture called *Casablanca* – the usual spy film set in PICTURESQUE North Africa – but quite enjoyable I suppose . . .') might seem galling to a wife stuck with a baby in the country, so he tried to play down his enjoyment: 'You know ALL THAT BORES ME STIFF . . . I simply can't help it. It's such DREARY FUN . . . God, what a life. But I find I have to make *some* show of not being incurious as to what's going on.'

What he could not hide, and must have been particularly tormenting to those in England, was his unconcealed delight in the abundance of food – not just the bacon and two eggs for breakfast, but the solitary dinner at the 21 Club 'where I had – shall I tell you? – 1st of all Tomato Juice . . . *Then* I had Alligator Pear. *Then* I had ooh such tender ribs of beef, & spinach en branche and fresh lima beans – and then a strawberry ice with real strawberries.'[218]

Before opening in New York, *Flare Path* went on tour in New Haven, Connecticut. The opening night, on 16 December, 'went well I think. Not a big house – but friendly and fairly enthusiastic.' Alec was pleased with his own performance. 'It's extraordinary acting again,' he wrote to Chattie. 'I've developed beyond belief in the two year interval. And I like acting!!! Very much! What's more, I think I do it rather well. The cast seem to think I'm terrific – that's dangerous.' And to Merula: 'I'm bloody good in *Flare Path*, considering. Wish you could see it. I don't do a single trick – I promise you. It's the most simple thing I've ever done and by far the best.'

The play opened in New York on 23 December and the first night seemed promising. 'I made a success and most people liked the play.' But it was poorly received by the critics. Lewis Nichols of the *New York Times*, while commending Alec's 'nervous energy and bounce', thought the play itself was 'sentimental, slow and confused'. 'But you should see the notices,' Alec wrote to Merula. 'They STINK!!! Really, out of all proportion. Three or four haven't been quite so bad and three have been actually good – one of them a rave. But it's all been v. depressing.'

Flare Path closed after two weeks but Alec did not feel that the play's failure would affect his career. Quite to the contrary: '20th Century Fox came round to see me and have asked me to go to Hollywood to star in the film!' One of the reviews said 'Come back Mr Guinness' – and on a radio broadcast: 'I was described as "witty, handsome !!!!!! English Alec Guinness". So EGO, dear, has had FUN.'

seventeen

In mid-January 1943, Alec left New York for Quincy to take delivery of his landing craft – LCI(L)* No. 124. He was full of misgivings about his abilities to command a ship. 'What is bad and I must endeavour to find some solution to,' he wrote to Merula:

> . . . is the lack of confidence I have in myself as an officer. If I was going as an ordinary seaman I'd be as happy as a lark . . . But this officer business – accepting responsibility, *having* to think about things that bore me and putting up that artificial barrier between myself and other men – well, I just can't manage it. At least, I *can* manage it, on the razor edge of unhappiness and insanity.[219]

In mid-February, he received his sailing orders and spent a last few days in New York going to farewell parties given by his New York friends

---

* Landing Craft Infantry (Large).

and stocking up on liquor, wine and a library of classics in the Modern
Library edition: Dickens, Jane Austen, Tolstoy, Dostoevsky, Proust,
Boswell, Meredith, Waugh, Greene; and anthologies of Shakespeare
and Milton.

It would seem from Alec's letters to Merula that he thought, until
the last moment, that he would be returning to Britain. 'God how I
look forward . . . to the day when I put a continent behind me and aim
at you,' he wrote on 14 March 1943. 'I hope we haven't got to bear this
separation much longer.' In fact, the flotilla which included LCI (L) 124
set course not for Britain but for North Africa, putting in at Bermuda,
Gibraltar and finally, after the sixteen-day crossing of the Atlantic, at
the small port of Djidjelli on the North African coast.

There, Alec settled down to a relatively undemanding life of naval
exercises, practice landings and the art of concealment by night to
avoid the occasional bombing and strafing raids by German planes.
'Apart from work,' he wrote to Chattie:

> I'm living a v. dull life. I play Backgammon in the evenings either with
> my 1st Lieutenant, an *excellent*, sweet, reliable, rather common young
> man, or with a very pretty, vivacious young Canadian officer who tells
> me the 'plots' of the plays he wrote for his university Dramatic Club –
> 'plots' which *astonish* me with their pointlessness. Or I offer drinks to
> American naval officers who drop in to '*yarn*' – a very yawn making
> pastime. And I read quite a bit. And I look at the pictures in my cabin
> (I've gone rather mad about painting.) And I make jokes with my crew.
> I'm *devoted* to my crew. There are about three of them who bore me
> or whom I *can't* take much notice of – but the others I find
> enchanting. I believe I must have quite the best crew over here. They
> are inclined to be a bit grubby and I bawl at them until they look
> smart, but they are all so cheerful and gay. I take them for P.T. in the
> mornings before breakfast and in the afternoons we often have awful
> games and tug o' war – all incredibly hearty you see – and somehow
> it all seems quite enjoyable. I suspect that I'm becoming awfully bossy
> and shall *hate* making my own bed at home more than ever. Most of

my fellow officers are incredible dullards, bores, shits and oh just unspeakable. Half a dozen are really nice. And that's all there is to say about life just now.[220]

This active duty in charge of a crew, sometimes in dangerous circumstances, dispelled the self-doubt from which Alec had suffered in New York. He found that he enjoyed being in command: 'All my nasty desires to *manage* other people's lives come surging along and I get quite a glow from it.' He also liked the idea that he would be cool under fire. Soon after arriving in North Africa, shortly after his twenty-ninth birthday on 24 April, Alec's ship was caught in a storm at sea and was blown off-course into a minefield during the night. 'My birthday,' he wrote to Chattie:

> . . . heralded a series of hair-raising days which I enjoyed *in retrospect* – though at the time I thought, if I was capable of thought, well this is the end and I regret that it is, and who would have thought that I would make such an undramatic, badly timed, *silly* exit from life. But here I am. And here's my ship. And all is lovely sunshine and excitement. I had the greatest compliment of my life paid me by one of my subordinates, who said, 'I hope, when the time comes, that I go into action with you' which made me burst into tears . . .

Alec, who had come close to pacificism prior to the war, was now a patriot:

> I think what England has stood for, in spite of much rottenness, *more* stupidity, *greater* smugness, and a horrible amount of guile, is still a good basis for taking a stand in the war. America has so little compared with us. I find myself fighting [for] more – democracy, what have you. I suppose being *away* from English cities, hedgerows, trees, people, customs etc makes one re-value them. I value them perhaps too lightly at the moment. As for people serving *art* rather than their country, I think that's just high falutin nonsense. The opportunity for experience

which is lost is incalculable. Redgrave* is finished as an artist, I swear. So is Gielgud. If artists are worth anything they must set their country an example in honesty, valour, nobility and vitality – the other is just decadence.[221]

Peter Bull, though perhaps not the embodiment of honesty, valour, nobility and vitality that Alec had in mind, was proving a competent and courageous naval officer and, to Alec's delight, was also in command of an anti-aircraft vessel berthed in the port of Djidjelli. One of their first escapades together was a dash across the desert to Bougie where Vivien Leigh and Beatrice Lillie were entertaining the troops at the garrison theatre. After only twenty minutes backstage in the company of the two actresses, Alec and Bully became anxious about the return journey to Djidjelli. Vivien Leigh buttonholed an Admiral and, caressing the lapels of his uniform, admiring his campaign ribbons, she suddenly asked him what he was doing for the next few hours. His eyes danced with excitement as he blushingly replied, 'Nothing.' 'Then,' said Vivien, 'you won't be needing your car.' The two Navy Lieutenants were driven back to Djidjelli in the Admiral's staff car.[222]

An outsider's glimpse of Alec's life while at Djidjelli comes from the diary of Augur East, an officer in command of a unit of the Eighth Army that was ferried from Djidjelli to Sousse on the LCI (L) 124:

Embarked at DJIDJELLI in a clean L.C.I. – most unusual – and sailed at 1700 hours for a thirty-nine hour voyage to SOUSSE. Very decent skipper called Cuffe – Lt. Commander, RNVR – who offered us the run of his cabin, alcohol and food. The cabin was immaculate with chintz-covered bunk and porthole curtains to match, and a tiny bookcase filled with Shakespeare and the classics. He spent most of his time on the bridge but I had several meals with him in the course of which he told me that he was an actor by profession, that his ship had been built in

---

* Michael Redgrave had been enrolled in the Navy but had been released after an injury to his arm.

New York and while he was there supervising its construction he had been lucky enough to get the lead in *Flare Path* on Broadway. When I said that I reckoned I ought to but didn't recognise his name he said, 'No, I use a stage name, I call myself Guinness – Alec Guinness.'[223]

In Djidjelli itself, Alec relied on Peter Bull to relieve the tedium. 'Nothing very funny has come my way – except when Peter comes on board. We put our ships alongside each other yesterday and had a party.'[224] Whether or not fun for the homosexual Bully involved dallying with sailors or Arab boys is not known. Sam Beazley, who served in the Army, recalled that, 'If you were an officer, you couldn't have homosexual relationships with your men, and most people didn't, but on leave, probably – that was what leave was for . . .'[225] And George Melly, who served on HMS *Dido* during World War II, wrote in his memoir of the time, *Rum, Bum and Concertina*, that:

Sex on the *Dido* was comparatively low-key but uncensorious. There were a few obvious homosexuals, the doe-eyed writer for one, many heterosexuals, and a fair number of those who would, on a casual basis, relieve sexual pressure with their own sex . . . Sex was not really an issue on the *Dido*. There was much the same atmosphere as at a fairly easy-going public school.[226]

Given the long period of absence from their wives and girlfriends, a degree of 'facultative' homosexuality is hardly surprising. Alec, when he read Melly's book, judged it to be 'unnecessarily brave'. His own experience in this respect is also unknown. The diary he kept at the time was lost at sea, and the only source for the period are his letters to Merula and Chattie. He occasionally writes of his 'gross sinfulness' but does not list the gross sins. Reading between the lines of his letters home, we get a glimpse of a kind of homoerotic flirting that seems to have gone on at Alec and Bully's parties. 'I've doled out Manhattans & Martinis and Old Fashioneds to people who visit me,' Alec wrote to Merula:

Do I sound as if I'm 'leading a life'? It's not that at all – I hardly drink. But I'm trying to get my 1st Lieut. tight to see what he talks about when he feels quite uninhibited. He's such a nice person but a bit prudey I think – takes his inner life v. seriously. He's admirable – but I wish he would FART or GIRK or say FUCK or kneel to say his prayers at night and refuse all drinks. I like him very much, don't mistake me, and I'm not even irritated by him – But God if only he would pick his nose or eat his toe-nails or do something which would enable me to unlace my corsets. I've tried him with very stiff drinks and it just begins to work on him and he begins to sprawl a bit and giggle and then I see him purse his lips and make an effort and he closes up. I suppose he thinks he's sinning, poor lad.[227]

Alec had taken to his first officer, John Bostock, from the first, even if he considered him 'common' because he wore a 'fountain pen clipped in his outside breast pocket'. 'He's practically a saint and has nearly all the qualities I envy in a man – friendliness, goodness, calmness, bravery – everything I lack so shockingly . . .'; and at first the Lieutenant seemed to have admired Alec in return, but then he seems to have changed his mind by mid-July. Alec wrote to Merula:

I'm a bit upset today because my 1st Lieut has announced he wants to leave the ship. This was bound to come sooner or later. But he's being rather tight-lipped whistling schoolboy about it. We've got on very well on the whole but recently he resented me telling him anything. I'm much to blame I have no doubt. Two men living on top of each other for a long time and with nothing in common is difficult . . .[228]

Ten days or so later, we find Alec giving 'a little dinner party' to celebrate the redecoration of his cabin (the chintz curtains). His guests were the commanding officer of another landing craft 'with whom I get on very well':

. . . and a young man called Bilson who showed me great hospitality a few nights ago on his ship. A pansy boy (an ex of Harry Andrews') – I can't remember his name – he visited once or twice at the Queens if I'm not mistaken. Well, ANYONE who links, however oddly, with home, is pretty welcome, and apart from his bright green ring and the fact that he stands with his knees touching and legs sagging and pushes up his hair now and then he was very agreeable. The Welshman and I had awful jokes about him with my First Lieutenant who was terrified that he would have advances made at him.[229]

It was this same fear, perhaps, that prompted Bostock to ask for a transfer from LCI (L) 124. But his fears may have been groundless. 'During the 1939–45 hostilities,' Alec wrote some years later, 'I was impressed by an officer who, I surmised, was possibly attracted to his own sex. The only indication was his almost parental concern for the welfare of the men under his command. No bad thing.'[230]

At the end of April 1943, Alec was promoted to the rank of full Lieutenant and wrote to Merula telling her to make sure that she received the increased allowance. By mid-May, after the capture of Tunis and Bizerte from the Germans, all North Africa was in Allied hands. It was known that an invasion of Europe was planned but not where it would take place. In June, Alec and Bully, together with the other landing craft commanders, were summoned to a top secret conference where they were shown photographs taken by a submarine of a coastline and told to study a particular section with a small white lighthouse. Returning to No. 124, Bully flipped through *The Mediterranean Pilot* and identified the lighthouse: it was on Cape Passero on the extreme south-eastern tip of Sicily.

In early July, under the overall command of Vice-Admiral Sir Roderick McGrigor, LCI (L) 124 sailed from Djidjelli via Sousse to Malta. Suffering from a cracked rib after a fall from the bridge, Alec sailed with the flotilla to Malta and put in to the harbour at Valetta – much changed by the German bombers since he had visited it on the Old Vic tour in 1939.

On 9 July, LCI (L) 124 set out again with sealed orders in the ship's safe. Thanks to Bully's deductions, Alec knew what the orders were and so made straight for the beach on Sicily's Cape Passero. After the protracted and hazardous off-loading of two hundred soldiers from a troop ship, Alec led half-a-dozen other LCIs towards the shore. No. 124 dropped its kedge-anchor as prescribed in order to keep the craft at right angles and winch itself off the beach when the men had landed. However, before Alec could lower the ship's ramp, another boat crossed too close behind him and cut the cable, with the result that the stern of No. 124 drifted towards the shore, the ramp could not be lowered and the soldiers had to let themselves down over the side with ropes.

Alec had failed to receive a message telling him that the invasion had been postponed by an hour: as a result, the barrage of rocket and gunfire to destroy the island's defences started *after* Alec had landed his two hundred men. However, the shells passed harmlessly over LCI (L) 124 and the soldiers who had taken up positions in the olive groves inland. Alec and his crew were to remain on Cape Passero for the next ten days, waiting for a destroyer to tow their boat off the beach.

Alec's role in leading the flotilla of landing craft towards the beaches of Sicily, and perhaps the fact that inadvertently he had been in the vanguard of the invasion, seems to have been appreciated in high places. Alec, at any rate, heard rumours to this effect. 'I have some funny and embarrassing news for you,' he wrote to Merula on 23 July. 'Well, it's all foolishness and you reading this I accept as a PROMISE that you will NOT TELL A SOUL . . . I have been recommended for a decoration for recent services.' However, Alec also wrote an account of his role in the invasion of Sicily – 'a v. dull *indeed* piece about my personal lack of activity in it' – which he sent to John Gielgud, and Gielgud to the *Daily Telegraph* where it was published on 20 August 1943 under the headline: 'I took my Landing Craft to the Sicily Beaches'. This was *mal vu* by the naval authorities and no doubt scuppered Alec's chances of a decoration. He was later summoned to 'explain' his conduct 'to their Lordships of the Admiralty. Nuisance. I think that £10 from the *Telegraph* had better go to the Red Cross as you suggested [or] an Actor's Orphanage or something.'

By 17 August 1943, the whole of Sicily was in Allied hands and on 3 September came the first landings on the Italian mainland. Mussolini, whom Alec had so narrowly missed meeting for tea four years before, had fallen from power and on 7 September Italy surrendered. The German army moved into northern Italy, occupying Rome on 10 September. The advance of the Allies from southern Italy was halted.

Alec's LCI (L) 124 was now stationed at the liberated ports on the Adriatic – Bari, Brindisi and Barletta – and was given the task of taking supplies to the partisans fighting the Germans in Yugoslavia and returning with their wounded and refugees. 'I live,' he wrote to Susy Salaman, 'on the edge of the only funny and exciting part of the war – the cloak-and-dagger warfare. Incredible and silly things happen and I get first hand knowledge of a side of the war which I hardly knew existed.'[231]

On the last day of 1943, Alec was ordered to sail for the Yugoslav island of Vis to evacuate four hundred women and children in advance of an anticipated German invasion. That night, off Vis, they were hit by a hurricane and the ship was lit up by St Elmo's fire. An electrical discharge created 'ribbons of blue fluorescent light' on the guard rails and rigging 'until the whole ship was lit up like some dizzying fairground side-show'. Alec found it 'beautiful and strangely comforting . . .'[232]

Earlier that day, resting in his cabin, Alec had woken to hear a sinister voice say, 'Tomorrow.' Convinced that this was a premonition of death, he navigated during the hurricane as best he could but with a sense of doom: the main worry that recurred in his mind was that Merula would have to care for his mother. The premonition of death proved false: of course Alec survived, so did his crew – but his ship was thrown onto the rocks as it entered the small Italian port of Termoli.

He gave the order to abandon ship and then he himself, with some regret, took leave of that cabin with the chintz curtains, and abandoned all the souvenirs of his stay in North Africa, as well as the diary he had been keeping and all the books in his much-prized library, except for a paperback thriller.

eighteen

No blame was attached to Alec for the loss of LCI (L) 124. 'I have been absolutely completely exonerated and there is to be no Court of Enquiry, let alone Court Martial,' he wrote to Merula. However, it meant parting from his 1st Lieutenant, John Bostock, and the crew he had come to regard with such affection, and led to a backwash of exhaustion and depression.

Writing to Merula from Malta, where he had been sent to await a new command, he confessed that 'I am a bit over-weary . . . and have been, for a week or two, at the lowest vitality I've ever known.' To Chattie, too, he confided the sense of dejection that followed the loss of his ship. 'I've felt ill – mentally rather than physically – throughout January – and although I'm getting back to normal now I want a complete change and rest. Rather ashamed of myself really, for I thought I possessed a nervous energy that would never let me down, and here I am pretty cracked up without a decent excuse.'[233]

A consequence of this dejection was an increasingly bleak view of human nature. In a letter to Tony Guthrie, Alec described how the sailors threw bread dipped in acid to the seagulls. Even the beauty of the landscape was merely a veil concealing corruption. 'Here we are approaching a sunny port at ten in the morning,' he wrote to Chattie. 'The sea is like mother of pearl and the mist is all gilded and there is a huge fishing fleet with patchwork sails sitting on the water – it's all very idyllic – and yet I know the town smells, the children are covered in scabs and the middle of the street is a river of shit.'[234]

The war itself was gruesome. 'I've seen a few dead lads floating about, all blown up and unimaginable,' Alec wrote in the same letter, 'but as I have a strong distaste for that sort of horror I've always neglected my duty by them. One is supposed to go and chop off their identity discs etc and search their pockets, if any. I simply couldn't.'[235] However, Alec could be calm in a crisis and quietly courageous. Accepting the invitation of a fellow-officer to go on a jaunt to Corsica, he found himself caught up in the bungled invasion of Elba. With no helmet or flak-jacket, Alec took over the controls of an Oerlikon gun and fired on the German positions on the island until the gun jammed. Sailors were cut down around him by the machine-guns or were burnt by the phosphorous shells.

Alec was often angered by the sneers of regular naval officers at those in the RNVR who were actors in civilian life. Not just Alec but a number of his friends had proved their valour: Tony Quayle, impatient in his comfortable berth as ADC to the Commander-in-Chief in Gibraltar, had volunteered to fight with the partisans in Albania; Bobby Flemyng had been awarded the MC in Eritrea, and was to win a military OBE when fighting the Germans in Italy; and Peter Bull was awarded the DSC.

Alec continued to disapprove of those whom he felt had shirked their duty. He was disconcerted to hear that John Rotton, his great friend from his training on Loch Fyne, had left the Navy 'because he has been judged by psychologists as an "obsessional neurotic". Apparently it all arose from him feeling he had to tell the Admiralty that nothing would persuade him to be parted from Polly . . .'[236] Later, it appeared that a further pretext had been an eye ailment, like Michael Redgrave's damaged arm – neither of which Alec thought an adequate excuse for opting out of the war. How good it would be, Alec wrote to Merula, 'if Michael Redgrave pretended there was nothing wrong with his arm – or, let me face it, John Rotton with his eyes.' Yet he also felt ashamed of his bitter feelings towards the skivers: 'I hope you will always rap me over the knuckles,' he said to his wife, 'if I drop harsh remarks about . . . anyone at the BBC or Michael Redgrave or Frith Banbury, Alec Clunes or the others . . . [but] when I think of the WOMEN who have joined and the MEN who haven't it is difficult. We are so short handed.'[237]

Alec's feeling that women should do war work rather than pursue their careers on the stage certainly applied to Chattie, whom he thought of as a second-rate actress anyway*; but his disapproval of Merula's professional endeavours was less patriotic than personal – even paranoid. He had already been slightly taken aback when in New York to hear that her book, an illustrated alphabet for Eusty and Mary's son Christopher, *Christopher's ABC*, had been published by her cousin Denis Cohen at The Cresset Press, and by the end of 1943 had sold 20,000 copies. 'HOW VERY AMAZINGLY CLEVER of you to have sold 20 THOUSAND books . . .! Good show old girl . . .'

The book's success, however, did not deter Alec from a patronising, school-masterly criticism of some of the drawings she enclosed with her letters. 'I had some not good drawings of Matthew. You must learn to construct better. Now that you know people like your drawing and that your sheer spontaneity makes money there's no excuse for carrying on in the same slap-dash way. You are like, in your drawing, some chit of a girl who has made an overnight theatrical success.'[238] And, a year later: 'I'm SORRY – but it's useless for me to pretend that I like them [three drawings of Matthew by Merula]. I

---

* Chattie later worked on coal barges on the Grand Union Canal.

suppose that if I was a NICE husband I'd just leave it at that or perhaps not quite as far as that! But I don't even think they are good drawings.'[239]

Alec continued his relentless assault on Merula's poor spelling: 'Your SPELLING my love is WORSE – if that is possible . . . You ought to be put in gaol, my sweet, until you can spell the word CINEMA – which is not even pronounced as CINERMAR.' Her failure to date her letters continued to irritate him: 'Even if you can't remember the actual date you can at least supply me with the *month*, which in the circumstances is often helpful'; as did her general impracticality – 'Thank you for Air Letter Cards. But you goose to have stamped them! and you goose again to have stamped them with 6d [pence] stamps instead of 3d!!'

Alec was as critical of Merula's literary endeavours as he was of her painting. In the summer of 1944 she enclosed a poem, which he returned with a line by line critique that amounted to a comprehensive demolition. 'A page from "Cuffe's Guide to Poesy",' he begins. Then:

> Here, my love, is the poem you sent me. This is not for your instruction, neither to praise or blame, but that you may know more truly what I think of it (I have some uncertainty) or rather what it suggests to me. So on the left you will find your own poem, in the centre my criticism or process of thought or whatever, and on the right how I would endeavour to reshape it. This is only for amusement . . . my sweet, and I hope you won't take it as an offence.[240]

Most disconcerting for Alec was the news that Merula, in his absence, was pursuing her acting career. 'I haven't seen Merry for ages,' Judy Guthrie wrote from England, 'but Tony . . . has because she was up seeing Bronnie about *Great Expectations* & said she was in excellent form.'[241] This was *not* what Alec wanted to hear. 'I hate you leading a life about which I know nothing, and don't even know the surroundings,' he wrote to Merula. 'I'm hoping nothing has come of the Liverpool offer. I'm sorry darling but I'd loathe you to tat about on the stage up North.'[242]

Three days later, he wrote again to try and dissuade Merula from accepting the job:

I don't want you to go off acting in the provinces. Or anywhere without me, really. (I can almost hear Michel's [St Denis] words that I have ruined your career being confirmed.) I have told you my opinion of your capabilities as an actress often enough; I think you are quite exceptional. Also, and this is V difficult to say, I don't think you can learn much from professional actors. You, like others of your family, inherit a brilliant amateur talent. Why do you want to heap unhappiness on your head by struggling with your pure quality against all the artificiality and cunning of the professional theatre?

It is conceivable, of course, that one of Alec's anxieties was that Merula might hear stories about his past; or that she might somehow be corrupted by that 'artificiality and cunning'. Inevitably, any man separated from his wife for a prolonged period will worry that she might succumb to another man's advances. He dithered about how he would deal with such a predicament: 'If you fall in love with someone else,' he wrote to Merula, 'as long as you chuck him when I reappear, I'll forgive you with all my heart'; but later, in response to a letter from Merula about free love, he changed his tune:

Darling, don't think your charmingly simple theories about marriage and divorce would get far or mean much . . . Supposing we weren't married – just living your 'free love' (free for all?) life – well, I might feel a bit uneasy that when I get home I might find you living with Bannerman and in the world's eyes you'd be quite justified. Whereas, AS THINGS ARE, if I get back & find you living with B'man I shall take a TERRIBLE REVENGE and MOST RIGHT THINKING PEOPLE will SYMPATHISE with ME. So leave free love speculations to your dear DAD and be V. CAREFUL. All my legitimate love, Alec.

Alec's worry about a lover, however, took second place to his fear that Merula might develop a successful career in the theatre. Clearly, he realised that he was inconsistent and unreasonable in praising her talent yet asking her only to act if she could act with him. 'Oh, darling love all this is probably wildly unwise and is obviously interfering. You have your own life to lead as well as a married life, and honestly all I'm interested in is yours and M.'s happiness. If it's going to make you happy to act, then act.' And he later came to regret his intervention:

> It was thoughtless of me to try to influence you not to go to Liverpool. Anyway I was glad when I heard that you had gone. I had a very sweet letter from Marti saying how important she thought it that you should feel free and active. So you must forgive me. And I hope you will always do what appeals to you and what you feel you will be most happy doing.

Alec also acknowledged that wanting to keep her off the stage and at home had more to do with his own neuroses than with any objective considerations:

> However bad and stupid all that has been, and it *has*, it must at least be said for me that I've never wanted you sheltered just because you were my wife . . . I think that, particularly since Matthew's birth, I've been so determined that he should have some sort of *family* life and not lead the bitty existence I did as a child.[243]

No letters survive from Merula to Alec from this period of the war, but it is clear that she showed a certain imperviousness to his school-masterly critique of her drawing and writing, and she ignored his attempt to prevent her returning to the stage. Of course, his letters also contained repeated assurances of his love, and there were other imperatives governing Merula's decisions such as her desire to escape, every now and then, from the intense and often quarrelsome atmosphere at Wadlington.

There was one decision that she made, wholly on her own initiative, that gave Alec great pleasure: she was confirmed into the Church of England:

Well love, fancy being confirmed! Couldn't admire you more for the plunge. Very glad . . . I wish I was going to be there to hold your hand but I shall pray for you as much as I can, that you won't get the giggles, or walk out an atheist, as I did at the age of sixteen.[244]

But even here, Alec could not resist reminding Merula of her duties as a Christian. Their friend Marriott Longman had married her fellow student from the London Acting School, Pierre Lefèvre, and she had asked Merula to be the godmother of their first child, a daughter, Andrée. 'Have you insisted on your godchild Andrée being christened?' Alec wrote to Merula. 'Because I think you should.'[245]

On 2 April 1944, Alec celebrated his thirtieth birthday. 'I spent a pleasant birthday yesterday,' he wrote to Merula, 'but was horrified to realise that I *am* now *30*. Oh, God I hope I spend the next 30 years less stupidly. Perhaps by then I shall have written 30 plays and speak three languages fluently and have 3 grandchildren????' On 12 April he was suddenly sent to Algiers to investigate a charge that naval stores were being sold on the black market. He was delighted to escape from Malta where he had felt in a rut, and to be back in North Africa. 'I find people in rags and robes and fezs, and the silliness of French hats, and rather wonderful smells, and goats in the main street, all rather romantic and lush.' He envisaged a journey into the desert to find the hermitage of Charles de Foucauld. His investigations were inconclusive, but before he could return to Malta he was press-ganged by 'a rather fussed Admiral' to take a stinking old boat to Messina in southern Italy.

There, he learned that he had been given a new command – LCI (L) 272. Although he could not feel quite the same affection for this

new ship, and his much-loved 1st Lieutenant, John Bostock, was
replaced by a tall Canadian, John Keys, it is clear from his letters to
Merula and Chattie that he was delighted to be back with a crew. As
captain, he had a pastoral role. 'I'm having to be rather paternal
with one or two of the crew these days.' He felt he was liked by his
men:

> I suppose it's because I gossip with them on the bridge when at sea, and
> show them the sun & stars through a sextant and make them talk about
> their home life . . . I'm horribly sentimental about all these young lads.
> Even after I had gone to bed (on the upper deck) one or two of them
> came & sat down near me and poured out their ambitions or just talked
> about their 'mums' and 'dads'. It's so awful when they start on cricket
> or football though . . .[246]

Alec had his favourites. One of his crew was 'a young R.C. lad from
Northern Ireland' who he thought was 'a *saint*. He's a devoted R.C.,
doesn't drink or smoke or swear, is clean, polite, alert and altogether
something of a novelty'. Overall, he was happy with his new ship and
liked the crew, with two exceptions:

> A fearfully handsome lad with a sulky expression who is frightened of
> me and 2 – a tiny little lad with a lascivious face, who has dirty tricks –
> runs round the deck at night with his cock out, and sticks his arse over
> the side of the ship for a shit . . . The others are grand lads.[247]

As before, it could be said that there seems to be an erotic tinge to his
appreciation of the different young men – a kind of horror, which we
come across later, of both the handsome lad, who perhaps tempted
him, and the sailor with the lascivious face who sensed that he was to
be tempted. Alec's letters to Merula occasionally reveal a streak of self-
loathing. 'I'm sure I have a passion for acting,' he wrote, 'because I've
got a pretty good hate of what I really am . . . I am so full of the most
dreadful hypocrisy – I simply stink of shallowness and beastliness.'

On 24 April, he told Merula how he had made his confession – the first since August the year before – not to his 'new friend', the naval chaplain, 'an Anglo-Catholic and obviously an intelligent, good and upright man, and what is a little unusual for a high churchman married and with a large family which I think is *good*' – but to another priest from outside the Navy 'who had the horrible job of listening to my sins and forgiving them in Christ's name and was a sort of saint:

> I couldn't have felt more *sure* about his genuineness or fineness. So, dear sweet Merula, it's a happily clean and rather gay husband you have writing to you tonight – all new, though I look just as stupid and old and dandruffy . . . I feel goodish, having had no chance yet to be spiteful or wicked or unkind – and with the good Lord's help I shall make more of an effort about myself from now on than I have during the past thirty years.[248]

'Spiteful or wicked or unkind': it may well be that Alec's conscience was troubled not by sins of the flesh, or even lascivious imaginings of sex with the young sailors of whom he was so fond, but simply from the harm done to others by his sharp tongue. St Francis of Sales had written in his *Introduction to the Devout Life*, one of the books that Alec carried constantly with him, that, 'Derision or mockery always involves contempt and so is gravely sinful, so that theologians rightly hold mockery for the worst sin of the tongue we can commit against our neighbour.'[249] Alec could be cold and dismissive. Polly Rotton had told him that he showed '*dislike* more than anyone she'd ever met'. There can be little doubt that Alec did not conceal the disdain he felt for some of his fellow officers, or 'the wretched WRENS' he was obliged to partner at the occasional naval ball. Mockery, putting people down, even those whom he loved most, was to remain for Alec a besetting sin.

But there was a work by another Christian writer very different from St Francis of Sales, which Alec was reading at this time and which must have heightened his sense of his own soul as a battlefield for good and evil. This was *The Brothers Karamazov* by Fyodor Dostoevsky. Already, in July 1941 while training to be an officer, he had asked Merula to send him this book. 'Pappa said he had a copy,' she had written, 'and I could descend on that but after he had gone I could only find one vol and that 2 so 1 will have to wait till I go to Middle Lodge . . .'[250] A month later he had written to Chattie: 'I've been awfully stimulated and churned about by *The Brothers Karamazov*'; and now, in May 1944, he told Merula that he had been reading and making notes on the novel with a view to adapting it as 'a long long play done in two halves'.* The original drama about the young man with the stigmata he had started in New York had not worked: 'The Brothers K,' he wrote, 'answers I believe my desire for a play about a saint. Of course I'm casting it in my mind already . . .'[251] In June he wrote that 'I continue with the Karamazov jottings'; in July that he hoped to reduce its length to four and a quarter hours; on 20 September that 'Last night was quite a red-letter night for me – *I finished the first act of Karamazov*! Rereading it today I see quite a lot of loose ends and possible cuts and mosaic-like work to be done but it's something of an achievement and encourages me about the rest of the play – and what's more I think it very actable . . .'; and on 11 October: 'Tonight I FINISHED KARAMAZOV !!!!! Isn't it INCREDIBLE! Mind you, it's a bit scrappy and will have to [be] gone over carefully, and maybe half a scene will need scrapping here and there to be replaced by something else – but the play exists – it could go into rehearsal tomorrow . . .'

Tony Guthrie, to whom he had written telling him of his adaptation, was lukewarm. '*Brothers Karamazov* sounds interesting but I wish you'd write something original – or something contemporary.

---

* *The Brothers Karamazov* had in fact been adapted by Jacques Copeau and staged at the Théâtre du Vieux Colombier in 1911. It is unclear whether or not Alec was aware of this: even if he was, Copeau's adaptation would not have been available in Malta; nor, though he was trying to teach himself the language, could Alec read French.

Did you ever finish that memoir of your childhood? I thought it had great quality.'[252] Guthrie also asked Alec: 'You do want to come back & act, don't you?' which was a more pertinent question than he realised.

That Alec wanted to come back was beyond question, but the sense of a higher vocation that had led him to consider taking Holy Orders had returned, though exactly what he felt called to do was not clear. In a letter to Merula at the time he was first embarking on his adaptation of Dostoevsky's powerfully Christian novel, he wrote abjuring an ambition which, as it would turn out, quite accurately predicted the kind of life he would lead in his later years:

> I know so well what I *used* to want. I wanted happiness – and that
> consisted of you & me & our children being a *family*, and having a
> small place in the country (where it was always Spring!) and a flat in
> town (which would be a centre of rather successful smart clever artists)
> and sufficient money not to have to think of money, and I wanted to
> be *thought* a great actor – and to be a great actor.[253]

Now Alec rejected this as 'a nauseating daydream'. He was not sure what he wanted to be, 'but I *am* beginning to feel that I have a more important job to do than just being a successful actor.' The quest was not so much for a profession that was better suited to his talents, but something of greater *spiritual* significance. He felt this with particular force after hearing all the theatrical gossip over lunch at the Officers' Club in Valetta from Nigel Patrick, 'London's most actorish actor'. 'When I had finished my gossipy wicked lunch I thought: How difficult it is to move among such people *and* lead the life one would like to lead. And that depressed me.'[254]

This contradiction in Alec's nature – the split between the man who loved 'gossipy wicked' lunches and the man who yearned for the serenity that came when he felt filled with the Grace of God – was never to be resolved. But he had come to understand that the Devil was never idle, and that he was pulled away from a state of grace by the gravity of worldly preoccupations and delights, even as he conversed with God:

> I have discovered, or *realised* for the first time, such a simple simple truth that I'm almost ashamed (I mean I've *realised* it in my life rather than just in my head). That is that one can ask for something in one's prayers and not quite mean it – one can ask for *faith* out of a sort of *politeness* for instance – one can ask to be shown the awfulness of one's past sins just because one is told to – a sort of formality. etc. etc. Or one can ask for these things and *mean it desperately* – and one's prayer is answered – almost unexpectedly – but quite terrifyingly recognisably . . .[255]

Or, as the King puts it in *Hamlet:* 'My words fly up, my thoughts remain below. Words without thoughts never to heaven go.'[256]

As the commander of LCI (L) No 272, Alec saw further action in the Mediterranean theatre of war. He made a run to the Allied beachhead at Anzio and made trips across the Adriatic to Yugoslavia. In Malta, but also when posted at the Adriatic port of Barletta, he saw a surprising number of his friends from the theatre, either serving in the armed forces or touring to entertain the troops. He was based variously in North Africa, Italy, Malta, back briefly to North Africa, and again in Italy. Shortly before the end of his tour of duty, he was given leave to visit Rome, where he met up with Tony Quayle and had an audience with Pope Pius XII:

> No ceremony. He's an extraordinary personality. He darted in, all in white fur, and sat on a throne, and two or three very dressed up officers with golden helmets, and one or two bishops, stood at each side of him and the Swiss guard closed the doors. He didn't smile and then quickly spoke in English & French. I couldn't catch all of it, but it was to the effect there will never be peace in the world or our hearts unless we make God the centre of our lives – to refer all things to Him. When he

spoke of God he looked up and raised his exceptionally beautiful hands a little, palm upwards. I *never knew* a man *could* do that with *such* simplicity and sincerity as he did. Then he left his throne and walked rapidly up to people and had a word with them – and seeing him close one was practically bowled over by his gentleness and charm – one of the loveliest smiles I've ever seen. He sort of exuded something of what one feels some of the more lovable saints must have had. We all knelt – quite a few hundred of us – and he blessed us – and then we left. But a very impressive man indeed.[257]

To his great subsequent regret, Alec *failed* to see Padre Pio, the saintly Capuchin priest living near Foggia on the Adriatic coast, reputed to have the stigmata.

By September 1944, Alec had been serving abroad for two years and would have been due for home leave had not the period for a foreign tour of duty been extended for a further six months. Both he and Merula had grown apprehensive about what they would make of one another when they were reunited. Merula, now working as a Land Girl, was afraid that living in the country with only the company of women had made her dull and that she was not clever enough to share Alec's intellectual pursuits. Alec sought to reassure her:

If you are duller than you were two years ago – and you probably aren't – I don't think it matters much. We'll be a fine dull couple together. I'm not only duller – and I certainly am – but I'm also HORRIDER. I'm just a horrible bald snapping school-maam. And I'm not 'INTERLECKTOOL' (intellectual please) a bit. I'm afraid I do write much too much about BOOKS etc in my letters but that is simply because I cannot write about my life.[258]

Alec's main anxiety about his homecoming was focused not on Merula but Matthew. Time and distance had led to a certain detachment: 'I'm far less concerned about him than I used to be,' Alec wrote to Merula. 'He's a comparative stranger, and although I wish him every good and pray for him night and morning and laugh when I think about him sometimes – he is no longer very *real* to me.' Was Alec jealous of Matthew? Merula wondered. 'No, I'm not jealous of Matthew. At least I would never admit it if I were. I don't think one can be jealous of anyone I love as much as I love him.' Alec loved him yet 'I can't help dreading meeting him again. I'm not so worried now about him not liking me, but about me not liking him.'[259]

There are a number of touching letters from Alec to Matthew – considerately written in capital letters – which reveal, despite the misgivings expressed above, an enormous residual affection:

> It is a long time since I have seen you but I have some photographs and except that you are bigger they look much the same as when I saw you last. One day I will come back and Mummy and you and I will live cosily on our own and have lots of laughs. I don't like being away from you but I have to be.

> For your information:- the driver of a ship is called a quartermaster usually. I am the *captain* of a ship but I don't drive it – I just say where it has to go and consequently I am very important indeed. On the other side is a picture of my ship. Lots of love. Daddy.[260]

There was a touch of Alec's tactless candour in some of these letters: 'It's nice for me to know you are a good boy, and I like lots of things I hear about you, but I'm very tired of trains. I prefer balloons and ships' – but Matthew was as yet too young, and too far away, to be wounded by his father's admonitions. Never having had a father, and with Dr. Gilbert, the Headmaster of Roborough, his only role model as a child, a school-masterly approach to Matthew's upbringing was only to be expected. Certainly Alec, although his son was only three, had started to plan Matthew's upbringing and education. 'Is he being nice to you or does he take after his pappa and treat you cruelly?' he asked Merula when Matthew was only six months old. 'Don't let him grow up wilful but break all resistance. He'll love you for it in the end.'[261] 'Does he say grace before his meals? I think he should,' he wrote to Merula in May of 1944 when Matthew was not yet four. He did not want him to grow up as a 'nancy boy': 'Don't you think M ought to have his hair cut? It's too long & feminine in his photos.' And he worried that Matthew might be too innocent and guileless: 'He'll never cope with the BRUTAL WORLD at such a rate – I dread to think of his disillusionment.'

But Alec's chief anxiety seemed to be that his own faults – of which he was only too aware – would reappear in Matthew. 'I find it so awful when I recognise myself in him – even by hearsay . . . That *teasing* – a horrible horrible fault – and that biting and horror of kissing – and the general desperate independence all come out of love that's twisted – not free & simple & generous as it should be.' He worried that Matthew was being raised too indulgently and that he would have to counteract Merula's influence with sternness:

My fear of your laxity perhaps drives me to the opposite extreme. I hope not, but I'm prepared to be told that. And I know you aren't really lax. And discipline doesn't mean being sharp & snappy – that's bullying. It means leading – hence disciples 'followers' – and a child must be led out of his passion and selfishness. It's a work that is begun in childhood & lasts all one's life, as we are beginning to see. And if it doesn't begin in childhood then it's TERRIBLE because all sorts of self-will will have taken charge.[262]

Alec even became preoccupied with where Matthew should go to school:

Soon Matthew will have to be educated – oh, Lord. I think I'm in favour of the Jesuits. What's the Jesuit school at Windsor? And I wonder if it's anything to do with the S.J.'s that old Sir Sydney thinks so highly of? And do you think one has to put his name down or anything like that?

I suppose Michel would be fairly obstructive about any information on that score?[263]

The preferred school of the Salaman family was Bedales, a progressive and co-educational boarding-school in Hampshire; and Merula seems to have suggested that Matthew might be happier to be educated with girls. Alec preferred the idea of something more virile:

> I think your surmise about the Bedales kind of education is probably right – except that I don't think unhappiness or happiness has much to do with it – obviously a child should be made as happy as possible. Good principles have always been handed down from men to boys, and my only real bone about education is that good principles are not found by boys for themselves but have to be handed down if they are to continue. And this continuance is desirable.[264]

The Jesuit college near Windsor esteemed by Sydney Cockerell was Beaumont and it was there, around ten years later, that Matthew would be sent to school.

Towards the end of 1944, in anticipation of his return, Alec started to make a large model boat with a hull carved from one block of wood as a present for Matthew. Alec was skilled with his hands. On New Year's Day 1945, he described to Merula how he had melted down some old lead soldiers to provide ballast for the bottom of Matthew's boat. On 18 February, however, as he was packing up for his journey home, Alec realised that the boat:

> . . . was much too heavy for the post and far too cumbersome to bring with me. So at sunset yesterday I put an envelope in it with 'Matthew's' written on it and the weather being what it is I should imagine it is still sailing very slowly and rather lop-sidedly across the Adriatic! I'm terribly sorry – and will of course buy him one in England however much it costs me.[265]

At noon on 18 February 1945, in the port of Barletta, Alec handed over the command of LCI (L) 272 to 'a pimply Scotsman' and was free to return to England. He had done his packing, shaved off his beard, destroyed the diary he had been keeping and given up smoking – throwing all his pipes into the sea. He hoped to visit Malta on his way home and perhaps travel overland through France, but 'will probably end up lounging round Naples for a bit. Jeremy* is there, which will make that bearable.' He was driven to Naples from Barletta, arriving 'covered with dust and jogged to death'. He loathed the city, was lodged in a 'HIDEOUS hotel that they appear to be still building', and found that the troopship's departure had been delayed for ten days; but his stay was eased by the presence of Jeremy Hutchinson, Tony Quayle and Peter Bull. Quayle was serving as ADC to an American Admiral and lived in great comfort in a villa that had been occupied by the Italian foreign minister – also Mussolini's son-in-law – Count Ciano, and the German Reichsmarshal, Hermann Goering. At Alec's instigation, Quayle invited Bully to dine with the Admiral: Alec got the giggles and Bully disgraced himself by getting drunk.

'I shan't attempt to write again!' he wrote to Merula on 27 February 1945. And then, clearly apprehensive about their reunion: 'Oh, dear – it feels very strange in my stomach. I've got so bald and BAGGY under the eyes, and quick-tempered and lazy (even lazier) and oh Lord I'm horrible and awful and when you see me you'll say Oh, Go away.'

---

* Jeremy Hutchinson, then married to Peggy Ashcroft, who was serving as Assistant Signals Officer at the Allied Naval Headquarters at Caserta.

part four

guinness is good for you

nineteen

Alec disembarked from his troopship at Liverpool almost two and a half years after he had left for America on the *Queen Mary* from the Clyde. He went to the Adelphi Hotel where the Guthries were waiting to greet him. The warmth of their welcome abated when they discovered that the timid young actor was now a handsome, battle-hardened British naval officer, mature beyond his years. 'You have become very grand and veddy Briddish,' Judy mocked; both the Guthries remained 'rather cool and censorious' until Alec's departure on the London train.

Before leaving Liverpool, Alec had telephoned Merula and asked her to come up to London to meet in Martita Hunt's flat in Upper Wimpole Street. Merula had been speechless when she heard his voice; but had then washed her hair and taken from the wardrobe the cherry-coloured coat and skirt that she had bought when she was acting in Liverpool and had kept for this occasion. She arrived at Martita's before Alec and waited for him, sniffing and spluttering because she had 'a streaming cold'. 'I sat in Martita's little lobby and waited for that creaky lift. It seemed an eternity – and then there he was. We couldn't speak. We just clung to one another and the world swam'.[266]

Merula had come up to London from a cottage where she had been living with her sister-in-law, Mary Salaman, on the farm belonging to the Salamans' neighbours, the Elwes. For some months in 1943, despite Alec's disapproval, she had acted in rep. at the Liverpool Playhouse, and it was there that she had decided to be confirmed into the Church of England. Her sponsor had been George Melly's mother, Maud, who had a large house in a smart part of Liverpool which was open to those who came to the Playhouse: Maud was a particular friend of Bobby Flemyng, Harry Andrews and the Redgraves.

For a while after her return south, Merula and Matthew had lived with Mary and Eusty Salaman in a converted windmill on Langstone Harbour: Eusty had returned to take a gunnery course on Hayling Island. When he was once again posted abroad, Merula and Matthew went to live with her other, Russian, sister-in-law, Natasha; and in the summer of 1944 moved yet again to Oakdale Farm to help her childhood friend Nutty Elwes with the harvest.

They remained there for a year, Merula working as a Land Girl – milking the cows, raking up the hay and taking the heifers to market. When Mary Salaman became desperate yet again to escape from her mother-in-law at Wadlington, the Elwes offered Merula and Mary their uninhabited cowman's cottage: 'Most of the windows were broken and the boiler was cracked; the floors were strewn with dead squirrels and birds, and an owl had been living in the bath and it was inches deep in owl droppings.' Merula painted the walls with distemper and Mary arrived from Wadlington with Merula's furniture from Middle Lodge, her son Christopher and a new baby, Toby.

This was the home to which Alec returned and, although Mary moved out of the cottage into the farm, it was not an environment that eased the re-establishment of the conjugal life of the fastidious Naval Lieutenant and his farm-hand wife. 'Shambles there. Pig sty,'[267] Alec wrote in the diary he started soon after his return to England.

However, it was not just the discomfort of their home that made Alec's return problematic. 'Alec was afraid of getting too close to us and I felt hurt and uneasy at the distance between us,' Merula later recalled. Each had got used to life without the other and was afraid of abandoning that self-reliance, particularly since Alec's return did not mean that he was free of the Navy: the war was more or less over in Europe but continued in the Far East and it was quite possible that, after a month's leave, he would be once more posted abroad.

Alec and Merula's feelings for one another vacillated as they struggled to adapt the fond images stored in the heart during their separation to the reality of their new familiarity. 'My relationship with Merry has been causing me anxiety – but that has eased. All all my fault,' wrote Alec less than a month after his return. Though at one point he noted that Merula was looking increasingly like her mother, Alec had not ceased to find her attractive. 'Mary went to the pictures with Nutty & Merry and I left happily on our own. Sat in silence by the fire and made love.' On the eve of VE Day*, Merula baked a victory cake and 'in the evening we giggled over Lear's limericks'. However, on 10 May, Alec wrote in his diary:

All afternoon have been obsessed with this idea of the flatness, staleness, and lack of depth in my relationship with Merula. I attach no blame at all to her. I feel a tenderness for her which would prevent me trying to hurt. But why doesn't she take pains with her appearance? And why doesn't she shut the door and clean out the bath after use? And why is it *funny* to be dressed shabbily rather than revolting. Feeling as I do, can I say that I love her? I can't say that I don't. My selfishness and laziness blur my vision.

These sour thoughts had been brought on by Alec's returning home at 6.30 p.m. to find the house locked and empty; he had to climb in

---

* The public celebration of Victory in Europe.

through the window; and even as he wrote in his journal, he acknowledged that his self-pity was irrational. 'I will wait, knowing how hasty and stupid and unchristian I am; and try not to think that I'm martyring myself. For she is a good and thoughtful woman and always generous minded. I would never find another like her.' And, a little later that evening: 'Had a bath. – Merry & Matthew back at 1900 with bunches of bluebells, having been at Aunt Hettie's.' And later still: 'Happy with Merry – how ridiculous my earlier resentment seems.'

A month after his return to England, Alec's leave came to an end and he was posted to Southampton to take up a desk job and occasionally sail landing craft to and fro across the English Channel. Alec and Merula therefore stayed on occasion with Merula's aunt and uncle, Sir Henry and Lady Beaumont, in their house in Fawley on the Solent. They were not made to feel particularly welcome. 'Aunt Hetta had a double dose of the Wake stinge,' wrote Merula. 'We had all our own separate rations set out in little pots.' Alec and Merula also considered Merula's aunt to be a snob. 'Aunt Hett's near approach to an asylum just before the war,' wrote Alec, 'seems to have been caused by the tussle between her snobbishness and religion. Apparently she was brought to her senses by finding a priest who assured her it was quite OK to go on being a snob. Which she does very successfully.'[268] And a month later: 'Aunt Hett's horror of the lower orders extends to animals – "Horrid horrid mongrel. It ought to be shot".'

It would appear that the Beaumonts did not take to Alec, or at any rate reported back to the Salamans at Wadlington that he bullied Merula – gossip which came back to Alec through Chattie. 'Yes, poor Merry,' he wrote in a sarcastic rejoinder to Chattie in the middle of May:

I've reduced her to a helpless, gittering, cringing creature with no personality at all. And I have been equally successful with Matthew. Great fun it has been for me, as you can well imagine. After all, if you don't love a person it's the simplest way of feeling a hate that will lead to separation, isn't it. And about time too, I can hear most of my in-law family saying. After all, it was desperately dull for all the gossipers, tellers of tales and scandal searchers to have a young man and woman living together without fuss for seven years. So I thought, well, Tease, Tease, Tease – (it has even been suggested by some of your friends that I beat your sister – and of course I married her for her money – none of which I will dare to deny) – and she is notoriously unhappy and pale in my company, and so free when I'm away – so I know you will be delighted to hear I expect to bury her next week.[269]

Alec found getting used to life with a five-year-old son as difficult as his readjustment to living with Merula. He had thought long and hard about his role as a father, and there can be no question but that when he thought about Matthew, he did so with great love. There can be no doubt, either, that he wished to make up for lost time by playing his paternal role to the full.

First and foremost came Matthew's religious formation but that got off to a bad start. 'Tried to tell Matthew about the crucifixion and showed him my rosary,' wrote Alec in his diary a week or two after his return, 'but he was only struck with its resemblance to an aeroplane.'[270] There was also his education. 'Tried to get into Science Museum for Matthew – but shut. Afterwards took little M on the tram that dives underground at Holborn. Walked in St James to see the pelicans.' Alec delighted in dressing up and playing roles to entertain Matthew and his friends: on his son's fifth birthday, back at the cowman's cottage at Oakdale, Merula baked a cake with cherries on the top and Alec came in and out of the house in different disguises – 'a clown, a blackamoor and a curious creature with a long nose, and then a giant dressed in a striped nightshirt and fez who stole the cake and ran away – that was all delightful, the children loved it . . .' Later, Merula did drawings of the occasion which were published as *Christopher's New House*.

Above all, Alec liked to build models for Matthew, not just to make up for the boat that he had been unable to bring back from Barletta, but because he enjoyed making things with his hands. He constructed a model aeroplane for Matthew and a model boat for his cousin Christopher. 'To Horsham for glue,' he records in his diary for 6 April 1945. Ten days later: 'Matthew slipped with the windmill and smashed it. Howls. Started to make a cottage out of the remains.' In May Alec made a castle and drawbridge from balsa wood bought in Horsham and wrote with pride that, when painted, it 'looks just like a shop model'.

However, there were subconscious passions at work in both father and son. Matthew, though he was to remember events in his life prior to Alec's return, had almost no memories of the months that followed. It seems likely that, while proud to have a father at last, he resented having to share his mother's attention. 'Matthew in good boisterous form, but deteriorated greatly after his supper, and ended up by pinching me without provocation and got a consequent spanking.' 'Caught 1730 ferry home. Matthew decided not to recognise my presence on my return.' Alec sometimes descended to his son's level:

> Teased Matthew too much at tea-time by pretending to eat his last three chocolates. This resulted in tears, him saying 'I don't like you' – with great feeling, and climbing under the table to pinch me. But within half an hour we were buddies again. I fear I don't pay him enough attention, for he's a good and loving boy. But such a chatterer.[271]

One event which Matthew *did* remember was Alec's launch of a beautiful model boat that he had built for Matthew and Christopher. Alec pushed the boat onto a pond but as it drifted on the still water it suddenly exploded: he had hidden a firework in the boat and lit a short fuse with his cigarette. 'Matthew and Christopher watched it go with horror.' Then he made a house, two storeys with furniture and little people, and set that alight. 'Tears from Matthew and Christopher.'[272]

Alec's strange moods came not just from the difficulties in readjusting to family life, but also from his intense frustration at being obliged to continue in the Navy. After the dropping of atom bombs on Hiroshima and Nagasaki, and the subsequent surrender of Japan, there was no longer a risk that he might be sent to the Far East; but he had to clock on for duty at Southampton, either to transport men and *materiel* across the Channel or, more often, to sit idly in an office. 'My life dribbles along,' he wrote to Chattie:

> . . . with the occasional trip to Le Havre, which lets Merry catch up on the enormous quantity of rations I eat when at home. I read history, keep a diary, stumble through some perplexed and rather ungracious prayers, regret the sordidness of much of my past, regret the wasted hours of sleep, regret that I can so easily divert my creative energy to useless ends, such as writing dull letters like this . . .[273]

Alec made better use of his inactive solitude than this letter suggests. He reworked certain scenes of his stage adaptation of *The Brothers Karamazov*, delivered the manuscript to a typist, and immediately started work on a short story about his experiences in the hurricane on New Year's Eve, 1944. His first title, 'Money for Jam', he later changed to '31st December 1943' 'which has more dignity'. Its completion inspired him to write more: 'Characters & incidents for short stories keep cropping up in my mind.' He wrote a story called 'Wiggie' which he read to Merula and 'she seemed to like. Think I must make a collection of stories, rather similar, and call it "Fee-Fi-Fo-Fum" – the blood of Englishmen crying to heaven.'

The reaction of Alec's friends to these literary endeavours was mixed. 'Telegram from Edith S about the storm narrative saying "Profoundly impressed and moved". Letter from Sir Sydney about same – who does not seem to have been so impressed and he requires more art and working up of "awe".' As for *The Brothers Karamazov*, Chattie 'was obviously disappointed' while the Guthries 'who are very sensible and dear to me and usually think I'm "wonderful" couldn't raise more than "Very interesting. Now would you like cocoa or coffee?"'[274] However, Alec sent a copy of his story to John Lehmann who said he would publish it in the next issue of Penguin New Writing under the title Alec had first thought of, 'Money for Jam'.

Alec also read anything he could lay his hands on – fiction, history, theology, literary criticism. The list of titles that he notes in his diary following his return include essays by Auden and Eliot – 'What's in a Classic?' too academic for my taste' – Berdyaev's *The Meaning of History*, Gore's *The Body of Christ*, Montaigne, Raimond de Sebard, *Rasselas* – given to him by Fr Cyril Tomkinson, now reassigned to a parish in London; Kirk's *Moral Theology*, a copy of which he sent to John Rotton, and *The Vision of God*; Trevelyan's *England in the Age of Wycliffe*; Huxley's *Time Must Have a Stop*; Dostoevsky's *The House of the Dead*, and Coleridge's translation of Schiller's *Wallenstein* which Alec attempted to adapt for the modern stage. He liked to share his enthusiasms with others: he sent Marriott Lefèvre a copy of Trevelyan's *English Social History*; and he would read to Merula when at home. 'After dinner read *Little Gidding* aloud – well, but too emotionally.' Eliot's poetry remained a passion.

But his reading was not just for pleasure: Alec was always in search of a subject for a new play. At first he thought that a drama could be made from Tolstoy's life and death. 'Horrified reading of the last years of Tolstoy's life – the terrible story of the son Leo tearing up his father's letters – the Countess' attempt to extract royalties – it's all so grim . . . Is there material for a play there?'[275] He ordered every book by Tolstoy, and *on* Tolstoy, as well as 'all the diaries – both his and hers' – from Bumpus in London. But in early June he was distracted from his reading of Tolstoy by a 'Terrific write-up by Desmond McCarthy for Evelyn Waugh's new novel, *Brideshead Revisited*', which he promptly ordered from Zwemmer's; and also 'a lively novel recommended by Tony in Rome' – Joyce Cary's *The Horse's Mouth*.

Despite making good use of his long hours of leisure in this way, Alec remained frustrated that the Admiralty would not release him even though it was known that he was an actor of some eminence: he was given leave to play Admiral Nelson in a patriotic pageant held in the Albert Hall in April of 1945 called *Hearts of Oak*. However, his duties at Southampton were light and he had frequent opportunities to pop up to London to do some shopping and see his friends. 'To Norton's for a hair-cut, to the Bank for money, to Harrods for a toy penguin for Matthew, to Zwemmers for lunch.' 'Tea with Tony Quayle in the Garrick Club, dined with Martita.' 'Called on the Lavers . . .*, then Fortnums, Simpsons and lunch with Veronica at the Café Royal. Then to the Nat. Gal. . . . Then to see Peggy† at Haymarket where she was presiding over a giant tea-party . . . Then to Emlyn's *The Wind of Heaven*‡ which was stimulating . . . Pleasant supper at Pruniers.'[276]

Alec re-established contact with all his pre-war friends – Edith Sitwell, Edith Evans, Sydney Cockerell, Cyril Tomkinson. 'To Kew. Tea with Lady Cockerell & then a session in Sir Sydney's study – looking at his £4000 Kingsford Chaucer, letters from Henry James, Shaw's manuscript of *John Bull's Other Island*, illuminated manuscripts etc.'[277]

To All Saints Vicarage to see Father Cyril. Stayed ¾ of an hour. Looked around Bumpus. Then lunch at the Café Royal with Peggy, Jeremy, Michael Redgrave and Rachel**. Jeremy – wearing Labour Party colours for his Westminster constituency – in good form, having canvassed at No 10 Downing St†† – Michael v. self-conscious. – Left early for a sleep before his matinée‡‡ – surely height of affectation. – Rachel sweet as usual . . . Bought a good edition of *Little Dorrit* and some fine cigars from Dunhill.[278]

The appearance of Jeremy Hutchinson in Labour Party colours is

---

*   James Laver, author and curator of costumes at the Victoria & Albert Museum, was
     married to the Irish actress, Veronica Turleigh.
†   Peggy Ashcroft.
‡   Emlyn Williams played Ambrose Ellis in his own play.
** The actress Rachel Kempson, Michael Redgrave's wife.
†† Hutchinson was a barrister in civilian life but had Bloomsbury connections through
     his mother, Mary Hutchinson, born Barnes.
‡‡ Michael Redgrave was directing, and playing Colonel Stjerbinsky in *Jacobowski and the
     Colonel* at the Piccadilly Theatre.

one of the few references in Alec's diaries to the 1945 General Election
which led to the fall of Winston Churchill and a Labour government
led by Clement Attlee coming to power. Alec had no great interest in
politics but had strong feelings about particular issues. He had been
horrified by the poverty he had witnessed when stationed at Barletta,
as he revealed in a moving letter he wrote to Merula around five
months before his return:

> If only people at home knew – and it is only recently that I have begun
> to realise – what great agony some parts of Europe are in – an agony
> that puts all the sufferings of England to nothing – but nothing –
> children who are raw – red raw – and bleeding and scabby – because
> they have to be washed in sea-water because the only fresh water has
> to be used for drinking, it's so scarce. Children dressed in sacking, and
> that scantily, because there is nothing else – that sleep in straw – and are
> unable to write. Families from which every piece of furniture &
> crockery has been stolen – and who drink from any old broken tin or
> bottle. Five thousand people who for four years have lived solely on
> black bread, olive oil and an occasional lettuce. And with it all have lived
> in fear and hate.[279]

Alec was mildly patriotic and critical of conscientious objectors, feeling
as he did that England was not just worth fighting for but that the
British had some right to rule the world. 'I know there's a lot wrong
with us – and the Americans – and we suffer from a smug, Philistine,
money grubbing soul – but I do think we are entitled, by our
punctuality, to boss the world.'[280]

On the other hand, he had low expectations of the 'common man':

> The dream of so many people is longer hours in bed and longer hours
> in the cinema – a complete indifference to the gift of being alive and
> having a perception of right and wrong. I see it so much in the lads in
> my ship – nice lads they are – but in some ways tragic – for they are just
> existing – and the way they tackle their pints of beer and their ten

minutes with a whore lacks all the sweep and bigness of even a wicked life.[281]

Alec had even thought about emigrating after the war:

Sometimes I feel I'd like to clear out of England (and if out of England then out of Europe – unless perhaps Ireland) but I don't think I could bear to leave so many good friends behind. And where to anyway – I can only think of three places – Canada, New Zealand and U.S.A. And the latter is the only place where I could earn a living as an actor. But I wouldn't live in America without becoming an American citizen – and I think I'd rather not do that.[282]

What particularly enraged Alec from time to time was the vengeful feelings in the victors. 'In the evening the radio announced the shooting by the Allies of 2 German youths, 16 & 17 years, for espionage . . . Drafted a rough letter to the *Times* & *Telegraph*. Merry & I both upset by it'.[283] He was appalled by a call from the Archbishop of York to 'Shun the Hun'. 'The press is determined we shall not be "soft" with our German victims, but it seems unnecessary for the official spokesman of the Church to seek popularity by pandering to public desire for revenge.'[284]

Alec thought that trials for 'war crimes' were no more than 'victors' justice': 'Most memorable thing in news to-day has been refusal of King of Denmark to sign death warrants of collaborators.'[285] He was particularly incensed at the vengeance taken by Communist partisans. 'I'm terribly distressed about the Greeks,' he wrote to Merula:

It was so obvious, though, it would happen. And it will happen elsewhere too. This loathsome 'revenge' business is seen in practice. It's curious that the people who desire the whipping or shooting of collaborationists – and how can a girl of fourteen or boy of ten be considered a collaborationist! – are all people whose social theory is one of Fraternity, people who oppose war, and who, in clamouring that the people don't get sufficient food, withhold food from men and old women who don't belong to their party organisation . . . Dear me, I find myself more and more in the opposite boat to your dear mamma* – I think our most precious possession at home is the monarchy . . .'[286]

Alec's encounters with Tito's partisans in Yugoslavia had given him a lasting antipathy to Communists: 'I have taken a violent dislike to all commissars and am bored to tears with hammers and sickles'[287]; and, while he cannot have believed that the Labour Party would bring about a proletarian revolution, he feared socialistic regulation. 'We have had a terrific discussion this morning about the Post War World – and in principle we have agreed – that of all things we loathe above all REGIMENTATION and the BOSSING ABOUT of our lives.'[288]

As a result of this mix of political attitudes and emotions, Alec seemed undecided as to how to vote in the 1945 election. 'I've told the government you can have my VOTE while I'm away,' he wrote to Merula from Barletta, 'and if you don't want it that Susy can have it!' Back in England, in the run-up to the election, he listened to 'Attlee's campaign speech – which was reasonable enough, but he lacks personality or drive.' Alec was more impressed by the Liberal Party broadcast but 'one does feel that the Liberal Party is a minority – and consequently ineffective'.[289] But in the end, after listening to a broadcast by Beveridge, he cast his vote 'as a Liberal on the ballot paper'.[290]

With Merula and Matthew still living in the cottage at Oakdale Farm, Alec had no base in London and when on leave from Southampton used to spend the night on friends' sofas or in their spare beds – after dinner with Martita, for example, or John Gielgud. He would also, on

---

* Big Chattie professed to be a Communist.

occasions, spend the night in Turkish baths which, since they were well known as a place for homosexual encounters, raises the possibility that Alec went there for more than a steam bath and a good night's sleep. 'At midnight to Russell Hotel Baths for bed only,' he records in his diary on 18 July 1945. And, two days later, 'Went to the Baths in St James's Street, Ernest Milton wandering around them like a ghost.' Ernest Milton was an actor, a Roman Catholic and a homosexual. On 28 October: 'To All Saints for Evensong and good dinner. Left 10.45 and stayed night at Jermyn St Turkish Baths – revoltingly dirty. But slept undisturbed.'

None of these entries amount to an acknowledgement of homosexual encounters but it suggests that Alec was, to say the least, and to use a phrase he must have been familiar with from the Catholic Catechism, failing to avoid 'occasions of sin'. There can be no doubt but that he was a prey to sexual temptation. 'Lascivious thoughts stream in and out of my head, like the mist,' he wrote in his diary on 19 May 1945. 'A result perhaps, of seeing, scribbled on a lavatory wall yesterday "Wanted a MASTER. I will be his slave for life for £1 a week".' And on 11 June: 'All day my thoughts running on lascivious lines. This sort of thinking poisoning my mind & will lead to the asylum unless well checked NOW.'

It seems unlikely that these lascivious thoughts involved images of women. He describes inviting a Wren officer to tea at Hythe on 8 July, picnicking 'in the heather on edge of forest', and then walking her back to Hythe, but there is no intimation that she was either attractive or unattractive, nor any suggestion that anything improper occurred. His eye more often alights on young men. 'Talked to a young sailor outside the Empire and bought his ticket for *Henry V.*' 'Charming French sailor on board with our loading instructions.' 'Drinks with . . . handsome stage manager.' And, very soon after his return: 'Swiss Cottage by 2230. Followed by young man.'

In Alec's letters to Merula there is, understandably, nothing to suggest that he might be attracted to men. Indeed, he talks about homosexuals as if he were definitely not one of their number. Writing from Italy in May 1944, he describes a man who 'wished to make advances to me in the back of the car, which took me fairly by surprise. However all embarrassment was saved as I pretended not to notice – which was impossible – and changed my position & the conversation. – Perhaps I'm not as bald as I thought.'[291] And earlier, in September of 1943, he told her that a friend he had made in New York, a British diplomat, Val Stavredi, was now in London. 'You won't like him much but he has his points – a great many. Remember what I told you about him? He is very brilliant and worldly and cooks as well as Marti . . . I'm sure he'd like to see you and take you somewhere. He's a pansy, so I feel quite safe.'[292]

Alec came much closer to revealing himself to his sister-in-law, Chattie, who had confided in him about her own problematic love affair and had thought she might have shocked Alec by admitting that she had slept with a man out of wedlock:

> I'm the last person on earth who would care to damn myself with passing a moral judgement on such a subject, so please don't think I had pious horrors. I reserve my horrors for my own awfulnesses – and there are so many of them, and have been of such an unpleasant intensity – that really if I lived as a saint from now to my death I would still be unable at the end of my life to lay down the law about such things. Which of course, dear Chattie, is not quite the same thing as grasping what one believes to be right or wrong on such matters: it just means that for similar reasons that prevented me taking a pacifist stand I am prevented by the past and present from criticising anyone's sexual arrangements.

Despite this reluctance to judge other people's behaviour, Alec seemed to find the idea of sex without love repugnant. Two naval officers had 'got pretty stinking last night and invited some Italian girls on board,' he wrote to Merula during the war, 'who were, I suppose, little better than whores. They were prepared to do anything, I'm told, for a lb [pound] of sugar'. He went to bed, he assured Merula, 'and I hope I don't have to tell you ALONE – earlyish, because sitting with a forced grin on my face for hour after hour is exhausting'. This was not just to reassure Merula; he need not have mentioned the incident if he had slept with a whore; but because he thought sex divorced from love demeaned the divine spark in men and women.

Alec defended the strictness of the Church's teaching on sexual morality in his letter to Chattie:

> The Church, when she points her finger, says in fact 'you are wrong in doing that. Our civilisation, our belief in the godhead in man, is founded on such and such principles. If you oppose them or break them you shake the whole fabric of our civilisation'. What else would you have her say or do? Tell you you are doing fine when you are doing rotten? It is almost impossible for us not to deceive ourselves, we must do our level best to minimise the deceit, to reduce it and whittle it away until we know ourselves for what we are.[293]

Alec's acceptance of the Church's teaching that sex outside marriage is sinful, and his consequent feelings of guilt and remorse when he sinned, combined with a refusal to condemn others – even Christians – who took a different view was to remain with him for the rest of his life.

twenty

In the summer of 1945 Alec found a *pied-à-terre* in London in the Guthries' flat which they had sublet to Anthony Quayle. Tony Guthrie was producing a play in New York and Quayle, who had recently separated from his wife, Hermione Hannen – Ophelia to Alec's Hamlet in Guthrie's modern-dress production before the war – had not yet married his second wife, Dorothy Hyson. The flat itself, at the very top of 23 Old Buildings at Lincoln's Inn (near the office of Arks Publicity) was as chaotic as the Guthries' house in Ireland. It is difficult to imagine the fastidious Alec, who complained that Merula never cleaned the bath, living among the discarded galoshes, books, scripts, and spilt cat food on the sloping floors of this garret where the bath could only be reached by a ladder, and was 'balanced on some beams . . . with one leg missing and in its place, supporting the bath . . . the great sponge' that Merula and Alec had bought for the Guthries in Malta on the Old Vic Tour. But no doubt Alec was glad to have the company of Quayle and a bed in London because an opportunity had arisen, which he was keen to grasp, to appear – not on the stage – but in a film.

David Lean, the young film editor who had been brought by his wife, Kay Walsh, to see Martita Hunt as Miss Havisham in Alec's stage adaptation of *Great Expectations*, had decided to adapt the novel for the screen. Lean was around ten years older than Alec, and had worked his way up in the British cinema industry to become a distinguished editor on films such as *Pygmalion*, an adaptation of the play by George Bernard Shaw, and *French Without Tears*, with a script by Terence Rattigan – both of these directed by Anthony Asquith, the son of the Liberal Prime Minister, Herbert Asquith.

Lean had been excused from duty in the armed services during the war to work on propaganda films such as *49th Parallel* and *One of Our Aircraft is Missing*, both directed by Michael Powell. In 1942 he had graduated from film editor to co-director with Noël Coward of a naval saga, *In Which We Serve*; and in 1944, with Coward as producer, directed a screen adaptation of Coward's play, *This Happy Breed*, taking sole credit as director for the first time. In 1945, he had directed film versions of two further Coward plays, *Blithe Spirit* and *Still Life* – the latter reincarnated for the screen as *Brief Encounter*.

Brief Encounter had not yet been released when Alec heard about the planned film of *Great Expectations*. Although Lean and Kay Walsh both acknowledged that it was Alec's stage adaptation which had given them the idea of putting Dickens' novel on the screen, and although the play had been performed at the Liverpool Playhouse during the war, there was no approach to buy the rights to Alec's play. Lean, and the team he had brought together to produce his earlier films in a company called Cineguild – which included a baronet, Sir Anthony Havelock-Allan and a cinematographer, Ronald Neame – first approached the successful playwright Clemence Dane to write a screenplay. 'Apparently Clemence Dane is doing the script,' Alec wrote in his diary. 'And they are using a Reader – which appears unnecessary and suggests plagiarism.'

Dane's script proved unsatisfactory, and so Lean and Neame retired to a pub in Cornwall and wrote the script themselves. When it came to casting, they acknowledged the film's provenance by hiring Sophie Harris and Margaret Harris of the Motleys to design the sets, Martita Hunt to play Miss Havisham, and Alec to repeat his stage role as Herbert Pocket. It is a credit to the impact he had made on Lean six years before that he could envisage Alec, now a bald thirty-one year old, playing a much younger man. Alec took a screen test on 9 August 1945, at Highbury Studios. 'Ronald Neame & David Lean – can't get the right names – both charming. So was make-up man. Disastrous wig in Denham. So was toupée all fluffed out – a patched up affair but didn't look so bad for period. Wrong colour & character that's all. – Dried up a lot during my test. But quite enjoyed it in a strange way. Finished at 1445.'

Lean and Neame were sufficiently impressed by the screen test to offer Alec a 'shark like' contract, but it remained unclear as to whether or not he would be released by the Navy. His immediate superiors were helpful but the Admiralty bureaucracy was intransigent. In early September it was proposed that Alec be transferred to the naval base at Westcliffe and would then be sent on leave – though there was always a chance that the leave would be cancelled. On 12 September, Alec was telephoned by Neame to say that Cineguild were prepared to take the risk; three days later, Alec took the train to Rochester and started filming on 19 September:

Up at 6.30. Make-up at 7.00. Eyebrows plucked & bleached. Make-up a success. Wig needs a bit more vitality – but is very beautiful. – Rain in early morning. On the set by about 9.45. Long shots of rowing and beaching the rowboat – a bastard of a thing. John Mills & I quite exhausted. Shot of Finlay* and me running from the boat to the inn was done over and over again – couldn't get it right. – Finished at lunch-time. Back to Rochester and looked for rooms for Merry.

---

* Finlay Currie who played Magwitch.

Alec got no pleasure from the experience of filming. 'Can't remember day – except utter boredom,' he wrote in his diary on 11 October. He got fed up with the pampering of John Mills who was playing Pip. 'Filmed after lunch – rowing. Must confess I'm intensely bored. And a little fed up with Johnny this, Johnny that – Johnny are you getting blistered, Johnny do you want a rug to sit on – poor Johnny.'[294]

Given that Alec's screen performance in *Great Expectations* was to prove the beginning of a spectacular film career which outshone, though it did not eclipse, his standing as a stage actor, it is striking how fortuitous it was. His two previous experiences of film acting – as an extra in Victor Saville's *Evergreen* more than ten years before and playing in a propaganda film during the war – had been unpleasant. He rarely mentions going to the movies, though many must have been available to the armed forces: he much preferred to read. In New York, he had been to Lean and Coward's *In Which We Serve*: 'It is very good but one recognises every face that flits by.'[295] But it seems unlikely that Alec would have considered going for a part in a film directed by David Lean or anyone else had he not felt that to dramatise *Great Expectations* was somehow *his* idea and Herbert Pocket *his* role.

His mentors, after all – Gielgud, Guthrie, St Denis and Komisarjevsky – were dedicated to the stage and felt disdain for the screen: in Komisarjevsky's case, more than disdain – contempt:

The commercial cinema is an entertainment or pastime for illiterate slaves of an up-to-date 'business civilisation' founded on Mammon. The sham naturalism, the treacly romanticism, the sentimentality on the one hand with its psychological complement – brutality – on the other, the tinned literature and language and music of the cinema have had their big share in the debasement of the idealistic significance of theatrical performances and workmanship.[296]

Lean's film that preceded *Great Expectations*, *Brief Encounter* – the story of an unconsummated love affair conducted amid swirling steam on a provincial railway station to the strains of Rachmaninov – was not

short of all those qualities that Komis despised. Alec went to a preview
in Rochester on 3 October 1945, and noted only: 'Celia Johnson quite
lovely in it.' However, the film when it was released was an astounding
success with both the critics and the public and became, in the words
of Lean's biographer, Kevin Brownlow, 'one of the most famous and
fondly remembered of all British films'.[297]

By the time Alec had seen the preview of *Brief Encounter*, he was
well into the filming of the exterior scenes of *Great Expectations* on the
Thames estuary, uncomfortably close to the naval base at Chatham
where he had spent the vilest moments of his National Service. In
November 1945, this finally came to an end. Alec was demobbed. On
20 November he went to the Chiswick Food Office to collect a civilian
Ration Card, coupons and an Identity Card. He chose this moment to
abandon the name of Cuffe which he had been obliged to use
throughout the war. 'Registered in the name of Guinness. This will be
official in six months' time.' He then went to Olympia to collect the
civilian clothes provided by the government – 'a waste of time except
the mac'. He went up to Piccadilly to order a suit from Fortnum &
Mason, and another from Benson, Perry & Whitley. After a drink with
Michel St Denis at the Waldorf, he dined alone at the Café Royal.

In January 1946, the filming of *Great Expectations* moved to Denham
Studios for the interior scenes. By now Alec had come under the spell
of the 'lithe and handsome'[298], 'enchanting, affable, exciting'[299]
director, David Lean, and had grown to respect his meticulous
cinematographic technique. 'He was very good,' Alec later told Lean's
biographer, Kevin Brownlow:

I was overawed. It was the first proper film job I'd done. He didn't tell
one how to perform. He just knew when something was not quite
catching. He didn't know how to put anything right, he just knew what
wasn't right . . . I had a close-up in which I had to laugh out loud and
this is always difficult. Difficult laughing in the theatre, but suddenly I
thought, on film you will see that this is manufactured and I am not
remotely amused. We tried it once or twice and David said, 'Let's forget

the whole thing for a moment. Let's just wait twenty minutes' and so he sat by my side and I hadn't seen that he had made a little signal to the camera to start turning in the course of the conversation and then he said something which made me laugh and he said, 'Cut'. So he got his shot on a totally false premise . . . but thank God. I was so grateful. I don't think I would ever have achieved it otherwise.[300]

Alec makes a brief reference to this incident in his diary on 28 February 1946: 'To Denham by 8.45. David Lean tricked me into laugh for close-up. Home by 9.15 p.m.'

Home by now was a pretty eighteenth-century house called 'The Brook' on Stamford Brook Road in Chiswick into which Alec, Merula and Matthew had moved on 4 December 1945, renting it from Orovida, the granddaughter of French impressionist painter Camille Pissarro. Thanks to *Great Expectations*, and despite his 'shark like' contract with Cineguild, Alec could now afford the rent of this substantial dwelling: on 25 October 1945 he noted in his diary that '£81 + £27 + £243' had been paid into his bank account, but remembering 'that at least 1/3rd of income goes in tax'.

'The Brook', however, was only a temporary solution, and in May 1946 the Guinnesses took the lease of one of the large, elegant houses on St Peter's Square, Hammersmith, that had been built for Wellington's generals after the Napoleonic Wars. Alec had to ask his father-in-law, Michel Salaman, to help them pay for it. 'Called on Michel to discuss raising £2000 for house,' he noted on 14 February. And on 10 May: 'We've got the house in St Peter's Sq. – No. 7. Very nice. We won't have enough stuff to fill it.' It was to remain their home for the next eight years.

Alec's career as an actor was now back on course. 'Have written to *Spotlight* to re-start my advertisement and to Equity to get up to date there.' Alec rushed around town fielding offers and making suggestions. Edith Sitwell wrote to say that she and Osbert were writing a play with him in mind. He showed his own adaptation of Schiller to Michael Redgrave. He became interested in a play called *Heloise* and tried to get Glen Byam Shaw to direct it. 'Glen to dinner. Read him 1st act *Heloise*. He can't do it. Suggests Glenville.'[301] And the next day: 'Lunch with Peter Glenville to ask him to produce *Heloise*. Like him and think he'll do it well.' In the event, nothing came of *Heloise* but Glenville was to become one of Alec's closest friends.

Dostoevsky was all the rage. Frith Banbury came to tea to try and interest Alec in his adaptation of *The Idiot* and John Gielgud asked him to direct a stage version of *Crime and Punishment*. And, of course, there was also Alec's own adaptation of *The Brothers Karamazov*, which had interested a powerful new consortium of theatrical managements, the Company of Four: it had been formed by Binkie Beaumont of H.M. Tennent, John Christie and Rudolf Bing at Glyndebourne, Tony Guthrie at the Old Vic and Norman Higgins of the Arts Theatre at Cambridge to by-pass the log-jam caused in London theatres by long-running musicals. Their plan was to stage contemporary plays that would rehearse for four weeks, tour for four weeks, and run for four weeks at the Lyric Theatre in Hammersmith.

In March of 1946, when Alec was still filming *Great Expectations*, the Company of Four agreed to stage his adaptation of *Karamazov* and Alec dropped all other offers. On 26 March he lunched at the Gargoyle with a twenty-year-old Oxford graduate, Peter Brook, who had shown exceptional promise as a director at OUDS. 'Decided on *Karamazov*,' Alec noted in his diary, 'if Tony will produce – or possibly P.B. or self?' He telephoned Gielgud on 1 April to turn down *Crime and Punishment* and the next day Peter Brook telephoned to accept the offer to direct *Karamazov*. It was now a question of casting. Alec himself would play Mitya, the Czech actor Frederick Valk was approached to play Karamazov and Alec took an actor he particularly admired, Ernest Milton, to lunch at Rules to try and persuade him to play the mystic Fr Zossima. 'Like him a lot – fantastic, witty.' Milton was a Roman Catholic and Alec successfully played on this by saying that, if he played Fr Zossima, he would be 'mercilessly attacked by the anti-clerical press'.[302]

Milton accepted and Alec also recruited, for the lesser parts, his friends from the London Acting School, Pierre and Marriott Lefèvre; James Laver's wife Veronica Turleigh, and Jehane Ingram (now Jehane West). Rehearsals started on 6 May and the production was not without problems. 'Ernest a bit happier today,' Alec recorded in his diary on 8 May, 'but having him & Valk in the same play is nearly impossible.' And on 21 May: 'Am desperate about my own part. Freddie tells me I'm playing myself and not Mitya.' The play opened in Cambridge on 27 May and transferred to the Lyric Hammersmith on 4 June, its running time reduced from three hours, ten minutes to two hours, thirty-five minutes. 'Quite a good reception and fairly glamorous first night. Little party at home afterwards . . .'

The reviews the next day were mixed. 'One could perhaps best describe Mr Alec Guinness's adaptation,' wrote the all-powerful critic of the *Sunday Times*, James Agate, 'by saying that it is one of those colossal mistakes which are tremendously worth doing . . . As Mitya Mr Alec Guinness disappointed in the first two acts . . .; when he got down to bare feet and convict's garb his playing took on the required intensity.'

Alec, who later described his adaptation as loose and lopsided, had no time to withdraw to lick his wounds but at once started to rehearse for the role of Garcin in *Huis Clos*, a play by the French existentialist, Jean-Paul Sartre, translated as *Vicious Circle*. It was also directed by the young Peter Brook and staged at the Arts Theatre Club. Alec's diaries suggest that he had little interest in Sartre's existentialism but he was, together with Ernest Milton, one of the few actors who actually believed in the play's setting – Hell. It is *Huis Clos* that has the famous line: *'l'enfer, c'est les autres'* ('Hell is other people').

Already in April of 1946, Alec had been approached to rejoin the Old Vic Company which was planning to stage another series of plays at the New Theatre. His first role was to be the Fool in *King Lear*, directed by Laurence Olivier who would be playing the title role. 'Decided in my mind on the Vic – the Fool being the great attraction – if Larry will let me play him as a clown and give me a freeish hand,' Alec noted in his diary on 4 April, going to see Olivier the following evening 'to talk about the Fool'. Laurie Evans, whom Alec had engaged as his agent, negotiated a salary of thirty-five pounds a week.

Alec's attitude towards Laurence Olivier was a mixture of admiration and dislike. He had closely watched his performance as Romeo and Mercutio in *Romeo and Juliet* before the war and, as we have seen, thought that 'his Romeo was as arresting and beautiful as his Mercutio was vulgar and gimmicky'. Olivier's superficial approach to a play itself – it was said that he would only read his own part – was in marked contrast to Alec's intelligent and meticulous study of a play as a whole. Olivier was just what Alec did not want to be – an actor who was *merely* an actor – 'technically brilliant'[303] but humanly shallow.

He also saw how Olivier would undermine other actors to boost his own standing and, though he would write at the time of Olivier's death that 'he was certainly patient with me when I was rehearsing the Fool to his Lear', his diary entry for 21 September 1946 reads: 'Dress rehearsal with Larry. Misery.' He may have suspected, as John Mortimer maintains, that Olivier did not rate him highly as an actor; that like Gielgud he thought Alec should stick to 'those little parts you do so well' – one of which was, he no doubt thought, Lear's Fool: but, as Alec told Mortimer, he benefited from Larry's vanity in this post-war production because, he noticed, Olivier's directions ensured that the stage lights were raised whenever Lear came on stage and lowered when he left it; and Alec was only on stage with Lear.

King Lear opened at the New Theatre on 24 September 1946. Alec received twenty-eight telegrams of congratulation, a decanter from Martita Hunt and 'flowers from Larry & Vivien. All very gratifying'. The first act was slow but the production delighted the audience. 'Hysterical reception. Stood next to Larry for call, who mentioned me in his speech.' Alec dined that night with Merula and Peter Bull.

The reviews reflected the audience's enthusiasm and a number singled out Alec for praise. 'Mr Alec Guinness played the teasing, transient part which always promises more than it yields better than

I have ever seen it done before,' wrote Ivor Brown in the *Observer*. 'Few actors succeed in getting through the incongruity to the enormous pathos behind,' wrote Eric Keown in *Punch*, 'but Mr Guinness does this brilliantly. His Fool is infinitely sad and infinitely humorous and for once Lear's affection for him can be understood.'

The critical acclaim for Alec's acting continued with the contrasting roles he played in the Old Vic's repertory: Eric Birling in J.B. Priestley's *An Inspector Calls*; the Comte de Guiche in Edmond Rostand's *Cyrano de Bergerac* – this directed by Tony Guthrie and with Ralph Richardson playing Cyrano; Abel Drugger in Ben Jonson's *The Alchemist*. 'This player creates (or recreates) every part he touches,' wrote Brown in the *Observer*. 'A glorious piece of playing,' wrote the veteran critic of the *Sunday Times*, James Agate, of Alec's Abel Drugger; 'I name him the best living English character-actor,' wrote the new *enfant terrible* among the British theatre critics, Kenneth Tynan.

This last was a double-edged compliment because Alec's ambition was precisely to escape from the confines of character acting into the amplitude of a major role. This came in the following year when he was cast in the title role of Shakespeare's *Richard II*, directed by another of the leading actors in the Old Vic troupe, Ralph Richardson. This was a challenge not just in itself, but because the standard set by the 1946 season at the New Theatre was high and he had been singled out as one of its stars. 'A distinguished English actor,' wrote Harold Hobson, a critic who was to replace James Agate at the *Sunday Times*:

> . . . recently returned after twelve years in America, told me a few days ago that since 1939 the London stage has done wonders. Broadly speaking, this is true. An abundance of new talent has been showered upon us in the serious theatre . . . At the Old Vic a young player has recently given such performances that I, a confirmed passenger on the water-wagon, can now, for the first time in my life, echo with sincerity, 'Guinness is good for you'.[304]

But, as Hobson made clear, the very success of previous productions such as Olivier's *Lear* had raised the public's expectations. The season starting in November 1947, was:

> . . . to be the Old Vic's critical season. Ralph Richardson and Laurence Olivier have put the Old Vic on a pinnacle; and pinnacles, like bayonets, are hard things to sit on. Neither of these great men is in this year's company. Whether the newcomers – Trevor Howard, Patricia Burke and Celia Johnson – together with Alec Guinness, can replace them in the affections of the Old Vic audience, is a question to which the answer is most eagerly awaited.

Alec was not just a newcomer; he was also an actor who appealed to the mind, the ear and the eyes of those who watched his performance; but he did not set up a throb in the hearts of young women:

> One complicating factor is that the Old Vic audience, which used to be the most intelligent in London, is probably now the least. It replaces knowledge and judgement with sex and hysteria. It has enthusiasm; but the enthusiasm is for getting autographs and rubbing shoulders with film stars. During the intervals hordes of gallery girls rushed down into the stalls. Most of them were very young – fifteen or sixteen. Fat girls, thin girls, pretty girls, and girls not so pretty. Many of them were intent on capturing Richardson's autograph: he and Lady Richardson were in seats next to me. The girls pushed and shoved, but were quite polite. 'You don't mind, do you?' they said, with winning smiles, as they stamped on my toes.[305]

However, Shakespeare's Richard II, like the Richard II of history, is not heroic in the muscular way that might appeal to the gallery girls; he is thoughtful, poetic, melancholy, and – by the standards of the mediaeval warrior caste – a wimp. It was also a role that called for a beauty of speech and one of Alec's already established strengths was his diction. But, as with his Hamlet before the war, Alec was acting in the shadow of John Gielgud's Richard, given in the Queens theatre ten years before. Here again, Alec felt that he had been unable to escape from that shadow, describing his performance as 'a partly-plagiarised, third-rate imitation of Gielgud's definitive Richard'.[306]

This self-criticism was almost certainly unduly harsh: the audience attending the first night, which included Harold Hobson, received the play with 'great enthusiasm, but no hysteria'. Hobson also noticed that 'there were several seats empty, and the usual frenzied autograph hunters did not seem to be present either in large numbers or ferocious mood. I left the theatre at the end with toes untrodden.' However, his considered view of Alec's performance was admiring: 'I have never heard the great speeches more beautifully delivered. In the scenes in Wales in particular that music which at first only Mr Guinness hears surges through the theatre. He has a whole orchestra in his voice: the wailing violin, the thundering trumpet, the lamenting 'cello. Mr Guinness's is one of the three best performances in London.'[307]

There were other complimentary reviews but, as so often with thin-skinned artists, it is the adverse opinions that matter most. 'The speeches were spoken with the keenest intelligence,' wrote Ivor Brown in the *Observer*, 'but with something less than magic.' The influential James Agate firmly returned Alec to his pigeon-hole: 'Mr Guinness's genius is for the rueful comic, a note which this play never strikes.' Kenneth Tynan blamed Alec's failure on the play's director, Ralph Richardson. 'Sir Ralph . . . tries to make Mr Guinness bellow, which is like casting a clipped and sensitive tenor for Boris Godunov; he would have him speak at the top of a voice whose peculiar quality it is to have no top.'[308]

The reviews rankled, and continued to rankle for many years. 'The *Manchester Guardian* once started a review of my *Richard II* by saying "Guinness has no music in his voice",' he wrote to a friend in 1961, 'but by the end of the column said it was like listening to Bach!'[309] They also made him chary of reading reviews in the future: 'Since then I have rarely read the critics, except for amusement.'[310]

The setback, more imagined than real, of Alec's *Richard II*, did not cramp his style in his three remaining roles in the Old Vic season at the New: the Dauphin in Shaw's *St Joan*; Hlestakov in Gogol's *The Government Inspector* and Menenius in Shakespeare's *Coriolanus*. In *St Joan* he was playing with Celia Johnson, whom Alec had admired in David Lean's *Brief Encounter*, and generally esteemed as an actress, though he did not consider that she mastered the opening scene – 'embarrassing in itself . . . The only actress I have seen deal successfully with that opening,' he wrote later, 'was Eileen Atkins in 1977.' Sybil Thorndike was the only Joan who had convinced him that she heard the bells. 'That couldn't be said of Celia Johnson's Joan; I fear she only heard a tinkle, like that of a silver bell on a cat's collar.'[311]

twenty-one

In the short speech Alec made from the stage after the first night of *Richard II*, he had told the audience that 'for the past three months I have been working in what is known as the Industry; but I can't tell you how glad I am to be back with the Profession.' The sentiment expressed was probably sincere enough; the stage, with its live audience, was an exhilarating stimulant at each performance; but the implication that Alec had been *reluctantly* drawn back into 'the Industry' – viz. movies – was misleading. The role that he had been acting on film, that of Fagin in David Lean's second Dickens adaptation, *Oliver Twist*, had been given to him, with some misgivings, at Alec's request.

Great Expectations had been released in 1946 to great critical acclaim: the *Daily Express* headlined its review, 'Britain makes her greatest film'. Starting with a script that had efficiently reduced the essentials of Dickens' long novel to a taut visual narrative and giving it, as a bonus, a happy ending that was also dramatically more satisfactory, Lean displayed real artistry – particularly in his use of the wide landscapes of the Thames estuary. The *Sturm und Drang* of the opening scenes, and the theatricality of the cobwebbed wedding feast for the jilted Miss Havisham, were more reminiscent of pre-war German cinema than the Pathé-Pictorial style of the British studios at that time. Lean had also elicited fine performances from his actors, catching the caricature found in many of Dickens' fictional creations without provoking a suspension of disbelief, and never losing his audience's enrapt engagement with the fate of Pip.

While the performance of John Mills as Pip, however, produced no surprises, Alec, as Pip's friend and mentor Herbert Pocket, brought unique verve and charm from the moment Pocket appeared on the screen, carrying a bag of vegetables to the door of his lodgings. Given his age – Alec was now thirty-one – it was astonishing that he could be so convincing as a much younger man. With the long floppy lock of his wig falling over his face, his 'posh' voice, and the gentle manner that so exactly matched the courtesy implicit in his lines, Alec created a memorable character in this supporting role.

Although widely advised that it would be a mistake to attempt to repeat the success of *Great Expectations* with another Dickens adaptation, Lean remained obsessed with Dickens' earlier novel, *Oliver Twist*. Alec, too, had loved this classic since boyhood: Oliver's unhappy childhood, like that of Pip, seemed to have parallels with his own. But he had also been fascinated by the character of Fagin, the villainous Jewish master of a band of apprentice thieves: at Roborough, when staging shadow plays behind a sheet, he had played Fagin using 'handkerchiefs and rags and things off a barrow' and speaking in 'some sort of funny voice'.[312]

Alec now decided that he wanted to play Fagin in Lean's film. Clearly, it would be an audacious casting and, realising that Lean might be reluctant to take the risk, Alec put it to him over lunch at the Savoy. The director rejected the idea out of hand. Alec then told Lean that his reaction was typical of the unimaginative and unadventurous nature of the British film industry: everyone was typecast. This provoked

Lean to agree to a screen test, which Alec took along with the actor Robert Donat who wanted the role of Fagin's murderous deputy, Bill Sikes.

Before taking the test, Alec had studied the illustrations by the nineteenth-century engraver and caricaturist, George Cruikshank, for the original editions of Dickens' novels and had made himself up, in his dressing-room at the New Theatre, to resemble Cruikshank's portrayal of Fagin. He also adopted a rasping, lisping tone with a particular accent, and rehearsed a mincing, shuffling walk. This careful preparation, following a long consideration of how the role should be played, paid off. Lean was astonished when Alec appeared on the set. 'I was bowled over by it and he got the part without another word.' Robert Donat was less convincing as Bill Sikes: the part went to Robert Newton.

Alec's idea of Fagin, and the make-up for the screen test, were his own; but when it came to filming, his initial conception was meticulously fulfilled by the make-up artist, Stuart Freeborn. He, too, had imagined a Fagin like Cruikshank's and Cruikshank's vision, it should be noted, matched Dickens' own description of Fagin in his novel; but, when first preparing Alec for the role, Freeborn had tried a 'toned-down' version with fewer wrinkles and no hooked nose. This, in Freeborn's view, made Alec look more like Christ than Fagin and Lean, too, preferred the wrinkled, hook-nosed version.

The process of preparing Alec for a day's shooting demanded exceptional patience from both actor and make-up artist. Alec would arrive at Pinewood Studios at five-thirty in the morning, and Freeborn would work on him for the next three hours. The result might well have seemed an exaggerated caricature had it not fitted with the stylised sets – even more reminiscent than those of *Great Expectations* of expressionist German films of the Weimar era, starting with Robert Wiene's 1919 classic, *The Cabinet of Dr Caligari*.

Unfortunately, another film made six years earlier in Nazi Germany had also caricatured the stereotypical Jew: this was Veit Harlan's film of Lion Feuchtwänger's *Jew Süss*. Werner Krauss, who had acted in *The*

Cabinet of Dr Caligari, not only played multiple roles in this film – as Alec was to do in *Kind Hearts and Coronets* – but had shown a Guinness-like thoroughness in preparing himself for these roles: he 'steeped himself in a Jewish ambience and, with macabre dedication, walked about his villa in a greasy gabardine with a stocking pulled over his head, while the objects of his mimicry were being killed in the ghettos of the East'. Ferdinand Marian, blackmailed into playing the title role by Goebbels by the threat of losing his exemption from military service, committed suicide at the end of the war.

Ironically, this story of a Jew in Würtenberg in the Middle Ages had been filmed in Britain in 1934 by Lothar Mendes, with the Jewish Michael Balcon as producer, to ridicule anti-Semitism; but the German version, in which the malign Süss rapes an Aryan girl, was 'the cinematic curtain-raiser for the Final Solution'[313] – 'highly recommended for its artistic value' by the Nazi Minister of Propaganda, Dr Paul Joseph Goebbels.

Clearly, neither Alec, Stuart Freeborn nor David Lean had seen Harlan's film, and any suggestion that there was an anti-Semitic intent in their depiction of Fagin cannot be sustained. It showed, however, a certain insensitivity to the enormity of the fruits of anti-Semitism on the continent of Europe; or simply how long it took for the enormities of the Holocaust to sink into the contemporary mind. As a result, when *Oliver Twist* was first shown in Britain in 1948 there were complaints from some Jews, but no widespread objection. In the United States, however, the film ran into grave trouble. It was attacked by a number of Jewish organisations and, as a result, was withdrawn from circulation. *Oliver Twist* was not shown in the United States until 1951, and then with twelve minutes cut. Sadly for the Americans, these twelve minutes were among the most enchanting of Alec's film career – Fagin's elegant cavort in which he demonstrates the art of pick-pocketing to Oliver, revealing with his smile and the twinkle in his eye that even the worst villains can possess humour and charm.

However, *Oliver Twist*'s troubles in the United States did not prevent a widespread acknowledgement that David Lean had made a fine film and that Alec had once again almost stolen the show. He had certainly demonstrated to 'the Industry' what was already known in 'the Profession', that he was a superb actor, and one whose performances were particularly effective on the screen.

Michael Balcon, the able and energetic producer who had made the British version of *Jew Süss* for Gaumont in 1934, had, since 1938, been the head of a film production company based in Ealing Studios in a suburb of west London. Balcon had, like other British Jews from the time of Benjamin Disraeli, and including the Hungarian-born film-maker Alexander Korda, a quasi-ideal, quasi-sentimental, but wholly patriotic vision of what was best about Britain, the British people and the British way of life. His expressed aim at Ealing Studios was to build up 'a native industry with its roots firmly planted in the soil of this country . . . making British film production . . . a significant part of our national life'.[314]

In 1987, when complaining in his diary about how much he disliked reading screenplays, Alec recalled that the script that was now sent to him by one of Balcon's team of directors, Robert Hamer, was one of only two that he had actually enjoyed reading. This was *Kind Hearts and Coronets*, an adaptation by Hamer and John Dighton of a novel by Roy Horniman, *Israel Rank*. It was, as the film demonstrates, a particularly literary script, with allusions to Chaucer and quotations from Tennyson: and the film that came from it was not as *visual* as dedicated cinéastes hold that films should be.

It was, however, a beautifully balanced, understated black comedy, which played with great delicacy and even greater cynicism upon the themes that are of perennial interest to the English – class and sex. Though the latter may have been of lesser interest to Alec, the plight of Louis Mazzini, the product of a *mésalliance* of a daughter of a ducal family, must have struck a chord with a man whose illegitimacy was still a shameful secret – the terrible uncertainty, still acute in many in England in the 1940s, as to whether one should present oneself at the front door or at the servants' entrance.

Dennis Price, who played Louis Mazzini, systematically and with charming *sang-froid* murdering all members of the d'Ascoyne family who stand between him and the succession to the title of Duke of Grafton, did so with a faultless panache. But once again – it was becoming professionally hazardous to appear in a film with Alec Guinness – Alec upstaged him, playing eight characters – in all of Mazzini's victims so brilliantly that distinctive personalities emerge from characters superficially the same. The banking d'Ascoyne, who at first rebuffs but later employs and befriends Louis Mazzini, though old and grey-haired like the rector, is not at all the same man; nor is Ethelred, the gruff and blinkered Duke.

Who were Alec's models for his brilliant impersonations? One can imagine the arrogant young Ascoyne d'Ascoyne as a junior officer encountered by Alec as a naval rating, and in *Blessings in Disguise* he describes an obnoxious naval captain on Loch Fyne as a model for Admiral Lord Horatio d'Ascoyne. The young photographer, Henry D'Ascoyne, has a touch of Herbert Pocket who in turn has a touch of Alec himself. General Lord Rufus d'Ascoyne is perhaps the nearest to a predictable caricature; Lady Agatha makes a brief appearance, and was the first but not the last role Alec would play dressed as a woman; and it is perhaps possible to surmise that there was something of the bibulous Reverend Cyril Tomkinson in the Reverend Lord Henry d'Ascoyne.

Alec acknowledged that much of the credit for his success in *Kind Hearts and Coronets* was due to the director, Robert Hamer, a man still under forty who had studied Economics at Cambridge and 'looked and sounded like an endearing frog'.[315] He retained a life-long devotion to Hamer: only to take calls from the United States and from Robert Hamer would Alec rise from table, leaving his food to grow cold. He would go on to make three other films under Hamer's direction – *Father Brown* in 1954, *To Paris With Love* in 1955 and *The Scapegoat* in 1959 – none of which were, or deserved to be, as successful as *Kind Hearts and Coronets*. Alec made five further films for Ealing Studios – *A Run for Your Money* in 1949 directed by Charles Frend; *The Lavender*

Hill Mob in 1951 directed by Charles Crichton; *The Man in the White Suit* in 1951, *The Ladykillers* in 1955, both directed by Alexander Mackendrick and *Barnacle Bill* in 1957.

Balcon ran Ealing Studios in the manner of a company whose products happened to be films: a team of writers, directors and editors were his staff and actors were treated as casual labour hired for seasonal work. Later in his life, Alec would look back with mild umbrage at the off-hand treatment of actors at Ealing – this, perhaps, in contrast to the deference shown to him subsequently by the Hollywood studios. He hardly came across Balcon. He also never forgot the casual attitude taken by the studio towards his physical safety when acting certain hazardous scenes.

For the scene in *Kind Hearts and Coronets* where Admiral Lord d'Ascoyne goes down with his ship, saluting and standing to attention as the water rises, Alec had his feet attached by wire to the base of the tank. Hamer wanted the camera to linger on the swirling water long enough to show the Admiral's cap floating away. This required Alec to hold his breath for at least half a minute: Alec, having taken up yoga, told Hamer that he could hold it for up to four minutes. The scene was duly shot at the end of a long day and, considering it satisfactory, the members of the production team began packing up their equipment and preparing to go home. Only well into the four minutes was it remembered that Alec was still tethered underwater and one of the crew had to dive into the tank with wire-cutters to set him free.

For the scene when Lady Agatha d'Ascoyne rises in the balloon, Alec was mocked by the production team for insisting upon a double: sure enough, the balloon drifted away and the double was lucky to return alive. In *The Man in the White Suit* he had to be suspended by a wire which he recognised, from his time in the Navy, was likely to snap. When he pointed this out to the technicians, they laughed and told him to mind his own business. Sure enough, the wire snapped and it was only good luck that saved him from death or serious injury. And for the final scene of *The Ladykillers*, when Alec, as the Professor, is killed by the railway signal falling onto his head, the production crew made sure that this would not in fact happen by placing a metal pin half an inch above the level of Alec's head. Lines were drawn in chalk to mark where he should stand for the shot. When it came to the take, however, the signal sheared the metal pin and tore the back of Alec's jacket. He had been standing an inch or two in front of the chalk marks – a mistake that saved his life.

During the 1950s, Alec made other films for other studios: the *Last Holiday** and *The Mudlark* in 1950; *The Card* in 1952, directed by Ronald Neame, David Lean's deputy on *Great Expectations* and *Oliver Twist*; *The Malta Story* and *The Captain's Paradise* in 1953; *Father Brown* in 1954; *To Paris with Love* in 1955 and, also in 1955 and most significant in Alec's own estimation, *The Prisoner*, directed by his friend Peter Glenville; but none of them endeared him to the British cinemagoers in the same way as the Ealing comedies had done. Those were an exceptionally happy conjunction of script and actor that caught the public mood in the grim post-war years and, a vindication of Balcon's gamble that the British industry should play to its strengths, appealed by their very Englishness to Americans too. There were films aplenty coming out of Hollywood with virile heroes, but as Kenneth Tynan wrote in his study of Alec published in 1953:

> In the Ealing pictures there is no hero in the generally accepted sense of the word, but only a whimsical hero-impersonator . . . We see little of the boudoir, the bagnio or the American bar, and much of the police force, the Civil Service, and the small shopkeeper – strata of society to which Guinness is easily adaptable.[316]

In 1950, when *Kind Hearts and Coronets* was released in the United States, the American Board of Review declared Alec the best actor of the year. The film established him as a star: it also made him moderately rich. In

---

* This was directed by Henry Cass who, when Alec had auditioned for a part in *Antony and Cleopatra* in 1934, had shouted: 'You're no actor. Get off the fucking stage.'

1946 his agent, Laurie Evans, had agreed a wage of £35 a week with the Old Vic; by 1952 he was asking, and getting, from Alexander Korda and Rank, a fee of £15,000 for a single movie; and by 1955 MGM was offering Alec a fifteen-year contract at $1,000 a week.

Of course, as Alec so often complained in his diary, and in letters to his friends, the rates of Income Tax were high: when he noted in his diary in 1945 that at least a third of his income would go in tax, that was of the modest income he would earn at the Old Vic. As he earned more, so he paid higher tax, rising to a marginal rate of eighty-five per cent. He did the Football Pools every week: 'If only I could win the Pools I would be set up financially,' he wrote in his diary after Korda's offer. 'The fifteen thousand means nothing by the time tax is taken off. When one dies in poverty, I can see the papers commenting "and he earned £15,000 a picture" – with no comment on paying away nearly all of it on armaments one doesn't approve of, and social services one doesn't use.'[317]

Alec's Ealing comedies received accolades from both sides of the Atlantic and are still the films which, if not the most widely known or the most admired of his long career, are remembered with the greatest affection. But Alec himself, though he remained grateful to directors such as Robert Hamer who had brought him fame and fortune, and became a personal friend of Charles and Sonja Frend, was ambivalent about his achievement. 'Disappointed with *Ladykillers* script,' he recorded in his diary on 12 April, 1955. Alan Bennett recalled that he 'was scathing about the Ealing comedies'. 'Of the old Ealing films I think *The Man in the White Suit* stands up best . . .' he wrote to his friend Dame Felicitas Corrigan in 1979, 'though I don't think my performance adds up to much . . .'[318] And in the same year he noted, '*Lavender Hill Mob* was being shown on TV but I didn't look at a single frame of it.'[319] Yet in 1986 he was infuriated when Bridget Boland said that Robert Hamer and Sandy Mackendrick were fifth-rate directors and retaliated by saying *Gaslight* (which she scripted for the 1940 version) was a bore. 'I think she's a bit mad – with loneliness.'[320]

What Alec feared, perhaps, was that his very success in these comic roles confirmed Gielgud's condescending judgement that he was best in 'those little parts that you do so well'. When interviewed by Melvyn Bragg for *The South Bank Show* on London Weekend Television in 1985, he expressed his irritation that Ealing Studios had promoted him as 'a man of a thousand faces'. It riled him, he said, because in films such as *The Man in the White Suit* and *The Card*, there were no facial props other than the inevitable toupée. But his irritation also masked two areas of anxiety – the first, that his success in minor roles suggested that he could not master a *major* role; the second, that behind the grease-paint and false whiskers, he *was* a man of a thousand faces – and none.

twenty-two

Two major theatrical roles that Alec played in 1949 and 1950 can be seen as keys to an understanding of his state of mind in the 1950s. The first was that of the 'Unidentified Guest', subsequently identified as the psychologist Sir Henry Harcourt-Reilly, in T.S. Eliot's *The Cocktail Party*, produced by Henry Sherek and directed by E. Martin Browne at the Lyceum Theatre in Edinburgh.

T.S. Eliot had been Alec's favourite contemporary poet since his youth. It was Eliot's 'Burnt Norton' that John Rotton had produced from his duffel coat for Alec to read in the warm funnel of the warship during their naval training in Scotland. Alec's later recitals and recordings of *The Waste Land* and other of Eliot's poetic works showed an exceptional feeling for the cadences and meaning of the verse. Alec, as we have seen, had even written a fan letter to Eliot after his wartime broadcast.*

---

* See Chapter 14.

Now he actually met his literary hero. Eliot attended rehearsals of
The Cocktail Party and impressed Alec with his humility:

> He was very unobtrusive at rehearsals. I remember one day saying to
> the director – 'I think I've said this speech before. Or am I being silly?'
> Then Eliot came down, looked at the script, and crossed out the
> speech. Not many playwrights are capable of that. Another time, I said
> 'I cannot get from that side of the stage to the other unless I stop
> speaking – couldn't I have something to bridge me?' He wrote four
> beautiful lines straight off. Without a query.[321]

With hindsight, one can see traits common in the personalities of the
great poet and the great actor. Both were devout Christians who were
drawn to sanctity and tormented by their failure to achieve it. As
Lyndall Gordon has shown in her perceptive study of Eliot, there was
in him, even prior to his conversion to Christianity, in his
unpublished 'First Debate between Body and Soul' 'a fierce disgust of
the flesh, its masturbations and defecations' that reappears 'again in
The Waste Land's ruthless "Burning burning burning" of the sexually
polluted flesh'.[322]

It was through Eliot that Alec had discovered and come to admire
the fiercely ascetic Charles de Foucauld, and Eliot's exercise in
mortification in an urban setting is similar to Alec's:

> There he lived the introspective life of a solitary, like Jeremiah in the pit
> or St John of the Cross in the dark prison. There, under the crucifix, he
> observed strict religious rules, some given, some of his own devising.
> He memorised passages of the Bible, said the rosary every night, and
> kept the fasts. During Lent he denied himself gin, and limited his
> favourite game of Patience to one pack.[323]

Some of Eliot's petty sins were also like Alec's. To his friend Mary
Douglas, writes Lyndall Gordon, Eliot 'was often fussy,
hypochondriacal, self-obsessed, and capricious. She was appalled by

the suddenness of his fury, and would beg him to control it for both their sakes. He would get out of her car, and slam the door. Few saw Eliot from that semi-intimate perspective'. Few saw Alec from that semi-intimate perspective either.

The Cocktail Party, superficially a drawing-room comedy of the kind commonly staged in the West End, is in fact a Christian morality play: 'The tactic was to get an indifferent, largely atheist audience to take in a moral message without realising it.' Sir Harcourt-Reilly, the role played by Alec, 'is really more like a priest than a psychiatrist', and one of the lines he delivers expresses a moral nostrum that was to remain with Alec throughout his life: 'Your business,' Harcourt-Reilly tells Celia Coplestone played by Irene Worth, 'is not to clear your conscience,/ But to learn how to bear the burdens of your conscience.'

The critical reception of *The Cocktail Party* was varied. Blank verse drama, as written by Christopher Fry and now Eliot, was briefly in the ascendant but the difficult and unfashionable ideas evinced some puzzlement and even derision: Alan Dent in the *News Chronicle* called the play 'a finely acted piece of flapdoodle'. That it was finely acted seemed beyond dispute: Harold Hobson wrote in the *Sunday Times* that it established Alec as one of the nation's leading actors. 'The triangle of Gielgud, Olivier, and Richardson is visibly changing into a quadrilateral.'

Since no theatre was available for a transfer to London, Henry Sherek took *The Cocktail Party* to the Henry Miller Theatre in New York. Once again, Alec embarked on the *Queen Mary* but in very different conditions from his earlier voyage. He had a stateroom all to himself and, rather than the company of naval sub-lieutenants, he kept that of the other passengers travelling First Class – among them Peggy Ashcroft's first husband, the publisher Rupert Hart-Davis, and Ian Fleming's wife, Ann.

New York once again had an electrifying effect on Alec. The play, opening in January of 1950, was an instant success. 'No one understood the play, but everyone assumed it was important,' wrote Brooks Atkinson in *Broadway*.[324] 'Packed to the ceiling again last night,'

Alec wrote to Merula from the Meurice Hotel, 'and queues all day at the box office':

> At 3.30 yesterday it BEGAN for me – photographers, interviewers and the general hurly-burly of being a success in the American sense. I didn't get to bed until 4.00 a.m. and didn't sleep much then. Was up at 10.30 this morning and had an interview with the *New Yorker* – a charming man did it who was v. intelligent about the play. But God knows what they'll write, as they have now cottoned on to the fact that I was Fagin . . .[325]

When they did, Alec ran into trouble. At a party given for Olivia de Havilland and Carol Reed at the Rockefeller Centre, 'My *hostess* – a little old lady – not Jewish – greeted me sweetly with "Why, Mr Guinness, I *must* tell you that I think your performance in *Oliver Twist* was just simply *too disgraceful* to *Jewry!*'[326]

In general however, Alec was made welcome – even by Jews. 'I had a delicious little adventure to-day' he wrote to Merula on 2 February:

> I went to a dullish lunch party & left with Peter Glenville, with whom I walked a few hundred yards afterwards. We stopped at a crossing for the traffic and a rather cherubic bright old gentleman eyed me sharply. Then he crossed to me & said 'Aren't you in *The Cocktail Party?*' When I said yes, he seized my hand and held it, patting it. Then he said, 'I saw it last night. It is the greatest experience I've ever had in the theatre. It is the most superbly acted play I have seen, and will you please tell all the cast that I think you are all wonderful. My name is SAM GOLDWYN!' I was delighted to have Peter as a witness as no one would have believed me otherwise!

Not only was Peter Glenville in town, but also Noël Coward who at a grand dinner-party on Park Avenue given by a 'fluttering old queer who is mad about the theatre . . . sat at the piano and played all the songs from his new operetta, which were v. gay and funny. I made a social success, for once, by doing an imitation of John & Peggy in (the) ballroom scene from *Romeo* . . .'[327]

Alec's stay in New York with *The Cocktail Party* laid the foundations of important lifelong friendships with other members of the cast, particularly Bobby Flemyng who played Edward Chamberlayne and Irene Worth. 'I had a lazy day. Bobby came to spend the week-end with me and we pottered about in dressing-gowns until lunch-time, when Irene came to help me make tit-bits.'

In April Merula came to New York with Matthew to enjoy not just the exhilaration of the city but also the luxuries still unknown in post-war Britain. Alec had worried about the expense: 'I shall be able to let you and M have $150 to spend on clothes etc. when you arrive (*between* you I mean) but living will have to be simple.' But when they returned to England, he felt bereft:

> I was very depressed and lonely when you went. I *hated* coming back to the apartment, and it was sick-making finding a forgotten sock of Matthew's and a blouse of yours and a packet of hair-pins (no use to me). I dried up twice during the show on Friday night and cut a great chunk yesterday but I'm OK again now. It was quite delicious having you both here. Now it seems impossible that I managed Jan Feb & March without you. But I did.[328]

Alec, though he was now 'sick of being able to have everything and anything, sick of the grandeur', and longed to see the dog's dirty paw marks on the carpet, kept himself busy at the New York Public Library studying the life of Disraeli for the role he had been offered in the film, *The Mudlark*; but also planning a foray into classical acting, back in London, that would establish once and for all that he was, as Harold Hobson had said, in the quadrilateral of great English actors: he would finally master the role of Hamlet in a production that he would direct himself.

The attempt failed – catastrophically – and this marked Alec for life. 'We sat up, after M's excellent kedgeree, until 0200 talking theatre talk,' Alec wrote in his diary on 3 September 1979. 'I got on to the theme of my own theatrical disasters – the awful first night of my 1951 Hamlet . . . As a result – theatrical nightmares, which I haven't had for quite a time.'

The production was financed by Henry Sherek, flushed with the success of *The Cocktail Party* in New York. For the first time in his life Alec, like Gielgud at the New Theatre in 1934, was given *carte blanche*. His casting was original, with roles given to actors with little experience of Shakespeare: Lydia Sherwood as Gertrude, Ingrid Burke as Ophelia, Robert Urquhart as Horatio, Walter Fitzgerald as Claudius, Alan Webb as Polonius and, as Laertes, the young actor he had first met when staying with Edith Evans, Michael Gough. In a diary entry in 1976, Alec was defensive about his choice: 'at least ten of the company (picked by me) *became* stars of stage, screen or TV even if not all for ever'.[329] But clearly their future celebrity was not thanks to their appearance in his *Hamlet*.

The choice of a designer, too, proved to be a mistake. Having been impressed by Salvador de Madariaga's essay *On Hamlet* published three years earlier, which insisted upon the pervasive Spanish influence in Elizabethan England, Alec chose the Spanish designer Mariano Andreu, instructing him to avoid permanent, semi-permanent or realistic sets: he had disliked the rostrum erected on stage for Richardson's production of *Richard II*, saying that he could have conversations on the stairs in his own home.

A young actor, Robert Shaw, was given the role of Rosencrantz. It was later said that Alec had become infatuated with Shaw after seeing him play a page in *Much Ado About Nothing* at Stratford-on-Avon, and had paid him over the odds to appear in his *Hamlet*. The homosexual flirtation, if that is what it was, led Alec to slap Shaw on stage. John Warner, who played Osric, said that the slap was in response to the line: 'Will't please you go, my lord?' delivered with lewd innuendo; but Warner was in the wings whereas an eye-witness, the director James

Roose-Evans, sitting in the stalls for the matinée when the incident occurred, remembers the slap as a response to the more provocative line, '"My lord, you once did love me", which Shaw delivered in a startlingly suggestive tone, whereupon Guinness, as Hamlet, slapped him in the face, rebuking this insolent courtier'.[330]

A second piece of casting, that of Kenneth Tynan as the Player King, was an even better example of what Tynan himself called Alec's 'exuberant oddness' in his choice of actors. Tynan, then aged twenty-four, had been at Oxford where he had staged his own version of *Hamlet*, taking the role for himself of the Third Player. Alec had seen this production when it was staged at the Rudolf Steiner Hall. Tynan's fledgling career, however, was not as an actor but as a critic yet he accepted the role and became a caustic observer of the becalmed rehearsals and 'the fiasco of the opening night'.

To assist him in the direction, Alec took on a young director, Frank Hauser, whose chief experience had been in dramas for BBC radio. Hauser was only too aware of his own limitations, yet Alec showed 'a curious deference in his conduct of rehearsals' towards him and would agree to Hauser's suggestions. This bifurcation in the play's direction proved fatal. 'Relentless direction might have extracted more from the players,' wrote Tynan. 'Guinness's reluctance to commit himself to solo direction worked its own downfall.'[331]

Alec's dithering also infected his playing of Hamlet. He had a clear idea of how he did *not* want to play Hamlet but, though some of his positive notions were considered by Tynan to be 'dazzling', they did not amount to a coherent whole. He wanted to avoid the traditional 'sweet and gentle prince', bringing out the nasty side of Hamlet as demonstrated by his brutal treatment of Ophelia; yet the positive side of his hero eluded him. 'It was a failure,' wrote Tynan, 'born of indecision, and fostered by the cancer of Guinness's humility. Unwilling, on the one hand, to work within the framework of tradition, he was fearful, on the other, of abandoning it entirely. This bred a fatal ambiguity, both in the production and in his own performance.'[332]

The production did not make a preliminary provincial tour but went straight to the New Theatre in London. Tynan describes how, on the opening night, Alec arrived too early at the theatre and so retired to the Garrick Club, where he went around touching the busts of the illustrious thespians of the past to bring him luck. They did not. The New Theatre had been fitted with a sophisticated new lighting system which malfunctioned, with the result that court scenes were acted in obscurity while the Ghost appeared on the battlements in a blaze of light.

But this glitch was simply the bitter icing on an inedible cake. There were boos from the gallery at the final curtain and the reviews in the next morning's papers were mostly severe. 'It is the custom of genius to do things in a big way,' wrote Harold Hobson in the *Sunday Times*, 'and the cropper that Mr Guinness came on Thursday night was truly monumental.' Beverly Baxter, the *Evening Standard* critic, considered it 'the worst production of *Hamlet* I have ever seen' and, for good measure, wrote that Kenneth Tynan 'would not get a chance in a village hall unless he were related to the vicar'.

After the fall of the final curtain on the first night, Alec turned 'to the rest of the company and said, very softly: "It was my fault. Don't blame yourselves. I gave up in the first act".' He also appeared, in the weeks which followed, to give up on the whole endeavour: 'It is still difficult to understand,' wrote Tynan a few years later, 'why no further rehearsals were called, after the first performance, to put things right.'[333] Such had been the blow to his self-confidence, that Alec felt nothing could be salvaged from the wreckage.

Yet was the play such a wreck? Edith Sitwell was vocal in her defence of Alec's Hamlet, which was perhaps an expression of the loyalty one might expect of a friend: but even some of the reviewers after that catastrophic first night saw exceptional qualities in Alec's performance. W.A. Darlington, the *Daily Telegraph* critic, conceded that Alec's Hamlet lacked 'all romantic colour and much emotional force', but judged that he achieved as a result 'an admirable sardonic quality which underlines and lights up everything he does, giving the performance as a whole the unmistakable stamp of individuality'. Frank Hauser, too, thought that Alec had given 'a remarkable, magnificent performance which never got properly credited'; and James Roose-Evans, who had been at the matinée when Alec had slapped the cheek of the insolent young Robert Shaw, still remembered the impression Alec's playing of Hamlet had made on him more than fifty years later:

> I saw the performance twice and on the second occasion I took with me Eleanor Farjeon, who had seen many Hamlets including Henry Irving's, and she insisted on going round to Guinness's dressing-room afterwards to tell him how superb she considered it. For me, it remains the most definitive performance of the role that I have seen, and one by which I judge all others . . . His speaking of the role was for me a revelation, brought up on the music of Gielgud's speaking of Shakespeare. When it came to 'To be or not to be' he started upstage centre and simply moved slowly downstage, speaking the lines quietly. It was as though he were new minting the words, thinking them there on the spot . . . His declaration of friendship to Horatio was the most moving I have ever heard. Again, a simple declaration, no gestures, but an intensity of feeling which was only surpassed at the graveside of Ophelia when a great cry was wrenched from him, 'I *loved* Ophelia!' It was a cry that still haunts me.[334]

The chief beneficiary of Alec's *Hamlet* was Kenneth Tynan, who first wrote a damning review in *Harper's Bazaar* under an assumed name; then ousted Beverly Baxter as the theatre critic of the *Evening Standard*; and finally drew on his experience of the whole fiasco for a chapter of his study of Alec, published two years later. Tynan described him as an actor who, 'were he to commit a murder, I have no doubt that the number of false arrests following the circulation of his description would break all records'.[335] Alec remained the man with a thousand faces – and none.

Alec was to play two more Shakespearean roles within two years of his 1951 *Hamlet* but not in England. In 1952 Tyrone Guthrie was invited to Canada to found a Shakespearean Theatre at Stratford, Ontario. He immediately asked Alec to join him. 'A long and inspiring letter from Tony G. in Eire re Canadian project,' Alec wrote in his diary on 12 September 1952; and then, eleven days later, 'Must refuse Canadian job as I feel Tony's contempt for stars (particularly those concerned with films) would undermine me completely. This is a hard decision to make but I'm sure the right one. Binkie, of course, delighted at any discomfiture for Tony.'

Alec went to the Guthries' flat in Lincoln's Inn to discuss the project, telling Guthrie that he felt he 'hadn't confidence in me as an artist . . . It was all rather unpleasant.' The next day, however, he changed his mind and, over lunch at the White Tower, 'settled up our differences of yesterday & started planning – for *Hamlet* & *Julius Caesar*. All quite gay.' He was offered $5,000 'for the whole thing' which he thought was good, but both his agent, Laurie Evans, and his friend Peter Glenville, advised strongly against the venture. 'Peter G . . . begged me not to go to Canada next summer. Said all my friends and Laurie felt strongly about this but had never dared say anything. Agreed with him about danger of working 3000 miles away with Tony Guthrie. Don't see how I can possibly withdraw my support now.'[336]

Alec spent the summer of 1953 in Stratford, Ontario. He appeared as the King of France in a modern-dress production of *All's Well That Ends Well* and played the title role in *Richard III*. Apart from one or two tiffs with Guthrie, his stay in Canada provided an agreeable interlude which brought back his confidence in his ability to play Shakespeare but did not expunge the memory of his disastrous *Hamlet*.

twenty-three

When Alec celebrated his fortieth birthday on 2 April 1954 he was, to all appearances, one of the most enviable men in the world. He was rich, famous and esteemed by his peers. He had an intelligent and devoted wife, a son who charmed all who knew him, numerous friends from both within and without the profession and a handsome house on St Peter's Square.

Yet the nine years which had followed his return from the war and saw his astonishing professional success had also seen Alec struggle with depression and self-doubt. 'I can't drive a car or speak French,' he wrote in his diary on 11 September 1952:

> I have written nothing, thought nothing, created nothing, wrapped my talent in a napkin and let it grow dim. I'm not deeply sad about this, only contemptuous. It isn't a matter of the years now, but the decades. I'm too experienced, too familiar with my own sloth to say, 'Oh, but next year.' I can only hope in greater spans that my life will achieve

some meaning and make some kindly good mark. – In Algiers, in '41,
at HMS *Raleigh*, even picking bacon rind out of rubbish heaps in
Inveraray, it seemed to have some direction, a certain amount of
energy and proper self-discipline & self-correction.[337]

Alec suffered, as he himself recognised, from bouts of paranoia. He felt
he was 'in danger of persecution mania setting in, or rather the
wretched feeling I have sometimes that my personality is anathema to
people. Of course it must be to some people, and I'm ready to face
that, but it's dreadful when you experience it on-stage.'[338] In 1954,
some six months after his fortieth birthday, he records a session of
pessimistic introspection. 'Searched my heart depressingly and decided
I'm leading a visionless, pointless, selfish life – no objective, no
ambition (other than to keep on earning money – though only for the
tax situation).'[339] A week or so later, in mid-October 1954, he shared
his sense of self-loathing with his friend, Peter Glenville. 'Peter and I
vied with each other in the stupidity, failure etc. of our lives as human
beings.'

What was this life as a human being? The household at St Peter's
Square, besides Alec and his immediate family, included at one time or
another his mother, two young Canadian drama students, the 'daily'
Mrs Parker, Mollie Hartley-Milburn, a former drama teacher who
worked as Alec's part-time secretary, Johnny the chauffeur, a South
African Grey parrot called Percy, two dogs, Tilly and Vesta, and a cat
called Zossima.

When Alec had returned from his wartime service in the
Mediterranean, his mother, Agnes, had been living in Guildford and
Alec had been paying her an allowance of thirty shillings a week. She
came to London to see him on 5 August 1945, and Alec gave her lunch
at the Café Royal. There is no reason to suppose that he had revised
the opinion of her that he had expressed to Merula towards the end of
the war: 'I feel a great pity for her, but no love, no fondness . . .'; but
he was scrupulous in doing his duty as a son and perhaps decided that

she might be less likely to get drunk, fall into debt or be arrested for shop-lifting if she lived with him at St Peter's Square. She also acted as a babysitter until the night when Matthew, then aged seven, was woken by the sound of his grandmother screaming. She was lying on the floor drunk. Her nightdress had been singed by the small electric fire in her room and her legs were trapped under her bed.

Matthew met his parents when they returned and told them what had happened. Alec 'shot upstairs, shouting and yelling', Matthew recalled, 'and threw his mother out of the house in her nightdress, throwing a suitcase with her belongings after her'. Agnes was banished to Brighton, where she lived in lodgings until Alec bought her a flat. 'Have been down to see her a couple of times during the past week and think I have found her a ground-floor flat in Hove. Looked at about six,' Alec noted in his diary on 1 February 1955. After he had bought the flat in Brunswick Square, Hove, he went back and forth. 'To Brighton in morning to fix up Mother's flat. Carpet & curtains there already.' 'Finished the flat except for a draining board and a lamp. Mother greatly cheered up and forgot all about her illness.'

Agnes's great-niece Jane, the granddaughter of her sister Eileen, was a lodger. She was a drama student at the Connaught Theatre in Worthing and had fond memories of Alec's mother:

She would get up every morning. She'd make sure I had a breakfast and she'd pack me a little packet of sandwiches to take with me. And she'd wash my sweaters and she'd put them under the carpet to dry so they wouldn't shrink. And she was always welcoming and concerned for my welfare and had I got enough pennies and had I eaten and if I wasn't very well – you stay there in bed. She was a really kindly giving person. I loved her.

Alec was her life. Oh, Alec did this, Alec did that . . . Before I was living there, Granny Lou and Aunt Anne [Agnes] would take my brother and me to London to the Globe Theatre. We used to get matinée tickets. It was always 'Alec sent us tickets'. We weren't very interested in the matinée but we loved going to London and hailing a

taxi and going to the Lyons Corner House. And we were always going
to go backstage to see Alec but we never did. There was always a
message: sorry, I've got an appointment or I've got to go out or I can't
this time. He always gave us the brush off.[340]

Alec's fame had other disagreeable consequences beyond the
attentions of unwanted cousins. 'An anonymous letter,' Alec noted in
his diary on 17 February 1955, 'saying "I'm one of the trades people
who your mother owes money to. She trades on your name and is a
menace in the pubs and shops here." Very sickening – made me feel ill
and weary for the rest of the day.'

Merula's career was a casualty of Alec's meteoric rise to fame. In 1948,
the actor Stuart Burge formed a travelling repertory company and
invited Merula to join it. She was inclined to accept but Alec forbade
it, saying that their marriage would not work if both pursued their
careers. She had to choose. Recognising that to work in a *travelling*
repertory company would indeed be incompatible with her duties as
a wife and a mother, Merula turned down Burge's offer; but she had
not resigned herself to abandoning her theatrical career altogether. In
1952 she was offered an irresistible role and was prepared to defy Alec
but Matthew fell ill with polio and the confrontation was postponed.

The crisis came a year or so later, after Matthew had recovered,
when again Alec told her that if she took a part she had been offered
it would mean the end of their marriage. Percy Harris told Jonathan
Croall, the biographer of Gielgud, that he had said: 'Either you are an
actress or you are my wife.' This precipitated a breakdown: Merula
was always in tears. Alec acted decisively. Matthew was sent away to
a riding school and Merula was booked into a suite in the Ritz. 'Alec
was working. He left her alone in a suite in the Ritz. She cried for three
days – then it was over. She decided not to consider acting again. He
had left her to lie on her bed to weep – and weep and weep. All her
mental illness was rolled into one. She buried all the things she had
suffered. Tore it all up. She later said it was a liberation.'[341]

Alec's subsequent justification for his brutal *diktat* was not that his career was more important than hers, but rather – as he had suggested in his letters during the war – that Merula was somehow *too good* for the theatre. Writing to her from Asheville, North Carolina, where he was filming *The Swan* in September 1955, he presented a *post-facto* explanation for what he had done:

> I know that so often with my shallowish enthusiasm I'm so liable to lay things on with a trowel or bang down the law, that often I hesitate to encourage you to come out *in words* with what you are feeling or thinking – I always have a fear of *contaminating* you my darling . . . I always have the feeling of protecting *your* integrity, and it's stupid of me because your integrity could withstand anything. That is one of the reasons – well the only reason really – why I was happy when you gave up the theatre. You had talent – exceptional I think – for the theatre – but you are too good for the theatre and I always feel, rightly or wrongly, that it would *distress* you in the end and force you to lower your standards.[342]

Whether or not Merula accepted this justification or not, one cannot tell. What seems clear is that Merula's decision was indeed a 'liberation'. It freed her, not just to devote herself to Alec and develop talents as a visual artist that did not threaten him, but also to achieve an inner strength that others would remark on throughout her life.

Merula's ideas on how to raise a child came from her own experience as a child, when her father had earned her undying love by beating her with a riding-crop, supplemented by what she had learned about breaking in horses while working for the equestrian trainer, Major Faudel Phillips. Merula frequently beat Matthew with a belt and – having been told by Major Phillips that you should never beat an animal in anger – when he was a little older, would wait until bath-time to beat him for some transgression during the day.

Alec beat him only twice – once when Matthew, aged six or seven, was happily emptying jugs of water over the side of his bath, which then cascaded through to the room below; and, on the second occasion, whacking him on the head from behind when the boy had been rude to his mother, after which Matthew retired to his room and would not speak to Alec for several days.

The actress Veronica Turleigh told her daughter Bridget that she considered Alec and Merula were too strict with Matthew: so too the Redgraves, who were the Guinnesses' neighbours in Hammersmith. Well into his adult life, Matthew was known to involuntarily shy away when sitting at table if his father picked up a spoon because Alec, like Mrs Joe in the film of *Great Expectations,* would shut him up at meal-time with a crack on the head with a large spoon.

An element of naval discipline was brought into the Guinness home: Alec would come to 'inspect' Matthew's bedroom and 'get cross if there was so much as a sock lying on the floor'. Matthew was afraid of his father, not so much because of the crack on the head with a spoon, but of a verbal dressing down. Alec called Matthew 'the fat arse of Chiswick'; he would say, 'your arse is enormous' and 'a fat arse is the sign of a knave or a fool'.

Alec had a small rowing-boat on the Thames. He made models and fish flies in his workshop at 7 St Peter's Square and practised casting on the lawn. He loved making board games: 'Started to plan an "Attack" game of Shakespearean characters,' his diary tells us in November 1952. 'Tragedy versus Comedy, with Francis Bacon and Earl of Oxford as spies, poor dears. It looks quite promising.' On 3 December 'Started to make snakes & ladders set – with theatrical implications.' And on the sixth, 'Started to teach Matthew chess'.

Alec chain-smoked, coughing and spluttering as he worked on model gliders and the toys which he then blew up. He made an aluminium diesel-powered racing car and Matthew's toy train had a real steam-powered locomotive. Alec's diaries record his determination to be a good father, taking Matthew up to town for a haircut, then to a model theatre exhibition, and teaching him how to play chess. Merula would paint and perhaps Matthew resented his mother's distraction: one day he took a razor-blade and cut a cross in the canvas of one of her pictures. When Alec saw what he had done, he went straight to his work-bench, smashed the balsa-wood launch he had been making, and never again made another model for his son. 'Love him as I do,' Alec wrote to Merula many years later when Matthew was twenty, 'my mind keeps going back to that day as a small boy when he ran a razor blade over one of your paintings.'[343]

One of the few occasions when Matthew remembered being alone with Alec was when his father took him to have his hair cut in Bond Street. Afterwards, they walked down Burlington Arcade and looked at the toys in Hamley's. He also recalled being taken to a Marx Brothers film by his father in a cinema in Hammersmith, which Matthew found unfunny but made Alec laugh so much that he collapsed between the rows of seats onto the floor.

Sadly, despite these outings, no intimacy was established between father and son and Matthew sometimes felt envious of the warm embrace that other boys received from their parents. Alec's intense sensitivity – that rawness remarked upon by Merula – led him to withdraw if he felt rebuffed. Matthew, later in life, had a clear memory of the occasion when, at around the age of eight, he was returning from an outing with his father and they were both laughing after 'some remark about dog-shit on the road which I thought hysterically funny – about it being like apple crumble; and he put his hand on the back of my neck and said something about "my chicken" and I shook him off and said "I'm not your chicken" and Alec never touched me again'.

Number 7, St Peter's Square became a focus for Merula's relations and the Guinnesses' friends. Chattie, who had married an actor, John Blatchley, came to live in Chiswick and Blatchley worked for a while as Alec's secretary. Marriott Longman, married to Pierre Lefèvre, and with a daughter, Andrée, three years younger than Matthew, came from Notting Hill: Alec records in his diary, soon after his return from the war, pushing Andrée in her pram around the Round Pond in Kensington Gardens. Among the Guinnesses' neighbours were

Anthony and Jocelyn Lousada whose daughter Jenny was Matthew's first love; and Michael Redgrave and his wife, Rachel Kempson with their children Vanessa, Corin and Lynn. 'Matthew Guinness came to play with Corin,' Rachel Kempson wrote to her husband. 'Adorable about his father – he'd been to see him as Hamlet and he *loved* it. I just wanted to hug him, he was so glowing with pride and loyalty and had obviously minded *so* much *for his father*.'[344]

'The atmosphere in the Guinness household was quite contradictory,' Corin Redgrave recalled:

. . . because Alec was a very strict father – even by the standards of those days; and Matthew was very strictly brought up. He had to ask permission to play with his train set, chiefly because it was such an expensive train set and Alec liked to play with it by himself. It was a real miniature steam train; you had to put methylated spirits under the boiler which would heat it up and off it would go. It was beautiful – a big train set. But Alec had to be asked permission. And there was a very, very bad atmosphere if Matthew did something that he wasn't supposed to or had forgotten something that he was supposed to do. And I remember Merula as a very benign person but not someone who would intervene on Matthew's behalf with Alec, saying, 'No, Alec, not that.' Alec was gracious but I would have found him an alarming father except that he was perfectly delightful to Matthew's friends – chiefly me. I think I was the only friend that Matthew had at that time; extremely polite and thoughtful and kind. 'Would you like some lemonade? I think you'll rather like this, we made it ourselves.' He used to sit in a leather-backed chair and he was utterly sweet.[345]

A charming glimpse of what Matthew looked like at this period comes not just from the photographs in the Guinness family albums but the few frames at the start of *The Card*, the film directed by Ronald Neame based on the novel by Arnold Bennett, in which Alec played the role of 'Denry' Machin and Matthew appeared as Machin as a child. Off-screen, at home, Matthew was dressed-down in the Salamans' style which horrified the Redgraves' nanny. 'Matthew did look scruffy. He wore country clothes – a Viyella shirt that was slightly frayed and baggy shorts that looked as if they had been passed on by a cousin . . . We had a nanny and would go down and see our parents just after tea before going to bed.'[346]

In the summer of 1952 Matthew fell ill and was found to have the viral disease, poliomyelitis or, as it was more commonly known at the time, 'infantile paralysis'. For a time, Matthew was paralysed from the waist down and it was unclear as to whether or not he would be permanently disabled. Merula nursed him at St Peter's Square: Alec lit votive candles 'in the little church in Maiden Lane'. Walking home from working on the interior scenes for the film of *Father Brown* in the Riverside Studios in Hammersmith, he would drop into a small Catholic church 'just to sit quietly for ten minutes and gather what peace of spirit I could'.[347] He did not 'pray or plead or worship' but eventually made a negative pact with God: if Matthew recovered, he would never put an obstacle in his way if he, Matthew, wanted to become a Catholic.

On 9 September 1952, the Guinnesses were told by Matthew's consultant that 'apart from competitive team games, he can lead a normal life again'. The next day, Alec lit three more candles in the Catholic Church of Corpus Christi in thanksgiving. It would appear that God had kept His side of the bargain although, given what we now know about Alec's High Church Anglican beliefs, and his leanings towards Rome, it seems unlikely that he would have raised objections had Matthew chosen to become a Catholic. Moreover, Alec made such an eventuality more likely by deciding to send Matthew not to Westminster, the ancient and elite public school for day pupils where Corin Redgrave was to go, and for which Matthew had been entered, but to Beaumont, the Jesuit boarding school near Windsor. And, when Alec and Merula had taken Matthew for an interview with Beaumont's Rector, they had been specifically warned that it was highly likely that

Matthew would convert to Catholicism if he went to this Catholic school.

It would therefore seem that Alec was not sacrificing much – or indeed anything – in the 'bargain' he made with God, but rather that he liked the idea of behaving like a character in a novel by Graham Greene. The denouement of this anecdote, in Alec's autobiography, comes when his Jesuit-educated friend, Peter Glenville, suggests Beaumont: '"But it is Catholic!" I said: then remembered my promise in the little Hammersmith church.' Yet as we have seen from Alec's wartime letters to Merula, he had proposed sending Matthew to Beaumont as early as 1944 because the school had earned the esteem of Sir Sydney Cockerell. Memory is, perhaps, selective and authors, even autobiographers, write for effect.

twenty-four

The decision to send Matthew to a boarding school was taken partly because Alec and Merula had decided to move out of London and live in the country. The colony of actors living in Hammersmith and Chiswick was, in any case, breaking up. Chattie and her husband, John Blatchley, together with Marriott and Pierre Lefèvre went to join Michel St Denis in Strasbourg where he was running one of five theatrical centres set up by the French government. 'John Blatchley in to say farewell,' Alec noted in his diary on 18 January 1955. 'Off to join St Denis in France. Madness.' Subsequently, the Lefèvres followed, and later the Blatchleys moved to the grim coal-mining town of St Etienne to provide theatre for the working classes under the aegis of Copeau's son-in-law, Jean d'Asté. And Michael Redgrave was forced to sell the beautiful Bedford House to pay his income tax.

While living in St Peter's Square, Alec's feelings towards Michael Redgrave had changed. He had known him since they had both played

in the Old Vic season at the New Theatre in 1936; they had both gone
to stay with Edith Evans in Kent at a time when Redgrave was her
lover; Alec's presence was cover for the adulterous affair. Redgrave was
older than Alec but the two men had had equally unsatisfactory
childhoods: Redgrave was the illegitimate son of two actors, George
Ellsworthy 'Roy' Redgrave and Daisy Scudamore; his father had
emigrated to Australia the year after Michael's birth but his mother,
whom he adored, married a rich and respectable banker who had
given Michael a gentleman's education.

During the war, as we have seen, Alec had suspected Redgrave of
malingering but that was no reason for the Guinnesses to avoid the
Redgraves socially and, on 20 March 1946, Alec and Merula went to
watch the Oxford and Cambridge boat race from Bedford House, and
'in the evening to Michael Redgrave's birthday party . . . all elegant and
meaningless. We felt that none of the people there were any greater
friends with Michael than we were'.[348] But, on 6 October 1946, 'to
Redgraves' for drinks at noon – Matthew spent afternoon with them.
Michael in for drinks at 5.30 and we had a fascinating heart to heart &
hair down talk. Came round to him with a bang.'

Thereafter, Michael Redgrave would often drop in at 7 St Peter's
Square and the two men became close friends. What no doubt helped
to bring Alec round to the older and more celebrated actor was that
Redgrave greatly admired Alec's acting both on stage and screen: he
thought, like Garrick, that 'you can fool the town in Tragedy, but
Comedy will find you out'. But there was also a personal rapport:
Corin Redgrave judged that both Alec and his father were shy,
inhibited men who found refuge in one another's company:

They would sit up talking late into the night and my father would
walk home. My father was a great dropper-in. Dropping-in is a good
thing because if people say they are busy, it's not a rebuff. I imagine
that they probably confided in one another quite a lot. My father
always carried quite a burden of guilt vis-à-vis my mother and us
children.[349]

The burden of guilt came from Redgrave's homosexuality. As an undergraduate at Magdalene College, Cambridge, in the late 1920s, Redgrave had belonged to a group of homosexual aesthetes formed around the economist John Maynard Keynes and John Gielgud's friend, George 'Dadie' Rylands, a young English don at King's College. Anthony Blunt, the art historian and future Soviet spy was also part of this circle that Blunt's biographer, Miranda Carter, called 'the Cambridge outpost of Bloomsbury'.[350] Redgrave, Blunt and Robin Fedden founded a literary magazine called *Venture* in 1928; and the following year Redgrave wrote a pastiche of Virginia Woolf's *Orlando* which was published in the undergraduate magazine *Granta*, illustrated with a photograph of Blunt in drag.

When Michael Redgrave married Rachel Kempson he had told her of his homosexual leanings and later wrote: 'I cannot feel it would be right – even if I had the will power which I have not – to cut off or starve the other side of my nature.'[351] They lived amicably together and produced three children – Vanessa, Corin and Lynn – but Rachel Kempson had a long-term lover, Glen Byam Shaw, and Michael a male lover, Bob Mitchell, who worked as his chauffeur, and lived around the corner from Bedford House.

It is not known whether Michael Redgrave confided in Alec about the intimate details of his private life. 'Michael Redgrave phoned asking me down for a drink,' Alec wrote in his diary on 7 October 1952. 'Went at about 12.00. Michael & I exchanged notes on our drunken mums – but nothing of great interest.' Alec felt a deep compassion – and hence fondness – for those men such as Redgrave, Ernest Milton and Bobby Flemyng who found themselves married to women they loved but were sexually attracted to men. All might have wished it were otherwise: Michael Redgrave told Frith Banbury that he thanked God his children were not queer. And Redgrave, too, felt great compassion for fellow homosexuals: when the actor Max Adrian was arrested for importuning in the gentlemen's lavatory at Victoria station, Redgrave went to visit him in prison and helped him financially on his release.[352]

Michael Redgrave could drive, but only did so on his honeymoon. Alec, though he had learned to manoeuvre the notoriously tricky LCIs during the war, never learned to drive a car. He did take some lessons with Merula in Michel Salaman's car but drove it into a tree. Throughout his life he relied upon others to drive him – either Merula or the men he employed, sometimes with the dual role of chauffeur and dresser and a substitute, perhaps, for the company of sailors that he had liked so much during the war.

Johnny, the driver Alec employed when living in St Peter's Square in the 1950s, was a married man. Another member of Alec's crew was a young Norwegian who worked in the Norwegian ski resort where the Guinnesses and Marriott Lefèvre went on holiday in 1951. Marriott told Matthew, towards the end of her life, how painful it had been to see 'how smitten' Alec had been by the young man. Marriott also told Matthew that she had been in love with Alec: she had been surprised that he had proposed to Merula, not to her. Now, on the skiing holiday, she had caught Alec looking adoringly at the ski instructor, and then intercepted a glance from Merula which intimated that she too had seen and understood.

Some months after their return to England, the Guinnesses invited the young Norwegian to stay with them at St Peter's Square to look after Matthew, now half-paralysed with polio, carrying him to the lavatory and to his bath. But by 9 September 1952, Alec had grown tired of his company. 'We're a bit sick of [him] still being with us.' And, on the twenty-seventh of the same month: '[he] left this morning. Gave us a wooden carving of a Norwegian fisherman. He was very touching – reluctant to go, I believe, and yet excited at the idea of home.'

Two further members of the crew were the young Canadian drama students, Timothy Findley*, nick-named 'Tif', and Richard Easton. Alec had met both Findley and Easton at Stratford, Ontario, where

---

* later a distinguished Canadian novelist.

Easton had played Sir Thomas Vaughan in *Richard III*. Matthew recalled that Merula was motherly towards the two young men. After Dicky Easton had moved out into a 'grubby little mews flat', Alec invited him to dinner but was stood up:

> Dicky Easton phoned to say he wouldn't be coming tonight. This angered me unreasonably. After the months he spent in this house last year with Findley he can't have thought seriously that his virtue would be in danger. Scribbled off an indignant letter and then destroyed it. Much better that way.[353]

Around a fortnight later, both Easton's reticence and Alec's huff seemed to have passed. 'Dicky Easton to supper at 11.30 – in great good humour. Lectured him rather heavily.' Lectured him about what? The diary does not say. Nor, when Alec writes: 'Dropped into Corpus Christi before matinée. What's the use when I carry on in the same way' does he elaborate on what 'the same way' is. A rumour circulated at around this time that Alec was arrested for importuning in a public lavatory in Liverpool but escaped the attention of the Press by giving his name as Herbert Pocket or, according to Binkie Beaumont's deputy, Kitty Black, his real name of Cuffe. Attempts by an earlier biographer, Garry O'Connor, to substantiate the rumour by trawling through the police records and press cuttings turned up nothing.[354] The rumour is possibly a conflation of stories about Alec's 'cottaging' and the arrest of John Gielgud, in October 1953, in a public lavatory in Chelsea after dining with the Guinnesses at St Peter's Square.

Alec later told Matthew that he had been aware that evening that Gielgud was in an agitated state and, after he had left, felt he should go after him but failed to find him when he did. Gielgud was charged with soliciting, pleaded guilty under a false name before a stipendiary magistrate in a police court, was fined £10 and instructed to consult a doctor. However, he had the misfortune to be recognised by a court reporter. Gielgud faced down the subsequent scandal with the

sympathetic help of his thespian friends, and when he opened in
A Day by the Sea in Liverpool shortly afterwards, was applauded when
he made his entrance.

It was partly as a result of Gielgud's arrest and conviction that, on
24 August 1954, the Home Secretary set up a committee under Sir
John Wolfenden, the Vice-Chancellor of Reading University and
formerly the headmaster of Uppingham and Shrewsbury schools, 'to
consider . . . the law and practice relating to homosexual offences and
the treatment of persons convicted of such offences by the courts'.
Alec was emphatically in favour of greater tolerance towards
homosexuals: he commended Terence Rattigan's *Separate Tables*, after
the first night, as 'a noble gesture' and 'a bold plea from the theatre for
liberal minded tolerance towards sexual waywardness'.[355] There is only
one direct reference to Gielgud's conviction in Alec's diaries, and that
lighthearted:

> Peter told hilarious story of Noël Coward and Terry Rattigan at some
> hotel after John G's unfortunate episode last year. Noel saying 'We
> must be very very discreet' – (wagging his finger) – and then saying to
> Terry in the lounge, apropos the previous night's play, 'You gave me a
> wonderful night' and kissing him.[356]

There are one or two intimations in the diary that, after Gielgud's
troubles, caution was the order of the day. 'Great parade of queens,'
Alec noted on a visit to Brighton. 'Gaunt little things with swift little
walks and rather heavy bald Jewish gentlemen draped in their
overcoats. Two navvies greatly interested. Beautiful sad looking youth,
nearly down and out, sitting staring at the sea from a shelter. Wanted
to give him £1 and say 'Go and eat and get a bed' but didn't dare, for
obvious reasons.'[357] And again, ten days later: 'A curious advance made
to me by a very tall school-boy at Stamford Brook station. Well, thank
God it wasn't the other way round.'

It seems reasonable to deduce from such entries that Alec was, to
say the least, alert to the possibility of fleeting sexual relations with

anonymous men. But these entries are cryptic – 'Walked to St James's station. The Park very busy. Not home until after midnight' – and it is therefore difficult to delineate with any precision Alec's sex life at the time. Watching the films he made during this period – and, indeed, throughout his life – one is never convinced that Alec is sexually attracted to his leading ladies. 'When we kissed,' said Petula Clark who, at the age of eighteen, was kissed by Alec in *The Card*, 'I don't think the earth moved for either of us.'[358] The prim unworldliness of Sidney Stratton in *The Man in the White Suit* made him a good foil to the sexy sultriness of Joan Greenwood as Daphne Birnley; and he was credible as the husband of sexually repressed wives as played by Valerie Hobson in *Kind Hearts and Coronets* or Celia Johnson in *The Captain's Paradise*: but the limits to Alec's ability to get under the skin of his characters are shown when he has to play the passionate Lothario to such beauties as Muriel Pavlow in *Malta Story*, Yvonne de Carlo in *The Captain's Paradise*, Odile Versois in *To Paris with Love* or, to leap ahead to the end of the decade, Nicole Maurey in *The Scapegoat*. He wholly fails to persuade the audience that he longs to make love to these beautiful women.

Conjugal relations with Merula, she later told Matthew, continued until they were both aged forty. The second child that had been planned in the wartime letters did not appear and though Merula, prompted by Alec, ascertained that she was quite capable of conceiving, Alec could not face a similar investigation. An entry in his diary on 14 September 1954, while he and Merula were on holiday in Italy, suggests that he was still attracted to his wife: 'The beast with two backs – happily.' But in October of the same year Merula went into hospital for an operation and, if she was correct in saying that they stopped making love after the age of forty, then they may not have had sexual relations after her surgery. Possibly Alec used the operation as a pretext to prolong indefinitely the celibacy that her temporary condition had made necessary. Merula, predictably, blamed herself for being a dull lover.

Though it may sometimes be unnecessary for a biographer to linger

over his subject's sexual predilections, they would appear to have some
relevance to Alec's particular quality as an actor. As the critic Michael
Billington puts it:

> The sexuality in one way becomes a kind of metaphor or clue to his
> art. Some actors' art is based on a naked, breast-baring self-revelation;
> but his art was an act of mimetic skill and behaviourist detail which
> meant a cancellation of himself. There are endless stories of people
> failing to recognise him as he walked down the street. That says
> something – that his whole life and career is based on concealment and
> disguise, so there is something in himself that he is hiding and not
> wishing to acknowledge. So it is not prurient to investigate his sexuality
> because sexuality is often the clue to what they were like as actors.[359]

The exact nature of Alec's sexuality, however, is not at all clear.
Certainly, within his family circle, he always spoke of 'queers' as if he
was not one of their number: writing to Merula from New York in
1950, he mentions meeting 'J.G's two rather dear young pansy actor
friends who I find very cosy and intelligent I must say, and although
they are as queer as queer they don't throw it at one.'[360] It did not
occur to many of Alec's closest friends that he might have had
homosexual inclinations until the question was raised after his death.

Yet Alec was quite open about the power to attract of a handsome
young man. Emlyn Williams brought the young Richard Burton to St
Peter's Square where he was introduced to Ernest Milton who 'could
scarcely take his eyes from the beauty of Burton's head'.[361] And there
is no doubt that he himself was equally affected by virile good looks.
In Malta, where he went to film *The Malta Story* in October 1952, he
'stood rum to a couple of the most handsome bearded sailors I've ever
seen'. Malta was still a major base for the British Navy and Alec, who
would have been familiar with Valetta from his wartime service, spent
much of his time chatting to sailors in the bars. He offered a bed in his
room to a 'not very attractive creature' called Harold who, after they
had retired, 'said – in the middle of the night – a propos of no

conversation – "Do you think homosexuality hurts?" I laughed too loudly & asked him what he meant. He said he didn't know and I settled down for sleep again. Not for long – as he snores . . .'[362]

Besides his work on the film, Alec was drawn into the social life of the naval establishment on Malta – he was now a celebrity, after all. 'Earl Mountbatten came over & chatted to me for five minutes which I thought most civil. He has enormous charm, and it was clever of him to have learned that I'd been in LCIs. Said he'd designed them on the back of an envelope.' Merula flew out from England for a holiday, returning to London on 24 October: and on the very night of the day she left, after extricating himself from the company of his filming friends, Alec:

> . . . went for a short walk and then sat in a bar. Three jolly sailors, not in uniform, invited me to drink with them and wanted to take me out in ten days' time! Tiresome male whore – Tommy – greeted me as a long lost friend. Gave him a whiskey. Asked him what he was going to do when he came out of Fleet Air Arm and he said dress designing. Didn't believe a word of it but thought it an obvious implication that he was prepared to do anything – right there and then. Didn't encourage him much. To bed at 12.30.[363]

Thus Alec, while attracted to handsome young men, remained repelled by the kind of man who was willing to respond to his desires. He had written with a fascinated horror of the 'tiny little lad with a lascivious face' in the crew of his new LCI in 1944; and it was the same in the Turkish Bath in Jermyn Street, as in the bar in Valetta:

> Went to the Imperial Turkish Baths, but not for a sweat – just got hot in the steam room & then slept after a massage . . . The boy who served tea had the wettest reddest mouth & sulkiest expression I've ever seen in a male. It all revolted me.[364]

A resolution in Alec's attitude to his own sexual nature seems to have taken place on a trip he made with Peter Bull to Tangier in February

1955. Passing through Paris on the way, they had gone to see 'Clouzot's *Les Diaboliques*. Disgraceful and often boring melodrama – finely acted by Signoret – which doesn't hold water at all.' In Tangier, it poured with rain and Alec suffered from an 'uncomfortable tummy'. Bully took him to meet an aristocratic English homosexual, the Hon. David Herbert, and his American friend James Caffery, at a bar 'run by a queer coloured man'. They went on to lunch at Herbert's 'pink villa'; but the next day we find Alec cancelling a trip to Fez and trying to change his Air France ticket for a British European Airways ticket to return to London from Gibraltar. 'They all say fly to Marrakech where the sun *will* be shining – but I've settled for Spain, where if it's raining presumably we can sit in the churches or visit interesting places.'[365]

'Woke up in the bright sunshine (and great wind) to find I had such fearful stomach cramps that I must stay in bed. Very gloomily lay there until 2.00 p.m. – constant visits to the loo. Peter had suffered a bit last night but was better to-day.' Alec was unamused when 'an elderly Englishman with a high-pitched voice asked me if my "friend" was a film star'. It was not just his upset stomach, the bad weather or the desire to see churches that led Alec to flee from Tangier. 'I hate this place and have taken a big turn against queers.'

Alec and Bully left Tangier on the last day of February and reached Gibraltar by four in the afternoon. There they hired a car but discovered, at the Spanish border, that Bully 'had *two* visas for Spanish Morocco but not one for Spain. It was a sad thing – both of us v. upset. Eventually decided I should come on & P return to Tangier.' Alec was later to write that Bully had failed to get a Spanish visa 'accidentally on purpose'. He was delighted to return to have fun in Tangier away from Alec's disapproving eye; and Alec equally pleased to go on alone into Spain. 'Very beautiful – fine mountains behind and gorgeous sunset. The cicadas chirruping a little. Have a tiny chalet with blazing wood fire – clean & pretty & comfortable.'

Staying a night at the Rock Hotel in Gibraltar on his way back to England, Alec overheard a conversation at the next table. 'Chinless lady from the Rock Hotel, at lunch table, said to green velvet hatted lady opposite me "I hear Alec Guinness was at The Rock". To which her companion replied, "I know. And at Tangier – staying with David Herbert." How nonsense starts.'[366]

It would seem, then, that by the mid-1950s Alec came to settle for a celibate life. To join Bully as a fully paid up member of what W.H. Auden called 'Homintern', though it might have been true to his sexual nature, would have put at risk the marriage and family life which, after his rootless childhood, he valued so highly. It might also have jeopardised his career: there was still a widespread revulsion against homosexuality among the general public and Alec was now so well known that sooner or later he would have been bound to be caught out.

Above all, however, such wayward passions and desires offended against Alec's sense of order. Again, because of his chaotic childhood, order was essential to his sense of well-being. Disordered behaviour led to self-disgust, and self-disgust to depression. Alec had known the peace and serenity that is the fruit of a good conscience and longed for it to return. As he reached the middle of his life, he sought to leave behind the tormented, unstable Hamlet and become a sage patriarch like T.S. Eliot's Sir Henry Harcourt-Reilly. All he needed was to find a mechanism that would make him the kind of man he wanted to be.

twenty-five

In the summer of 1953, while Alec was performing in Stratford, Ontario, the sale was completed on five acres of land on the edge of a hamlet in Hampshire, Steep Marsh. The property, Kettlebrook Meadows, had beautiful views over wooded countryside towards the South Downs and a line of hills, called the Hangers, was a mile or so from the small town of Petersfield, fifteen miles or so from Wadlington and about sixty miles from London.

The property was registered in Merula's name. Eusty Salaman, Merula's much loved brother, was asked to design a house. He lived near Midhurst and had an architectural practice in Petersfield. His first project had been a house for his mother on the beach at Selsey: now he drew up plans for something modern, with one large room incorporating living room and dining room and picture windows to make the most of the view.

It took a good eighteen months to build the house. Postwar shortages and planning restrictions still bedevilled life in Britain. 'Eusty spent the night with us – to discuss details of fixtures for the house,' Alec wrote in his diary on 24 August 1954, 'but I was so horrified and angry at the possibility of an 18 month delay for electricity, that I couldn't discuss anything seriously.' Alec went up and down from London to follow the progress of the house. 'Went down to Petersfield to see the house. Gorgeous day. Delighted with it all now weather boarding is up and the roof completed.' On 4 November: 'Caught 1.50 to Petersfield. Collected Eusty and went up to the house. Slow progress but most of the plastering is done now, and the glazing. Variety of small hold-ups. Was able to walk around upstairs, which was pleasant. Our bedroom bigger and bathroom smaller than I expected.' On 19 January 1955: 'M and I off to Heal's in the morning where we spent nearly £700 on beds, bedding etc. Terrifying. But like what we bought – particularly the candlewick bedspreads'. On 1 February: 'We've been down to Kettlebrook Meadows two or three times. With luck we shall be able to camp in the house by the end of the month'; and finally on 21 March: 'Spent this week at Kettlebrook – first night, Friday, by myself, because Merry wasn't feeling well, then she joined me for Sat and Sunday. Much to be done still but it looks ravishing.'

Kettlebrook Meadows was modern in design. The first storey was partly white-painted brick, partly faced with flint; the second clad with cedar weather-boarding; and the shallow roof was tiled with slate. There was a wide balcony reached from the main bedroom; in the early years Alec would often sleep out on the balcony in a feather-down sleeping bag. Separating the back of the house from the front, there was a redbrick wall with an arched doorway. On the south-facing side there was a stone-flagged terrace and, outside Alec's study, white pillars to support a Russian vine. In due course, Alec and Merula would plant numerous specimen trees; make a pond about twenty metres long and three metres wide with a fountain and statues of herons, and build a stone Japanese shrine. Further from the house, there was a croquet lawn and wooden outbuildings incorporating a room that would serve at times as a study for Alec and sleeping quarters for the chauffeur.

The front door led into a hallway with a curved staircase to the first floor. To the right was a door leading to Alec's study, which was later made larger with a curved glass-block wall. One door from the study led out onto the terrace, another into the large living-space which could also be approached from the hall. The living room had a sofa and armchairs at one end and the dining-table at the other. Against one wall was a large marble-topped bookcase which curved out to become a tiled peninsula housing the fireplace.

The kitchen was small and there were only three bedrooms: one for Alec and Merula, a spare room and bathroom, a small room for Matthew, and a studio for Merula. In later years, there were a number of additions: a small conservatory on the south side of the house, extensions to Alec's study and the kitchen, and a staff flat built over the garage. But, even if the postwar limitations meant that some of the materials were not of the first order, the original house built to Eusty's design was an agreeable and manageable dwelling in a beautiful setting, close to the homes of Merula's family and within easy reach of London.

Alec and Merula also kept a pied-à-terre in London – first a house in Ennismore Garden Mews, subsequently a flat in Smith Square. However, Merula had long yearned to return to the life amidst animals that she had known at Ruckmans in her childhood and at Ockley during the war. She had remained a shy and private person, who never particularly liked London and felt ill-equipped to be the wife of a star. She loathed the kind of glamorous life that others considered one of the rewards of celebrity and success. Merula was happiest wearing scruffy clothes, mucking out loose boxes, nursing sick dogs, goats or horses, or, with dirt under her fingernails, digging weeds out of the ground. Moreover, it suited her to live near her brother Eusty, his wife Mary, her parents, and the unfortunate Susy because Matthew was away at boarding school for more than half the year and Alec was so often either working in London or abroad.

Alec had filmed in Malta for *The Malta Story*, in Morocco for *The Captain's Paradise*, and in France for *Father Brown* and *To Paris with Love*. The latter two, though directed by Robert Hamer, had not approached the brilliance of *Kind Hearts and Coronets*. In fact, both films were poor. In *Father Brown*, Alec played G.K. Chesterton's holy sleuth as a myopic simpleton with a script that was full of holes. He was duly cut down to size by at least one critic: 'Alec Guinness is a small-part player forced into stardom,' wrote Robert Ottaway in the *Sunday Graphic*. 'He is, in the last resort, a little man blown up beyond his true proportions.' And in *To Paris with Love* the combination of a fatuous screenplay and the lack of sexual electricity between Alec and his female co-star led to a flop. 'Forced by the script to declare his love for a 20-year-old shop assistant,' wrote the *Evening Standard* critic of Alec, 'he fails to give the remotest indication that there is any more love for her in his heart than you would find on an East Coast fishmonger's slab'. It was no better off-screen. Odile Versois, who played the shop assistant, annoyed Alec by turning up late on the set. 'I told her I thought she was a great actress with a great career but that she was the most selfish girl I had ever come across. Floods of tears.'[367]

Alec's own performance, as he swallows a shuttlecock and gets entangled in the badminton net, was pastiche Chaplin. He shot the scene back at Pinewood Studios on a cold, drizzly day 'clad in sports shirt and thin trousers only, climbing and re-climbing a very prickly, draughty fir tree. It was one of those days when I thought I am worth every penny they pay me.' When he finished filming *To Paris with Love* at the end of the month it was 'Good riddance. Not much of it has been happy, though it's had its gay and pleasant moments.'

In September 1955, Alec went to the United States to make his first major Hollywood movie, *The Swan*. This was not his first contract with an American studio: he had appeared as Disraeli in 20th Century-Fox's *The Mudlark*. But *The Mudlark* had been made in England: now, on 18 September 1955, he flew to Los Angeles on a 'Flying Viking Ship' under contract to MGM.

From the first moment that he set foot in California, Alec was treated as a major star. 'Charming but rather flustered reception,' he wrote to Merula. 'Grace Kelly came to meet me & seems sweet and simple.' He was taken to the Beverly Hills Hotel where he was given 'a gorgeous bungalow suite – with a kitchen with an electric stove just like ours. And my bathroom has a *square* bath.' There followed a succession of glamorous parties where he was introduced to a bevy of stars. 'Went to Grace Kelly's barbecue party – one or two *tennis* stars (v. nice) and Michael Wilding & Elizabeth Taylor, and the Nivens as nice & attractive & amusing as ever . . .' 'Deborah Kerr . . . talks just like Maggie Leighton but with K. Walsh's vocabulary . . .' 'Ginger Rogers is, I should think, about the nicest person here – in fact she exudes something of a Saint – very simple, very calm, sweetly gay, generous – oh, she's an adorable person.'[368] Alec found James Mason 'nice and sweet but pretty shy' and found it hard to talk to him: and he was 'moderately' rude to Mason's wife because she 'kept saying how much she loathed England'. 'Tonight I go to Hitchcock's just to dine with James Stewart and Grace Kelly, which ought to be pleasant.' 'Today I take Marlene to lunch.'

The director of *The Swan* was a Hungarian, Charles Vidor, 'who sounds like Korda'; the screenplay was adapted by John Dighton (who had written both *Kind Hearts and Coronets* with Hamer, and *The Man in the White Suit*) from the play of the same name by the Hungarian dramatist, Ferenc Molnar. Alec played Albert, the Crown Prince of a Ruritanian kingdom, who comes to visit his aunt and great aunt to see if his cousin, Princess Alexandra (Grace Kelly) would make a suitable wife.

For the external scenes of the film, MGM had chosen a huge pseudo-Versailles built by George W. Vanderbilt at Biltmore near Asheville in North Carolina. It was therefore to Asheville that Alec travelled with his co-stars at the end of September. He had become fond of Grace Kelly and Louis Jourdan, who played the role of the royal tutor: 'I can't tell you what a sweet lot they are – absolutely easy and fun without being bitchy and gay without getting drunk . . .'

Alec clearly felt a twinge of guilt that he was enjoying the high life in the United States while Merula vegetated at home: it was now that he wrote to her saying how it was for the sake of her 'integrity' and to save her from 'contamination' that he had made her give up acting.

The jolly company of his fellow stars in Asheville was enhanced on 9 October by the arrival of Peter Glenville. When Alec was excused by Vidor, he and Glenville made a quick tour of the American South. 'Well – *here* I am,' Alec wrote to Merula from New Orleans, 'and delighted I came, and it's fun having Peter around who is determined to go everywhere and see everything . . .'[369]

Alec was back in Los Angeles by the middle of October to work at the MGM Studios on the interior scenes of *The Swan*. Once again, he was caught up in the social round. Angela Lansbury gave a birthday party for Peter Glenville but, Alec wrote to Merula on 30 October, 'last night was *the* party night – at Gary Cooper's. Apparently there has not been such a Hollywood party for at least a year':

> This is going to read like some ghastly gossip column or film magazine – but there it is. Anyway, Coopers have superb low house quite nearby . . . The party was held in the garden, which was entirely covered by a vast purple and blue and dull gold silken tent, hung with illuminated stars, and *heated* for the evening (which was warm anyway) . . . Gary Cooper who is quiet and unassuming and nice and probably a tiny bit of a bore – and Elizabeth Taylor (wearing a tiara) and the Princess of Belgium (who is married to the Prince of Belgium and is *only 15* but looks a very pretty 28) – and a millionaire of 25 who has never done a stroke of work in his life . . . and Fred Astaire. It's tedious going on about how sweet people are here but they just are.

The glamorous life continued throughout the autumn. 'Lunch at the Nivens' . . . Dine with Claudette Colbert and her funny doctor husband next week . . .' Mike Todd asked Alec to make a cameo appearance as a Chinese bartender in *Around the World in 80 Days* but MGM would not allow it. Alec met Groucho Marx, Jennifer Jones, 'rather liked Kirk Douglas' but fell head over heels for Glenn Ford:

> Monday night I dined with Glenn Ford and I've made, I suspect, a life-long close friend. We're dotty about each other. He is absolutely

enchanting – simple, genuine, and somehow very moving. I'm not sure that after a bottle of wine and three brandies I didn't ask him and his son (aged 12) to come and spend a month with us next year – I must check up on that . . . But there we are, in the throes of a friendship and as I think he's just about the nicest man I've ever met I do hope it lasts.[370]

The friendship did last for some years; Alec kept a framed photograph of Ford at Kettlebrook Meadows, but it would seem that Ford either was not as fond of Alec as Alec was of him, or was made uneasy by Alec's devotion. 'We spent a lot of time together when I was making *The Swan*, dining at least once a week,' Alec recorded in his diary on 20 November 1975, after running into Ford buying a magnum of champagne in New York:

I was very caught up in his friendship and mysteriousness, but we had nothing in common really. We met once or twice in New York, lunched, went to see *The Pleasure of His Company* one matinée – and I always had the feeling I was being deceived in some way. And I was right. One evening we had a dinner date and he called me up to say he must put me off as he had to go to Washington for some important Presidential dinner. Fair enough, though I was disappointed. I can't remember the restaurant I went to that night, but there was Glenn sitting with a girl. It would have been so easy for him to have told the truth and made another date.

While in Hollywood making *The Swan*, Alec met James Dean outside an Italian restaurant. Dean showed him his brand-new sports car. 'The sports car looked sinister to me,' Alec wrote in his autobiography:

Exhausted, hungry, feeling a little ill-tempered in spite of Dean's kindness, I heard myself saying in a voice I could hardly recognise as my own, 'Please, never get in it.' I looked at my watch. 'It is now ten o'clock, Friday the 23rd of September, 1955. If you get in that car you will be found dead in it by this time next week.'[371]

Dean had laughed and ignored Alec's warning. At four in the morning on the following Friday, Dean crashed the car and was killed.

At a party given by John Wayne at the Beverly Hills Hotel Alec met Lauren Bacall, who was to become a lifelong friend. He also got into a fight when:

> . . . a well-known Hollywood agent said you shouldn't be seen talking to that Limey so I clocked him and flew out in a rage, went back to my room and back to bed – ashamed of myself and angry; but Wayne rang and told me to come down again so I went back and a lot of people gathered round and he said: I want you to shake hands with this man. So we shook hands coldly but solemnly and there was applause whereupon I clocked him again. Something else he'd said drove me mad. But John Wayne was marvellous. I got a huge box of cigars the next day.[372]

Alec was clearly fond of, and also intrigued by, Grace Kelly. 'Here I sit,' he wrote to Merula on 14 November, 'having just dismissed P. Glenville & Louis Jourdan who have been having drinks in my bungalow. I've spent the evening with Louis and his wife, just the three of us, in scandalous gossip, mostly about Grace Kelly, who for all her sweetness we think is Miss Enigma 1955–1975.' And clearly Grace Kelly was fond enough of Alec to continue with a long-running practical joke: before leaving Asheville for New Orleans, he had bribed the hall porter of the hotel to put a tomahawk that had been presented to him by a visiting troupe of Indians between the sheets of Grace Kelly's bed – he had judged it too heavy to put in his suitcase. Grace Kelly, however, took it with her trousseau when she married and managed to return the tomahawk to Alec between the sheets of his bed in London. The tomahawk was passed to and fro in this way over the next twenty-five years.

While in Hollywood, Alec was the subject of tittle-tattle in the newspapers. 'One of the scandalous magazines here called *Whisper*,' he wrote to Merula, 'announces that I am about to marry Yvonne de Carlo !!!!!!!!!!!!!! Just in case you didn't know.' Equally fanciful, but seemingly real enough at the time, were the bids put in for Alec's services in the future:

> Spent an hour at MCA today talking to Lew Wasserman – who is head now. Stein is semi-retired and is a really brilliant and sensitive & nice man. Talked of many plans about which he was most sensible but primarily an MGM offer which is *really* fascinating. Apparently they are prepared to pay me $1000 a week (about £325) for *twelve years* if I will make four pictures of my own choice with them during that period. Am going to go into that one carefully as it sounds too good to be true.[373]

Financially and socially, Alec's first trip to Hollywood was a great success; professionally, it was less satisfactory. Alec was not happy with his role in *The Swan*. 'I simply couldn't see eye to eye with Vidor over anything,' he wrote to Merula, 'and although we didn't squabble we both sulked a bit and button-holed other people to complain. The result has been lousy performing on my part – neither one thing nor the other.'[374] He suffered from one of his periodic bouts of self-doubt. 'I am a fraud, a phoney, and with a second-hand talent.' His unconvincing performance, however, came not from his inadequacies as an actor but from the contradictions of his role. Nonetheless, when the film was released, it was a box-office success. *The Swan* was the last film to be made by Grace Kelly before she gave up her career to marry Prince Rainier of Monaco, and people went in their thousands to see, in Cinemascope and Technicolor, Hollywood's beautiful ice-maiden play a Ruritanian princess.

twenty-six

While Alec was in Hollywood he received a letter from Matthew at school at Beaumont to say that, as the Rector had predicted, he had asked to be received into the Roman Catholic Church. 'Very touched by Matthew's letter,' Alec wrote to Merula on 15 October 1955. 'I do hope he's not doing it all on an emotional splurge – though no doubt that is to be expected too at his age . . . It *is* a bit of a shock – this sudden independence and growing up. But a good and nice thing as well.'

Alec was annoyed to hear that Merula's family were upset:

How silly and mean of your family to be embarrassed by M's reception into the Church. I partly expected that reaction, but certainly not from Mary & Eusty. *Don't* let it upset you please please *please*. God knows I've had a mental falling off from Catholicism here (also anticipated by me) but I still know it makes a million times more sense than all that wishy-washy thinking or clutching at straws round and about Wadlington.

And it's sad that strong and definite and not ignoble decisions should distress people one's fond of.[375]

Alec's letters suggest that he felt mildly upstaged by Matthew's decision because he himself, before leaving England, had been receiving instruction from the parish priest of the Catholic church in Petersfield. One Saturday afternoon during the summer of 1955, he had bicycled 'almost aimlessly' from Kettlebrook Meadows to the Catholic Church of St Lawrence and told the priest, Fr Henry Clarke, that he thought he might like to become a Catholic. He also describes a retreat he made at the Cistercian Abbey of Mount St Bernard, Leicestershire – the Cistercians being those of 'the Strict Observance' (known as Trappists from their mother house of La Trappe) – before leaving for California to make *The Swan*, his baggage heavy with books on Catholic theology.

Fr Clarke had recommended that he go to Mass each Sunday while in the United States. He did so with Grace Kelly on his first Sunday in Los Angeles. It was not a happy experience. 'I left after the sermon,' he wrote to Merula:

> . . . primarily because of the heat – I had foolishly gone in my tweed suit – but the sermon speeded me on my way because it was one of those aggressive self-satisfied Catholic affairs about which one hears so much. This country, I'm sure, is a grim test of faith – I expected it to be so, and so far I'm right. It makes no difference to the doctrine I know, and I cling to that, but dear oh dear I long already for European tolerance – or even European peasant simplicity and even superstition – no, not superstition – but they are ignorant here of what other people feel and believe.[376]

A week later, he went to Mass again: 'same dreadful age-long sermon – but it being cooler I stuck it out and was pleased I went'.

Despite the helter-skelter life in what he called 'the flesh-pots of Los Angeles', Alec continued his religious reading. He regretted bringing only one volume of a history of the Catholic Church which, he told Merula, 'is fascinating and I'm getting all those ancient heresies sorted out – and at last see why they were so dangerous for civilisation – it has greatly increased my respect for the ancient church – the attitude to heretics has always fussed me'. And, in another letter he wrote: 'One of the things I like about the Catholic Church is that it has so deeply explored all this side of God's gift and is so hard-headed and adamant in not letting anything phoney pass off for the real thing.'[377]

Merula and Matthew flew out to California to spend Christmas with Alec, and in January 1956 the three returned to England. Alec completed his instruction with Fr Clarke in Petersfield and on 24 March 1956, with the actress Veronica Turleigh and her son Patrick Laver as his sponsors, he was 'reconciled with the Holy Roman Catholic and Apostolic Church'. Prior to the ceremony, he made a 'general confession' to Father Clarke, repenting of the sins of a lifetime. A few days afterwards, as he recorded in his diary eighteen years later, 'I began to think my general confession had been totally inadequate and went to see him again to discuss it; the first signs of scrupulosity which assailed me for a few years.'[378]

Later in life, in his autobiography, Alec dismissed his years as a member of the Church of England as 'a brief period, at the beginning of the war, during which I got up in the early hours of winter mornings to bicycle in the dark to Holy Communion at a country church'; and further on he says how he had 'embraced, very briefly, not to say flittingly, Anglo-Catholicism . . . It was, I suppose, a psychological bulwark against the uncertainties of war and fear of the future and it stood me in good stead while it lasted.'[379]

This was, as his letters and diaries make plain, a retrospective belittling of his religious sentiments at the time. Alec had, after all, considered becoming an Anglican priest, and had remained a believing and practising member of the Church of England throughout the war. We find him, in late 1945, visiting the Lady Abbess at St Mary's Abbey, West Malling; confessing his sins at St Michael and All Angels, and

taking Martita Hunt to the Kissing of the Cross on Good Friday. His
Anglicanism was so high that the practice was barely distinguishable
from Roman Catholicism; and his letters to Chattie in 1941 suggest
that he regarded the two denominations as two regiments in the same
army: 'the crack one – the Roman one – has expensive uniforms which
I can't afford – but which I think I ought to belong to but can't quite
manage'.[380] At the end of the war, in June 1945, he and Merula had
discussed Roman Catholicism while on a walk. 'My inclinations today
very much that way. Resolutions about saying the Rosary.'[381] When he
took Ernest Milton to lunch at the Savoy to persuade him to play the
part of Zossima in the play of *The Brothers Karamazov*, Milton – a
Catholic and a homosexual – 'told me I ought to be an R.C. and kept
clutching my hand. "I'm only doing Zossima because I love you".'[382]
Yet Alec had not, at this time, followed his 'inclination' towards
Catholicism. When the Guinnesses moved to St Peter's Square
Matthew was educated with the vicar's children, and when Chattie
decided to become a Christian Alec persuaded her and her son, Patrick
Blatchley, to be baptised in the Church of England. Alec's main
concession to his years as an Anglican was the use of the word
'reconciliation' to describe his conversion to the Catholic Church.

Alec's doubts about Christianity seem to have started soon after his
return home. 'The past ten days have been mentally bad – very bad,'
he wrote in his diary on 14 August 1945, 'but light began to creep in
again on Monday. With the reading of Fr D'Arcy's book on Love*,
begun yesterday, I feel a quiet strength growing.' Faith was an antidote
to depression. 'My deep melancholy fit has passed slightly,' he wrote
on 27 October 1954. 'My self-depreciation reached a new low during
the past few days. My soul, my body, my brain longs for a religion. The
world is too bleak and blank without a sense of worship.'[383]

Clearly, Alec found that the Anglican Church did not meet his needs.
He found it too easygoing, its discipline too lax. It was, as he had said
to Chattie back in 1941, 'full of wise and good nice, good and friendly

---

*   Rev. Martin D'Arcy was an eminent English Jesuit.

men' but was 'a bit of a rabble, and it's so easy to get lost . . .' However, Alec's reasons for erasing his Anglican years in his autobiography can only be surmised. While writing *Blessings in Disguise* he had been reminded by the Benedictine nun Dame Felicitas Corrigan that, because of his celebrity, this presented a wonderful opportunity to promote the Catholic Church, and he may have thought the impact of his conversion would be diluted if it was presented merely as a lateral move from one Christian denomination to another.

Alec may also have judged that excising his Anglican years from his narrative would create a better literary effect. He preferred to ascribe his conversion in *Blessings in Disguise* to the deal he made with God that resulted in Matthew's sudden recovery from poliomyelitis; and the incident during the filming of *Father Brown* in Burgundy when a little French boy had taken Alec's hand as he walked along a country lane, mistaking Alec, in his soutane, for a real priest. This had led Alec to conclude that the Catholic Church could not be 'as scheming and creepy' as he had hitherto supposed if it could 'inspire such confidence in a child, making its priests, even when unknown, so easily approachable'. Both these passages provide charming vignettes* but they give no inkling of the complex influences that led Alec on the road to Rome.

The first factor leading to his conversion was his need for an intellectual, institutional and sacramental structure that would enable him to keep the dark side of his personality at bay. To his friend, the actress Jehane West, 'he talked about his faith; his need for it; the black hole without it'. 'Alec converted to Catholicism,' said Edward Herrmann, also a Catholic convert, who acted with Alec in *A Walk in the Woods*, 'out of a need to contain and manage his emotional life: confession was a crucial safety valve. It was a mechanism that kept him sane.'[384]

---

* The second, somewhat less charming after the scandalous revelations in later years about paedophile priests.

A second factor was Alec's innate superstition. He believed in ghosts and premonitions, and both he and Merula were convinced that Middle Lodge was haunted. Alec was deeply impressed by the predictions of a fortune teller – 'a blowsy American woman with black velvet in her hair' – he consulted in New York in 1942. 'I must say the old girl worked out some pretty amazing things, considering she knew nothing of me,' he wrote to Merula. 'She said the war would be over in 1944 but I wouldn't be out of uniform until 1945 . . . There are no major worries but no more children . . .'[385] 'She also told me one or two definite things about my past that I dislike and don't discuss with anyone. I was *very* impressed.'

There was also the mysterious voice that had predicted his death – 'penetrating, gloating, undoubtedly evil' – prior to the hurricane which wrecked his ship on New Year's Day, 1943. While filming *Great Expectations* he had tried to contact the spirits of the dead by table rapping with David Lean and John Mills. While in Tangiers with Peter Bull he had bought a pack of Tarot cards for forty pesetas. 'After a sleep P and I told our fortunes, terribly sketchily, with Tarot cards. Mine promised honours and said I would build a home in the country and plant a quince tree.'[386] Alec became obsessed with his Tarot cards until suddenly one evening, 'I got the horrors about them and impetuously threw cards and books on a blazing log fire.'

There was also the premonition of James Dean's fatal accident in his sports car; and, nine months prior to that, a lesser incident involving a motor car and the supernatural. Alec and Merula were on holiday in Scotland. 'Bad puncture at the Trossachs. Couldn't get the wheel off. After nearly an hour's effort said a little prayer to St Anthony and they [the nuts] came loose the very next time I tried – and with only a small effort.'[387]

Paradoxically, despite this attachment to the magical powers of Catholic saints such as St Anthony, which was to grow more powerful after his reception into the Catholic Church, the most serious rival to Catholicism was the more nebulous teaching of the Buddha. He had shown some interest in this before the war but had been taken aback, when going to see a Buddhist monk, to find him packing his suitcase to leave town to escape the Blitz. His interest revived in the autumn of 1954:

> Have been very taken up during past 24 hours with Buddhism – result of reading rather indifferent Penguin book on the subject. In 1938/9 I was taken up with it – but I think I could understand more easily now, and could easily have more compassion. If I could find the right guide and mentor, guru, instructor, what-have-you, so that I didn't have to struggle on my own and fall into some hazy theosophical outlook, I believe it could be the religion for me.[388]

In early November 1954, Alec bought 'one or two books on Buddhism' and felt 'increasingly drawn to the Buddha'. 'My own desperate weaknesses begin to pale, though they are as lively as ever. I suppose it's utterly idle to think they will pass without effort, but the mere substitution of positive thoughts of peace and good will have their effect I am confident.' Alec discussed his spiritual search with Chattie and John Blatchley; he 'read some of the Upanishads' and found them 'beautiful'; but then decided that it was a less suitable faith for an actor than Catholicism:

> The last day or two – through what means I don't know – have resurrected my interest in Catholicism. So much I don't like, so much of the historical background I hate, but for an actor it appeals. What liberality of thought I could entertain as a Catholic I don't know – but something there fits the actor. Buddhism would logically mean a change of profession.[389]

The tone of Alec's religious investigations suggests that he was not searching for the truth as such, but for a system of belief that would be psychologically therapeutic; asking not what he could do for God but what God could do for him. It was this that led the then Archbishop of Liverpool, John Heenan, to say in a BBC broadcast after reading a profile of Alec in *Time* magazine, that Alec gave the impression that his need for faith was like 'needing a haircut', which provoked Alec to write in protest and Heenan to apologise and 'by way to reparation . . . say Mass for me every day for a week'.[390]

A Devil's Advocate could think of other self-serving motives for Alec's conversion. 'I've discovered that there's a specific Englishness about being a Catholic,' said the American Edward Herrmann. 'It's a very upper-class thing to do. Especially if you convert. A Waughish thing. This maybe was a motive for Alec. He strove mightily after gentility.'[391] It is undoubtedly true that there was, in the 1950s, a multi-faceted sense of election – or, more simply, snobbery – found among English Catholics. There were not just the Recusant families which had retained their loyalty to the Catholic Faith, despite persecution, since before the Protestant Reformation. There was also an *inverted* snobbery: Protestantism in Britain had largely fragmented along class lines with Methodism appealing to the working class and Anglicanism to the middle class – whereas in a Catholic church a duchess knelt at the same communion rail as an Irish navvy. This attitude pervades Evelyn Waugh's novel, *Brideshead Revisited*, which Alec had bought at Zwemmer's bookshop after reading Desmond McCarthy's enthusiastic review in 1945.

Catholicism at that time also managed to combine that sense of social as well as geographical universality with an aura of *intellectual* superiority. Evelyn Waugh and Graham Greene, two of Britain's most admired and successful authors, wrote novels saturated with Catholic values: plots that involved miracles are found in best-sellers such as Greene's *The End of the Affair*. Greene's Catholicism, like the Russian Orthodoxy of Rasputin, held that God *preferred* the repentant sinner – the Prodigal Son – to the man or woman who avoided sin, while the Anglican culture in Britain, coloured by the Protestant concept of predestination, tended to equate virtue with respectability. A religion which held that God became man precisely to save the most sinful and depraved had an enormous appeal to the naturally lascivious or uncharitable such as Oscar Wilde, Evelyn Waugh – or Alec Guinness.

Catholicism at that time was also seen as the intellectual bulwark against the two secular ideologies perceived as threatening to engulf the civilised world. Soviet Communism was the most obvious danger – not just as a military threat but as an ideology widely accepted among academics, artists and intellectuals. However, there were Christian writers – not all of them Catholic – such as Christopher Dawson, C.S. Lewis, Hilaire Belloc, G.K. Chesterton and T.S. Eliot who were equally alarmed by the materialistic consumerism championed by the United States. One of Alec's favourite quotations from Chesterton was: 'The Church is the one thing that prevents a man from the degrading servitude of being a child of his own time.'

Alec shared the dismay of these conservative sages at the spread of American values. 'Eliot was alarmed at the dominance of the United States in post-war Europe,' wrote Joseph Pearce in his book *Literary Converts: Spiritual Inspiration in an Age of Unbelief*:

. . . and began to feel that he was witnessing the collapse of that culture which, more than thirty years earlier, he had left America to find. To his evident dismay it appeared that the world had rejected tradition for modernity, culture for ease and spiritual comforts for material luxuries.

Ironically, it was this very development that was to be the cause of the greatest number of conversions to Catholicism in the second half of the century as those alienated by the vacuity of consumerism sought sanctuary, sanity and depth in the faith, culture and tradition of the church.[392]

Among the *Literary Converts* included in Pearce's study were Alec Guinness, and his friend Edith Sitwell who, at the end of July 1955, summoned Alec to attend her reception into the Roman Catholic Church. Alec duly turned up shortly before noon on 4 August at the Jesuit Church of the Immaculate Conception in Farm Street, Mayfair. Her godfather was Evelyn Waugh who was dressed in a check suit and straw boater with a red-and-blue ribbon. Waugh described the ceremony in his diary:

At 11.45 to Farm Street where I met Father D'Arcy and went with him to the church to the Ignatius chapel to await Edith and Father Caraman.[393] A bald shy man introduced himself as the actor Alec Guinness. Presently Edith appeared swathed in black like a sixteenth-century infanta . . . Edith recanted her errors in fine ringing tones and received conditional baptism, then was led into the confessional while six of us collected in the sacristy – Guinness and I and Father D'Arcy, an old lame deaf woman with dyed red hair whose name I never learned*, a little swarthy man who looked like a Jew but claimed to be Portuguese† and a blond youth who looked American but claimed to be English.[394]

After the ceremony, the party retired to the Sesame Club where they sat down to a lunch of 'cold consommé, lobster Newburg, steak, strawberry flan and great quantities of wine'. Waugh was agreeably surprised by the fare – he had heard 'gruesome stories' about the Sesame Club – but not by his fellow guests: 'Very odd company,' he wrote to Nancy Mitford two days later, 'none of whom I had seen before, only one I had heard of – the actor Alec Guinness, very shy & bald.' 'I liked Alec Guinness so much', he wrote to Edith Sitwell when thanking her for choosing him as her sponsor, 'and will try to see more of him. I have long admired his art.'[395] Waugh then went on to warn her that she should expect to find, among her fellow Catholics, 'bores and prigs and crooks and cads. I always think of myself: "I know I am awful. But how much more awful I should be without the Faith".'[396] This is a judgement, as we shall see, that might also be made of Alec.

'Perhaps Leonora was right,' says John Dowell in Ford Madox Ford's novel, *The Good Soldier*. 'Perhaps Roman Catholics, with their queer, shifty ways are always right. They are dealing with the queer, shifty thing that is human nature.'[397] One of the aspects of Roman Catholicism that

---

* Identified as Evelyn Weil by Victoria Glendinning in her biography of Edith Sitwell.
† Alberto de Lucada: Glendinning op. cit.

impressed Alec was its ability to attract and to hold both the saint and the sinner, as exemplified by two of his closest friends from within the acting profession.

The first – the saint – was Veronica Turleigh, who came from an Irish Catholic family in Donegal and had a degree from the Catholic University in Dublin. Alec, when writing to Merula from Buxton in Derbyshire, had described her as 'one of the greatest, but *greatest* mathematicians in the country!' She had been mocked within the profession for her 'Mediaeval mind' but in a letter to Merula written in May 1942, Alec said she was 'one of the six nicest women I know'; and in another, two years later, he said she was the only one of his friends to have escaped his malicious tongue. 'There's hardly one I haven't said a wretched unkind word about at one time or another. Except Veronica. I've never slandered her.'[398] She had played Gertrude, Hamlet's mother, to Alec's Hamlet in Tyrone Guthrie's modern-dress production. If the second child that he and Merula had hoped for at the start of the war had been a girl, her name would have been Veronica.

If Veronica Turleigh exemplified the virtuous, observant Catholic, Peter Glenville belonged to the Church that was 'a refuge of sinners'. His background was bizarre. Sean Glenville and Dorothy Ward were a highly successful double act in that uniquely British theatrical institution, the pantomime. Dorothy Ward, with famously beautiful legs, played the principal 'boy' and Sean Glenville the 'dame'. It was hardly surprising, Glenville used to say, that he was queer. His father became an alcoholic but the couple's success brought money: Dorothy Ward wore diamond bracelets from her wrist to her elbow; and, since she was a Roman Catholic, provided the funds to send Peter to Stonyhurst, the public school run by the Jesuits in Lancashire.

From there Glenville went to Christ Church, Oxford where he joined OUDS. 'The OUDS at that time was a distinctly homosexual society with some very good-looking young men, among them Peter Glenville, Robert Flemyng and Rattigan himself, all of whom were keen to cluster around the visiting star.'[399] The 'visiting star' was John

Gielgud who, in 1932, came to direct *Romeo and Juliet*. In 1934, Glenville was elected president of OUDS, and after graduation made his first professional stage appearance at the Manchester Repertory Company in Louis Jourdan's role as the tutor, Dr Agi, in Ferenc Molnar's *The Swan*. His early career was as an actor (he replaced the irretrievably intoxicated Cyril Cusack, who had insulted Vivien Leigh, as Louis Dubedat in Shaw's *The Doctor's Dilemma* in 1942): he turned to directing only after the war. He was an intimate member of the circle of John Gielgud's and Binkie Beaumont's friends. Glenville was remembered by Kitty Black, whose translation of Sartre's *Les Mains Sales* he directed in 1947, as 'a bit hawk-faced, not particularly good-looking, but with a strong personality and great charm'.

Alec had first met Glenville before the war: he received 'a letter, a very nice one', from Peter Glenville on 5 April 1941. On 12 March 1946, he took Glenville to lunch to ask him to direct *Heloise*, but their close friendship began only when, in the early summer of 1948, the three Guinnesses were on holiday on the island of Ischia with Ernest Milton. At a particularly difficult moment, when Milton was in despair at having spilt sun-tan lotion over his new suit, they had 'stumbled across Peter Glenville and William Hardy-Smith, also holidaying on Ischia'.[400]

Peter Glenville, like Peter Bull, was a man with very many friends so there is no need to look for any other reason for Alec taking to him beyond a shared sense of humour and delight in bitchy gossip. Matthew remembered that during Glenville's visits to Kettlebrook Meadows there was non-stop laughter. Of course, Glenville had, like Peter Bull, the social assurance and poise of a public-school and Oxford-educated 'gentleman'; and, also like Bull, no apparent anxieties about his homosexual condition. He had family money – enough, at any rate, to have a house in Brompton Square. Another of Alec's closest friends, the actor Richard Leech, recalled being taken to a party given by Glenville where he was 'quizzed by G. Greene about Eliz. Bowen'. Glenville was in New York in 1950 when Alec was playing in *The Cocktail Party*, and took Alec to 'a wildly social weekend [on] some millionairess's estate – can't remember the name – it's frightfully well known – as is the fact that she murdered her husband'.[401] He also appeared in Asheville, North Carolina, as we have seen, when Alec was making *The Swan* and accompanied him on a jaunt to New Orleans.

Glenville was the perfect travelling companion, 'determined to go everywhere and see everything', as Alec had told Merula; but the two men had in common not just their love of the theatre but their fascination with the Catholic Church. 'Peter G & Bill Smith . . . stayed talking mostly of Pd. Pio, who has caught our imagination, and of Sts. Therese and Teresa* until 1.30 this morning,' Alec wrote in his diary on 12 September 1952. 'Went to Burns & Oates to get Peter G St Teresa of Avila's autobiography,' he notes on 9 December of the same year. 'Peter Glenville to dinner, quiet happy evening ending up playing Gregorian chants on the gramophone,' he records on 28 November 1954.

When Alec was confirmed into the Catholic Church some months after his reception, Peter Glenville acted as his sponsor: the ceremony was performed by Archbishop Henry King, Bishop of Portsmouth, in an attic in his residence in Winchester. How Glenville reconciled his life-long liaison with Bill Smith with the Catholic Church's teaching on the sinfulness of sexual relations outside a marriage between a man and a woman is unclear. There were to be found then, as there are now, confessors who take a lenient view of sexual sins. A close friend of Alec's in the later years of his life, Quentin Stevenson – a homosexual and once a Catholic – describes 'the sort of Farm Street talk: "oh, you shouldn't have gone to confession there, you should have gone to Farm Street because Fr So-and-so is sweet about that sort of thing" . . . The very people who go on about how wonderful it is being a Catholic because of the Church's authority will, ten minutes later, tell you about the private arrangements they have made with God.'[402] In Catholic parlance, absolution – the forgiveness of a penitent's sins

---

* Saints Teresa of Lisieux and Teresa of Avila.

by the priest, acting on the authority of Christ who had told his disciples that those whose sins they forgave were forgiven – depended not just on an Act of Contrition made before the priest in the confessional, but also on a 'firm purpose of amendment' – a determination not to commit the sin again.

Yet even where the purpose of amendment might seem to be feeble, and even where living with a man to whom one is sexually attracted might seem contrary to the Church's injunction to avoid 'occasions of sin' – even, indeed, where a sinner seems to take advantage of the sacrament in a most cynical way – the very fact that he deems the sacrament necessary for his salvation suggests faith in Christ and acceptance of, if not obedience to, the disciplines of the Church. And it is also quite possible that a man in Glenville's position, like the large number of heterosexuals who find themselves living with women they cannot marry in Church, might postpone amending his ways in the hope that God would grant him the opportunity to repent before he dies.

Alec's friendship with Peter Glenville first led to a professional collaboration when Glenville directed Sam and Bella Spewack's mediocre play, *Under the Sycamore Tree*, at the Aldwych in 1952 with Alec playing the role of the Ant Scientist and Peter Bull in the cast. Kenneth Tynan, by then the *Evening Standard* critic, wrote that Alec played 'the Ant Scientist with rubber-soled charm, mincing stealth, and unfailing wit'. The audience, however, were not always so appreciative:

> When I got to the theatre I found a letter from a Mr Day asking for his money back – 24 shillings – as he was a tomato seller and if he sold rotten tomatoes his clients asked for their money back. 'If you are a gentleman you will return me the price of my seats' was his expression. I took enormous pleasure in writing back, at rather too much length, suggesting that with growing tomatoes he also cultivate a sense of humour.[403]

A further collaboration two years later gave rise to what Alec was to consider one of his finest performances, that of the title role in Bridget

Boland's play *The Prisoner*. The drama had been inspired by the recent arrest by the Communist authorities of the Roman Catholic Primate of Hungary, Cardinal Mindszenty. (Alec was invited by Cardinal Heenan to meet Cardinal Mindszenty some years later when Mindszenty came to London but Alec declined – still resentful, perhaps, at the 'haircut' jibe.) Bridget Boland had written five previous plays and was much liked within the profession. Kitty Black thought she was 'wonderful – the head girl of the school on which all other girls had a crush . . . The front of her hair was dyed flame-coloured because she always had a cigarette in her mouth. Her top-knot was dyed with nicotine . . . Like many women of her generation, she lost out because of the dearth of men after World War I.'

Boland, a lapsed Catholic, had worked on propaganda films during the war but *The Prisoner* was more than a dramatised documentary. The Cardinal, played by Alec, starts off confident in the integrity and holiness that has made him beloved by the people; but inexorably the Interrogator, played by Noel Willman, whose task is to get his prisoner to confess to crimes against the state, breaks through this facade, forcing the Cardinal to own up to baser motives for his religious zeal – a wish to cleanse himself of the shame of his mother's life of prostitution. The Interrogator's brain-washing proves effective: the Cardinal, a broken man, pleads guilty to the charges of treason.

Since Alec kept no diary during this period – the play was staged in April 1954, and he re-started his diary only in August – the effect of playing the Cardinal must be a matter of conjecture. Some of the critics had misgivings about the play: Robert Tanitch, in his study of Alec Guinness, thought that the subject matter deserved more than Boland's 'Freudian conclusion'; and Philip Hope-Wallace, in *Time and Tide*, 'longed for Arthur Koestler or Dostoevsky to take a hand': but Hope-Wallace went on to say that 'Mr Guinness's study of the prisoner held me right to the end; there were gestures of fatigue acted here, which one has seen a thousand times in real life but seldom, consciously, on the stage. Such is the mark of transcendent genius in acting.'

True to the training of St Denis and Komisarjevsky, Alec would have done his utmost to get into the mind of the East European Cardinal; and the preoccupation did not end with the play's last night at the Globe Theatre. Plans were already afoot to make a film of *The Prisoner* for Columbia. Alec would again play the Cardinal, Glenville would direct, but there were differences as to who should play the Interrogator. Alec turned down 'the outrageous idea' that he should play *both* roles. James Mason was unavailable; Trevor Howard turned down the role 'because of billing difficulty'; Alec wanted Paul Scofield but Glenville thought him 'too costumy'. Gielgud was approached but 'he has to toss off Clarence for Larry's *Richard III* film'. The role was finally played by Jack Hawkins.

What seems to have concentrated Alec's mind on the question of his own beliefs was Columbia's suggestion 'that the Cardinal shouldn't be Catholic. Couldn't he be a kind of non-denominational Billy Graham? Also wanted to cut the Cathedral scene, which is best in the script. Firmly said No. What their next move will be I can't imagine. But without its Catholicism it would be meaningless.' Then Alec adds: 'How strange the subjective working of the actor! Yesterday, or was it the day before, I had a sudden pull to Rome again – having spent six violently anti-Catholic, almost anti-Christian months. The inner workings getting ready for *The Prisoner*, I suppose.'[404]

Finally, one must add to the list of those things that led to Alec's conversion, the effect of his spiritual reading – of the New Testament, of course, but also the biographies of saints such as the two Saints Teresa, ascetics such as Charles de Foucauld and, above all, his adopted patron, St Francis de Sales. 'Consider the nobility and excellence of your soul,' wrote St Francis:

> Endowed with reason, it not only knows this visible world but also knows that there is a heaven, that there are angels, that there is a God and that he is supreme, ineffable and good; reason which knows that there is an eternity and understands how to live in this world in order to live for ever in company with God and his angels in the next.[405]

From the time of his conversion to Christianity before the war, Alec had never been without a copy of St Francis de Sales' *The Devout Life*. The first had been lost in the wreck of his landing craft. 'Two or three years ago I was given a St F. de S.,' Alec had written to Chattie towards the end of the war, 'and adored him & promptly lost the book':

> Now I have been sent another, and have returned to his friendly wisdom and greatness with more understanding and a better resolution, I hope, to follow his methods. The most comfortable of saints – a man who does not raise his eyebrows at balls and theatres and picnics – in moderation. I come and go in fits and starts – so to speak – in my religious life, but it deepens I believe and pray and trust.[406]

'No one,' wrote Joseph Pearce in *Literary Converts*, 'has been able to describe a conversion in terms which are objectively appropriate. As in the language of mystics, analogies which give only a shadow of the substance have been used.'[407] Alec became a Catholic because he accepted that the Roman Catholic Church was the Church founded by Jesus Christ, the Second Person of a Trinitarian God. But long before Alec's formal 'reconciliation' he had been living the life of a Catholic, more conscious than most Roman Catholics that the Church was a community of both the living and the dead. He prayed to Mary, the Mother of God, said the Rosary, and conversed with his favourite Catholic saints, calling for their intercession in the greatest and smallest of causes – a votive candle lit so that Matthew might walk again, or a request to St Anthony of Padua to loosen the nuts on a wheel.

But Alec also felt that he had had a direct *experience* of God Himself, and of God's grace; and in the final analysis this was the point of departure of his conversion. 'I think most . . . human beings have that once in their lives,' he wrote to Merula from Los Angeles:

> . . . in greatly varying degrees of course. And *of course* it's the most supreme, happy, and important moment of life. I believe it is . . . God giving each man and woman, according to their capacity, a glimpse of

his promise to them, an impression of what eternity could mean, a glimpse of their *adoption* as Sons of God, and by its *withdrawal* a realisation of what the Fall of Man means. We are all left with a feeling of exhilaration and yet at the same time, hand in hand with its happiness, a sadness that we are unlikely to encounter it again in this life. It's a golden carrot held up to donkeys – who could be gods . . .[408]

part five

faith, fame and failure

twenty-seven

In May, 1956 – a month after his reception into the Catholic Church, and as if to demonstrate that religious convictions can go with a sense of fun – Alec appeared in a French bedroom farce at the Winter Garden Theatre in London. This was *Hotel Paradiso* by Georges Feydeau and Maurice Desvallières. Alec starred as Monsieur Boniface, a hen-pecked husband who takes the wife of his best friend, Mme Cot, played by Irene Worth, to a seedy hotel where the planned seduction is thwarted by a sequence of preposterous and unpredictable events. The play – London's first taste of Feydeau – was directed by Peter Glenville; Billie Whitelaw and Kenneth Williams played supporting roles. It was chic and witty and a great success. Alec flourished in his clowning role. When the police raid the hotel in the second act, Mme Cot says she is there with her husband, M. Cot, and Boniface that he is there with his wife, Mme Boniface. The police search for M. Boniface and issue his description. Michael Billington, the future theatre critic of the *Guardian*, then a boy of sixteen and seeing one of his first plays, remembers his astonishment at Alec's demonstration of elasticity in his mime. When the police say M. Boniface is 'a very small man, Guinness suddenly puts on inches; then someone says, no, he was a very tall man, and Guinness shrinks like a concertina into absolute nothingness. This showed his genius for reinventing himself in front of you on stage'.[409]

'Perhaps,' Alec reflected in his diary, after watching the less successful film version almost a quarter of a century later, 'I should have been some sort of clown rather than an actor who has fallen between half a dozen stools.'[410] An aspect of Alec's distinctive quality as an actor was his love of clowning and his skill at mime. One thinks back to how, in the school dormitory, he had tried with a pillow case to imitate the turn he had seen at the London Coliseum where a man had seemed to disappear into a sack; and one thinks, too, of the demanding tutoring in mime by Michel St Denis in his production of *Noah* and the classes Alec took in the London Acting School.

An actor's success or failure in a role, or in a series of roles that make up a career, often depend upon his ability to choose not just a good play or script, but also to discern in the character he is to play qualities that resonate in his own personality. Of course an actor, like anyone else, may lack the self-knowledge that would allow such discernment; or he may want to play a character on the stage or the screen who expresses some repressed traits. A project that Alec had been trying to get off the ground since 1954 was a film of Joyce Cary's novel, *The Horse's Mouth*, in which he – the precise, punctual, modest, conventional, buttoned-up Alec Guinness – would play the anarchic, amoral, boastful, egotistical painter, Gully Jimson. Alec had adapted the novel himself; Ronald Neame had agreed to direct it and John Bryan to produce it; and, while in Hollywood making *The Swan*, Alec had been told that MGM would put up the money.

Then as now, however, the Hollywood studios proved fickle, and by the summer of 1956 nothing had been agreed. And now another script was sent to Alec with a role that corresponded more precisely to the kind of man he was than the kind of man he might like to be. The character was an army officer similar to one that Alec had himself created in a play he had started to write during the war. 'I'm hugely enjoying [writing] a rather sad-funny part for myself,' he had written to Merula, 'of a fearfully common and lonely bank clerk who was a major in the war (this war) and got the M.C. and whose only happiness in life had been the war.'[411]

Nicholson, the role now proposed for Alec, was a colonel rather than a major, but he was 'common and lonely' and his only happiness in life had been the British Army. He was the creation of a French novelist, Pierre Boulle, who had based his character on two British Army officers he had come across in Indo-China during the war. In Boulle's novel Nicholson, the commander of a battalion of British soldiers taken prisoner by the Japanese after the fall of Singapore, refuses to obey the orders of the Japanese camp commandant, Colonel Saito, that British officers should work alongside their men building a bridge for a railway through Burma. Saito's attempts to coerce him fail; the prisoners cannot be made to work effectively by the Japanese and so, because it is imperative that the bridge be built by a certain date, the commandant, Saito, gives way to Nicholson who, for the sake of his men's discipline and morale, not only builds the bridge but one in which he and his men can take pride – thereby contributing to the enemy's war effort.

The novel was translated into English and published in Britain in 1954 with the title *Bridge on the River Kwai*. It came to the notice of the American scriptwriter Carl Foreman, author of the screenplay for the highly successful *High Noon*. At the time, Foreman was living in exile in Britain, having been blacklisted in Hollywood as a result of Senator McCarthy's persecution of suspected Communists in the film industry. He was employed as a writer by London Films, the production company of Alexander and Zoltan Korda. Foreman saw the potential for a movie in *Kwai*. London Films bought an option and Foreman wrote a script.

After reading the screenplay, however, Alexander Korda decided that the story of a British officer who collaborates with the Japanese could not possibly succeed and sold the rights to Horizon Films, a production company that had been set up by director John Huston and the powerful, charismatic producer, Sam Spiegel, to make *The African Queen*. Like Alexander Korda, Spiegel was a Jewish emigré from Eastern Europe who, though based in London, was a citizen of the United States and had won an Oscar two years before for Elia Kazan's masterpiece, *On the Waterfront*.

Spiegel and Foreman, looking for a director for *Kwai*, failed to interest such major figures as Howard Hawks, Fred Zinnemann and John Ford and so turned, *faute de mieux*, to David Lean. Lean, since directing Alec in *Oliver Twist*, had made five further films, among them *Hobson's Choice* starring one of the actors Alec most admired, Charles Laughton. In trouble with the British tax authorities and in the process of divorcing his second wife, the actress Ann Todd, Lean liked the story but loathed Foreman's screenplay. The question of who wrote, or co-wrote, the final script for *Kwai* was to become a matter of dispute – with claims and counter-claims by Foreman, Lean and others. When the film was released the credit went to Pierre Boulle.

Equally disputed – and now part of movie folklore – was which actors were approached to play the part of Colonel Nicholson. Charles Laughton was proposed, but rejected because he was too fat to be credible as a half-starved prisoner of war. Noël Coward, Ralph Richardson, Anthony Quayle, Ray Milland, James Mason, Ronald Colman and Douglas Fairbanks Jr. were all suggested but were either unavailable, considered unsuitable or turned down the role. In the project's early days Alec was approached by Spiegel but he too turned it down. His name came up again after Lean had become involved but Lean was unenthusiastic. 'I don't think he will give us the "size" we need. He could do it, of course, but in a different way from what we have visualised.'[412] However, Spiegel persisted and over dinner persuaded Alec to change his mind. 'I started out maintaining that I wouldn't play the role and by the end of the evening we were discussing what kind of wig I would wear.'[413] There was also the inducement of a substantial fee. The agreement signed on 14 November 1956 between Horizon Pictures (GB), Lustre Films Ltd and Alec Guinness c/o Lustre

Films MCA guaranteed Alec £150,000* to be paid in twelve instalments, $10,000 dollars a week after the twelfth week of shooting; and first-class travel and hotel accommodation.[414]

After considering sites in Thailand, Spain and Yugoslavia for the film, Lean and Spiegel settled on a stretch of river running through jungle near the village of Kitugala, sixty miles from Colombo, the capital of Sri Lanka, then called Ceylon. Taking a short holiday with Merula in Rome *en route*, Alec flew out to Colombo on 9 November 1956. Lean met him at the airport and drove him into Colombo:

Passed a baby elephant on the road, walking while eating its breakfast. And lots of *tiny* oxen. And *huge* magnolia trees, and the breadfruit trees are tremendous and very lovely. Apart from that it's all rather hideous, what I've seen. David says that out in the country it is dramatically beautiful and I mustn't get too depressed by Colombo itself. Enchanting wicked black children crowd round me and pull at my clothes saying, 'You plenty money! Give me for beer!' The hotel is a large bright red ramshackle monstrosity which might be at Troon or some lesser Scottish resort. The sea bangs outside my window and big fans in the ceiling whirr silently all the time . . .

Arrived too late to go to mass, of course, but did look in the Catholic church close by – terrible pink and blue statuary but rather touching somehow and completely open all round with small boys playing football.[415]

Alec took time to adjust to 'the piping heat and terrifying humidity'. 'Have spent most of the day in bed,' he wrote on 24 November:

Had my 2nd T.A.B. injection last night and found the sun too bright & dizzying to-day. Feel much better now, though pretty bored. Reading keeps me going a bit – I'm still on Romano Guardini† – but

---

*   Alec always insisted that he made no money from *Bridge Over the River Kwai*.
†   *The Lord* by Romano Guardini.

apart from that there is nothing to do. I haven't the energy to learn my
lines – anyway I know them for the next week's work. Rather dread
the start of this film – I've decided I'm horribly bad at acting.

Alec's main preoccupation, almost as soon as he arrived, appears to
have been Merula and Matthew's plan to come out to Ceylon for
Christmas:

> Heaven knows what you are going to do with yourselves. It won't be
> a bit like the Hollywood visit – and I can't even think of any
> Christmas presents – the shops are more or less confined to Yardley's
> Lavender Water, ebony elephants and general junk . . . Honestly, I
> can't find a thing for you or Matthew except a ruby which I can't
> afford. You'd better bring your own Christmas presents and send me
> the bill!

The Third World conditions that prevailed in Ceylon grated on Alec's
penchant for punctuality and order:

> Things to be prepared for: – Servants who are so silent you don't know
> they are in the room with you. Trains leave anything up to two hours
> late. Trains arrive anything up to five hours late. Air Ceylon arrives
> anything up to two weeks late. Waiters putting the menu for the next
> course between your mouth and what is on your fork as you are just
> popping it in. A phone call to Kandy (70 miles) has to be booked 3
> hours before wanted. A phone called to Mt. Lavinia (7 miles) takes 20
> minutes to organise. The ugliest white people you have ever seen. It's
> very *un* S. of France . . . I'm sorry if all this sounds depressing. I'm not
> *really* depressed – it's just the wretchedness of Colombo which gets one
> down.

In his letters to Merula, Alec said little about the making of the film.
'The place is beginning to fill up with actors,' he wrote on
21 November:

James Donald*, and a couple of small-part people, and a Japanese star† (very Hollywoodised and grand) and another Japanese who looks interesting and is quite chit chatty. The latter has brought a Japanese flute and a tiny pair of Japanese scissors with him, as *props*, he explained – 'if you put those on the set then people will know we are Japanese and you won't need anything else' – which I like as an approach to film-making very much.

To enhance the film's potential in the American market, a role had been created for an American character, a naval POW, Shears, who escapes from the camp but is subsequently wrested from the arms of a WREN while recuperating in Ceylon by the British Major Warden, played by Jack Hawkins, to return as part of a commando unit to blow up the Kwai bridge. For this romantic role Spiegel had hired William Holden for a fee of $300,000 plus ten per cent of the profits, making him the most expensive actor in the profession. Holden, who had been nominated for an Oscar for his performance in Billy Wilder's *Sunset Boulevard*, worked well with Lean but irritated Alec. 'Our life here has received the influx of Holden (who does love to pontificate),' Alec wrote to Merula. And later: 'I do wish Bill Holden would stop boasting of the famous actors he has employed in his company, or indeed of the fortunes he has lost. And he talks as much about *Sunset Boulevard* as Martita did of *The Mad Woman of Chaillot*. Isn't that an extraordinary habit that certain actors have.'[416]

The objection raised to the casting of Charles Laughton as Colonel Nicholson might also have been made of Holden who, though certainly not fat, seemed too fit and well-fed in the opening scenes of the film to be credible as a prisoner-of-war. Lean was later to commend him for his professional approach to the job, by which he probably meant that Holden went along with everything that Lean suggested.

---

* Donald played the British medical officer.
† Sessue Hayakawa who played Colonel Saito.

Alec was less amenable: he had, in his usual obsessive way, *become* Colonel Nicholson and felt he knew him better than Lean did. 'If you and I were having dinner with him,' Lean told Alec, 'we'd find him an awful bore.' Alec took umbrage. 'Oh, I see. You're asking me to play a bore . . . No, I don't want to play a bore. I'll pay my own fare home.'[417] The difference between Alec and David Lean was about whether or not an element of tongue-in-cheek humour should enter into Alec's portrayal of Nicholson. Alec thought it should – partly, no doubt, to make Nicholson a more sympathetic character. He clearly identified with the character: Nicholson's line – 'Without law, there is no civilisation' – might well have come from Alec in real life. It was therefore natural that he should want to incorporate into the character something of his own sense of humour; and equally inevitable that Lean should dispute this if, as Alec later suggested in a letter to Lean's biographer, Kevin Brownlow, Lean *lacked* a sense of humour. 'Such humour as he displayed was usually dyspeptic and cynical.'

There was another area of sensitivity which, looking back from the twenty-first century might seem obscure, but was real at the time. Was *The Bridge on the River Kwai* anti-British? The war against the Japanese had ended little more than ten years before and, because of the cruel treatment of the British prisoners-of-war by the Japanese in the building of the railway through Burma, it was a delicate matter to make a film which made British and Japanese colonels equally pig-headed or, as they say of one another in the film, equally 'mad'. Certainly, if the film played down the Japanese atrocities (because it was thought gruesome detail would frighten off audiences), it reflects some of the lingering prejudices of the British at the time: for example, that the Japanese engineers were less competent than the British at building bridges.

Alec was a patriot and no doubt wanted to avoid the anti-British slant that some saw in Boulle's original novel. Lean later claimed that James Donald decided that Lean was making an anti-British film. 'He told the rest of the cast, including Alec Guinness, who I think went

along with it.' Lean therefore took against the British actors and had
a bitter dispute with Alec in one of the last scenes in the film where
Nicholson, proud of his achievement in building the bridge, ruminates
on his life against the setting sun. Lean filmed the scene from behind,
showing not Alec's face but the back of his head. And when he had
finished with Alec and was to film with Holden, he said: 'Now you can
all fuck off and go home, you English actors. Thank God that I'm
starting work tomorrow with an American actor. It'll be such a
pleasure to say good-bye to you guys.'[418]

The making of *The Bridge on the River Kwai* was an unpleasant
experience for all concerned. The heat, the humidity, the poisonous
snakes and centipedes, the logistical demands of building such a
complex set in the middle of the jungle, were compounded by ill-
temper and bad luck. It was a time when the British workforce,
particularly in the film industry, was at its most 'bolshie'. When one
of the two-man crew working the generator fell sick, and the second
man did the work alone, the unions at once called a strike which had
to be settled in London.

There were also strokes of bad luck. 'One of the assistant directors*
was killed this morning in a car crash,' Alec wrote to Merula on 3
December 1956, 'and my make-up man has broken his back and
another assistant† is badly cut and bruised. I saw the results of the
smash and it was awful . . .' The make-up man was Stuart Freeborn,
who had so painstakingly prepared Alec for the role of Fagin in *Oliver
Twist*. He survived the accident but left hospital an inch or two shorter
than when he had gone in.

At one point during the filming of *Kwai*, Alec's relationship with
David Lean degenerated to a point where they were not on speaking
terms. Teddy Darvas, the assistant film editor, dining with Lean one
evening, pointed out that Alec was eating alone. Lean said: 'We're not
speaking.' Darvas replied: 'It seems silly after all these years – here you

---

*   John Kerrison
†   Gus Agosti

are in the same hotel and you don't speak'. Lean agreed and went to
sit with Alec. 'They made it up,' wrote Darvas. 'That lasted forty-eight
hours.'

Both Alec and David Lean were strong-minded men and while Alec,
when making *Great Expectations* and *Oliver Twist*, had felt sufficiently
beholden to the older man to fall in with his wishes, he had, by the
time of *Kwai*, developed a greater confidence in his own abilities and
judgements. Alec would later write of 'David's extreme unpleasantness
in later years', saying that 'he depended so much, it seemed to me, on
sycophants' and had no sense of humour. 'David Lean told me, in
Ceylon, that swimming in the river one evening, he came face to face
with a cobra swimming in the opposite direction. They both turned
and fled. I should have commented, "Wise cobra"!'

There can be little doubt but that Alec was a difficult actor to direct:
success had made him imperious and sure of his own view of how a
role should be played. No doubt he missed the easygoing rapport he
had had with Peter Glenville, and he grew tetchy even when praised.
Matthew remembers that when he and his mother came out to Ceylon
for Christmas:

> David was always very nice and he would say things to my mother
> when we were meeting for drinks on the veranda of the hotel just
> outside Colombo. David would say 'Alec has been absolutely brilliant
> today.' And that would make my father cross. I don't know why
> because David Lean was being nice. But it would annoy my father.

Yet Alec later recognised that many of Lean's decisions on how
Nicholson should be played turned out to be right. Lean describes how,
during Merula and Matthew's visit, he took them into the hotel room
which he had converted into a cutting-room, and showed them rushes
of the film for an hour, including the long, staggering walk from the
corrugated iron coop – the 'oven' – where Nicholson had been
imprisoned. Alec had disliked the shot, telling Lean that it was 'an
awful, terrible walk – much too long . . .'[419] The three Guinnesses said

nothing after seeing the rushes, returning to their hotel room in silence; but later, according to Lean, Alec came to his room and said that he and Merula and Matthew had discussed the scene 'and before going to sleep tonight I ought to tell you that all of us thought it was the best thing I've ever done'.

While Alec was on location in Ceylon, Merula was considering whether or not to follow her husband and son into the Roman Catholic Church. She had seen how Alec, after his reception, had become calmer. 'My mother,' Matthew remembered, 'said there was a big change . . . His demons had gone.' Matthew, paradoxically, remembered the time between his conversion to Catholicism and his father's as the best there had been between them. Alec had loved Matthew's stories 'out of school' about the Jesuits at Beaumont; and while Matthew had wanted Alec to become a Catholic, he had not felt the same about Merula:

> I didn't particularly want my mother to become a Catholic. And that was a real problem. And when she was under instruction I was very worried for her. I felt it was breaking her spirit . . . She was subjugating something in herself and I thought it was a mistake. She had subjugated herself to my father and now she was being broken.

There was something original and idiosyncratic in Merula that made it difficult for her to assent to the dogmas of an institutionalised religion; but she felt that unless she became a Catholic she would always be the odd one out. She was already an Anglican, of course, and the doctrinal divide between the High Anglicanism that she had practised since before the war was not *so* different from Roman Catholicism: but particularly at that time the Roman Catholic Church – the 'crack regiment' as Alec had called it – expected a higher degree of training and discipline than the Anglican home guard.

Merula's sister-in-law Mary remembered that the main stumbling block for Merula was the Church's teaching that animals did not have souls but 'eventually a Jesuit from Farm Street convinced her that they did'. Alec had advised Merula to discuss her doubts with a Jesuit priest, but he put no pressure on Merula to follow him into the Catholic Church:

> Whatever you do don't force yourself to take the plunge – I'm positive it's got to feel the *obvious, natural, happy* thing. I would be wretched if you jumped into the Church and then felt rebellious. I think one *does* feel rebellious about certain things – and I'm sure there's lots of it I don't understand and don't particularly want to understand. In fact I don't understand half of it and in my lazy way I don't suppose I'll ever bother to know more – and yet I feel I did the right thing and am happy that some instinct (which one is so wrong in thinking is blind) steered me along that particular path.[420]

By the beginning of December, Merula was still undecided and wanted Alec to help her make up her mind. But Alec insisted that the decision must be hers alone:

> I can't help you my love. All I can suggest is three things (1) whether you feel as I'm sure you do that Christ was true in his claims and is God (2) whether you are satisfied that the claims of the Catholic Church are reasonably justified. And then (3) – probably more difficult for you than for me, as it's a question of temperament to start with – whether in a Catholic Church you feel a sense of worship. For me this last grows. I find it less and less a difficulty – in fact none really – except through my own fidgetiness and distraction and general crossness with people & things – but I accept absolutely now and with no effort that I am in the actual presence of God on the altar. There have been very few days this year when I haven't paid a visit – even if only for three minutes – to a church, merely to kneel and be astonished at the humility of God. My prayers are always full of my requirements and not true prayers at all – but somehow I can feel a *steadying* from the Blessed Sacrament. (How one winces at using these Catholic expressions – but that's just a silly

pride) – and one day perhaps before I die I shall have managed to make a decent unegotistic prayer.

Alec wrote that 'the sheer *kindness* of God is quite staggering – the easiness, the childlike way one is led in the first few months – *years* I *hope*'; and he envisaged that Merula's vision of the divine would be distinct from both Matthew's and his:

> For each of us God must look different and I suppose each of us will walk round and round God for all time gaping at just how different he is. I don't think I ask any more than that – except it would be nice if you and Matthew and I had at least *recognisable* views of him so that while we may be seeing different aspects we at least know we are gazing at the same fundamental. But if you choose not to – and heaven knows what Matthew thinks – I promise you most solemnly that I wouldn't think for an instant that you had been blind or foolish or done anything that wasn't wise and right for you. If you *are* to come in to the Church then it'll be useless your trying to resist – all the horrors that have been and are perpetrated in Christ's name will be so skilfully outweighed by God.
>
> One final word in the 'Yes' side – one of the *recent things* I've discovered is that now there is *always* something to *think* about. Never a dull moment in heaven or hell.[421]

Some time in December 1956, Merula resolved her doubts and was received into the Roman Catholic Church. She told Alec only when she and Matthew joined him in Ceylon, where the three celebrated their first Christmas together in the same church.

The shooting of *Kwai* went beyond the scheduled twelve weeks: 'my presence here,' Alec wrote to Merula after she had returned to England in mid-February, 1957, 'is costing Sam S an extra $10,000 dollars a week.' But even this inducement did not tempt Alec to linger and when he was released he left for England on the first possible flight. The experience of making *Kwai* had been an ordeal for everybody involved, but the end product, which Alec saw in September of 1957, made it more than worthwhile. 'I think it's TERRIFIC,' he wrote to Lean:

> 'I was gripped, moved, stimulated and all the right things. It has real authority behind it and eye and ear are constantly alive and fascinated. I do congratulate you. Anyway, I'm vastly proud to be associated with it.
>
> I liked Jack* . . . Bill† I liked too . . . Liked Geoffrey‡ – very appealing. Even liked Guinness – though I thought he was a bit flat here and there (at moments you suggested to him he was and he didn't believe) and only regretted his playing the Pied Piper Hospital scene with a hand in his pocket and not being definite enough at his death. The only thing I didn't care for was the girl on Mount Lavinia beach. Thought the Siamese enchanting. A wonderful film. Thank you for having me. As ever, Alec.'[422]

And seventeen years later, after a turkey dinner on Christmas night, Alec and Merula watched *The Bridge on the River Kwai* on television:

> I hadn't intended to but having switched it on some ten minutes after it had started we became hooked. Although I had always thought it a fine exciting film, in spite of thinking my own part in it rather unbelievable, almost laughable, I have also had a slight resentment about it, thinking it almost too well made; shot after beautifully composed shot looking like the cover of some Eastern *Country Life*. Last night on TV, the colour poorly reproduced, the composition of the shots thrown for a loop by being reduced to the square of the box from the wide screen, both Merula and I found it compelling. Both the story and characters took on a new intensity. The concentration remained on

---

*   Jack Hawkins
†   William Holden
‡   Geoffrey Horne

essentials ... Of course some things got lost or diminished – particularly my mad spastic walk from the 'oven' to the Japanese commander's hut. That walk was, quite unconsciously, an imitation of Matthew's walk when he was first recovering from polio at the age of twelve. That it was so only dawned on me when I ran some 16 mil. film I took of him at Selsey. Merula and I had persuaded ourselves that his walk was quite normal, just a bit stiff: the self-deception of parents. While not admitting the walk was odd it must have burned itself into my unconscious to reappear, unawares, in a film three years later. Seventeen years ago the film was made. I was also surprised at what a minor impact the Colonel Bogey tune made last night, it having been associated with the film so very strongly through the years, to a degree that depressed and nauseated me.[423]

twenty-eight

Soon after his return to England from Ceylon, and before the release of *The Bridge on the River Kwai*, Alec returned to Ealing to make the studio's penultimate film, *Barnacle Bill*. It was the story of a naval captain who, because of chronic seasickness, cannot go to sea. Instead, he converts a derelict pier into a shore-based cruise liner. The film was directed by Charles Frend, who had directed Alec in *A Run for Your Money* in 1949, and the screenplay by T.E.B. Clarke had some of the ingredients of Ealing's earlier successes: Alec plays multiple roles as in *Kind Hearts and Coronets* – not just the present-day sea captain but also a number of his sea-faring ancestors; there are conflicts with authority in the form of the local council as in Ealing's *Passport to Pimlico*. There was plenty of scope in Alec's role for clowning, dancing and the kind of anarchic behaviour that appealed to the suppressed side of his nature: he joins a gang of teddy boys in smashing up a theatre and jives with a pony-tailed girl; but the film was judged a pale imitation of the Ealing classics and Alec subsequently regretted making 'the wretched, boring *Barnacle Bill* – which I never wanted to do and only did out of friendship to Charley Frend.'[424]

The failure of *Barnacle Bill* went unnoticed, however, beside the stupendous success of *The Bridge on the River Kwai*, which opened in London on 2 October 1957 and in New York on 18 December, and was acclaimed by the critics on both sides of the Atlantic. It had cost almost $3,000,000 to make but by 1980 was estimated to have grossed over $30 million, with ten per cent of the profit going to William Holden and ninety per cent to Sam Spiegel. The 'Colonel Bogey' theme music, as Alec noted ruefully seventeen years later, topped the charts throughout the world. The film received eight Academy Award nominations and won seven of them at the Oscar ceremony in March 1958 – including Best Film, Best Director and, for Alec, Best Actor: he received his Oscar at a dinner in London, having come straight from the set of *The Horse's Mouth*.

Alec also won Best Actor awards from the New York Film Critics' Circle, the National Board of Review, the British Film Academy and the Golden Globe award. He had won awards before for *Kind Hearts and Coronets* and *The Lavender Hill Mob*: and, for his role in *The Prisoner*, a prize from the Office Catholique International du Cinéma; but none of these came anywhere near the international prestige of an Oscar.

'Undoubtedly,' wrote John Russell Taylor in his study of Alec, '*Kwai* was the real turning-point in Guinness's career, making him at one fell swoop into an international celebrity rather than merely an actor known internationally by a discriminating minority.'[425] Accompanying the Oscar was that other definitive seal of American approval: the cover of *Time* magazine. Alec's picture was accompanied by a profile that declared him 'the most gifted character actor in the English-speaking theatre' and, together with Gielgud, Olivier and Richardson, one of the four greatest actors in Britain.

Fame brings power, particularly in the film industry, and Alec now had the big-time producers and Hollywood studios at his command. His screenplay of *The Horse's Mouth* was taken off the shelf and went into production with John Bryan as producer and Ronald Neame as

director – Neame, who had been David Lean's assistant director on
Great Expectations, had directed Alec in *The Card*. Alec was also in a
position to influence the casting: there were parts for Lean's first wife,
Kay Walsh, who had brought her then husband to see Alec's stage
adaptation of *Great Expectations* – the genesis of Alec's screen career –
and who had appeared with him in *Oliver Twist*; Veronica Turleigh,
Alec's mother in *The Card* and sponsor at his reception into the
Catholic Church; and two other friends, Ernest Thesiger and Michael
Gough, both of whom had been in *The Man in the White Suit*.

Alec had first come across Joyce Cary's novel at the end of the war
after it had been recommended by Anthony Quayle. 'Bought a *David
Copperfield*,' he recorded in his diary, 'and *The Horse's Mouth* – a lively
novel recommended by Tony in Rome.'[426] Alec had got bogged down
in it on first reading and it was Merula who first suggested that the
novel might make a good film. Perhaps she saw something of the artist
idolised by the Salaman family, Augustus John, in the character of
Gully Jimson. Perhaps, too, she recognised that the character of Gully
Jimson would appeal to the anarchic artist trapped inside her
conventional, punctilious husband; or that he would see in Gully not
just the dedication of an Augustus John, a Paul Gaugin or a Vincent
van Gogh, but also of those uncompromising saints he so admired
such as Charles de Foucauld or Teresa of Lisieux.

Alec had embarked upon his adaptation of *The Horse's Mouth* in the
spring of 1954:

> On both train journeys scribbled a suggested opening sequence for *The
> Horse's Mouth*. Rather pleased with it. Read it to Merula; she thought
> it moved along at a good speed and was true to the spirit of the book,
> but was doubtful about letting Gully steal Nosey's bike. Personally I
> think this, though dangerous for sympathy, good.[427]

Four years before the film was made, in August 1954, Alec was in
conversation with John Bryan and Ronald Neame. On 30 August he
'Lunched with Ronnie and John and read them my suggested opening

for *Horse's Mouth*. Think they were surprised and mildly impressed.' They met again the next day. 'Lunched and talked H's M with Ronnie – quite constructively, I think. I slightly fear his sentimentality – as he slightly fears my harshness – but we can talk freely and easily together. If only I could genuinely like a few more of his suggestions!'

Kay Walsh was also involved at this stage. 'To Kay Walsh's for dinner – which was superb. Escargots and then tournedos. Very happy she & Elliott looked. After dinner read the H's M script – which was a far bigger flop than I expected. She feels I've missed Gully's importance. So far as the script is concerned I think she's right – though his size has always been clear to me as an actor.'[428] And, a year later, came the false dawn while Alec was making *The Swan*, with MGM and Alexander Korda vying for the privilege of making the film. 'Korda is now trying for *The Horse's Mouth* as MGM say they are prepared to do it,' Alec noted on 14 November 1955; then, five days later: 'MGM *are* going to do *The Horse's Mouth*!!! The news came through yesterday and final details will be discussed and probably settled on Monday.' *The Bridge on the River Kwai* and *Barnacle Bill* intervened but finally, in 1957, *The Horse's Mouth* went into production.

The finished film is, in a sense, all performance – there is only a tenuous plot. It opens as Gully Jimson, an avant-garde artist approaching old age, is released from Wormwood Scrubs prison where he has served a month's sentence for threatening the life of the millionaire, Hickson. Jimson is penniless but a second millionaire, Sir William Beeder, has asked to purchase one of his early paintings, a nude in the bath. Jimson no longer possesses any of his early paintings: his former mistress and model, Sarah, sold them to Hickson to pay off his debts. She kept one canvas for herself and this Jimson now tries to retrieve, with the help of his current mistress, Dee Coker (Kay Walsh).

There are some comic scenes, particularly when Jimson takes over the apartment of Sir William and Lady Beeder (Veronica Turleigh) to paint a mural while they are on holiday in the Caribbean – there to be joined by the sculptor, Abel (Michael Gough). In his portrayal of Gully Jimson, Alec gave a wholly convincing performance of a man who, like

Colonel Nicholson in *Kwai*, was likeable and unlikeable in equal measure. Jimson is rude, callous, and selfish, but nonetheless endearing thanks to Alec's mesmerising performance, replete with his grimaces, his idiosyncratic shuffle, and the rasping voice that he had first used for Fagin, and was to use again some years later in *Hitler: The Last Ten Days*.

The *Horse's Mouth*, which Alec regarded as among his finest works, had a lukewarm reception by the British critics. Inevitably, some felt that he had failed in his attempt to recreate Joyce Cary's Gully Jimson on the screen, reducing the novel, as Dilys Powell put it in the *Sunday Times*, to an 'intellectual Ealing-type film in which the artist . . . becomes the comic gimmick'; others that Alec's performance was self-indulgent – more fun for him to act than for his audience to watch. But both his performance and his adaptation were acclaimed abroad – the former winning him the top acting award at the 1957 Venice Film Festival, the latter earning an Oscar nomination for Best Screenplay adapted from another medium. It also won an award in Moscow where the story of an artist exploited by capitalists went down well.

After *The Horse's Mouth* Alec went straight on to *The Scapegoat* – a second film which, if not so directly his inspiration, saw him again in control. Its genesis was a successful novel by Daphne du Maurier about a young English teacher of French, John Barratt, who, while on holiday in France, is duped by his double, a Comte de Gué, into impersonating him while the count disappears. Reluctantly, Barratt grows into the role to the point of falling in love with de Gué's mistress, Bela. It turns out that de Gué intends Barratt to be the scapegoat when he murders his wife.

How anyone ever believed that a plot which so stretches credulity on the printed page could be made believable on film is difficult to comprehend, but it is clear that Daphne du Maurier had received substantial offers for the rights to her book. She had decided, however, that if there was to be a film, Alec must play the double role. She had approached him, and the two formed a company to produce the film, taking the project to Michael Balcon – now Sir Michael Balcon – at Ealing Studios.

Balcon's script editor at the time was none other than Kenneth Tynan who, in a memorandum to Balcon written on 24 October 1956, judged the novel:

> . . . a cut above Daphne Du Maurier's usual stuff, and one can see in it a very plush box office vehicle. But it will need very careful handling. The big obstacle is, of course, the basic postulate of two identical human beings. It is further complicated by the coincidence that one is a Frenchman who speaks perfect English and the other an Englishman who speaks perfect French. If the picture is shot in a wholly realistic style I can't see any audience swallowing this easily . . .

Tynan had misgivings as to whether or not Alec was up to the role. 'I can't help thinking,' he went on:

> . . . that the role of Jean is going to be a very big test indeed for Alec. The early sequences, when he walks blindly into a series of comedy situations, will be easy for him. The question will be: can he keep pace with the almost tragic later developments of the plot? In other words: will the audience ever recover from the initial impression that the film is a comedy about an impersonation? This will need deeper emotional playing than Alec has yet given us on the screen . . . A director with a strong romantic style and the ability to squeeze hitherto undiscovered passion out of Alec would solve all the major problems.[429]

Tynan was writing this, of course, before the making of *Kwai*. He had seen *The Prisoner*, but his anti-clericalism may have clouded his judgement on Alec's performance in that role. The point for Balcon, however, was not whether Alec was suitable for the role but how to hang on to an actor who, because *The Ladykillers* had been a great success in the United States, was likely to ensure the success of any film he chose to make. 'Ealing for some time have not been making forward contractual commitments with artistes except for specific pictures,' he wrote to Alec's agent, Laurence Evans, on 12 December 1955, 'but we are very interested in doing so with Alec Guinness if he is of the same mind.'[430]

Balcon, though determined to produce *The Scapegoat* even after his departure from Ealing Studios, was aware of the hazards of a project where an actor and the owner of the source rights – Alec and Daphne du Maurier – had so much power. '*The Scapegoat* is going to be a very difficult matter to handle at the outset,' he wrote to M.G. Muchnic at Loews Incorporated in New York. 'I repeat that none of the parties concerned know anything about production and they are trying to do everything they can to handle the production without outside control.'[431] Alec, certainly, seems to have brought a number of his friends on board, suggesting that the screenplay be written by Bridget Boland, that the film be directed by Peter Glenville, and that the role of de Gué's brother-in-law be played by Peter Bull.

Alec also tried to cast Andrée, the daughter of his friend Marriott Lefèvre, in the role of the twelve-year-old Marie-Noel de Gué. Andrée was then a pupil at the Ballet Rambert School in Notting Hill and was in a sensitive condition because of her parents' recent divorce. She was angry at being taken out of school at her mother's request to see Alec at her nearby home on Ladbroke Grove; she felt she was being taken for granted; and, while she did not refuse the job, made a sufficiently bad impression to oblige Alec to look elsewhere.

Alec had no better luck with his friends Peter Glenville and Bridget Boland. Glenville loathed the first draft of Boland's script and, wrote Balcon, 'has convinced himself that nothing good can possibly emerge from Bridget Boland'. He also asked for the stupendous fee of $100,000 which, given that he had only as yet directed one film, *The Prisoner,* and that both Alec and Daphne du Maurier were taking fees of £20,000, suggested a certain over-estimation of his worth. Nor would he commit himself to the project – to Alec's exasperation. 'My feeling two or three nights ago,' Alec wrote to Michael Balcon, 'was that Glenville should be asked to say Yes or No definitively – within twenty-four hours. As you know, I am most anxious for him to do the film but not if we are all going to be exhausted by dramas before we even start. There have been too many occasions when he has involved himself in preparing a picture and then withdrawn for me to feel comfortable with the way things stand.'[432]

Peter Glenville would not make the required commitment and the search started for another director. Kenneth Tynan suggested Ingmar Bergman, then unknown to the British. Approaches were also made to George Cukor and Vincente Minnelli, and Michael Balcon wrote to MGM, who were financing the film, that he had 'a promising young director', Guy Hamilton, standing by. In January, however, Balcon settled on Robert Hamer, who agreed to direct *The Scapegoat* for a fee of £10,000 – rather less than the sum demanded by Peter Glenville. However, Hamer was having drinking problems, and it is possible that rumours of this had crossed the Atlantic and brought misgivings at MGM. On 17 January 1958, Balcon wrote to a Mr Silverstein:

I would remind you that Robert Hamer is the ideal director from Guinness's point of view. He has never wanted anyone else and, in point of fact, when he was told of the decision, he said it was the best day's news he had had in years. Any change at this point would bring it into immediate trouble with Guinness and with Daphne du Maurier.[433]

Hamer went to work on the screenplay – not with Bridget Boland whose three drafts had all been deemed unsatisfactory, but with a bright young American writer, Gore Vidal. Although Alec had disliked a screenplay Vidal had written on the Dreyfus affair, Vidal had been sent for from the United States, arriving at Southampton on the *Queen Mary* on 4 November 1957. Hamer, even before he had signed up to direct the film, had worked with him and their joint script was completed by the middle of February.

When Daphne du Maurier read this adaptation of her novel, she was horrified. 'I read the script at the week-end,' she wrote to Michael Balcon:

. . . fully prepared to like it (except perhaps for dialogue) and find it
exciting, and well worked-out, with the characters well-drawn. I was
frankly *appalled*. And indeed, for a time, I almost wondered if the whole
thing was a joke or leg-pull, just to see how the story would seem if it
was played as a farce. Then I began to get angry. The whole point of
the original story had gone . . . Bridget's efforts seemed to me like
Shakespeare in comparison. Seriously, I do not believe for one moment
you and the rest of the studio can consider going ahead with this script.
I had a word with Alec on Monday night and I feel sure he felt the same
way.'[434]

Du Maurier said she was sorry 'if this letter comes as an added shock'
but assured Balcon that it could not be as big a shock to him as 'the
Gore Vidal script' had been to her. She may have sensed the young
Vidal's contempt for the source material with what he called its 'rich
tautologies, gleaming oxymorons and surreal syntax': if so, she
returned it with a vengeance. 'If the studio's opinion, and yours as
well, is that the script can be used as a foundation, then we none of us
talk the same language, and we are in for a disaster.'

Balcon showed this letter to Hamer who was incensed. He
telephoned Alec to say he thought Du Maurier's letter was a
disgraceful document – 'a compound of stupidity, egomania and
gross bad manners'. In a memorandum to Balcon, he referred to the
script as 'the results of the combined efforts of you, Gore, Ken,
Dennis* and me,' and that the trespass against professional good
manners was so vast as 'to go over the frontier into personal bad
manners as well'.[435]

In the event, the production went ahead with this screenplay and
Du Maurier's predictions of disaster were proved right. Seeing the film
today, the audience is hard-pressed to suspend disbelief. It is expected
to accept that only de Gué's dog senses that John Barratt is not his

*   possibly Dennis van Thal.

master; and de Gué's mistress, only after she has made love to Barratt and found him gentle rather than cruel.

But even if one swallows the implausibility of the premise, the script has a number of glaring non-sequiturs. It is not clear why John Barratt suddenly decides to accept the role of Comte de Gué; nor how Gué, who has contrived the imposture to be able to blame the murder of his wife on Barratt, had hoped to overcome the cast-iron alibi provided by Barratt's chauffeur and mistress.

Alec is wholly unconvincing as the malevolent count, and plausible as his double, the English don – his existential loneliness established by a few Graham-Greeneish voice-overs – only until, as in *The Captain's Paradise* et al, he plays the love scenes with de Gué's mistress and, as always, gives the impression that kissing the sumptuous Nicole Maurey is something of an ordeal.

Alec is far more convincing as the pretend parent to de Gué's daughter, Marie-Noël, played by Annabel Bartlett who, despite her pure Kensington tones (in contrast to the sexy French accent adopted by Irene Worth as de Gué's wife), conveys the vulnerability of a lonely child in an unhappy marriage and elicits from Alec a tenderness that he had shown towards her on the set.

Annabel Bartlett, a pupil at the Notting Hill and Ealing High School, came to Hamer's notice through friends of her parents, Basil and Mary Bartlett. Her audition for the part had been conducted by Alec; she had read her lines sitting on a trolley at Elstree Studios. Her father Basil accompanied her as chaperone to Nagent-le-Retrou, near Le Mans in western France, where the exterior shots of *The Scapegoat* were filmed. In her hotel bedroom she found waiting for her a book, *Histoire de France*, inscribed: 'This book – just a present to welcome you to the film – is in French, I'm afraid, but I thought you might like it all the same. I hope you will be happy with us and enjoy pretending to be Marie-Noël. Alec Guinness.'

She was also made welcome by Peter Bull: 'Wherever we went, Bully would find the best ice cream.'[436] Irene Worth did Annabel's washing while Alec kept her amused, drawing mazes for her in a notebook and once, while they were waiting for an early-morning shot, drawing a huge maze with a stick on the muddy bank of a lake. However, he warned her against a career in the theatre.

There was constant unease during the making of *The Scapegoat* because of Hamer's drinking. A bender was precipitated by the arrival of the enormously celebrated American actress, Bette Davis, who played de Gué's mother. It was therefore left to Alec to take charge. 'I loaded her with flowers – which she accepted,' he recalled in his diary at the time of her death:

> . . . but she refused all invitations to dinner etc and had no desire to chat. She despised all the British film crew, told me Robert Hamer wasn't a director and knew nothing of films (admittedly Robert was on the way down and deep in drink trouble) and she obviously considered me a nonentity – with which I wouldn't quarrel greatly. But she was not the artist I had expected. She entirely missed the character of the old Countess, which could have been theatrically effective, and only wanted to be extravagantly over-dressed and surrounded, quite ridiculously, by flowers. She knew her lines – and spat them forth in her familiar way – and was always on time. What is called professional. A strong and aggressive personality. After the film was shown (a failure) she let it be known that she considered I had ruined her performance and had had it cut to a minimum.'[437]

The misfortunes of *The Scapegoat*, as Alec recalled, did not end with the last take. Hamer was incapable of applying himself to the editing, and the version accepted by Balcon was rejected by MGM. The American studio recut the film and had Alec record a voice-over narration. 'I have to state,' Balcon wrote to Sol Siegel after seeing the MGM print, 'the reconstructed version of the film shows great ingenuity indeed and in my view a worth-while mystery picture will result, but, alas, not *The Scapegoat*.'[438] The *Sunday Times* film critic, Dilys Powell, concurred. 'The film has an air of a thing cut and then cobbled together again; one would like to know at whose suggestion and with whose agreement.' And Daphne du Maurier was saddened to see the disaster she had predicted. 'I am glad *Scapegoat* is doing good business,' she wrote to Michael Balcon. 'I admit I did not see the finished version, and though cutting obviously quickened the pace I gather certain cuts made nonsense of what was left of the original story. I don't think even the fairest critic had a good word for the "trick" ending, which I knew was hopeless from the start. However, the poor old film got off on the wrong foot from the word go, and I think when that happens ill-luck seems to cling.'[439]

And Alec's final verdict on the 'unfortunate *Scapegoat*', delivered in his diary in 1974, was that it was a film 'we should never have done with the lamentable script we had, nor with dear Bob Hamer directing'. Yet at the time he had exerted a greater power and influence over the production than anyone else: if it had failed, Alec himself was largely to blame.

twenty-nine

Towards the end of the summer of 1958, Alec returned to Kettlebrook Meadows after two trips abroad – the first a holiday in Venice with Merula, Matthew and Peter Bull; the second a film festival in Mexico City. Among the letters that awaited his attention was one from the personal private secretary of the Prime Minister, Harold Macmillan, to say that he was minded to recommend Alec for a knighthood to the young Queen, Elizabeth II.

In his autobiography, Alec wittily linked this offer of a knighthood with his bravura performance before a hostile audience in Mexico City at a time when the British were unpopular in South America for selling arms to the Cuban dictator, Batista. In reality, the knighthood was a proper and inevitable recognition by the British government of Alec's exceptional accomplishments and worldwide fame. Already, three years before, he had been made a Commander of the British Empire; and if, in the usual order of things, he might have been expected to wait for a knighthood until he was rather older than a mere forty-five,

Alec with Matthew and Merula, peeling potatoes for lunch with other company members during the filming of *Great Expectations* (1946).

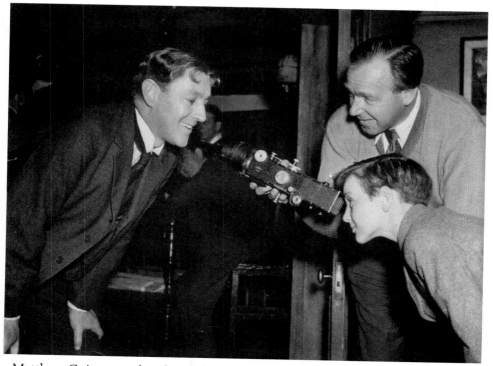

Matthew Guinness, who played the young 'Denry' Machin, looking at his father through a viewfinder held by Ronald Neame during the filming of *The Card* (1952).

Alec as eight different members of the d'Ascoyne family in *Kind Hearts and Coronets* (1949), which earned him his first award. The American Board of Review declared Alec the best actor of the year.

Alec with co-star Joan Greenwood, during the filming of his favourite Ealing Comedy, *The Man in the White Suit* (1951).

Alec with Albert Finney. They later appeared together in the film *Scrooge* (1970) – a musical adaptation of Charles Dickens's *A Christmas Carol*.

Alec in the stage version of Bridget Boland's *The Prisoner* (1954). Playing a cardinal from behind the Iron Curtain, the play influenced Alec's conversion to Roman Catholicism. 'Yesterday, or was it the day before, I had a sudden pull to Rome again – having spent six violently anti-Catholic, almost anti-Christian months. The inner workings getting ready for *The Prisoner* I suppose.'

Alec as Prince Albert and Grace Kelly as Princess Alexandra in *The Swan* (1956).
'For all her sweetness we think she is Miss Enigma 1955–1975.'

Alec as Colonel Nicholson in David Lean's *Bridge on the River Kwai* (1957). Alec quarrelled with Lean over the interpretation of the part but the film was a triumph. Alec won an Oscar as best actor.

Alec as Major Jock Sinclair in *Tunes of Glory* (1960), considered by Merula to be his finest performance on screen.

Alec as Captain Crawford in *HMS Defiant* (1962). 'I look like Edith Evans at a party in an unsuitable hat.'

Alec's photograph of friend and colleague Anthony Quayle, during the filming of *HMS Defiant* in Spain. 'A good man of integrity, fine intelligence and abounding courage.'

David Lean photographed by Alec in Seville, during the filming of *Lawrence of Arabia*.

Alec as Prince Feisal in *Lawrence of Arabia* (1962). Alec was considered too old to play the role of Lawrence.

Photographed by Alec, Omar Sharif during the filming of *Lawrence of Arabia*.

Peter O'Toole in conversation, photographed by Alec on the Gulf of Aqaba. 'He's marvellously good as Lawrence.'

Alec as Adolf Hitler in *Hitler: The Last Ten Days* (1973). Alec considered this to be one of his three best film performances. 'I don't think that in the whole of my professional life I have put so much into a part.'

Alec as George Smiley in 1979. *Tinker, Tailor, Soldier, Spy* revived Alec's screen career after decades in the doldrums.

it would have seemed churlish if this prophet, lauded by the American Academy of Motion Picture Arts and Sciences and acclaimed by *Time* magazine as one of the four greatest actors in Britain, was not recognised in his own country.

Alec's knighthood was principally an official acknowledgement of his talent and achievement as an actor and he told Matthew that he accepted it 'for the good of the profession'. However, like his commission in the Navy, it also established that he was the gentleman he had always wanted to be. Britain at this time was on the threshold of significant social changes but it is important to the understanding of certain aspects of Alec's character to recall the prevalence of class consciousness and class distinctions at that time: disdain for those beneath them in the social hierarchy found among the 'upper' and 'middle classes', and residues of deference in the 'lower' or 'working classes' towards the aristocracy. Both Alec and Merula used the word 'common' to denote the kind of vulgarity and bad taste associated with the lower-middle class to which Alec's mother and his Cuff cousins belonged. Alec's private education at Roborough – 'you're quite wrong,' he wrote to Merula from Buxton in 1938, 'that I didn't go to a public school' – followed by his commission in the Navy during the war had been the necessary *institutional* prerequisites of his status as a 'gentleman'; but there were subjective qualities that were equally important – above all one's *accent*, that could so easily betray the origins of an upstart.

Alec's accent on leaving Roborough would not have been 'common'; Beryl Daniels, the headmaster's daughter, recalled the high quality of his poetry recitals, even as a boy; but it is possible that his lessons from Martita Hunt were not simply to enable his voice to carry into an auditorium but also to distance himself from his common cousins. At times, he tried too hard. 'There's no "r" in "vanilla", Alec,' Gielgud had once said to him in a restaurant in the early days after Alec had asked for a vanilla ice cream, thus humiliating him in front of his friends. But by the time Alec had got to the Navy he was able, with his friend Peter Bull, to assume an upper-class drawl, and later to remark pityingly to Merula on a fellow officer 'who is ashamed to *speak* because his voice is so common, so he *signals* – even when a few feet away'.[440]

Throughout his life, Alec attached great importance to the habits and dress of an English gentleman. Even when he could barely afford to pay his domestic bills, he had his suits made to measure in Savile Row and bought his shirts in Jermyn Street. He employed a chauffeur and, later in his life, banked with the Queen's bankers, Coutts. Corin Redgrave recalled that his father, Michael, was 'in awe of the way Alec adopted the ways of the aristocracy with alarming ease'. Michael Redgrave even suspected that Alec, like Ralph Richardson, was slightly ashamed of being an actor because he did not think it was 'a proper gentleman's profession'.[441]

It is not uncommon for those with a sense of a superior destiny to reinvent themselves: the English shires are thick with pseudo-squires. The process can cause harm, however, to those such as Alec's mother, Agnes Cuff, who cannot be accommodated in the new dispensation. Alec was, throughout his life, a dutiful son in that he provided for his mother and would visit her whenever he could; he would even correspond on the question of her welfare with a Cuff niece who kept an eye on her, but there was never any question of introducing her to his friends.

Alec was also, at times, exasperated that Merula who, though she undoubtedly came from the upper classes, appeared utterly indifferent to the trappings of privilege and ascendancy that meant so much to him. As a child, Merula had been a tomboy; she had never taken a delight in feminine adornments and attire. Alec, now that he was rich, would buy her couture dresses and expensive jewellery which she wore awkwardly. Nicholas Blatchley, Chattie's eldest son, judged that 'Alec would have liked Merula to be more stylish', and Marriott Lefèvre told her daughter Andrée that Merula 'had been like a circus act, going through hoops to be the person that Alec wanted'. Yet, as we have seen with her failure to date her letters despite Alec's persistent pleading, this was not always so. A friend and neighbour of the Guinnesses, Henryetta Edwards, noticed that when Alec and Merula went shopping together in Petersfield, Alec would walk on the other side of the street because Merula was so shabbily dressed.

Also vulnerable to Alec's high standards was his son. Matthew was by nature more like his mother than his father – gentle, easygoing, unworldly, good-humoured. 'One of the remarkable things about him, all his life,' Alec noted in his diary in 1978, 'is that he has never asked for any money. Even as a small boy there was never a request for half-a-crown and [he was] always touchingly grateful when he was given something.'[442]

Matthew was popular with his Salaman cousins when they saw him with their grandparents at Wadlington, or at Eusty Salaman's farmhouse, Slong. He had grown into a marvellous raconteur. 'One evening at Wadlington,' his cousin Nick Blatchley recalled, 'Matthew came by and we sat around the fire in the sitting room and Matthew started telling me this story about a spy and it was *The Spy Who Came in from the Cold* and he told it from beginning to end without drawing breath; it took him four or five hours. We sat there and just listened until two or three in the morning.'[443]

Matthew's career at Beaumont was academically unspectacular. His father told him he had chosen the school because he disliked schoolteachers and wanted Matthew to be raised by men with a higher vocation. Catholic public schools at the time, however, shared the same educational ethos as better-known Anglican institutions. Matthew got his school colours in boxing, was captain of rowing, company commander in the Cadet Force and, in his last year, one of the six captains of the school. Alec followed his progress with a father's usual mix of pride and anxiety. 'Enchanting letter from Matthew this morning informing he'd got 95/100 for autobiographical essay,' he noted in his diary on 26 September 1954. On 13 November: 'Down to Beaumont with Matthew for tea and to see the school play – Ron Williamson's *Gunpowder, Treason and Plot*. Poor play – interesting history lesson . . . The play dragged on and we didn't leave until after 8.00 p.m. Early to bed.'[444]

During the holidays, Matthew was largely left to his own devices. There were occasional joint ventures between father and son. 'Last night Matthew and I devised and made a 75 ft 16mm film about an egg that cracks itself open and only feet marks come out – to meet feet marks from a split onion. Finished this morning. M back to school this evening very cheerfully. He's been excellent company these holidays.'[445] And at the end of the Easter holidays in 1955: 'Matthew returned to school to-day. Think he has been brighter and handsomer and altogether more charming these holidays than ever before.'[446]

These warm feelings, however, and the joint ventures of the mechanically-minded father and son, did not make up for that fear of rebuff that inhibited a physical demonstration of Alec's affection, nor alleviate Matthew's constant fear of the sharp, denigrating remark that would cut him down to size. Alec's own self-esteem necessitated a son he could be proud of, and he could not help comparing Matthew's progress with that of the sons of others – Eusty's son Christopher, for example, who was Matthew's exact contemporary and constant childhood friend; or Michael Gough's son Simon; or Michael Redgrave's son Corin, who had been sent to Westminster, the school at one time envisaged for Matthew.

'Corin turned up from Westminster – very well-mannered, tall, sophisticated, with a slightly patronising air,' Alec noted in his diary on 26 September 1954. Matthew remembered this visit, first because he and Corin detonated a bomb in the garden (each in adulthood remembering the other as reckless and wild); and second, for the change that came over Corin when, having dressed for dinner, he refused to speak to the younger Matthew and when asked by Alec what he meant to do in life, replied: 'I'm going to be Sir Corin Redgrave with my name blazoned in lights all over Piccadilly.'

Alec would have liked Matthew to show the same poise, sophistication and ambition and, like Corin Redgrave, to have gone to Cambridge University. In fact, Matthew's academic aptitude was modest: he failed to pass any Advanced Level exams. He was good at boxing and the Master of an Oxford College offered him a place as a potential Boxing

Blue; but Alec refused to allow Matthew to accept it on the grounds that it would be unjust to deprive an academically more deserving candidate of a place. Later, when there was a chance of Matthew going to Harvard, Alec vetoed it on the grounds of expense. Instead, at the suggestion of Christopher Fry, he proposed that Matthew learn languages, starting with a course at the Italian University of Perugia.

Perugia was a success but failed to give Matthew a clear sense of direction. He spent some months in St Etienne, working with Jean d'Asté's troupe of actors touring in a circus tent. He lived with Chattie, her children, Nick, Jo and Claire, and fell deeply in love with a French girl, Frédérique. 'I've heard nothing from Matthew, have you?' Alec wrote to Merula in April 1961:

> Oh, dear, I do hope he's not just drifting. Love him dearly as I do when nothing happens my mind keeps going back to that day as a small boy when he ran a razor blade over one of your paintings. I'm beginning to find I have to make excuses for him when people ask after him – 'oh, he's in France' – and leave it at that. It's a tiny bit humiliating.[447]

Merula defended her only offspring in a letter that does not survive, to which Alec answered:

> Yes, I am sure Matthew is remarkable, and very good in his heart, but my fear is that unless he holds down a job – and one he likes, preferably – for at least a couple of years – he will distrust himself and his ability throughout life and this will make him unhappy and restless. Well, we shall see. I hope he doesn't get caught up in the theatre – unless it's to write. If he was really interested in the theatre he would be passionate about it, and we would have seen signs of dedication. He's too short for an actor, and he hasn't much sense of timing in telling a story – but when he writes it is all vivid.[448]

Alec had told Matthew to his face that he was too short – above all, that his neck was too short – for him to be an actor. Always appreciative of beauty in the male of his species, one cannot escape the impression that Alec was slightly disappointed that Matthew had inherited the broad shoulders and stocky figure of his grandfather, Michel Salaman. Alec loved Matthew; he was always welcoming when his son turned up at Kettlebrook, and wrote letters full of fine sentiments and good advice; but there was a certain caution in their relations.

Alec was aware that he was the cause of Matthew's wariness. 'It's awful,' he wrote to his son:

> . . . if any horrid mocking tongue has been (or is) a barrier between us or something you fear – it's something I *hate* and don't at all mean – but which I can recognise in myself as the defence barrier I so often put up to either cover my emotions or because it springs naturally from the hurts and pitfalls of my own youth. I hope it is diminishing – and will one day vanish. But believe me, it is *never* intended to hurt or embarrass – and if it has done, I'm sorry, and try to blame my silliness and not me.[449]

Alec confessed to the same shortcomings vis-à-vis his son to a new friend, the Benedictine nun, Dame Felicitas Corrigan. 'He's a good and darling boy,' he wrote at the beginning of May 1962, 'but for all his quiet and rather tough manner I suspect he's a turmoil of fears and indecisions within. I have never helped much because I'm impatient and sometimes caustic tongued – and oh dear, oh dear – the sins of the fathers are visited on the sons in curious ways. Please spare him a prayer.'[450] He feared that he had bequeathed some of his own weaknesses to his son and warned against them even as he tried to build up his confidence:

> I think you are *terribly* forgetful, exasperatingly 'last minute rush' – which is impolite – but you must stop, *forthwith*, thinking yourself useless etc. etc. It *may* take you years to find the feet you want or a direction you want to go in. There is nothing odd in that. And nothing

to be ashamed of. Your French and Italian are small achievements perhaps, but useful ones. And you will add to them. If you have inherited my slothfulness, well I suppose that's my poor example and you can get out of it. I assure you, my dearly loved son, whether you work, or drift, or pass exams or fail them, whether you mend roads, sail ships, invent ridiculous machines, fell timber, take care of the poor, write unpublishable poems – *whatever* you do, or cease to do, you will leave a worthwhile mark on the world. So please, no more of this diffidence. You have a great capacity for enjoying life, so for God's sake enjoy it. The melancholy fit will come and go. I have it now and then, though far less these days.

And he recalled his own fits of depression at Matthew's age:

I seem to remember a time, before I married, when I would lie on my bed reading, perhaps, nearly all day, or walking the deserted London streets half the night out of a melancholy search of I didn't know what. And I was 42 before I found a certain sort of spiritual stability in Catholicism. You will never escape yourself, nor must you try – all you can do as a human being is to *be* yourself and develop. And you will. I write as if you were in distress – I hope you are not, and that if you were the fit has passed.[451]

Merula ascribed her son's unhappiness to the fact that he felt 'that Alec was disappointed in him, and on top of it his girlfriend has turned him down'. Her secret hope, she confided to Dame Felicitas Corrigan, was that Matthew might become a monk. 'For some time I have prayed that he might find some sort of vocation in the worldly sense,' she went on:

. . . but just lately I have dared to express (in a whisper) that he might be led to *a* vocation . . . He is such a darling, gay and funny and warm hearted [person], but he seems incapable of hooking himself on to any line of life, and has the maddest wildest dreams of inventing something to reverse gravity, etc. His mind is always roaming around such subjects . . . Actually, I have always had a thought that he would be a monk since I first clapped eyes on him, but I have no faith in any premonitions. They are mostly wrong.[452]

Matthew was wholly unaware of his mother's pious hopes, and Alec acknowledged that they were unlikely to be fulfilled. 'There was a time when we thought he might have a vocation to the priesthood,' Alec wrote to Dame Felicitas, 'but no, that doesn't appear to have materialised.' If Matthew was not going to be a priest, Alec hoped he might have something to do with the sea and Matthew went to work as an apprentice to some fishermen at the small port of Christchurch in Dorset. When he had learned the rudiments of navigation, he was hired by Tony Quayle to pick up a yacht he had had built in Scotland and sail it to Almeria on the south coast of Spain. Half-way across the Bay of Biscay, however, Matthew decided to give up the sea and try the stage. He would rise above his father's misgivings and be an actor after all.

Alec's reaction to this news was relief that Matthew had finally settled on a profession and only stipulated that he should train in a reputable acting school. Later that year, Matthew joined his father in Ireland: Alec thought he might buy a house there and wanted Matthew to drive him around. It was the first time they had been alone together for more than a few hours since Matthew was a child. Alec judged this time with his son a great success. 'In evening M & I to Redback for excellent dinner & walk along Liffey & its back streets,' he wrote in his diary. 'Felt closer to him than I ever have – since he was a baby anyway.'[453]

A year later, Matthew enrolled at LAMDA and returned as Marriott's lodger to 14 Ladbroke Grove.

thirty

Alec's success as a screen actor in the 1950s led to a decline in the number of his appearances on stage. Apart from his time in the Navy during World War II, not a year had passed between his first appearance in *Queer Cargo* in 1934 and *The Prisoner* in 1954 in which he had not appeared in at least one play – and in some years, as many as half a dozen. After *The Prisoner*, however, four years passed with his only theatre performance being Monsieur Boniface in *Hotel Paradiso*.

It would fill a book to enumerate all the offers that came his way. 'Wrote to Priestley saying I wouldn't do *The Fool* play. Can't give real reason for not doing it.' 'Lunched with Binkie at Scotts. Full of plans . . . He suggested Malvolio in prod. of *12th Nt* . . . *The Little Hut* in N.Y. – *Charlie's Aunt* next Christmas – a tour of *The Apple Cart* – some new play. And so on.'[454] 'To lunch with a man called Legge who wants me to make gramophone record of Eliot's *Practical Cats* . . .' 'Preston Sturges and entourage from Gaumont Francais to see me – asking me to do *Les Carnets du Major Thompson* in Paris.' 'Lot of TV offers from New York – none interesting.' 'To-day I received an offer of $500,000 to play – you'll never guess – Christ . . . I've said No to *Elephant Hide* with Susan Hayward.'[455] 'In the evening Chat & John in for coffee and read aloud first act of *Waiting for Godot*. Do so like this play.' 'In the evening Donald Albery phoned to ask me if I'd start rehearsing *Godot* in a week's time for an eight-week season. This all depends on postponing *The Ladykillers* film for 2 weeks. Maybe.'[456] 'No, I won't be doing *Becket** – I don't believe in it as a film. Warners have offered me *The Devil's Advocate* for next June in Italy which does interest me.'[457] And, on 17 January 1962: 'Declined *Death in Venice* for Zeffirelli.'

Alec later regretted not appearing in Samuel Beckett's *Waiting for Godot* but the film offers came with substantial inducements – and not just cash. Alexander Korda, who wanted Alec to appear in his remake of *The Four Feathers*, tempted him with a painting by Boudin:

> To Korda's office at 10.30 – Alex indicated I could spend a couple of thousand on a picture if I'd do the 5 days in *Four Feathers* for him. May need some sorting out on account of clauses in my Rank contract – but I *do* want the Boudin of Finistère in the Marlborough and I *do* want the big Vuillard at Delbanco. The last price of the latter, when I went in with Vivien Leigh this summer, was £1800. Last year they only asked £900![458]

Alec had acquired a taste for art: the next day he returned to:

> . . . the Marlborough Gallery to see the Boudin again. Like it immensely. They want £2700 for it. Badly framed. Then to Delbanco to see the big Vuillard again. They now ask £2500 for it – but it is

---

*   *Becket*, an adaptation of the play by Jean Anouilh, was produced by John Bryan and directed by Peter Glenville in 1964 with Richard Burton, Peter O'Toole, Donald Wolfit, John Gielgud, Martita Hunt and Sian Phillips. Edward Anhalt won an Oscar for his script and there were a number of Oscar nominations, including for Best Picture.

splendid, and would be fine on the cottage wall which Eusty wanted to have a flint panel. Bought a little Vuillard pastel – of a line of trees. £220. Too much, but it saved me buying a minute Renoir oil sketch for £550.

Five days later, on 20 October, 'At 6.00 p.m. a taxi drew up and two men arrived. They announced "The Picture – from Sir Alexander Korda". And wheeled in the Boudin "Finistere". Unexpected, unarranged for – feel this is bribery and corruption.' Alec hung the picture on his wall. 'The Boudin looks divine – even in this grey depressing light.' However, over lunch at Les Arcs, his agent, Laurie Evans, said 'that the Boudin must go back to the Marlborough Gallery at once – that it's wicked of Korda to have sent it. I agreed – but will probably hold on to it for another day.' On 22 October, 'Took the Boudin back to the Marlborough Gallery. Caused quite a stir, and I was heartbroken to see it go. Called on Korda and explained. He wasn't too bad about it. Suggested I should have *two* pictures – Boudin not enough.'

It is not clear why Laurie Evans was so insistent that Alec should *not* accept the Boudin since Alec was contracted to Korda to appear in four films for a guarantee of £15,000 – one of them an adaptation of Robert Graves's *I, Claudius*. Korda's death in January 1956, Alec wrote to Matthew, placed him:

> . . . in a very tricky professional position for, as you know, I was contracted to do four pictures for him and built Kettlebrook with the money and I haven't done *one* film yet. Well, we'll see what horrors are ahead during the week. Unofficially I've been asked to do a film about Lawrence of Arabia in the autumn, and officially I've been asked to do a film in Hong Kong for April – I want to be able to do the Lawrence, and *perhaps* the other.[459]

Alec's fascination with T.E. Lawrence had followed his reading of Lawrence's *Seven Pillars of Wisdom* and the playing of Ransom, a

character based on Lawrence, in *The Ascent of F.6.* in 1939. The project
he alluded to in this letter to Matthew was not Sam Spiegel's and David
Lean's, but a screenplay by Terence Rattigan for a film that was to have
been produced by Anatole de Grunwald for J. Arthur Rank. Lean, after
Kwai, had planned to make a film about Gandhi with Alec in the title
role. Alec had at first refused on the grounds that Gandhi should be
played by an Indian 'and preferably a Hindu'; but was eventually
persuaded by Lean that 'Indians can't act'. 'Of course, I'm with you
over Gandhi,' he wrote to Lean, 'as you really think I can play it. I'm
not sure I can, but I feel I'm ready to play something big and it might
as well be Gandhi and I could only pull off a really big thing with you
I believe – and that's God's truth. So count on me.'[460]

Meanwhile, while waiting for Lean, Alec accepted the role of
Wormold in *Our Man in Havana*, adapted by Graham Greene from his
own novel and directed by Carol Reed. Greene and Reed had
collaborated on the enormously successful *The Third Man*. Alec liked
Greene and greatly admired his work: his novels were among the
books he kept close to his desk at Kettlebrook Meadows. *Our Man in
Havana* was what Greene at the time called 'an entertainment' (he
dropped the distinction between his entertainments and the more
serious novels when some critics judged the former superior to the
latter) – a witty story of a seedy Englishman selling vacuum cleaners
in Havana who augments his income by selling the concocted fruits of
his supposed espionage to the British Secret Service.

Before the start of filming in Havana, Alec and Merula flew to the
Caribbean with Noël Coward who played Hawthorne, the man from
MI6, for a short stay at Firefly, Coward's house on the north coast of
Jamaica. The visit was not a success. The atmosphere was too
flamboyantly camp for Alec's taste; there was a scorpion by the
swimming-pool, Alec's watch and precious fountain pen were stolen
from the Guinnesses' bedroom; and Coward had a stand-up row with
one of his guests during dinner.

The filming in Havana took place shortly after the city had fallen to
the revolutionary army of Fidel Castro. 'Merula had difficulty getting

a hair-do in the hotel salon as it was always crowded with Castro's officers having their shoulder-length hair permed and their beards curled while they sat, with sub-machine guns across their knees, being flattered and cosseted by adoring Cuban hand-maidens.'[461]

This brush with history was entertaining but the work was professionally unsatisfactory. Alec's concept of Wormold differed from that of the director, Carol Reed. 'We don't want any of your character acting,' he was told. 'Play it straight.' As a result, Alec hardly plays it at all – 'he glides through the picture, colourless, ordinary, negative – a ghost of the Guinness of previous films,' wrote Anthony Carthew, the critic of the *Daily Herald*.

Alec appears to have realised that he was giving a lacklustre performance. 'We plod on in the usual way,' Alec wrote to Merula, after she had returned to England:

> Ernie Kovacs, sweet natured as he is, is driving me mad with his endless jokes about TV stations and general asinine behaviour between takes. Jo Morrow is quietening down a bit – in my presence anyway. I think Carol must have said something to her. There are still a few loud screams of Hi! and O-Daddy-O etc . . . but she's getting better. And the girl has some talent, even if it's not the kind that appeals to me. Burl Ives arrived yesterday, complete with wife, guitar, and personal press agent! He seems very sweet and real. So does the wife. But I have a horrid feeling that as soon as Ernie has finished with his jokes Ives will be singing to me. I've been feeling very glum and down but am better to-day.[462]

It was not just Alec's acting that hampered the film: it was flawed in both its script and direction. It begins as an ironic comedy in the style of *The Lavender Hill Mob* or *The Ladykillers*, and Alec plays it as such; but, with the murder of the loveable old German, Dr Hasselbacher, played by Burl Ives, it turns into an unconvincing Hitchcock-style thriller. Milly, Wormold's pony-mad daughter, was played by an American actress, Jo Morrow, presumably for commercial reasons, and – even though

Wormold is given a line early in the film bemoaning the fact that she has picked up an American accent – is unconvincing. Noël Coward, the old pro, playing Hawthorne, performs with great panache. There were no doubt some sniggers by those in the know during the scene in which Hawthorne tells Wormold to follow him into a gents' lavatory. Coward, too, looks amused: Alec, less so.

The interior scenes for *Our Man in Havana* were shot at Shepperton Studios. 'On 19th May 1959 we started studio work on *Our Man in Havana*, having returned from Cuba on the 13th. Didn't enjoy that film either, except for making friends with Ernie Kovacs. Odd that I should have started two bad and one unsatisfactory film on nearly the same date three years running.'

This was Alec's verdict on *Our Man in Havana* on 19 May 1973, when looking back through his diaries to see what he had been doing on that date over the years – the two bad films being *Barnacle Bill* and *The Scapegoat*. However, he was now shown a script which, with *Kind Hearts and Coronets*, was the second of 'only two I have read with pleasure as something to read'.

This was *Tunes of Glory*, adapted by the author James Kennaway from his novel of the same name. The screenplay was shown to John Mills who at once recognised its potential but realised that it would only raise sufficient backing if he could bring in another star. It was sent to Alec, who committed himself to the project before it had been decided which actor should play which of the two leading characters, both of them Army officers. The first, Major Jock Sinclair, is a brave, crude, heavy-drinking Scot who had come up from the ranks during World War II, temporarily in command of an elite Scots regiment; the second, the upper-class Oxford and Sandhurst Colonel Barrow who is sent to replace him. John Mills, in his autobiography, wrote that he and Alec first thought to toss a coin to decide who should play which role, but then agreed on what he called 'off-beat' casting – Alec as the swaggering Scot, Mills as the gentlemanly Barrow.

The choice of director and the casting of *Tunes of Glory*, however, suggests that, as with *The Scapegoat*, Alec had considerable influence over the production: despite the mediocrity of his last three films, he still retained what Hollywood termed 'muscle'. The unflamboyant but highly competent Ronald Neame (who had directed *The Horse's Mouth* and *The Card*) was engaged to direct *Tunes of Glory* and a part was given to Alec's friend Richard Leech. Kay Walsh, Nancy in *Oliver Twist*, was cast as Sinclair's some-time mistress, Mary; Dennis Price, Louis Mazzini in *Kind Hearts and Coronets*, played Sinclair's unctuous friend, Captain Charles Scott. With Price and Mills in these lesser roles (because, despite Mills's contention that Sinclair and Barrow were dramatically on a par, Sinclair's is a far more challenging role and hence has the potential for a virtuoso performance), it almost seems as if Alec – despite having upstaged these actors in the earlier films – was here intent on driving home his triumph over his rivals.

If this was so, it was no doubt unconscious, but it gave a frightening edge to Alec's performance. Jock Sinclair, the military upstart, hiding his sense of inadequacy and insecurity behind a facade of brash and bullying bonhomie, undermines and finally drives to suicide, his neurotic, pedantic rival for the command of the regiment, Lt. Colonel Basil Barrow. Mills is good as Barrow but Alec is astonishing as Sinclair. Mills twitches to suggest the damage done to his nerves as a prisoner-of-war in World War II; but Alec, with a ginger moustache and toupée, exudes the inner rage of the insecure *parvenu* in an officers' culture that rates the Etonian Barrow's Oxford degree over Sinclair's natural qualities of leadership and courage in the field.

Kennaway's script – balanced, tight, efficient – is reminiscent of *The Caine Mutiny*, which Alec had seen in the summer of 1954 and greatly admired; and there were qualities in Major Sinclair comparable to those in Colonel Nicholson in *Kwai* – and, indeed, in Alec. Both officers had Alec's 'chippiness': and, just as the pedantry in Alec's character enabled him to give such a convincing performance as Nicholson, so the dark, domineering side to his nature was given free rein in the role of Jock Sinclair.

The quality of the acting in *Tunes of Glory* was recognised by the critics when the film was released though some, such as Ellen

Fitzpatrick in *Films in Review*, thought that Alec should have played Lt. Colonel Barrow and John Mills Jock Sinclair. 'I understand such casting was the original intention. Whoever wacked it around certainly wacked the profit-potential of the film.'[463] John Mills won the award for the Best Actor at the 1960 Venice Film Festival, which Alec had won for his Gully Jimson two years before.

If Alec felt any disappointment, it must have been mitigated by a letter of congratulation from Laurence Olivier. 'I do think it is a wonderful and illuminating study and the Scots conveyed so superbly in gesture and bearing as well as accent gave an extraordinary truth to all of it – particularly passages of extravagant or high flown expression and the superstitious side of him came to life in an extraordinarily clear and true way . . .'[464] And, more importantly, by the enduring judgement of Merula that it was the best thing he had done:

> I was absolutely thrilled with *Tunes of Glory* last night – it must be the best film ever, and your very finest perf. I can't remember if it's the 3rd or 4th time I've seen it, and each time has been more exciting than the time before. I think it's because the direction is so straight forward, with no fancy tricks, it doesn't date, and the story and the acting are so strong. I was as spellbound as if I had never seen it before, and could have sat it through again . . . Oh I do love you, and admire you, over and over. There, I've had my rave. Don't forget I love you more than the whole world – sometimes I don't think I let you know well enough. Merry.[465]

Alec, too, felt that this had been his best screen performance to date. What he could not have anticipated at the time – he was still only forty-six – was that he had reached the summit of his career as a film actor. In no subsequent leading role in a feature film would he approach, let alone surpass, his inspired characterisations in his mid-forties of Colonel Nicholson, Gully Jimson or Jock Sinclair.

thirty-one

On 14 May 1960, Alec returned to the London stage to play Lawrence of Arabia in *Ross* by Terence Rattigan, directed by Glen Byam Shaw. Ross was the name taken by T.E. Lawrence, Lawrence of Arabia, when he attempted to escape from his fame and from himself by joining the RAF as an Ordinary Airman. Alec was, as Bernard Levin, then the theatre critic of the *Daily Express* wrote at the time, 'the only possible choice for this strange, contradictory ascetic . . .' There was not only a passable physical resemblance but Lawrence had long been the object of Alec's interest and admiration. Like Alec, he had been born out of wedlock and, like Alec, had been tormented by his unacknowledged homosexuality. That, at any rate, was the hypothesis put forward by Rattigan's play. And Lawrence had qualities that Alec would *like* to have had: he was learned – fluent in Arabic and Ancient Greek – and, as he showed with his memoir, *The Seven Pillars of Wisdom*, a considerable writer. The worship by Rattigan's Lawrence of 'a false god . . . the will'[466]; his love for his young Arab servant, Hamed;

the diplomat Ronald Storrs's view that Lawrence was 'strongly introverted, withdrawn and self-conscious, and will never allow anyone to see his true nature'[467] – all had parallels in Alec's character and condition.

To prepare himself for the part, Alec went to talk to some of the people who had known Lawrence – Alec's old friend, Sydney Cockerell ('He was a terrible fibber'), Robert Graves, David Garnett and Siegfried Sassoon.* With the help of these reminiscences, and by his own easy identification with the character of Lawrence, Alec gave a memorable performance. The play itself had started as a screenplay, and came across on stage, in the view of Robert Tanitch, 'like some discarded film script in which the locations have been left out';[468] but it had one or two nice ironies, and a few dramatic moments such as the close of Act I when Lawrence announces the capture of Aqaba. The most arresting scene, which had all London talking, came in Act II, Scene IV, when Lawrence, a prisoner of the Turks, is beaten and buggered by his captors off-stage.

The play's premise, somewhat far-fetched, is that this is done on the orders of a Turkish general who has discerned the homosexual masochism that Lawrence has been hiding from himself: rather than create a myth and a martyr by executing Lawrence, he intends to precipitate his psychological breakdown – 'bodily integrity violated, will broken, enemy destroyed'. Credible or not, the dramatic effect caused the requisite stir. The young Tom Courtenay saw the play three times: 'Alec was extraordinary . . . The main thing was his powerful presence. You could read his thoughts.' John Mortimer long remembered the 'extremely vivid walk of someone who had just been buggered' and even Donald Wolfit, the extrovert actor much mocked by the Gielgud circle, was impressed by Alec's performance:

---

* Alec wrote to Sassoon asking to pay a second visit but received no reply 'so I assumed,' he wrote to Dame Felicitas Corrigan, a friend of Sassoon's, 'that I was *persona non-grata*' – AG to Dame Felicitas Corrigan, 6 June 1963.

I set myself to do a theatre round. 2.30 'Ross' at the Haymarket where I saw some of the worst settings (by Motley) and some of the worst acting I have ever seen at the Haymarket. Dear oh dear – but Guinness redeemed all as I told him afterwards – it's a film scenario of a play – 4 good scenes. But the climax was buggery you know.[469]

Alec's admirer Evelyn Waugh was dragged to see *Ross* by his daughter Teresa. 'She made me go to a play about Lawrence of Arabia,' he wrote to Nancy Mitford. 'All the actors except Sir Alec Guinness were comic buggers & the plot was all buggery – as far as I can gather false to history.'[470]

On the first night of *Ross*, Rattigan came to Alec's dressing-room while he was making up and gave him 'the Eric Kennington portrait of Ali Ibn el Hussein which was reproduced in *The Seven Pillars of Wisdom*, and a beautifully leather-bound manuscript of the play.'[471] Alec was touched to receive these gifts but, hating to be encumbered by memorabilia, he passed them on at the time of Rattigan's death – the manuscript to the actor Simon Ward who had played Lawrence in an Old Vic production of *Ross*; and the portrait of Ali Ibn el Hussein to Rattigan's 'intimate friend for many years', who was none other than the 'pansy' friend of the Salamans, the ballet dancer Billy Chappell!

That a play with a 'plot that is all buggery', as Evelyn Waugh put it, should be staged at the Theatre Royal, Haymarket, in May of 1960 shows the extent to which the parameters of what was acceptable to a West End audience had changed. The law dating from the mid-eighteenth century which required that all plays be licensed by the Lord Chamberlain was still in force – it was not abolished until 1968 – but the days were gone when a play that made so much as a fleeting reference to homosexuality could only be staged in a private theatre club. Though nothing was explicitly stated, the off-stage anal rape of Lawrence was as clear to members of the public as it was to Tom Courtenay, John Mortimer, Wolfit and Waugh.

In taking the part of Lawrence, Alec must have been aware that he was not only portraying a historical figure with whom he felt some degree of affinity and whom he greatly admired, but also that he was conveying to the public – which was still, by and large, averse to the idea of 'queer' sex – that the homosexual condition is to be found in heroes like Lawrence, and that the condition itself is not something to which one should attach blame.

In this regard, Alec was a man of his time. The Home Office committee under Sir John Wolfenden that had been set up in 1954 to consider the law relating to homosexual offences had published its report in 1957. Of the thirteen members of the committee, twelve recommended that homosexual behaviour between consenting adults in private should no longer be a criminal offence. Its recommendations were accepted and passed into law by a Labour government in 1968.

However, Alec was determined that *he* should not be taken for a homosexual. He was furious when his friend Richard Leech told him that actress Coral Browne had said that he 'had been cottaging again'. 'Cooked bacon and eggs for Richard Leech. Upset at him repeating to me gossip about me put out by Coral Browne. More cross in my heart with him than Coral.'[472] The next day, after going to confession in Westminster Cathedral, and perhaps soliciting the priest's advice, he lunched with Binkie Beaumont and his agent, Dennis van Thal (he had by then left Laurie Evans), after which the three went to see Coral Browne in her dressing-room where Alec threatened her with legal action. She did what she could to wriggle out of her predicament by saying that she had been totally misunderstood: she had merely said that Alec was doing up a *cottage* in Ennismore Garden Mews.

Coral Browne, and her reputedly homosexual husband Vincent Price, subsequently became two of Alec's closest friends, as did Tom Courtenay, who had so admired Alec's performance in *Ross*. A year or two later, when he was making *King and Country* for Joseph Losey, Courtenay came across Alec in Paris in the company of a louche homosexual film producer, James Woolf. 'Alec was very fond of Jimmy Woolf because he was very camp, wicked. I remember Jimmy Woolf saying; "Oh, he'd much rather be shacked up with some nice young man".' Courtenay spent an evening with Woolf, Noël Coward, Peter Glenville, Alec, and some other good-looking young men who became 'the object of their camposity – their jokes . . .'; but Courtenay was never afraid that Alec would make a pass at him, if only because of his religious convictions. Jimmy Woolf and the actor, Vernon Dobtcheff, both referred to Alec as 'a certain Holy Person'.

Thus it would seem that Alec enjoyed the company of homosexuals, and a degree of voyeuristic flirtation with handsome young men. There is an undated letter from Peter Bull in the Kettlebrook archive which suggests a continuing interest in sailors:

> . . . in re Not very ordinary seaman caplin. nocaps caplin I call him . . . Please (and now I'm being pompous) don't get too taken up with him because although he is, in my opinion, one of the most remarkable people I've met in my life, some of his letters even shock me, with their complete lack of discipline, and though the actual phrases used and experiences related are so vivid that you can't forget them, he is perfectly liable to do something quite dotty which may embarrass any of us without his meaning to. He might easily break ship and swim to Plymouth and announce to a delighted Press that he loves Sir A, and wants to show it.

It is difficult to ascertain whether Alec, who had read so widely in the fields of Christian theology and church history, accepted the Church's teaching that sexual intercourse is only licit between a man and his wife – and then only where the act is open to the creation of new life. If Satan's fall was, as some theologians have suggested, caused by envy of man, then the great Adversary and Prince of Lies takes particular delight when the procreative end of the sexual act is thwarted. The Catholic Catechism describes sodomy as a sin 'crying out to Heaven for Vengeance', while Pope Paul VI's 1968 Encyclical, *Humanae Vitae*, which gets no mention in Alec's diaries, described contraception as 'intrinsically evil'.

The difficulty faced by Alec when it came to sexual relations between members of the same sex was that, though it was condemned by the Catholic Church and all monotheistic religions, it was so prevalent among those he loved in the acting profession that he could not see it as intrinsically evil. He accepted that mortal sin meant death to the soul and consequent damnation; he went frequently to confession to receive forgiveness and absolution for *his* own sins; but, while he acknowledged that Christ told his disciples '"be ye perfect" . . . common sense shouts that this is not an overnight or, for most of us, even a lifetime's achievement'.[473]

In his wartime letter to Chattie Alec had defended the Church's teaching as the bulwark of order, but his greater experience of life, and perhaps of his own weaknesses, had made him indulgent towards his friends' disordered desires. Faith might be the first of the three 'theological' virtues, and Charity the greatest, but there was also Hope: and Alec did not seem to believe that John Gielgud, Peter Glenville, Peter Bull, Val Stavredi, Terence Rattigan, Michael Redgrave, Binkie Beaumont, Jimmy Woolf, Quentin Stevenson, Keith Baxter, or any other of his many homosexual friends were evil people destined for Hell. Quite to the contrary, he saw only too clearly that the life of the homosexual, far from being a riot of delighted debauchery, was more often one of loneliness and confusion. He had a particular sympathy for those who, like Ernest Milton, Michael Redgrave, Bobby Flemyng and Alec himself, wrestled with disordered passions while trying to keep their marriages, their families and their homes intact.

Nor did Alec believe in the traditional concept of Hell. 'I believe time ceases for the individual at death, so there can be no after-life (as there was no before-life) but that probably the personality lives in God's keeping,' he wrote in his diary on 14 December 1976; and, on 2 January 1982:

I get very put off by people who look at the after-life – if it exists – as a cocktail-party attended by one's dead friends and billions of others, where one waves happily to Mary Queen of Scots, Shakespeare,

Socrates and a few Catholic saints. Very exhausting for the VIPs to be continually on show. The vision of God, whatever that may mean, seems to get by-passed. Perhaps he is expected to just put in an appearance now and then as some giant genial host. 'Let me introduce my Son!' No, none of it will do. And yet I believe in the existence of a heavenly state and a hellish one. And why is eternity always thought of as length of time, when presumably time will no longer exist – if that is imaginable . . .

Alec showed little interest in the cause of the homosexual condition. During his lifetime the Judaeo/Christian view that homosexual intercourse was an offence against both divine and natural law was undermined by the perception of homosexuality 'as a "biological" rather than a psychological condition, as a destiny rather than a choice'.[474] Between these two, was the view that homosexuality was a psychological disorder: however, Sir John Wolfenden's committee had rejected the virtually unanimous evidence presented by psychiatrists and psychoanalysts that homosexuality should be regarded as a disease on the grounds that 'in many cases it is the only symptom and is compatible with full mental health in other respects'.

There was then, and there remains in Britain, considerable scepticism about psychoanalysis as a science. The authors of the 1957 Wolfenden Report, particularly Sir John Wolfenden himself, whose son was homosexual, were predictably reluctant to accept a hypothesis that saw the cause of homosexuality in the failure of a child in the first eighteen months or so of its life to establish a gender-defined identity because of an absent, passive or otherwise unsatisfactory father. In Alec's case, however, sexual attraction to other men was not the only symptom of a disordered condition. Others were depression, boredom and an exaggerated need for approval from others. Alec 'was so touchy,' Matthew recalled. 'Hypersensitive. He could take umbrage or offence at the smallest thing.'[475] 'He was like someone without an outer skin,' wrote Merula. 'He bled . . . If our daily lady forgot to say good morning he would be convinced that she was about to give notice.'[476]

While some homosexuals may identify with their mothers and develop a gentle, 'feminine' persona, others, some psycho-analysts suggest, fear 're-engulfment' and see their mothers as a threat. Alec's dislike of his mother appears pathological: 'The most depressing thing I have to do nowadays,' he wrote to Dame Felicitas Corrigan shortly after appearing in *Ross*, 'is to call on her, in her little villa in Winchester, because I know I can never make contact and my heart becomes a stone whenever I see her.'[477] Matthew recalled how, when he drove his father to Winchester to see Agnes, Alec would never sit down but would wander around the room looking at her pictures and knick-knacks while she followed his every movement with adoring eyes. His lines as the Cardinal in Bridget Boland's play, *The Prisoner*, might have been his own: 'I never learned to pray for her;' 'She is supposed to be someone I love.' 'I do not love my mother. I never have.' 'The flesh . . . weak . . . Unclean flesh . . . my body . . . of her flesh and blood . . .' 'I became a priest because I wanted to feel clean.'

Boland's psychological insights into her character may seem unsophisticated but Alec was able to recite his lines with some conviction. He was, Matthew recalled, embarrassed by his body. While Merula had inherited the Salamans' lack of inhibition, Matthew never saw his father naked. The only full-length mirror at Kettlebrook Meadows was in the guest bathroom.

Alec had many friends who were women: Chattie, Marriott, Bridget Boland, Margaret Leighton, Mu Richardson, Annie Gough, Leueen MacGrath and her step-daughter Anne Kaufman, Percy (Margaret) Harris, Veronica Turleigh, Ros Atkinson, Jehane West, Eileen Atkins, Jean Marsh, Jill Balcon, and the Benedictine nun, Dame Felicitas Corrigan – yet he had a strong streak of misogyny and would sometimes express a prejudice against women that Eileen Atkins found baffling and irrational. 'Now I've known that ever since I started doing *A Room of One's Own,*' she wrote to Alec:

. . . that you disapproved of Virginia Woolf and anything she might have written, *that* you made abundantly clear. Being polite you booked to come but must have been very relieved that a rail strike excused you. It makes me sad to think that you can't appreciate her brilliance & wit but why you should take so against so many women of brilliance and wit is a mystery. You, of course, mention the three that I have played, or in Vita's case adapted, but in the past you've said you didn't want to read George Eliot (mainly because of her looks apparently) and some months ago you burst out on the 'phone to me 'I'm *sick* of women.' As you were speaking to one I thought this rather rude but held my tongue. (You are also married to a remarkable woman whom I presumed you weren't sick of!)[478]

Merula *was* a remarkable woman, as Eileen Atkins realised, and she was right to presume that Alec never grew sick of her. She was the only woman Alec said that he loved, and there can be no doubt that he meant what he said. Even if they stopped sleeping together ten years or so after Alec's return from the war, there remained an exceptional intimacy between them. In the 1950s, Matthew recalled, they used to dance to gramophone records at Kettlebrook Meadows, and in the 1970s they became keen on opera: they would listen to an opera as they ate supper in the evening. Theirs was a true marriage of minds. Alec relied on Merula in choosing his roles and was particularly nervous on-stage when he knew that she or Matthew were in the audience. He was more open-minded than Merula when it came to choice of friends but usually deferred to her judgement. They would read the same books so that they could discuss them, and shared a love of plants, animals, music, travel and, above all, the theatre.

However, Alec's treatment of Merula was frequently cruel. It was not only that he forced her to abandon her career. Almost all his friends testified to the way he frequently humiliated her in front of others. Jehane West ascribed it to his lack of confidence in himself. 'Alec's cruelty to Merula . . . that again is insecurity. Striking out. Striking everyone away except me.' Jane Cornwell (wife of John Le Carré): 'He was so disparaging of Merula. He would say, "Merula, who understands nothing of my life".' Jill Balcon: 'If she hesitated over something that she was trying to say, he would pitch in . . . He would pounce. And he was horrible about her cooking.' Anne Kauffman-Schneider: 'He was occasionally rude to Merula. He was rude about the food. The food was fine.' Eileen Atkins: 'When I first knew him he used to be vile to Merula, and to Matthew. I can be like that – we're twin souls, somehow. He'd say to her "the dinner is disgusting, it's uneatable". And it wouldn't be at all.' And according to Alan Bennett:

> He always put her down. The first two or three times I stayed there, he would always disparage the food – 'I'm sorry about this' – when in fact she was a good inspirational cook; she could conjure something up out of nothing; and I used to have two or three helpings which proves that it wasn't just politeness, and gradually he stopped being like that. It was sheer nerves. I am sure that it extended to other departments – about the way she dressed and so on.

Bobby Flemyng, who appeared with Alec in *The Cocktail Party* in New York, told Sam Beazley that Alec 'was awfully sharp with Merula and that she was rather frightened of him when they were in America. I found that most distressing'. Richard Leech told Matthew that he was 'sometimes quite appalled by the things that Alec said to Merula'. Natasha Harwood recalled a painful dinner at Kettlebrook:

> It was Shrove Tuesday. He rang up and said come over, we've got eggs and pancakes. Eggs meant a huge bowl of caviar. And champagne. And vodka. And all that may not have helped his mood. And afterwards, Merula had gone to get this filet of beef. It wasn't overcooked – brown and crusty on the outside and pink on the inside; but Alec got in a state and so started mimicking like a schoolboy bully. He was doing it on purpose – needling her and embarrassing her in front of us.

On one occasion, when he was aged fifteen or sixteen, Matthew was so appalled by his father's verbal bullying of his mother that he intervened, saying, 'Don't talk to my mother like that' – using exactly the words and tone that Alec might have used to him. Alec immediately went up to his bedroom, packed a suitcase and left for London. Merula was distraught and begged Matthew to apologise to his father, which he did when Alec returned the next day.

Alec consistently demeaned Merula's attempts to develop her talents as an author and artist. He effusively thanked those who bought Merula's embroidered pictures as if they could only possibly have made the purchase from the kindness of their hearts; and accused Merula of putting pressure on their guests to buy her wares. 'It wasn't very kind of Alec to say I foist my works on all our guests,' Merula wrote to Anne Kauffman, 'it's not a BIT true, there are very few who even *know* I have been *published* and that I have a store of works that never come out of their hidey hole. Of course, he was embarrassed, poor darling, he gets particularly embarrassed by my efforts for juveniles. Maybe because of his unhappy childhood, or maybe just because he doesn't like them.'[479]

A psychoanalyst would no doubt concur that Alec's cruelty to Merula was 'because of his unhappy childhood', though by 'childhood' he or she might mean the first two or three years of infancy rather than those later years in boarding-houses and residential hotels. The absence of a father with whom he could identify in his formative years would, at least from a Freudian perspective, explain not just Alec's misogyny but also his homosexual tendencies – and his ambivalent attitude towards that homosexuality.* The analyst might also see some connection between Merula's docile acceptance of Alec's occasional cruelty to her passion for her father that followed the beating with a riding crop. She herself attributed it quite simply to her unquestioning, unconditional love of Alec. 'My darling,' she wrote to Alec on the occasion of their fiftieth wedding anniversary:

For 50 years I haven't been able to say I love you, I love you, I love you,

---

* See Charles W. Socarides, M.D., *The Pre Oedipal Original and Psychoanalytic Therapy of Sexual Perversions*. International Universities Press, Inc., Madison, Connecticut, 1988.

it sounds silly before it comes up into my mouth, and I am grateful for
your care, and trust, and consideration, and constancy and for you just
being you, and somehow with all the partying I haven't had time to say
thank you for marrying me, and staying with me, and I am not
worthy . . . Forgive this – I just feel FULL – and don't want you to feel
depressed. Always always yours forever most beloved spouse.

'I had a wonderful talk with Merula once,' Eileen Atkins recalled:

I used to go out for a walk with her – with three dogs and four goats –
we were chatting on about the theatre . . . I was probably moaning a
bit. And she said, 'Oh, you're all so unhappy in the theatre. You're
always worrying, rushing about, thinking you should be doing
something else' . . . And I said, 'But Merula, that's what we're
enjoying . . . that's part of it. And I had heard that you were a
wonderful actress. Doesn't it in any way infuriate you that Alec made
you give up? You might have turned out to be the better actor.' And she
said, 'It made me very unhappy for a long time. I wanted to act. Then
one day I thought, Well, Merula, either you can spend the rest of your
life being unhappy because you're not acting, or you can give in and
decide to be happy.' And she said, 'I gave in and I've been very happy
ever since.'[480]

thirty-two

'A happy life between us,' Alec wrote in his diary on his fifty-ninth wedding anniversary, 'but I often feel M has had a raw deal.'[481] Alec was aware not just of his everyday shortcomings but also of the disordered and destructive impulses latent in his character. Like T.E. Lawrence, he believed in the ability of the will – Dr Jekyll – to contain the amoral libidinous drives of Mr Hyde. One mechanism of control was his practice of the Roman Catholic religion: its strict code of conduct showed the path to follow, however steep and stony it might seem; the sacrament of confession salved his conscience when he sinned; and the saints to whom he prayed interceded for him. He experienced moments of almost mystical ecstasy in the presence of the Blessed Sacrament:

> . . . I was walking up Kingsway in the middle of an afternoon when an impulse compelled me to start running. With joy in my heart, and in a state of almost sexual excitement, I ran until I reached the little

Catholic church there (St Anselm and St Cecilia) which I had never entered before; I knelt; caught my breath, and for ten minutes was lost to the world.[482]

There were other ways, too, in which Alec sought to enforce and monitor his self-control. The first was his handwriting which, he tells us in *Blessings in Disguise*, his friend Sydney Cockerell had deemed 'unformed' – urging him to develop an italic script and sending him as a model the handwriting sheets of a Benedictine monk at Ampleforth, Dom Patrick Barry.* Cockerell himself had a tiny, neat italic hand which Alec greatly admired. In fact, the handwriting Alec had learned at Roborough was clear enough; but it did become, by dint of practice, exquisite. Alec frequently copied out poems or passages from spiritual works such as St Augustine's *Confessions*. He was always buying new pens and liked nothing better than to sit down before a clean sheet of paper. All his many letters were hand-written and there is rarely a word crossed out. His italic script was a means both of concealing his character from an imaginary graphologist and of confirming to himself that he was in control. When he went through an occasional spiritual crisis as, say, towards the end of January 1971, when he 'felt very feeble mentally and spiritually', he would practise his handwriting to regain his composure.

Alec's second further means of monitoring his own behaviour was to start keeping a record of his daily activities in a small leather-bound diary, measuring around four by five inches with a page for each day. The first diary, bought from Fortnum & Mason in 1961, contains only a record of his expenses while abroad. On 1 January 1962, however, he begins – as did Queen Victoria and Sir Sydney Cockerell – with a record of the weather: 'Snow as from yesterday morning – three or four inches, six in part': most entries start with a record of the weather. Alec liked to look back through these diaries to see what he had been

---

* Dom Patrick Barry, OSB, later both headmaster and Abbot of Ampleforth.

doing on a particular day over the years. The last entry was made on
22 July 2000, just two weeks before he died.

He had kept an intermittent journal since the war, and that too – as
he wrote on 9 September 1992 – was 'an attempt to discipline myself
a little'; but from the very start he failed to record incidents or thoughts
that might prove shaming on later reading: 'This diary is no longer
objectively true as I intended it to be,' he wrote on 10 September 1946.
'Omissions creep in.' Almost thirty years later he described his diary
disparagingly as his 'disjointed, self-conscious rather prissy, fairly
reticent "journal" or whatever'. The reticence was because Alec
wanted it to be a mirror in which he could see the man he wanted to
be – devout, sagacious, ironic, observant, cultivated, well-read. He
drew on the large diaries for *My Name Escapes Me* and *A Positively Final
Appearance* – his published Diary and Journal.The rare references to
anything awkward are found in the Small Diaries' record of day-to-day
events.

It was the same with most of Alec's letters that have come to light,
in particular his long correspondence with Dame Felicitas Corrigan. He
had first met her through Sydney Cockerell who, though not a
Catholic, had been a friend of the Abbess of Stanbrook, Dame
Laurentia McLachlan. He had introduced Dame Laurentia to George
Bernard Shaw and a celebrated correspondence between the Catholic
nun and the atheist playwright had followed. A selection of Cockerell's
own correspondence with famous people, including Alec, had been
published in 1956 as *The Best of Friends*:* Cockerell's biographer, Wilfrid
Blunt, though he conceded that Alec's letters revealed him as 'the
possessor of a serious and searching mind', also felt that some of
Cockerell's correspondents whose letters were *not* included in his book
'were all more worthy of inclusion, if being "the best of friends" was
the criterion of admission, than many of those who bore a more
illustrious name but whose letters were, in fact, often less interesting'.

---

* Later dramatised and staged in the West End with Gielgud as Cockerell, Alec having
  turned down the role.

Alec was aware of Cockerell's weakness. 'It's impossible,' he had written to Merula towards the end of the war, 'not to come to the conclusion that the nice old boy was a ferocious Lion Hunter, and that his entry card to the private lives of the great was largely a matter of pointing out niggling "errata" in their works.'[483] But in his new role as a serious-minded Roman Catholic, he was glad to make the acquaintance of Dame Felicitas, this remarkable nun who was a friend of the poet Siegfried Sassoon, the novelist Rumer Godden (whose novel *In This House of Brede* depicted an abbey like Stanbrook); and who, Cockerell judged, 'is a very wonderful woman' with 'a livelier sense of humour and a wider outlook than Dame Laurentia'. It was Dame Felicitas who appears to have initiated the correspondence: the first letter to her from Kettlebrook was from Mollie Hartley-Milburn, Alec's secretary, and began 'Dear Father Corrigan'! Alec himself wrote to her from the Imperial Hotel in Tokyo: he and Merula had travelled to Japan both to take a holiday to see Alec's old friend from wartime New York, Val Stavredi, and above all to absorb Japanese culture for the role Alec was to play in Hollywood in *A Majority of One*. He would write more than eight hundred letters to Dame Felicitas over the next forty years.

A second cleric befriended by Alec following his reception into the Roman Catholic Church was the Jesuit priest who had received Edith Sitwell, Fr Philip Caraman. The son of an Armenian banker and an Italian mother, Caraman was educated at the Jesuit public school in Lancashire, Stonyhurst, where a fellow pupil was Peter Glenville. On leaving school he joined the Society of Jesus and became a protégé of the Jesuit provincial, Martin d'Arcy, whose book on Love had helped lift Alec out of a depression in August of 1946. As editor of the Jesuit Order's learned journal, *The Month*, Caraman came to know Catholic writers such as Edith Sitwell, Evelyn Waugh and Graham Greene. In 1959 he was asked to promote the canonisation of forty English and Welsh martyrs during the reign of Elizabeth I. To assist him in this work he recruited Evelyn Waugh's favourite daughter Margaret, her sister Harriet, and a number of other young ladies.

In the early years of the 1960s, Alec spent long periods of time abroad. The spring of 1961 saw him in Hollywood filming *A Majority of One* for director Mervyn Le Roy. Once again, he rather enjoyed mixing with the stars. He met Groucho Marx and Marilyn Monroe. 'She's a bit dippy but there's no doubt she has charm and appeal and personality. Saw Zsa-Zsa* to-day who has got so stout I didn't recognise her. But she was as funny as ever.'[484]

He was less amused by an item in a gossip column that he was having an affair with the actress Merle Oberon. 'The *Hollywood Reporter*,' he wrote to Merula:

> . . . an idiotic local daily film rag – had a paragraph last week implying that Merle was trying to break up my home. Great foolishness – and I've never even seen her alone. They didn't mention names but the paragraph read 'Ex English film beauty star tries to trap English knight thespian currently here' – so two and two were rapidly put together to make sixteen. But the people who matter know it's nonsense and I only hope poor old Merle isn't damaged by it . . .[485]

Alec became involved in a fracas at a party when:

> David Selznick accused me of being anti-Semitic because I did *Oliver Twist* and then offered to punch Peter Glenville on the nose for being 'sophisticated' and 'not caring about six million Jews having been exterminated'. Eddie Goetz† rolled his eyes to heaven, breathed hard and clutched my hand . . . Mr Louis Jourdan made things worse by pretending to calm everyone. I was rather loud and flushed to begin with but did keep fairly calm. I can't remember how it managed to simmer down. Never seen Peter loudly angry before. It all caused

---

*   The much-married Hungarian movie star, Zsa Zsa Gabor.
†   David Selznick and William Goetz were the sons-in-law of the head of MGM, Louis B. Mayer.

quite a stir. This is the first time this visit that I've seen that sort of ugliness. But Selznick is a sort of mad man and a huge ego maniac.[486]

Alec became a support to the family of Gary Cooper as Cooper lay dying. 'He came out of a coma yesterday morning and asked his wife to send me a message, which was just "please get hold of Alec Guinness and tell him in my opinion he is the greatest actor in the world" . . .'[487] After Cooper's death, Alec went to his Requiem Mass with Peter Glenville, Eddie Goetz, Mel Ferrer and Audrey Hepburn:

> It was at the expensive beige carpeted Church of the Good Shepherd. Very sweetly and impressively done. Singing was good, the Bishop who spoke the Eulogy was very striking and I would judge a good and sincere man, and for all the rich black Paris models that were being worn it had an odd simplicity and was most moving. The most remarkable feature, I suppose, was the discretion of the press photographers and the quiet un-pushing, un-pointing un-hysterical nature of the rather large crowd gathered outside the church.[488]

The filming proved unsatisfactory. The screenplay of *A Majority of One* had been adapted by Leonard Spigelgass from his stage play that had enjoyed a successful run on Broadway. It is the story of a romance between a Japanese widower, played by Alec, whose daughter died in the American bombing of Hiroshima, and a Jewish-American widow, played by Rosalind Russell, whose son had been killed by the Japanese in the Pacific. Laurie Evans, Alec's agent, had negotiated a fee for Alec of £70,000, and Alec was later to say that he did it for the money; but the fact that he had gone to Japan to prepare for the role suggests that he saw playing a Japanese as an opportunity to extend his range. However, he found the director, Mervyn Le Roy, incompetent. 'It's the WORST DIRECTED FILM I've ever been in,' he wrote to Merula, 'and Mervyn *doesn't know* it. He's well satisfied. The set of my Japanese house is good, and the garden charming, and it's all pretty accurate – but believe it or not Mervyn has had it all bathed in green, pink and blue light to *give it colour* – so it looks like an Oriental brothel.'[489]

When the filming was finished, Alec concluded that he was sure 'the film is tedious to a degree, but I must admit I have enjoyed it'. However, the reviews when it was released were damning, singling out in particular the miscasting of Alec as the Japanese Koichi Asano. Alec looked for a scapegoat for this setback and found one in his agent, Laurie Evans. He dismissed him and moved his custom to Dennis van Thal.

Alec returned to England on 8 June. At the end of the month, feeling the need for spiritual replenishment, he made a retreat in the Trappist Monastery of Mount St Bernard. In July he took Merula to the Holy Land and then, while she returned to London, he went on to Aqaba where David Lean had started filming *Lawrence of Arabia*.

Despite his success as *Ross*, Alec was deemed too old to play Lawrence by both David Lean and Sam Spiegel, who was producing the film. The part went to the young actor Peter O'Toole, and Alec was offered the smaller role of Prince Feisal after Laurence Olivier had turned it down. Although he had balked at playing an Indian – Gandhi – and had fallen flat on his face as the Japanese Koichi Asano, Alec seemed happy to try his hand as the Arab Feisal. He had learned from *Kwai* that Lean, however difficult, could elicit a fine performance and produce an outstanding film. He was also happy to be working with old friends in the profession such as Jack Hawkins, Anthony Quayle and many of the technicians. '50% of the unit I know,' he wrote to Merula, 'which is nice, either from *Kwai* or *Havana* days and even *The Ladykillers*'.

The part, as written by the playwright Robert Bolt, was admirably suited to Alec's particular talent. As Kenneth von Gunden put it in his *Alec Guinness. The Films*, Feisal 'the consummate politician, is also a minimalist, just as Guinness is a minimalist actor. Acting, like politics, is about revealing only what is necessary. Emotion and expression must be parcelled out sparingly. To give away too much too soon is to overplay one's hand; what is left unsaid is as important as what is spoken aloud.'[490] No other role would fit his style and character so well until he came to play John le Carré's George Smiley; but Feisal was essentially an impersonation – one of the small parts he played so well.

Alec spent two and a half weeks in Aqaba for the exterior scenes, shot in the desert, in which he is seen mainly on a horse. 'I'm now at Aqaba – however it is spelt,' he wrote to Merula on 23 July 1961, 'and the Red Sea is lapping my shoes fifty yards away. I've been lent David Lean's comfortable and air-conditioned Nissen hut but the conditioning packed up a couple of hours before my arrival'. Six days later, Peter O'Toole arrived with his wife, Siân Phillips:

> I'd only met him for a few minutes before, after *The Long & The Short & The Tall* – and I must say I'm very impressed by him. He has great wayward charm and is very striking in eye and carriage. Wife seems nice too. There's a charming and most intelligent Egyptian actor here as well called Omar Sherif [sic], who is the matinée idol of the Middle East. The few others are a bit nondescript and uninteresting . . .
>
> I have now done the first and most essential of the two scenes I have to do here. I enjoyed it a lot. *I* think I look quite too gorgeous and very like Feisal. Two old Bedouin who were in Feisal's entourage started to prostrate themselves when they saw me, thinking a Resurrection had taken place, and I don't think they quite believed it when they were assured I was only a singer and dancer. Auda's grandson – aged about sixty – is a charming small hawk, all wrapped around in deep but dirty black, and is the star camel rider of the desert. He speaks no English but then one great golden smile coming out of the beach and he grasped my right hand in both of his and held it to his heart yesterday which was most touching . . .[491]

To play the Prince, Alec had to take riding lessons 'with a v. nice Etonian type called Maj. Jeremy Taylor'. However, after five one-hour sessions Alec still found trotting 'well nigh impossible for more than a few paces – I bounce around like mad – but a tiny canter or two I did this morning I found, surprisingly, rather more comfortable . . . Anyway, I've stayed on to date. But it's clear to me – and must certainly be to the gallant major – that I shall be unable to do the full requirements of the film and a clever double will have to do the galloping over the desert.'

Alec's relations with Lean were good:

I find David much less knotty and more cosy than in *Kwai* days. Mind you we haven't had much of a chance yet to get to loggerheads, but for the moment all goes swimmingly between us and there is no doubt about it – he is a truly *great* director, and is becoming a rather great man I think. I suppose it's the new wife has relaxed & humanised him . . .

I like O'Toole *very* much – and his wife. He's marvellously good as Lawrence. He's dreamy good to act with and has great personal charm and gaiety. He obviously goes off the rails every now and then and I should think his wife – who has a sort of strength & wisdom about her – has got as much as anyone could handle, but he has a good heart and wit as well . . .

After completing his external scenes for *Lawrence of Arabia* on 10 August 1961, Alec returned to England for a mere ten days before leaving for Spain to film HMS *Defiant* (called *Damn the Defiant* in the United States). This was a naval adventure in the C.S. Forester tradition, set at the turn of the nineteenth century, and was widely regarded as unworthy of one of England's greatest actors. Alec played a Captain Crawford who attempts to mitigate the sadistic impulses of his second-in-command, Lieutenant Scott-Paget, played by Dirk Bogarde. There is a battle, a mutiny, and conflicts between discipline, patriotism and natural justice, but the sum of the parts is mediocre. Quite what attracted Alec to the project – apart from the substantial fee that he could now command for any role he chose – is unclear. He liked the sea, liked working with friends such as Tony Quayle, and perhaps saw more in the character of Captain Crawford as an embodiment of the best traditions of the British Navy.

As usual, things started well. 'I've done my first day on the new film,' he wrote to Merula:

> I look rather gorgeous, I think, in my uniform; it's a pity I'm just playing a dummy. It's a pleasant unit and the actors seem a fresh lot, and I like Brabourne* & Lewis Gilbert – though the latter is not going to be my favourite director. He's very sweet and alive and good-natured and enthusiastic, and I imagine is a good technician, but no ideas (I suspect). Ah well, I knew these things before I started and I don't think I shall be unhappy except for the knowledge of the feeble perf. I must give.[492]

Little more than a week later, Alec's spirits sank further:

> I feel very gloomy about the film. Lewis Gilbert and Brabourne are very sweet but have a sort of old pro attitude whereby anything is o.k. and it's all very sloppy and my part is too dull & gloomy for words. Dirk is quite sweet but he bears no resemblance to any naval officer and is totally un-period in manner and looks. He's gay and amusing but pretty silly.

And by the end of August, they had sunk further still:

> The film itself doesn't bear thinking about. All concerned are pleasant enough, but the script is so awful and ignorant and the dialogue so fake and the whole thing, direction, production, clothes, everything, so utterly careless, and Brabourne & Lewis Gilbert are smugly delighted with the horrors they are perpetrating. It's the worst I've ever been involved in. And I look like Edith Evans at a party in an unsuitable hat.

---

* John Brabourne, the producer.

Alec was no happier when, back in England, he came to the end of shooting the interiors. 'Goodness this film is tedious,' he wrote to Matthew, 'and I'm at my most feeble worst. Never again shall I play a "straight" part. Dirk is good. And Tony Quayle. But it's such rubbish I blush at what I have to say and do. Ah well, only a few more hours. There's a slight end of term feeling to-day. I must now go and get blown up – again.'[493]

At least, while back in London that autumn, Alec could see his friends. He was compulsively hospitable, giving dinner – mostly at the Connaught or the Caprice – to personal and professional friends. In the autumn of 1961 he entertained Eusty and Mary Salaman, Omar Sharif, Kay Walsh, Marriott Lefèvre, Peter and Natasha Brook, Jimmy Woolf, Anthony and Dot Quayle, Charles and Sonja Frend, Robert Graves, Richard Leech and Fr Philip Caraman, Peter Glenville and Bill Smith, and Coral Browne. On 19 November he gave a small cocktail party at the Connaught to which he had invited Albert Finney, Peter Bull, Robert Graves, Graham Greene, T.S. Eliot, Veronica Turleigh, and her husband James Laver. After the party, he gave dinner to Peter O'Toole, Martita Hunt and Jimmy Woolf.

The cost of his constant and lavish hospitality was carefully noted in his diary: the cocktail party cost £38, the dinner £36 and tips for the staff at the Connaught came to £8. His bill at the Connaught, he noted ruefully when he checked out on 20 November to return to Kettlebrook Meadows, was £227, 'not chargeable to expenses' – in today's money, around £3,000. Alec always paid the bill and made it plain in his diary that he did so; it was always 'dinner to a friend', never dinner with. Only rarely would he allow others to pay a restaurant bill, or for anything else. He also gave money to his nephews and nieces and old friends who were down on their luck. After lunch with Ernest Milton on 22 October 1954, Alec noted: 'He's in a very bad way all round – morally, financially. Gave him a cheque for £100 and a copy of The Wilder Shores of Love.' In Ceylon when filming Kwai he gave £50 'to an English soldier whom I liked v. much and found in a sad state waiting for a plane to take him home to his mother dying of cancer'. When Sydney Cockerell fell ill, he sent him 'an enormous bunch of expensive pink roses'. On 2 January 1962: 'To bank and drew £100 for Robert Hamer . . . Lunch with Robert at Pruniers. Pale, but rather smartly turned out for him and in not bad form.' When he visited Dame Felicitas Corrigan at Stanbrook Abbey and saw that the rheumatism in her hand was preventing her from playing the organ, he insisted that she have private treatment: 'I will pay for the consultations and treatment . . . I have no idea what it might cost me initially but anything up to £250ish will leave me undisturbed, and if it's more than that I can find more – with ease.'[494]

'When I rattled off to you the other day a list of people whom I had helped financially in 1962,' he wrote to Merula on 12 January 1963, 'I left some out but realised later, with disquiet, that I had included Mike Gough. Can't think why – haven't had to help them in years. What awful tricks the brain plays.' He sent a cheque out of the blue to Corin Redgrave when he was at university, sent 1,000 francs to Marriott when she was going to Paris with a list of restaurants where he recommended it be spent, and put a hundred dollars into a Chase Manhattan bank account for his nephew Toby Salaman when he heard he was going to New York. Also, after lunch in a smart restaurant to which Toby had turned up wearing a polo-necked jersey, Alec – after writing a cheque to pay the bill – had written a second one for £100 made out to Toby, which he passed under the table, saying, 'Buy yourself a decent suit.'

In Alec's *Commonplace Book*, published posthumously, there is a quotation from William Blake: 'He who would do good to another must do it in minute particulars. General Good is the plea of the scoundrel, hypocrite and flatterer.' This sentiment coloured his attitude towards the high rates of taxation levied in Britain at the time to pay for the Welfare State. 'It's hideously too much,' Alec remarked of a 'Supertax' demand in 1952. He had seen Michael Redgrave forced to sell Bedford House in Chiswick to meet his tax demands and Robert Newton made bankrupt by the Inland Revenue, owing £46,000.[495] He kept a close watch on his own expenditure, noting the cost of each item in that 1961 diary, listing his regular monthly payments to Merula and Matthew; and his annual Standing Orders to the Athenaeum and Garrick Clubs, the Automobile Association, the London Library, Actors' Equity and the Actors' Orphans' Fund, and a summary of the state of his finances on 20 November 1961: £11,000 in his current account, £47,722 in his deposit account and, in a second tax reserve deposit account, £115,180 – the equivalent, in 2003, of £1,500,000.

Alec's generosity in this period, the cost of running two houses – Kettlebrook Meadows and Ennismore Mews – the salary of a gardener, a cleaning lady and Fred the chauffeur, together with the need to have the best of everything himself, would all have been affordable thanks to the enormous fees that Alec was paid by the film industry, had it not been for the high marginal rates of tax: as much as eighty-five per cent on high incomes, with a fifteen per cent surcharge on 'unearned' income such as dividends or interest. His expenses were just affordable *after* tax but Alec, who had seen the luck turn of so many actors, had no confidence that he would continue to command such large sums of money. It was for this reason that, in the last months of 1961, he planned to take a 'tax holiday' by becoming non-resident in the United Kingdom for the tax year 1962–1963. 'So from early January,' he wrote to Matthew, 'I shall be out of the country until May 1963. Sad, but if it enables me to keep even half of the money I've earned this year, worth it, as I shall never earn like this again.'[496]

thirty-three

In the first three months of 1962, Alec travelled to and fro between London and Seville, where David Lean was using the Moorish palaces for the interior scenes of *Lawrence of Arabia*. 'Jack [Hawkins] is here,' he wrote to Merula on 20 January 1962:

> . . . and I think in rather a poor way, poor old thing. He's so very shaky – his hands tremble all the time, and having had the top of his head shaven to play Allenby (it looks like a blue egg – rather flat though) he looks wounded in his pride. Claude Rains is here too, and is a dear.
>
> O'Toole's Arab servant Shufti as well, looking (and probably about to use) daggers at Mrs O'Toole. I haven't seen *Mrs* Lean – she leaves next week I believe – but that is all v. sad I gather.* She won't go out

---

* Lean's marriage to his Indian wife Leila was breaking up and he was having an affair with the continuity girl – a New Zealander in her early forties, Barbara Cole.

because she will wear saris and that makes the Spanish stare. Tony is very fond of her and distressed for her. David seems OK and less beady-eyed than usual – though not exactly cosy; I mean I would have thought a drink might have been offered or an introduction made to his wife or something on my first day. On the other hand he did have a vast bowl of dead carnations sent to my funeral parlour . . .*

Alec's admiration for Peter O'Toole had cooled, largely because of O'Toole's excessive drinking. On 3 March Alec, O'Toole, Tony Quayle and Jack Hawkins were entertained to dinner by a Spanish grandee at Domeque's new bodega in Jerez. O'Toole got drunk, quarrelled with his host, and threw a glass of champagne in his face. 'O'Toole could have been killed – shot, strapped or strangled – and I'm beginning to think it's a pity he wasn't.'[497]

When the filming moved to Almeria on the south coast of Spain for more location shooting, Alec shared a villa with Tony Quayle. Fred, his chauffeur, had driven out from England and Alec planned a motoring holiday up the coast of Spain to Barcelona and on to the South of France. 'I long for you to join me in France,' he wrote to Merula on 20 March, 'or indeed anywhere – but NOT here.' He took against Almeria – 'its rubble, its dirt, its puddles flecked with petrol, its hawkers of second-hand umbrellas, etc. etc. and oh etc.'[498]

Alec was assiduous in his Catholic devotions, always going to Mass on Sundays and frequently during the week. In Seville he went to confession:

. . . an enchanting young middle-aged priest who said he spoke English. That was a bit of an exaggeration and we got in such a muddle & slightly giggly that we had to almost abandon the grille and lip read each other. I was somewhat startled by my penances! I was expecting a few simple Hail Marys – but no – he said, 'For two hours when you next are filming, you will make mental reparation for all the bad films'.

---

* Alec's room in the Hotel Alfonso XIII.

That is when we had to start lip reading. I've rather abandoned trying
to work out what he means and will do my own penance.[499]

24 March was the sixth anniversary of Alec's reception into the
Catholic Church. 'It seems a long time when I look at myself,' he
wrote to Dame Felicitas, 'and view my impatience, my sharp tongue,
my sloth, deceit, weakness and grosser sins; and it *is* a long time when
I consider my total ignorance of so many ecclesiastical and spiritual
things. Yet I think I am as happy about it as if it were only last
week.'[500]

On 6 April, Alec finished filming and set off the next day, driven
by Fred, for the South of France, stopping for three days in
Barcelona. He reached St Jean Cap Ferrat on 12 April and moved into
a 'rather creaky ramshackle hotel which belongs to friends of ours
in England', the Hotel Voile d'Or*. Unable now to return to England,
Alec remained there for just under a month, whiling away the time
reading the four novels of Lawrence Durrell's Alexandria Quartet:
'They are not for nuns, I fear,' he wrote to Dame Felicitas, 'and often
barely escape pornography.' Merula came out from England with his
dinner jacket, and Matthew joined him from Almeria after delivering
Tony Quayle's yacht. On their last evening, he and Merula went for
drinks in Tony's Riviera villa with Alec's old friend Glenn Ford.

On 10 May, Fred and Matthew went back to England and Alec and
Merula embarked on the yacht *Clonsilla*. This belonged to Honor
Svejdar, formerly Honor Guinness, whom Alec had met on board the
Queen Mary when she invited him to 'take tea with your cousin': she
was quite convinced that Alec was the son of her uncle Walter
Guinness, Baron Moyne.

The *Clonsilla* was a far cry from LCI (L) that Alec had commanded
during the war. '*Very* impressed by the yacht,' Alec wrote in his small
diary. And to Dame Felicitas:

---

* The hotel was owned by British film director, Michael Powell.

I always like prayers for those in peril on the sea – but the private and luxurious yacht I was in is a tiny liner – with stabilisers and every modern navigational aid and splendid radar instruments which show you the outlines of coasts up to 48 miles away, other ships, rocks and even very large waves. And there are other gorgeous instruments which draw you pictures of the sea bottom as you peer over it. And the clever thing steers herself, if you can tell her where to go.[501]

It was while on this cruise that Alec heard from Dame Felicitas of the death of Sydney Cockerell and how, when in a coma, the determined agnostic had been baptised, or had received the Church's sacrament of Extreme Unction.* 'I received your letter about Sydney's death just before leaving St Jean Cap Ferrat. What you told me I will not repeat, though I feel I must say it's the sort of thing I can't say I approve of. I feel the mercy of God is more embracing than any ceremony. Is that my old Protestant upbringing poisoning my Catholicism?'[502]

In the same letter he described to Dame Felicitas a semi-mystical experience when, in the small Corsican port of Bonifacio, he had gone into a tiny church on the quayside on a Saturday evening:

> . . . and knelt in a dark corner where I could see the Tabernacle. I started to say the Glorious Mysteries on my rosary. I became aware that I was near a hideous plaster statue of St T. of Lisieux. Gradually my senses were overpowered by the scent of roses. I looked round the church – there were some lilies before Joan of Arc, and some Sweet William and droopy carnations on the altar, and some wild flowers in a jam jar near Our Lady but no *roses*. I thought, 'I'm *imagining* things.' This curious awareness of roses came over me four or five or six times – I'm not sure. I was very happy with my meditation. On leaving I saw that I had been at the side of a very dark smokey painting – which I could barely make out – in which I could dimly see three white roses floating. I went back

---

* This is a deduction from Alec's letter to Dame Felicitas: her letter to him does not survive.

on board. A little later Merula went into the church (I hadn't told her what had happened) – and she said that while she was there bunches of roses were brought from the sacristy to place at the feet of St Joan. So my 'experience' was no more than the scent of roses brought on a draught from the sacristy. And yet. And yet. And yet I am not totally satisfied with that explanation . . . There have been times when I have thought I could easily 'catch' the numinous; some have been true, I am sure, and others self-deception. It is for me, I suspect, a dangerous area.

The cruise ended on 26 May at Catania, from where Alec and Merula flew to Rome where Alec said a 'rather melancholy au revoir to Merula' who returned to England. Bridget Boland, now a close friend of Alec's, had a flat next to the Palace of the Grand Master of the Knights of Malta overlooking the Forum of Trajan; and his agent, Dennis van Thal, was visiting the city with his wife Mary.

On 11 June, he flew from Rome to Boston where he was to receive an honorary doctorate from the Jesuits' Boston College. 'The Jesuit Fathers here have been most kind and jolly and relaxed and attentive and hospitable,' he wrote to Dame Felicitas. 'I had a lobster dinner with a dozen of them at a ramshackle beach-house last week.' However, as so often, Alec was distressed by aspects of American Catholicism:

> I felt *obliged* to complain to one of them, a good friend of mine, of how Mass was said at the St Francis Xavier chapel. Seven minutes flat from the opening of Mass until the end of the Gospel and nine minutes from the beginning of the Credo to the end! . . . The sign of the cross was reduced to a hurried scratching of the stomach and the 'elevations' were so blasphemously hurried that I thought there might easily be an accident. Oh dear oh dear oh dear. And why why why? I found it very disturbing. I wrote an angry note to the priest in charge and then tore it up as useless as well as uncharitable.[503]

During his year in tax exile, Alec missed the theatre. 'I'm doing something rather surprising,' he wrote to Merula from Boston:

I'm learning *Lear*. I don't know whether I want to play him or not. I think I do, but in a very *small* and obscure theatre – somewhere where the critics couldn't or wouldn't descend with their pre-conceived ideas, and a first night audience wouldn't arrive pre-bored. I still cling a bit to my post-atomic war idea so far as clothing is concerned. I'm not *in love* with the idea but cannot loose it from my mind and the imagery it carries – old tweed suits and Edward VII type hats. And why is Lear always presented un-bonneted? It is clear in the text it is unusual and outrageous for him suddenly not to have his bonnet. A niggly thing – which would be as tiresome to an audience as Hamlet's beard. People don't listen. More and more I know people don't listen and very rarely look. And if they do they leap to conclusions that were already in their minds *before* they looked and listened. The innocent eye and ear must be hard to come by.'[504]

From Boston Alec flew to Dublin where he was joined by Matthew and the two set off to look at properties in Connemara. Alec envisaged 'a simple house in good repair, with 20 or 30 acres at the most, a fine view and fishing near-by' but found that 'the houses the Irish build are so hideous, unless they are Georgian mansions, or they have so many hundreds of acres attached that they become not only prohibitive financial but moral responsibilities.'[505] Towards the end of June, he flew to Berlin to receive the David O. Selznick Gold Laurel Award, for adding to international understanding, at the Berlin Film Festival – somewhat ironic, since David Selznick had accused him of anti-Semitism – then back to Paris where, on 1 July, the Feast of the Most Precious Blood, he went to confession, Mass and communion at the Madeleine church:

Walking back down the aisle I was hailed by Graham Greene. This is the second time we've met in a strange church within the year.* Joined

---

* The previous occasion had been at the Jesuit church at Farm Street eighteen months before.

him at noon for drinks at his flat in Blvd Malesherbes. A pleasant large room but very bare. Then we lunched at the Lancaster – caviar & champagne and got a bit high & confidential. All very enjoyable.[506]

The two men also talked business: Alec agreed to play the priest in a film of Greene's play *The Living Room*.

Alec went back to Ireland and, for most of July, stayed in the Old Courra Hotel at Bray, near Dublin, serving at the Mass said each morning by an old friend, Canon Cathal McCarthy, in his room – 'altar on chest of drawers, screen around the bed – all very touching'. He kept in touch with his agent, Dennis van Thal. 'The rain falls softly,' he wrote to Dame Felicitas. 'A lamb is bleating. An obviously coarse-minded and over lengthy film script called *The Fall of the Roman Empire* has just been dropped like a load of turf by an express postman. They ask me to play Marcus Aurelius. In Madrid. In November. The money would be good. But I would prefer Greene's legless priest in *The Living Room* . . . But the Crash of the Roman Empire will have to be waded through I suppose.'[507]

Merula joined Alec in July and they paid a visit to the Guthries at Anna-ma-kerrig, before going to stay with Honor and Frankie Svejdar on her estate in Phibblestown, Co. Dublin where Fr Philip Caraman was a fellow guest.

Honor Svejdar was a recent convert to Catholicism. Enormously rich, even by the standards of the Guinnesses, she had first married the Conservative politician, 'Chips' Channon – an amusing diarist and a homosexual. Honor was obsessive: her son Paul recalled how, when she had developed an enthusiasm for horse-racing, he had not seen her for six months and then, suddenly, when he asked after her race horses, found that she had lost all interest.

It was in her horse-racing phase, during the war, that Honor Channon had set out from London to take the boat train to Ireland, discovered at Paddington station that the Holyhead ferry had been cancelled because of bad weather, and returned home to find her husband Chips in bed with Terence Rattigan. She had turned on her heel and left both the house and her husband. Her son Paul, to whom Rattigan had dedicated his play *The Winslow Boy*, was sent to the United States to live with the Astors. It was said that during the war Honor Channon had had a number of passports made out in different names so that she could spend the night in hotels with different lovers. On VJ Day, so the gossip ran, she had been to a victory celebration at the officers' club of the Czech air force at their base at Northolt which had turned into an orgy. She woke the next morning with a Czech navigator, Flight Lieutenant Franztec Svejdar, the man she subsequently married.

The story of her conversion to Catholicism begins in Victoria Street in London where, leaving the Army & Navy department store after doing some Christmas shopping, it started to rain. Honor took refuge in the nearby Roman Catholic Westminster Cathedral and there had a vision 'probably of the Virgin Mary – which left her certain that there was truth in religion. She began to investigate religion with the same single-mindedness she had shown in learning Ancient Greek or taking up horse racing'.[508]

One of those who helped her with her researches was her 'cousin' Alec. Writing to Merula about his failure to bring Marriott Lefèvre into the Church, Alec claimed that 'the only person I have been able to help or do anything for in this direction has been Honor, and God knows what blunders I may have made there – though she will be received this summer.'[509] One of Alec's ways of helping Honor was to introduce her to Fr Philip Caraman, and it was he who received her into the Church.

A second cruise on the *Clonsilla* was planned for September 1962, but Alec's exile had led to a state of religious elation – 'a sort of second spring spiritually,' he wrote to Dame Felicitas, despite 'coming ghastly croppers every half hour or so, snapping at taxi drivers, snubbing gushing women, smoothing my wounded pride, etc.' At the end of July, he cabled Dame Felicitas to ask for a letter of introduction to the Abbot at Subiaco in Italy. There, besieged by journalists, he made a

four-day retreat which he describes in *Blessings in Disguise*. From
Subiaco Alec went to Rome, having been lent Bridget Boland's flat. He
went to Mass and communion every day.

Merula joined Alec at Athens on 3 September; four days later they
flew to Rhodes to join the Svejdars, Fr Philip Caraman and two friends
of Honor's, Janet Vigors and Anne Feversham*, on board the *Clonsilla*.
The yacht was a welcome refuge from the journalists and paparazzi
who pursued Alec wherever he went. But a month on the yacht
brought irritations of another kind:

> We spent a couple of rough and dangerous days – terrible winds
> beating down from the mountains – but more distressing by far has
> been a growing dislike I have found for my host, whom I find so rude
> to his wife that it is embarrassing and who is a fibber to put it mildly
> and, oh, oh, oh – *my* lack of patience and charity have come whizzing
> to the surface. It got so acute a few days ago that Merula and I
> wondered whether we shouldn't leave the boat at Athens – but all is
> calmer now and I pray that all will remain so. I *do* find it hard when
> very rich people don't say 'thank-you' for small services rendered by
> fishermen, or simple people ashore. A question asked, the answer
> charmingly given – and no 'thank you'. I rush around after them
> bowing, scraping and smiling saying 'Efharisto'. It's depressing . . . It's
> good for me, no doubt, to see a glimpse – in caricature – of my own
> failings – or at least a few of them, and to guess, shamefacedly, how
> often I have been rude to people, often quite deliberately. And then
> their suspicions about being cheated in the markets etc. etc. – and how
> often I detect myself suspecting people of taking advantage of me.
> *Fortunately* I have the *Imitation*† with me so I get some nasty jolts about
> myself each day almost. I don't want to carp, I hope, but any account

---

*   Anne, Countess of Feversham, was the daughter of the Earl of Halifax, High Church
     Anglican, Foreign Secretary and British Ambassador in Washington during World War
     II at the time the embassy was asked to give Alec leave to appear on Broadway.
†   *The Imitation of Christ* by Thomas à Kempis, a 15th-century work of spiritual guidance.

of my luxurious travels wouldn't be *quite* true without an indication of the occasional distress and unpleasantness of the human element.[510]

It particularly pained Alec that the Svejdars should treat their captain, an ex-naval officer, as a servant: it pained the captain, too, who was driven to resign. At one moment, Alec was obliged to take command of the boat. The cruise came to an end when the *Clonsilla* reached Malta on 6 October. Two days later Alec and Merula saw Honor and Frankie Svejdar off at the airport. 'I wonder if they feel as relieved at seeing the back of us as we do them. It feels like a weight lifted.'[511]

thirty-four

Alec and Merula remained in Malta for another week, giving a holiday to Bridget Boland. 'We enticed her to Malta for a few days,' Alec wrote to Dame Felicitas. 'She is in low spirits . . . a lapsed Catholic. She is always most loyal . . . about the Church but, as she says, she "just doesn't believe". And her lack of belief is distressing her.'[512] Then Alec flew to Rome and Merula to England to face a domestic crisis. Fred, Alec's chauffeur, had been rude to Merula on her return. 'Merry on phone distressed about Fred's behaviour,' Alec noted in his diary, 'so sent a telegram sacking him on the spot. Sad after 6½ years but it's very much his own fault and maybe he needs the change and companionship. Felt beastly all afternoon . . . An odd disjointed and sometimes tearful evening.'[513]

Fred was an orphan – a Barnardo boy – from Portsmouth who had been a submariner during the war, and had served in the Merchant Navy. He had a rough, working-class accent and lived in a shed about three hundred yards from the house, using the lavatory and wash basin by the utilities room in the main house. He acted as Alec's dresser and chauffeur. The Guinnesses' first car was a modest, second-hand Standard Vanguard, the second a brand new Triumph Renown, followed by a Triumph Mayflower and finally a Bentley. Merula refused to drive the Bentley, thinking it too big and grand, and later Alec changed it for a three-litre Rover. There was also a Riley, which Merula liked to drive at high speed.

Fred had great charm. He would spend his evenings playing darts at the Harrow, a pub a short walk from Kettlebrook Meadows. Matthew, whom Fred taught to drive, remembered him as 'very gregarious in a pub kind of way: his life off-duty was down at the Harrow. He charmed the pants off American middle-aged ladies; my father would send Fred to pick them up at the airport and they raved'. Merula got on with him well enough but 'was always nervous when Alec was away for any length of time'. When Alec was at Kettlebrook, Fred would never dare ask to borrow the car; but when he was away he would come to Merula and ask, 'Would it be all right, Lady Guinness, if I took the car to Portsmouth?'. Matthew was fond of him, but when Alec and Merula were away on their cruise of the Mediterranean he came home unexpectedly to find Fred sitting in the drawing room drinking whisky with half-a-dozen villainous-looking friends. He cabled his parents and when Merula returned, Fred behaved insolently towards her and was dismissed.

Since Alec had to remain abroad until at least 5 April 1963, he was in no hurry to replace Fred; but in June the post was filled by a member of the crew of the *Clonsilla*, a young man from Glasgow called Rob*. Alec seems to have taken to Rob and kept in touch with him after the cruise. Photographs in the Guinness family album taken on the *Clonsilla* show him to be slim and pleasant-looking. He was young – around Matthew's age – and one of his first tasks, other than driving Alec up to town, was to build a hay barn near to the shed that had been Fred's living-quarters and was now his.

---

* Not his real name.

Alec would retire during the day to an office adjacent to the
chauffeur's room, which he called 'the hut'. 'He used to write in the hut,'
recalled his friend Mark Kingston. 'Alec would say "I'm going to the hut"
and no one would have dared disturb him there . . . It used to be full of
LPs.' Alec now had, as it were, a small shore-based boat with a one-man
crew that was not only a refuge from the domestic life within the house,
but also from what he referred to as his 'alleged' secretary, Molly Hartley-
Milburn. 'She used to be an actress (no talent)', Alec told Dame Felicitas:

> . . . and she was largely responsible for my getting my drama-school
> scholarship at age of 19 or 20 as she was one of the 'Judges'. Didn't know
> me. But she was good to me as a student. She fell on evil times and some
> 11 years ago I offered her a temporary part-time job and a flat at the top
> of our house in London. That lasted a couple of years. Then 4 years ago
> I offered her a job again – as secretary – with only a 2 year guarantee. She
> is a *hopeless* secretary and I'm afraid horribly bossy to anyone else we
> employ, putting their backs up, and like all lonely people she talks and
> talks and talks, and is very jealous of some of our friends and her
> CATHOLICISM is really ST. JUDISM* and sends us up the wall. She is
> tactless (in front of Protestant or atheist friends) and often uncharitable
> and is off to Mass & Communion almost every day. She is also, I may say,
> devoted to us – though perhaps a little frightened of me. Matthew can't
> stand her gush . . . Well, that's poor Molly Milburn, an ornament of the
> Church, a battle-axe for every rumour of the improbably miraculous.[514]

Alec's last months as a tax exile in the spring of 1963 had been spent
in Spain filming *The Fall of the Roman Empire*. In this story of the long
and gory vendetta of Marcus Aurelius' son Commodus against the
Roman General Livius, Alec played the stoic Roman Emperor Marcus
Aurelius. His daughter Lucilla was played by Sophia Loren.

Alec took the role because he had withdrawn from the proposed

---

*   St Jude, one of Christ's apostles, is traditionally the patron saint of hopeless causes.

film of Graham Greene's *The Living Room* and, if he had to remain out of the country, he might as well spend the time making more money. He shared the billing with Christopher Plummer, Mel Ferrer, James Mason, Eric Porter, Omar Sharif and his old friend, Tony Quayle, with whom he made himself comfortable in a seventeenth-century farmhouse. But the script did not improve in the acting: he found it 'painful rubbish, and if only I *liked* Marcus Aurelius'.[515] The exterior scenes were shot in bitterly cold conditions and, though he told Merula that he had 'quite a regard' for the American director, Anthony Mann, who did not sell himself 'as "the great director" in the way David too often does', he thought the script 'contemptible', and found it 'not uninteresting to be in the worst film ever conceived'.[516] Together with *A Majority of One*, he judged it 'absolutely shaming' and claimed that he had never seen more than twenty minutes of the finished product.

Alec took to Sophia Loren – 'Very warm and sweet-natured and professional and fun,' he wrote to Merula on 15 February; and, five days later: 'Sophia Loren is a *dear* and you'd like her a lot. Quite the nicest and straightest of those film gals I've ever met. *Fairly* good at the acting – but should be a comedienne.' Alec as the world-weary Emperor was considered by Penelope Gilliat, the distinguished film critic of the London *Observer*, to be 'perfect casting for the part, a natural stoic if ever our neurotic age possessed one'; and the film received some favourable reviews in London but was slammed by the critics in New York, where Alec happened to be when it was released. *The Fall of the Roman Empire* ran for over three hours; the Roman forum built in Spain was the largest set to date in the history of the cinema; it lost over $18,000,000 for its producer, Samuel Bronston, and did little to enhance Alec's reputation.

Alec's own financial position, he confided in Dame Felicitas, was affected by 'the news that £60,000 which should have been mine has been trickled down by American Big Bizniss into something nearer £13,000 – after eight years' work in a 50–50 partnership with an American film enterprise. Wicked stuff, but I can't, legally, say they are *dishonest* – only sharp and over business-like. Clearly I have thought too much of money during the past eight months – well, there it is.'[517]

As a result of this débâcle, Alec was tempted to avoid tax on the money he earned from *The Fall of the Roman Empire* by remaining abroad for a second tax year but, as he told Dame Felicitas, Providence advised him against it during Mass:

> I went to Mass and Communion last night . . . and just before going to the altar rail came to a swift and happy conclusion . . . to return to England mid-April. For months now I have been turning over and over in my mind, ad nauseam, the advantages of staying on a further year. By not staying out I shall have to pay £30,000 in taxes which I could avoid if I did remain on the continent, or in the USA. But it was as if Our Lord said, 'You'll be happier if you go back to England, and what is £30,000 anyway.' A great burden was lifted – and I became very light-hearted and silly and gay afterwards . . .[518]

Alec returned to England on 8 April, the second day of the new financial year, flying from Cherbourg to Bournemouth after a meandering journey with Merula and Matthew through France in their Citroën Safari. He asked to be dropped at the church at Petersfield and walked the last stretch to Kettlebrook Meadows. 'Delighted with the new additions to house,' he wrote in his diary. 'Study particularly pleasing. M's curtains in living room disastrous.'[519]

One of Alec's reasons for returning to England was to give up his well-paid but tedious film work and return to the stage. He had therefore turned down an offer from the Italian director, Franco Zeffirelli, to play Gustav von Aschenbach in an adaptation of Thomas Mann's novella, *Death in Venice** and 'two weeks' work in *V.I.P.* with Liz Taylor &

---

* The film was eventually made by Luchino Visconti, not Zeffirelli.

Burton . . . for about £30,000'; and he resisted the 'near blackmail' of
priests of the Salesian Order to make a film about their founder:
'"How much more good you could do in the world by making this
film instead of the ones you do," etc. etc.' Instead, he committed
himself to two plays: 'I accepted to do Ionesco's new play (to be called
Exit the King),' he told Dame Felicitas. 'Then on November 7th I sail to
New York to start rehearsals for a play on Dylan Thomas.'

Alec had regretted turning down Samuel Beckett's *Waiting for Godot*
back in 1954 and saw in *Exit the King* by the Rumanian Eugene Ionesco,
exponent of the 'Theatre of the Absurd', a chance to demonstrate his
talents in a drama that was neither classical such as *Hamlet* nor
conventional such as Rattigan's *Ross*. *Exit the King* was directed by
George Devine, who had directed Alec's adaptation of *Great
Expectations* in the Rudolf Steiner Hall before the war, and was staged
first at the Lyceum Theatre in Edinburgh as part of the Festival, and
subsequently transferred to the Royal Court in London.

The play is a meditation on death, which is inevitably hard to make
entertaining, and it lacks the wit and casual brilliance of Ionesco's
shorter plays such as *The Bald Prima Donna*. Alec's admirers were
delighted to see him back on the stage and his interpretation of King
Berenger was admired, but the play itself received adverse reviews and
had a limited run. However, it proved to be the genesis of a friendship
between Alec and a much younger actress that was to last for the rest
of his life. Eileen Atkins, then in her mid-twenties, had been cast by
George Devine in the role of the Queen. Though Devine had initially
assured her that he did not want her to act the part older than she was,
in rehearsals he kept suggesting that she adopt the voice and gait of an
older woman; and when Atkins said that she could not do it, decided
that he would replace her with someone else.

Alec intervened. 'I want you to know,' he told Atkins – it was the
first time he had talked to her – 'that you're not going under any
circumstances. I've spoken to George and I will direct you from now
on. I think you're going to be wonderful . . .'[520] Why did Alec step in
to over-rule his director? Atkins believes that he was impressed by her

professionalism and by the trouble she took, in a scene where she was pushing him in a wheelchair, to make sure that he 'found his lights'. And the reason for this professional collaboration developing into a close friendship she ascribed to the common bond of a wretched childhood and, in particular, her hatred of her mother. 'I was talking to him about my mother, once, and I was really being vile about her – someone said, you don't sound as if you like her, and I said, I actually hate my mother. Alec heard this and I think he was so relieved to hear someone say this, and that you *could* actually say it.'[521]

While still in Spain making *The Fall of the Roman Empire*, Alec had heard disturbing rumours about the state of mind of his Jesuit friend, Fr Philip Caraman. 'Merula and I are worried about Fr Philip Caraman,' he wrote to Dame Felicitas, 'because *obviously* he is ill and tired and very very low and he won't say *what* it is; time those 40 martyrs did something for him – he's given these past few years to them, unstintingly.'[522]

The reason for the priest's dejection was his dismissal as editor of the Jesuit journal, *The Month*. Fr Caraman was an early victim of the fierce struggle between conservatives and liberals that followed the Second Vatican Council, a historic gathering that was to change the Church that Alec had joined in many fundamental ways. The Society of Jesus, in particular, was to alter its sense of mission from scholarship, teaching and ministering to the upper echelons of society to a 'preferential option for the poor' – frequently expressing this option in radical, even revolutionary, political terms. Fr Caraman – whose solicitude for the souls of celebrated and aristocratic Catholics had led him to be seen by some as a snob – came to be regarded by the growing number of 'progressives' in the Society of Jesus as an unsuitable editor for their intellectual journal.

Fr Caraman was also told that he had become the object of the affections of Evelyn Waugh's nineteen-year-old daughter who had been working as his assistant. Margaret was, at the time, about to marry an eligible young Catholic, Giles Fitzherbert, and therefore the charge that she was in love with the fifty-three-year-old Jesuit was far-fetched. The truth, in fact, was the inverse: it was Fr Caraman who was infatuated with Margaret Waugh but had not realised it until the idea had been put into his mind by members of his Order.

The explosion of this unexpected passion and his ousting as editor of *The Month* brought about a grave nervous breakdown. Fr Caraman was sent for treatment to a refuge for priests in trouble and, when he was deemed well enough, posted to a parish in Norway. 'I think there is something wrong with the Society of Jesus that continually brings on these near-breakdowns,' Alec wrote to Merula. 'Rumour has it that Philip Caraman is being exiled to Norway for the rest of his life! Actually I think that's what he'd like, but I should think the cut off from his friends would be a strain.'[523]

thirty-five

In August 1962, Alec had been sent 'an extraordinary and wildly worded and rather blasphemous play on Dylan Thomas's last year in America. I rather want to do it though I am foolish casting.'[524] This was *Dylan* by Sidney Michael. Alec accepted the role and sailed for New York from Southampton on the *Queen Mary* on 7 November 1963. The play, directed by Peter Glenville, opened at the Plymouth Theatre in New York on 18 January 1964, and was a great popular and critical success. Alec's performance was particularly admired. 'You will want to see *Dylan*,' wrote the critic of the *New York Herald Tribune*, 'for the sorrow in Alec Guinness's face.'

The play toured in New Haven and Toronto prior to opening in New York – on Christmas Eve Alec went to midnight Mass in Toronto – and ran until 12 September of the following year. For eight months Alec rented Sybil Burton's apartment at 300 Central Park West. His letters home suggest that he disliked living on his own. 'I lead a fairly lonely and totally unprofitable life,' he told Marriott Lefèvre:

. . . just a sort of exile in New York. The money I earn, which is considerable, all goes to tax authorities, and I haven't the energy to do anything. I don't even read much . . . At night I usually take one or two people out for supper to a black leather room, a tinkling piano at the far end, and drunken ladies lolling on the hearts of their paunchy agents . . . I long for the green of K'brook, and a line of hills I can trust, and Shem's wet doggy smell, & Percy's squeezes*, and croquet . . . [525]

In fact, two of his closest friends were in New York with him – Val Stavredi, and Peter Glenville with his companion, Bill Smith; on most days, they met up for lunch or dinner at Sardi's. Merula visited before Christmas and again in May, bringing Matthew and Chattie at Alec's expense. He also invited Rob, his chauffeur, for a fortnight's holiday in New York. To Merula he gave the impression that he regretted this generous gesture. 'What the hell am I going to do with Rob,' he wrote. 'How stupidly "kind" I am.'

Alec went to meet Rob off the *Queen Elizabeth* on 30 June, but missed him in 'the screaming crowd and steam bath heat'. Rob found his own way to 300 Central Park West. On 1 July, Alec stayed up talking with Rob until 3.00 in the morning. 'Oh, how right you are about Rob,' Alec wrote to Merula:

He's a good and willing boy but I'm not sure I wouldn't rather have Mollie around, St Jude and all . . . I patted him on his enormous behind *en passant* and I thought he was going to pass out – he looked at me as if I was making some wild pass at him. I've taken him out twice with members of the co . . . I said we would *consider* buying a cottage nearby and renting it to him . . . How I can ever have thought he might be able to do secretarial work I can't imagine . . . [526]

'I do hope Rob is not being a drag,' Merula wrote back on 6 July. 'If

---

* Percy, the parrot, would hold Alec's finger in his beak and then gradually increase the pressure.

you are sad and lonely, I can always leave everything.' Alec discouraged
her from returning to New York. He took a summer break of ten days
or so, during which he went with Rob and Jimmy Ray, one of the
company, to Fire Island, which 'did me good to get away for 24 hours,
and have a bathe, and have to jump the Atlantic waves, and get a bit of
sun and a lot of wind'; but, he assured Merula, 'you and M would
loathe it – as I did'.[527] Fire Island is a resort favoured by homosexuals.

Alec's 'exile' in New York saw one of his occasional crises of faith.
He had been assiduous in his devotions, he told Dame Felicitas on 31
January 1963:

> For eighteen months, now, I have been to communion twice a week
> (excluding Sundays) – until two months ago, when it became physically
> impossible. But now I think I am back to *one* weekday, at least. And I
> say the Rosary every day. And I read a chapter of the New Testament
> and probably a bit of something else of a spiritual nature, each day. And
> that's about it. Oh, and I usually manage to drop in on the Blessed
> Sacrament for a minute or two four or five times a week. Nothing to
> hold my head up about, you see. But I do believe I remember to express
> my gratitude to God for all things, in a few words each day. C'est tout.
> And every night before the curtain goes up . . . I say 'God rest the soul
> of poor Dylan Thomas and accept this performance from me'.[528]

Alec even persuaded the 'Jewish theatre management' to have no
performance on Good Friday, which 'raised eyebrows throughout New
York and caused a certain amount of happiness: apparently *only once
before* in recent years has an actor made a bit of a stand about Good
Friday and managed to get a performance cut'.[529] But these devotions
did not save him from doubt or self-doubt. 'Fifty this week,' he wrote
to Dame Felicitas in the same letter, 'and just as nasty as I was at
fifteen.'

Among the causes of his spiritual crisis was the experience of
American Catholicism. 'After a few months in the arch-diocese of
Archbishop Spellman,' he told Dame Felicitas, 'I have a lot of

sympathy with anti-Catholicism.' And in a later letter: 'Oh, American Lady Catholics! If *only* they wouldn't wander round St Patrick's Cathedral with *gloves* on top of their heads, or a piece of Kleenex paper, to conform to covered heads rulings.'* His doubts had started after midnight Mass in Toronto, where he had found the sermon dispiriting, and by the beginning of January, he confessed to Dame Felicitas, had:

> . . . decided, quite calmly, regretfully but it seemed to me sanely, that my place was not within the fold of the Church. Too much to be taken 'on faith', too little reconciliation with scientific knowledge (physical and psychological), too cramping in ideas, etc. etc. – oh, and ETC. I was worried how to break this to Merula (who arrives in New York next week) and my friends, lay & ecclesiastical. So there I was – a letter started to you, and me, for the first time, having deliberately turned my back on obligation and Mass. And then there was your letter, with its superb quotations and your fine comments right on the fringe of where my mind had been wandering in distress. I really do think it was an act of Providence, arriving when it did.[530]

Dame Felicitas's letter, which does not survive, saved his faith and by the end of June Alec felt able to tell Merula that he had 'been having a "religious" or irreligious, rather, turmoil in my mind but all is well again'.[531]

Alec returned to London, again on the *Queen Mary*, reaching Kettlebrook Meadows on 22 September, but within little more than a month left for Munich to appear in a film directed by Gottfried Reinhardt, *Situation Hopeless – But Not Serious*, a lame comedy about an eccentric German who hides two American pilots during World War II and fails to tell them when the war is over. Alec loathed Munich,

---

* Women at the time were required to cover their heads in church 'because of the Angels': see St Paul, 1 Corinthians 11: 2–6.

loathed the film and loathed his own performance. 'I'm awful, a sort of lifeless doll impersonating myself in *Lavender Hill* or *Fr Brown*,' he wrote to Merula; and to Marriott he confessed, 'I've often suspected I'm a not good actor and with the lack of energy of passing years and my technical accomplishments being pretty old-fashioned now, I know it. Can't act comedy any more anyway.'[532]

The critics would confirm Alec's assessment of his own performance: '*Situation Hopeless – But Not Serious*,' wrote the film's reviewer in *Time* magazine, 're-establishes that Sir Alec has taken leave of his sense of humour.' He also seemed to have lost his ability to judge a good script: *A Majority of One*, HMS *Defiant*, *The Fall of the Roman Empire* and now *Situation Hopeless* were all mediocre. Had he turned down offers to appear in better films? Graham Greene's *The Living Room* might have been more interesting, and he was offered 'a rather effective part' in *The Spy Who Came in from the Cold*; but the greatest missed opportunity was surely his rejection of Franco Zeffirelli's offer to play Gustav von Aschenbach, the hero of Thomas Mann's *Death in Venice*.

This is the story, it will be recalled, of a celebrated German writer who, on holiday on the Venice Lido, becomes infatuated with a beautiful Polish adolescent, Tadzio, staying at the same resort with his family. First of all, as Kenneth Tynan had written in 1953, Alec was 'one of the few people alive who could play a genius convincingly. How seldom one sees an actor playing an author, whom it is possible to imagine constructing a coherent sentence, let alone a masterpiece'.[533] When the film was finally made in 1971 by Luchino Visconti, not Zeffirelli, Aschenbach was played by Dirk Bogarde who, though in fact a talented writer himself, was unconvincing as a German genius – albeit now changed into a composer. 'If it had starred Alec,' in the view of Tom Courtenay, 'it would have been a greater film. You would have felt that he *was* a great writer. With Dirk, you didn't.'[534]

However, the affinity between Alec and Aschenbach, as with Aschenbach's creator, Thomas Mann, was in their highly complex characters and sexuality – so often more effectively depicted by novelists than by psychologists, historians or biographers. '"You see, Aschenbach has always lived like this" – here the speaker closed the fingers of his left hand to a fist – "never like this" – and he let his open hand hang relaxed from the back of his chair.' Just as Alec was proud of his knighthood, so Aschenbach is gratified to have been ennobled, entitled 'since his fiftieth birthday' to add the prefix 'von'. He was, like Alec, a man 'of transcendent gifts [who] outgrows his carefree prentice stage, recognises his own worth and forces the world to recognise it too and pay it homage, though he puts on a courtly bearing to hide his bitter struggles and his loneliness'.[535]

But, above all, what Alec shared with Aschenbach was his love of physically beautiful young men. 'Aschenbach noticed with astonishment the lad's perfect beauty. His face recalled the noblest moment of Greek sculpture – pale, with a sweet reserve . . .' In Aschenbach's case it is Tadzio, of course, but it could have been any of the several young men who captured Alec's tender attention. We are now inclined to consider such strong and intoxicating emotions as merely the cerebral manifestation of sexual desire, and so condemn it as a sin or extol it as an appetite; but Mann catches the far subtler and paradoxical mix of sensuous yearning and paternal solicitude: 'his heart was stirred, it felt a father's kindness: such an emotion as the possessor of beauty can inspire in one who has offered himself up in spirit to create beauty'.

The feelings towards Alec of the young men who became the objects of his affections is a matter of conjecture but was in all probability a respectful fondness – the 'sort of relationship and acquaintanceship . . . set up between Aschenbach and the youthful Tadzio; it was with a thrill of joy the older man perceived that the lad was not entirely unresponsive to all the tender notice lavished on him . . .' and '. . . in his infatuation he cared for nothing but to keep Tadzio here, and owned to himself, not without horror, that he could not exist were the lad to pass from his sight.'[536]

It seems puzzling that Alec, so intellectually curious and a reader, if not of Freud, then of Jung, never seems to have inquired as to

whether or not his passing passions for handsome young men had a
psychological cause, and so whether there might be a 'cure', for his
condition. 'The truth may have been,' writes Mann of Aschenbach:

> . . . that the ageing man did not want to be cured, that his illusion was
> far too dear to him. Who shall unriddle the puzzle of the artist's
> nature? Who understands that mingling of discipline and licence in
> which it stands so deeply rooted? For not to be able to want sobriety is
> licentious folly. Aschenbach was no longer disposed to self-analysis. He
> had no taste for it; his self-esteem, the attitude of mind proper to his
> years, his maturity and single-mindedness, disinclined him to look
> within himself.[537]

An ingredient in what made a young man attractive to Alec seems to
have been the element of hierarchy and service such as existed
between the naval officer and able seaman. Thus, though he liked
them, Alec did not fall for either of the two young American actors
who appeared with him in *Situation Hopeless*, Robert Redford and Mike
Connors. 'The two chaps I like. Redford is interesting – bit of a chip
on the shoulder – but amusing and alert and probably an original.
Connors is charming and obviously v. nice but not interesting – just
"show biz" talk. Anyway I'm sure they will be good to work with and
Redford is going to be a big star one day I am positive.'[538]

Instead, Alec seems to have taken to the young man who had been
employed to drive him around, Wolfgang Lettau.* 'I'm bringing my
rather nice chauffeur (who is an architectural student) Wolfgang back
for a week as a tip-cum-leaving present,' he wrote to Marriott from
Munich. 'He's an East German refugee and either gloomy and
whipped-looking or rather childishly excited. But pleasant enough,
though table manners are Bavarian.'[539] For Christmas, Wolfgang drove
Alec, Peter Glenville and Bill Smith to Salzburg. 'Peter & Bill . . . got

---

* Not his real name.

on my nerves a bit by being just so theatre gossipy all day,' Alec noted on Christmas Day. On 29 December Alec and Wolfgang took the night train from Munich to Ostend, arriving at the Connaught at four in the afternoon. Alec then popped down to Harrods where he bought a seal-skin coat for Merula, before returning to take Wolfgang to dine at the Guinea Grill in Mayfair.

Wolfgang came for the New Year to Kettlebrook where they played Mah Jong. Alec sent him to London on 4 January 'for a couple of nights' and, the next day, took him 'to Olympia circus which was very tatty'. On 6 January, he took Wolfgang to lunch at the Tiberio; the next day they were back at Kettlebrook where Merula, Wolfgang and Rob went for a walk 'along the coast at Langston'. The next day, 'up to town by train with Wolfgang' and on 9 January 'saw Wolfgang off to Munich'.

What did Merula make of Wolfgang, Rob, or any of the other young men whom Alec brought into her home either as lodgers, chauffeurs or guests? Though she and Matthew noticed that Alec's tone changed when he told them about a good-looking male actor – there was a catch in his voice which he used to disguise with a little cough and, when hiding strong emotions, little bits of spittle would appear at the corners of his mouth – they never discussed Alec's infatuations. However, Merula was wise and intuitive and it seems likely that she understood, more or less, what was passing through Alec's mind. But she was not without spirit and, if prepared to show no curiosity about what Alec got up to in London, there were limits to what she could endure in her own home.

It was particularly hard for Merula that she was left to deal with the staff chosen by Alec during his long absences abroad, and in time her patience gave out – first with Alec's secretary, Mollie Hartley-Milburn, then with his chauffeur, Rob. Mollie was hard to sack because of the long history of her friendship with Alec, but Merula found her increasingly irritating and suspected that she was one of the chief reasons why Matthew was losing his Catholic faith. She wrote to Dame Felicitas:

It's very worrying that about the only people I don't like are pious
Catholics – what do you do about people you don't like? – there's one
in my life and for years I've been telling myself that she's really good
and really I like her and I get more irritable and strung up, and then
suddenly two days ago I said to myself – I am a liar and I HATE her and
she's a bore and not even good-hearted and I felt MUCH better and
more relaxed in her presence. And she's a VERY pious lady and goes to
Mass every day and it seems to me it means nothing at all. I know it is
partly or mostly her piety which has turned Matthew. She makes one
hate everything one loves, and I automatically use bad language in front
of her, though it's not one of my usual faults, and I am sick to death of
going to confession on her account – I can't believe it's my fault any
more. I don't know why I am writing this except it must be a problem
which crops up in convents . . .[540]

Mollie was eventually told to go, and went to work for the Harvill
Press; but Merula must have realised that it might be more difficult to
get rid of Rob. Indeed, when Rob became engaged to be married, Alec
proposed to lodge him not in a nearby cottage but in a flat built on to
the house. On 1 February 1965, Alec complained to Dame Felicitas of:

. . . the constant hammering of the three old men working on this
house – erecting (eventually I suppose) a flat over the garage for my
chauffeur and his bride-to-be. The bride-to-be, Merula has just told me,
is *horrified* to hear she is going to live in the wing of a house occupied
by Catholics. (She is a Scottish Presbyterian.) And apparently my
chauffeur has told Merula that our Catholicism has to be kept secret
from her strict parents in case they try to put a stop to the wedding. It
sounds odd, doesn't it, in these ecumenical days? And if they only knew
what a doubting Thomas I have become would they be encouraged or
even more appalled?

Rob went off to Glasgow to get married at the beginning of April 'so
motoring jaunts are out until the end of his honeymoon' and when he

returned with his bride, since the flat was not yet ready, moved into the Guinnesses' spare room. On 22 July, Alec and Merula went to Paris where Peter Glenville was, finally, to film *Hotel Paradiso*, with Alec once again in the role of Monsieur Boniface. While they were away, in a repetition of the incident with Fred, Matthew turned up unexpectedly at Kettlebrook to find that Rob had invited his parents-in-law to stay and had taken over the house.

This was the pretext that Merula had been waiting for, but her description of the incident to Dame Felicitas suggests a long-standing dislike of Rob:

> I have sacked the goody goody methodist king boy-scout Glasgow boy who was working for us for two years and we have built a really super new flat onto the house for him and his bride – and he was one of those fresh clean living young men with a constant smile and always walked on Tip Toe, and as soon as we were well away in Paris those little mice were playing helter skelter and the place was a shambles – so I'm back where I was last year wondering how to get it sorted out in the confessional as really it's my own fault . . . Anyway its blissful having our house to ourselves again though we shall have to get somebody soon.[541]

Finding a replacement for Rob did not prove easy. 'A new chauffeur handy-man (very temporary) arrived yesterday,' Alec wrote to Dame Felicitas on 18 November, 'and has to be shown the ropes. This afternoon we interviewed a Marine corporal, who could come to us with his wife and small daughter in March . . . We want a couple, if possible, as I think it's time Merula had more free time for her painting and life generally. When she married me she never bargained for being cook-housekeeper etc. etc. and has been marvellously uncomplaining all these years.'

thirty-six

In the spring of 1965 Alec returned to Spain yet again, this time to play Yevgraf Zhivago in David Lean's film of Boris Pasternak's *Dr Zhivago*. Alec disliked the novel: 'I couldn't get on with it at all,' he later confessed to Dame Felicitas, 'although I tried three times. There are fine things in it, but I don't think it is a novel at all.'[542] He had dithered about accepting the role of Yevgraf. 'I have said NO to *Dr Zhivago*,' he wrote to Merula on 2 November 1964. 'I just don't somehow feel like it.' But, ten days later, 'David Lean is putting pressure on me over *Zhivago*[543] and I must say, re-reading the script as a whole, I'm tempted.' On 14 November, he gave way to the temptation:

I have just sent David Lean a wire saying Yes to *Zhivago*. I thoroughly object to supporting Omar Fred Sharif and, with the exception of Tom Courtenay, I don't like the rest of the casting much. And the part, for me, is enigmatic and the commentary stuff is irritating, but David persuades me the commentary will work. Anyway for £90,000 it's worth turning up in Spain, I think . . .'[544]

Merula had misgivings. 'I am afraid I feel awfully sad about you being sucked into another monster epic,' she wrote to Alec in Munich, 'even if it is David Lean – they seem to me to totally smother the actor however good, and one comes away with a wonderful impression of desert or forums or some such and the human element disappears in the vista.'[545] Nevertheless, Alec went ahead and met up in Madrid with some old friends such as Ralph Richardson who had directed him in *Richard II* and had appeared with him in *Lawrence of Arabia*. 'Ralph a bit pissed' appeared in Alec's Small Diary; and later, 'Ralph very pissed.' There was also Omar Sharif who, Alec told Merula, he found 'very charming and unaffected and asked politely after you'. On 29 April, Alec 'took Tom Courtenay and Julie Christie (who plays Lara) to dinner. She's a beatnik sort of girl and very intelligent and rather sweet I think. We stayed up nattering until nearly 2.00.' And he told Merula that he was 'dotty about tiny Rita Tushington [sic*], and so would you be. She performs exquisitely – same sort of blushing honesty that Celia Johnson has – or had. She has unfortunate teeth but it doesn't seem to matter. And she's a dear, gay, lightly amusing and tender girl.'[546]

Alec's only difficulties were with David Lean who not only, in Alec's view, played 'the great director', but, feeling that he had more or less made Alec as a film actor by casting him as Herbert Pocket, showed none of the deference that by now Alec had come to expect from directors. On one occasion Lean had the temerity first to tell Alec that he thought he was too old for the part – there is a scene in which Alec plays Yevgraf as a young man – and later to telephone him 'to say my face was too fat on screen'. They disagreed on how Alec should play Yevgraf: 'David threw me by suggesting big emotions for final shots which are written lightly & tenderly. I begin to almost dislike him and

---

* Rita Tushingham

his egoism he assumes everyone else has as well.'[547] Eight years later
Alec was to look back on his 'unhappy stint on *Dr Zhivago*. David Lean
and I had fallen out quite a bit during that film, he having become so
very intense, slave-driver, tetchy and humourless, and after one lot of
rushes, in which my face had appeared scarlet, accused me of drinking
too much, which was not really so, I felt.'[548]

As always, Alec's performance as Zhivago's half-brother, the Soviet
general Yevgraf Zhivago, was accomplished, but it was a peripheral
and dramatically unnecessary role and the whole world knew it.
During a press conference given in Madrid, Alec wrote to Merula:

> A loathsome newspaper columnist – Canadian – asked me how I
> enjoyed being a 'bit' player after having been a star. Aren't people
> extraordinary. I wasn't quick enough to say I had always been a bit
> player – playing one bit Monday, another bit Tuesday, a third bit
> Wednesday and so on. Such callous nastiness nearly makes one want
> to do a big star stuff career all over again and *snub* them all. But I think
> I'm going to have more interesting fish to fry.[549]

*Il n'y a que la verité qui blesse:** it was John Gielgud's jibe all over again.
Though the film was a great success, winning a number of Oscars and
making many millions for David Lean, his producer Carlo Ponti and
MGM, it was for Alec a painful reminder that his acting career was
becalmed.

As to 'the more interesting fish' he had to fry Alec, remembering John
Gielgud's successful season at the Queen's Theatre before the war,
decided that the time had come for him to try and do the same.
'Binkie, apparently, is biting quite hard at the idea I put up of me doing
a season of plays in London next year,' he wrote to Merula in April
1965. 'Ralph would like to pool. I expect John as well. But you can't

---

* It's only the truth that hurts.

have 3 thespian knights of a certain age all whooping it up together. But it would be rather nice to do something not state-aided. I hate to be beholden to Mr Wilson or any Trade Union movement.'[550]

Alec's dig at the Labour Prime Minister, Harold Wilson, was aimed as much at those actors who appeared in the state-funded National Theatre. This had evolved after World War II from Lillian Baylis's Old Vic, and was placed under the direction of the first among equals of England's theatrical knights, Sir Laurence, later Lord, Olivier. Although the personal feelings of Alec and Olivier for one another would fluctuate, both had reservations about the other's talents. 'Larry was very dismissive of Alec,' John Mortimer recalled. 'He said: "We thought we had a star in this young man but he never succeeded"'; and Alec's judgement of Olivier, as we have seen, was that he was 'technically brilliant but he always left me rather cold'. Given this mild antipathy, it is hardly surprising that Olivier should not have pressed Alec to appear at the National or that Alec, so busy with his successful film career, should not have wanted to do so. It was said that Olivier once summoned Alec to the National to offer him a part, kept him waiting for forty minutes, and then offered him the minor role of Antonio in *The Merchant of Venice*. However, a letter in Alec's archive suggests that Olivier offered him a more significant role in 1969, which he turned down. 'I absolutely and entirely appreciate the reasons for your decision,' wrote Olivier. 'That "worried, jaded" phase has had me putting off *Lear* year by year. I hope both you and I snap out of it alright before too long otherwise we shall find ourselves yielding the ghost at the woeful realisation that we have wished our lives away.'[551]

Before Alec could put his grand plan for a season of plays into action, he had to fulfil a few existing commitments. The first, dating back a number of years, was the film of *Hotel Paradiso*, which was made in Paris in the summer of 1965. From the end of July to the end of October, Alec lived in a flat in the rue Bonaparte, and had the company of Peter Glenville, who both directed and appeared in the film, and Glenville's companion, Bill Smith; but although the filming may have been enjoyable, the end product was not. Alec, never persuasive as a heterosexual lover, was now too old to lust convincingly after Gina Lollobrigida on the screen. The failure of the film, however, was not due only to Alec's shortcomings. 'Glenville as Glenville,' wrote the reviewer in *Time* magazine when it was released in the United States, 'hasn't the faintest idea of how to get the fun on film.' *Hotel Paradiso* was not released in Britain until 1971 and, in the opinion of Peter Buckley in *Films and Filming*, 'it should have stayed on the shelf. It is a dog, a mangy mongrel of the lowest order, and an insult to all involved.' Alec later judged it 'not good – very flaccid and mistaken construction and Peter G's appearance in it a mistake'.[552]

Alec's next commitment was to play an Austrian prince in Arthur Miller's play, *Incident at Vichy*, put on at the Phoenix Theatre in January 1966. Though Alec's role was largely a matter of reacting to what was essentially a debate on the Holocaust, he was not always malleable in the hands of the director, Peter Wood. 'Peter Wood started re-shaping beginning of play,' he wrote in his diary on 5 January 1966, 'spoiling it I thought. Eventually I blew my top in a quiet way and said what was on my mind.' The play, in which Tony Quayle starred as the Interrogator, had poor reviews and a short run.

Back to film, his third commitment was a Cold War thriller, *The Quiller Memorandum*. He played Pol, the MI6 officer controlling the secret agent Quiller (George Segal). The screenplay, based on Adam Hall's *The Berlin Memorandum*, was by the playwright Harold Pinter, and the film was directed by Michael Anderson who had made *The Dam Busters*. Alec was fascinated by Berlin – the city divided into different zones with its wall separating the central and eastern parts of the city, which were under Communist rule, from the capitalist and democratic sectors in the west. Alec was entertained by senior officers of the NATO garrisons, but his work was undemanding. He had only four short scenes in the film and his performance, though highly competent, did nothing to further his career. In 1973, he referred to the film in his diary as 'the unmemorable *Quiller Memorandum*' and, after watching it on television in November 1980, as 'a very cliché-ridden story and Pinter's script no better than I remembered it. I was surprised to find myself thinking I wasn't too bad in the rotten little part I played.'[553]

The 'season of plays' planned by Alec for 1966 had, by the summer of 1966, been reduced to a single production – Shakespeare's *Macbeth*. As John Russell Taylor pointed out in his study of Alec, this was a strange choice for someone as superstitious as Alec. *Macbeth* is so famously unlucky that many in the theatrical profession will never mention it by name, referring to it simply as 'the Scottish play'. Alec further tempted fate with an audacious piece of casting: for Lady Macbeth he chose the French actress, Simone Signoret. Alec had first met Signoret and her husband, Yves Montand, when he was in New York in 1959 to act in a CBS television production of John D. Hess's *The Wicked Scheme of Jebal Deeks*. He had taken to them both and thought highly of Signoret as an actress.

To direct the play, Alec again demonstrated a certain audacity in approaching the thirty-six-year-old director, William Gaskill, recently appointed the artistic director of the English Stage Company which ran the Royal Court Theatre in London's Sloane Square. Though Gaskill had directed both *Richard III* and *Cymbeline* at Stratford-on-Avon, he had made his name by staging new works by radical young playwrights such as John Arden and Edward Bond, and by their mentor, Bertolt Brecht. Brecht was in high fashion at the time: Michel St Denis directed his *Squire Puntila and his Servant Matti* at the Aldwych in July 1965, and that summer four of his plays in German had been staged by Brecht's own Berliner Ensemble at the National Theatre. Matthew had told his father of the superb quality of the Ensemble's acting.

It was an exciting time for the English theatre, not just with the advent of abrasive new English playwrights, but also avant-garde dramas coming from Europe, such as Peter Weiss's *The Persecution and Assassination of Marat as Performed by the Inmates of the Asylum of Charenton under the Direction of the Marquis de Sade*, which Peter Brook directed at the Aldwych in November 1965. And there were much discussed reinterpretations of classic Shakespearean roles such as

David Warner's *Hamlet*, staged a month later, again at the Aldwych and again directed by Peter Hall.

Alec hoped, no doubt, that by catching the tide of this modernity, the demeaning if lucrative bit parts in Hollywood films would be forgotten and he would re-establish his reputation as one of the four greatest classical actors in England. In August he started to go to a gym twice a week 'to get myself fit for McB' but had a disagreeable sense of foreboding. 'Ghastly fears and horrors about *Macbeth*, feeling it must be called off,' he wrote in his diary on 9 July 1966. 'All fears were for myself rather than Simone. I was going to suggest it was postponed for a year.' He was also uneasy about his choice of director. 'I am expecting, for the day, the young man who is to direct my *Macbeth*,' he wrote to Dame Felicitas on 2 August, 'and it is all going to be tiresome and tetchy, I feel, and I am going to have to call on more patience than I can muster. I am rather hoping it will all fall through.' Three weeks later he gloomily predicted to the Benedictine nun that 'it will be a greatly disliked production and performance so I must take a big breath to prepare myself for the critical ducking I am bound to receive. A prayer for my courage and integrity please.'[554]

Alec had some old friends among the cast such as the Scots actor Gordon Jackson and his nephew, Eusty Salaman's son, Toby, who played Seyton; but Alec, try as he might *not* to pull rank, found it hard to accept the changes that had come over the profession in recent years. When he had started out, young actors had dressed respectably and addressed the lead players as *Miss* Evans or *Mr* Gielgud; and during rehearsals they would sit quietly in the stalls, studying the performances of the masters of their craft. But as Toby Salaman recalled, many of Gaskill's recruits to the cast were:

. . . a new breed of young actor – working-class lads. On one occasion, they sat with their feet up when Alec was working on-stage with the director, Bill Gaskill. Alec hated playing the 'grand old actor' but on this occasion he exploded: he couldn't concentrate on his work and said,

'When I was a boy we would have been studying a great actor at work.'
Giggles in the bar afterwards.[555]

Jack Shepherd, who played the Porter, became Alec's 'bête noire'.
Some years later, Alec read in a profile of Shepherd by Sheridan
Morley that 'the entire company lined up with water-pistols intending
to shoot me' but was assured by his friend Gordon Jackson that this
was 'insane rubbish. Well, I hope so, and am inclined to think so . . .
Anyway, by the end of the day I relaxed, went to Mass and forgave
Shepherd, but with more difficulty forgave Morley . . .'[556]

Macbeth opened at the Royal Court Theatre on 20 October 1966.
Frith Banbury thought that the production was 'a disaster' and Joss
Ackland that Alec was miscast. The then young director, Alan
Strachan, who would subsequently direct Alec in two plays, regarded
it as a failure on several fronts:

> It wasn't good – not just Simone Signoret. Some people said that it was
> ahead of its time but I'm not sure about that. It was very Brechtian –
> directed by William Gaskill – and he, like all the Royal Court boys,
> were greatly influenced by Brecht, and the idea that everything
> superfluous must be pared away. So he did a *Mother Courage* job and
> directed that play at around the same time at the National. It was a bare
> set with bright light; no shadow or darkness; after the murder, the stage
> was more brightly lit. I didn't object to that but it left an enormous
> onus on the actors: and Alec – though he didn't give a disastrous
> performance, in fact it was a fascinating performance – but it was a
> study in miniature. Everything was very finely etched. And I don't
> think you can bring off *Macbeth* without some very broad strokes. Even
> the fight at the end was a bit decorous. There was no sense of people
> knowing that one of them was going to die. He was wonderful in the
> scene with the witches; he made you see them in his mind's eye.[557]

The greatest handicap, however, was Simone Signoret. She had
promised Alec that she would take lessons in English but she had failed

to keep the appointments with her tutor. Alec told Matthew that she was lazy but he believed, nonetheless, that she would convey the sexual magnetism that might hold a husband in thrall. But her husky voice and voluptuous figure proved insufficient and her heavy accent a liability. 'The play was a disaster,' Toby Salaman recalled:

> . . . largely because Alec had insisted on Simone Signoret playing the role of Lady Macbeth. She couldn't speak English. Alec felt responsible but he abandoned her. She was very unhappy. Alec didn't help her. On the first night, Signoret 'dried'. Alec whispered her line 'If we should fail . . .' Still she said nothing. He repeated it in a louder voice. She picked it up and continued. On the first night, through the open door, I saw Simone Signoret weeping in her dressing-room.

It was in fact the second night. 'Simone dried up and nearly fainted,' Alec recorded in his diary, 'and said out loud "I'm OK now" and went back over a speech. Ghastly experience.' Signoret may well have been affected by the reviews of *Macbeth* which Alec had not read. With the exception of *The Times*, they were uniformly damning, with credit for the fiasco divided evenly between Alec and Bill Gaskill. 'At every point it cries out for just the pompous wardrobe and mobs of stage-listeners Gaskill has banished,' wrote Ronald Bryden in the *Observer*. And B.A. Young, in the *Financial Times*, felt that 'it must have taken a great deal of work to persuade Alec Guinness to give a performance so totally colourless as his Macbeth'.

'My eyes couldn't see properly or my mind register after reading the terrible notices,' Merula wrote to Dame Felicitas, 'excitingly bad, as the director's friend (ex-monk) called them. Alec doesn't read notices, which is wise and strong-minded of him.' She reassured Dame Felicitas that Alec was 'in good fighting form, though the hole [sic] venture has been a great strain – it is the very devil of a part – physically and spiritually and one can't help getting sucked into the disturbance and evil of the thing. Neither of us has been sleeping properly and the world seems full of frightening destructive forces.'[558]

Alec's own post-mortem to Dame Felicitas after *Macbeth* had closed on 19 November was measured:

It created something of a furore and violent headlines in the popular or gutter press. Most people disliked it, a small percentage championed it, and the Sunday press and weekly papers treated it with respect. So far as I am concerned the people whose opinion I value think it is the best thing I have done, and I suspect they are right. But it was an uphill fight and I had to carry completely (and impossibly) my French leading lady – no featherweight! It was excellent for me physically, vocally, mentally – but I doubt if my soul benefited. Well, it's over and out of the system. Deo Gratias.[559]

In his Small Diary, after the last night, Alec noted: 'Have rarely finished anything with less regret.'

part six

private lives

thirty-seven

At a time of growing public interest in the private lives of the stars of stage and screen, Alec and Merula Guinness fiercely resisted any intrusion into their privacy. In the interviews that Alec was obliged to give from time to time to promote a play or a book, he gave away nothing. Merula never spoke to the press. Their friends, their neighbours and the Salaman family all exercised total discretion, respecting their desire for privacy but also aware that any breach of the *omerta* would bring friendship to an end.

The private life of the Guinnesses in the middle period of their relationship centred around their home, their family, their friends, their pets and their travels; and there was that area of their life that was private to Alec – his befriending of one or two young men.

Alec and Merula Guinness lived at Kettlebrook Meadows from 1955 until their deaths in the year 2000. Merula remained, by and large, content with the house, designed by her brother and close to his home, Slong Farm and her parents at Wadlington, and with sufficient

land around it for her ponies, goats and dogs. Alec found at
Kettlebrook the stability that he had never had as a child, but within
his mind he was always restless and planning to live elsewhere. 'He
kept wondering whether or not they shouldn't sell Kettlebrook and
move away,' Matthew recalled:

> He was restless . . . there was an estate on the Hebrides . . . my mother
> said, that's fine for you, you'll be in the West End doing a show and I'll
> be stuck on this little island. She wanted to stay at Kettlebrook. My
> mother liked Kettlebrook because she was such a country person – she
> had horses, she liked all that – and really my father's only interests
> outside town were fishing, boats and water. There was something sad
> that they hadn't got somewhere by a lake or a river or the sea.[560]

At one point, Alec proposed living in California: 'you can certainly live
there,' Merula had said, 'but not with me.'

A good reason for looking for another house came in 1963 when the
Hampshire County Council put forward three alternative routes for a
by-pass around Petersfield for the A3, the main road from London to
Portsmouth: one of the routes would pass within a few hundred yards
of Kettlebrook Meadows. Though Alec was prominent in the battle to
stop the by-pass, he also began to consider moving house. Over the
next years they looked at numerous properties in Hampshire, Essex,
Ealing, Putney, East Sussex. Time and again they embarked on a
purchase, only to pull out before contracts were exchanged. They
asked Daphne du Maurier to find them a house in Cornwall,
considered a priest's house on the island of Eigg; a 'simple cottage in
Pembrokeshire'; the Redgraves' house, 'Wilks Water'; a number of
farmhouses around Petersfield and 'a small Georgian house in the
Meon Valley'.

Finally, in June 1985, Alec 'spotted a house at Steep, a little way up
the Hangers, for sale for £200,000. Three and a half acres. In
photographs it looks like Eusty's design. Obviously a superb position.
It is well out of the way of the Green route, should it come.'[561] This

was Ashford Cottage, which had indeed been designed by Eusty Salaman, and was well away from the by-pass, surrounded by woods. It seemed just the thing. For once, Alec and Merula did not get cold feet: Ashford Cottage was bought and Kettlebrook Meadows put on the market. Alec gave a tour of the new property to Alan Bennett and Peggy Ashcroft after a Sunday lunch at Kettlebrook: none of them liked the name. Alan Bennett suggested changing it to 'Dun-Filmin'.

But in October came a change of heart. Kettlebrook was withdrawn from the market. 'We want to think more seriously about moving or not,' Alec wrote in his diary. 'Our emotional feeling is to stay where we are and re-sell Ashford Cottage. This has been home and no other place could be that for the last years of our life.'[562] To get rid of Ashford Cottage, Alec first tried to sell it to his friends Mark and Marigold Kingston but, much to Alec's displeasure, the Kingstons declined. 'Our new house is still on the market (at £140,000) and no bidders,' he wrote to Dame Felicitas. Then, with the house still unsold at the end of March 1986, he 'suggested, or queried, with Matthew whether he . . . would like to rent, for a peppercorn, Ashford Cottage . . . We would retain possession of the house and leave it to him in our will'.[563] Three weeks later, he and Merula decided to *give* Ashford Cottage to Matthew.

The restlessness had come to an end. The Petersfield by-pass was finally built, almost thirty years after it was first planned, opening on 9 July 1992. 'The government department responsible had the impertinence to invite me to the cutting of the ribbon ceremony,' Alec complained to Edward Herrmann, 'as if I could stand and applaud the inconvenience and distress caused to my life'.[564] And after the by-pass had opened, he noted in his diary: 'The hum and roar of traffic is with us for the rest of our lives.'

One of the reasons for remaining at Kettlebrook was Alec and Merula's love of the garden they had created over forty years. Alec loved nature, and the entries in his diary recorded not just the weather but what he could see from his study window – the changes brought about by the seasons, the behaviour of birds. 'Five baby wrens, about the size of kumquats, and who can barely fly, have been trying to post themselves through our letter box,' he wrote to Anne Kaufman. 'They would be welcome, as nothing particularly agreeable – other than your letter – has fallen on our mat recently.'[565] At one time, Alec had an aviary with humming birds and tropical finches. On 25 October 1980, he observed in his diary:

> This, I think, is the prettiest autumn we have ever had here. The last few days have been mild, though fresh in the mornings, bathed in sunlight, golden, pink and green. The cherry outside the kitchen rarely lasts long once its leaves have turned but this year it has been spectacular for a week and still rich in colour. Many trees are still quite green.[566]

Life at Kettlebrook was particularly agreeable in summer and they would eat out whenever they could. 'Apart from family anxieties life here is being pretty well idyllic,' Alec wrote to Dame Felicitas on 15 July 1989:

> We are up by seven, sometimes earlier, on these idyllic mornings. I have my coffee and then feed the Koi Carp and then drift into the day. Nearly all our meals have been taken out of doors. We have an arbour, greatly sheltered by a fig tree and vine, where we often lunch, and a patio on the other side of the house, where we dine and can listen to the gramophone as dusk falls. All that and a glass of wine – what more could a man desire?

By and large the garden was Merula's domain. Alec planted crocus bulbs, and occasionally trees, but his chief interest was a pond he had made in the garden, '60ft × 10ft – set in a cloister of evergreens', which he weeded in waders and which became home to nine Japanese carp. Their well-being preoccupied Alec: 'A blustery, unsettled day with a cold wind,' he noted in his diary on 3 June 1984. 'Two of the Japanese carp have now died and a third appears to be going.' By the end of the week, all were dead – poisoned, he thought, by oil leaking from the electric pump.

Perhaps the strongest strand in the bond that bound Alec and Merula together was their love of animals. While Alec's only responsibility was to feed his birds and his carp, Merula had a whole menagerie which included, at different periods, horses, dogs, cats, goats, a parrot and two visiting crows; but Alec was as devoted to them as she was. 'He loved all animals,' his friend Jehane West recalled. 'With them he didn't feel the need to protect himself because they don't judge . . . His attitude to animals was trusting. They couldn't utter any scathing remarks or have unkind thoughts because they don't. Most of their life at home was based around the animals.'[567]

Alec and Merula's first pet had been Trotwood the dormouse who, placed on top of a radiator at Ruckmans, had been reduced to a 'thimbleful of dust'. In St Peter's Square days they had had a collie called Dingo, bought from the Battersea Dogs' Home; Zossima, a Siamese kitten bought at Harrods, and Percy, the South African grey parrot who could recite the first line of a soliloquy from *Hamlet*: 'Oh, what a rogue and peasant slave am I . . .' Percy came with them to Kettlebrook where there was a succession of dogs: Tilly and her daughter Vesta; Bluebell, Japhet, Dido and Flora; Shem, a black and white shih-tzu, and Dorcas, 'a beautiful and rather alarming Belgian shepherd'; Seraphina, an Abyssinian cat; a horse, a couple of Shetland ponies, and Perdita, the first of Merula's herd of goats.

Merula had been brought up with animals at Ruckmans and, being shy, found it easier to relate to them than to human beings. Like St Francis of Assisi, or the Guinnesses' friend Jehane West, her love of animals was almost a religion and encompassed 'all creatures, great and small'. Alec's love of animals had its limits. 'The struggle with moles continues and gets more desperate on my part,' he noted in his diary on 26 May 1974. Five years later, almost to the day: 'The moles are driving me mad and each smoke bomb costs 29 pence.' 'I have now used about thirty Murphy smoke bombs against our plague of moles and still they come.' 'It's nine o'clock and a quite beautiful morning. But a mole hill has appeared on the lawn . . .' He finally had to call on professional help. 'It is now nine days,' he noted on 14 March 1980, 'since Mr Blank, the moles man, put down his poisoned worms and all seems clear.'

In January 1974, Alec bought a double-barrelled shot gun, 'mostly for rabbits and pigeons – but Vanessa Redgrave had better beware': this was the time of IRA bombs in London, the coal miners' strike, and the 'three-day week', and Alec had received a letter from Peter Glenville in New York 'asking if I think it likely, as reported in your press, that the military are about to take over here.'[568] The rabbits were never defeated: towards the end of his life, Alec threatened to infect them with myxomatosis in the company of Merula and the actor Keith Baxter. '"If you do that",' Merula said, '"I've got a stick upstairs and a knapsack and I'm going to walk down that path and I'll never come back". And it was only half a joke.'[569]

In July 1974, Alec bought a three-month-old Dandy Dinmont puppy from a breeder in North Harrow, Mrs Burt. He paid £40 which he thought a bargain: 'In the shops, where obtainable, which is rare, I believe the price is around £85. He has seven champions among his forebears, is beautifully marked but has a slight kink in his tail.'[570]

'*The* event in our lives is the arrival of a Dandy Dinmont puppy,' he wrote to Anne Kaufman, 'called Walter after Sir W. Scott who had a couple. Walter is very low on the ground and is likely to stay there, I imagine.'[571] Alec also announced the advent of Walter to Dame Felicitas:

He is quite ravishing but *very* destructive and inclined to cast himself into the pond. And also to decorate my study with vast quantities of pond weed. It's good for us to have someone very young around again. Also it's delicious for me to have one of the animals devoted (apparently) to me rather than Merula, who grabs all their affections always (and rightly).[572]

Merula confirmed what Alec had written. 'We have a new dog, about a yard long and four inches high, he is called Walter, and is Alec's dog, and Alec is head over heals [sic] in love with it. I have never seen him so besotted before, it's really touching.'[573] Though Merula was not one to think before putting her thoughts down on paper, she was probably right to say that Alec had never loved any creature as much as he came to love Walter. In his diary and his letters to his friends, he describes Walter as if he is a human being:

Walter was brought to see me in London last weekend but chose to pretend that he barely knew me. Much tossing of the head and staring in the opposite direction.[574]

Walter had a bad day Wednesday. He bit the postman on the ankle in the morning and one of the kids on the nose in the afternoon – unheard of behaviour for him. He was greatly ashamed and contrite and when I returned home on Thursday evening he was obviously anxious as to whether I knew or not, just like a child who has been naughty.[575]

Walter had great hopes of being elected Pope and was very dispirited by the result. He's not sitting at the next conclave because he's got a small abscess on his bum. Apart from those setbacks he's in good form and increasingly dear.[576]

Walter has just walked in very slowly, muddy and drenched and is pretending to be deaf to avoid bathing or drying.[577]

When planning a holiday in the summer of 1975, Alec told Anne Kaufman that Merula was keen on a trip to Mexico, 'but can I face not seeing Walter for over three months? If only he could read letters instead of eating them I wouldn't feel so fussed at leaving him.'[578] Walter was 'all that gives me a pant to be home', Alec wrote when filming in California. On 15 January 1978, Alec 'Joined M at Mass at St

Lawrence, where she told me Walter had been run over by milk van in
our drive yesterday, but is still alive, in the vet's surgery. Deeply upset.
Left Mass immediately and went home. Couldn't speak for an hour or
so. Near tears all day.'[579] Walter's pelvis was crushed, a leg broken and
his stomach split open. He remained at the vet's for ten days 'and
Merula and I were in deep gloom'. Alec was acting in Alan Bennett's
play *The Old Country* at the time and Bennett remembered how after
Walter's accident 'he was so upset he nearly didn't perform that night'.

In June 1985, Walter became terminally ill. 'My mother has had a
slight stroke – her second,' Alec wrote to Dame Felicitas, 'but seems
quite bright and talking more sense than usual. My beloved Dandy
Dinmont (Walter) has got leukemia but puts a brave face on it and a
slightly wagging tail. He has massive injections each week and there
is hope he will get through the next year.'[580] In fact, Walter barely
survived the next month:

It is 0900 on a beautiful morning and apprehensively M and I wait for
the vet, Mr Rodgers. We had half expected him yesterday evening.
Walter hasn't eaten for two days and is in a very bad way. We think he
may have had a stroke which is affecting his back legs, and he is
obviously in distress with his glands. All yesterday we were resigned
and nearly tearful. He gives a minute wag to his tail when he sees M.
I have had to carry him in and out and up and down stairs. It must have
been painful for him – and he is a great weight – but he has been
sweetly patient. He has been with us for over eleven years now and a
close and loving friend. So often I've said that when he dies I shall die
as well. Apart from anything else we have been bound by the same
birthday. His absence will mean a new kind of life.
(Later)
It's now 12.45. Walter died 2½ hours ago – eased out of life by the vet,
who behaved charmingly, kindly and correctly. I spent a difficult hour
digging his grave, close to where Tilly and Vesta are buried, right
behind the Atlantic Cedar. He was wrapped in a blue blanket and I
didn't look at him after death. My last contact when he was alive was

to kiss him on the ear just before he received the first injection, to make him dopey. Carrying his wrapped up and very limp body to his burial plot was the most trying part of it. I found myself, ridiculously I suppose, talking to him, explaining where he was – past the three cypress trees, past the end of the pond, to the spot which is shady but where a lot of daffodils will bloom in the spring. And we shall still be here, I imagine, when the daffodils are out next year. I'm glad he had a sniff round Ashford Cottage grounds last week. I don't know where Merula is. Turning hay I expect.

I've put some logs on Walter's grave, to prevent its being disturbed, until we can get a paving stone to mark it.

'This past week has seemed interminable, mourning for Walter each day,' Alec wrote in his diary on 13 July 1985. 'I have visited his grave morning and evening and always found a tear in my eye. But I reflect on his happy life and the jumble of emotions begin to quieten.' In his Small Diary, on 16 July: 'First day I haven't shed a tear for Walter – but I have visited his grave each morning and evening.' 'We miss our Walter's jolly jokes and smiles,' Merula told Dame Felicitas in a letter dated on the last day of October. And, referring to their indecision over Ashford Cottage, she added: 'Of course, one of the reasons why we can't leave Kettlebrook is that Walter is buried here – and Alec's heart, or a large piece of it, is in Walter's grave.'

thirty-eight

The depth and sincerity of Alec's love for Walter contrasts with his awkward and inhibited feelings for his human relatives. Agnes Cuff, Alec's mother, lived in a small house in Winchester with one of her sisters as an occasional companion. In October 1965, Alec 'had a letter from a cousin full of anxieties about my mother. I've had anxieties, of one sort or another, about my mother all my life,' he wrote to Dame Felicitas:

It looks as if I have to find someone to live with her – and she's not easy – and as she has always refused to have anyone else in the house (which is small enough, heaven knows) I am non-plussed as to what to do. I feel if I *move* her, to a hotel or easy flat or something, she will just *give up*, and apart from fading away make a nuisance of herself . . . Oh, what to do about lonely people? And, what to do about old people? As I have never (since the age of 13) been close to my mother, I often felt angry and resentful about her behaviour, and am therefore far from dutiful. I feel now a bit guilt-ridden and yet helpless and hopeless. A subject for prayer, I suppose.[581]

Five years later, little had changed:

My mother is a constant worry and moral problem and is unwell. She drinks *far* too much, falls down, cracks her head or bruises herself and then there is no one to look after her properly. She lived with us for a year and I won't have that again. If I give her more than the necessary cash it goes on the bottle. She either antagonises people who *do* stay, briefly, in the little house I have bought for her in Winchester, or takes against them and they go, and then, naturally, complains of loneliness.[582]

In 1970, Alec moved his mother from Winchester to a small house in Petersfield:

She is too lonely in Winchester and it's as much as I can do to get over there once a week which I *usually* do. Heaven knows I don't want her too near us – she runs up bills in the shops, makes trouble, causes a bit of scandal with drink, throws my name around, and is far from wise. But she will be so next week, and it will make her feel happier, I hope, to be within ten minutes' drive of me. I have never been able to love her – not since about the age of nine and much of my life has been greatly poisoned by her – but I've been quite content this afternoon choosing carpets and curtains and wallpapers etc. for the new place. I expect to get her in there in late January.

In 1972, 'through the good offices of Brompton Oratory', Alec found 'an elderly, impoverished, likeable, but virtually stone deaf ex-nurse gentle-folk sort of old lady to come down for five weeks to look after my mother', but he and Merula found that 'it was almost as exhausting as having them here. Shopping, lost keys, boilers expiring, ovens exploding, fuses and forgotten dog's meat, etc. etc.' 'Looked in on

Mother,' he noted in his Small Diary on 14 December, 'and grumbled about her never thanking us for anything. Which left her in tears, I'm afraid.'

When in England, Alec tried to behave as a conscientious son but Agnes managed to exasperate him in all the old ways:

> The milkman informed me that my mother owed £30 for milk and wouldn't pay. It's only a matter of weeks since she refused to pay her paper bill of £40. So I suppose that means £70 has gone on gin and Guinness recently. When I taxed her with the milk bill she said they were all cheats, it wasn't true, they owed her money for empty bottles etc and then pretended collapse and a tear.

In September 1978, Agnes had been found with a broken ankle, lying on the floor near her bed. 'She managed to get to a telephone when she sobered up.' Alec and Merula decided that she could no longer go on living alone and contemplated moving her into the annexe at Kettlebrook built for Rob and his wife: they had also offered it to Bridget Boland who had 'understandably but foolishly' declined.

Fortunately, a room became available at the Sue Ryder residential home near Petersfield, Bordean House, and Agnes was taken there when she was released from hospital where she had been treated for her broken ankle. Some of the old problems persisted: 'Sister James from Bordean telephoned this evening to say my mother had fallen over three or four times to-day with drink.' On 9 December 1979, when Alec and Merula went with a cake to celebrate Agnes's ninety-first birthday, they found her 'flat out on her bed mumbly drunk. A nearly empty bottle of Bristol Cream sherry was on her dressing-table and the room stank of sick.' Agnes had a 'small transient stroke' in January 1980: 'The poor old thing was, I think, a little frightened and ruminating about it.'

Agnes's ninety-second birthday was 'celebrated in Bristol Cream sherry. She was in bright good form.' By January 1982, she was 'declining rapidly' but made a quick recovery and, visiting her in

March, Alec found her in 'bright chatty form but not talking much sense. If Mother said, with a sigh, "Oh well! Such is life" once, she said it ten times.' Four years later, in February 1986, Alec came away from visiting his mother feeling:

> . . . awful at the thoughts I half-entertained; wishing she would die now or immediately after I return from New York. It will be very fussing if she goes while I am away or after I have started filming in late March. Very unfilial thoughts. I feel so sorry for her and the wretchedness and silliness of her wasted life but I don't see what I can do. She doesn't take in much of what is said to her and keeps repeating, with a sigh but meaninglessly, 'Such is life.' Some old piece of pub chat with her drinking cronies of forty years or so ago. And yet I wouldn't mind betting that when I go to see her next, probably at the end of the week, she'll be momentarily quite bright and bright-eyed.[583]

Agnes Cuff, or Agnes de Cuffe, as she had preferred to be known, died ten days later, taking the secret of Alec's paternity with her to the grave. 'She was unconscious during her last day and mostly so the day before,' Alec told Dame Felicitas. 'She died peacefully, thank God. I was with her some of the time during her last three or four days. She is buried in a peaceful little churchyard quite near where she spent the last six years. The C of E funeral service was simple, excellently conducted and the parson was good and spoke well. Just Merula, Matthew, our granddaughter*, a friend of hers and some nurses and staff from the home.'[584]

The day after his mother's funeral, Alec returned to her room in Bordean House 'to collect the pictures and an oddment or two. There was about £25 in cash in a drawer. Everything else was rubbish and to be destroyed – except her fur coat which I have suggested should be given to the Sue Ryder shop.' He gave the administrator £1,000 as a

---

* Sally Guinness

donation in appreciation of their kindness to Agnes, then returned to Kettlebrook feeling 'rather dream-like, remote, dull' and exhausted. 'When I was finally home, in the early evening I felt almost light-headed and frivolous. Opened a bottle of champagne.'

Because Alec had been so often away, either on-stage in London or filming abroad, much of the day-to-day preoccupation with Agnes had been left to Merula. Merula had also to share with her siblings the care of *her* ageing parents, Michel and Big Chattie, and, because she lived closest to Wadlington, of her older sister, Susy, who remained in a limbo between adult and infantile states of mind. Between 1967 and 1971, many of Merula's letters to Alec are about her trials dealing with her parents and Susy.

Michel Salaman died on 18 May 1971. 'Her mother,' Alec told Dame Felicitas, 'was in the same hospital and has now been removed to a nursing home, from which she will not come out alive, I'm sure. We all expect her to die within weeks. She is 96. My father-in-law was 94.'[585] Big Chattie lived on for another year, dying on 29 April 1972. 'Merula telephoned me at the theatre in the evening,' Alec told Dame Felicitas, 'and said, "I shan't come up to London tonight. I have a feeling I ought to spend the night at Mummy's nursing home". She arrived there at 9.00 p.m. and her mother died just after midnight. No other members of the family were there.'[586]

The death of Big Chattie did not mean the end of the *Sturm und Drang* of the Salaman family's lives. 'My family is like a whirlwind,' Merula wrote to Dame Felicitas:

One gets sucked into the middle and blown round and round in circles. When I say my family, I mean the Salaman family. Ever since my Pa died it's been a series of traumatic dramas – no – one drama in three acts. I had no idea that death is not the end but the beginning of events . . . we have just been living the third act – the disposal of family furniture and effects – wildly exciting and exhausting . . .[587]

Alec remained detached. His relations with his brothers and sisters-in-law had been mixed. He was closest by far to Chattie and had treated her to a trip to New York. Mary Salaman felt that Chattie was the bravest of the Salamans when it came to standing up to Alec. Like her mother, Chattie had strong left-wing convictions which she had put into practice by taking theatre to the proletariat in St Etienne and would argue with Alec about politics. 'Violent political argument. I was too rude to Chattie,' Alec wrote in his Small Diary on 13 July 1967; and, the following day, 'Ashamed of treatment of Chattie, but re-read Communist Manifesto and thought how right I was.'

Alec would have judged Chattie's life 'disordered'. Her marriage to John Blatchley, which had suffered a knock when she had had an affair with Jean d'Asté in St Etienne and given birth to his daughter, Claire, stumbled on for a year or two but then finally came to an end. 'Chattie is very low indeed,' Matthew had written to his father when visiting his aunt in France, 'and the whole atmosphere is one of sadness and disintegration. Only five of the old company are left.' Chattie returned to England in the early 1970s and worked in the theatre in the East End, then in Hammersmith, trying to bring the ideals of Copeau, St Denis and d'Asté to English theatre. She taught at the Guildhall School of Drama and lived in a small house in Acton.

Merula's brothers and sisters had all followed artistic vocations: Jill became a potter, Mikey a painter and Eusty practised as an architect in Petersfield until, in the mid-1960s, his partnership got into financial difficulties and finally went bankrupt. The Salamans blamed his partner for this fiasco but it was also acknowledged that Eusty had no head for business. He was a gentle, amiable, outspoken, gregarious fellow, a good cricketer, and loved by all. He and his wife Mary had three delightful children, Christopher, Toby and Chloe. It was Christopher who had been like a brother to his cousin Matthew.

Most of the Salamans were in awe of Alec because he was so

successful and they were not. In some the awe was mixed with a measure of resentment: they felt that his fame had made him aloof. He was also rich, whereas the Salaman fortune had been dissipated after the war. Alec and Merula's Catholicism was a further alienating factor: though Chattie became an Anglican and her husband, John Blatchley, a Charismatic Catholic; Eusty's wife, Mary, a lapsed Catholic, felt that Alec and Merula were too dismissive of anyone who did not share their beliefs. 'Merula became very intolerant. Anyone who wasn't a Catholic was a pagan.'[588] Mary also judged that her husband, Eusty, was 'wary of Alec, but not wary enough'.

When Eusty's practice got into financial troubles, Merula wrote to Alec, then filming in Spain, to ask if she could give him some money. 'Oh dear, what sadnesses,' Alec wrote in reply:

> I won't grudge your letting Eusty have a couple of thousand pounds if you wish to do that, but my own feeling is very strong that it is useless to pour money into that business. Certainly while Peter McEver* is anywhere near it. He strikes me as having the same disruptive, destructive, muddling, false-hoped, idiot-whatever-it-is that my mother has had all her life . . . My own feeling would be to not help business-wise – after all, we are totally ignorant of business matters – but be in a position to help Eusty personally when the whole thing collapses, as I fear it is bound to do. Then, if this financial haul of mine† comes off successfully, we might be able to help substantially.[589]

'I sent Eusty £200 two weeks ago and no word from him,' he wrote to Merula on 12 June 1962. 'I *suppose* he received it.' Two years later, when Alec learned that Eusty and Mary were finding it difficult to go on paying their children's school fees, he sent them a cheque for a thousand pounds. Mary wrote to thank him, saying how wonderful it

---

* Eusty's partner in the architectural practice.
† This was the year Alec remained abroad to avoid UK income tax.

had been to be able to pay off their debts and still have enough money left to buy a piece of furniture she had coveted for some time – an antique chair. This provoked a letter 'of seismic vitriol' from Alec which he subsequently regretted. 'My dear Eusty,' he wrote from New York where he was appearing in *Dylan*:

I should have written weeks ago to apologise humbly for the unpleasant tone of my angry letter. I do so now. I am terribly sorry to have upset you and deeply regret my letter. I was angry and felt madly frustrated being so far away and not knowing what was going on – and working under great pressure – but all that is no valid excuse. So you must do your best to forgive me.[590]

Alec liked to be thought generous but did not want to be taken for granted. 'Chattie told us that Nick is in a worried state financially so I have sent him £500,' he notes in his diary on 7 October 1978. But, six years later, he reacted less favourably when Nick Blatchley asked for help with the cost of his further education:

A long letter from Nick Blatchley asking me if I would loan him £10,000 to help him undertake a course in Higher Mathematics. Or any sum of money. Sent him, as a gift, £1000 with no assurance that there would be any more to follow next year . . . I feel very well off at the moment, with well over a million in the bank, but after taxes this will probably be down to £350,000. And there is £6000 p.a. towards Sally's education, over £5000 p.a. to my mother and I expect about £3000 p.a. to Matthew. I find it mounts up. It's good that I am the only extravagant one in the family.[591]

Eusty's son, Toby, felt that his parents 'lived in terror of Alec'. There was palpable tension when they came to dinner. They knew he hated ceremony and sycophancy but he also loathed over-familiarity. 'Shy people like me didn't have a chance.'[592] Merula would only invite members of her family to Kettlebrook when Alec was away. Toby

Salaman and his then girlfriend, Nerissa Garnett*, having tea with
Merula at Kettlebrook, noticed Merula turn pale when Alec
unexpectedly returned from London. They quickly departed. On
another occasion, it was Alec who fled from a Salaman. Matthew,
walking up from the Harrow, the pub at the bottom of the garden, saw
his father running from the house, his head down. Jill Salaman had
come to call and he was escaping to London.

---

*   Daughter of David Garnett, granddaughter of the painter Duncan Grant who had
    used Chattie, together with Mary and Angelica Bell, as models for his mural on a
    church near Lewes.

thirty-nine

When Matthew received the news that he had been accepted as a drama student at LAMDA, Alec had been delighted. 'Did Alec tell you that Matthew has gone to LAMDA i.e. drama school – and seems thrilled with it,' Merula wrote to Dame Felicitas. 'I can't tell you what a relief it is to have him settled at last, and he looks as if he has dropped a load of bricks. I think this all stems from Lourdes.'[593] Alec was also relieved: 'It *does* seem as if he is happy and busily making up for the indecisive and lazy year,' but, he told Dame Felicitas, 'I don't think he *is* an actor but anyway the training will give him all sorts of confidence I hope.'[594]

However, Alec's relief that Matthew was doing *something* was mixed with apprehension that he might not do it well. Alec's protective feelings for his good-natured but unworldly son were combined with fear that any failure would reflect badly on *him*. During a performance at LAMDA of Bernard Shaw's *Fanny's First Play*, Matthew peeped through the closed curtains and saw Alec sitting in the auditorium with his face hidden in his hands. 'Both of us were embarrassed. It was a terrible production.'

Both Alec and Merula, having secretly hoped that Matthew might become a priest, now began to fear that he was losing his Catholic faith. 'We are fairly anxious about Matthew's religious life now,' Alec wrote to Dame Felicitas:

> Apparently he goes to Mass (at any rate when his mother is there, one doesn't know about other times) but always seeks an excuse for not going to communion – by taking a bite from an apple just before leaving for mass*, or some other such device. It's unlike him to be deceptive or devious and we fear he has lost – what *other* word can we use? – or turned away from his faith and is only going through a form and ceremony so as not to distress us. I have suspected this for a year or more now. And apparently he is bitter (perhaps too strong a word, as he's not that sort of lad, but *very* critical) about this Jesuit education and no longer has any time for the Order at all. Maybe it's all youthful reaction. I don't know. But a bit worrying.[595]

Matthew's doubts had first arisen when he had been living in Italy. They increased when he read *The Phenomenon of Man* by the Jesuit philosopher and palaeontologist, Teilhard du Chardin – a work given to him by his father. It had helped Alec, he had told Dame Felicitas, to weather 'the worst spiritual crisis that has ever come my way':

> A climax was reached and for four days I decided I had abandoned not only the Catholic Church but Xtianity as well. I contacted various priests and considered I received nothing but sympathetic clichés – But God was good and kind and gently led me home again. And I thank God, too, for Fr Teilhard de Chardin. I wonder what on earth, or in heaven, he and your St Jerome could possibly say to each

---

*   Catholics have to fast before going to Communion.

other. I know which I think the more generous-minded and better-minded.[596]

Alec's own doubts made him sympathetic when, on 25 June 1964, he received a letter from Matthew 'full of doubts and complaints about LAMDA, of course, but very sensible, and also giving out some clue as to his religious feelings at the moment'. Matthew also told his mother about 'his religious dilemmers [sic] and things we have never had in the open before'. 'I think you will find,' Merula wrote to Alec, 'that he has matured and relaxed and opened up a great deal since you saw him last.'[597]

However, Alec continued to worry that Matthew was too fragile for real life – an echo of the reasons he had given Merula for persuading her to give up her career, and an acknowledgement, perhaps, of the steel in his own ambition. He wrote to Dame Felicitas just before Christmas 1966, to solicit:

. . . special prayers for my dear Matthew. Can't explain why – couldn't even if I had the time – but I am *worried* about him. He is dear and good and charming, but deep down I sense a great distress and a sort of not quite facing up to life which frightens me. He chooses to live (he is in Nottingham) in grim and filthy surroundings (not necessary financially) and in squalor. I know he is in love with a girl we like very much (and who would suit him) but she has turned him down so far though they remain friends. He has said *nothing* of this and we are supposed not to know. But I suspect he's in a sort of hell . . .[598]

On 4 February 1967, Alec told Dame Felicitas that '*secretly* we keep our fingers crossed that he is going to announce his engagement to a girl we like very much – though we know – again secretly – that she turned him down nearly a year ago. But he seems to remain faithful and they see a great deal of each other.' A fortnight later, Matthew told his parents that he was engaged to be married to Andrée, the daughter of

their friends from the London Acting School, Pierre and Marriott
Lefèvre.

Merula was Andrée's godmother but, despite the close friendship
between the parents, Andrée had seldom seen Matthew as a child.
Marriott went on holiday with Alec and Merula without her; Andrée
saw more of Chattie and Eusty than Merula and if she ran into
Matthew, it was with his cousins, Christopher, Toby and Chloe
Salaman at Slong Farm. Andrée had gone to the Ballet Rambert School
close to her home in Ladbroke Grove. Matthew and his cousin Toby
had lodged in the Lefèvres' house while at drama school. Matthew was
three and a half years older and Andrée adored him. 'He used to be
very, very funny . . . He was such a lovely, warm, open, generous,
funny, humble person.'[599] Because Marriott now spent some of her
time in her house in Essex, the young people were left on their own,
entertaining Andrée's friends from the Rambert School and talking late
into the night.

When Matthew told his parents that he was to marry Andrée, they
were delighted. 'I do see that she is a very sweet and attractive girl,'
Alec wrote to Matthew from Paris after the engagement had been
announced, 'but I have thought so for a long time.' Then, inevitably,
Alec tried to take charge:

Go to Sullivan & Woolley (18 Conduit Street). Ask for Mr Peters. I will
have written to him to expect you. Order yourself three suits as a sort
of pre-wedding present from me. I *know* fittings are tedious – but you
will bless me in the end. I suggest you get yourself a dark blue or dark
grey formal evening suit, a lightweight tweed or grey flannel suit and
a summer suiting of some sort. And also, to go with that, go to
TURNBULL & ASSER in Jermyn Street and order yourself a dozen
white or cream shirts of good material. Again you will bless me. And
again it's a gift and they will have to be pre-warned. *They* don't need
fittings – just measurements. With all that in hand you should be as
sparkling as a band-box by your wedding day.[600]

To Andrée, Alec wrote 'a most loving letter' accompanying a beautiful necklace. But Alec was not wholly in control. Matthew and Andrée 'are getting married in a Registrar's office . . . and have begged that none of us be present,' Alec reported to Dame Felicitas:

They have also refused any kind of party. However her mother is providing a small luncheon party for the family and them, and Merula and I are doing a small dinner. I had wanted to do something gayer and more amusing – like hiring a Thames Steamer and taking them all down river with a tiny band – something memorable – but they have said No.[601]

With money provided by Alec, Matthew and Andrée bought a cottage in Mortlake, close to Richmond Park and, Alec reported to Dame Felicitas, 'seemed gorgeously happy and relaxed. What a wonderful generation those young ones are – when they aren't beatnik. Much truer than we were at that age, I feel.' 'Rejoice with us,' Alec wrote, again to Dame Felicitas, on 12 June 1968. 'Andrée gave birth – swiftly and easily – to a well set up boy. Matthew is inordinately proud. Merula and I drift around with smiles and moist eyes. I keep raising my heart to God.'[602]

Matthew and Andrée called their son Samuel and in 1971 Andrée gave birth to a second child, Sally. As so often between generations, differences about how to bring up the children caused some tension. No doubt in reaction against his own strict upbringing, Matthew was an indulgent father and Andrée, as she later recognised, projected onto Alec and Merula her resentment at her own mother's dominating personality, continuing with them 'the fight against her for my own independence'. She saw in Alec and Merula the kind of disdain that had led her mother to reject her father: the dismissive 'terms used by that generation were, "oh, but they're so *boring*". "Common" as well came up.'

In 1973 Matthew and Andrée moved into a larger house at 19 Claremont Road in Twickenham. Alec hoped that the extra space would alleviate the difficulties which he could see they were facing in their marriage: 'Apparently Andrée is now off to marriage-guidance people and group-therapy a couple of times a week and always returns emotional and tearful,' he wrote in his diary on 10 May 1974. He could not understand why Andrée 'who hates housework, refuses to have anyone' to clean the house. 'She seems not to mind a muddled piggy existence.'

Alec, with his loathing for disorder, was appalled by the chaos of his son's household which he witnessed on a visit to 19 Claremont Road, noting in particular a broken fence at the bottom of the garden. During dinner, when they next came to Kettlebrook Meadows for the weekend:

I made an innocent enquiry about M & A's broken fence with their neighbours & Andrée said she liked it that way. And her garden being overgrown with weeds. Which I said she couldn't. Then she had screaming hysterics, shouting at me, 'You silly old fool! Etc.' So I caught the 9.45 train up to London. Matthew came down to the station, stared at me and turned on his heels. So that's that as far as I'm concerned.[603]

This account, from Alec's Small Diary, was written up more fully in his journal six days later:

Last Sunday evening was terrible. The day had been very enjoyable, hot and sunny, lunch out of doors and the children playing around and in the big pond. But I had an odd feeling, from time to time, that Andrée was bottling up something. During dinner, having accused Matthew – fairly lightly I thought – of not having thanked me for paying some forgotten insurance on his house (he said he had thanked me) I changed, as I thought, the conversation by asking if their garden fence was still in a state of collapse. Matthew said wearily, it was. Andrée, who was sitting opposite me, stared at me with sullen eyes and said, 'I like it that way!' I said, 'You must be joking!' Then she went on to say she liked the garden to have weeds and be a mess etc. It was so dotty that I suppose I showed my disbelief and contempt. Then all hell broke loose. She screamed at and abused me, thumping the table and waving her arms above her head. It was all quite horrid. Matthew got into a white rage with me; so I changed my clothes and got Mr Jones to drive me to Petersfield station. Matthew followed me down there, came on to the same platform and just stared at me. I spoke to him quietly and then he abruptly turned on his heel and walked away. I thought it was unlikely I should ever see him again. My heart was thumping so heavily that I had to deliberately calm myself and walk very slowly. It was a miserable night at Smith Square, and a miserable return home next day. Merula, naturally, in a state of distress and depression. On Wednesday I had to return to London, where I found a letter from Matthew – an attempt at opening a door to reconciliation – and ending up 'I hope it's only au revoir and not adieu.'[604]

Matthew's recollection of this incident is slightly different.

I was here for the weekend with Andrée . . . and he said something dismissive to Andrée about our house in Twickenham. 'Nice house; pity it looked like a gypsy encampment and a pity about the dreadful fence.' He had come to see the house. And the fence wasn't ours. We were trying to reach an arrangement with the landlord to change the fence. Andrée flipped. She lost her temper. Alec said in a calm voice, 'My dear Andrée, if you can't learn to behave, I shall have to ask you to leave my house.' Alec was very formal. Samuel was asleep upstairs. I was astonished: it was a bolt from the blue. I said: 'Don't be such a pompous ass.' So Alec left.[605]

Three days after this fracas, Alec received a letter of apology from Matthew and Andrée: 'There is no doubt that I am quite desperately sad,' he noted in his diary. However, Alec did not see his son for another two months. Matthew was then asked to meet him for dinner in a grand London restaurant and found that there was a third person present – a stage manager whom he had never met before – and nothing was said about the row. After that, things returned to normal although it was some time before they spent another weekend at Kettlebrook.

Alec had an ambivalent attitude towards Matthew's acting career. He appeared on stage with him only once, in the play *Time Out of Mind* by Bridget Boland which had a short run at the Yvonne Arnaud Theatre in Guildford in July 1970: it was an awkward experience for them both. Alec was delighted if Matthew made a success of a part but was always afraid that a failure might reflect badly on him. This was true socially as well as professionally. 'He didn't like it if in company people got interested in what I was doing. He would shut that off pretty sharply . . . "don't ask him about that"'.

It is possible, of course, that Alec was afraid that Matthew might *bore* his friends. 'Matthew talked far far too long,' Alec recorded in his diary on 2 April 1981. '1 ¼ hours non-stop during dinner.' Matthew had, every now and then, tremendous enthusiasms – on the subject of pheromones, for example, or the Californian movement for group therapy, EST – which Alec received with a measure of scepticism. 'Matthew sweetly turned up. He talked for about two hours solidly about his EST experiences. All a bit mad, uncouth and suspect, I thought. But he was very dear and stayed the night.' Though Alec liked long telephone conversations with friends such as Robert Hamer or Mark Kingston, he would answer a call from Matthew abruptly and pass him straight on to Merula.

Alec was generous towards Matthew and Andrée's children. There was Beluga caviar on Matthew's birthday and a cheque for £1,000. He paid his granddaughter Sally's school fees at Bedales. He tried to be a good grandfather to Samuel and Sally but as often as not failed: 'Found the children irritating all day and fear I showed it.'[606] 'Samuel and Andrée came down for the day yesterday. What had been quiet and agreeable turned into a bear-garden of chaos and noise.'[607] One of Andrée's grievances against Alec was that he spent more time in the grand houses of his rich friends than he did at his grandchildren's home in Twickenham, which he visited only three times.

Matthew and Andrée's permissive upbringing had produced uninhibited children. Sally recalled that, as a teenager, Alec was irritated by her mumbling, but she loved to spend her holidays at Kettlebrook. She called Merula 'Merula' because she did not like to be called 'Granny' and Alec 'Grandfather Alec'. She remembers her nervous anticipation when Alec emerged from his study at mealtimes, partly because she knew high standards were expected at table, but also because he would often come out playing some funny role. She was not afraid of him but was conscious that Matthew was uneasy about how she and Samuel would behave. Sally adored both her Guinness grandparents but particularly Merula.

Sally was equally fond of Marriott, Andrée's mother, and would stay with her at her house in the country, The Old Stores at Elmdon, near Saffron Walden. The deteriorating relationship between Matthew and Andrée, however, led to a brief coldness between Marriott and the older Guinnesses. In January of 1982 Marriott turned down an invitation to join them on holiday. 'At present I can't cope with great love for both of you, mixed with inevitable restraints and silences about our children and our grandchildren – like great chasms . . .'[608] And, when Alec protested: 'Do you not know that you (separately and/or together) overpower me? If this makes either of you angry or offended, put that anger into trying to understand the effect you both have on me: I don't know, I think that this is perhaps too hard to do . . .'[609]

In an incoherent way, Marriott perhaps wanted to convey to Alec that his powerful, domineering personality had contributed to the failure of her daughter's marriage, both because his poor opinion of Andrée as wife and mother had further lowered her self-esteem; and because he and Merula, by their disciplinarian approach to Matthew's upbringing, had led to their son's passivity as a parent. As Alec had written to Dame Felicitas à propos of Matthew almost twenty years before: 'Oh dear, oh dear – the sins of the fathers are visited on the sons in curious ways.'[610]

Matthew and Andrée were divorced in December, 1985. 'All very amicable,' Alec reported to Dame Felicitas, 'and now he is here with his lady friend . . . *Quite* like her – but not enough, I fear, to feel cosy and truly welcoming.'[611] Matthew's recollection of Alec's first meeting with Helen gives us an idea of what it meant when Alec did not feel cosy and truly welcoming. 'He sat next to Helen but held up his hand to shield her from his sight. He did not speak to her. He was incredibly rude.'

In 1982, Matthew decided to take a sabbatical from acting; moved to Ashford Cottage in 1986 and was married to Helen in 1989. 'My beloved Matthew is marrying his lady friend of four years' standing this Monday,' Alec told Dame Felicitas, 'which pleases Merula and me greatly. In a register office, of course.'[612] Four years later, Matthew's second marriage ended. Ashford Cottage was sold, Matthew went to live on a boat on the Thames, and in August 1996, married for a third time.

forty

In 1964 Alec and Merula bought a small house at 30 Ennismore Gardens Mews as a pied-à-terre in London. Alec was always in two minds about the advisability of having two houses: he worried about the expense, and in April 1969 he sold it to his neighbour, Kay Walsh: 'Too much responsibility,' Alec told Dame Felicitas. To replace it, he bought the lease of a flat beneath Percy Harris in Smith Square, Westminster. When the lease expired in 1977, Alec arranged to move to a 'gorgeous flat next door . . . rather above our station' but then changed his mind. 'A hunch on Christmas Eve,' he told Dame Felicitas, 'said to me "don't" so tomorrow I start back-pedalling and, as nothing has been signed, I hope it's not too late to withdraw. In fact we have decided to have nowhere in London and when I have to work here I'll stay in a hotel. Cheaper in the long run.'

Thus started Alec's Connaught years. The quiet, discreet and expensive hotel in Carlos Place, facing the Jesuit church at Farm Street, became Alec's second home until shortly before he died. A

small suite was always at his disposal. Alec referred to the church at
Farm Street as his 'private chapel in London' and the Grill Room at
the Connaught became his canteen. He loved the comfort, the
discretion, the luxury: it became a home from home. He entertained
there – not just one or two friends in the Grill but, on rare occasions,
larger groups in a private room. 'Tuesday we gave a champagne party
in our suite for about 22 people,' he noted proudly in his diary on 19
December 1982:

> . . . followed by dinner for 10 in a private dining-room. We thought it
> all a great success. Liz Frink* and her husband were there (and for
> dinner, as were Margaret and Giles Fitzherbert, Jocelyn Herbert, Alan
> Bennett and Ron Eyre.) At the party David and Jane Cornwell†, the
> Kingstons, Nan Munro‡ (who kept addressing Frink, DBE as Miss
> Frisk), the Van Thals, Lindy Dufferin**, Peter Bull, Tony Quayle (who
> stayed for dinner) and the Bernard Heptons††. The dinner menu was
> (a) smoked salmon (b) Noisette d'Agneau a l'Estragon and (c) fabulous
> crêpe soufflées Belle Epoque. The wines Chardonnay Bourgogne
> (1978) Château Fonplégade (1976) and Château Suduiraut (1972). It was
> all extremely good.

On 21 April 1994, Alec gave 'a glamorous luncheon for John Gielgud
who was 90 last week. I owe him my theatre career and have always
wanted to make a gesture for him. So I took a private room at the
Connaught and we sat down fourteen.'[613] Besides John Gielgud, the
guests included Keith Baxter, Wendy Hiller, Anna Massey, Eileen
Atkins, Judi Dench, Maggie Smith, Dorothy Tutin, Lindsay Anderson,

---

*   Elisabeth Frink had sculpted a head of Alec for the National Portrait Gallery.

†   John le Carré and his wife.

‡   South African actress whom Alec would have first seen as Fräulein von Dordeck in
Children in Uniform at the Haymarket Theatre in November, 1934.

** Marchioness of Dufferin and Ava, the daughter of Loel Guinness, one of Alec's
'cousins'.

†† Bernard Hepton appeared with Alec in *Smiley's People.*'

Jocelyn Herbert, Percy Harris and Alan Bennett. Martin Hensler, Gielgud's companion, declined the invitation. 'He says he can't leave the house empty with the birds and dogs,' Gielgud told Alec, 'and I think he feels he sees too much of me already.'[614]

As a general rule, Alec disliked receiving hospitality from others, preferring all social engagements to be on his terms and on his terrain. He would occasionally dine with neighbours such as the Harwoods or Jill Balcon, and in London with close friends such as Leueen MacGrath. He accepted invitations from, and became friends with, 'society hostesses' such as Brooke Astor in New York or Maureen Littman in London; and became greatly attached to Drue Heinz, publisher of the *Paris Review*. The wife of Henry John Heinz and a discerning patron of literature, she endowed the Hawthornden Prize.

Alec also allowed himself to be taken up by his 'cousins', the grand Guinnesses – not just by Honor Svejdar, but her son Paul Channon; Lindy, Marchioness of Dufferin and Ava and the granddaughter of Benjamin Guinness, one of the candidates for Alec's natural father; and her mother-in-law, Maureen, the dowager Marchioness of Dufferin and Ava. On 6 July 1978, Alec dined at Apsley House, the London home of the Duke of Wellington, with the Duke's son and daughter-in-law, the Marquis and Marchioness of Douro – the Marchioness being both a Guinness and the granddaughter of the last German Kaiser – before going on to a party given by the Channons for Prince Charles. Merula loathed such grand occasions and avoided them whenever she could.

Alec had mixed feelings about the different members of the royal family. When filming *Hotel Paradiso* in Paris in 1966 he was taken by Peter Glenville to 'some rich house on the Left Bank' where he had enraged the Duke of Windsor by bringing him whisky in the wrong glass: '"I said a *small* glass!" he screamed at me. "A small glass, a small glass, a small glass! You fool".' Alec had searched for a small glass but there was none to be found. Later the Duke apologised for his rudeness. '"I don't know what came over me. I am so sorry"'.[615]

Ten years before, Alec had received his CBE from the Queen Mother, whom he adored. In 1975 he was invited to a reception at Buckingham Palace given by the Queen. 'I'm impressed,' he wrote to Anne Kaufman, 'but Merula is indifferent.' The event was written up in detail in Alec's diary. In 1978, he sat next to the Queen Mother at a dinner given by Maureen Dufferin and had a conversation with 'H.R.H. Prince of Wales . . . in which he informed me that he thought Shakespeare wrote much of *Macbeth* as a joke.'[616] In 1979 he once again was invited to meet the Queen Mother at dinner with Maureen Dufferin. Again, the evening was described in detail in Alec's diary:

> Thursday was Maureen Dufferin's dinner-party for the Queen Mother. Arrived at Hans Crescent at 19.40. A very warm night. HM arrived wearing an emerald green chiffon dress printed over with mauve cabbages. She was also sporting magnificent dark emeralds. At dinner – I think we were eighteen – I sat between Maureen and Lady d'Erlanger. Quite easy going. After dinner talked for ten minutes with Duke of Grafton. Upstairs Maureen invited me to come and talk to HM but I declined, saying she must have had quite enough of me last year, when we were left in the dark when the lights fused. So I was put with HM's lady-in-waiting whose name I never fathomed . . .[617]

This dinner became an annual event until 1986 when Alec began to find it a little too much. 'Maureen Dufferin has changed dates of her dinner to the Queen Mum . . . and so I have felt obliged to decline: I think M would be a bit hurt at my being unnecessarily away from home on my birthday.'[618] He then seemed to regret it:

> Weather was lovely for my and Walter's birthday. Dinner to Matthew and his lady friend and Jill Balcon. Caviar followed by black Boudin and fruit salad. It was a pleasantish evening but somehow didn't go with a swing. I suspect it was my fault as I heard myself being rather harsh about some of Merula's relatives. Perhaps because I could have been with Queen Mum but turned Her down for my own party.[619]

One of Alec's favourite words was 'chuffed', and there is no doubt that
he was 'chuffed' at being lionised by select members of the aristocracy,
plutocracy and the royal family. In 1987, he went to the Cannes Film
Festival accompanied by Mark Kingston and sat next to Diana, Princess
of Wales at a gala dinner. His natural deference was shaken when he
came up against Prince Charles's views on Shakespeare or Princess
Margaret's comment, on coming backstage after attending *A Walk in the
Woods*: 'Oh Alec, what a lot of talking.' On New Year's Day, 1992,
depressed by the civil war in Yugoslavia, he lashed out at everyone in
high places – 'Major seems nice but bland, Kinnock windy and
opportunist, Carey of Canterbury gap-toothed and vulgar, the Queen
mostly grumpy (anyway in her photographs) and the Prince of Wales
asinine and opinionated – well, as quoted in the press.'[620] But all were
forgiven when, in May 1994, Alec received a letter from 10 Downing
Street asking if he would be agreeable 'to be appointed a Member of
the Order of the Companions of Honour'. He accepted and received
special 'telemessages' of congratulation from the Queen, the Duke of
Edinburgh, Prince Charles and Princess Margaret, conveyed by her
Private Secretary. On 28 July, Alec was received in private audience by
the Queen to receive his badge as a Companion of Honour.

Alec had an unsophisticated and inconsistent attitude towards money.
When he had thought of selling Kettlebrook Meadows in the mid-
1970s, it was not just the prospect of the by-pass but because of the
cost of running a country house. 'We know that within a very few
years,' he wrote to Dame Felicitas on 13 March 1971, 'we shall have to
give up Kettlebrook, which is far too expensive to run these days.'
Again, on 7 July 1975, he wrote to her that:

> We can hang on here for a bit if we let all go to seed in a Chekhovian
> way – and indeed we are already letting that happen partially – but in
> time we shall have to dismiss our gardener/odd-job man and then it *will*
> be a sad sight. Next year I must have the *woodwork* of the house re-
> painted, and that will cost over £1,000. And so it goes on.[621]

Yet Alec himself recognised that he was inconsistent: 'For all our talk of the necessity of leaving Kettlebrook we are now contemplating spending about £4,000 on enlarging the kitchen there.'[622] Even as he was complaining to Dame Felicitas that the running costs of Kettlebrook were too great, he was negotiating a fat fee for appearing in the film *Murder by Death*: 'They started off by offering $50,000 for ten weeks' work, which is ludicrous. I am holding out for a hundred and considerable weekly expenses.'[623] And it seems that Merula paid very little attention to his financial worries: 'I've had a lovely spending spree,' she wrote to Anne Kaufman, 'starting with baby tractor through new television, new deep freeze to washing machine. There's nothing like Alec saying he's broke to get me throwing the money around – of course it's all *investment* and helps towards self-sufficiency year.'[624]

In an era of rapidly rising property prices, the best investment by far would have been a house in London but, though Alec worried about money and loved earning large sums, he showed no interest in investment or capital growth. He spent his single tax-avoiding year abroad, but never took steps to avoid tax through such devices as off-shore companies and trusts: he loathed paying money to lawyers. He bought no stocks and shares which, in this inflationary period, showed consistent and often dramatic growth. Alec did not, as some said, keep his money in a Post Office savings account, but he did little better by leaving most of it in a deposit account where it earned interest which was taxed at the highest rate – up to ninety-eight pence in the pound.

Alec did avoid income tax by making tax deductible contributions to a number of pension funds: National Provident, Equitable Life, Norwich Union. These were limited by law to a percentage of his income, which increased as he grew older; since his income in some years was substantial, so were the sums salted away. However, in the late 1960s he saw a considerable drop in his income. 'Columbia are discontinuing my contract,' he noted in his Small Diary on 31 October 1969. 'So I shall be reduced to approximately £4,000 a year instead of a steady £12,000 for the next nine years.' On 13 March 1971, he told

Dame Felicitas – in whom he confided his worldly as well as his spiritual preoccupations – that 'no work that I want to do comes my way . . . I *may* do a bit of filming, just for the cash, in May. In the last financial year I have earned £90! Not the usual £80,000 I am used to over a decade.' 'Depressed by my current account being so low,' he wrote in his diary on 17 February 1972. 'Must economise.' When his finances *were* given a fillip, it was not by a film but by a play – Alan Bennett's *Habeas Corpus*. 'I haven't counted up what I made in cash from it, but I suppose probably £30,000, which would be far the greatest sum I've ever made from a play.'[625]

Alec vacillated between frugality and extravagance. After receiving an offer of $150,000 in January 1976, to appear in *Star Wars*, and in February, £10,000 to do a forty-five-minute commercial for Concorde, he records that an 'electricity bill this morning for the past quarter nearly gave me a seizure – £176, of which £133 was the "inexpensive" night-storage system. As we primarily heat with Calor gas this seems absurdly over-charged'.[626]

That a world-famous film star should heat his house with night-storage heaters and Calor gas stoves struck the Guinnesses' friends as bizarre. Kettlebrook Meadows had been built with a modern heating system with ducted hot air but the system malfunctioned in 1970. Alec and Merula awoke in the middle of the night, Merula told Dame Felicitas, to find:

> . . . our oil fired central heater belching fumes all over the house and we were nearly exfixiated (sp?) in our beds. We've had the whole thing ripped out and workmen are all over the house blocking up the air vents, and to Hell with central heating from now on . . . Paraffin stoves, Calor gas, plug ins from now, and two vests if necessary.'[627]

Merula was as good as her word. No new central heating was installed and the house in winter became very cold. For guests, particularly Americans, a week-end in winter could be an ordeal. Anne Kaufman-Schneider, used to well-heated American apartments, could hardly sit on the seat of the lavatory because it was 'a cake of ice'. Eileen Atkins and Ronald Eyre, staying at Kettlebrook during the coal miners' strike and the subsequent 'three day week', when good citizens were enjoined to save electricity, were told by Alec to switch off the radiators in their bedrooms when they came down to dinner:

> Well, Ron and I met going downstairs and we both said that there was no way we were going to turn off our heaters, it was freezing. But we'd been downstairs for about ten minutes when Alec disappeared for a moment and then returned saying: 'You both forgot to turn off your heating.' Then it came round to eating time, and Ron said, 'I can't smell any smell of anything cooking. Are we going to get anything? Go out and ask if you can help Merula cook.' I went to the kitchen and asked Merula if I could help. She said, 'No, no, it's all over there,' and she pointed to an awful old suitcase in the corner. I said, 'Where?' She said, 'There, in the suitcase. Alec made me make a hay box.' We were having Bollito Misto which is slightly disgusting. She said, 'I didn't have any hay. It's mostly Alec's underwear.' She'd put the casserole in the suitcase surrounded by clothes. Of course, it wasn't cooked and was disgusting and he was rude to her, but it was his idea.[628]

Alec was, however, compulsively hospitable, not just entertaining his friends in expensive restaurants in London, but also inviting them down for the weekend. Neither he nor Merula felt comfortable with live-in servants so it was left to Merula to do the cooking. Guests, by and large, were not allowed to help. Jill Balcon, who lived nearby and was a superb cook, was never allowed into the kitchen – 'perhaps if Merula was alone'. Alan Bennett, who became a regular weekend guest, was allowed to make himself tea. Anne Kaufman-Schneider, who once insisted on doing something to help, was given the task of cleaning the silver. Her husband, Irving, was allowed to help with the goats. There were always exquisite toiletries in the guest bathroom and, with some guests, Alec liked to give the impression that there was a discreet staff at work behind the scenes. After a muddy walk with Merula, John le Carré was told by Alec to leave his shoes outside his bedroom door at night: le Carré, an early riser, went down at six the next morning to find Alec, in a green apron, cleaning his shoes.

Alec kept a set of tools in his desk which he used to hang pictures, attach plugs to lamps and make minor repairs. He had higher standards than Merula when it came to outward appearances: it was he who would plump up the cushions and arrange candles on the dining-table. It was Alec's job to lay the table and he did the washing-up until they bought a dishwasher. Occasionally, he would do the cooking, particularly when he was alone in the flat in Smith Square: his specialities were the actor 'Vincent Price's chicken with garlic'*, Haddock Monte Carlo, Bollito Misto, Caesar Salad, Apple and Curry soup (a recipe he adopted from Hilaire's restaurant in the Brompton Road) and *paella*. Alec's love of good food meant that he put on weight and often went on the Scarsdale diet.

For cocktails Alec would make Danish Marys (tomato juice and aquavit). He loved good wine. 'I remember him telling me about a certain wine,' said Sam Beazley. 'I knew nothing about wine. He bought wine from King Bomba in Soho – this was before the war. He was an epicure even then.' Did he drink too much? 'I may be a bad husband,' he wrote to Merula towards the end of the war, 'but I don't think you need fear ever that I will take to the bottle to drown my sorrows. On the whole the bottle, far from drowning, just swells them.'[629] 'Although Alec liked to have a drink in the evening,' Eileen Atkins recalled, 'none of us ever saw him drunk. He drank properly; a drink before dinner; wine with dinner; but I have never seen him drunk or even slightly pissed.'

'I do find entertaining guests quite hard work without you,' Merula wrote to Alec when he was in India making *A Passage to India*. 'Not

---

* Price was a known gourmet who published cookbooks and appeared as a TV chef.

having you do the drinks and coffee and dishwasher makes it a bit of a scramble.'[630] Merula was shy and relied on Alec to entertain their guests. Kitty Black, who went down to Kettlebrook when she was producing a play Merula had written for children, remembered him as 'ebullient, outgoing and endlessly entertaining'. He was a wonderful mimic and loved gossip. His guests were almost all from the worlds of theatre and film. Among his neighbours were his old friend Bridget Boland, the actress Mai Zetterling and her husband, the author David Hughes; Margaret Leighton and her husband, the actor Michael Wilding; the playwright Ronald Harwood and his wife Natasha; and the actress Jill Balcon, daughter of the head of Ealing Studios, Sir Michael Balcon; she was married first to the poet Cecil Day Lewis and subsequently lived with the military historian, Antony Brett-James. Outside the profession, among the neighbours whom he saw from time to time, were the author and former officer in SOE,* Selwyn Jepson, and Blake Parker, a retired naval captain.

A source of transient guests was the annual season at the Chichester Festival Theatre. Eileen Atkins 'practically lived with them' when she was acting at Chichester. Omar Sharif came to lunch from Chichester and when Alec himself played Shylock in *The Merchant of Venice* there in 1982, he gave a dinner at Kettlebrook for the entire cast. There were also the regular visits from close friends from London – Marriott Lefèvre, Peter Bull, Peter Glenville with Bill Smith, the actress Leueen MacGrath; and those who lived abroad – Jehane West from Greece and, from the United States, Anne Kaufman, with her husband, Irving Schneider, and Edward Herrmann, Alec's co-star in the play, *A Walk in the Woods*.

Alec was possessive of his guests. After lunch at Kettlebrook, the Schneiders accepted an offer from Jill Balcon to go sightseeing. 'I found myself feeling rather stupidly cross with Jill for taking them off to Selborne without consulting me,' Alec wrote in his diary. 'It doesn't

---

*   Special Operations Executive.

matter an iota – I just felt irritated with Jill grabbing at one's friends. Somehow it wasn't a 100% satisfactory weekend'.[631] Ronald Eyre, who directed Alec in *Voyage Round my Father*, *Habeas Corpus* and *A Walk in the Woods*, was well aware of Alec's sensitivities: when he went to stay at Kettlebrook with Eileen Atkins, he said he could drive her down but, "'I can't give you a lift back because Alec wouldn't be able to bear seeing us leave together, because he'd think we were talking about him. So you'll have to go back by train".'[632]

Alan Bennett became the Guinnesses' most regular and privileged guest:

> I'd go down on a Saturday afternoon and would have tea with Merula and Alec would be having his nap; and then we'd have supper and I'd stay through to Sunday supper and leave after that. He always wanted you to stay until Monday morning and try and bend you to his will. I'd go for a walk with Merula on a Sunday afternoon. He never went for walks.[633]

Alec had first met Bennett when Ron Eyre offered him a part in Bennett's *Habeas Corpus*. Bennett describes how he:

> . . . went with Ron to see him at the flat that they had at that time in Smith Square . . . I was very, very nervous. It was made far worse because I'd had a cold and so I'd taken about five of the fizzy Vitamin C without knowing that they were very strong emetics. So I had stomach cramps and had to go to the loo, but the loo at the flat in Smith Square had a glass door and you could see that there had been problems with this door because there were bits of paper stuck across . . . and so my first meeting with the great man, I was there in the loo . . . but we survived that.[634]

Alec greatly admired Bennett's writing and was the progenitor of his play *An Englishman Abroad*: Coral Browne had told Alec about meeting

Guy Burgess in Moscow; Alec had repeated the story to Bennett; Bennett had then asked to meet Coral Browne and, after hearing her account, had gone off to write the play. Alan Bennett twice went on holiday with Alec and Merula – once to Italy and later to stay in John le Carré's house, Tregiffian, in Cornwall. Neither was a particular success. In Italy, Bennett became exasperated by going everywhere in a chauffeur-driven car, and in Cornwall by Alec's high standards. 'It was a strain going on holiday with Alec. You couldn't just go into a tea-shop.' The visit to Cornwall was particularly difficult. 'The house felt spooked. I didn't like deep black water. We didn't go on expeditions.' Alan offended Merula by refusing to lift Walter over a fence. He had left after three days:

> Alan went back to London on the night train on Tuesday. He seemed rather edgy and discontented during his short stay. A taxi took him to Penzance and I paid for it before he got in. He didn't see me do so but when he found out his only comment was 'You treat me as if I was the stage-door keeper,' which I thought pretty ungracious. M thinks he is going through some personal crisis. He made some sadly cynical remarks about suicide.[635]

Two years later, when Alec and Merula invited Alan to stay with them in a villa in Greece, Alan prevaricated – to Alec's irritation. 'Alan wouldn't say Yes or No to the invitation to Greece we made him a couple of days ago. Obviously he won't come but I didn't want to say "Well don't!" That makes five people who have either accepted or half accepted and then shilly-shallied and finally called off . . .'[636] But Alec's annoyance was quickly forgotten and Alan became, in the view of Alec's friends such as Jill Balcon, Anne Kaufman or Drue Heinz, 'the son that Alec wished he had had'.[637]

There were limits to the intimacy between Bennett and the Guinnesses. Merula would not discuss Alec with Bennett: 'I think I once tried to talk about him but felt that it embarrassed her'; and though Bennett would confide in Alec about his emotional crises, Alec never once revealed that he might have been through the same sort of thing himself. Once, when they were driving past roadworks one summer, Alec nodded towards the workmen, stripped to the waist, and said: 'Very disturbing.' This was a unique intimation that Alec was attracted to his own sex. The two men shared a scepticism about the value of sexual fulfilment. Anne Kaufman recalls a winter walk at Kettlebrook:

> It was beautiful with a huge moon, crunchy snow, and Alan . . . Somehow, Alan got on to sex. He said that he thought that sex was highly over-rated. He said something about 'the docking position'. And Alec was laughing in the field and it was great. We were like five children aged six . . . standing laughing in the snow. It was a moment of Alec that I had never seen. Totally relaxed.

It was not always so relaxed. There were times when Alan Bennett was embarrassed by Alec's beastliness towards Merula. 'He was always putting her down' – not just her cooking but also, subtly, her writing and embroidery. When Bennett bought one of Merula's embroidered pictures, Alec thanked him profusely as if he was making his purchase as a favour to Alec. Bennett greatly admired Merula's work and wrote an introduction to her book, *Heaven is Like* . . .

It was the same when it came to Alec's treatment of Matthew. 'Alec treated Matthew badly. I once left the room because I couldn't bear the way he was talking to Matthew.' He was also irritated by Alec's inability to accept gifts or hospitality. 'I once took him out and it was so disastrous so I didn't even ask, ever again . . . He was a host, not a guest, and you knew he would be deeply unhappy if you paid for anything.' Bennett once brought a jar of caviar to Kettlebrook but Alec made such a performance out of thanking him that the next time he simply hid the pot at the back of the fridge.

Alec, despite his trickiness, retained the lifelong devotion of many friends. To Peter Glenville he was 'Dearest Alecco'; to Peter Bull,

'Dearest Alec'; to Richard Leech, 'Beloved Alec'. Michael Gough called him 'McSir' and Alec and Anne Kaufman used a variety of nicknames. Alec was devoted to Gordon Jackson and would talk to Mark Kingston on the telephone every Sunday morning. Kingston was one of the few who could tease Alec and get away with it and, with Richard Leech, was an executor of Alec's will. Alec's closest women friends were his sister-in-law Chattie, Marriott Lefèvre, Bridget Boland, Eileen Atkins, Anne Kaufman and, above all, Anne Kaufman's stepmother, the actress Leueen MacGrath.

Leueen was the daughter of a distinguished British Army officer, Walter MacGrath, DSO, MC, Croix de Guerre, and was educated in Catholic convents in Lausanne and Brussels. After studying at RADA at the same time as Frith Banbury and Rachel Kempson, she had a moderately successful career as an actress. She replaced Jessica Tandy as Jacqueline in Terence Rattigan's *French without Tears* in 1937, appeared very briefly in Anthony Asquith's film of Shaw's *Pygmalion*, and played the wife of the Flight Lieutenant in Rattigan's *Flare Path*, in the London, not the Broadway, production. Leueen's greatest success came in 1947 when she played Eileen Perry in *Edward, My Son*, by Robert Morley and Noel Langley. 'I remember the first time I saw her on the stage – the second act of *Edward, My Son*,' Irene Worth wrote to Alec at the time of Leueen's death. 'She threw herself onto Robert's ample landscape and covered his head with a cascade of silk blonde hair – very, very long, beautiful, erotic beyond anything else ever done again on stage or screen.'[638]

When *Edward, My Son* transferred to Broadway, Leueen went with it and there met the celebrated playwright, George S. Kaufman, whom she married. He was Leueen's third husband. Kaufman, around twenty years older than she, had also been married: his first wife, Beatrice, had died two years before. Anne, their adopted daughter, was only around ten years younger than Leueen and had been used to taking care of her father. Now she had also to take care of Leueen. 'She was like the daughter and I was like the mother. She was always getting things wrong; she couldn't remember where she was meant to be going; she missed appointments; she was always late.' The marriage to Kaufman lasted eight years.

Leueen was beautiful. 'Everyone noticed if she came into the room. She had real allure,' Anne Kaufman recalled. Jehane West, who knew both actresses, compared Leueen's beauty to that of Vivien Leigh. She too remembered how 'Leueen couldn't enter a room without everyone falling silent.' Sheridan Morley remembered her as 'breathtaking, she had waist-length hair . . . It's hard to find a modern equivalent. She had a fey manner, rather like a young Mia Farrow. A Peter Pan. Androgynous. Gay men always liked her.' Jill Balcon judged her 'irresistible – a *femme fatale*. She was adorable, outrageous.' She also remembered how, in her childhood, Leueen's name had struck terror in the heart of many an actor's wife. Leueen's five husbands were a small fraction of her lovers.

Alec first met Leueen MacGrath in New York in 1964 when he was appearing in *Dylan*, most probably through Peter Glenville who knew everyone. Their close friendship seems to have started in 1971 when they appeared together in John Mortimer's play, *A Voyage Round My Father*. She seems to have endeared herself towards Alec by teasing him: when Alec told her to write a hundred lines 'I must not laugh on-stage,' she embarrassed him by doing what he had asked. She was elegant, flirtatious, temperamental, beautiful and glamorous – everything, in fact, that Merula was not – and Alec adored her. Did they have an affair? Leueen, who did not like to admit that any man had escaped her clutches, told her stepdaughter Anne that, when on tour, she and Alec had gone to the brink but that he had finally desisted, saying that he could not betray his 'little wife'; but Anne Kaufman judged the story was probably untrue.

John Mortimer, who had attended the rehearsals of *A Voyage Round My Father*, felt that he was cold-shouldered by Alec – he was eventually told by the theatre manager that Alec had asked that Mortimer stay away from rehearsals because he was in the course of leaving his first wife, Penelope, for a second Penelope, Penny Gollop. Mortimer made things worse when, after three months of the run, he and Penny received an invitation from Alec to dine with him at Leith's restaurant in Notting Hill Gate. Alec was a stickler for punctuality* but John Mortimer had got the time wrong and turned up half an hour late. Alec, in a cold rage, told him how he had given dinner to the director, the other actors, the stage manager and the electricians, as if this evening with the Mortimers was the last chore of the run. John, searching for something to say, and having been to that night's performance, asked Alec if he did not think that Leueen had rather strange diction. 'If you'd had your lips around as many cocks in your life as Leueen MacGrath,' Alec answered, 'then you'd have rather strange diction.'[639]

Some felt that Merula might have resented Alec's fondness for Leueen but it seems likely that she knew her husband well enough to be able to feel confident that nothing untoward was going on. She could recognise that Leueen, so very beautiful and elegant, was more of an accoutrement for Alec than a rival for his love. She had the glamour, and wore the kind of expensive bangles and couture dresses that Alec so pointlessly bought for Merula. But Merula no doubt noticed how her fey femininity also irritated Alec. 'Leueen said to an uncomprehending young waiter "Just bring me a watercress salad and I may play with it,"' Alec noted in his diary on 26 January 1974. 'Almost on a par with her enquiry, on the rotten economy flight (BEA) we made from Stockholm, when the steward was offering round cigarettes and little bottles of whisky, "Have you any Madame Grès Cabochard bath oil?"'

Leueen was not afraid to stand up to Alec and she matched his moodiness with her own. 'Had blazing row with Leueen during dinner,' is Alec's first mention of her in his diaries. 'Tears and all. Rather gloomily to bed at 11ish.'[640] She constantly exasperated him with her fads. 'Leueen got tiresome asking for an oriental herb brew

---

*   Alan Bennett, having arranged to lunch with Alec in a restaurant at one o'clock, had suggested meeting earlier because Alec had to do a matinée. 'You're quite right,' said Alec, 'let's say five to one.'

which she insisted was called Gin Sling,' he wrote in his diary; and, to Anne Kaufman, at the end of August 1986:

Lulu was here last weekend . . . She did get on my nerves a bit one evening with her tiny, fastidious, very minor culinary demands which meant M or I had to keep jumping up searching while our food got cold and *then* she barely picked at whatever she wanted. Love her as I do I find that streak in her – spoiled over the years I suppose – rather irritating and my impatience is barely disguised, I fear.

Alec was also impressed that Leueen's self-absorption almost equalled his own. 'Lulu has been to us for two weekends running,' Alec wrote to Anne Kaufman on 17 September 1975:

. . . in excellent form except for losing her favourite glasses. (Merula found she had *six* pairs in her (Lulu's) car, apart from *another* pair in her bag, but Lulu wasn't interested in any of them.) It took from 4.p.m. Sunday to 11.am Monday *not* to find them. This included trudging through Durford Wood for an hour, going over an old path – on which Merula found a *button* which had fallen off Lulu's skirt (unknown to Lulu) the previous day.

Unlike many of Alec's other friends, Leueen was quite prepared to fall out with Alec. 'Leueen in good form and suddenly had a rage with me – for replying too loudly to a question she had asked twice,' Alec noted in his diary on 2 August 1985. 'She flounced off to bed. M and I were astonished.' The two were constantly having little spats. 'I have spoken to Leueen daily,' Alec wrote to Anne Kaufman on 20 August 1989, 'but yesterday she slammed down the receiver on me in one of her blind rages.'

Alec was frequently instrumental in getting parts for his friends. His extraordinary and early success in film and theatre, and the 'muscle' this gave him when it came to raising finance for a play or a film, also gave him the power to influence the casting. Peter Bull crops up, in larger or smaller roles, in a number of the films in which Alec was a star: *Oliver Twist*, *The Captain's Paradise*, *The Scapegoat*. We find Richard Leech in *Tunes of Glory*, Eileen Atkins and Michael Gough in *Smiley's People*, Leueen MacGrath and Michael Gough in *The Gift of Friendship* and Mark Kingston in *Hitler: The Last Ten Days*. All were, of course, wholly up to the roles they played. But his recommendations were not always accepted. Writing to David Lean in September 1982 about who should play Fielding in *A Passage to India*, Alec wrote: 'I think you should have a look at Mark Kingston. He's a good actor and a good man. Believe you would like him. Hard-working, intelligent, nice-mannered.'[641] The part went to James Fox.

Although there can be no suggestion that any of Alec's friends 'kept in' with him simply because they hoped he might bring work their way, this power of patronage, combined with his domineering personality, meant that many found him intimidating. 'What I can't remember with Alec,' recalled Ronald Harwood, 'is laughing together genuinely because one was so nervous of him that I affected it.' 'Everyone was intimidated by Alec,' said Edward Herrmann. 'He seemed to want to accept people on his terms . . . he always wanted to define the pitch.' Eileen Atkins was intimidated by him but fought against it. 'Something in me always says, you are not to be intimidated, you will not be intimidated, you will answer him back, you will not pretend anything . . . I tried very hard but didn't always succeed.' Whenever Alec asked her out to dinner, Eileen would feel she had to prepare amusing anecdotes or bits of gossip and dress up to his standards: she and her friend Jean Marsh, also a friend of Alec's, had a special wardrobe for going out with him. Mark Kingston, too, often felt that 'I should sing for my supper.' Marriott Lefèvre felt that she had to dress up when Alec asked her out to dinner. 'She loved him to bits,' recalled Matthew, 'but she was frightened of him.' Alec was always scrupulous about including the husbands or wives of his friends in any invitation to dinner: Marigold Kingston, the wife of Mark, sometimes felt *de trop*. 'Is that an *old* dress,' Alec would ask; or 'Those

are very nice shoes you are wearing. Have you had them quite a time?'
When Eileen Atkins married Bill Shepherd, Alec gave him a hard time.
'He used to give Bill looks of such deep contempt that that made my
husband behave badly so that in the end they were both as bad as one
another; but I have to say that Bill did try so it was always Alec who
started it.'

Even Alec's parish priest at Petersfield, Monsignor Murtagh, realised
that 'You sort of had to remain in your mould with him. I was the
parish priest, and a friend, but I knew that that was where I stood.' And
Alan Bennett who, like Leueen, could be sharp with Alec, would, after
seeing a film with Alec, wait until Alec had given his opinion before
venturing his own. 'That was the way in which he controlled you in a
funny way . . . But by the end, I just didn't bother. I took no notice.'

'I rarely take offence,' Alec told Dame Felicitas in 1965, 'except at lazy
shopkeepers or London's Kensington lady-shoppers who don't say
thank you when you hold a door for them.'[642] This was not quite true.
There had been the punch-up at John Wayne's party in Beverly Hills
in 1955, and the contretemps with David Selznick in 1961. The
telephone had been slammed down on him by Kay Walsh as well as
Leueen MacGrath: 'Couldn't make head or tail of it, being quite
unaware of my rudeness.'[643] There were constant spats with insolent
sales people and recalcitrant waiters. In 1980, he told Anne Kaufman,
he 'had a smashing row with a customer in Heywood Hill's, who kept
saying of Evelyn Waugh that he was a conceited shit. "Do you know
him, sir?" "No, sir, – but I met him once". "I expect that was quite
enough for him, sir." "What do you mean, sir?" etc. etc. Pistols in Hyde
Park at Dawn.'[644]

Alec had a row with the gentle Ronald Eyre over Alec's perceived
rudeness to the actor, Alan Bates. Alec had gone to the first night of
John Osborne's *A Patriot for Me*, directed by Eyre at the Chichester
Festival. After watching Bates's performance, which was generally
acknowledged to be superb, Alec went backstage and pushed open the
door to Bates's dressing-room where the actor was taking a shower.

'Alan, it's Alec. You must be absolutely exhausted.' And that was all. He said nothing to Eyre who, meeting Mark Kingston at a party given by John Osborne at Edenbridge, said: 'You tell your friend Alec Guinness to be more fucking generous in his remarks after a play.' An angry correspondence ensued but, Eyre concluded, 'my mind is quite set on wanting to remain friends' – and they did.

Feminism was a constant source of friction with Eileen Atkins. She was a great admirer of Virginia Woolf, herself adapting Woolf's works for the stage; whereas Alec thought that 'Virginia Woolf's writing is no more than glamorous knitting'.[645] One evening, when he was dining with Eileen, her husband Bill Shepherd, and Jean Marsh, at the Rue St Jacques restaurant, Alec became incensed when Eileen criticised the Catholic Church for teaching that birth control was sinful. 'I was deeply into this book about women in the Third World and circumcision,' Eileen Atkins recalled, 'and their not being allowed birth control – and that was when he went berserk. "Who do you think you are, you western women, telling these women what they should or should not do?"'

The argument raged on and finally Alec lost his temper. 'He got up and said, "I'm not sitting at this table with you any more. You're a very, very wicked woman." And he threw his chair so hard back into its place that it hit my shin.'

Alec describes the incident and its aftermath in his Small Diary for 1991:

July 10. In evening to Rue St Jacques for dinner to Eileen, Bill & Jean. Food OK but evening a disaster as Eileen & I rowed about reduction or not of families in the Third World. I felt she had become Mrs Pankhurst & Virginia Woolf and Women's Lib all rolled into one – and she gets very ugly in the face when angry. I paid the bill (£340) and left them there.

July 17. No letter from Eileen acknowledging my apology. I suspect she's wiped me off her slate.

July 23. Letter from Eileen acknowledging my apology. Wrote back to her. All fairly all right I think, but her letter a bit spikey and madly over-sensitive ('You must have been relieved that a train strike gave you an excuse for not seeing *A Room of One's Own*'). There's a very big wounded Ego there. However, I'm sure we shall be fully reconciled.

July 26. Longish letter from Eileen and all seems well again.

forty-one

Most of Alec's friendships were conducted either face to face in London restaurants or at Kettlebrook, or over the telephone; however, he kept up a steady correspondence with two of his women friends – one, Dame Felicitas Corrigan, enclosed at Stanbrook Abbey; the other Anne Kaufman, living in the United States. Each elicited a different aspect of Alec's character: the Benedictine nun appealed to the learned, devout, sagacious and solicitous Alec who strived for the salvation of his soul; the Jewish New Yorker drew out the witty, ironic, sophisticated, hedonistic, sharp-tongued Alec who loved to gossip and have fun.

Anne Kaufman had first met Alec at a dinner given in London by her stepmother, Leueen. 'He thought I was funny. It was all very easy. And when we left the flat that night, it was quite cold – and he had a big long muffler – a sort of a red cashmere scarf – and he gave it to me. I still have it.'[646] Like Leueen, Anne was not intimidated by Alec though she was aware of his shortcomings: 'he could be ungenerous –

never about money but with himself'. She was aware that Alec did not think much of her father's work. He walked out of *Once in a Lifetime* when it was put on at the Aldwych Theatre: 'He said, "Oh, it's commercial theatre".'

Anne Kaufman had married a man closely resembling Alec, Irving Schneider, who had worked in the theatre and now helped her run George Kaufman's estate. They came frequently to England, saw the Guinnesses both in London and at Kettlebrook, and once went on holiday with them to Greece. It was here, in a villa near Galaxadion recommended by John le Carré, that she had seen Alec at his worst. Before leaving England, Alec had told the Schneiders, and the other couple he had invited, Jill Balcon and her companion, Antony Brett-James, to bring one smart set of clothes:

> Alec had said on the phone: wear anything but bring something smart in case we go out. But there was nowhere to go. But one night the three ladies decided that we were going to dress up. It wasn't really dressed up but we each had a kaftan, so we decided to do the number, and we did. We all arrived on the veranda at the same time and Alec was furious. He took it to mean – he even said so later – that we were saying: we've brought all this stuff and you haven't taken us anywhere special. Merula didn't like to talk back and Jill would never talk back. I said: 'We just thought we'd look nice for you'. Nothing. It was a very unpleasant night.

Earlier in the course of her long friendship with Alec, Anne Kaufman had momentarily imagined that Alec fancied her, and later that she was in love with him. Perhaps incited by her stepmother Lulu's story that she and Alec had almost gone to bed together when on tour with *Voyage Round My Father*, she thought a pass might be in the offing:

> He was in *A Family and a Fortune* and Irving and I went to see it and he took us out afterwards to a multi-million pound bowl of spaghetti. We were staying in a little hotel which now costs a fortune. He used to call

every day – every morning. He sent flowers. One morning, he invited me to come to the matinée. He asked me to see the matinée by myself. 'Would you like to see the play again?' I went to see the play. I said to Irving: 'I don't know what this is about but I'll go.' I went backstage and he was in a terry cloth robe and when I came in he locked the door. And I suddenly thought . . . he was a very intriguing, charismatic man, and I thought – well, it would be nice – and the flowers which came, and the presents which came . . . So I thought, well, why not? I didn't know Merula well at the time. I had never been unfaithful to my husband but I thought – it'd be an experience.

He knelt in front of the fridge and said: 'What would you like to drink?' He knew I didn't like champagne. 'I have tomato juice, apple juice . . . No, no, you can't have the apple juice because I only have one bottle and *I'm* having that.' So I thought: Anne, forget it. And then we sat and talked for about forty minutes until he said that he thought he ought to have a rest before the next performance. Why did he lock the door? I don't know. He maybe didn't want anyone to come in. When I left, I felt dumb.

Alec was immensely fond of Anne and, to show his affection, he staged one delightful deception. Anne had told him that she adored the series *Upstairs, Downstairs* which had been running on American television, and in which Alec's friend, Gordon Jackson, played the butler. On one of their trips to London, Alec asked the Schneiders to supper at Smith Square:

When we got there, Merula was sort of dressed up in a kaftan. At the end of the big room, they had a dining table. Matthew was there. Anyway, there was a woman there on the sofa. So Alec took us in and introduced us in the kind of English way in which no one says who anyone is. But he said, 'This is Mrs Trossack.' Then, about five minutes later, he said: 'Has Hale opened the champagne yet?' In fact, I always used to drink Bourbon – I don't like champagne; but I sensed that there was a reason so I thought I'm not going to say that I don't want a glass of champagne. Then this butler came in with a tray. I took a glass and looked into the face of the butler, because I'm an American, and it was Gordon Jackson. I had a fit.

'Mrs Trossack' was in fact Gordon Jackson's wife, Rhona. Alec was delighted with his joke. 'I had asked Gordon Jackson to come,' he noted in his diary, 'conceal himself in the kitchen until after their arrival, and then appear as Hudson. He did it charmingly and it was a huge success.'[647]

With such attentions from so intelligent, talented and famous a man, who physically resembled her husband, it is hardly surprising that Anne should fall in love with Alec; and she wrote a letter to say so, slightly tipsy on a Boeing, on one of her return journeys over the Atlantic. She posted it when she reached New York. The reply she received from Alec put her firmly in her place:

My dear Anne,

Yes, this is written with my new italic calligraphic pen – partly to show off and partly because it may force me to write more slowly and think of what I am putting on paper. If you wish to – and I rather hope you may do so – show this letter to Irving. But not if you feel he would think it an impertinence or if it would cause deep emotional upsets. I refer to your last letter of course. Any man would be flattered, but this particular one can only be distressed for you and look on it as a passing aberration. Perhaps you have already forgotten it, come to your senses etc. etc. – in which case please forgive me for opening, or in any way scratching, a sore. I love – in the strict sense – only four creatures in this life; my wife, my son, my grandson* – and Walter. I have great affection, which one loosely calls love, for many more and you – and indeed Leueen – are very high on that list. It cannot and never will be otherwise. Can you accept that? And in doing so continue with a happy,

---

* This was before the birth of Alec's granddaughter, Sally.

gay, giggly and also, I hope, serious friendship? I certainly hope that.
You are a rare bright bird; I greatly enjoy your company; and selfishly
I want you to continue to be part of my experience of life. Cannot we
let it drift and develop in that way? If you can't then you must put me
out of mind. I would not hurt Merula for all the tea in Boston Harbour,
and you should do your best not to hurt Irving. He is a gentle, humble
good man and exceedingly sensitive and likeable. I think sometimes
you ride a bit rough-shod over him. Like me you have a quick and
perhaps harsh tongue. I feel you could make things happier for
yourself, and I assume so for him, if you showed him greater
consideration. You could, for instance, collect your own unguents, and
help him, in his shyness, to come more out of his shell.

So that was that. Anne replied to Alec's letter on 5 July 1975:

Let me say at the outset, that as long as I felt compelled to make a fool
of myself, I thank Heaven that I was lucky enough to have chosen you.
I have reread your letter at least a dozen times; it is the kindest, most
thoughtful, most face-saving-for-me, letter I've ever read. And your
hand-writing is wondrous to behold! What an unlikely thing for me to
have done! Do you think the altitude – or the speed of the 747 – had
anything to do with my taking leave of my senses? I, who have never
even had too much to drink, for fear of losing some sort of control? . . .
If I'd taken the letter home I might have reconsidered and torn it up.
I wish I had. But I didn't, and now there's nothing to do but to thank
you for being so understanding – and to beg you to forget the whole
matter. Look on it as a momentary surge of emotion from a lady-
about-to-be-fifty, who was swept off her feet by all your attentions.
They were not misconstrued – and I don't want them to stop! Please
consider the matter closed . . .[648]

The matter was closed. The incident was never again mentioned and
Alec and Anne Kaufman did successfully continue their 'happy, gay,
giggly' and serious friendship for the rest of Alec's life. Whether or not

Anne began to collect her 'own unguents' is unknown, but what is clear from the correspondence is that she was used repeatedly by Alec to obtain those things that could only be found in New York. 'My dear Royal Anne – a laundry list and not a letter. Could you please send us to Kettlebrook the following: 5 largest *double* non-iron (and non-fitted) sheets . . .'[649] 'A small tiresome commission, which I hope you won't object to in spite of your SILENCE. Would you please send me 4 NOXEMA *LATHER* SHAVING CREAM and 4 NOXEMA *BRUSHLESS* SHAVING CREAM. I enclose a cheque for $40.00 which I hope will cover request plus postage. Any dollars left over please spend on daisies or gerbera for yourself.'[650] 'Dearest Anne, I enclose a check for $120. Would you buy yourself, say, forty dollars worth of flowers to brighten your life and with the remainder send me some decent paper table napkins? Here one can only get, now, feeble little two-ply things, not much better than Kleenex. What I'd like, if obtainable, is some largish plain white, four ply napkins . . .'[651]

But Alec repaid Anne's favours in his favourite currency. Three years before he died, after Irving Schneider's long terminal illness, he treated Anne to four days at the Connaught:

There will be a car from Miles & Miles to meet you and take you to The Connaught . . . Now, strict instructions: I do not want you to pay for *anything* (other than your flights) so at the hotel you will order what meals etc you want, either in your room or The Grill Room. *All* extras will be paid including telephones, papers etc. When you leave you just march out of the hotel saying the bill has been seen to. *But* you'll have tipping to do – perhaps £10 to concierge, £5 to your room maid, and £5 to porters. All that adds up and taxis are fiendishly expensive now but necessary – so there will be a bulging envelope waiting for you at the hotel with £150 in it to cover the above. *Please* ask anyone you want to dinner or lunch and have it slapped on the bill.[652]

Alec's instructions to Anne Kaufman on tipping demonstrate not just his generosity towards the Connaught staff, but his failure to move with the times when it came to such notions as a service charge or credit cards. At the Connaught Grill, or any of the other restaurants he patronised, he would take out a folded five or ten-pound note, from a supply he had secreted in a waistcoat pocket, and slip it discreetly into the palm of the head waiter, the wine waiter and the man at the door. He would pay for his dinner with a cheque; he obtained a credit card only very late in life. When he was abroad he paid his restaurant bills in cash. His favourite restaurants in the 1940s were Chez Victor, the Ivy, Prunier, the Café Royal, the Savoy, and Les Ambassadeurs. In the 1950s he had started patronising the Connaught, and had a transient passion for an Indian restaurant in South Kensington, Jamshid's, where he took the young Corin Redgrave and also Charles and Sonja Frend.

The White Tower was in favour in the 1970s. Alec was there one evening 'as the guest of Ralph and Mu Richardson. When Ralph was shown the duck they proposed to roast for him, he took it off the platter and sat it on his head. Mu remained calm and cool.' Alec also patronised the White Tower until he was shown to a 'tiny table against which waiters would clearly brush us on two sides'. Alec protested and was told by the head waiter, '"But Sir Alec, this is the table where I always put our most important customers. It is the best table we have." Which it wasn't by any means. "Then why have you never given it to me in the last twenty-five years?" I asked. Shitty of me, and unchristian, but I couldn't resist it, and I have resisted the White Tower ever since.'[653]

Alec had high standards in service, cooking and value for money and frequently boycotted restaurants that let him down. He had 'an easy happy evening' with John Gielgud at L'Etoile on 15 March 1973, but on 11 November 1974, dined at the Mirabelle with Mark Kingston 'which cost me £38 for nothing very elaborate. That's the end of the Mirabelle for me.' During the run of A Family and a Fortune in 1975, he would slum it with other members of the cast in cheaper restaurants such as Giovanni's in Goodwin's Court off St Martin's Lane and Margaret Leighton's favourite restaurant, La Constantina. After one performance he booked a table for 10.50 p.m. at Ma Cuisine, 'a new restaurant in Walton Street which Jean Marsh had told me about' but, arriving five minutes early, was told that his table was not ready and there was nowhere for them to wait. 'I asked if it was the idea that we should walk the streets for ten minutes and the French lady owner, with a charming smile, said "Yes". So we said we'd walk elsewhere – and did so. Fortunately eating places abound in that area.'[654]

On 5 May 1979, Alec took the le Carrés and Sonja Frend to a new restaurant called the Arlington. 'Indifferent meal . . . made more irritating by poor service and a negro singer at the piano. I'm told the restaurant hopes to emulate the Caprice . . . Not a hope in hell, a totally wrong and inadequate approach. The evening cost £90.' He found Frederick's in Islington 'attractive but a bit noisy'; dining at the Dorchester, the cigar waiter 'managed to hit me on the head with the box. By way of apology he sqeezed my shoulder saying "Sorry, old bean". Such is the Dorchester now.'[655] Cecconi's, an Italian restaurant within walking distance of the Connaught, became a favourite. In 1981 he ended his boycott of the Mirabelle, dining there with the German actor Curt Jurgens and his wife. 'Over-cooked grouse and a falling-off of service. Shall give it a miss for some months.'[656] He gave a dinner for Peggy Ashcroft at Scotts in Mayfair in August 1983, but did not like the atmosphere 'which I find almost sinister. And the air-conditioning was too chilly'. Lunch at Orso's in Covent Garden prompted a spoof guide for Anne Kaufman in New York:

THE GUINNESS GUIDE TO INDIFFERENT FOOD
ORSOS 27 Wellington Street.
Situated in an unpleasingly shaped basement, decorated with white lavatory tiles and lacking strip lighting, this rendez-vous for American children bears very little resemblance to 46th St N.Y.C. . . . .

Alec returned to L'Etoile with the Goughs on 4 June 1987, finding it 'far too expensive for its quality but I like the atmosphere'. Bibendum, in the Michelin Building in South Kensington, he considered 'good for lunch. I found it rather too bleak for dinner. Food excellent but had to send back soup and coffee as they were both barely warm. And the price!'[657] After Laurence Olivier's memorial service Alec took Merula, Alan Bennett, Peggy Ashcroft and Jill Balcon for lunch at the Connaught. 'It was all a bit hugger-mugger, late and disorganised. Caviar again. Cost over £600.'[658] Alec sent a postcard from Paris to Anne Kaufman to report that 'le Train Bleu was une catastrophe'. John le Carré introduced him to Odette's in Primrose Hill, but that was a taxi ride from the Connaught, and Christopher Sinclair-Stevenson, first his publisher and subsequently his literary agent, to Hilaire's in the Brompton Road, from where he pinched the recipe for apple and curry soup. Leith's in Notting Hill was where John and Penny Mortimer kept him waiting, and his quarrel with Eileen Atkins happened at the Rue St Jacques.

The perfect restaurant proved elusive: as often as not, Alec returned to the Connaught Grill and, towards the end of his life, lost his taste for gourmandising in sumptuous surroundings. 'Could we not go somewhere simple?' he asked Christopher Sinclair-Stevenson two years before he died. 'I've gone off expensive places. Do you know anything of Pru Leith's new small establishment in Beak Street? Or somewhere near you? Or Al San Vincenzo in Connaught Street? Or anywhere, really . . .'[659]

One of Alec's dreams as an impoverished young actor was to have enough money to travel. His first trip abroad had been to Bruges in Belgium, where he and Merula had stayed in a cheap hotel with a 'green and pink and dirty restaurant and brass chandeliers'. For their honeymoon they had gone hiking in Ireland and, until middle-age, Alec had enjoyed modest outdoor holidays. He went fishing in the Lake District and, with Merula in 1968, took the holiday in Iceland that they had planned before they were married. He and Merula at one time owned two Volkswagen camper vans in which they made excursions into the English countryside. Matthew recalled that one of the happiest holidays had been in a simple cottage, close to the home of Robert Graves on the island of Majorca, where the only cooking facility was a charcoal stove.

But as Alec grew older and richer, he became more demanding. His holiday in Italy soon after the war with Merula, Matthew and Ernest Milton was successful; his trip to Morocco with Peter Bull was not. In 1954 Alec and Merula took 'an enchanting small house in Venice' for six weeks; that holiday was only spoiled when, Alec later suggested, he was poisoned in Asolo by Freya Stark.[660] Merula visited him in the United States; at the Ventana Inn at Big Sur they found that Steve McQueen and his wife were fellow guests 'showing themselves friendly and unaffected and sweet natured'.[661] Alec and Merula went to the Holy Land in 1961 and, of course, there was the uncongenial Mediterranean cruise on the *Clonsilla*, and they enjoyed a 'happy and delightful holiday' at Portmeirion in the summer of 1966.

Alec was always trying out expensive country-house hotels 'primarily to give M a rest from goats, dogs, puppy and stove' but usually the weather or the food or the service was disappointing. 'M and I got back to K'brook from Hunstrete at 1400 today – a day earlier than intended. It was a pleasant jaunt, the hotel very attractive, well run, prettily decorated and the food superb. But it was grey and cold outside and when, yesterday evening, snow began to fall we decided we wouldn't risk bad roads by staying the full time. Cost us £440.'[662] In January 1975, he and Merula spent ten days in New York:

A purely frivolous venture which I hope will snap us out of a rather gloomy rut, enable us to see old friends there, dodge the IRA bombs here, and buy odds and ends of small things it would be pleasant to have and which are obtainable only in the U.S. It's a fairly spur of the moment decision and as I haven't been there for about seven years I look forward to it greatly. But not to our flight in a Jumbo tourist class . . .[663]

They stayed with Peter Glenville, indulged in an orgy of shopping in the kitchen utensils department of Bloomingdale's and were entertained by 'Astors, Heinzs, Buckleys and Schneiders'.[664]

Alec never went on holiday with Matthew and Andrée or his grandchildren. If he invited a third person to accompany him and

Merula, it was usually a single woman – spinster, widow or divorcée –
such as Brigid Boland, Percy Harris or Sonja Frend. Marriott Lefèvre
went with them to Galaxidion in Greece in 1974: the weather was
terrible, the lens fell out of Alec's camera and it was clear from his
diaries that he was bored. 'Alec never had a successful holiday,' Alan
Bennett recalled. 'He would invite someone he felt sorry for and then
feel irritated. Sonja Frend, for example.'[665] In Venice in March 1979,
Alec complained in his diary: 'Sonja infuriated me by tapping her
fingernail on a 14th century painting to point out something and was
reprimanded, rightly, by one of the staff. Given a chance I think she'd
have lit up one of her endless fags. She's very dear but extremely
exasperating from time to time . . .'[666] 'We had a pleasant week there,
taking a widowed friend,' Alec told Anne Kaufman, 'but I've now *had*
Venice . . . The whole place is now, I find, noisily dead.'[667] However,
ten years later the Guinnesses returned with Mary Salaman. 'He made
the trip a nightmare by disapproving of everything; he kept saying they
were being ripped off,' Mary Salaman recalled. 'He wouldn't explore.
We stayed in a horrible expensive hotel. Posh friends of Alec's had
recommended it. There was a strike by the staff. All the thousands of
lire confused him and made him think that he was being ripped off.'[668]

'At a rough reckoning,' Alec noted in his Small Diary on 23
November 1989, 'I guess our rather unsatisfactory holiday cost, in all,
just under a pound a minute. Mary got on both our nerves – mine
particularly – as she behaved as if deprived about everything (On
menus – "Oh, what a bore! They haven't got so-and-so"). The holiday
cost me about £16,000. Quite absurd. Had thought we'd never see
Venice again. It was good to be out of season; but I'm not sure I'd
bother to go again.'[669] After the holiday in Venice, Mary Salaman
rarely went to Kettlebrook. 'Only when Alec was away in London.'

The Guinnesses were often unlucky with the weather. The 'weather
wasn't good . . .' in Santiago de Compostella. 'Glad we went but must
admit to being rather disappointed.'[670] It was the same on Lake
Annecy in the spring of 1988: 'Weather is rotten,' Alec wrote to Dame
Felicitas. 'Nothing to do except chug round the lake and get wet.'[671] In

1993 he returned from a holiday on the Isle of Wight close to Cowes where he had been conceived: 'Came back with a filthy cough . . . Given me, I suspect, by an idiot Italian girl with a drip on her nose who *blew* into the paper bag before putting the pasta in. I told her to start again – with another bag – but I think she dripped into that.'[672] In 1994 Alec and Merula went to Rome for Holy Week and got soaked with rain during an audience with the Pope. They were shown around by a priest, Fr Derek Jennings, terminally ill with cancer, who then accompanied them to Bressanone in the Dolomites. 'He said Mass daily at a convent nearby and we attended most days. He put a brave face on his situation but could not help referring to it constantly. Understandable, I suppose. But a little wearisome and dampening.'[673]

Among Alec and Merula's more successful holidays was a trip to India when Alec was filming *A Passage to India* – Matthew recalls them saying they achieved a spiritual serenity visiting Hindu temples that had eluded them in the parish church in Petersfield – and a visit to the Hanseatic cities of Hamburg and Lübeck with Marriott in 1992. In April 1997, Alec and Merula spent a week in the Brenner Park Hotel in Baden-Baden, recommended to them by the author and actor, John Wells. 'Have a gooden-gooden time in Baden-Baden,' wrote Alan Bennett on a postcard. Their penultimate holiday was at Le Prieuré at Villeneuve-lès-Avignon: 'Spacious and v. good food,' Alec reported to Eileen Atkins, 'but a puffer-puffer goods train makes itself heard every half hour.'[674] In October 1998, they spent a day and a night in Eastbourne. 'I was using it as Proust's madeleine,' Alec wrote to the poet and actor Quentin Stevenson, 'to jerk my memory about late twenties and early thirties.'[675] And in September 1998, they spent four nights at the discreet Tresanton Hotel at St Mawes in Cornwall.

The following year, 1999, Alec planned a holiday in a hotel on the Hebridean Isle of Eriska recommended by Maggie Smith but Merula called it off because of a pinched nerve in her shoulder. 'She *always* gets something inconveniently wrong when we are about to go away. Basically I think she doesn't like leaving the nest, even for a day.' But by the following year, 2000, even Alec had lost his appetite for travel.

'We can't think where to go on holiday this year,' he wrote to Jehane West just two months before he died. 'Lots of places we would like to visit or re-visit but the *travelling* is so exhausting and Heathrow & Gatwick make me feel sick.'[676]

forty-two

During the pre-London tour of one of the plays in which Alec appeared in his late middle-age, the provincial theatre provided him with a dresser who, for the purposes of this biography, will be known by the initial N. He was a young man from a modest background and, at the end of the week's run, Alec invited him to come and work as his dresser in London. It was noticed by the company that Alec was particularly kind to him and took him to supper in fancy restaurants.

Some time later, in the course of the play's London run, the director was telephoned by the company manager and asked to meet him in a pub near the theatre. He reported that the young dresser had given in his notice, saying that he had to return home at once. N. had claimed that Alec invited him back to his flat in Smith Square and, while giving him a massage, had made a sexual assault.

The director and the company manager both believed what N. had told them but persuaded him to go on working until the end of the

week, and then told Alec that he had resigned. 'Why?' Alec asked
sharply. 'What has he been saying?' Alec, thereafter, was noticeably
distant with the director. N. left the company and, so far as the director
knew, returned to his home in the provinces.

Alec referred to this incident in a letter to Anne Kaufman. 'My dresser
has left me, indicating he had suicidal tendencies (showing me some little
scratches on the *upper* side of his arm from which you couldn't bleed to
death in twenty years even if you prised them open'.) He makes no
mention of it in his diary as such, but there are a number of entries in his
Small Diary which suggest a growing involvement with the young man:

Oct 8. N. to tea.

Oct 9. After show took N. to supper at L'Epicure and put him up for the
night.

Oct 16. N. back to Smith Sq with me so as to come to Kettlebrook
Sunday.

Oct 17. N. and I got to Waterloo half an hour early . . .

Oct 21. Took N. to supper at 'Bacco 70'.

Oct 28. Took N. to La Poule au Pot. To bed at 2 a.m.

Oct 29. N. phoned, distressed and a bit drunk, from Finchley Road,
unable to get back to Upton Park. He eventually got a taxi and arrived
here at 3 a.m.

Oct 30. N. recovered by midday. Took him to lunch at Brompton Grill
and left him at Science Museum while I went to the theatre and slept.

Nov 4. [The company director] tells me N. has given a week's notice,
which I consider so much too short. I'm inclined to tell him not to
come back as from Monday.

Nov 5. N. arrived in a bad state not having got his job. He hung around
for a bit and then left us for good. Poor deranged boy. Told me he had 3
times in past year attempted suicide – but I wondered.

Nov 6. Keep thinking distressfully of N. and wondering if he'll pick up
another job with ease. I suppose I spoiled him . . .

Nov 17 . . . N. called at front door. Slightly drunk and very maudlin. Let
him sit here for 10 minutes and then pushed him off.

Dec 17. At 2 a.m. my buzzer went insistently but I didn't answer it. N.?
A drunk? Anyway, irritating.
Jan 23, 1978. N. and his girlfriend to see me (after show).

What seems clear from these entries is that N. did not return to his home in the provinces after his resignation, but continued to see Alec – on the last recorded occasion, with his girlfriend – and that Alec felt sorry for the young man, and that perhaps the pity was mingled with love. N. was by no means the only young man whom Alec took up in this way.

Alec suffered from solitude during the long London runs: 'I am a bit restless and unable to settle to anything except the nightly performances. It is lonely when Merula is away; yet she has nothing to do in town and at least at home she can paint, work in the garden, walk the dogs and do the things she likes doing; though she is a bit lonely too.'[677] It was therefore hardly surprising that he liked to see just the kind of young men whose company he had found so congenial during the war. At the end of the run of *A Family and a Fortune* Alec gave a fancy-dress party for the company – 'all of whom are preparing their gold lamé dresses. But unbeknownst to them Maggie L and I are going as lower deck sailors. I've got my costume – I had forgotten how good I look in R.N. bell-bottoms. Perhaps I should wear them always.'[678]

D., a stage carpenter and electrician, was clearly the object of Alec's affection between 1976 and 1978. 'D. had a couple of Bourbons in my dressing-room and . . . drove me home. Gave him bacon and eggs . . . Fascinated to find him reading Waugh and Graham Greene.' 'Gave the electrician lad, D., the 3 vol (paperback) of *Unconditional Surrender* which he had shown an interest in.' 'D. offered me a lift home in his father's van. Gave him grilled steak.' 'Gave D. supper and taught him backgammon.' 'D. drove me down to K'brook.' 'D. arrived 12.15 and drove me back to London leaving at 13.30.' 'Bought green wool shirt for D. at Dunhills . . . After the show took D. to La Poule au Pot.' 'D. drove me down to K'brook. Wandered with D. in the garden. He pushed off to London . . .' 'D. called at Smith Sq with Leueen's telephone attachment and had tea.' 'Cooked meal for D. and had longish walk on Embankment.' 'Took D. to supper at Germano.' 'Took D. to supper at Langan's. He stayed the night here.'[679] D. continued to visit Alec, in London and at Kettlebrook, sometimes with his girlfriend, later his wife, and was a beneficiary in Alec's will.

While there is no evidence whatsoever of a sexual relationship between Alec and this or, indeed, any other man, what seems clear is that such working-class young men satisfied some kind of emotional craving in Alec. An undated, and partly indecipherable letter from Bobby Flemyng, whom Alec describes in *My Name Escapes Me* as 'one of my closest actor friends', suggests some sort of emotional breakdown at some point in Alec's life brought on by an unhappy passion. Bobby Flemyng, Sam Beazley recalled:

> . . . had a difficult time because he was always queer but had a wife. He married his wife because they were having an affair; then the war started and he thought he'd better marry her because then she'd get a pension; he was sure to get killed. We all thought we'd get killed. He was queer all his life. Bobby had this terrible disaster which was to fall in love with a younger man in middle age. He had a nervous breakdown and then a stroke and had a really terrible time. He went through what others go through when in their twenties or earlier. And Alec was very kind and arranged for him to go to some Catholic place for a retreat but it didn't do any good. He was out of his mind with love for this young man.[680]

A letter from Bobby Flemyng referring to this crisis was written in response to a letter from Alec in which he seems to have told him that he was disillusioned with acting and intended to give up the stage. Bobby recalled Alec saying how, as one matured and grew old, it was impossible to sustain the child-like 'let's pretend' that was the source of all acting, and how, when he, Flemyng, was acting with John Gielgud in *Forty Years On*, Gielgud had told him that he had come to hate acting. Olivier, he thought, had escaped the dilemma by becoming an administrator.

Flemyng then told Alec how, in middle age, he had felt disappointed by the course his career had taken and had hoped 'above all to find passion – an ignoble and selfish ambition, I fear, given the circumstances and with my responsibilities'. He had found passion, he wrote – but too late, too unsuitably and, some would say, 'too falsely'. He said he wished he had had the courage either to pursue this passion, thereby hurting his wife and daughter; or reject it and spare them. In the event, he had tried to do both, which had caused the greatest possible distress to all concerned. The past three years had been a time of great suffering: if there was an alternative to sexual jealousy, he wrote, he'd like to hear of it.

In these unhappy circumstances, Flemyng went on, 'the one anodyne' had been his work on the stage; and, if this was true for him, it would surely be all the more true for Alec. Alec knew him too well, Flemyng wrote, to suspect him of flattery when he said that Alec's talent was far too great to be laid aside. 'You are a God-given actor, and you have so much still to do by example in the profession, and by renown outside it.' Concluding his letter, Flemyng adds 'to be flippant', that the wish of his chauffeur's wife to move away is 'no occasion for you to leave the stage'.[681]

The reference to *Forty Years On* would date this letter some time *after* 1968 which means the chauffeur to whom he refers cannot have been Rob. The tone of the letter suggests that it was Alec who was in trouble at this time but, on 31 August 1968, Alec noted in his Small Diary: 'Bobby Flemyng 'phoned, in distress, asking if I knew a monastery he could go to. I offered to take him to Quarr on Sept 12th and fixed this up.' On 5 September 1968, Bobby Flemyng wrote to Alec from the Garrick Club:

> I feel I behaved with great cowardice and lack of will power, and I have caused damage to others besides myself, which is terrible. Also I've been a great fat bore to boot.

All the same my heart really has been broken however stupid that may be, and I need courage and discipline and I suppose acceptance. Anyway bless you for your kindness and I look forward to it much.

Both men visited the Benedictine Abbey between 12 and 14 September. Alec makes scant reference in his Small Diary to what went on. On the Friday they walked into Ryde where 'Bobby . . . did endless telephoning'. They did the same on Saturday. 'Strolled on front – all rather tedious.' After their retreat, Alec seems to have put his troubled friend in touch with Fr Philip Caraman: a letter from the Jesuit to Alec, dated 23 September 1968, says that, 'Before I can answer your question about Robert Flemyng, I should really meet him. It is difficult to recommend a person to help him without knowing a bit about him.'[682]

No doubt, Alec hoped that Flemyng, like him, would find an answer to his suffering in the Catholic Church, but there is no mention of his friend's conversion. Thereafter, the only references to him in Alec's diaries are when he visits him in hospital in 1985 and 1989; and to his death in 1995.

It would seem, then, that Alec felt disordered passions could be controlled, if not cured, by prayer, repentance and the Grace of God. Yet he was never able to detach himself altogether from his homosexual alter-ago. He was fascinated by the trial of the Liberal leader, Jeremy Thorpe, charged with seducing and then attempting to murder a young man whom he called Bunny. Alec also showed great interest in the artistic depictions of unusual, mostly homosexual, forms of sexual expression, and often found them disturbing. In Rome in 1962, he bought Jean Genet's *Thief's Journal*, a novel that vividly depicts homosexual liaisons in the criminal milieu, but later in the day destroyed it: 'too sad & unwitty a book. But elements of truth shine through it. But not good for me.'[683] He had the same ambivalent reaction to the memoirs of the homosexual politician, Tom Driberg: 'Read Driberg's book –

absorbing but pretty disgusting.'[684] After reading George Melly's graphic depiction of homosexuality in the Navy he noted in his diary: 'Bought George Melly's *Rum, Bum & Guitar* [sic]. Very funny and well written – and unnecessarily brave I'd think.'[685] He was disturbed by an explicit homosexual novel by Alan Hollinghurst: 'Have decided to get rid of *Swimming Pool Library* – too unsuitable,' he wrote in his Small Diary on 2 March 1988; and, the next day: 'Burned *The Swimming Pool Library*, having only dipped in it. Well written but unhealthy and not a book to leave around.' In 1998 he 'watched *Queer Street* film on Ch 4. I had no idea such 90% pornography was allowed on our boxes. Disturbing.'[686]

To the puzzlement of Matthew and Andrée, Alec sent Matthew a copy of *The Gamecock* by Michael Baldwin, a novel set in the Peninsular War in which Arthur Wellesley's Spanish manservant is buggered by the future Iron Duke as he writes his dispatches. Alec warned them of the strong subject matter but praised the quality of the writing. It occurred to both Matthew and Andrée that Alec was possibly testing the water to see how they would react if he were to admit to homosexual leanings. Alec became obsessed by another novel, Robert Nye's *The Late William Shakespeare*, a fictional account of Anne Hathaway's visit to her estranged husband, William Shakespeare, in London, during which he takes her to the bed bought with a thousand pounds paid to him by the Earl of Southampton. 'What did you do that was worth a thousand pounds?' Anne asks him. 'Why, I buggered him, my dear,' Mr Shakespeare said softly. 'And what is that?' Anne asks. Shakespeare demonstrates – to his wife's delight.

Alec ordered a copy of the novel to be sent to Eileen Atkins. 'I am halfway through it and am totally riveted. It is gloriously made in a surreal way, very funny and sometimes moving and quite brilliantly written, in my opinion . . . I shall be disappointed if you don't like it but do let me know what you really feel . . .' He suggested that Eileen Atkins might like to do it 'as a one woman show'. 'Long talk with Eileen,' he noted in his Small Diary on 1 February 1993, 'who liked

Mrs Shakespeare but fearful of its filth'. He also tried but failed to
interest Patrick Garland in adapting it for Chichester. He sent it to his
Catholic American friend, Edward Herrmann, who was baffled.

It was the same with the theatre and cinema. He went to see the
film *La Cage aux Folles* at least three times – the first time with Peter
Glenville and Bill Smith, the second with Val Stavredi, and the third
time with Merula and Marriott. 'M loved it but Marriott, I think,
unimpressed'; and to Lindsay Kemp's ballet *Flowers* six times – once
with Merula and the Harwoods. Ronald Harwood recalled:

> We had dinner at Prunier's which he loved and then we went to the
> Oxford Polytechnic; he took us there. They made a great fuss of us. We
> took our seats. The curtain went up on men with great phalluses
> masturbating. Eight of them. Alec covered Natasha's eyes. When it
> stopped, he took them away. He was so embarrassed – he'd forgotten
> quite what it was he'd enjoyed. The rest of the evening was a lot of
> naked men swinging around. And afterwards, we went around to see
> Lindsay Kemp who curtseyed to Alec. It was very embarrassing. There
> he was with his old married neighbours and his wife. He hadn't
> thought it through. Wrong casting.[687]

On 24 December 1974, Alec was asked by London's *Evening Standard*
to name a man or woman who had most impressed him during the
past year. He chose Lindsay Kemp 'for which no doubt I shall be
dismissed as frivolous and camp. But in a way it's true; anyway I went
to see *Flowers* four or five times in spite of disliking its masturbatory
opening, its blasphemy and some of its nudity.'[688]

'He loved the camp world, the gay world,' Ronald Harwood
recalled. 'He loved gossip and indiscreet stories.' Right at the end of
his life, Alec engaged in 'a playfully risqué and indiscreet'
correspondence with a homosexual friend, S.: 'S. sent me four nearly
feelthy p.c.s which arrived yesterday. He gets curiouser and curiouser.
They don't even make me laugh. But he is obviously a kind man.'[689]
Many of Alec's friends were homosexual and there was no tinge of

disapproval for those who had lovers. Bill Smith, Peter Glenville's companion, remained a close friend even after Glenville's death. Keith Baxter was welcomed to Kettlebrook and when his former lover, Richard Warwick (who played Antonio to Alec's Shylock), was dying of AIDS both Alec and Merula offered to visit him. Yet Alec disliked 'vociferous "Gay" groups' and disapproved of Ian McKellen who 'has become as aggressive and militant as Vanessa Redgrave – seeking (nobly, no doubt) assistance for AIDS victims but also marching hundreds of gays down Whitehall . . . flaunting homosexual causes. Very tiresome and it is bound to create a horrid backlash.'[690] He did not believe in 'gay rights'. 'BBC announced they were giving £75 "wedding" gift and a week's "honeymoon" holiday to each of their homosexual staff. Madness.'[691]

While Alec persisted in presenting a non-homosexual persona to the outside world – even to many of his close homosexual friends – he seems to have aroused the attention of other, anonymous, homosexuals. 'To Ladbroke Arms for a drink. Accosted by a persistent male . . . while walking home,' he noted in his diary on 25 June 1981 when he was sixty-seven years old. On 18 May 1987, when he was seventy-three, 'A youth (18–19) made an advance to me while changing trains at Haslemere. Astonished – and pretended I hadn't noticed. Such a thing can't have happened to me for 30 odd years.'[692]

Alec never arrived at a settled view on homosexuality. Merula once shocked Jill Balcon by saying, in Alec's presence, that she thought homosexuals were treacherous: Alec, behind her back, simply shrugged his shoulders. 'Had a vivid dream about being asked my attitude to homosexuality . . . Made a brilliant and true reply contrasting love and lust but for the life of me cannot recall what it was.'[693] The vivid dream was perhaps closer to a nightmare: Alec would never discuss homosexuality with either his heterosexual or homosexual friends. He always managed to avoid topics of conversation that might expose his latent proclivities. The Catholic priest, Derek Jennings – known as 'Dazzle' Jennings in his Anglican days – the intimate friend of Princess Margaret who had arranged Alec and Merula's audience with the Pope in 1994 and then accompanied them for a stay in the Dolomites, had irritated Alec by constantly reminding them that he had cancer, but also, two years earlier, by bringing up the subject of homosexuality. 'Took Fr Derek Jennings to dinner at Les Saveurs. Wish he'd drop his constant references to homosexuality. It's becoming an obsession.'[694] 'Derek Jennings for dinner in The Grill. Found him rather arrogant and tiresome and endlessly on about homosexuality.'[695]

Yet in the confessional, homosexual fantasies were almost certainly on the list of Alec's sins. 'I went to confession to Fr Murtagh,' Alec noted in his diary on 17 November 1974, 'who recounted the story of the old priest who said to the young man in the confessional, "Do you entertain lascivious thoughts?" to which he replied, "No Father, they entertain me." But my trouble is that they are unwelcome guests whom I have difficulty in pushing out of the house.' He never wholly succeeded. 'Had a sleep plagued by lascivious thoughts.'[696] 'Sudden attack of near lascivious thoughts, why, suddenly?'[697] 'My mind plagued by very unwanted lascivious thoughts – first time for about 3 years. Why? Can't account for it.' This entry in his Small Diary was made on 31 May 1996 when Alec was eighty-two years old.

The explanation, for a Catholic, is that the Devil never tires of tempting those souls he thinks worth having, and that the temptations are often more devious than we can anticipate or imagine. 'The anguish of life is, that a good man finds that he is doing things with mixed motives', Alec quoted from a book by the Jesuit, Fr Martindale, in his diary in February 1975. As with Thomas Mann's Aschenbach, *eros* and *agape* became confused. Almost certainly, Alec's initial impulse in the case of N. was one of compassion; but, as Thomas à Kempis warns in one of Alec's works of spiritual reading, *The Imitation of Christ*, 'Not every desire comes of the Holy Spirit, though it may seem right and good; for it is often hard to judge whether a desire springs from good or evil motives, or whether it arises from your own inclinations. Many are deceived in the end, who at first seemed to be led by the Holy Spirit.'[698] The entry for 5 December 1976 in Alec's Small Diary – the day after N. had accused Alec of a sexual assault – reads: 'Bright chilly day. Sore throat. To Farm Street to confession – first for six weeks. Good kind priest . . .'

part seven

indian summer

forty-three

'I believe my talent, whatever it was, has gone for good,' Alec wrote to Merula from Dahomey in West Africa in July 1967. 'Surprisingly this doesn't distress me, though it is rather humiliating. Deep down in me, I can't be bothered quite enough to trouble or care.'[699] Still dejected after the failure of his *Macbeth*, Alec was now playing the role of a bogus ex-Army officer, Major Jones, in a film of Graham Greene's *The Comedians*. The project might have been a tonic to revive him; he was among old friends. Peter Glenville was the director; Graham Greene had adapted his own novel; Peter Ustinov, an actor Alec greatly admired, was playing the Ambassador Pineda; the delectable Elizabeth Taylor was the Ambassador's wife, and her husband, Richard Burton, played her lover, Mr Brown.

Alec had first met Richard Burton at a party in London in 1949, after which Burton had been an occasional dinner guest at St Peter's Square where they would read Shakespeare together. It was Burton who introduced Alec to the poetry of Dylan Thomas. Now, in Dahomey,

Alec wrote to Matthew, 'I hardly find him the same person. Although he's a bit dour at the moment, he can be amusing and is highly intelligent and not uninteresting. But drink has taken a bit of a toll, I fear.'[700]

At first, the Burtons 'kept themselves very much to themselves' but, after dining with them in their villa in the presidential compound at Cotonou hired by the company for the filming, Alec wrote approvingly to Merula about Elizabeth Taylor:

> I do find her most sweet and warm-hearted. Her language is foul, in that Hollywood way, and I suppose she is not frightfully intelligent – well, maybe yes – certainly not intellectual – but she is shrewd and straightforward and kind. Richard is bright (when he chooses) and amusing and indeed interesting, but he tells the same story over and over again, worse than I do.[701]

Alec was drawn in to the Burtons' quarrelsome marriage. 'Had a difficult day with the Burtons . . . She sat in my room weeping most of the afternoon because he was so drunk and beastly to her. Which he was. But all patched up in the end.'

'I am enjoying the film,' Alec wrote to Dame Felicitas, 'and think it the best part that has come my way (other than Macbeth) in quite a few years.' However, the film, an undisguised indictment of the ruler of Haiti, 'Papa Doc' Duvalier and his Tonton Macoute, was said to have been cursed by Voodoo witch doctors at the request of Duvalier – something which stimulated Alec's latent superstitiousness. 'Goodness, I was glad to leave Dahomey!' he wrote to Dame Felicitas when the filming was over:

> Although I was comfortably placed, and with pleasant and good friends, I was beginning to suspect that if I had to spend another week there I would succumb to one or all of the various illnesses prevalent along that coast. Breathing became almost difficult and a mysterious *map* of Africa appeared on my chest, lasting four days. I couldn't help

Kettlebrook Meadows, designed for Alec and Merula by Eusty Salaman in 1953. Alec and Merula remained there until they died.

Merula and Matthew Guinness in the drawing room of 7, St. Peter's Square, around 1949. The parrot, Percy, could recite the first line of a soliloquy from Hamlet.

Alec photographs Merula at work in the garden at Kettlebrook.

John Gielgud, the actor who, at the height of his fame, helped the penniless would-be actor and gave Alec his first significant role as Osric in his 1934 production of *Hamlet*.

The French theatre director, Michel St Denis, whose uncompromising approach to acting, and belief in mime, greatly affected the development of Alec's technique.

Tyrone Guthrie, the Irish director, who chose the 25-year-old Alec for the title role in his modern-dress production of *Hamlet* at the Old Vic in 1939.

Peter Bull photographed by Alec at Kettlebrook Meadows.
Alec and 'Bully' both underwent basic training at HMS Raleigh,
the naval induction centre at Torpoint in Cornwall. 'Thank
Heaven for Peter Bull.'

Peter Glenville, described by Alec as 'probably my closest friend',
at Kettlebrook Meadows. A Roman Catholic and a homosexual,
Glenville directed Alec in a number of plays and films.

Fr Philip Caraman, S.J., a close friend of both Alec and Evelyn Waugh.

Fr Clarke, Parish priest of Petersfield in 1956, who received Alec into the Roman Catholic Church.

Alec with Canon Cathal McCarthy, his 'tame saint' in Dublin.

Leueen 'Lulu' MacGrath, who appeared with Alec in John Mortimer's *A Voyage Around My Father* in 1971, and became one of his closest women friends. The third of her five husbands was George Kaufman.

Honor Svejda, born Guinness, at Kettlebrook Meadows. She was convinced that Alec was the illegitimate son of her cousin, Lord Moyne.

Anne Kaufman-Schneider, the daughter of the US playwright George Kaufman and stepdaughter of Leueen MacGrath. She briefly imagined that she was in love with Alec.

Merula and Alec with Jack Hawkins at La Voile d'Or in St Jean Cap Ferrat in April, 1962. Alec spent 1962–1963 abroad to avoid UK income tax.

Alec and Merula on board the Clonsilla, 1962.

From left to right: Chattie Blatchley, Matthew, Merula and Alec. Taken in Sybil Burton's apartment in New York, 1964.

Walter.

Photograph taken by Alec's granddaughter, Sally, of Alec and Merula with their great-granddaughter Natasha and great-grandson Otis.

Alec Guinness: 1914–2000.

feeling it was sinister. No, not really, but ideas of Voodoo are never absent from one's mind there. Peter Glenville, an intimate friend, very nearly drowned under my eyes. A moment before it happened something said to me 'where is your Rosary?' It was in the pocket of my shirt. I had just got out one Hail Mary when he shouted for help. It really was a miracle and inexplicable how he got ashore again; the only rational possibility was an extra large wave washed him to where he could get a grip on the sand with his feet. And the identical thing happened to his and my friend William Smith, who was washed in three minutes later. They were both totally exhausted. When they had sufficiently recovered and had a sleep we sought out the nearest church to give thanks, kneeling on the concrete and sand outside as it was locked, but we could see the sanctuary light burning through some elaborate iron work.[702]

The Comedians was only a moderate success. 'I think he is inclined to rush a bit and to be a bit too mechanical,' Alec wrote to Merula of Glenville's directing. Michael Armstrong, addressing Glenville in a review for *Films and Filming*, thought it 'a bore . . . an insult to your theme and the many talented people who expressed it'. As was so often the case, Alec's Major Jones was the only character to alleviate the tedium of the drama: Graham Greene considered the film 'not very well directed' but thought 'there was one outstanding scene – one of my favourites in the cinema – in the cemetery with Burton when the whole weight lay with you.'[703] Running for almost three hours, *The Comedians* was much too long and, after its initial release, was cut by half an hour, leaving many of Alec's scenes on the cutting-room floor.

On his return from West Africa in the spring of 1967, the producer Michael Codron sent Alec a play for his consideration. It was by an unknown young university lecturer, Simon Gray, whose agent, Clive Goodwin, had shown it to Codron, who had initially sent it to Alec's agent, Dennis van Thal; but Van Thal had decided that showing the play to Alec would be a waste of time. It is easy to see why. *Wise Child* is a scabrous comedy, set in a seedy boarding house run by a homosexual with religious leanings where a criminal hides out disguised as a mother with a grown-up, mother-fixated son. The role proposed for Alec was that of the criminal, who spends much of the time in drag.

But Van Thal was wrong. Cautiously, Alec considered whether this was not in fact a role that would break the mould and rejuvenate his career. Because there were parallels between Simon Gray's play and the work of Joe Orton, a flagrant homosexual, Alec wanted to make sure, before he took the part, that he could not be accused of collaborating in something that might corrupt and deprave. Gray, who had initially written the play for television and had only adapted it for the stage because he had been advised that it was too outrageous for broadcasting, was summoned back from a holiday in Portugal to be looked over by the great theatrical knight:

> It was so that Alec could make sure that I wasn't like any of the characters in the play, and that I was a respectable person. And indeed I was: I was a lecturer in English at London University, married with two children. I had dinner with him; he spent most of the time in a ghastly competition quoting from the *Four Quartets*. He was intoning away at me and I was trying to come up with couplets. We both drank much too much. It was in his flat . . . I got drunker and drunker – and so was he – but he boomed sedately. I managed to get away and tumbled into the gutter. I looked up and saw this moon-like face watching behind the curtains . . . It was a very odd evening. It was my first experience of the big time.[704]

Simon Gray passed the test of respectability and Alec accepted the role. He ensured that the part of the homosexual hotelier was given to his friend Gordon Jackson and that of his 'son' to Simon Ward. The director was John Dexter. 'On September 11th,' Alec wrote to Dame Felicitas, 'I start rehearsals for a new play (a very strange, wayward, outrageous play, but of great quality, I think, and for all the offences it will give and raised eyebrows it will cause, a compassionate and interesting one).'[705]

Simon Gray was also nervous – it was his first stage play – and was made uncomfortable by what he witnessed during the rehearsals:

> It was directed by John Dexter who was a brilliant man. But he was a bully – a hateful man; and I was distressed in rehearsals because he used to pick on Gordon Jackson who was in it because of Alec. He was absolutely marvellous but John Dexter couldn't leave him alone. John hadn't been to university, but he was far more intelligent than most people, and he also hated closets – closet queens – which Gordon was; as was Alec. Some overt homosexuals hate secret homosexuals. He had to take it out on someone and he couldn't take it out on Alec. He was notoriously a bully – sex was always in it somewhere. I liked him very much and got on with him well but I couldn't bear all this stuff and I didn't like Alec for letting it go.

Gray also became exasperated because Alec was ignoring a clear stage direction at the end of the first act:

> It was clearly written that the Guinness character should give the Ward character, after the initial shudder of revulsion, an embrace – should put his arm around him because he had realised that this was one very sick child. And Alec wasn't doing it. What he was doing was giving the shocked, disgusted look and then waiting for the curtain. I said this wasn't right. He should find something in him of love. I mentioned this to John and he said: 'You tell Alec.' So I did. And he listened, solemnly, and took it in. Half an hour later, John came and said: 'Alec thinks it would be better if you left rehearsals.' And he ignored what I had said.

Gray perceived, quite rightly, that Alec was in danger of losing his nerve. 'I am in the midst of hectic rehearsals for my strange disturbing funny absurd and rather ill-making play,' he wrote to Dame Felicitas on 23 September. 'Have never been so nervous in my life.' He was afraid that acting in drag in a black comedy would upset a number of his traditional admirers, and there is no doubt that it did. The American cartoonist, David Levine, was present on the second night when 'as the curtain was coming down, a viewer, standing in a side exit, shouted, "It's filth, Sir Alec, and beneath you".'.[706] Gray felt that Alec was trying to have it both ways. 'Alec was always trying to tell the audience that this wasn't him. He wanted to dissociate himself from it yet act it with great skill and panache. He didn't let himself into the passions of the play. It was a play about feelings and he didn't like the feelings when he got close to them.' Gray thought that Donald Pleasence played the role more convincingly on Broadway.

The first night audience, however, was enthusiastic and after the final curtain Merula went up to Simon Gray, flung her arms around his neck, and said, 'Thank you, thank you, you've saved his career.' And, while the play itself was regarded by some critics as an attempt to jump on to the Joe Orton bandwagon, Alec's performance received good notices which he, of course, did not read. *Wise Child* ran for four months at Wyndham's Theatre. 'Alec is in a new play and all is going very well – it's a SUCCESS,' Merula wrote to Dame Felicitas:

> . . . and poor old gloomy is nosing around for a grumble and can't find one. It's a marvellous play I think – though pretty peculiar, and not for Aunt Edna and the kiddies, and I don't think for you either really, but in spite of its roughness and creepiness, it is a compassionate play, one does really *care* about the odd characters and Alec is sublimely and outrageously funny – all the cast is V.G. and so's the production and the public comes – and he enjoys it – so what CAN he grumble about?[707]

'Poor old gloomy' was, perhaps, suffering from another of his hopeless 'crushes' – this time on the pleasant-looking young actor whom he saw daily during the run, Simon Ward. Gray, also a friend of Ward and his wife Alexandra, recalled that Alec used to invite Ward to stay at Kettlebrook and was always irritated if it was proposed that Alexandra might come with him. Alexandra, a friend of the Waughs, remembered a small dinner she gave for Alec where the other guests were Margaret Fitzherbert and Father Philip Caraman, now back from his exile in Norway. Alec spent the evening looking moon-eyed at her husband; the Jesuit, similarly, had eyes only for Margaret. Alexandra felt somewhat left out.

No such friendship was formed between Alec and Simon Gray:

On the first night Alec gave me a really expensive silver goblet on which was written nothing. It was a completely purposeless gift. For a first-night present it was meaningless. If he had had engraved 'Alec Guinness, *Wise Child*' or something like that it would have had some point. I never saw him after that. Once we sat in an epicure restaurant. He was on his own eating quietly in a corner. He was alone. I was with someone. Our eyes met but we didn't acknowledge one another. Then, a few years before he died, I ran into him in the street. He was on his way to see an actor friend who was dying – perhaps Bobby Flemyng, or Ralph Richardson's widow – and I saw this man whom I didn't recognise moving unsteadily along the pavement and we just happened to turn towards each other. His face was terrible. He looked as if every sin he had ever dreamed of committing was expressed there in his face. His face was swollen and lumpy. We had a few courteous words and then went our different ways.

In March 1968, Alec returned to Shakespeare for the first time since his *Macbeth*, playing Malvolio to Joan Plowright's Viola in a television production of *Twelfth Night* directed by John Dexter. Laurence Olivier, by then married to Joan Plowright, came to Elstree Studios to see the run-through of the play and whispered to Alec: 'Fascinating, old dear. I never realised before that Malvolio could be played as a bore.'[708] After this, Alec was 'a little put out; I would hear the word "bore" running through the rest of my performance'. Dexter's production, which was not screened until 1970, was judged unsatisfactory and left Alec 'on the verge of a breakdown – physically, mentally, spiritually'.

To recover, he spent twenty-four hours alone in a suite at a grand hotel in Brighton.

In April, however, he returned to safer theatrical terrain by staging a revival of T.S. Eliot's *The Cocktail Party* at the Chichester Festival. Alec directed the play himself and again played the priest-like Sir Henry Harcourt-Reilly. 'The work has been happy, on the whole, and I have enjoyed it,' Alec wrote to Dame Felicitas, 'but I can't see the wood for the trees and don't know whether what I have done is sheer foolishness, just plain dull, or maybe quite good.'[709] It turned out to be more than good. Eliot's verse drama might have gone out of fashion, but the modesty and clarity of Alec's performance was praised. In the autumn, the production transferred to the West End, first to Wyndham's and later to the Haymarket, with Alec's friends Eileen Atkins and Mark Kingston joining the cast. 'Splendid notices from Hobson in *S. Times*,' Alec noted in his Small Diary on 10 November – noting, too, the less favourable reviews in the *Observer* and *Sunday Telegraph*. Clearly, there were times when Alec *did* read reviews.

In 1969, Alec joined John Gielgud in a BBC television production of a duologue, *Conversation at Night*, by the Swiss playwright, Friedrich Dürrenmatt: Alec played the executioner and Gielgud his victim. Alec had done numerous broadcasts for the BBC, starting with *Doctor Faustus* in 1938. That summer, he went to Spain to play King Charles I in the film *Cromwell*. Once again, Alec was playing a secondary role but one more substantial than the 'bit parts' he had been accused of taking in Lean's recent films – so substantial, in fact, that Richard Harris, who played Cromwell, objected to the director, Ken Hughes, that it was too strong:

Richard Harris is complaining that he thinks my part is better than his (which it certainly *isn't* – though neither could be called distinguished) and wants his part re-written before he works in the studio. Oh, and etc. etc. I think it will all blow over but I have pointed out to Ken – who is a dear – that I will happily withdraw if they want and they can find an actor who will play Charles the way Richard would like it – as a villain. All very silly. It'll be forgotten by next week.[710]

Alec's performance as a world-weary King Charles was entirely convincing and – contrasted to Harris's egocentric, stagey and 'actorish' playing of Cromwell – showed once again how self-effacement contributed to Alec's genius as an actor. This was the fourth of six Heads of State he was to play on film – seven if one counts a Prime Minister, Disraeli, in *The Mudlark* – and he had prepared for the role with his usual professionalism. He had written to Anthony Blunt, the Keeper of the Queen's Pictures, he told Anne Kaufman at the time of the spy's disgrace, 'to study a particular portrait of Charles I at his trial, which HM owns. I had a curt refusal so he's *never* been popular with me. If I'd sent a p.c. to her I bet she'd have said, "Yes, and come to tea".'[711]

Ronald Harwood was hired to work on the script. The filming got behindhand. Richard Harris missed his flight to Spain and so hired a private jet. 'The hanging around is fearsomely boring,' Alec wrote to Merula. 'Nothing to write about, except wind and cold and drizzle . . . The young actors around are probably quite pleasant but strike me as being rather arrogant and uppity. One of them was complaining that the company hasn't put a Rolls at his disposal as they had on his previous film. He's all of 23 and this is his 2nd picture.'[712] As when playing Prince Feisal in *Lawrence of Arabia*, Alec had to ride a horse into battle. 'I spent yesterday on my tall white sensitive horse and did a rather wobbly canter over a ridgey bit of ground right up to camera. I was somewhat doubtful as to whether I, my hat, my wig, beard and moustache would make it but they all seem pleased – and rather surprised.'

Alec had old friends such as Robert Morley in the cast, and he made new ones, such as Nigel Stock and Michael Jayston, but he took violently against Timothy Dalton: 17 June, the last day of filming, 'was so slow,' Alec wrote in his Small Diary, 'and Tim Dalton such a pain.'[713] The director failed to film the movement of Alec's hands at the moment of Charles's execution – a gesture Alec had seen as the defining moment of his whole performances. On 6 August of the following year, 1970, Alec took Merula and Leueen to see the finished film. 'Oh dear, oh dear. A very depressing experience. Felt the audience was violently anti-Charles. But it's a heavy, boring film.'[714]

Cromwell was Alec's last film for Columbia, marking the end of a contract that had guaranteed him £12,000 a year. He now began worrying about money and, in July 1969, sold a number of his paintings at auction – works by Howard Hodgkin, Edward Burra, Keith Vaughan and Felix Kelly. He agreed to appear as John in *Time Out of Mind* at the Yvonne Arnaud Theatre, Guildford as a favour to its author, his old friend Bridget Boland: both Matthew and Mark Kingston were in the cast. And in 1970, he played Marley's Ghost in *Scrooge*, a musical version of Dickens's *Christmas Carol*, directed by another old friend, Ronald Neame, with Dame Edith Evans also in the cast. Albert Finney, who played Scrooge, Alec knew already: 'Took Finney and Bully to supper at La Reserve,' he had noted in his Small Diary on 10 January 1962. 'Finney without a tie.' However, if this unsuccessful attempt by Leslie Bricusse to exploit the success of Lionel Bart's *Oliver*, a musical adaptation of *Oliver Twist*, was a small blip in the career of the young up-and-coming actor, it was a low point for Alec.

forty-four

'I am now blissfully out of work,' Alec wrote to Dame Felicitas after finishing *Scrooge*. 'Alec is wonderfully well,' Merula wrote, also to Dame Felicitas. 'He looks younger and better than he has for years. Idleness does him good, but he is getting rather restless and if work doesn't come along soon we will be packing our bags and trailing off to places, I have no doubt.'[715] In fact, appearances were deceptive. Three days later, Alec collapsed while cashing a cheque at his bank in London. 'I had to be whisked off to The Clinic,' he wrote to Dame Felicitas:

> . . . from which I returned on Saturday. I'm fine again now. Apparently it was inner-ear trouble . . . If I had died there and then, what a wasted and sinful life I would have had to account for – and no doubt it will be much the same in the future. But the funny thing is that as I keeled over, and wondered to myself if it could possibly be death (I had been feeling so terribly well up to that moment), I had an odd feeling of

happiness and forgiveness even. Merula flicked through my mind with
slight anxiety and regret and yet the word or idea, GOD, was gaily and
lightly overwhelming.[716]

Until then Alec's health had been good but his collapse, which had
been accompanied by vomiting, gave him enough of a shock for him
to try and give up smoking. He was addictive by nature – a compulsive
gourmand and shopaholic – and found it difficult, particularly when
Merula continued to smoke up to forty cigarettes a day. Alec would
prick Merula's cigarettes with a pin to reduce the intake of nicotine.

The inner-ear trouble was the first of a number of minor ailments.
In April 1970, he had surgery for a double hernia; there was a gallstone
in June 1971; he had 'near bronchial pneumonia' in 1973 – his excuse
for a long break in his correspondence with Dame Felicitas – and high
blood pressure in 1974; diverticulitis was diagnosed in 1975; a further
hernia operation in 1977; a haemorrhage in the retina of his left eye in
1979; and two more hernia operations – the fourth in 1982 when Val
Stavredi, Faith Brook, Leueen MacGrath and Mu Richardson came to
visit him, and 'the Leans arrived bearing half a pound of Beluga caviar.
Very spoiled I felt.'[717]

Alec suffered from hypochondria: 'For three days now,' he noted in
his diary on 26 November 1975, 'I've been struck every few hours by
a sharp headache. Immediately, of course, I think it's a tumour on the
brain or an imminent stroke.' He could be flippant about his health:
'If I've got AIDS,' he told Matthew and Merula, 'I hope I die of
something else,' adding hastily, 'and I can't think how I might have got
it.' Alec's insistence on having the best of everything extended to
medical practitioners: while Merula trusted her health to the local GP
at Petersfield, Alec went to a private doctor in London, Dr John
Janvrin. Advised to lose weight, he went on the Scarsdale diet with
some dramatic effects: 'Lost between eight and nine pounds,' he
boasted in his diary on 1 June 1980, which, Merula told Dame Felicitas,
did him 'a *great deal* of good, looks ten years younger and has much
more energy'.[718] But Alec remained an incorrigible gourmand and, as

the years passed, his girth showed the effects of the rich eating in expensive restaurants. He also suffered from gout and, like Merula, continued to smoke. 'My non-smoking New Year resolution was quickly and easily broken.'[719]

In 1971 Alec played John Mortimer's blind and irascible father in *A Voyage Round My Father*, a performance that for B.A. Young, the *Financial Times* critic, was 'beyond praise' and for Frank Marcus, writing in the *Sunday Telegraph*, Alec's 'best performance in recent years'. But John Mortimer found Laurence Olivier more convincing: 'My father was rather frightening. Alec was a masochist playing a sadist. When Laurence Olivier played my father, he was much more like my father because Olivier was genuinely frightening.'[720] For Alec, however, his success in the play seemed to arrest the decline in his professional fortunes; and there was the bonus of two new friendships: Leueen MacGrath, and the play's director, Ronald Eyre.

'I come out of *A Voyage Round My Father* on Easter Saturday,' Alec wrote to Dame Felicitas. 'I had hoped to leave last night, so that I could have an uninterrupted Easter, but the management wouldn't play. So no Easter vigil for me this year . . .'[721] No longer did Alec have the muscle to dictate terms, as he had in New York when the Good Friday performance of *Dylan* had been cancelled at his request.

The Italian director Franco Zeffirelli, who had failed to persuade Alec to take the role of Aschenbach in *Death in Venice*, recruited him for a cameo role in a film he made in 1972 about St Francis of Assisi – a saint admired, indeed venerated, by both Alec and Merula. Alec appeared, right at the end of *Brother Sun, Sister Moon*, as the magisterial Pope Innocent III who, against the advice of his Curia, sanctions Francis's rule of absolute poverty and devotion to the poor. In effect, Alec was Marcus Aurelius in vestments instead of a toga but, despite the rococo theatricality of his scene, the folksy soundtrack with Donovan's hippy ballad, and the homoerotic tinge to the film, Alec's Innocent is credible and moving. 'I'm not worried about the St Francis film,' he wrote to

Dame Felicitas on the eve of its release, 'because it is really ravishing to look at, has an innocent charm and I play such a tiny part in it. The dialogue is rotten throughout and the acting not up to much, but its visual beauty brought a tear to my eye when I saw it.'[722]

Laurence Olivier, who had turned down the role, concurred. 'Dearest Alec,' he wrote on 26 January 1973:

> Zeff treated me to a showing of 'Sun & Moon' yesterday and I must just tell you how great you are in it – Absolutely nobody else in the world could have handled that very tricky problem as you did . . . Every split second full of meaning and information. Franco really owes you a great great deal (I think I'd have been a worried friend about the film without you) . . . Bravo dear boy. Best get yourself a quick ordination & they'll just have to make you the next Pope – the only Latin word you have to know is *Volo* & I can teach you that! Love Larry.

Numerous film roles, both major and minor, were suggested to Alec in the course of the 1960s and 1970s: the Mahdi to Charlton Heston's Gordon in *Khartoum* (the role was played by Olivier); Pope Pius XII in a film of Rolf Hochhuth's play *The Representative*; the Emperor Claudius in an adaptation of Robert Graves's *I, Claudius* to be directed by Tony Richardson; the composer Wagner in Visconti's *Ludwig*; T.S. Eliot's *The Elder Statesman* for BBC television; and a part in *The Rocky Horror Show* – 'Do you think my varicose veins would show through the fishnet stockings?' he asked Anne Kaufman. Alec either rejected the offers or the projects fell through.

In 1973, however, another Italian director, Ennio de Concini, offered Alec a unique challenge – the title role in *Hitler: The Last Ten Days*. The screenplay was based on an eye-witness account of Hitler's life in the bunker beneath the Chancellery in Berlin during the final days of the Third Reich. Alec thought it was superb and saw a chance to astonish an audience once again with a leading role. However, it was dangerous for Alec, who struggled to repress his cruel, predatory and domineering alter-ego, to summon it up by entering imaginatively into the mind of the paranoid German dictator. 'Restless about film and mental state,' he noted in his Small Diary on 23 July 1971. 'Fascinating and alarming stuff,' he wrote to Dame Felicitas. 'And a very good script. I keep my fingers crossed.'

Alec did his usual meticulous research, listening to recordings and watching newsreels of Hitler's speeches, and living the character. Merula, who told Ronald Neame how exhausting it had been living with Alec as Gully Jimson, remarked upon how nasty he was while preparing to play Hitler. By the time filming started, empathy with the dictator had brought the tyrannical side of Alec's personality to the fore. A number of his friends were among the cast – Mark Kingston, Simon Ward and Eileen Atkins's former husband, Julian Glover. During the filming Alec became 'irritated with John Bennett . . . and bawled him out one afternoon which resulted in a good old row. Sort of made it up in late afternoon. First time in my life I've ever bawled out a fellow actor.'[723]

'There was too much arse-licking during the filming of Hitler,' Joss Ackland, one of the cast, recalled. 'Everyone was obsequious towards Alec'. Working together in an ersatz bunker at Shepperton Studios for eight weeks, the company began to realise that the film was going to be a disaster. Some blamed Alec. 'Alec was bad as Hitler,' said Ackland. 'It was ridiculous casting.' Julian Glover, on the other hand, judged Alec 'indistinguishable from the original'.[724] There were those who, after the film was released, thought that Alec had done something immoral in making Hitler so 'human'.

'I have been working exceedingly hard – to near breaking point – as Hitler,' Alec wrote to Dame Felicitas ten days after shooting finished, 'in a film, the script of which I thought was really first rate but the final result of which is, sadly, somewhat disappointing. I don't think that in the whole of my professional life I have put so much into a part – so I feel rather sour and cheated. Probably I have largely myself to blame.'[725] And, also to Dame Felicitas, five months later as the film was about to be released:

The Hitler film, I'm afraid is a mess. Very sad for me as I am sure it's quite the best piece of acting I've done in my life, but it has been chopped about, forty minutes removed from it (it *was* ten minutes too long) and all bitty and meaningless now. So I expect I shall have to carry the can pretty unpleasantly for that . . . Between you and me I don't much want to ever make another film; so many of the wrong people are in charge of the industry and actors are being used more and more as puppets.[726]

By 1979, when *Hitler: The Last Ten Days* was shown on television, Alec had downgraded his performance as Hitler from the best thing he'd ever done to 'one of the three best pieces of work I've done on the screen'.[727] As a bravura impersonation, he was probably right. Despite adopting Gully Jimson's rasping voice, Alec does manage to suggest the monstrosity behind the mask of trite politeness and to convey the banal ordinariness of the tyrant's daily life. The critics, however, were savage. The *New York Times* thought Alec 'looks right as Hitler, and that's about all'. The *New Yorker* thought he looked exactly like Alec Guinness and judged the film 'flippant'; and the critic of the magazine *Commonweal* thought that Alec's Hitler, like his Malvolio, was a bore.

In late 1972 Ronald Eyre, who had directed Alec in *A Voyage Round My Father*, sent him *Habeas Corpus*, a new play by a young playwright, Alan Bennett. Alec had been to see Gielgud on the first night of Bennett's first play, *Forty Years On*, but could not make up his mind about *Habeas Corpus*. 'I re-read Bennett play and still cannot decide. Spoke to Kenny More* about Bennett. He loathes him.'[728] The play, Alec later wrote to Dame Felicitas, as if justifying his decision to play a lecherous GP, 'has the air of a Restoration play – a semi-permissive near farce which may offend some – but has literary merit, I feel, and tucked deep down in it, for those with ears to hear, it is honest and

---

* The actor Kenneth More had appeared with Alec in *Scrooge*.

searching'.[729] Even well into rehearsals, however, he was in two minds about it. 'I'm in the midst of rehearsing my v. strange piece. I have seldom been more bewildered professionally,' he wrote to Anne Kaufman. 'One day I think it really *is* funny, and another a load of boring rubbish. Whatever it may be I *don't* get the message lightly wrapped inside it. But it's a pleasant cast and I love working with Ron Eyre (who directs it) and I find Alan Bennett (who wrote it) good-natured and amusing. I give it about three weeks in London and predict a critical panning.'[730]

Before opening in London, *Habeas Corpus* played for two weeks in Oxford. On the first night of the tour, most of the laughing was inspired by the antics of a young actor, Andrew Sachs. As so often after a first night that he judged to be a fiasco, Alec was thrown into despair. After the performance, the cast returned to the Randolph Hotel for a late supper with producer Michael Codron, Alan Bennett, Ronald Eyre and, with Alec at his table, Merula and his agent, Dennis van Thal. There was polite chatter until, in a lull in the conversation, Alec was heard saying to his agent: 'Well, Dennis. *This* time I mean it. You're going to have to get me out of this one.'

In fact, Alec himself had had some influence over the play's direction. 'Ron Eyre would be submissive to Alec up to a point,' Alan Bennett recalled, 'and then he would blow up.' It was Alec's idea to perform a little dance at the end of the play: 'It skewered the play but made it more palatable. I wouldn't have let anyone else do it.'[731] But Alec seems to have felt that both the part and his performance were never quite right. 'I was never satisfied with my performance,' he wrote in his diary, 'and often grumbled inside myself at the unfortunate placing of some of Wicksteed's speeches. It seemed to me I was always having to make an entrance on someone else's round or laugh, and consequently lowering the temperature.'[732] But the play was admired by the critics and Alec was praised. 'The latest batch of reviews,' Alan Bennett informed him, 'all seem to say what a silly person I am, and how, despite that, you manage to salvage the play. So I feel a bit that I may have done you a disservice. I hope not.'[733] And,

at the end of the run in March 1974: 'You've made the play much more
than I could ever have dreamed of and I owe you a great debt. It
doesn't seem long since I first came, very nervously, to Smith Square.
The time since has been one of the happiest and most fruitful in my
life.'[734] For Alec, too, despite his professional misgivings, *Habeas Corpus*
'has been just about the happiest theatre venture I've had'.[735] It also
made him, as we have seen, more money than he had ever before
made from the stage.

In August 1974, after a holiday in Greece, Alec played Jocelyn Broome
in a television production of John Osborne's *The Gift of Friendship*,
directed by Mike Newell and starring his old friends Leueen MacGrath
and Michael Gough, and Alan Badel's daughter Sarah. It was a slight
script – prescient in the sense that Broome keeps a daily diary as he
prepares for death – but Alec feared that his own 'performance was
trapped into an element of pretension'. 'Your step-mum seems in good
order,' he wrote to Anne Kaufman. 'We are both being driven cynically
demented by our tall pretentious young director – to a point where
yesterday I forced myself to ask whether the commercials, which will
interrupt our thespian efforts from time to time, will have the same
subtlety as ourselves.'[736]

   In the same year, Alec broadcast *King Lear* on the radio from 'the
gloomy beige halls of Broadcasting House'. 'It was, on the whole, a
pleasant assignment with a very agreeable cast,' he recorded in his
diary, 'but I suspect the result may be worthily hum-drum.' 'I failed
hopelessly in the storm sequence,' he noted after listening to the play
on the radio, 'but feel I was rather good in the last scenes. A good
production, in which Robert Powell was outstanding as Edgar, Cyril
Cusack excellent as Gloucester, and Eileen as Regan, as also was Sarah
Badel as Cordelia.'[737]

Alec's next big project for the West End stage was a theatrical
adaptation by Julian Mitchell of a novel by Ivy Compton-Burnett, *A
Family and a Fortune* in 1975. Michael Codron, who had produced Alan

Bennett's plays, first suggested that Alec should both direct and appear in the play, but after flirting with the idea Alec decided that it would be too much: instead, he told Anne Kaufman, he 'would breathe down the young director's neck'. The young director in question was Alan Strachan, then aged twenty-six, who had made his name directing Shaw's *John Bull's Other Island* at the Mermaid Theatre. Like Simon Gray and Alan Bennett, Alan Strachan was summoned to Smith Square to be looked over:

The flat was not at all what I expected. It was very 'hip'. In those days – the '70s – there was a huge vogue for Peacock chairs from Habitat. There was no sofa but lots of enormous cushions on the floor. One wall was lined with cork, à la Proust. There was no single bit of theatrical memorabilia; there was one drawing by Merula which she had done for Noah in the hall. The main sitting area was almost hippy; Alec was always into fashion; he liked to be *au courant*. He was a truffle-hound of trend.[738]

The cast included two of Alec's old friends – Margaret Leighton and Rachel Kempson, and the sets were designed by Percy Harris who lived above Alec at Smith Square. Rachel Kempson had been reluctant to take the part of Blanche Gaveston because, after a wretched time playing in Peter Nichols's *The Freeway* at the National Theatre, she had lost her nerve about appearing on-stage. Strachan, whom she already knew, persuaded her that she would be among old friends, and Alec was enlisted to win her round. When the play went into production, Alec went to great lengths to reassure her. 'I really am getting over my nerves on stage,' she wrote to her husband, Michael Redgrave, who was on tour in the United States:

. . . and only have a moment of 'butterflies' just before I go on. Alec who stands near me just before my entrance in Act I, the start of the play, always says, 'All right?' and I say, 'Yes, I think so,' and he says, 'Of *course* you are.' I adore Maggie and she likes me to visit her during

'making up' & so I take my make-up & sit by her. Alec calls it 'The
Girls' Dorm'. I find him very special with that blessed thing of no
sexual feelings between us.[739]

In *A Family and a Fortune* Alec played the second son of an
impoverished upper-middle-class English family. Alan Strachan
thought that he liked the part:

> . . . as one he could invest with a lot of slyness and wit. I also think Ivy
> Compton-Burnett's odd Buddhist-like wisdom appealed to him; a very
> bleak world; an unforgiving view of human nature, one which Alec
> rather shared. I think he had quite a low opinion of human behaviour
> and I think Compton-Burnett's world isn't pretty; people are motivated
> by avarice, lust . . . and all sorts of distinctly unworthy motives which
> they try not to admit to themselves or to other people; and I think he
> was fascinated by the veneer of civilisation which we all put on to
> disguise what Ivy Compton-Burnett calls our Nature to which she
> usually gives a capital N.

The play went on tour before it opened in London. 'Merula says it has
a mesmeric quality,' Alec wrote to Anne Kaufman from Bath, 'which
is what I hope. But I feel she doesn't care for all the acting, including
mine. She has said nothing, which bodes not much good.'[740] The
reviews, after the London opening, were mixed but, Alec assured
Dame Felicitas in July, the play, 'in spite of the fact that by no means
all people like it, and it must be Treble Dutch to foreigners, continues
to do better business than any other play in London. It is a sweet-
natured agreeable company, so it's a pleasure to get down to the
theatre each night – in spite of the heat.'[741]

In the course of the run at the Apollo Theatre, Strachan noticed
certain Compton-Burnettean traits in Alec's own character. The actor
Anthony Nicholls who played Edgar Gaveston became Alec's
'whipping boy':

For some reason during the pre-London run, Alec began to disparage him – not to him but to other actors and to me – which I didn't like because I thought Tony was good. He was going through a difficult time; his marriage was breaking up; he was also ill – he died of cancer a year later. He was sleeping very badly and so became absent-minded. On one occasion, in Brighton, he missed an entrance which is appalling; it threw everybody because everybody is waiting on-stage for an actor to enter, especially in a play with such verbal precision as Ivy Compton-Burnett's. It was only a half-minute or so but it threw things into disarray. It was Tony's fault. He had lost concentration backstage. Alec – and it was the only time when I felt he had behaved badly – said to Tony in front of everyone else, after the curtain came down: 'Make sure that never happens again.' It undermined his confidence. Tony never did do it again; it was quite unnecessary for Alec to say that. Thus, there was a streak of cruelty in Alec.

But, by the same token, there were acts of great kindness. Maggie Leighton's understudy, a rather sad, lonely person, lived for two things; the life of the theatre and her dog. The dog died. Alec found out and bought her a new one – a Dandy Dinmont.

The success of *Habeas Corpus* would lead Alec to appear in Alan Bennett's next play, *The Old Country*; and Alec's satisfaction with the young director of *A Family and a Fortune*, Alan Strachan, led the two men to collaborate on *Yahoo*, an 'entertainment' based on the life and work of the eighteenth-century satirist, Jonathan Swift. Alec was already working on a script for *Yahoo* when, in October of 1975, he returned to Hollywood to play a blind butler in a Neil Simon comedy, *Murder by Death*.

The film, produced by Ray Stark and directed by Robert Moore, was a send-up of classic detective films – the characters included Hercule Poirot, Charlie Chan and Miss Marple – and a bevy of big names had been recruited to the cast from both sides of the Atlantic. They included Peter Falk, Peter Sellers (who had been with Alec in *The Ladykillers*), Estelle Winwood (who had appeared with Alec in *The*

Swan), Elsa Lanchester, David Niven, Maggie Smith and the author, Truman Capote. Estelle Winwood, Alec recalled when she died in 1984, 'was always trying to inveigle me into playing bridge. She had a dangerous tongue.' He found Maggie Smith 'a nice, sensitive woman under that brittle camp. A relapsed Catholic, I find.' David Niven, of course, he had always liked but, as on *Cromwell*, he found the pretensions of the younger actors exasperating. 'So much time is spent accommodating Peter Falk's and Peter Sellers's moods and feelings that I am skimped for time.'[742] Stories later circulated of how Peter Sellers sent a sidekick to take the measurements of Alec's caravan, fearing that it might be larger than his. There is also the story, originating from the film's author, Neil Simon, and passed on by Alec to John le Carré, of how, during the shooting, the telephone rang in Simon's room:

> 'This is Alec Guinness. First of all, what a marvellous script this is. I am afraid there is a problem on page 24 . . . I do think it's not quite right . . .' Second week, he rang again: 'Could we look at page 48.' And so on, week after week; until on the eve of shooting, Alec said: 'I'm afraid Merula can't come and I wonder if you could arrange, for want of a better expression, a piece of fluff.' So Neil Simon drew himself up to his full 4 foot 4 and said, 'I am not a pimp.' And put the 'phone down. And it had been Peter Sellers all the time.'[743]

Alec's complaints are less about Sellers's pranks than his egotism:

> Yesterday's work was a bit thrown as Sellers was reported to be ill with the bug that's going around. When I took Eileen to dinner at La Scala, Peter entered, apparently bright as a button and saying he was recovered. And he was reported as being seen at the Bel Air in the early afternoon, so it would appear he hadn't been ill for very long. I suppose that's the behaviour which gets you the 'superstar' label and passes for the attribute of genius. In my experience all bad behaviour which has been excused as genius has been childish tantrums, egomania and downright shitty selfishness.[744]

There was a scene in the screenplay of *Murder by Death* in which the butler is found naked on the kitchen floor. Alec refused 'to appear in the nude. After all, we don't want screams, only laughter, and that of a seemly sort'; and he was too august for the producers to insist so a substitute was found. 'Today they are photographing my naked body at the kitchen table,' Alec wrote in his diary on 20 November 1975, 'a scene I said I would refuse to do when accepting the part. Modesty? No. Shyness, I suppose, and a desire not to advertise my sixty-two-year-old fleshiness to the world. I have a suspicion that they have chosen a stand-in to do it who is about a stone heavier than me and totally round in the middle.'

Overall, Alec wrote to Anne Kaufman from Los Angeles, the film was 'pleasant and quite fun to do but I'm bored at doing so little and so infrequently'.[745] Nor was the engagement as lucrative as he had hoped. 'I shall be almost out of pocket,' he told Dame Felicitas, 'from my American venture in spite of having earned good money – taxes have eaten it nearly all away.'[746] The producers did well enough; the film was commercially successful in the United States, but it did little for Alec's reputation. 'I have had an abusive letter about *Murder by Death* from some fellow countryman of yours,' Alec wrote to Anne Kaufman on 8 August 1976. '"Now you are past it, why don't you retire? Why not give readings from great literature instead of trying to act in drivel etc. etc.".'

forty-five

'I don't know for sure what I shall do next,' Alec had written to Dame Felicitas after his return from Los Angeles at the end of 1975. 'There's talk of a film I'd rather like to do, which would take me to Tunisia for a couple of weeks and the rest of it would be in London. That would be in April. I continue to tinker at my work on Swift and greatly hope to have it on in some theatre by the end of the year. And there are schemes, which involve me as an actor, for a dramatisation of Evelyn Waugh's *Ordeal of Gilbert Pinfold*.'[747]

A play based on *The Ordeal of Gilbert Pinfold* had originally been suggested by Ronald Harwood, the playwright whom Alec had first come across during the filming of *Cromwell* and who was now his friend and neighbour in Hampshire. Evelyn Waugh's son Auberon, also a friend of Alec's, agreed to release the rights if Alec liked the adaptation and would appear in the play. 'A rather tricky situation,' Alec wrote to Anne Kaufman. 'I like and rather admire the people concerned but hate to be put in a position of moral decisions.'[748]

One of the things that seemed to attract Alec to the idea of *Pinfold* was the possibility that it might lead to the conversion to Catholicism of Ronald Harwood. Harwood had asked for Alec's advice as to where he could pick up some Catholic atmosphere to understand the character of Pinfold, and Alec had suggested a visit to Quarr Abbey on the Isle of Wight – a place he had been to on retreat. 'If you want to go to Quarr Abbey,' he wrote to Harwood:

> I would be happy to take you there and stay a night or two; almost any time. If, on the other hand, you wish to go non-professionally, so to speak, you would prefer, obviously, to be quite alone – but you still might like to be taken and introduced, and I'd be happy to do that also. I hesitate putting this to you, as I don't wish to intrude, but want you to know that I'd be a happy guide – and I'd waive my usual fee.[749]

Harwood, a Jew, seems to have felt that Alec might be under a misapprehension because, on 6 January 1976, Alec felt he had to reassure him that he knew he was not a Catholic:

> No, of course I know you are not a Catholic. I hadn't even assumed you are a Christian (in the orthodox sense), though very much so I think in the moral sense. I don't think you would find the Benedictine monks fussing and certainly not proselytising; just accepting. And a bit strange, perhaps. What one has to bear in mind is that the sense of calm and peace one experiences . . . is the result of their fight against tensions and evil. Or so I am led to believe. And do believe. It is possible you could be repelled by or feel melancholic in the atmosphere there but I think not. Anyway you can always pack and politely go home. No questions asked.[750]

On 15 March 1976, with *Yahoo* firmly scheduled for the autumn, Alec wrote to Harwood that, 'My professional commitments are likely to take me until early next year; when free of them I would be happy to attempt Pinfold.' By July Alec was having cold feet. 'I'm committed

morally I suppose,' he wrote to Anne Kaufman, 'to do it for a month
in Manchester, at the new theatre* which opens there shortly, *sometime*
in 1977 – at my convenience. It was a tricky position I was put in, by
a friend and neighbour, and I would rather like to back-pedal.'[751]

Alec did not back-pedal and Michael Elliot, the director of the Royal
Exchange Theatre, announced at a press conference in Manchester
that the great actor would appear in a new play by Ronald Harwood.
Alec wriggled and squirmed. He noted in his diary on 3 December
1976, that doing *Pinfold* would mean closing *Yahoo* in April 1977, when
Codron had assured him that it might run until the early summer.
However, there arose another, more pressing, reason for pulling out.
'Professional *confidence* please,' he wrote to Anne Kaufman on 7
November 1976:

> I have read a most remarkable play, by Alan Bennett. The second half
> of the second act is a bit of a mess – but he knows that and, hopefully,
> can rectify it – but I will go so far as to say it is the most distinguished
> piece of writing I have read in a decade. I don't know why I bother to
> say decade. The best English writing since the flowering of Evelyn
> Waugh . . . It is quite clearly (to my mind) about Philby and the
> defectors to Russia. An erudite, amusing, character-probing spine-
> chilling piece – doomed, I'd say, to instant failure because it's too clever.
> Codron wants me to do it later next year.[752]

'Re-reading Pinfold dramatisation and wondering how to get out of it,'
Alec noted in his Small Diary on 30 October 1976. On 16 February
1977, Ronald Harwood sent Alec for his perusal the agreement he had
signed with Auberon Waugh giving Harwood the right to stage the
play if Alec appeared in the title role. Alec could not do both *The
Ordeal of Gilbert Pinfold* and *The Old Country*. He ditched *Pinfold*, giving
a hernia operation as an excuse.

---

*   The Royal Exchange.

Ronald Harwood was profoundly disappointed by Alec's decision and Michael Elliot was outraged when it became known that Alec was going to do *The Old Country*. Rehearsals of *Pinfold* were due to start in less than a month. He demanded from Alec a doctor's certificate to establish that his operation was not just a pretext. This enraged Alec. 'Angered still by Manchester wanting a doctor's certificate – when I don't even have a contract with them,' he wrote in his Small Diary on 11 February 1977. And, two days later: 'Ron & Natasha Harwood to coffee after dinner. As we were leaving I expressed my annoyance at Manchester requiring medical certificate, but he said (huffily) that it was for the Waugh estate.' The story was leaked to the *Guardian*, provoking Alec to write a letter correcting 'the impression given in the article that this was a sudden unexpected decision which has left the company with only twenty-seven days in which to find a replacement before rehearsals start'. He itemised the warning shots he said he had fired across the bows of the Royal Exchange Theatre regarding his health, concluding that Michael Elliot had had 'sixty-two days in which to re-cast the play'.[753]

The last word came from Auberon Waugh in a letter to Alec dated 22 July 1977:

I was sorry to hear from Ronald Harwood of your illness. I have never had an operation for a hernia although I have had most other operations and, for my own part, enjoy them very much indeed. Of course, my tastes are peculiar, but I hope nevertheless you do not find the experience disagreeable.

I am very sorry you will be unable to play Pinfold as a result. I was looking forward to this very much indeed. Whoever now takes it on will be a poor shadow of yourself. Harwood is understandably mortified; I secretly hope that he will find nobody else and that you may yet emerge triumphantly from your hospital bed and from Alan Bennett's play in June to take the part.[754]

'I've got you *Journal to Stella*,' Alec had written to Merula on 11 November 1940. 'It's jolly decent of me to send it and not read it myself.' This was the beginning of Alec and Merula's long absorption in the work of Swift that resulted in Alec's 'entertainment', which he had more or less completed by the end of 1973. 'Temporarily calling it "Yahoo",' he wrote in his diary on 1 January 1974.

The collaboration with Alan Strachan had started over supper one evening during the run of *A Family and a Fortune*, and had got underway when Alec returned from making *Murder by Death*. 'Yesterday evening I took Alan Strachan to dinner at L'Etoile so we could discuss the Swift project,' Alec wrote in his diary on 6 January 1976. 'We seem to be thinking along the same lines. I wish I felt easier with him. I like him, know him to have humour and to be very intelligent – but I can't quite get through to him. Perhaps it's because he's a trifle alarmed by me.' Alec was pleased with Strachan's contribution. 'He has done painstaking research and if we can knock some life into the linking material I think we shall be on to something good.'

'The collaboration with Alec on Swift . . . started well,' Alan Strachan recalled. 'I went down to Kettlebrook virtually every weekend for the whole spring and early summer. We would work in the little study by the stairs. Sometimes we would work in Smith Square but it became very hot and Alec didn't like that.'

However, Strachan gradually came to realise that there was not a meeting of minds:

There was no way in which he was going to tackle any of the scatological stuff, which is fine . . . I don't think it desperately matters if you don't do 'Celia, Celia, Celia shits' and all that; but I was very, very keen to include the letter on a young lady going to bed – that nightmare poem about a whore, her taking off her clothes, full of self-disgust; and I could see a way to stage it. Alec said 'well, I don't know where that would fit in'. He had been fine about a huge chunk of *A Modest Proposal* . . . but I knew right away that this might be a problem. In the very first draft, that poem was in but he summoned me down to Kettlebrook. Merula wasn't there. He said – 'I hope you don't mind, I read through the first draft of *Yahoo* to Merula and she said you can't possibly do that poem.' There's no way of knowing whether Merula really said this or not. I should have insisted but we were pretty far in to it. Codron had booked two touring theatres; it would have been very difficult to have backed out; and also he was still absolutely set on that huge chunk of *A Modest Proposal* so I thought that was enough.

As a result of Alec's fastidiousness, Strachan felt that their script was 'fatally compromised, partly because of my reluctance to force the issue with Alec'. However, he thought that Alec's performance had moments of genius:

The best bit in the play was a staging of verses on the death of Dr Swift which was played as a card game with Alec playing a society matron – he always liked to get into drag – and Angela* and Nicola† as two other society matrons, and Mark‡ as a rather maidenish man. Mick Hughes, who lit the show, devised the wonderful lighting which made it look as if it was lit by candlelight. The whole thing was surreal. And Alec was wonderful in that, and in *A Modest Proposal* – chillingly good – which is Swift's masterpiece.

Yahoo opened in the provinces, playing first in Cambridge and then Bath. Michael Codron had thought that an academic audience in a university town would appreciate an entertainment based on Swift but he was mistaken: the audience, Strachan judged, did not want to see Alec playing a querulous, irritable old divine. In Bath, the audience seemed to like it even less. Strachan invited Alec out to lunch for which

---

* Angel Thorne
† Nicola Paget
‡ Mark Kingston

Strachan, after a long tussle, made it clear that he would pay the bill. Alec wanted to cut *A Modest Proposal*: Strachan said that it would ruin the show and Alec backed down. It opened in London at the Queen's Theatre to mostly favourable reviews. Bernard Levin in the *Sunday Times* judged that 'It was not Swift complete . . .; the misanthropy is there, but not the loathing of the body which provoked it and eventually destroyed him,' but reported that 'a huge chunk of the *Modest Proposal*, delivered by Guinness with a majestic ferocity . . . froze the first-night audience into a trance of horror.' *Yahoo*, he judged, '. . . does not provide an evening of delight, nor yet of hope . . . But something even rarer in the theatre: true satisfaction'.

Mollie Panter-Downes, in her 'Letter from London' in the *New Yorker* – sent to Alec by Anne Kaufman – also found *Yahoo* 'one of the rare entirely satisfying bits of nourishment to be had in the present disappointing theatre season' which, since many of London's theatregoers were American tourists, accounted for the play's commercial success. '*Yahoo* has recouped its investment,' Alec wrote to Anne Kaufman on 7 November 1976, 'so now we are all into the money.' However, there were also Japanese tourists in the audience who, with an inadequate grasp of English, failed to laugh at the jokes.

At one performance, early in December, the whole first row consisted of Japanese. The first joke in the play was Alec as Swift, preaching to a congregation of one in a country parish in Ireland, saying: 'Dearly beloved Roger, the Spirit moveth both you and me.' An English audience laughed at this: the Japanese did not. Under his breath, but perfectly audibly, Alec muttered: 'Jesus Christ.' 'From then on,' Alan Strachan recalled, 'things went from bad to worse.' Without telling the cast, Strachan had slipped into the theatre to watch the performance:

> I didn't go round at the interval; in the second half, and in the Gulliver excerpt, he changed the staging so that he came downstage and had his back to the audience but his face to three other actors; he clearly started

pulling faces and Mark Kingston corpsed* and so did Nicola and the whole scene crumpled into idiocy. After that it was dark and all went more or less all right.

The curtain fell at the end and I slipped down the side of the auditorium and through the pass door to the wings. After the last curtain call, but before they had time to disperse – I was so angry – I went on-stage and yelled at them. I shouldn't have done it. I should have waited until they were in their dressing-rooms. The stagehands were still around and the dressers. But it was something that needed to be said to everybody. I did shout and said it had been a disgrace and if people were paying the top price in the West End – £9 or whatever it was in those days – they should get value for money. I said I was too angry to give notes that night but would they come in early the next day.

Alec was furious. He might have been all right if I had done it in the privacy of his dressing-room, but because it was in front of the stage-hands, etc. I just didn't think. I was angry as a member of the audience. Mark was very embarrassed. I did go the next night; Alec had come in early and had already started putting on his make-up so I had to address him in the mirror. He was so calm – preternaturally calm: it was his way of saying 'You have sinned, I am going to let you know that you have sinned, it would be cheapening for me to be angry. I'm going to be very, very calm and make you feel about 2¼ centimetres high.' His dresser was in the room which made it more difficult. I got through the few notes and then said I was sorry, but that I had felt very, very strongly about it. He said, 'Well, perhaps you should think of us, acting eight times a week before audiences who don't even speak the language.'

He never referred to it again. And I was not asked to direct him in his next play, *The Old Country*. Our friendship continued but it was never quite the same.[755]

---

* Actors' terminology for uncontrolled giggles on-stage.

'Last night's performance and audience were lousy,' Alec noted in his Small Diary on 4 December. 'Alan slapped us all on the wrist as soon as the curtain fell, which I was in no mood to accept, and said so, harshly. Of course he was quite right – but there was a school-masterish white-faced tone to what he said which I couldn't tolerate after a wretched show.'[756]

forty-six

While Alec was in Los Angeles making *Murder by Death*, a screenplay was sent to his hotel by a young director, George Lucas, who in 1973 had won Oscar nominations as both writer and director for his film *American Graffiti*. His new project, entitled *Star Wars*, was a science-fiction adventure with a role for Alec as Ben (Obi-Wan) Kenobi, a 'Jedi knight'. Alec was 'attracted to the idea of the film', reputedly because it was a fable of the battle of good and evil in which good is triumphant. On 19 December 1975, five days before he flew back to England, he took George Lucas to lunch at a restaurant near the studio, Sorrentino's. 'He is a small, neat-faced young man with a black beard,' Alec recorded in his diary the next day:

> . . . with tiny well-shaped hands, poorish teeth, glasses and not much sense of humour. But I liked him. The conversation, which was about the part he'd like me to play, was divided culturally by eight thousand

miles and thirty years; but I think we might understand each other, if
I can get past his intensity.[757]

'I have been offered a movie (20th Cent. Fox),' Alec wrote to Anne
Kaufman on 22 December, 'which I *may* accept, if they come up with
proper money. London and N. Africa, starting in mid-March. Science
fiction – which gives me pause – but it is to be directed by Paul [sic]
Lucas who did *American Graffiti*, which makes me feel I should. Big
part. Fairy-tale rubbish but *could* be interesting perhaps.'

Back in London, on 12 January 1976 Alec's agent, Dennis van Thal,
informed him that 'Twentieth Century Fox came through with an offer
of $150,000 plus a small participation. This is double what they offered
last week (when I turned it down because of money).' The 'small
participation' was two per cent of the producer's profit. The filming
started at EMI Studios in March where, after lunch with George Lucas
and Gary Kurtz, the film's producer, Alec rehearsed his duel as Ben
(Obi-Wan) Kenobi with Darth Vader using 'light' sabres – 'Darth Vader
being played by a giant of a man called Dave Prowse, whom I suspect
of not being an actor, though he is a member of Equity'.[758] 'Can't say
I'm enjoying the film,' Alec wrote to Anne Kaufman on 18 March:

. . . new rubbish dialogue reaches me every other day on wadges of
pink paper – and *none* of it makes my character clear or even bearable.
I just think, thankfully, of the lovely bread, which will help me keep
going until next April even if *Yahoo* collapses in a week . . . I must off
to studio and work with a dwarf (very sweet – and he has to wash in
a bidet) and your fellow countrymen Mark Hamill and Tennyson (that
can't be right) Ford. Ellison (? – No!) – well, a rangy, languid young man
who is probably intelligent and amusing. But Oh, God, God, they make
me feel *ninety* – and treat me as if I was 106. – Oh, *Harrison* Ford – ever
heard of him?

Merula accompanied Alec to North Africa for filming in Djerba and
Tozeur: they were there between 20 March and 5 April. He wrote

cheerful and enthusiastic letters to Matthew but he was uneasy about his role. 'The setups and costumes etc all looked good. I put on my basic costume and boots to give myself an hour of walking and moving across rough ground, trying to get the feel of the character. Not much comes to me I must confess; there is an indecisiveness in the script which troubles me. And I cannot yet find a voice which I think suitable.'[759]

George Lucas also seemed to have his doubts about Alec's role. 'Irritated by George Lucas saying he hadn't made up his mind whether to kill off my part or not,' Alec wrote in his Small Diary on 12 April. 'A bit late for such decisions. And Harrison Ford referring to me as the Mother Superior didn't help.' On 16 April, Alec complained that a week's filming at Borehamwood 'has been tedious to a degree – hot, boring and indecisive. Apart from the money, which should get me comfortably through the year, I regret having embarked on the film. I like them all well enough, but it's not an acting job, the dialogue, which is lamentable, keeps being changed and only slightly improved, and I find myself old and out of touch with the young.'[760]

'The film plods on,' Alec wrote to Anne Kaufman on 14 May. 'I've had a week off while they all blow themselves up electrically etc. etc. I *could* finish by 1 June but suspect 10 June to be more likely, although I only have three brief scenes more to play. Play? *Drift* through, aimlessly. I *like* Harrison Ford but doubt if he's going to fire the Thames or the East River.'

Alec finished filming *Star Wars* on Wednesday 16 June 1976, and 'since then have been more or less flaked out, not ill, just physically incapable of an ounce of energy. Spent most of Saturday and yesterday in bed. Usually I am very resilient after a film, but this one has left me numb.'[761]

Towards the end of May 1977, when Alec was recovering from his hernia operation and learning his lines for *The Old Country*, *Star Wars* was released in the United States. 'George Lucas telephoned from San Francisco,' Alec noted in his Small Diary on 22 May, 'to say trade reviews of *Star Wars* excellent and wanting me to accept another quarter per cent.' On 27 May: 'Splendid news of reaction to *Star Wars* continues to come in.' On 3 June: 'Am pinning my hopes on *Star Wars* percentage which could bring me in £100,000 or more if it does *Jaws* business, as predicted.' On 13 June: 'Kurtz telephoned and came up with a quarter per cent instead of half per cent Lucas had suggested. A bit of an Indian gift, but I said nothing as it's kind of them anyway.'

Alec's story that Lucas offered to up his percentage from two to two and a half per cent, and subsequently reduced the offer to an extra quarter was told during his interview with Michael Parkinson on BBC television but it is contradicted by his own diary where Lucas's offer, made on 22 May, is clearly marked as a quarter per cent. Whether Lucas subsequently increased it, then reduced it again, or whether Alec's memory was faulty, is not known. What is clear is that it was a gesture of unique generosity which, Matthew recalls, astonished and delighted his father: Alec had never before been offered an unsolicited benefit of this kind.

At the beginning of June 1977, Alec received a letter from his beloved Peter Glenville in New York, starting as always, 'Dearest Alecco':

Well, I've seen *Star Wars* and it is everything you had heard. Thousands of people milling around the theatre (it's playing in four huge monster theatres here), and police on horseback controlling the crowds. All this on an early afternoon (2 p.m.) showing the day after Memorial Day holiday weekend which is usually a terrible day. Finally and uniquely the *N.Y. Times* reports today that the Dow Jones shares have gone up as a result of 20th Century prospects on *Star Wars* which has given a lift to all motion picture shares and prices! All tickets are four dollars each! It's a financial happening.

Furthermore the picture is a delight. Thrilling, innocent, spectacular, engaging, original, and the effects are astounding. People clapped & cheered during the movie itself . . . Also has a zippy *Boys Own* humour which manages to be both seraphic and sophisticated . . . You are lovely in it. A most attractive and convincing Prospero figure, and the idea of magic overcoming science & technology is splendid. And full marks for the creation of two adorable mechanical objects which become a science-fiction apotheosis of Don Quixote & Sancho Panza, and they make you laugh and care desperately. Our austere friend Noël thinks you give one of your most attractive performances ever. I would not go that far in view of the limited vocabulary of the role, but it is very imaginative and endearing. Meanwhile, for heavens sake, go abroad or do something to ensure that you will keep something of the considerable fortune that will undoubtedly come your way.

When Alec himself saw the finished film, he too was impressed:

It's a pretty staggering film as spectacle and technically brilliant. Exciting, very noisy and warm-hearted. The battle scenes at the end go on for five minutes too long, I feel; and some of the dialogue is excruciating and much of it is lost in noise, but it remains a vivid experience. The only really disappointing performance was Tony Daniels as the robot – fidgety and over-elaborately spoken. Not that any of the cast can stand up to the mechanical things around them.[762]

By the end of July, it had become apparent that Alec's two and a quarter per cent would make him 'a temporary fortune'. 'It had better,' he told Anne Kaufman. 'The British Government is taxing what little I have in the bank that I can call my own at 98 pence in the pound. So it's a few tuppences I have to live on. Everyone says clear out of the country and reside in U.S. for a year or two but I can't bring myself to do that – and what about Walter!'[763]

'Bank telephoned to say they'd received £308,552,' Alec noted in his diary on 1 February, 1978. 'First *Star Wars* money.' Another £131,700 followed on 10 November. Alec remained convinced, however, that George Lucas and Gary Kurtz had reneged on their promise of an extra *half* per cent. He took the two men to lunch when they were in London in May, 1979:

They were agreeable and a touch boring – George very enthusiastic about some film study / recreation centre he wants to build on a ranch near San Francisco. There was never a breath about the quarter per cent extra on *Star Wars* they promised me. It started, when first mentioned, as an extra half per cent – Gary referred to it as 'Oh, the quarter per cent' when I asked if it could be in writing. Now I wonder if it will prove non-existent. They have been so generous I can hardly complain if that proves to be the case – but presumably it's about £80,000 and I could be tempted to give them some jokey and unwanted publicity.[764]

Moreover, the gush of money brought on protracted quarrels with Alec's tax inspector. 'The tax authorities here are being quite awful about my *Star Wars* earnings,' Alec complained to Anne Kaufman, 'and it now looks as if I have to employ a top Tax Counsel and fight them in the law courts . . . I'm not sure that I'm not going to be *out* of pocket for having neared a rough million pounds and only spent six thousand (on the new kitchen – already shabby).'[765]

Another disadvantage of the film's great success, for Alec, was Lucas's plans for a sequel. Over lunch at Cecconi's, Lucas asked Alec if he would consider doing 'a couple of days' work on *Star Wars II*. I said I'd re-read the script. The idea doesn't attract me'.[766] A week later, Alec 'said yes to a day's work on *Star Wars II* – for, as far as I know, no money but perhaps a minute percentage of the profits. It's dull rubbishy stuff but, seeing what I owe to George Lucas, I finally hadn't the heart to refuse. Also he was clever enough not to plead his cause. I have insisted on no billing and minimum publicity.'[767]

Alec did his half-day's work at EMI Studios for *The Empire Strikes Back* at the beginning of September 1979. 'I hear that *Empire Strikes Back* has probably taken $120,000,000,' he noted in his Small Diary on 3 November 1980. 'So I think I can expect to receive, one day, about £20,000. But I'd be happy with just £5000.' Less than a year later, he was invited back to Cecconi's with George and Marsha Lucas. 'He was sounding me out, of course, about appearing in *Star Wars III*. I was non-committal but said I couldn't see myself in it if I had to expound the Force or any phony philosophy. I left them saying "I'm an unreliable character".'[768]

However, Alec finally agreed, again accepting as payment a small percentage. 'It's a rotten dull little bit but it would have been mean of me to refuse.' 'I do a couple of dreadful days on the horrible *Star Wars III* the first week of March,' Alec wrote to Anne Kaufman on 19 February 1982. 'I cannot bring myself to learn the wretched lines,' he reported, also to Anne, on 18 March 1982. 'It was a dreary *boring* job but I liked the director (Richard Marquand) and had nothing to do with any other actors – thank God – except Mark Hamill, who is pleasant.'

The few days of tedium were well-paid. In his Small Diary on 8 November 1983, Alec recorded: 'DVT* telephoned me with news of an unexpected windfall from *Star Wars* – $250,000. That will pay for Sally's schooling, our Italian holiday and our pre-filming holiday in India before I start filming there.' To Anne Kaufman, from Bangalore, while filming *A Passage to India*: 'I was told there were two letters waiting for me. The other was news of £100,000 just in from *Star Wars* so my post was *good* but yours even more welcome than the other.'[769]

The extraordinary success of *Star Wars* and its offspring made Alec wealthy – though the extent of his wealth was exaggerated in the Press. 'Talked with Mark†. He says *The Times* reports I've made £4½ million in past year. It is monstrous they can say such things. Where do they get hold of such nonsense?'[770] It also made him known to a new generation of moviegoers and spread his fame worldwide. Yet while Alec, as he had always done, loved making money, he was depressed that his celebrity was based on work that he himself did not esteem. When a mother in America boasted of how often her son had seen *Star Wars*, Alec made him promise that he would *never* see it again. His hut at Kettlebrook Meadows grew cluttered with unopened sacks of fan mail. '*Stars Wars* people ask me for an interview – I

---

* Dennis van Thal
† Mark Kingston

continue to refuse,' he noted in his Small Diary on 16 January 1997. 'They are ghastly bores.' 13 February: 'Was unpleasant to a woman journalist on *Telegraph*, who wanted to know how much I earned on *Star Wars*. Oh, I'm sick of that film and all the hype.' 12 March: 'Head waiter (at Dorchester Oriental Room) said, as I was leaving, "Now *Star Wars* is to be shown again, you'll be famous once more".'

forty-seven

A lec would live in the shadow of Ben (Obi-Wan) Kenobi for the rest of his life, and felt demeaned by the tinselly nature of his worldwide fame. However, to his peers his life seemed quite enviable. 'I have always been somewhat envious of the brilliant way you adapted to films and television,' John Gielgud wrote to him in 1980, 'both of which baffled me greatly for many years. But I thank God I am no longer camera-shy as well as having gained respect for the other media which I used not to have in the old days when live theatre seemed so much more worthwhile in every way.'[771] Alec had almost always been able to pick and choose his roles whereas financial necessity obliged the great John Gielgud, towards the end of his life, to take almost anything he was offered.

Prior to *Star Wars* Alec had played Julius Caesar in a television production of Bernard Shaw's *Caesar and Cleopatra*, which was released only in 1977 and was, Alec judged, 'a *not* satisfactory venture'.[772] More satisfactory – indeed, a resounding success – was Alan Bennett's

The Old Country, with Rachel Kempson playing Bron and Alec as Hilary, the exiled English spy. John Peter in the *Sunday Times* judged it one of Alec's finest performances: 'Both erect and crumbling, he conveys a sense of tenacious indecision and dignified self-disgust.' More significantly, Hilary, a fictional character based upon the real-life traitor Guy Burgess, was the herald of another role set in the world of espionage – John le Carré's George Smiley.

John le Carré is the pen name of David Cornwell. Deserted by his mother as a child, and raised by a father at one stage imprisoned for fraud, Cornwell had gone to university in Switzerland and become fluent in German. He had worked for a time as a schoolmaster at Eton, then for the British Intelligence Service. By the age of thirty-two he had written three novels under the name of John le Carré. His third, *The Spy Who Came in from the Cold* published in 1963, became a best-seller on both sides of the Atlantic. Le Carré's fourth novel, *The Naive and Sentimental Lover*, with which he sought to extend his range beyond the idiom of the spy story, had disappointing notices and sales: reviewers tend to be envious of success and readers want more of the same. With his fifth novel, *Tinker, Tailor, Soldier, Spy*, the novelist returned to the world of espionage and made George Smiley, a plump, seedy, donnish intelligence officer, the central character.

Tinker, Tailor, Soldier, Spy, though it did well in the United States, was not particularly successful in Britain. It was seen as too subtle and complex for the genre and there remained a residue of critical envy: le Carré was thought to be too clever by half. However, Jonathan Powell, the Head of Drama at BBC Television, thought that the novel would make a good serial and approached le Carré for the rights. At their very first meeting, le Carré told Powell that only one actor was right for Smiley – Alec Guinness – and was delegated to write to Alec to suggest it. In due course he received a cautious reply, acknowledging that Alec knew and admired the novel, expressing doubts as to his ability to do television, but agreeing to meet for lunch as a first step.

A lunch was duly arranged with le Carré, Powell and the writer chosen to adapt the novel, Arthur Hopcraft. Alec outlined all the reasons why he could *not* play Smiley: Smiley was too passive; everything happened around him; it was no role. He was only playing hard to get. 'I have agreed to do a seven-part TV serial of John le Carré's . . . *Tinker, Tailor, Soldier, Spy* starting in October, for BBC and Paramount,' he noted in his diary on 1 April 1978. 'Have met Cornwell a couple of times and like him very much. M and I are to go to his Cornish home . . . in early June for a fortnight.'

Alec and Merula spent the first five nights of their holiday in Cornwall at the Lamorna Cove Hotel, close to the Cornwells' house, Tregiffian. 'The hotel here is beautifully clean, friendly (though perhaps some of the staff too garrulous) and a touch pretentious. The young bearded porter tells us he is an actor (professional) and is about to play Dylan with the Redruth amateurs. The first three draft scripts of *Tinker, Tailor* were delivered to the hotel by David Cornwell.'[773]

The next four or five days were spent with Alec reading Hopcraft's scripts, visiting the Cornwells for lunch and supper, and taking walks along the cliff-top – 'rather wearying for my left knee. Walter's damaged leg a bit stiff too'. On the Monday night:

> David came over to dine with us and discuss it all. We had champagne in our 'Tree Tops' sitting room followed by an indifferent meal. He was very enchanting and entertaining. He told remarkable hair-raising tales of his father's financial dishonesties and imprisonments – without bitterness but with a wry sadness. My mother's petty pilfering and cheating was very mild stuff in comparison. It was a good evening and I felt we had got to know each other quite well, easily and sympathetically, in the course of a few hours. We certainly see eye to eye on *Tinker, Tailor* scripts. I feel I have made a friend. His and Jane's easy-going generosity over lending us Tregiffian is truly remarkable. We move there tomorrow morning.[774]

'Walter seemed very pleased with the set up,' Alec noted after the move to the le Carrés' house, Tregiffian. 'The house is very electrified, warm, comfortable and rather odd. The outside is somewhat forbidding.' On the Thursday 'at 9.00 a.m. the telephone rang and a very English woman's voice said, "This is the British Embassy, Bonn. The Ambassador wants a word with you." "I doubt if he wants a word with *me*," I said. "St Buryan 339?" "Yes." "Well, he wants a word with you." Then I gave my name. "Not Mr Cornwell?" "No." Pause. "The Ambassador will write to Mr Cornwell." It struck us as mildly inefficient on all counts.'

The Guinnesses had planned to spend a fortnight in Tregiffian but by the end of their first week, they were planning their escape. 'I feel we've had the best of the weather and benefited as much as we can. By the middle of next week we shall be ready to push on.' Alec rang John le Carré in London to say, 'We so adore it here but very dear friends of ours have turned up in London and we have to go back to look after them.' So they left, leaving behind a case of vintage Krug and 'a mountain of caviar'.[775] By Sunday 18 June they were happily back at Kettlebrook: 'Peter and Bill are lying out on the garden seats, M weeding, Walter peering from the dark red dwarf maples. I have scrubbed down the kitchen patio table.'

John le Carré concluded that Alec's premature departure from Tregiffian was because Alec had already become, in his own mind, a member of the British Secret Service; and that after the call from the British Ambassador in Bonn and a chance meeting with a neighbour of the Cornwells's on the cliff path who, by way of a joke, had suggested that Alec and Merula conduct any private conversation a good two hundred yards from the house, had decided that the house was bugged.

Back in London, Alec worked on Hopcraft's script with both le Carré and the thirty-eight-year-old director chosen by Jonathan Powell, John Irvin. Irvin had recently directed Charles Dickens's *Hard Times*, with a script by Arthur Hopcraft for Granada Television, which had won a number of awards. Alec took to Irvin, and approved of some of Hopcraft's adaptation, but complained in his diary that 'much of Smiley's dialogue in the scripts I find incomprehensible and I certainly wouldn't be able to put it over to an audience'.[776] There were times when he would draw a line through the dialogue, assuring le Carré and Irvin that he could convey what was said by the expression on his face. 'He was amazing,' John le Carré recalled:

> . . . in that he not only knew his own lines, he knew everyone's lines, and he had a clear idea of how a scene should play. What the dramatic energy was. What story point was being made and where the camera would be looking. And he would write himself out of the dialogue if necessary – he could steal a scene with his back. You couldn't take your eyes off him. I found him hypnotic on stage or on the screen.[777]

To provide Alec with a real-life model for the character of Smiley, le Carré arranged for him to meet the former chief of MI6, Sir Maurice Oldfield. The Secret Intelligence Service, which had allowed le Carré to publish *The Spy Who Came in from the Cold* because it was thought so *unlike* the reality of the Secret Service, had become irritated when the public – until then given only the fantasies of Ian Fleming – came to believe that it was an accurate portrait of Cold War espionage. They had particularly disliked *Tinker, Tailor, Soldier, Spy* because it implied that the Secret Service was fallible and penetrable which 'of course was true'.

Maurice Oldfield had by then retired, and was himself under a cloud after a scandal involving rent boys in Belfast. A lunch was arranged for 29 August 1978, which Alec described in his diary the following day:

> Yesterday David Cornwell took me to lunch, at la Poule au Pot, to meet Sir Maurice Oldfield, on whom he based much of Smiley*. Liked him. A bit plumper and shorter than me but not very different physically. An execrable tie, tatty shirt, good suit, flashy cuff-links and bright orange shoes. David had warned me that he would be shy, possibly silent and,

---

* 'Maurice was emphatically *not* the model for George S, though he shd. have been . . .' John le Carré to the author, 3 May 2003.

in any case, would make no reference to his Secret Service work. Wrong on all counts.

John le Carré introduced the two men, but later left them 'getting together across the table. They were cuddling up and I was an intrusion.' The most tangible consequence of this lunch was Alec's decision to model Smiley's clothing on Oldfield's – 'the awful orange suede boots and improbably large cuff-links which Oldfield had been wearing. And then spectacles; he had trays of spectacles from Curry & Paxton. We watched him trying them on.' Other mannerisms and characteristics were taken from le Carré himself: 'His hair piece and the way he wore it and the way he acted and the gestures he made bore strains of imitations of myself,' le Carré observed. 'The waddle was Oldfield's. He was a mixture of me and Oldfield and there was a lot of Alec himself.' The only failure was in making Alec look rumpled. 'When Alec was a young man playing those diffident parts, he could do it – he did look rumpled; but he was really very suave by the time we got him, and to rumple him down to make him look ill-dressed was really quite impossible. So the Smiley who came across was much more dapper than intended.'

Once Alec had agreed to play Smiley, John Irvin could cast at will. Among the other players were actors such as Joss Ackland, who had appeared in *Hitler: The Last Ten Days*, and Michael Jayston who had been in *Cromwell*. Alec took 'an instant dislike to Ian Richardson' but later decided that he had been mistaken and invited Richardson and his wife to dinner at the Connaught. Irvin also sensed an antipathy between Alec and Beryl Reid, who played Connie. 'He was very hard on her, particularly in rehearsal' and when Alec gave a party for the cast at Oxford, 'he did not ask Beryl Reid'.

As always, the other actors were somewhat in awe of Alec and for John Irvin, directing 'one of the finest actors in the world', was daunting. 'I was terrified, knowing that I had to spend a year with him.' On the first day of rehearsals, in a cavernous rehearsal hall off the A40, he made a suggestion which Alec rejected. Irvin coaxed Alec to play the scene in the two different ways and Alec came round to his point of view. 'Very good, John Irvin,' he said. 'Ten out of ten.'

Powell and Irvin were aware of Alec's misgivings about television drama; none of his earlier attempts in the medium had been a success and it was always possible that he might pull out. The production was delayed by work-to-rules and go-slows by the technicians and they knew that Alec could use these as a pretext to jump ship. As rehearsals proceeded, Irvin could see Alec 'going deeper and deeper into his shell'. Three weeks after they had started shooting, Alec rang Irvin at three in the morning. He said that he 'hadn't found Smiley' and that it would be better for Irvin to re-cast the role now than in three months' time. Irvin told Alec both of them needed their sleep, and they would discuss the matter on location in five hours' time.

They were shooting on Primrose Hill and when Irvin got there he saw Alec walking up and down wearing his bowler hat and umbrella. 'Alec!' he shouted. '*That's* your start line. *That's* your finish line. We're going to do it in one take. Do you understand?' Alec nodded, did as instructed and that was it. Later, during the making of *Smiley's People*, when Eileen Atkins asked Alec why he had particularly liked being directed by John Irvin, he replied: 'Balls behind the camera.'

'Modern euphemisms,' Alec noted in his diary on 25 September 1974, 'to add to Birth Control, for Birth Prevention, how about Industrial Action, which means, of course, that no industrial activity is taking place?' Industrial action meant that it took eighteen months to make the seven episodes of *Tinker, Tailor, Soldier, Spy*. Alec was on call for six months from 10 October 1978, to 18 March 1979. His fee was modest, the work exhausting, and in the middle of filming he suffered from a haemorrhage in his left eye and lost fifty per cent of his vision. Yet he noted in his Small Diary, after completing his final scene: 'Think I've enjoyed it more than any job I've done, though probably feeble in the part.'

On 30 July, a showing was organised of *Tinker, Tailor, Soldier, Spy* at

BAFTA's* private cinema at 195 Piccadilly to which Alec invited Sonja
Frend and Leueen MacGrath:

> The screening didn't start until 10.00. I remained for only the first four
> episodes, leaving in mid-afternoon. It was a sweltering hot muggy day
> and no air conditioning was on. I was very impressed by what I saw. It
> has a mark of real distinction in all departments. In the first two
> episodes I am too ineffectual, sad and uninteresting, but I think I
> improve as it progresses. At the end of the month I shall see the last
> three parts, or maybe all of it again.[778]

For the second 'marathon showing of *Tinker, Tailor* for the cast and
technicians at 195 Piccadilly' on 18 August, Alec invited Merula, Val
Stavredi, Sonja Frend again, and the Schneiders whom he had not seen
for the past two years. 'They seemed well impressed by the film, as
indeed was I; though my eyes felt tired and buttocks stiff during the
last two episodes.' The first episode was screened on BBC 2 on 8
September 1979. 'M and I watched it and were pleased. The press, so
far, has been remarkably good.' 'Remarkably good' was an
understatement. Apart from a 'long snide notice by Clive James in the
Observer. And a dishonest one at that', the reviews on both sides of the
Atlantic were ecstatic. 'At this point in his career,' wrote Gerald Clarke
in *Time* magazine, 'Guinness, solid and elegantly thoughtful, is beyond
praise.' In Britain, thanks partly to a strike that put ITV stations off the
air, the audience rating on BBC 2, the supposedly intellectual channel,
soared to seventeen million. *Tinker, Tailor* became the talking point on
radio shows, in the public bars and at dinner parties around the
country. For the first time in almost twenty years, Alec was not just
rich and famous, but universally acclaimed for his fine acting of a
major role on film.

---

*   British Academy of Film and Television Arts.

forty-eight

As with *Star Wars*, there was a sequel – *Smiley's People*. Le Carré had been writing, or at any rate, revising this novel during the filming of *Tinker, Tailor* . . . and it seems to the reader that it was now Alec himself who had become the model for Smiley. Like Alec, Smiley buys his books at Heywood Hill and has his hair cut at Trumpers. It is said of Smiley that 'he had never known anyone who could disappear so quickly in a crowd'. 'Don't like being touched as a rule. Greeks do it. Hate it personally. Smiley said he hated it too.'

Arthur Hopcraft declined to write the screenplay while John Irvin, much in demand because of the success of *Tinker, Tailor* . . . had moved on to make movies in Hollywood. Instead of Irvin, Jonathan Powell suggested John MacKenzie, whom he introduced to Alec over lunch. MacKenzie told Alec that at the age of eighteen he had been in charge of the Shetland pony on the set of *Tunes of Glory* which Alec thought 'omens well'. The adaptation was undertaken by the writer John Hopkins but, by 6 December 1980, Alec noted that they 'have been giving great trouble and headaches but now all is more or less resolved. Apparently John Hopkins has graciously climbed down and David Cornwell is going to do a patching job with several re-writes . . .'

There were also disputes with the director, John MacKenzie, and he was replaced. 'There has been (is) a fine old rumpus over *Smiley's People,*' Alec wrote to Anne Kaufman:

> The scripts were, for the most part, no good and Le Carré is tidying at them between ski runs in Switz'nd. The director has been fired as incompatible. I quite liked him in his raw way but he and the producer got to non-speakers and he and Le Carré to sniping. The atmosphere was bad and boded ill for future work – so I threw in my vote, when requested, with producer and Le Carré. The man who did TV *Rebecca* and *Thérèse Raquin* has been approached – Simon Langton. I don't know him. But something tells me we may not have heard the last of MacKenzie, the sacked director. I suspect a litigious character there. Anyway the upshot is a postponement of six months.[779]

The delay in the filming of *Smiley's People* meant that Alec had to withdraw from playing the title role in an adaptation of Graham Greene's *Dr Fischer of Geneva.* Script conferences were held in February and March, 1981, in the le Carrés's house in Hampstead. 'I have a nasty feeling we should never have embarked on it,' Alec noted in his diary on 7 March. There was some conflict between Alec and Simon Langton over script and casting. Alec found 'the long Connie scene confusing and generally unsatisfactory' but was stuck with Beryl Reid. Michael Jayston was unable to play Guillam because he had taken a role in *The Sound of Music.* 'Can't blame him but it's a bit of a blow.' An approach was made to Simone Signoret to play Ostrakova but the fee asked was too high. Then the part was offered to Judi Dench but she was excluded because of an operation on her foot; 'so Ostrakova has to be re-cast. They're talking in terms of Rita Tushingham, Brenda Bruce or Eileen Atkins'.[780] In the event, the part went to Eileen Atkins, and another role to Alec's old friend Michael Gough.

Rehearsals for *Smiley's People* started at St James' Church Hall on Gloucester Terrace on 22 June 1981. By mid-July, the unit was filming in Paris. 'I am still a grass widow,' Merula wrote to Anne Kaufman, 'but *he* comes back on Fri week. He doesn't sound v. pleased with the work – he says it's dull and slow.'[781] Alec was finding his director unsatisfactory. 'I felt dubious about Simon's work. He's very pleasant and easy-going but he has no sense of irony or wit, which are essential for my part. I greatly miss John Irvin's grip and inner tension.'[782]

At first, Alec was delighted to be in Paris with his friend Eileen Atkins. 'We had rooms next to one another at the top of a wonderful hotel in Paris,' Atkins recalled:

Alec said, 'I would love to show you Paris on your day off. Knock on my door at ten o'clock.' I knocked on his door and – you know how immaculately he is normally dressed – he was wearing a rather awful pair of dark glasses, some flat shoes, a short-sleeved white shirt, a black beret, and he was holding a string bag with some bread in it. I said, 'Alec, what are you doing?' He said, 'I have to dress like this because if I don't we'll have a bad time. Everyone will recognise me.' But in fact, everyone looked at him dressed like that. The big treat was going to be the lunch but of course they wouldn't serve him because he was improperly dressed.

We did have a lovely time until my husband, Bill Shepherd, turned up. Alec took us to his favourite restaurant, or one of his favourite restaurants, but my husband spoke fluent French whereas Alec's was halting; and my husband knows Paris and the restaurant knew my husband, and though he's not remotely famous, the waiters knew him and called 'Ah, Monsieur Shepherd.' I could see Alec's face fall.

When the first episode of *Smiley's People* was broadcast on British television, it had, Alec told Anne Kaufman:

. . . an undeserved good press – only one lousy one so far – and some have been almost raves. It's good to look at and gets better as it

progresses, but for my money there are some lamentable things in it –
including, natch, me. As Noël Coward says in his phoney 'Diaries' just
published, and ad nauseam, 'dear Alec, so disappointing. I'm afraid just
dull.'[783]

But the critical climate changed as further episodes followed. On 8
October Alec wrote to Anne again that the 'Press almost unanimous
in saying that they have always hated the works of le Carré. Most of
them don't even mention me – just as well . . . Alan Bennett says it was
far easier to follow than the plot of *The Merry Wives of Windsor*.'

Given the financial security provided by the success of the *Star Wars*
trilogy, and the esteem that came from Alec's fine performance as
Smiley, it might seem surprising that Alec subsequently agreed to
appear in some mediocre films. He liked to work and, despite his
percentage of *Star Wars*, he found it hard to resist offers of huge sums
for a small amount of work. Three days as an old sailor in *Raise the
Titanic* in December 1979 earned him £45,000. He played Sir
Fennimore Truscott in *Edwin*, a television film (originally a radio play)
by John Mortimer in February 1983. He was 'mad about Rodney
Bennett as director'[784] but disappointed by his own performance.
'Watched *Edwin* on TV. Can't bear myself in it.'[785] *Little Lord Fauntleroy*,
made for American television but shown in cinemas in Britain, in which
Alec played the role of the Earl of Dorincourt, was directed by Jack
Gold and given a Royal Charity Première at which Alec and Merula
were presented to Princess Anne, but it 'didn't please most of the press
and I must say I was very disappointed when I saw it'.[786]

In the letter to Anne Kaufman, in which he described the reception in
England of *Smiley's People*, Alec told her that he had agreed to appear
in a film of E.M. Forster's novel, *A Passage to India*, adapted by David
Lean. 'David Lean's script of *Passage to India* is v. g. and I've said I'll do
it . . . It's absurd casting but attracts me. Money has not been suggested
yet . . .'

Given that Alec had told Lean, many years before, that it would be unwise to cast a non-Indian in the role of Gandhi, it is perhaps surprising to find that both men appear, simultaneously, to have decided that Alec should play the other-worldly Hindu, Dr Godbole, in *A Passage to India*. 'The other day I even thought of Alec Guinness playing the part,' Lean wrote to the Indian writer of the first screenplay, Santha Rama Rau, on 7 October 1981; ten days later we find Alec himself touting for the part. 'Took David Lean & Sandy to dinner at Mirabelle (very small helpings of caviar). Only half-seriously I said to David, re *Passage to India*, 'If you can't get a Hindu for Dr G (the old Hindu) you might think of me.' And he said, 'We've been discussing it.' By 21 December, Lean had offered Alec the role and now Alec began to play hard to get. 'David Lean has asked me if I'd play Mr Gobbledigook (that *can't* be right) in *Passage to India*,' he wrote to Anne Kaufman:

Well, *maybe*. But they should have a Hindu. Curiously enough it crossed my mind as soon as I heard he was doing the film – I rather like the idea of doing an Indian dance all by myself in pouring rain and making funny noises – but then I dismiss it as madness. But I refuse to wear contact lenses or stay in India for more than two months.

I've seen a lot of David in the past year. He is back to his old charming self, such as he was thirty years ago. He has married his v. nice girl, Sandy. But between ourselves he is getting *on* a bit, rather forgetful and slow-witted. Which suits me. Also he has become quite partial to a whisky or two of an evening – very different from the days he thought me an alcoholic for taking a dry martini.[787]

On 20 September 1982, Alec wrote Lean a long letter containing his thoughts on Lean's script. 'I think you have done a marvellous job, telling a difficult story with a complicated background truly, clearly and excitingly. However, I have a few unimportant *niggles* with which you probably won't agree, which I'll be bold enough to put to you.'

Alec's cautious, almost obsequious tone with David Lean suggests an awareness that the old prima donna had to be handled with care.

He wrote perceptively about the different characters – Mrs Moore, Fielding, Mrs Callendar and, of course, Godbole: 'I've left him to last because, of course, this interests me personally most.' Alec's observations are of interest only to those familiar with Lean's original script; what is clear, however, is that he had studied the potential of the role and seen in it an opportunity to do something exceptional and new. 'If this film gets made (d.v.) I'd love to play Godbole – it excites and intrigues me – and no other part in ages has so attracted me – but I might be embarrassing and just plain awful in it.'

In October 1982, *A Passage to India* was postponed for ten months. Lean, who had not made a film since the disastrous *Ryan's Daughter* fourteen years earlier, faced trouble raising the finance. 'I am slightly relieved,' Alec wrote to Dame Felicitas, 'but . . . I must pull my socks up and do some remunerative work.' This came his way with the offer to play a chimeric Sigmund Freud in an American film, *Lovesick*, with Dudley Moore. It was a small part but Alec was paid $300,000 for a month's work, flying to New York on Concorde in April, 1982. It was now forty years since, as a young naval officer, he had first seen the city from the deck of the *Queen Mary*, and the passing years had had their effect. 'For the first time ever,' he wrote to Dame Felicitas on his return, 'I got bored with the city.'[788] Alec thought *Lovesick* an amusing film with 'a funny line or two' and thought his wig for Freud 'a miracle' and was taken aback when the film failed to find favour with the critics.

The postponed *A Passage to India* still preoccupied Alec: on 30 March 1983, he wrote to Lean and his wife Sandy thanking them for the lavish flowers they had sent him somewhat prematurely for his birthday, and telling them of his 'rather brilliant (I think) but absurd (I know) idea' for the part of Fielding: 'not an actor at all – though he used to be and I bet he was a good one – but is now a film director – Richard Marquand. He directed the last – not yet seen – *Star Wars* epic. Nice man – fortyish – tough – bullet-headed – pleasant looks but broken-toothed.'[789]

Then, suddenly, only ten days later, Alec wrote to Lean in a much colder tone saying that he intended to pull out of *Passage to India*:

> I flatter myself that – sadly – you may be disappointed by what I have to say, though possibly Ld. Brabourne* and money henchmen may be relieved. Godbole is not for me. I love the part and the book and I think the script first class, but for some time now I have been uneasy at the idea of trying to tackle it. It shouts for a Hindu, and if there are other Indians in the cast – as there must be – I could feel at a grave disadvantage, even with you and Sandy to help me. And apart from those perfectly genuine artistic considerations there is the purely professional careerist (even at my age and with my *near* indifference to reputation and fortune) in me which tells me that I cannot afford to hang about on the off chance that my services *might* be required. Although nothing has been signed or sealed or even properly discussed at the time of writing, I am going to open discussions about doing a play in New York . . .
>
> You must know how I love the idea of working with you – and Godbole would bring, so to speak, Herbert Pocket full circle. If the management of *Passage* had made a tentative approach by now I might feel differently . . . So I am going after the theatre job – and if that falls through or doesn't materialise, well I shall comfort myself with the thought that I am not really right for an Indian. And you can comfort yourself with the knowledge that I'm too bloody expensive these days.[790]

The tone of the letter suggests that Alec felt that he was being taken for granted. His agent, Dennis van Thal, was clearly asking for a larger fee than the producer, John Brabourne, was willing to pay. 'Tell Dennis I'll do *Passage to India* if money fair (he wants to ask too much) and Peggy Ashcroft plays Mrs Moore,' Alec noted in his Small Diary on 16 April 1983; and, two days later, outlining his conditions in his journal:

---

*   Lean's producer.

On Thursday this week I lunched with Dennis Van Thal at Mirabelle
and told him I am prepared to do *Passage to India* – (a) if a line about
Godbole's colour and un-Indian features is put in the text and (b) if
Peggy Ashcroft will play Mrs Moore. Today DVT tells me Brabourne
and Goodwin have agreed; £30,000 a week with a guarantee of
£180,000 and they have offered to pay for M and me to have a two-week
holiday – to explore and keep eyes open – towards the end of the year.
Shooting for me won't start until late January 1984.[791]

Peggy Ashcroft was summoned to India before Alec and returned to
England for Christmas. 'Spoke to Peggy Ashcroft – just back from
India. She returns to Bangalore January 12th. She thinks David is
making the film on too big a scale and with insufficient intimacy.'[792]
'Peg told me that the crew of *Passage to India* refer to John Box (design)
and David as Arse-lick and Old Lace – which doesn't sound
encouraging.'[793] On 23 January, Alec and Merula flew to New Delhi to
take the fortnight's holiday provided for by his contract: apart from five
nights in Agra, they remained based in Delhi. On 5 February, Merula
returned to England and Alec flew to start work in Bangalore.

A terrible spectre haunted Alec's playing of Godbole – that of Peter
Sellers in *The Millionairess* – Anthony Asquith's film, based on Shaw's
play, in which a millionairess falls in love with a poor Indian doctor. The
film was feeble but Sellers's comic Indian accent was one of his best-
loved and best-known turns, and it was therefore near to impossible for
any other actor to adopt the sing-song tone of Indian English without
seeming to imitate him. Alec's star turn, which to him would lift the
role above a banal impersonation, was to be a song-and-dance routine:
Alec prided himself on his mime-like dancing, occasionally suggesting
it to sceptical directors, and in the case of *Habeas Corpus*, succeeding in
tagging one on to the end of the play. 'I've had ten days here so far,' he
wrote to Anne Kaufman from Bangalore on 14 February:

. . . trying to learn a Sanskrit song, or dirge, or chant and going daily
to hour's dancing lessons from a 70 year old Brahmin guru. But as from

to-day David Lean doesn't want my elegant dance, so I now shuffle around banging two huge cymbals I can hardly pick up. Easier anyway but not so showy-offy. I start work tomorrow night, have a few days off, and then get down to it. I'm pleased with my make-up – though I look like the Old Bill posters for 1914–18 war. And my frocks are severely attractive. I shall never learn to tie the 15ft of a turban – I might just as well have settled for a python.

The atmosphere (unit wise) is all right I think. My fellow actors are mostly dears but I am highly suspicious of Miss Judy Davis (*My Brilliant Career*) who is *very* chippy-on-the-shoulder. But she acts remarkably well.

I'm now off to dinner with Dame Peggy (whom I've loved for 45 years or more) and Herr Direktor – and I must consult him about possibility of wearing a Moonstone ring. Thank God the *gentlemen* don't screw diamonds into their nostrils.

It struck Alec almost at once that his playing Godbole was not going to work. 'Five weeks in India today,' Alec complained to Anne Kaufman on 27 February, 'and I've still only done 20 seconds before the camera.' He suggested to Richard Goodwin, the film's co-producer, that he should withdraw from the film but Goodwin persuaded him to stay on. 'Oh dear, you sound distressed about things to do with the film,' Merula wrote to her husband on 1 March, 'and the awful thing is that it doesn't come as a surprise.'

Normally, Merula took the view that when Alec thought things were going well the film turned out a disaster, and when he complained that things were going badly his performance would be superb. *A Passage to India* would prove the exception to this rule. The entries in Alec's Small Diaries record his increasing misery. 2 March: 'Very depressed by appearance etc and would love to get out of film even at this stage.' 3 March: 'New Godbole make-up. Eyebrows OK and moustache reasonable, but I look like an old turkey up for sale – disappointing.' 23 March: 'Had a row with David and told him much of what I thought and added, "An apology wouldn't be out of place."

"*Me* apologise to *you*?" he said. Too complicated to go into but it was inevitable we'd squabble. However, we found a way of getting through the evening – by abandoning the dance I'd rehearsed.' 2 April: '70th birthday. Srinagar.' 5 April: 'Tony Snowdon thinks David is actually mad, and Banerjee* the most arrogant and conceited man he's met.' 'Oh, it will be nice to give a performance without someone saying every half minute, "Could you move half an inch to your left? And now could you lean back a fraction? And would you mind reading the telegram holding it about two inches under your chin?" etc. etc.'[794]

Richard Goodwin later said that Lean 'knew he was wrong about Alec Guinness, but he couldn't get out of it. We begged him not to do it. He said, "I need my old friends around me. I've got to have Alec. I can't direct an Indian".'[795] 'Alec was terrified I was going to make him be a copy of Peter Sellers,' Lean was to say later:

> It never entered my head, actually. He should have played it dead straight, I think it would have been bloody good, but he didn't. I am not quite sure what he did with it. But if he'd played that part straight it would have been very good . . . It was a sort of dance, but it wasn't really a dance. Alec met somebody in Delhi and he learned all these eye movements. I didn't want eye movements and that caused a bit of trouble. It was an unhappy experience . . . He really rattled me on *Passage to India*.

With filming finished, and both Alec and the Leans back in London, Alec seems to have tried to patch up the quarrel. In October 1983, Alec had accepted a British Film Institute award on Lean's behalf at London's Guildhall. Now he sent it round to Lean's suite at the Berkeley Hotel, together with an expensive italic pen for Sandy Lean. A month passed with no note of acknowledgement, let alone thanks. Alec asked his agent, Dennis van Thal, to 'make enquiries as to

---

* Victor Banerjee, who played Dr Aziz.

whether something had gone wrong'. 'A few days ago,' he wrote to
Lean, van Thal 'informed me that he understood you had taken
offence at references to yourself in John Russell Taylor's book about
me.'

This was *Alec Guinness: A Celebration* written, without Alec's
authorisation, by the art critic John Russell Taylor who had formerly
been the film critic for the *Sunday Times*. Alec wrote to David Lean on
22 May 1984 – one of the only *typed* letters in Alec's archive – to say
that he had looked at:

> . . . all the references to you and, for the life of me, I can spot nothing
> that I would consider need offend you or your friends. If there *is*
> anything that upsets you I am sorry, but please don't lay it directly at
> my door, as I refused to co-operate in any way with the writing of the
> book . . . It seems to me very sad that, after an association of getting
> on for forty years, a rift should develop between us now. I have *always*,
> if you haven't noticed it, publicly expressed my gratitude to you for
> giving me my first film chances and subsequent rare opportunities . . .
> I have written this letter so that the air is cleared, at least at my end, and
> not necessarily to solicit a reply.[796]

Alec may always have expressed his gratitude to Lean for what he had
done for him earlier in his career, but he complained publicly about the
way Lean had treated him on *A Passage to India* in an interview with
Richard Findlater in the *Observer*. 'David never saw me do the dance,
and it dawned on me that he didn't really want me to dance'; Lean, in
reply, justified his decision by saying that 'Alec Guinness practically
ruined the film because of the dance'. Lean also pointed out, quite
rightly, that Alec was in two minds about what it might have achieved.
'He writes in newspapers,' Lean complained, 'that I ruined his part by
cutting out some of the dance and he writes me a private letter
thanking me for doing it.'

The letter to which Lean referred, which Alec wrote from New
York on 16 December 1984, was to congratulate Lean on the finished

film. 'It is expansive, handsome, gripping and yet somehow intimate. And the story – which we all know is somewhat complicated – comes over with simplicity. It didn't seem a minute too long.' Alec praises the performances of the other actors – particularly that of Peggy Ashcroft:

> For my part I'm afraid I thought I was sickeningly awful. I thought it was poor at the time we were doing it but I hadn't realised how wide of the mark I was. I don't in the least blame you, as you were helpful, but I do wish – when I asked Richard, very calmly and unfussily, in the first week, if you'd all like to get rid of me, he had taken me up on it. John Brabourne was right in his original objection.

When Alec saw Lean during the 'post-synching' of the film, he noted in his diary that 'all seemed well between us – no reference to our drawing aside. But when I asked after Sandy he seemed indifferent'.[797] It would appear that Lean simply could not be bothered with the niceties of human relationships that were so important to Alec. 'My song and dance have been entirely removed from the film,' Alec wrote to Anne Kaufman after seeing the final cut of A Passage to India 'and I suspect two other short scenes, which reduces my part to something totally negligible. Perhaps it's just as well. I'm probably awful in the film; the less seen the better and more easily forgotten. But I do think Sir D. L. might have sent me a p.c. explaining.'[798]

After attending the premiére in New York, Alec judged his performance as Godbole to be 'the poorest work I've ever done. Meaningless & irritating. Couldn't face the party at the end so took the Schneiders to Russian Tea Room.'[799] Back in England, Alec had to suffer the indignity of 'doing numerous TV interviews, press and radio too, from ten in the morning until late afternoon' to promote a film in which his own performance 'made me feel physically ill with embarrassment'.[800] When the film was released in Britain in March 1985, he was duly drubbed by the critics. 'Very bad notices indeed for me in all Sunday papers I have seen,' Alec noted in his diary:

In an odd way it hasn't disturbed me at all – not even an 'I told you so' attitude. I suppose I felt slightly miffed when I read that I played Godbole with a 'Peter Sellers accent' when I fell over backwards not to do so and checked up, when filming, with many people (including Indians) to make sure I wasn't doing that.[801]

And, four years later, after it was shown on television: 'Extremely bad notices for me in TV crits of *Passage to India*. "Embarrassing." "Miscast." "AG in blackface." Etc. Not really worrying – but I'd love them to know what I was up against.'[802]

forty-nine

In 1983, Alec had read Graham Greene's whimsical novel, *Monsignor Quixote*, which 'I found pleasing – but repetitive and tiresome at times – and the last chapter of it magnificent. I wish I had some good theology tucked inside me. I read, recently, Greene quoted as saying that the only reading he can stomach these days is theology. But what?'[803] He wrote to Greene to congratulate him on his novel and ask if he could recommend some theological reading. 'What a pleasure to hear from you,' Greene wrote back:

It's too long since we met. I'm so glad that you liked Monsignor Q. What about playing the part? Curiously enough I've had more letters from priests – especially Jesuits – than I've had for any other book of mine & it's gone down very well in Spain – even quoted in the Cortez by Canillo, the Communist ex-leader! I'm just back from two days at the vineyards of the Marques de Murrieta where they gave me their 1904 vintage to drink. I'm not a very great reader of theology these days, though I enjoy Hans Küng, but I would much like to read the Kelly on your recommendation. Affectionately Graham.[804]

In March 1985, Alec agreed to play the title role in a television film of *Monsignor Quixote*, adapted by Ronald Neame's son, Christopher, and directed by Rodney Bennett, whom Alec had liked so much when making *Edwin*. He also liked Leo McKern, who played Monsignor Quixote's friend, the Communist mayor, but he approached the project with his usual doubts. 'I think I'm past acting. My fly-away talent has dropped from the nest and is now just a bundle of twigs and dried feathers and no song sings.'[805] The most interesting part of the film, Alec judged afterwards, 'was working in the Trappist monastery of Osera and saying Mass, bare-footed and in pyjamas, at the high altar'.[806] 'Graham Greene turned up a few times when we were filming,' Alec told Dame Felicitas. 'As charming and kind as ever but his eighty-one years are beginning to tell. Typical of him (entre nous) but he has divided the proceeds from his Spanish sales (of film and book) equally between Osera Monastery and the rebels in Nicaragua.'[807]

The finished film received mixed reviews: there was, Alec wrote to Anne Kaufman, 'a slightly carping one in *Time Out* – with which I agreed 100%.'[808] Nancy Banks-Smith, writing in the *Guardian*, wondered whether Alec 'was quite the man to play this holy fool. That voice with the curves and polish of a cello. Those really terrifying eyes. Sometimes nothing moves in his face but his eyes and they do so with the heart-stopping click of a cocking-revolver.' Greene's Monsignor Quixote is supposedly a man incapable of evil and one who, in his own words, has never been tempted by the sins of the flesh. Alec took the view that sinful actors could more effectively play saints than virtuous ones, but he was no more successful in portraying a 'fool of God' in the character of Monsignor Quixote than he had been as Father Brown.

Monsignor Quixote was made for television but, in 1985, after initial misgivings, Alec succumbed to an offer of £180,000 to break his resolution never again to appear in a feature film. He agreed to play Mr Dorrit in Dickens's *Little Dorrit*, adapted and directed by Christine Edzard, and with the same producers as *A Passage to India*, John Brabourne and Richard Goodwin. As with *Tinker, Tailor . . .* Alec finished the filming saying that he had 'enjoyed it more than any film I've been in'. 'I'm rather sad at having finished the film as it was such a pleasant experience,' he told Anne Kaufman, adding presciently: 'A nasty something tells me that it can't possibly be a success and at 5½ hours may prove an interminable, even-paced, yawn.'

When Alec saw the film, he was not impressed. 'It is beautiful to look at but rather confusing. The narrative is very difficult to follow.' He was unimpressed by Sarah Pickering who played Little Dorrit and disappointed by his own performance. 'I don't think I can act any more and ought to retire. But I know I won't – yet.'[809] There were critics, however, who thought highly of Alec's Mr Dorrit. Alexander Walker in the *Evening Standard* thought it 'must be ranked among the six best performances he's ever given'.

In 1987, after initial reluctance, Alec flew to Venezuela to play Mr Todd in Charles Sturridge's film of Evelyn Waugh's novel *A Handful of Dust*. Here, unlike the holy innocent Monsignor Quixote, was a role that resonated in Alec's own character – the domineering half-caste, Mr Todd, who keeps the young English hero trapped in the Brazilian jungle to read him the novels of Dickens over and over again. It was a superb cameo performance giving credibility on the screen to a character created by an author whom Alec greatly admired.

Having once declined to play Aschenbach in a film of Thomas Mann's *Death in Venice*, Alec accepted the role of Mann's brother, Heinrich, in a television film of Christopher Hampton's play, *Tales from Hollywood*. It is an account of the German writers taking refuge in California during World War II, among them the Mann brothers and Bertolt Brecht. It was a highbrow entertainment with some good acting. Robin Bailey's Thomas Mann was rather more convincing than Alec's

Heinrich, partly because Heinrich was supposedly in thrall to his blonde barmaid wife, Nellie, played by Sinéad Cusack. Her father, the actor Cyril Cusack, wrote Alec a touching letter: 'To think your first film kiss was for my daughter Sinéad . . .'[810] This was not, of course, Alec's first film kiss: he had kissed a number of women in earlier films and his embrace with the much younger Sinéad Cusack in *Tales from Hollywood* was no more convincing than those that had preceded it.

Again, there were the usual doubts before filming started. 'I sometimes wonder if I have *ever* acted,' Alec wrote to Quentin Stevenson, 'and how I dare to ask for a salary.' When it was over, however, he was pleased:

I finished TV of *Tales from Hollywood* at 2300 on Dec 23rd, having got to TV Centre at 0900. Apart from the absurd scheduling, both for rehearsals and shooting, it was a pleasant assignment. Jeremy Irons was charming but interfered too much with Howard Davies's direction. Greatly liked Sinead Cusack; and surprisingly Jack Shepherd and I got along all right. At the time of *Macbeth* at The Royal Court he was my *bête noire*. He and Robin Bailey were excellent as Brecht and Thomas Mann.[811]

In his review of *Tales from Hollywood* in *The Times*, Benedict Nightingale praised Alec's performance as Heinrich Mann. 'The weariness, the sick misery, the increasingly debilitating attempts to sustain his self-respect and disguise his inner disintegration; they were all there, understated yet overwhelming . . . This was, I think, one of the great television performances.'

Alec's penultimate screen performance was in *A Foreign Field*, the story of a war veterans' reunion on the Normandy beaches. It was directed by Charles Sturridge who had directed Alec in *A Handful of Dust*, and the cast included many of Alec's old friends and colleagues – Lauren Bacall, Leo McKern, Geraldine Chaplin and Edward Herrmann. Alec played the role of Amos, a shell-shocked survivor of World War II. When he saw the finished film in February 1993, he was 'bitterly disappointed . . . I feel my part has been clipped to nothing and lost all impact'.[812] And on 7 February 1993, he noted in his Small Diary: 'My mind still runs on official retirement after *A Foreign Field*.' Alec's final television part was as the father of a Cambridge don in Jack Rosenthal's *Eskimo Day*, which was directed by Piers Haggard for the BBC in 1996.

Alec had begun his professional career as a stage actor, been drawn into film only because his adaptation of *Great Expectations* had inspired David Lean to adapt it for the screen, then let the two careers run in tandem – his stage appearances admired by the more discerning but also more limited theatre-going audiences. His film work reached a far wider public, equally admiring, but involved him in many more compromises with the high standards he set himself in the practice of his art.

In September 1982, five years after his last appearance on stage as Hilary in Alan Bennett's *The Old Country*, Alec was asked by Patrick Garland, the director of the Chichester Festival Theatre, whether he would consider playing Shylock in Shakespeare's *The Merchant of Venice*. The idea of staging this play had arisen in conversation between Garland and Eileen Atkins: he had asked her whether there was some part she would like to play and she had suggested Portia, adding that Alec might be persuaded to do Shylock. On 22 August 1982, Alec re-read *The Merchant of Venice*, in which he had played Lorenzo all those years ago, his lyrical interpretation inspired by his love for Merula, and 'wondered if I'd rather play Shylock or direct and play Old Gobbo . . . at Chichester. Eileen is a bit old for Portia, I fear. But it's her basic idea'.[813]

Patrick Garland revived the idea in mid-December 1983. In January 1984, 'in a cold and draughty pub in Chichester', Alec agreed to play Shylock and to be directed by Garland 'but was rather hoping for an approach to Lindsay Anderson':

Our main talk was of Portias. We both feel that Eileen is too old at fifty . . . I suggested that we would both be let off the hook if boys could be found for Portia and Nerissa. He seemed intrigued by the idea but is fearful of finding the right lads. Since then – and if no good boys available – I am going to put forward Peggy Ashcroft's suggestion of Felicity Kendal.[814]

On 9 January Garland came to Kettlebrook for lunch and told Alec that 'the idea of having fourteen-year-old boys for girls appears not to be practical and an approach has been made to Felicity Kendal for Portia'. Garland then had the disagreeable task of telling Eileen Atkins that Alec judged her too old to play the role. Eileen was outraged:

The morning post brought me a viperish letter from Eileen about *The Merchant of Venice*. 'Yes of course I was hurt and angry and surprised by your duplicity'.* I can't think where she finds the duplicity. I turned down Shylock last year (though the suggestion kindly came from her for me to play it) because I felt she was too mature for Portia, and I find all the Christians in the play unforgivable unless they are dewy-eyed young. She says in her letter the young can't act or speak verse. There's stuff about if she could play St Joan at forty-three she could play Portia at fifty, which is manifestly absurd. Anyway, I felt angry and telephoned her inviting her to lunch at Cecconi's. She could only come if Jean† came with her as they had a date. I went to Mass at Warwick Street and then met them at the restaurant at 1330. I took Eileen a shoulder bag (cost me £140 at Loewe) and Jean a pencil from Asprey. Lunch was awkward but polite. She now does accept that Patrick Garland asked me not to contact her until after he had. We parted with a vague show of amity but I felt there was poison in both our veins. I left in great dejection, pretty sure that I had said good-bye for always to two pleasant friends.[815]

---

* The letter does not survive. Eileen Atkins called Alec 'unnecessarily unethical'.
† Jean Marsh, close friend of Eileen Atkins, co-progenitor of the successful television series, *Upstairs, Downstairs*.

In the event, the role of Portia – rejected by Felicity Kendal and Diana Rigg – went to Joanna McCallum, the daughter of Alec's old friend, Googie Withers. For Launcelot Gobbo, Garland wanted Frankie Howerd:

> I found it very difficult to cast Launcelot Gobbo; I hate some of those clowns; I think everyone does. Feste is one thing; Touchstone is a bugger. It's all those Elizabethan in-jokes which have gone. Especially Launcelot Gobbo . . . I had seen Frankie do Bottom and he was good – ad libbing – which was true to Shakespeare . . . I rang Frankie up and spoke to him and there was the feeling that he might accept the part, and Alec's great name added great stature. But when I told Alec about it, feeling pleased with myself, Alec wouldn't have it at all. He said: 'oh, no, no . . .' And I could tell that if I pushed it, Alec would say 'you'd better find another Shylock' or, as Rex Harrison used to say, 'you'd better find yourself another boy'. They didn't have casting control but they didn't need it. So Frankie Howerd was dropped and we got a nice young man to act Launcelot Gobbo and Alec read me a great story about how lovely it was – it was beautifully written – but everyone else said the scene was awful . . . I did my best but you just sit there – the whole audience staring at this unfunny scene. Having said that, Alec never interfered in anything else.[816]

Alec had some reservations about Garland's direction but kept them to himself. Garland thought the rehearsals went well:

> Alec kept himself to himself. He used to have a sandwich for lunch and often I had it with him and he liked to sit in the rehearsal room. But he rehearsed with a cigarette in his mouth like a World War I soldier. He'd hold the cigarette in one corner of his mouth and speak the words. And whereas one would ask some actors not to smoke, being sloppy, one would not ask Alec because it was a means of concentration, a kind of prop. He was extremely concentrated at rehearsals and was very sweet.

Alec was sweet off-stage but menacing as Shylock. 'Shylock is indescribably awful,' judged Garland, 'and that was the kind of play I wanted to produce.' Alec concurred with Garland's interpretation, and 'this terrible leer came across his face – it was very malevolent. He didn't shrink from that':

He did one astonishing piece of business which was as valuable as anything I've ever seen on the stage – something you remember for life. I remember when he invented it. He used to think about it. He came very prepared to rehearsals. Very undemonstrative. He never experimented but actors of great talent don't. But he'd obviously thought about it. We'd both agreed that we didn't want a great big scimitar as there were in Victorian productions. Alec had said: 'I want a small surgical practical implement.' I saw the drift of it immediately. Something you would actually use if you were going to cut off a piece of a man's flesh. It was very workmanlike with string around it and a small blade and he held it in his fingers. Anyway: the business was that when he was about to do it, there was complete silence . . . He would never gesture, he would simply say: I wonder if . . . He came across. Antonio had bared his breast. Shylock came right up to him and put his ear right against his naked heart as a doctor would do. It was a horrible image, really awful, absolutely brilliant – and people drew in their breath and it gave a real frisson. No one else had done that and it was Alec's idea.

Despite the originality and effectiveness of this scene, Alec's performance – like his Hamlet and his Macbeth – was deemed to be too subtle and understated. 'Shylock is a small role,' wrote Michael Ratcliffe in the *Observer*, 'but in most performances his presence spreads throughout the play; not here, for when Guinness is not on the stage it is quite easy to forget Shylock is in the play at all.' 'Guinness has been away from the stage for seven years,' wrote Robert Hewison in the *Sunday Times*. 'He must be wondering why he came back.'

Commercially, the play was a great success. '*The Merchant*,' he told

Anne Kaufman, 'continues to play to full houses of blue-rinsed Sussex fascists. I thoroughly dislike the production but it seems to satisfy the unsophisticated customers.' Among the unsophisticated customers was Princess Margaret. 'Princess Margaret thought she was seeing *King Lear* and couldn't make out what had happened to all those daughters.'[817] He received an abusive letter 'from a woman in Reigate, writing on cheap ruled paper – complaining that I don't play Shylock as an "oily Jew" but walk through the part as Alec Guinness'.[818]

Midway through the production, Alec and Merula entertained the company at Kettlebrook. All were hoping that Alec would agree to a London transfer where, Garland believed, 'all the critics would have come again and would have said "we liked this at Chichester but it's got so much better now" and Alec would have gone down in theatrical history as creating one of the greatest Shylocks of our time.' But Alec had been deeply hurt by Hewison's review in the *Sunday Times*. 'The production is too irritating and my perf not all *that* interesting. I think it *very* unlikely I shall let myself go to the West End in it,' he wrote to Anne Kaufman. 'My agent (reliable) and Michael Codron both advise against it, as well as my instincts . . .' And, on 31 August over lunch at the Mirabelle, Alec and Dennis van Thal 'cleared the decks a bit, saying definitely No to *Merchant* transfer idea, No to *Lady Jane Grey** and a doubtful Yes/No to *Mgr Quixote*, to be decided later, and a probable Yes to narration of Lucas' Ewok film'.[819]

Three years after *The Merchant of Venice* at Chichester, the producer who had hoped to take it to London, Duncan Weldon, sent Alec a play for his consideration. 'Have received a play (American) from Duncan Weldon,' Alec wrote in his diary on 6 September 1987. 'A two-hander and so static and garrulous. But I like the part – of a Russian diplomat. It's called *A Walk in the Woods* by someone called Blessing. Well

---

*   A film role proposed by Trevor Nunn which Alec turned down a week later. 'He *can't* need the cash, so *why* is he doing Hollywoodised English history?': AG to Anne Kaufman, 4 September 1984.

written – but I have always frowned on plays which have a park bench for a setting. And a two-hander is too much work.'

Alec was now seventy-three years old. He had grown portly and was plagued with minor ailments and health scares. 'Janvrin telephoned with results of blood test: suspected diabetes, suspected enlarged heart, suspected prostate trouble. And yet I feel really well.'[820] He had sprained his hand filming *A Handful of Dust* in Venezuela, and had doubts about his ability to learn a large number of lines, yet was intrigued by the play. On 23 September 1987, he read passages aloud to Merula and Mu Richardson. 'M. has gone off it a bit, thinking it lacks substance and is only suitable for a fringe theatre. I see her point, to a certain extent, but still think it has distinction. Not sure what Mu felt; she says she will write a letter about it.'[821] Mu Richardson's letter, if she wrote it, does not survive.

Obtaining the rights from Lee Blessing seemed, at first, to depend upon Alec using the director of the New York production. Alec refused. He wanted Ronald Eyre or, failing him, Mike Nichols. *A Walk in the Woods* is a conversation between the senior American and Russian disarmament negotiators in a wood near Geneva. Alec's role was the Russian, Andrey Lvovich Botvinnik; for the American, John Honeymoon, Duncan Weldon wanted Christopher Reeve. Alec considered Christopher Walken. He asked Anne Kaufman to see the play in New York and it was Anne who suggested Edward Herrmann whom she had seen in *Eleanor and Franklin* and thought him good.

Herrmann, originally from Michigan, had studied at LAMDA and had played T.S. Eliot at the Royal Court Theatre, with Julie Covington as Eliot's first wife, in Michael Hastings's *Tom and Viv*. He was a tall, handsome, Anglophile who had in fact been considered for the role of Botvinnik for the New York production of *A Walk in the Woods*. In June 1988, he flew to London to be scrutinised by Alec. 'Yesterday I dashed to London to give lunch (lousy, at Le Caprice) to Ron Eyre and Ed Herrmann,' Alec reported to Anne Kaufman. 'I liked him a lot. He's obviously cultured and highly intelligent and sensitive. He's obviously keen to do the part and I don't think we need look any further.'[822] Herrmann was signed up and rehearsals started.

'I am very worried about my memory so far as *Walk in the Woods* is concerned,' Alec wrote to Anne Kaufman:

> I *think* I know a scene but when someone hears my *lines* a third of it has disappeared. Perhaps I should give it all up. I have always been so embarrassed by old actors floundering around and don't want to add to the number. Perhaps I'll hang on for another month. But I have signed my contract and there could be difficulties if I throw in my hand. It's nothing to do with the play – in which I see greater possibilities than I first thought – but just *me*.[823]

Edward Herrmann's recollection was that Alec also had misgivings about the play:

> In the process of rehearsals he suddenly came in and said: 'Ron, I don't know why I'm doing this play. It's absolute rubbish.' And it was rubbish. It has one argument and he makes it endlessly. In the first scene there's a wonderful patch and in the fourth scene there's a wonderful patch. And I quickly realised that the Russian had all the funny lines but nothing happens to him. At least the American has a sort of arc and transition and changes which is interesting. And Alec had run into the fact that there's not much there.[824]

An unexpected bonus, so far as Alec was concerned, was Edward Herrmann's interest in the Catholic Church. 'Great joy,' he wrote to Dame Felicitas. 'My American co-star in *A Walk in the Woods* is a delightful man, very intelligent and well read and a very good actor indeed. His name is Edward Herrmann. He told me two weeks ago that he intended to take instruction and he has started under Mgr. Leonard at the Cathedral. A prayer for him please.'[825] There was only one falling-out during the seven-month run. 'Ed fluffed, badly, and talked nonsense in 1st scene,' Alec noted in his Small Diary on

7 January 1989, 'and when he came to apologise in interval I snapped at him, saying I was getting bored with it. Sulks. He could hardly bring himself to say goodnight . . . Altogether a bad evening.' The next day, they made up. 'Spoke to Ed Herrmann and we easily reconciled ourselves after Saturday's tiff. Good.'

This tiff, Herrmann recalled, gave him an insight into Alec's character:

One night there was a bit of dialogue that was always a bit awkward and I'd screwed it up for about the fifth time. So I went round in the interval and said: 'I'm sorry about that.' And he said, 'Yes, it is a bit like Clapham Junction'. He just cut you right in half. I was devastated. And I called him over the week-end and he said: 'Oh, Ed, we must never quarrel, I'm so sorry.' And I said, 'No, you were right, I'm the one who's sorry, I've been fucking up that line for a long time.' He said: 'It's all right . . .' And I thought: what's he holding in? There was a savagery in him.

Alec and Herrmann gave their last performance of *A Walk in the Woods* on 20 May 1989. Though Alec had not announced a formal retirement, many sensed that this might be his last appearance on the stage:

It was a hot day and both Ed Herrmann and I gave a rather flaked out and sweaty performance in the evening. After our two usual curtain calls we strolled back to our dressing-rooms but the applause continued loudly, so, after a long interval, the curtain went up again. The lights were on in the auditorium and the entire audience standing and cheering. Ed picked up the discarded flowers from the last scene, divided them with me and we threw them at the stalls. It was all very surprising and invigorating. To my total surprise Matthew, Andrée and Samuel turned up in my dressing-room; I had no idea they were in front. Samuel was very sweet – a bit sheepish, unshaven, but looking quite handsome. I think I warmed to him more then than I have ever done.[826]

'I am sorry that you felt your last stage appearance could have been more distinguished,' Edward Herrmann wrote to Alec on 20 December 1999:

> . . . but I know what you mean about Blessing's play. Thin stuff. Why do we actors so often read more into a script than there is? Perhaps we think we can use it to showcase our skill – if we are egotistical enough – or perhaps that we can heal society in some small measure. People hardly credit such altruism but among actors I think it is very often true and has led me again and again into unsatisfying events.

For Alec, an unexpected benefit from the run of *A Walk in the Woods* was the friendship of Edward Herrmann – this at a time when many of his older friends were dying off – a bond strengthened when Herrmann was received into the Catholic Church. Less than two months before he died, Alec sent Herrmann a relic. 'This chip of bone from St Maria Goretti* was given me about thirty years ago in Dublin by Canon Cathal McCarthy – a *very* holy man. I would like you to have it. I have reached the time of life when I feel I should shed a few things.'[827]

---

* The fourteen-year-old Italian girl who in 1902 was killed because she refused to submit to rape. She was canonised in 1950.

part eight

sub specie aeternitatis

fifty

'Did you ever finish that memoir of your childhood? I thought it had great quality,'[828] Tyrone Guthrie wrote to Alec in September, 1944. By 1952, when Alec was not yet forty years old, the memoir of his childhood had become a projected autobiography. 'An irritating letter from the McGraw-Hill Book Inc. – so bloody patronising of British publishing – asking for the name of the publisher to whom I've promised my autobiography, if it ever gets written,' Alec wrote in his diary on 16 September 1952. 'Wrote back in a v. nasty vein.' Three days later: 'Have decided to transcribe what little of my autobiography is written into some splendid "counsels" notebooks I got yesterday – admirable for book writing, they seem to me – loose covered, foolscap sized and not too many pages.' On 8 May 1965, he 'tentatively re-started (for fifth time?) autobiography' but it was not until the beginning of 1982, when he was aged sixty-eight, that Alec finally entered into negotiations with a publisher: 'I have postponed by a week a luncheon date with Jamie Hamilton*, which is to discuss the much evaded autobiography. If only I could settle on a form for it I might make some progress.'[829]

Alec was in a quandary when it came to writing – in particular, when it came to writing about himself. He loved the whole process – the choosing of words, the crafting of sentences, the inscribing on a clean sheet of paper with a fine fountain pen in his precise italic hand. As a younger man he had tried writing fiction and drama, but had only succeeded with his stage adaptations of Dickens, Dostoevsky and Swift. He came to accept that he had no literary imagination or, if he did, was unwilling to open its lid for fear of what might leap out. 'He fussed about becoming a writer but he wouldn't let himself go,' was the judgement of his friend, Jehane West, 'and so all you got was the edited version with the juice taken out. I told him, just write for yourself, but he couldn't. Because then it was down on paper and someone might read it. He put that armour around himself. Any revelation was death.'[830]

Alec started the first draft of his autobiography cautiously with:

> . . . a series of chapters on various people who have influenced me. Today I plunged in to writing a few pages about Sybil Thorndike. So far as theatrical personalities are concerned I could do something similar on Gielgud, Edith Evans, Guthrie, St Denis, Alan Bennett (perhaps), Martita, and lump together Tom Courtenay, Albert Finney, Leueen (doubtful) Richard Burton, Glenville and, no doubt, some others. I have a tentative working title of *The Wild Geese Fly That Way*.[831]

The next working title, *A Half-Way Man*, was abandoned when John le Carré advised him that it was 'bad, with connotations which could be misunderstood'. 'Slow, laborious work,' he told Anne Kaufman on 27 January 1982. 'A thousand libels will follow it.' By mid-July 1983, Alec had completed '75,000 words – in first draft – of my famous book'.[832] 'The

---

* The publisher Hamish Hamilton.

trouble with all I have done,' he noted in his diary on 4 September, 'is a tone of rather sarcastic bitchiness, which I don't mean.' In November 1984, Alec delivered his book, 'now called *Blessings in Disguise* . . . Christopher Sinclair-Stevenson (now boss of Hamish Hamilton) expresses pleasure in it – and is editing it himself – but I am *very* dubious about the whole thing'.[833] He signed a contract which made him feel 'as nervous . . . as if I had signed a contract to sing at Covent Garden. They are to make a payment of £35,000 – half what Jamie Hamilton suggested a year or two ago. But it seems fair enough, considering the lack of quality and that it isn't strictly an autobiography.'[834]

Alec was wrong that his book lacked quality but right in saying that it was not strictly an autobiography. The first chapters describe his illegitimate birth, his peripatetic childhood and his early fascination with the theatre, but others are thematic: Chapter Four, 'The Quintessence of Dust', covers his religious beliefs from the atheism that followed his Anglican confirmation to his 'reconciliation' with the Roman Catholic Church. There is a long chapter on his service in the Navy, 'Damage to the Allied Cause' – written in the kind of 'non-swank' idiom found in Peter Bull's wartime memoir, *To Sea in a Sieve*. There is nothing abrasive or disturbing: it is a dance of the seven veils in which the strip-tease never takes place. Alec judged, quite rightly, that his admirers had no more desire than he to confront the seamy side of his life. He presents himself as a decent, witty, intellectually curious man whose besetting sins are irritability and a sharp tongue. The reader is seduced into believing that Alec has bared his soul but in fact he has given little away. It is a virtuoso performance – like that of the curtain-drawing workman in Komisarjevsky's 1936 production of *The Seagull* – in which Alec demonstrates that, with words as well as with mime, he can convince his audience that an illusion is real.

The first review of *Blessings in Disguise* was in *Harpers & Queen*. 'Says it's pompous & absurd in places. Surely not pompous? Pretentious perhaps.'[835] The *Harper's* review was atypical: by 4 October, Alec could boast to Anne Kaufman that 'the book is top of the bestseller list this week. They have had to print an extra 30,000 copies and are about to print more. Press here, on the whole, been v.g. Some carping in Catholic press – as I anticipated. But the nationals are excellent.'[836]

Alec went to Paris and New York to promote the French and American editions of *Blessings in Disguise*. The reading public were delighted with his elegant and witty memoir. Among the few dissenters was:

> . . . a Catholic lady (or so she said) quite unknown to me who wrote 'on almost every page of your book there is an obscenity. How do you, a Catholic, reconcile such filth with your faith?' I wrote back saying I had received no such complaints from Stanbrook Abbey, Mt St Bernard Abbey or the Fathers of Brompton Oratory or Farm Street. In any case I only used a rude word twice, I think – and in my opinion justifiably. One *very* nice outcome of my book – I have received three letters, again from strangers, each of which was from a lapsed Catholic. Two of them said that after reading the book they felt they must reconsider their position and one indicated that steps had already been taken. So the 'obscene' lady can take a jump at herself.[837]

A criticism made after the publication of his last book, *A Positively Final Appearance*, came closer to the bone. 'Pile of mail to deal with, including a violent attack on me from someone called Jane de Courcy Cato, possibly a cousin, saying how mean I had been to my mother. Nonsense, ignorant and unpleasant but I feel I must answer.'[838] Jane de Courcy Cato was indeed a cousin, the granddaughter of Alec's Aunt Louisa who had lodged with her Great-aunt Agnes in Hove – an unpleasant reminder for Alec of his mother's family which he had until then effectively excluded from his life. On 9 January 1998, Alec wrote an angry reply:

Dear Mrs de Courcy Cato,
Your letter, undated, reached me today.
    It is such an intemperate letter, and so ill informed, that my first instinct was to ignore it, dropping it in the wastepaper basket; but then

I thought that as you had gone to such trouble to show your ill will that perhaps I should put you right on a few points.

1. I never hated my mother as you state (on what authority I cannot imagine) though I must admit she nearly drove my wife and me mad from time to time with her dishonesty. Until I was fourteen I was fond of her – after that I didn't see much of her until I was about twenty, as I was in boarding school and in the holidays farmed out to various landladies.

2. She never had to support me in any way from the time of my birth. My father's solicitor paid all school fees, allowances, etc. and also supplied her with cash until my father died.

3. I couldn't assist her when I was earning thirty shillings a week but as soon as I received a proper salary I made her an allowance. In the course of her life I bought her two flats and two houses. For a time after the war she lived with my wife and me in London. That had to come to an end when we discovered there were occasions when, in a drunken stupor, she had dragged our small son into bed. And yet we never hated her.

4. At the age of eighteen I managed to save her from gaol by pleading with the very kind couple from whom she had stolen money. Again, during the war, friends of mine went to her rescue when she was had up before a magistrate. These pathetic things were, as you can imagine, hurtful, embarrassing and distressing.

5. Almost every week when I was in England I visited her, and if I couldn't my wife did.

6. She had charm, as we know, but she was more feckless than anyone I've known and a brilliant, convincing liar. Really, I suppose, she lived in a fantasy world.

7. I sat at her side while she was dying and found it in my heart to more or less forgive the injuries she had done me, and I tried to forgive myself the occasional harsh things I had said when exasperated by her dishonesty.

I have never written any of this down before. What little I wrote in my book was light-hearted but intended to give an inkling of what I

have been up against in childhood, adolescence and manhood. My
family know what it was like, and many friends, now alas dead . . .

It is unlikely you will think of apologising for your ill-considered
letter, but it would, of course, be acceptable.

Yours sincerely, Alec Guinness.[839]

Jane de Courcy Cato did write to apologise, but in the course of the
apology returned to the attack: 'I did not state that you hated your
mother – I asked the question (Why do you hate her so much?) which
to the average person after reading your biography seems a perfectly
reasonable question to ask. There certainly is no reference to any loving
or even fondness or kindlyness [sic] in them.'[840] 'Letter of apology from
de Courcy Cato,' Alec noted in his Small Diary, 'but it was unbalanced.
Replied politely saying this correspondence must end.'[841]

By writing an autobiography, Alec hoped to pre-empt any attempt at
a biography which, he quite rightly feared, might speculate about
aspects of his character he preferred to keep concealed. He was
shocked by Angela Fox's autobiography in which she described the
drug addiction of one of her sons; and, though he found Corin
Redgrave's book on his father, which disclosed Michael Redgrave's
homosexuality, 'interesting and rather touching', Alec wondered,
rhetorically, 'do we want to know such intricacies of a family?'[842]

In January 1982, Alec declined a request by the writer Jonathan
Croall to write his biography on the grounds that he was writing his
autobiography and in August 1983, did the same with Nicholas
Wapshott. In May 1983, he had told Anne Kaufman that 'some beast
is writing a book about me to be published on my 70th birthday and
I can't stop it legally.' This was John Russell Taylor's *Alec Guinness. A
Celebration*.

In October 1989, Alec gave lunch to the author Garry O'Connor
'who wanted to talk about Shakespeare. Don't quite know what he
was getting at and I talked foolishly – and I believe indiscreetly – Mu
says he's a dangerous man but I found him perfectly agreeable.'[843]

O'Connor, who had written a biography of Ralph Richardson, suggested to Alec that he should write his biography; Alec, of course, declined. In June 1992, O'Connor wrote to Alec to say that he was being 'pursued by daemons . . . to write a book about you, and I fear I must go ahead'. Again, Alec declined to co-operate. In July 1993, Alec heard that Jill Balcon had talked to Garry O'Connor. 'Not pleased. Alan B telephoned to say O'Connor had contacted him for s— about me and asked what I felt. I told him I was against the book. Jill very self defensive.'[844] O'Connor again approached Alec, asking him to validate the authenticity of some letters for his biography. Alec was advised by his solicitor that this might constitute a measure of endorsement and so declined. 'I continue to fret about existence of O'Connor book. Shall burn my copy,' Alec wrote in his Small Diary on 18 October 1994. And, on 19 October: 'Burned O'Connor book without looking at it further. It made quite a good blaze.'*

Alec followed his autobiography, *Blessings in Disguise*, with two volumes of diaries – *My Name Escapes Me: The Diary of a Retiring Actor* published in 1996, and *A Positively Final Appearance* published in 1999. The idea of publishing extracts from his diary had come from the editor of the *Spectator*, Charles Moore. Alec was aware that his writing, always elegant, and with some fine observations of nature as seen from his study window, was getting thinner and thinner. 'I've written 15,000 words,' he wrote to Edward Herrmann when he was engaged on *A Positively Final Appearance*, 'and they seem to me embarrassingly lame.'[845] He managed to drop some compliments about the work of his friends, and both books delighted the reading public, but occasionally the tedium of what he himself described as his 'Pooterish' existence frequently seeped into the prose.

In 1994, Christopher Sinclair-Stevenson and Jill Balcon had prepared a volume of tributes from a number of his friends which was

---

* O'Connor's biography suggested that Alec was attracted to men.

published as a 'surprise' present for Alec's eightieth birthday. Alec was not particularly grateful; indeed, he was annoyed; but one of the essays, 'A Mission into Enemy Territory' by John le Carré he thought 'remarkably perceptive' and he used it as a preface for *My Name Escapes Me*. Apart from a touch of irreverence in Auberon Waugh's memoir *Alec: A Birthday Present for Alec Guinness*, and the insights into the tricky side of Alec's character in le Carré's contribution, the birthday tributes were as respectful as one might expect for the eightieth birthday of such a great man.

Alec was now a national institution, laden with honours from the nation, the profession and the industry too numerous to mention – a knight bachelor, a Companion of Honour, and winner of two Oscars – one as best actor for *The Bridge on the River Kwai*, the second an honorary Oscar awarded in 1978 for 'advancing the art of screen acting through a host of memorable and distinguished performances'. He was made an honorary Doctor of Literature at Boston, Oxford and Cambridge Universities; was Man of the Year in 1980; was made a Fellow of the British Film Institute; had a bust by Elisabeth Frink commissioned for the National Portrait Gallery and a portrait by Derek Hill commissioned by Drue Heinz, also for the National Portrait Gallery. He won the BAFTA award for best television actor for *Smiley's People*, and, after the publication of *Blessings in Disguise*, the German Shakespeare Prize for services to English literature; and in 1988 an honorary Golden Bear award from the Berlin Film Festival. Alec was offered the French Legion d'Honneur but 'I have done nothing for France and have not been there in recent years, so I felt it best to decline. Greatly honoured, of course.'[846]

'Honours heaped on me recently don't mean much, I fear,' Alec wrote to Dame Felicitas in May 1989:

> One is expected to be grateful and impressed. I can't help feeling they are just scrapings at the bottom of the barrel – though kindly intended. Perhaps some actors like spectacular recognition – it should be, I suppose, part of their ambition. Not this one though. I know my own

2nd rateness too well to be hoodwinked by such things. And you *must* know that in saying that I feel I speak the truth. And without sourness.[847]

Alec was often accused of false modesty: John le Carré admired his ability to 'back into the limelight'. On the very first page of *Blessings in Disguise*, writing of himself in the third person, he said that he was 'well aware that he is not in the same class as Olivier, Richardson, Gielgud or the other greats'; that he was 'not at all proud of himself or his achievements'. Was this false modesty or a courageous confrontation with the truth? After his death, the judgements on Alec's standing as an actor varied. Reviewing Garry O'Connor's second biography of Alec in London's *Evening Standard*, Alexander Walker wrote that Alec's 'Catholicism bred caution, passivity. Thereafter, as O'Connor puts it, he acted "from within a safe perimeter".'[848] Michael Meyer judged that, after his conversion to Catholicism, Alec only ever acted the Pope. Although there have been some strange popes over the two thousand-year history of the Roman Catholic Church, the roles corralled within the 'safe perimeter' by this judgement include Colonel Nicholson in *Bridge on the River Kwai*, Boniface in *Hotel Paradiso*, Gully Jimson in *The Horse's Mouth*, Major Sinclair in *Tunes of Glory*, T.E. Lawrence in *Ross*, King Berenger in *Exit the King*, Dylan Thomas in *Dylan*, Mrs Artminster in *Wise Child*, Dr Arthur Wicksteed in *Habeas Corpus* and Adolf Hitler in *Hitler: The Last Ten Days*.

The letter to Alec from Bobby Flemyng urging him not to abandon his career shows the extent to which Alec's acting was admired by many of his peers. Gielgud, Olivier and Richardson were said to be baffled by the extent of Alec's success: Gielgud never really changed his view that Alec should stick to the little parts he did so well. It is probably true that, by the traditional measure of great acting – the playing of the major Shakespearean roles – Alec had been found wanting. His 1951 Hamlet and 1967 Macbeth were relative failures; his Romeo had been a fiasco; he could never have attempted Othello, and he played Lear only on radio.

However, Michael Redgrave admired Alec more than any other British actor of his generation: 'he said he had an invaluable key to great acting,' Alan Strachan recalled, 'the ability to convey that he has a secret.' Peter Glenville told the actor Peter Eyre that Alec's particular genius was 'to turn the stage into the screen'; and to the critic Michael Billington, while Alec may not have been among the greatest actors of his generation by the *traditional* definition of great acting, the traditional definition has become inadequate in a multi-media age. Even if Alec was not:

> . . . quite on the same level as Olivier and Gielgud – he was not a lion among actors – he was a formidable and fantastically inventive actor and one that was a pleasure to watch. He had an ability to enact spirituality and goodness and kindness which are normally hard to portray . . . And he could play characters with an obsession. Abel Drugger in *The Alchemist* – a dreamer – is said to have been one of the great cameo performances of all time. So many of his best performances are myopic characters – *Kwai, Tunes of Glory* – locked into some private fantasy; and this seems to carry through into all his work.
>
> There was also the plasticity of his body, and another quality which people do not mention much which is the quality of his voice, his speaking voice – the sheer beauty of it. I would say that Alec Guinness had a musical and beautiful voice which was part of his genius as an actor.[849]

However, Alec's dissatisfaction with himself had another cause: it was not just that he felt he had failed as an actor but that acting itself was not a major art. 'He is not at all proud of himself or his achievements,' he wrote in the preface to *Blessings in Disguise*. 'Deep in his heart he hankers to be an artist of some sort, but he is only an actor.' 'It's a foolish profession,' he wrote in his diary on 3 March 1991. 'Fun for the young, rewarding, if successful, for the middle-aged, and embarrassing for the old.'

Many readers of *Blessings in Disguise* were baffled that someone so successful and universally admired should belittle his own achievements in this way, and in *A Positively Final Appearance* he reassured his fellow-thespians that theirs was an honourable profession. 'In old age one may think, as I often do, "Oh, it has all been a load of rubbish"; but I can't remember ever talking to a proper actor – at any rate in his prime – who didn't rejoice in belonging to a profession that could boast Roscius, Burbage, Betterton, Garrick and Irving – and latter-day saints in the theatrical firmament' – and could perhaps boast Guinness who, 'sandwiched between 2 April 1934 and 30 May 1989 . . . played seventy-seven parts in the theatre, fifty-five in films, fourteen on TV. And during the Second World War put up the pretence of being a naval officer and a gentleman.'[850]

'I know so well what I *used* to want,' Alec had written to Merula during World War II:

> I wanted happiness – and that consisted of you & me & our children being a *family*, and having a small place in the country . . . and a flat in town (which would be a centre of rather successful smart clever artists) and sufficient money not to have to think of money, and I wanted to be thought a great actor – and to be a great actor.[851]

Was that not what he had achieved? Few people can have come so close to realising their youthful ambitions. Had he hoped for something more? Some of the names on his list of major actors meant nothing to those outside the profession, and even those like Garrick and Irving had left only their legend for posterity. On New Year's Day 1981, he wrote in his diary:

> How I regret never having seriously got down to French with all the opportunities I've had. But that applies to almost everything else as well as languages.* It makes me very aware of my wasted life as an artist; I

---

* The reader may remember the same regret at not mastering French in his letter to Chattie of 25 April 1944.

should have chucked security and settled for Bohemianism in which my
talents might have flowered more originally. Perhaps wife and child and
the desire for roots have been a mistake. I should have given an
adventurous Lear by now and invented a clown. Ah well. What I have
is a dear good wife, a dear good son and a house with views of rolling
downs, trees, grass, and open skies. And a pretty good collection of
books.

Quite what talents Alec had in mind is not clear. He was a gifted
cartoonist but never showed any serious dedication to pictorial art.
During the war, with his Modern Library of books in his chintz-
curtained cabin on LC (I) 124, he had perhaps dreamed of becoming
a great writer on a par with Dickens and Dostoevsky whose works he
adapted for the stage. Though he loved writing and his autobiography
was an accomplished work, it failed as great literature because, as
Jehane West had perceived, it was an edited version of his life 'with the
juice taken out'. Alec's letters to Dame Felicitas Corrigan, which he
became aware quite early on she was saving for posterity, have a
dullness about them that Dame Felicitas herself recognised, 'they
contained no surprises unlike those of Siegfried Sassoon':

> There were better letters from Merula. I don't think he wrote terribly
> good letters – interesting from such a man. A nice plain style. They
> were too – in a way – prosaic. You didn't expect anything that would
> thrill you. To begin with, a letter from Alec thrilled – you knew the
> writing, a style you had not met before, the mind you hadn't really
> met – and then you got used to it . . . He didn't want to give anything
> of himself away.[852]

His letters to Anne Kaufman, written carelessly – gossipy, bitchy,
ironic – are a better gauge of the kind of writer he might have been;
and his Small Diaries, with their scrappy record of how he passed his
days, are more vivid than the self-conscious and ponderous entries in
the canvas-backed journals which he wrote with such care. 'This diary

is no longer objectively true as I intended it to be – omissions creep in,'
he wrote on 10 September 1946. The omissions continued to creep in
so that, forty years later, Alec acknowledged they made tedious
reading. 'Basically it bores me. Why do I do it, I ask myself?'[853] 'My so-
called Journal (haphazard) is dull ditch-water and really only for my
eyes.'[854] 'This "journal" is so desperately dull . . . partly because I have
nothing much to say.'[855] 'Don't know why these jottings are so stiff and
desperately uninteresting. I suppose it is largely because it bores me to
enter them, and I curtail them with impatience.'[856] 'I don't know why
I ever started this casual journal/diary. I've just turned a few pages and
realise it is a monument to dullness. I have rarely entered what I have
felt, and it is often far from "frank"'.[857]

The 'frankness' that Alec eschewed would in all probability have
revealed his periodic passions for handsome young men; and by
'chucking security' Alec may have meant giving a freer rein to his
sexual desires. 'Came across this quote from Kipling,' he wrote in his
diary on 4 January, 1987. '"When your Daemon is in charge, do not try
to think consciously. Drift, wait and obey".'[858] However, Alec – with
the help of his Catholicism – had become someone quite incapable of
drifting, waiting or obeying his Daemon: when he did, he was wracked
by a remorse that even the sacrament of confession sometimes did not
assuage. 'To confession at Farm Street during the week but I continue
to feel gravely dissatisfied with myself and often night-marish. Dreams
during the past month have been very peculiar and alarmingly
vivid.'[859] Unlike his friend Peter Glenville, who had clearly reached an
accommodation with Catholic teaching and had formed a happy
lifelong bond with his companion, Bill Smith, Alec could never escape
the contradiction between his disordered passions and his self-image
as someone sage and devout.

There were occasional moments of self-knowledge. 'For a number
of weeks now my mind has run, willy-nilly, at unexpected moments
on all my sins and failings,' he wrote in his diary on 18 February 1990,
'with distress and shame. But what is most disturbing has been the

awareness that I am more grieved by my solecisms, ungentlemanly behaviour etc. than by my actual wrong-doing. That indicates a huge and stubborn pride. Is all this a warning and preparation for death? I somehow feel it can't be far off.' At times he seemed to feel that his hopes of peace, serenity, and even holiness following his conversion to Catholicism had been disappointed. 'Today is 34th anniversary of my reconciliation with the Church. Nothing, alas, to show for it. Except some Catholic friends.'[860]

Yet, in the last chapter of his last book, *A Positively Final Appearance*, Alec wrote:

> If I have one regret (leaving aside a thousand failings as a person, husband, grandfather, great-grandfather and friend – and my lazy, slapdash, selfish attitude as an actor) it would be that I didn't take the decision to become a Catholic in my early twenties. That would have sorted out a lot of my life and sweetened it.[861]

Both Alec and Merula remained remarkably loyal to the Catholic Church. Both were subject to tests of their faith and Alec went through periods of doubt. Both suffered from the radical changes that came about in the Roman Catholic Church as a result of the Second Vatican Council. Its decrees were in fact conservative, but they changed the emphasis from an internal, individual spirituality to a more communal approach; and post-Conciliar zealots for 'the spirit of Vatican II' urged Catholics to abandon their preoccupations with their private sins and instead atone for the 'structural sins' of unjust societies around the world.

Alec, as we have seen, was sceptical of collective benevolence, preferring to perform individual acts of charity – which he did, anonymously, many times over with gifts of cash to those in need: a fellow parishioner who wished to go to Lourdes, or actors or directors down on their luck such as Ernest Milton and Robert Hamer. He befriended a priest in west London who was suspended from his parish after an allegation was made in the *News of the World* that, many years before, he had made a pass at a young man. He was particularly solicitous towards the widows or divorced wives of his friends, sending money to Suria, the widow of Michel St Denis, and buying a wheelchair for Kay Warren, an old friend from Malta.

The most evident change following Vatican II was to the liturgy, and one of the greatest trials for those like Alec and Merula who had joined a church with a Latin Mass was suddenly to find it said in an English of great triteness and banality. The officiating priest, who had mysteriously re-enacted the sacrifice of Christ upon the Cross with his back to the congregation, now faced his parishioners from the other side of a table like a jovial scout-master serving orangeade and cupcakes in a village hall. The age-old plain-chant, or the melodious hymns of the pre-Conciliar church, were replaced by commonplace ditties or African dirges.

Two of Alec's Catholic friends reacted to these changes in different ways. Graham Greene managed to bend to this wind of change: his novel, *A Burnt-Out Case*, suggests a loss of faith in the mystical and magical Catholicism that had inspired some of his earlier works. Greene became a partisan of revolutionary movements in South America, likened the Soviet spy Kim Philby to the Elizabethan martyr, Edmund Campion and, towards the end of his life, told the world that the Vatican had much to learn from the Kremlin.

Evelyn Waugh, whose Augustinian Catholicism had so appealed to Alec, was at first optimistic that the Church would weather the storm. 'We live in a dark age,' he wrote to Alec on 2 December 1964:

> . . . and cannot hope to see more than a glimmer even in the Church. But there are few centuries when good Catholics have not felt this. Last Sunday, first in Advent, long foretold as day of doom passed easily in Taunton. In fact except for the unexplained omission of Confiteor it was unexceptionable. I am old enough to remember the Pope (Pius XI?) forbidding votive candles. No one paid any attention. St George's Taunton is like a Christmas tree all the time.[862]

Later, however, Waugh's optimism evaporated. 'A year in which the process of transforming the liturgy has followed a planned course,' he wrote in his diary on Easter Day, 1965:

> Protests avail nothing . . . More than the aesthetic changes which rob the Church of poetry, mystery and dignity, there are suggested changes in Faith and morals which alarm me. A kind of anti-clericalism is abroad which seeks to reduce the priest's unique sacramental position. The Mass is written of as a 'social meal' in which the 'people of God' perform the consecration. Pray God I will never apostatize but I can only now go to church as an act of duty and obedience . . .[863]

Waugh died a year later, after attending Mass on Easter Day.

Alec, too, continued to go to Mass but suffered from the liturgical changes. 'Latin was far from my strong point at school,' he wrote in *My Name Escapes Me*, 'and yet I miss its sonority in the essential and unchanging parts of the mass.'[864] 'I do think the *Gloria* in English is a mess in its present translation,' he complained to Dame Felicitas. 'It seems to me everything is back to front in the new mass.'[865] When Alec found pockets of pre-Conciliar Catholicism, he was overjoyed:

> I've found a delightful English-speaking French priest here, a M. l'Abbé Dupire, of St German des Prés. I only wish I had come across him earlier, though I have been impressed by the French priests I've watched, listened to, or who have heard my confessions. I wish all English, Irish and American priests (I exonerate Spanish and some German) could come and see the value of stillness, the economy of gesture, the simple strength of gesture, the concentration; and listen to the well measured phrasing, the pitch and correct volume and diction of these French priests.

L'Abbé Dupire was the priest who gave Alec the letter of St Francis of Sales to Madame de la Flechère which Alec had framed and hung in the hall at Kettlebrook Meadows.

Alec's moans and groans about the changes to the Liturgy were mostly directed to his Benedictine friend, Dame Felicitas Corrigan. 'Midnight Mass was pleasing but, oh dear, I do feel our dear parish priest has taken leave of his liturgical senses,'[866] he wrote to her on 25 December 1965. More than twenty years later, in 1987, after going to Mass at St Laurence's in Petersfield on the Feast of Corpus Christi, he wrote:

My spirits sink so low I can hardly bring myself to the Communion rail. All *my* fault I know – but my whole being winces at the congregation intoning introits etc. in dull English, slowly and badly – and the reading of the Epistle in a plummy voice, ill phrased and muddled, is a mortification I don't think I can stand any longer.

He and Merula planned to defect to another parish but Alec feared to offend the priest who had brought him into the Catholic Church:

The trouble about moving to a church slightly farther afield is that my *absence* from Petersfield will not only be noticed but commented on. Poor Fr Clarke has leukemia, and they say probably not more than six years to live, and as I'm a sheep of his pasturage I don't wish to pain him – *but* the drab liturgical goings on, and the rustle of folding 'missalettes' and the ghastly hymns are killing my soul. (Exaggeration! I just don't *like* it all). In my childish way I *want* a touch of mystery and strangeness in my worship. The present situation seems to me as insipid as bread and milk.[867]

Fortunately, what Alec called his 'private chapel in London', the Jesuit church next to the Connaught Hotel, avoided the more extreme measures of liturgical vandalism: 'I managed to get to Mass there a few times and very much liked their conducting of the New Rite.'[868] Alec, who had joined a Catholic Church in which parish hopping had been frowned upon as an Anglican weakness, now became as discriminating about church services as he was about restaurants and country house hotels, avoiding the kind of priest who, 'though obviously a good man . . . has a disastrous delivery and gives a chatty, jolly, facetious for the kiddy-winks homily . . . Personally, I think all this Social Get Together Religion is alienating the young as well as the old . . . Is it because they aren't getting it in Church that they are driven to Indian and bogus religions?'

Dame Felicitas Corrigan, to whom Alec mostly directed his complaints, was sympathetic. 'I agree wholeheartedly with pretty well every one of your strictures. You have suffered deeply from the Liturgical Revolution: so have I. And so have countless others. It looks to us as we view it at close quarters an unmitigated disaster of the first order.' However, she insisted on 'loyal obedience' and Alec, resolved to avoid carping from the sidelines, agreed to give a talk to the readers at his parish church in Petersfield. 'A bit tricky. All I'd like them to be is simple and clear, but how can they with some of the ghastly translations they have to read?'[869]

Alec was not alone in his dismay at the liturgical changes brought after Vatican II. In preparation for the role of Monsignor Quixote, 'Fr Philip Caraman took me through snatches of the Tridentine Mass, which I have to partially say in the Graham Greene film. I have entirely forgotten aspects of it (as indeed had Caraman) and I found it moving to rehearse those now forgotten gestures and ceremony.'[870] 'It seems to me,' Edward Herrmann wrote to Alec, 'that the state of the Church is so bad that we as practising Catholics must endeavour to build a strong inner voice and structure to withstand all the ludicrousness . . . around us. Bad priests are a fact of life – facts of life; bad theology is rampant, especially here in America, and worst of all perhaps the wretched performance of mass.'[871]

To all outward appearances, Alec and Merula both remained loyal and uncomplaining parishioners. 'He never criticised the liturgy,' recalled Monsignor Cyril Murtagh, the parish priest at Petersfield for the last twenty years or so of Alec's life. 'I had no sense that he was out of sympathy with the post-Conciliar developments. He certainly wasn't a Latin Mass Society type. Thank God.'[872] 'Why, why did we ever abandon a Latin liturgy?' Alec asked Dame Felicitas ten years before he died. 'It contained words weighted with 2,000 years of Christian theology, devotion and daily usage.'[873]

Alec was careful never to proselytise among his friends. Edward Herrmann was one of several friends who became Catholic but Alec did not convert him. 'He gave me a kind of comfortable atmosphere in which to continue my own search. It started before and ended afterwards. It certainly didn't interrupt it but he's not a key to it.'[874] Many years before, the actor James Cairncross believed that Alec 'gave me the final friendly shove through the door that led into the Roman Catholic Church in 1956.' Chattie, Merula's sister, balked at becoming a Catholic: she and John Blatchley were baptised as Anglicans. Chattie lost her faith in the 1950s; Blatchley became a Charismatic Catholic. On one occasion, when Anne Kaufman was on a visit to London:

> Alec said, 'I'm going to take you on a tour of churches'. He took me to the Farm Street Church . . . He took me to all these churches, and he was busy genuflecting, and he never said why he was taking me. He said, 'You might be interested to see this.' One of them was a secret church which was down a cul-de-sac. But he didn't try to convert me.[875]

'In no way did he ever make one feel uncomfortable or push it,' Eileen Atkins said of Alec and Catholicism:

> . . . but I knew he thought I was very fertile ground and I think he thought he was a failure that he didn't make it . . . One day on the stage when I was doing The Cocktail Party I was speaking my lines that were about faith and it was disgracefully unprofessional of me but I started crying and I couldn't stop. And Alec was so happy . . . he was jubilant. He took me to a restaurant afterwards, and said: 'It's happened, hasn't it?' And I said no. He said: 'But you were crying, I know something's

happened.' And I said: 'I'm afraid I've just broken up with my lover. That's all.'[876]

Eileen Atkins's close friend, Jean Marsh, became a Catholic when staying with Vincent Price and Coral Browne in Los Angeles. 'I wish you were here,' Jean Marsh wrote to Alec:

> . . . it would have been wonderful to have you as my sponsor. It does feel inevitable and I've known for a long time that it's what I should do. It hasn't been easy, it isn't easy now. But I'm absolutely sure of my faith! It's extraordinary I'm surrounded by doubters, there are three lapsed Catholics in my TV show but their doubts only underline my belief. They all blame Catholicism for all their problems, especially sexual ones. It makes them very cross when I say I have the same problems and my parents are atheists![877]

The only soul Alec ever claimed to have influenced towards Catholicism was Honor Svejdar (Honor Guinness). During the filming of *Tunes of Glory*, John Mills and his wife Mary had been impressed by Alec's description of his conversion. 'Prayers, please, for JOHN MILLS, the well-known actor – and a friend of mine – who tells me he is seriously considering taking instruction. His hesitation lies in the fact that he fears his wife won't follow him.* I know he has been *attracted* towards the Church for a few years'.[878] At the time of her divorce from Pierre Lefèvre, Alec seems to have hoped to bring Marriott into the fold. Sending her the work of St Thomas Aquinas he wrote: 'I feel I'm forcing you to embark on strange and unfamiliar waters – pushing you up a gangplank where you may not want to go. But if, as you said, you have recently come to realise a need for sorting things out, what else can a friend do?'[879]

---

*   Mary Hayley Bell (Mrs John Mills) had apparently been sexually assaulted by a Jesuit at the age of seventeen on a ship in the Red Sea. See *Kenneth von Gunden: Alec Guinness. The Films*. p. 316.

On 15 December 1983, Alec went to visit Laurence Olivier in St Thomas's Hospital in London, taking him sixty-four pounds worth of caviar from Fortnum & Mason:

The porter's Enquiry desk refused to have it sent up to him – 'Take it yourself' was the curt instruction. So I took it up to the 12th floor and handed it to a nice attractive nurse to deliver. While I was waiting for the lift to take me down again she came pounding back saying, 'Oh, he does so want to see you. He recognised your writing on the envelope.' So reluctantly – after all I'm not an intimate chum and he had had a kidney removed only four days previously – I went along. I found him sitting up in bed, frail and rather beautiful, but as chirpy as could be. He has a lovely room with spectacular views over the Thames and Houses of Parliament. It was about 1615 and the sky was absurdly dramatic, with dark blue clouds and flecks of orange sunset. Larry was most affectionate in his greeting. 'Thank God you have come. I've been thinking of you so much,' he said. 'Help me! Help me! I want to become a Catholic.' I intended staying only three minutes but sat down for a quarter of an hour. He re-iterated his statement about wanting to belong to the Church but I was cautious. Eventually I suggested he should see Fr Nugent from Farm St or any other sophisticated priest I could think of. (Later that night I wrote him a note with three possibilities.) He was brought up as an Anglo-Catholic (All Saints Margaret Street mostly) but was disillusioned by his curate father, it seems. I have an idea he thinks it is all just a question of acknowledging the Pope's supremacy. He said a couple of times, 'I believe in transubstantiation, you know!' He was very sweet and I felt easier with him than I have in 48 years.[880]

Distanced from death after his recovery from the operation, Olivier had second thoughts about embracing Catholicism and his funeral, in 1989, was in an Anglican Church:

Yesterday I went to Laurence Olivier's funeral, at a ramshackle little 12th-century church in West Sussex. I did not go on to the subsequent cremation. One or two rousing hymns, a couple of indifferently read readings, an embarrassingly fulsome address by a friend of his and some perfunctory prayers. A few years ago Larry quizzed me about becoming a Catholic and, rashly, I entertained hope. He was brought up a very high Anglican and, for all his waywardness . . . he retained a strong religious sense. I was sorry to see him fobbed off at last with something rather drab.[881]

Alec and Merula's son Matthew never returned to the Catholic Church and, in consequence, neither of their two grandchildren or three great-grandchildren were raised as Catholics. Merula shared Alec's distress at the liturgical changes but remained steadfast in the Catholic faith. Alec himself, despite periods of doubt, remained a convinced and observant Catholic until the end of his life. Even when frequent personal confession went out of fashion, he continued to make regular use of that sacrament, which embodies the promise of Christ to his disciples that those whose sins they forgave on earth were forgiven.

Was this a formula that enabled Alec to have his cake and eat it? To preserve the unity of the sagacious Dr Jekyll and the camp Dr Hyde? Graham Greene, in reviewing Evelyn Waugh's biography of the Catholic priest Ronald Knox, wrote of the difficulty faced by a biographer in describing the spiritual life of his subject: 'We have a sense of breaking into a life far more private and exclusive than a bedroom.' 'You must remember something about Alec,' Percy Harris told Alan Strachan after he had witnessed Alec's cruelty to another actor. 'He is a not very nice man trying to be a good one.' I said: "That's going a bit far." She said: "It's not. You must understand that and then you won't be so irritated by him".'[882]

In his attempt to be a good man, Alec shopped around for confessors in the same way as he did for a dignified mass. He had no regular spiritual director except, possibly, Fr Philip Caraman who, one suspects, was no more likely to say anything harsh to Alec than to Evelyn Waugh, and may have accepted the view of both men that, while the Grace of God may not have made them much better, its absence would have made them much worse. A rigorous spiritual director might have asked whether Alec was as scrupulous as he might have been in avoiding 'bad company' and 'occasions of sin'.

But equally, one must beware of the Anglo-Saxon tendency, coloured as it is by the Calvinist concept of predestination and the elect, to judge a man by the few occasions when he succumbed to temptation rather than the many when a temptation was resisted. 'To be credited with a vice or virtue the action must be protracted and habitual,' wrote St Francis of Sales. 'So it would be untrue to call a man bad-tempered or a thief because he was once angry or once guilty of stealing.'[883]

In the early days of his service in the Navy during World War II, Alec was ambitious to be a great actor, and perhaps a great writer, but he was also ambitious to be a saint. Was he disappointed, perhaps, in his later years that the Grace of God had not been more effective – that the Devil continued to tempt him until the very last days of his life? Was the genius that Alec felt had eluded him the genius of holiness that he had so admired in Francis of Sales, Augustine of Hippo, Charles de Foucauld, Julian of Norwich and his two beloved Teresas – of Avila and Lisieux? If so, it was a disappointment that he shared with T.S. Eliot, the poet he so admired. 'There remains the paradox,' wrote Lyndall Gordon, 'of a man who wished to be a saint above a poet, but who became all the greater as a poet for his failure to attain sainthood.'[884] Alec's failure to attain sainthood – the lifelong struggle with his weaknesses and contradictions – was part of what made him a great actor and, as an actor, faithful to a unique and fruitful call from God.

fifty-one

A lec lived longer than most of his friends. Sydney Cockerell died in 1962, Martita Hunt in 1969, Tyrone Guthrie in 1971: Alec travelled to Ireland to pay his condolences to his wife Judy. Merula's father, Michel Salaman, died in the same year at the age of ninety-four; her mother, Big Chattie, the year after. 'When I look at my address book these days,' Alec wrote to Dame Felicitas in 1973, 'I know more dead than living people. Convinced that I will die at the age of 64 and must, I suppose, make some serious effort about the next five years.'[885] Alec's headmaster, 'old D.G. Gilbert' and Ernest Milton, died in 1974; Margaret Leighton and Honor Svejdar in 1976. 'Our telephone book is now full of R.I.Ps,' Merula wrote to Dame Felicitas in 1982. 'I suppose it's what happens to everyone pushing 60 – I mean losing one's friends.'[886]

Peter Bull died in 1982. 'He became a close and dear friend and we usually spoke on the telephone every two weeks or so,' Alec wrote in his diary:

His circle of loving friends must be about the largest on record. He was fearful of death, I believe and in later years anxious about his health. (He had a previous heart attack about five years ago.) I couldn't follow his enthusiasm for teddy bears, which became obsessional and boring in the last decade – most of his talk became about 'teddies' and what Aloysius thought about things. He was emotional, gay and witty; an unfailing sender of birthday cards and a constant visitor to chums in hospital. Much of his character once he had grown up was, I'm sure, a sort of compensation for his miserable school days at Winchester – a school he could never forgive for its attitudes and bullying.[887]

'I am very depressed by the death of Margaret Fitzherbert (Evelyn Waugh's daughter),' Alec wrote to Anne Kaufman on 9 February 1985: 'Spent a few days with us last summer and I was fond of her. Knocked over by a car in London.' Eusty died the same year. Bridget Boland died in January 1988: 'She was a kind and brilliant woman,' Alec told Dame Felicitas. 'She died a lapsed Catholic and made a sign rejecting the idea of a priest.'[888]

In August 1988, Alec was told by Tony Quayle that Tony had cancer of the liver and only two or three months to live. 'He is, I suppose, just about my oldest friend,' Alec wrote to Anne Kaufman. 'A good man, of integrity, fine intelligence and abounding courage. I can't bear the loss of more friends.'[889]

Laurence Oliver died shortly before Anthony Quayle. 'A day or two ago,' Alec wrote in his diary, 'I thought I would make an entry about my feelings about God, death, etc. but it has all gone from my head – whatever I had in mind. Death has certainly been very much in the fore-front of my brain during the past weeks, probably from the time of Larry's death.'[890] In 1990, Alec lost two more friends: Gordon Jackson and the actor Ian Charleson. In the following year it was the turn of two of his dearest women friends, Coral Browne and Peggy Ashcroft.

'Too many of my friends are dying of cancer,' Alec wrote to Dame Felicitas on 26 March 1990. 'There are very few people left whom I can casually telephone to suggest lunch or to come here for a weekend.'[891] Mingled with Alec's grief was an irritation that illness and death should disrupt his ordered existence. He told Matthew that Leueen, during her terminal illness, became 'batty' and impossible to talk to. A dutiful friend in life, he seemed to some to abandon her in death. 'When Leueen got cancer,' Eileen Atkins recalled:

> . . . he pretty well left her alone. It was horrid. They had been such close friends. It was the same with me. When I got cancer, he left me alone for a year. He gave no reason for it. I got so upset. He'd call me and say 'how are you?' and he'd tell me who he'd had lunch with and who he'd had dinner with, and I'd think – when is he going to ask me out? But he didn't ask me until he knew I was clear – even though I'd made it clear that I was going out, even when I was having chemotherapy. He didn't like illness.[892]

Marigold Kingston formed the same impression when it came to Leueen:

> Alec who had written to her every day with funny drawings just stopped – the moment she took to her bed and was declared to be seriously ill. She never heard from him again. I know that because I was living with her on and off – and it was just awful. She said to me once: 'Why don't I hear from him?' And I said, 'I don't think that Alec is too well himself.' But he just wiped it off – she'd done wrong; she had become ill. She should have stayed bright and happy; and in a way he was right, she was a different person, she was a dying woman.[893]

In Alec's letters to Jehane West, also a close friend of Leueen's, who was living on the Greek island of Amorgos, he gave the impression of regular telephone calls to Leueen during her last months, but there is scant reference to either her illness or her death in his diaries. 'Leueen died at seven o'clock last night. John Janvrin telephoned me about it at 19.45. She had been expected to die about five days ago. It is amazing how that frail body held on.'[894] He seemed surprised that others among her friends were so upset.

Alec did, however, visit other friends such as Bobby Flemyng and Mu Richardson when they were dying, and therefore his apparent detachment at the time of Leueen's death may have been an exception rather than the rule. He had long been vaguely 'fussed' by Leueen's close friendship with Gavin Young, who had been with her when she died, and that may have been the reason for his failure to attend the small memorial service organised by Young and Frith Banbury, another of Leueen's old friends. Certainly, Alec had been working hard on *Tales of Hollywood* and neither his own nor Merula's health was good, but his absence was noted and baffled his friends – in particular, the Kingstons and Leueen's stepdaughter, Anne Kaufman.

Susie Salaman, Merula's brain-damaged sister, died finally, from pneumonia, in 1992. Cyril Cusack died in 1993. 'I admired him hugely and liked him very much.' Vincent Price died in the same year and Fr Derek Jennings in 1995. On 3 June 1996, Alec was telephoned by Marguerite Littman to say that Peter Glenville had died. Alec had described him to Dame Felicitas on one occasion as his closest friend but there had been a slight cooling of Alec's feelings in recent years. He had been offended when Glenville had turned down a weekend at Kettlebrook to stay with Alec's former agent, Laurie Evans. 'Asked them here for a night or weekend but they are too caught up socially. Naturally I think it is because Peter finds Kettlebrook too uncomfortable and draughty. Slightly miffed that he prefers to go to Laurie Evans's grandeur';[895] and, after a weekend when Glenville and Bill Smith *did* come to Kettlebrook: 'Peter & Bill left at 10.30. M and I decided that Peter has greatly changed – ill-mannered (which is surprising) and too snobby for words. And selfish. Bill remains as sweet as ever.'[896] Glenville's will stipulated that $300,000 should pass to Alec or Merula after the death of his companion, William Smith.

After Glenville's death, Alec organised a Requiem Mass at the Brompton Oratory, said by Glenville's contemporary at Stonyhurst, Fr Philip Caraman. Philip Caraman died in 1998 and John Wells in the same year. 'On Saturday I went to East Sussex to attend the funeral of John Wells, who was a dear good and witty man,' Alec wrote to Edward Herrmann. 'It was a well-heeled affair in a tiny village church. One of the particularly pleasing things about it was that there were no formal, florist flowers – but just rough little bunches of Sussex meadow flowers. Also a vagrant wasp.'[897]

Alec's grief at the death of his friends over the years was accompanied by a dread that he would be asked to give an address at the memorial service that followed. He read at the funeral of Veronica Turleigh, who had died after falling into a scalding bath; read passages from 'Ash Wednesday' and the 'Four Quartets' at T.S. Eliot's memorial service at Westminster Abbey; gave an address at the memorial services for Tony Guthrie, Tony Quayle, Martita Hunt, the playwright Benn Levy, Margaret Leighton, Edith Evans, Honor Svejdar, Celia Johnson, Percy Harris and Laurence Olivier.

'My life seems surrounded by memorial services (or celebrations as the agnostics call them nowadays),' Alec complained to Dame Felicitas. Each appearance was a minor performance and Alec was upset when, after his address at the service for Olivier, there were no congratulatory calls from his friends. 'Yesterday I was full of paranoia over the Abbey address but it has passed now. But I am slightly hurt that neither Eileen or Mu, who are so constantly on the telephone, have called.'[898] In 1991, Alec spoke at Graham Greene's memorial service at Westminster Cathedral and later in the year at a service for Peggy Ashcroft. As he was setting off to speak at a memorial service for Percy Harris, Alec heard of the death of his old friend, patron and mentor, John Gielgud. He went to his funeral but did not make an address. 'Priestess in charge,' he noted in his Small Diary. 'Donald Sinden read "For Whom The Bell Tolls". Scofield spoke a little and read a sonnet. Johnnie Mills – a tiny white bearded gnome – spoke about himself. Irene Worth read for 10 minutes, something from Thoreau but I couldn't hear.'[899]

fifty-two

'Wandered in grounds after lunch and sat sunning myself, thinking over past 80 years – 81 tomorrow,' Alec wrote in his Small Diary on 1 April 1995. 'Not much wanting to dwell on parts of my life but very grateful to Divine Providence for such a lot – well, for everything good.' On the next day, his birthday: 'As a young man I'd have thought reaching the age of 81 shatteringly awful. Now I'm quite pleased. How long? 3 months? Another year? Five years?' And on 12 April: 'Seemed to spend a lot of time rescuing bumble bee trapped by the windows.'

Slowly, Alec – orderly to the last – settled his affairs in this world and waited for the next. In 1993, he resigned his membership of the London Library and in 1997 from his two London clubs, the Garrick and the Athenaeum. Mary Salaman, Alec's sister-in-law, saw that he was bored in the last years of his life. His only literary project was a Commonplace Book – quotations from other writers interspersed with some observations of his own – which was only published after his death.

Alec and Merula's life in their final years was much like that of many another retired middle-class couple living in the south of England. Both would rise at eight. Helen Spurdle, who came to clean the house, would find Alec sitting at his desk in his dressing-gown with a cup of coffee, reading the *Daily Telegraph* and opening the post. Merula would be in the kitchen, also with a cup of coffee, and a bowl of cereal. The news in the *Telegraph* was invariably depressing. 'We feel very disturbed by the NATO bombings* which I believe can only worsen the situation,' Alec wrote to Dame Felicitas. 'Oh dear, when will we learn from experience? I find so much of life depressing these days. Hardening of arteries, I suppose. But there is another Easter upon us and I suppose one must summon up some hope.'[900]

While Merula went to her studio to paint, Alec, when he had dealt with his post, would go to his bedroom to dress. He and Merula would have a simple lunch together, after which Alec would rest. He would read or listen to music in the late afternoon, they would have a proper supper cooked by Merula, and then watch television. Alan Bennett recalled that Alec would drive him and Merula mad by constantly flicking from channel to channel.

A couple, Len and Helen Turrell, lived in the flat rent-free in exchange for small services: Len would bring in the logs, change the gas cylinders and keep an eye on Merula when Alec was in London. Their cleaner, Helen Spurdle, a fellow-Catholic, had been found through Fr Murtagh in the late 1970s and taken on first as a gardener, then as a domestic help and became an indispensable friend. 'I used to have coffee with Lady Guinness in the kitchen. We used to have chats – a lot of chats. She always listened. A quiet sort of person who took everything in. I confided in her and she confided in me. She used to talk a lot when he was away. She would talk about him and the work he was doing and what he was feeling . . . She would tell me about Matthew and the children and all their troubles.'[901]

---

* of Yugoslavia.

Alec's marriage to Merula remained much as it had always been. Merula had managed – cautiously but successfully – to develop her particular talents, first as an artist, making embroidered pictures of animals and scenes from the Bible; and then as a writer of plays for children; one of these was staged at Guildford at the same time as Bridget Boland's *Time out of Mind*, with Matthew in the cast of both, another at Stratford East by Kitty Black. Alec was made uncomfortable by her endeavours which, if unsuccessful might reflect badly on *him*, and if successful might steal his limelight. 'M accused me of being jealous of all her interests,' he wrote in his Small Diary on 14 July 1977. 'Not true.'

Other random extracts from Alec's Small Diaries give us a glimpse of their married life in their later years. 'Agreed to buy Devas portrait of myself (1948?) for £400.' 'Just before going to bed discovered M had turned the Devas portrait of me to the wall. Says she can't bear it. Felt very indignant inside about it. Slept fitfully.' 'Risotto with asparagus à la Harry's Bar but M neglected to wash the asparagus tips so it was spoiled by a lot of sand.' 'M thought the striped piece of ribbon which cost me £80 was a joke lavatory roll.' 'Poor chicken curry for dinner – curry is not M's strong point.' 'Tagliatelli Bolognese for dinner – somehow not satisfactory.' 'M refused to eat dried dolphin, saying it was cannibalism.' 'I rather snarled at M when she said I'm lazy. True, I fear.' 'Golden Wedding party. Much of the time I felt ill-tempered. M enjoyed herself. Food was good.' 'M slipped off to bed without telling me and I was cross. Also she has shown no interest or inclination to see *Handful of Dust*. Silly of me to feel hurt.' 'Cauliflower cheese. M had said she was doing a pasta dish. Getting very forgetful.' 'Snapped at M, regrettably, because of no milk in house & she'd forgotten who had telephoned me.' 'My curry-apple soup was wildly good, but M's chops on redcurrants seemed to go wrong.' 'M scratched her leg until she drew blood which spilled on sofa cover, which angered me. Poor dear.' 'M still writing away at some pre-history story. I fear plagiarism might be in the air.' 'Jill for dinner. I behaved tetchily towards M, who sat on sofa plucking hair from Bluebell and a bit slurred in speech. Went to bed feeling bad-tempered.' 'M very forgetful. I think that she hasn't heard, in last year or two, much of what I have told her but has pretended to hear. Went to bed feeling rather cross.'

'I need to jot down things that biographers and obituary writers wouldn't know,' Merula wrote to Christopher Sinclair-Stevenson after Alec's death:

> . . . things that have nothing to do with films or theatre or Alec's social life – the humdrum, homely, domestic pieces of everyday life . . .
>
> I think his strength came out of his weakness, and perhaps it's the humdrum that finds out one's weaknesses. His lack of self-confidence, his fear of the future, his need to be loved and his rejection of love, his need to give and rejection of gifts – he made it so difficult to be thanked.
>
> When we were first married, I was alarmed, having come from a big noisy family where one could hurl abuse at one's brothers and sisters without offence, that the tiniest pinprick could cause such pain for days. He was like someone without an outer skin. He bled. I felt I had to approach him on tiptoe with gloves on.
>
> We were opposite in all things: he was a towny, I a country girl; he shut windows, I opened them; he was physically lazy, I mentally lazy; he was a shopping addict whilst I hated shopping. We were Mr and Mrs Jack Sprat.
>
> His pessimism could get me down. If our daily lady forgot to say 'good morning' he would be convinced that she was about to give notice – she spoke in a whisper anyway. When our two-year-old granddaughter threw a tantrum he feared she would have an uncontrollable temper for the rest of her life. If one of the dogs made a mess in the kitchen then it was going to go on doing so forever, and so on.
>
> My crassness and stupidities were agony to him, until 'grounds for divorce' became a household joke.
>
> 'All shall be well, and all manner of things shall be well' was a motto he tried to adopt with difficulty after he came across the quote

from St Julian of Norwich. But the true motto of his life was 'the readiness is all' even to the point of dealing with his correspondence before breakfast. Being a split second late for anything was not tolerated: the hours of wasted time we spent cruising round London before a party or a first night, or sitting on railway stations are uncountable. Even Alec found it laughable, but it never altered. He couldn't help it.

Help for those up a gum tree was always immediate and practical, but sympathy for one's stupid mistakes was in short supply. His criticisms could be devastating, but a drop of praise or encouragement one could wallow in for days.

He didn't suffer fools gladly, nor the garrulous or the verbose or gushers. With all the contradictions of his makeup, there was always the rod of truth up the middle which was what I recognised when we first fell in love. I knew I could always trust him.

I think he was getting ready for death from the moment he finished *A Positively Final Appearance* or perhaps even when he started it, but on January 1st this year* I could palpably sense that he was packing his bags.

'When one was young,' Merula wrote to Dame Felicitas on 28 October, 1969, 'they used to give one to understand that one would get wise as one got older – what rubbish. Every birthday I wake up and think Today I am a year older, therefore I must be a year wiser – hurrah – but by lunchtime I have discovered that it's not so – alas – if possible even less wise – less and less wise every year. Sometimes I can't see the point of growing any older.'

To a number of the Guinnesses' closest friends, while Alec remained his old difficult self, it was Merula who gained in wisdom and goodness over the years, achieving the genius of sanctity that had eluded Alec. 'She impressed me as being even more extraordinary than

---

* The year 2000.

Alec – a tremendous spiritual force and the power behind the throne,'
Edward Herrmann recalled. Merula's innocence both baffled and
humbled Keith Baxter:

> Merula and I were sitting having lunch and Alec was bringing the dish
> out of the kitchen and we were talking about people going on about
> their past love lives . . . And I turned to Merula and said, 'Would you
> want to talk about your past love life, Merula?' And she looked at me
> and said, 'What do you mean? There's never been anybody except
> Alec.'[902]

To Baxter, Merula became the 'wise woman of Kettlebrook' and he
would call in to see her as much as to see Alec. Jehane West, too,
originally Alec's friend, came to feel a particular affinity with Merula.
'In some way,' she recalled, 'he didn't really like the fact that I was so
close to Merula. He was a little jealous. We used to go off for walks
with dogs and he would make snide remarks.'[903] It was the same with
Alan Bennett. Matthew recalled how, one day when he was at
Kettlebrook, he answered the telephone and told Alec that it was Alan
Bennett asking if he could come down for the weekend. 'Oh, he only
wants to see your mother,' Alec had replied. 'He doesn't want to see
me.'

Alec finally gave up smoking: Merula never did. Occasionally he
would steal a puff from her cigarette or smoke a cigar. He continued
his forays into London, driven by David Pike, to have his hair cut at
Trumpers, visit his doctor, buy delicacies at Fortnum & Mason, buy
books at Hatchards or Heywood Hill and see his dwindling number of
friends. There was a brief falling-out with the Connaught when a stay
coincided with a conference: Alec defected, briefly, to the Stafford
Hotel; but on 17 November 1999, the Connaught begged their most
revered customer to relent. 'Anthony Lee, under-manager at
Connaught, telephoned me to ask if I would return to the hotel and
said that there would be no more conferences until halfway through
next year, if then. So I said yes and booked for next Tuesday.'

Alec was determined to continue leading the life he had always led but age was taking its toll both on him and his friends. 'To Tate Gallery intending to see the Sargents but too fatiguing over tickets so withdrew. To Mu, by arrangement, but she couldn't open the front door. Lunch alone in Grill.' 'Drue,* in Oxfordshire, had forgotten about our arrangement for the evening. Luckily managed to get Piers & Emily for dinner. At Amandier, in Sussex Place. Drab décor but v.g. The Reads and I totally agree about Nato/Serbia.'[904]

Methodically Alec prepared for his death. He told Matthew that there was a letter he was to open only after his death: in the event, it contained only the names of his solicitors and a note to say where he had hidden the key to the safe. Alec often bickered with Merula over which of them would die first. Alec was convinced it would be him, and on 24 December 1999, wrote a short note to Merula to clarify her position in the event of his death. 'My darling. This is one of those tiresome letters to put you in the picture (of my affairs) when I drop off the twig.' He gave the names of his solicitor, accountant and bank, together with their addresses and telephone numbers, and described what her financial position would be after his death:

As you know, there is a retirement annuity which will operate until your death. The Annuities from Norwich Union, Standard Life and Eagle Star amount to £174,571 before tax. This should result in an income of about £105,000 paid in quarterly instalments to my bank.

At the time of writing I have approximately £1,974,000 in the bank but a big swipe of over £80,000 will have to be paid out in Income Tax before the end of January 2000.

From time to time I imagine some bits of money will come in from *Star Wars* or driblets from my books. These, I think, will go mostly to Matthew.

---

* Drue Heinz

I don't much care where I am buried. Move heaven and earth to
avoid a Memorial Service. I imagine there will be a Requiem for me at
St Lawrence. That is sufficient.

I hate to think of all the distress I may have caused you. Forgive me.
I love you dearly. I cannot imagine what life would have been without
you. All my love, Alec.

P.S. Take very great care – particularly in connection with electrical
appliances and cigarette ends.

A little under three months later, on 15 March 2000, Alec signed his
Last Will and Testament. The Trustees were Merula, Matthew,
Richard Leech and Mark Kingston. It stipulated that Alec should be
buried in Petersfield 'according to Roman Catholic rites and I
HEREBY expressly FORBID my Trustees allowing any Memorial
Mass Service or Celebration ceremony for me'. The Will divided his
estate into 398 segments, and made certain specific bequests. Around
forty per cent of the segments were left to Matthew, twenty per cent
to Merula, and a further twenty per cent to his grandchildren. There
were smaller bequests to his nephews Nicholas and Joseph Blatchley,
and Toby and Christopher Salaman; to Chattie's daughter by Jean
d'Asté, Claire Bernard; to Helen Spurdle, Leonard Turrell, David
Pike, Brian Beaumont, Keith Baxter and Wilfrid Wright; to the
Catholic Stage Guild, the Cardinal Hume Centre, the King George's
Fund for Sailors, St Laurence's Church in Petersfield and Steep
Village Hall.

From among his chattels, Alec left 'the Edward Lear water-colour
of Elephants in Bengal' and 'my Gold Pocket Watch with a quotation
from *Hamlet*' to Matthew; and paintings or leatherbound volumes to
Matthew's wife Jo, a neighbour, Captain Blake Parker, Richard Leech,
Anne Kaufman, Alan Bennett, Eileen Atkins, Mark Kingston, Tom
Courtenay, Michael and Henrietta Gough, Jill Balcon, Christopher
Sinclair-Stevenson, Ed Herrmann and 'my framed letter of St François
de Sales to Piers Paul Read'.

Alec left to Merula, 'and, if she shall predecease me, my son, all royalties which may accrue to my estate'. The value of Alec' s estate was around £2.5 million.

In February, 2000, Alec was diagnosed with prostate cancer. 'I have the old gent's disease – cancer of the prostate,' he wrote to Dame Felicitas. 'It doesn't trouble me – so far – and they tell me I'm far more likely to die from being knocked down by a train in Liverpool than from the disease. So I am avoiding Liverpool. If only they wouldn't do clever blood tests life would be more cheerful.'[905] He underwent further medical examinations, including a radiological scan and CT scan at the private Cromwell Hospital in west London, and a Histological Examination of tissue, undertaken by the Department of Histopathology at University College, London. 'My cancer thing is believed to be well under control,' he told Jehane West on 14 March 2000. 'Scans showed it hadn't got outside the prostate glands. If it had, my time would have been short. Now I am on some horrifically expensive injections at £140 a jab.'[906]

'My personal news is fairly good,' he wrote to Keith Baxter:

A few days ago I went to the Cromwell Hospital for a couple of scans and a consultation – an all-day affair. The results showed that the cancer is confined to the prostate and hasn't spread, as feared, to the bone or anywhere else. So, unless something untoward happens, my life expectancy has enlarged from ten months to a matter of years (or so they think). The bore is that I shall have to be on an alarming number of pills for the rest of life and have an injection (costing £300 a go) every three weeks. Well, I have a decent amount put aside which can take care of that for about four years. Long enough, I say, whatever Marcus Aurelius may have thought.

My doctor whispers to me, half smiling, that my pills may cause me to grow boobs. Like Victor Mature? If so, should I take to cross-dressing? A neatly pleated navy blue serge suit, I think, and a Nigger Brown cashmere jumper to show off a simple necklace of Ciro pearls.[907]

In April 2000, it was Merula's health that deteriorated gravely: Alec, who had arranged to dine in London with David Stewart, his old friend from the days of Arks Publicity, had to cancel his trip to town:

> If I had written three days ago I could have said all is well with us, but the evening before last Merula put her spine out in some way and is in excruciating pain (relieved of course by violently strong painkillers). We won't know until the doctor sees her again tomorrow what the next step is. Either looked after (very inadequately) here, or our little local hospital for a couple of weeks, or unpleasant surgery at Portsmouth.[908]

Merula returned to Kettlebrook and a bed was brought down to the living room so that she would not have to climb the stairs. 'It's six weeks since Merula was taken ill and life has been a drag,' Alec wrote to Keith Baxter on 19 May. 'But she is better in herself these last few days and I hope that tomorrow I can get her bed (with a lot of help) out of our living room and persuade her to sleep upstairs again. Our living room looks like a ghastly bed-sit.' On 23 May a hospital consultant's report was optimistic: 'Lady Guinness's blood test . . . shows that her liver tests have now returned entirely to normal.'[909] However, by 4 July her condition had deteriorated and she returned to a ward in the Queen Alexandra Hospital in Portsmouth: unlike Alec, Merula had always refused private health care, insisting on being a patient of the Petersfield general practitioner and receiving her treatment under the National Health Service.

Alec's legs had become swollen. It was thought that he had phlebitis and he was given pills to reduce the swelling. He grew listless and said he missed Merula: however, when he ceased to get up in the morning it became clear to Helen Spurdle, who came each day to clean the house, that it was not just his spirit that was ailing:

> He went to bed early; he rested a lot during the day. I would take his breakfast up to his bedroom, and he would not rise until mid-day. He

kept asking for fruit salad; it was the only food he would eat. I said to him: 'Sir Alec, you're not well'. He was a bit sharp. He said: 'I know I'm not, Mrs Spurdle.' 'Well, I think somebody should look after you.' He didn't make any comment. So I thought I would ring Matthew and say that I thought he should come down, and he did.'[910]

In early July, Matthew had broken his Achilles tendon jumping in a sack-race at his daughter Bethany's sports' day: his right leg was put in plaster and he was unable to drive. His wife Jo drove him from Twickenham to Kettlebrook where Matthew remained to care for his father: it was the first time he had been alone with Alec since they had driven around Ireland in 1962. He could only cook kneeling on the floor in front of the oven. Jill Balcon, a fine cook, would bring him dishes that she had prepared in her kitchen.

On 22 July, Alec was driven to Portsmouth by David Pike to visit Merula. By 28 July her condition had improved and she was transferred to the small hospital in Petersfield. On 24 July, the local GP, Dr Panton, called at Kettlebrook Meadows to see Alec, checked on the medication, and said that he would send for Alec's medical records from London. On 26 July, Sally, Alec's granddaughter, and her daughter Natasha came for a few days to relieve Matthew. Alec had become proud of his granddaughter. 'Sally looks as if she is going to be a really important potter,' he had told Dame Felicitas. 'Her work we have seen is most impressive.'[911] Now, for the first time in her life, Sally felt that she could establish an independent relationship with her grandfather. She cooked appetising dishes for him and Alec perked up. Alec's bed was moved down to the living room. They sat watching television together and chatted about the news.

Matthew returned to Kettlebrook on 28 July. On 31 July, Dr Panton's locum, Dr Wilders, called on Alec and Mark Kingston dropped in on his way to Chichester. On 1 August, Keith Baxter came by and shared with Alec a lunch of beer and sandwiches. On 2 August, the District Nurse came to take a blood sample: Alec was becoming anxious because he could not get up to London for his 'golden jab'. On 3 August, alarmed at his father's worsening condition, Matthew telephoned Dr Panton's surgery and spoke to Dr Frank Carter, who was standing in for the locum, Dr Wilders. Dr Carter told Matthew that he was on the way to the Petersfield Hospital to see Merula and suggested that Matthew meet him there. When Matthew arrived at the hospital, Dr Carter opened the file containing Merula's notes and, after reading them, told Matthew that Merula had liver cancer. He asked whether Merula would want to be told. Matthew said that she would.

Matthew then described Alec's grave condition to Dr Carter who, after considering what Matthew had said, and looking at Alec's file, told Matthew that his father might well be as critically ill as his mother, and that he would come and see him as soon as he had done his rounds. When he arrived at Kettlebrook, he found Alec talking with Alan Bennett who had arrived from London by train: he was trying to persuade Alec to employ a Macmillan nurse. After examining Alec, Dr Carter told him that he had advanced cancer of the liver, had only a short time to live and must have professional care.

An ambulance was sent for to take Alec to the King Edward VII hospital in Midhurst. 'Father wanted to get himself spruced up before the ambulance arrived,' Matthew recalled, 'and painfully dragged himself upstairs to get ready. I think that if he had had time he would have put on a suit but he was still in his dressing-gown when the ambulance arrived.' A stretcher was brought to the front door. Alec told Helen Spurdle that he would like to walk out of the house. 'Sir Alec said he would walk out and he climbed onto the stretcher at the front door. And they wheeled him to the ambulance. And his face was radiant. He was smiling and waving to me. And I thought: I'm never going to see him again. And it proved right. I think he must have realised that he was dying.'

Matthew accompanied his father in the ambulance and was brought back to Kettlebrook by his cousin, Toby Salaman. The next morning, on his way to visit his mother in hospital, he ran into Monsignor Murtagh, the parish priest, who was doing his shopping and gave him the news.

Monsignor Murtagh returned home and found a message on his answering machine summoning him to the King Edward VII Hospital:

That afternoon I set off for Midhurst with the Holy Oils and Holy Communion. I thought I would do that anyway, just in case. So I went into the King Edward VII and when I came into his room he said: 'They tell me I've only got a few hours to live.' So I anointed him, absolved him and gave him Communion. He levered himself up in the bed so that he could receive Communion in the hand. I didn't stay long with him because Merula and Matthew had arrived.[912]

Matthew, finding Merula in the Petersfield hospital out of bed and fully dressed, was told he could take her back to Kettlebrook for an hour or two to see the dogs. No sooner had they returned than there was a call from the King Edward VII Hospital to say that Alec might die within the next two hours. He had declined intravenous sustenance and had sent a message to say they should not bother to come to see him. At once, Jo drove Merula and Matthew to Midhurst:

Mother and I were both put in wheelchairs and trundled for what seemed miles to the Macmillan unit. Fr Murtagh was there . . . Mother and I were wheeled into his room and he said, 'Oh, so you did come,' and looked pleased. Then, with Mother on one side of his bed and myself on the other, each holding a hand – we were all in tears – he said: 'It's been a good life, and you've been a good wife and a good son to me. I'm sorry for all the mess and loose ends you'll have to deal with . . .'

My mother said: 'I won't be long behind.' And, smiling at her very tenderly, he said: 'I know.'

He said he was sorry for giving us all such difficult times and we had more tears and laughter. He still managed to give things an odd twist that made one laugh. 'Perhaps you should sue my doctor and that hospital . . . No, it wouldn't be worth the trouble – and the lawyers would take the lot,' he said. And: 'If a biographer called Garry O'Connor should approach you, tell him to fuck off.'

We were able to say how much we loved each other. He pulled my mother's hands to his face and kissed them, and said to me, 'Kiss me,' and gave me the firmest kiss I had ever had from him. Then he asked us to leave.

Matthew and Merula returned to Kettlebrook Meadows. The next day, Sally came down with her children. At ten in the evening, there was a call from the King Edward VII Hospital to say that Alec had died.

Alec's small private funeral service in St Lawrence's Church in Petersfield, at which few friends were present, was besieged by television cameras and the Press. Eulogies for the great actor appeared in every newspaper and on every screen. Obedient to the instructions in his Will, Merula rejected the many requests for a memorial service.

The funeral of Chattie Blatchley took place on 5 August, 2000, the day of Alec's death. Marriott Lefèvre lived on for another year. Merula returned to Kettlebrook. 'Either he or the Divinity who shapes our ends stage-managed the last hours myraculously [sic]' she wrote to John le Carré. 'We had a wonderful good-bye. There are no regrets and I fervently hope and have reason to believe I will join him before long.' 'I am living in the spare room and gaze out at the Hangers, and expect Alec to come striding over the hill to fetch me,' she wrote to Edward Herrmann. 'Please don't be sad – rejoice, he is with God and I hope to join him soon.'

On 18 October 2000, seventy-two days after Alec, Merula died. She suffered grievously in the last twenty-four hours of her life. Her funeral, too, was held in St Lawrence's Church, and she was then buried beside Alec in the cemetery above Petersfield.

NOTES

1 *Independent Magazine*, 1 October 1988
2 AG to Piers Paul Read: 1 October 1988
3 AG to Piers Paul Read: 27 May 1999
4 AG to Piers Paul Read: 21 December 1994
5 AG to Piers Paul Read: 24 June 1999
6 AG to Piers Paul Read: 16 December 1999
7 AG to Piers Paul Read: 24 February 2000
8 AG to Piers Paul Read: 14 June 2000
9 Coral Browne to AG: 15 July 1990
10 AG to Dame Felicitas: 27 June 1972
11 Diaries, 28 March 1945
12 Author interview with John le Carré

13 Author interview with Jane de Courcy Cato
14 Diary: 2 October 1984
15 Jane de Courcy Cato to AG: 28 January 1998
16 See Garry O'Connor: *Alec Guinness: The Unknown. A Life*
17 Diary: 30 August 1974
18 Diary: 30 August 1974
19 AG to Chattie Salaman: 31/10/1940. Author interview with Matthew Guinness
20 *Blessings in Disguise*, p. 1
21 AG to Merula: 8 May 1944
22 AG to Merula: 5 June 1944
23 Diary: 30 August 1974
24 *A Positively Final Appearance*, p. 152
25 *Blessings in Disguise*, p. 1
26 Diary: 28 March 1975
27 Diary: 5 December 1975
28 Diary: 27 March 1982

29   Author interview with Jane de
     Courcy Cato
30   Diary: 30 August 1974
31   Diary: 9 June 1981
32   Diary: 29 May 1973
33   *Blessings in Disguise*, p. 25
34   AG to Merula: 3 April 1944
35   *Blessings in Disguise*, p. 27
36   AG to Merula: 20 December 1941
37   *A Positively Final Appearance*, p. 228
38   AG to Dame Felicitas Corrigan:
     12 May 1982
39   see *Blessings in Disguise*, p. 1 et seq.
40   AG: interview with Michael
     Parkinson, BBC TV –
     18 December 1977
41   AG to Merula: 14 September 1943
42   Interview with Michael
     Parkinson, BBC TV –
     18 December 1977
43   Diary: 25 August 1974
44   Author interview with Jane de
     Courcy Cato
45   Diary: 11 February 1974
46   *A Positively Final Appearance*, p. 172
47   AG to Matthew Guinness: 27 May
     1967
48   Author interview with David
     Stewart
49   *A Positively Final Appearance*, p. 26
50   Diary: 3 March 1974
51   *Blessings in Disguise*, p. 25
52   Diary: 28 January 1975
53   Diary: 12 September 1982
54   *Blessings in Disguise*, p. 21
55   AG to Merula: 1 December 1943
56   AG to Merula: 9 January 1945
57   *Blessings in Disguise*, p. 30
58   Diary: 4 August 1982
59   Tribute to John Gielgud on his
     90th Birthday
60   See Sheridan Morley: *John G: The
     Authorised Biography of John
     Gielgud*, p. 95

61   Miranda Carter: *Anthony Blunt: His
     Lives*, p. 56
62   *Blessings in Disguise*, p. 54
63   Author interview with Sam
     Beazley
64   Author interview with Sam
     Beazley
65   Author interview with Frith
     Banbury
66   Author interview with Sam
     Beazley
67   *Blessings in Disguise*, p. 228
68   AG to John Gielgud: 8 May 1935
69   Michel St Denis: *Training for the
     Theatre*, p. 42
70   Anthony Quayle: *A Time to Speak*,
     p. 181
71   see Simon Callow in the *Guardian*,
     23 November 2002
72   Author interview with Sam
     Beazley
73   Merula Guinness: *Family Matters*,
     p. 55
74   Merula Guinness, op. cit., p. 55
75   AG to John Gielgud: 8 October
     1935
76   Diary: 12 July 1989
77   *A Positively Final Appearance*, p. 66
78   Quoted in Sheridan Morley, op. cit
79   Theodore Komisarjevsky, *The
     Theatre*, p. ix
80   Theodore Komisarjevsky, op. cit.,
     p. x
81   see Michael Holroyd: *Augustus
     John, Vol 1, The Years of Innocence*
82   Lois Lang-Sims: *A Time to be Born*,
     p. 53
83   *Blessings in Disguise*, p. 230
84   Merula Guinness: *Family Matters*,
     p.6
85   Lois Lang-Sims, *Flowers in a
     Teacup*, p. 95
86   Merula Guinness, op. cit., p. 13
87   Merula Guinness, op. cit., p. 55

88   AG to Chattie Salaman: 20 June 1938
89   Merula to AG: 1 September 1941
90   Merula to AG: 5 October 1941
91   Merula Guinness, op. cit., p. 60
92   John Russell Taylor: *Alec Guinness: A Celebration*, p. 25
93   Quoted in Robert Tanitch: *Guinness*
94   Merula to AG: 5 October 1941
95   AG to Chattie: 9 May 1941
96   Merula to AG: 5 October 1941
97   Diary: 20 June 1978
98   Diary: 20 June 1978
99   *Blessings in Disguise*, p. 79
100 Tyrone Guthrie: *In Various Directions: A View of the Theatre*, p. 14
101 Author interview with Jehane West
102 *Hamlet*, III.1
103 Merula Guinness, op. cit., p. 61
104 Merula Guinness, op. cit., p.62
105 AG to Merula: 24 August 1938
106 AG to Chattie: 20 June 1938
107 AG to Enid Bagnold: December, 1964.
108 AG to Merula: 31 August 1938
109 AG to Merula: 14 September 1938
110 John Gielgud to AG: August 1938
111 AG to Merula: 31 August 1938
112 Joan Wyndham to AG: undated
113 Unidentified to AG: 29 May 1991
114 John Gielgud to AG: undated
115 see *Blessings in Disguise*, p. 31
116 AG to Merula: 26 September 1941
117 Merula Guinness: op. cit., p. 71
118 AG to Dame Felicitas Corrigan: 24 March 1973
119 Anthony Quayle: op. cit., p. 195
120 Marcella Pavolini to AG: 30 August 1980
121 Anthony Quayle: op. cit., p. 195
122 Merula Guinness: op. cit., p. 111
123 see Wilfrid Blunt: *Cockerell*, p. 5
124 see Wilfrid Blunt: op. cit., p. 126
125 see Wilfrid Blunt: op. cit., p. 286
126 Merula Guinness: op. cit., p. 115
127 Diary: 22 April 1974
128 AG to Merula: 22 December 1941
129 Merula Guinness: op. cit., p. 137
130 AG to Merula: 29 August 1938
131 John Russell Taylor: op. cit., p. 32
132 *A Positively Final Appearance*, p. 18
133 James Cairncross to Piers Paul Read
134 AG to Merula: 4 September 1944
135 Merula Guinness: op. cit., p. 139
136 See Charles Duff: *The Lost Summer: The Heyday of the West End Theatre*, p. 8
137 AG to Merula: 11 June 1944
138 Merula Guinness: op. cit., p. 139
139 AG to Merula: 24 August 1943
140 *Blessings in Disguise*, p. 161
141 see Kevin Brownlow: *David Lean*, p. 206
142 Edith Sitwell to AG: undated
143 AG to Chattie: 26 June 1945
144 AG to Merula: 31 July 1941
145 see *Blessings in Disguise*, p. 101 et seq.
146 AG to Merula: 29 October 1944
147 AG to Jane de Courcy Cato: 9 September 1998
148 Merula to AG: undated
149 Diary: 6 June 1982
150 Merula Guinness: op. cit., p. 141
151 Diary: 6 June 1980
152 AG to Chattie: undated
153 AG to Chattie Salaman: 31 October 1940.
154 AG to Merula: 25 September 1940
155 AG to Merula: 3 October 1940
156 Merula Guinness: op. cit., p. 142

157 Victoria Glendinning: *Edith Sitwell, A Unicorn Among Lions*, p. 53

158 Mark Amory, Ed. *The Letters of Evelyn Waugh*, p. 163

159 AG to Merula: 11 November 1940

160 AG to Merula: 13 November 1940

161 Merula Guinness: op. cit., p. 144

162 John Mortimer: *The Rope Trick*, p. 72

163 AG to Merula: 29 July 1941

164 AG to Chattie: 30 January 1941

165 Merula to AG: 2 April 1941

166 Merula Guinness: op. cit., p. 146

167 Merula to AG: 22 August 1941

168 Merula to Eusty: 19 February 1945

169 AG to Merula: 11 February 1941

170 AG to Merula: 18 February 1941

171 AG to Merula: 14 April 1941

172 Edith Sitwell to AG: undated

173 Edith Sitwell to AG: 7 September 1941

174 Merula Guinness, op. cit., p. 146

175 AG to Merula: 9 April 1941

176 Cyril Tomkinson to AG: 8 February 1941

177 AG to Merula: 3 April 1941

178 AG to Merula: 19 April 1941

179 T.S. Eliot to AG: 9 April 1941

180 AG to Merula: 9 April 1941

181 AG to Chattie: 9 May 1941

182 The Warden of the Bishop's Hostel, Lincoln to Rev. G. Gater: 24 April 1941

183 AG to Merula: 28 April 1941

184 AG to Chattie: 9 May 1941

185 AG to Chattie: 9 May 1941

186 Mabel Wake to Merula: 19 September 1941

187 Eusty Salaman to Merula: 2 August 1941

188 Merula to AG: 1 August 1941

189 Merula to AG: 12 October 1941

190 AG to Merula: 28 August 1941

191 Merula to AG: 3 July 1941

192 *Blessings in Disguise*, p. 109

193 *A Positively Final Appearance*, p. 36

194 AG to Merula: 13 May 1941

195 AG to Merula: 21 August 1941

196 *Blessings in Disguise*, p. 109

197 AG to Merula: 31 July 1942

198 AG to Chattie: undated. c. July 1942

199 AG to Merula: 20 December 1941

200 John Gielgud to AG: undated, c. 1942

201 AG to Merula: 22 August 1941

202 AG to Merula: 18 April 1941

203 AG to Merula: 30 June 1941

204 Merula to AG: 1 September 1941

205 AG to Merula: 4 September 1941

206 Merula to AG: undated

207 Merula Guinness, op. cit., p. 151

208 Merula Guinness, op. cit., p. 152

209 Merula Guinness, op. cit., p. 155

210 AG to Merula: 14 September 1942

211 AG to Merula: 3 October 1942

212 AG to Merula: 15 October 1942

213 AG to Merula: 18 October 1942

214 AG to Merula: 31 October 1942

215 AG to Merula: 15 November 1942

216 *A Positively Final Appearance*, p. 123

217 AG to Merula: 12 January 1942

218 AG to Merula: 13 December 1942

219 AG to Merula: 12 January 1943

220 AG to Chattie: 8 April 1943

221 AG to Chattie: 8 April 1943

222 see *Blessings in Disguise*, p. 122

223 Augur East's unpublished diaries

224 AG to Merula: 24 June 1943

225 Author interview with Sam Beazley

226 George Melly: *Rum, Bum and Concertina*, p. 164

227 AG to Merula: 14 April 1943

228 AG to Merula: 19 July 1943

229 AG to Merula: 30 July 1943
230 *My Name Escapes Me*, p. 26
231 AG to Susy Salaman: 22 January 1944
232 *Blessings in Disguise*, p. 132
233 AG to Chattie: 4 February 1944
234 AG to Chattie: 4 February 1944
235 AG to Chattie: 1 March 1944
236 AG to Merula: 10 March 1944
237 AG to Merula: 2 May 1944
238 AG to Merula 27 August 1943
239 AG to Merula: 14 June 1944
240 AG to Merula: 27 June 1944
241 Judy Guthrie to AG: undated
242 AG to Merula: 3 August 1943
243 AG to Merula: 7 October 1943
244 AG to Merula: 1 December 1943
245 AG to Merula: 4 April 1944
246 AG to Merula: 4 June 1944
247 AG to Merula: 12 July 1944
248 AG to Merula: 24 April 1944
249 St Francis of Sales, *Introduction to the Devout Life*, p. 161
250 Merula to AG: 6 July 1941
251 AG to Merula: 29 May 1944
252 Tyrone Guthrie to AG: 5 September 1944
253 AG to Merula: 27 April 1944
254 AG to Merula: 9 May 1944
255 AG to Merula: 7 May 1944
256 *Hamlet*, III, 3
257 AG to Merula: 24 January 1945
258 AG to Merula: 12 August 1944
259 AG to Merula: 3 February 1944
260 AG to Matthew: 5 August 1944
261 AG to Merula: 1 January 1942
262 AG to Merula: 6 May 1944
263 AG to Merula: 22 May 1944
264 AG to Merula: 2 August 1944
265 AG to Merula: 18 February 1945
266 Merula Guinness: op. cit., p. 174
267 Diary: 1 November 1945
268 Diary: 3 June 1945
269 AG to Chattie: 14 July 1945
270 Diary: 30 March 1945
271 Diary: 2 June 1945
272 Merula Guinness: op. cit p. 175
273 AG to Chattie: 23 May 1945
274 AG to Chattie: 26 June 1945
275 Diary, 10 May 1945
276 Diary: 25 May 1945
277 Diary: 21 August 1945
278 Diary: 30 June 1945
279 AG to Merula: 8 October 1944
280 AG to Merula: 29 April 1944
281 AG to Merula: 5 October 1944
282 AG to Merula: 12 August 1944
283 Diary: 4 June 1945
284 Diary: 17 May 1945
285 Diary: 28 June 1945
286 AG to Merula: 10 December 1944
287 AG to Merula: 18 November 1944
288 AG to Merula: 25 August 1944
289 Diary: 6 June 1945
290 Diary: 28 June 1945
291 AG to Merula: 11 May 1944
292 AG to Merula: 14 September 1943
293 AG to Chattie: 9 August 1944
294 Diary: 6 October 1945
295 AG to Merula: 6 January 1943
296 Theodore Komisarjevsky: *The Theatre*, p. 175
297 Kevin Brownlow: *David Lean*, p. 203
298 *Blessings in Disguise*, p. 197
299 *My Name Escapes Me*, p. 91
300 Kevin Brownlow, op. cit., p. 219
301 Diary: 13 March 1946
302 *Blessings in Disguise*, p. 174
303 Diary: 12 July 1989
304 Harold Hobson: *Theatre*, p. 61
305 Harold Hobson, op. cit., p. 160
306 *Blessings in Disguise*, p. 20
307 Harold Hobson, op. cit., p. 169
308 Kenneth Tynan: *He That Plays the King: A View of the Theatre*, p. 89
309 AG to Dame Felicitas Corrigan: 13 December 1961

310 *Blessings in Disguise*, p. 20

311 *A Positively Final Appearance*, p. 49

312 quoted in Kevin Brownlow, op. cit., p. 231

313 Richard Grunberger: *A Social History of the Third Reich*, p. 377

314 quoted in Kenneth von Kunden: *Alec Guinness: The Films*, p. 25

315 *Blessings in Disguise*, p. 199

316 Kenneth Tynan: *Alec Guinness*, p. 67

317 Diary: 26 September 1952

318 AG to Dame Felicitas Corrigan: 31 December 1979

319 Diary: 8 September 1979

320 Small Diaries: 6 June 1986

321 Interview with Michael Parkinson – BBC Television, 18 December 1977

322 Lyndall Gordon: *Eliot's New Life*, p. 14

323 Lyndall Gordon: op. cit., p. 211

324 Quoted in Robert Tanitch: *Guinness*, p. 65

325 AG to Merula: 23 January 1950

326 AG to Merula: 30 January 1950

327 AG to Merula: 13 February 1950

328 AG to Merula: 30 April 1950

329 Diary: 11 February 1976

330 James Roose-Evans to PPR: 17 January 2003

331 Kenneth Tynan: *Alec Guinness*, p. 79

332 Kenneth Tynan: op. cit., p. 68

333 Kenneth Tynan: op. cit., p. 80

334 James Roose-Evans to PPR: 17 January 2003

335 Kenneth Tynan: op. cit., p. 11

336 Diary: 27 November 1952

337 Diary: 11 September 1952

338 Diary: 19 September 1952

339 Diary: 1 October 1954

340 Author interview with Jane de Courcy Cato

341 Author interview with Matthew Guinness

342 AG to Merula: 26 September 1955

343 AG to Merula: 24 April 1961

344 Rachel Kempson to Michael Redgrave: 29 May 1951

345 Author interview with Corin Redgrave

346 Author interview with Corin Redgrave

347 *Blessings in Disguise*, p. 37

348 Diary: 20 March 1946

349 Author interview with Corin Redgrave

350 Miranda Carter: *Anthony Blunt: His Lives*, p. 53

351 Quoted in Corin Redgrave: *Michael Redgrave: My Father*, p. 4

352 See Charles Duff: *The Lost Summer: The Heyday of the West End Theatre*, p. 50

353 Diary: 23 October 1954

354 See Sheridan Morley op. cit., p. 250 and Garry O'Connor, op. cit., p. 168

355 Diary: 22 September 1954

356 Diary: 8 October 1954

357 Diary: 1 October 1954

358 Quoted in Ronald Neame: *Straight from the Horse's Mouth*, p. 138

359 Author interview with Michael Billington

360 AG to Merula: 30 January 1950

361 *Blessings in Disguise*, p. 178

362 Diary: 13 November 1952

363 Diary: 24 November 1952

364 Diary: 19 September 1952

365 Diary: 25 February 1955

366 Diary: 6 March 1955

367 Diary: 1 September 1954

368 AG to Merula: 23 September 1955

369 AG to Merula: 12 October 1955
370 AG to Merula: 2 November 1955
371 *Blessings in Disguise*, p. 35
372 Interview with Michael Parkinson – BBC television, 18 December 1977
373 AG to Merula: 19 October 1955
374 AG to Merula: 14 November 1955
375 AG to Merula: 14 November 1955
376 AG to Merula: 24 September 1955
377 AG to Merula: 26 September 1955
378 Diary: 24 March 1974
379 *Blessings in Disguise*, p. 104
380 AG to Chattie: 15 November 1941
381 Diary: 17 June 1945
382 Diary: 4 May 1946
383 Diary: 27 October 1954
384 Author interview with Edward Herrmann
385 AG to Merula: 9 December 1942
386 Diary: 26 February 1955
387 Diary: 1 March 1955
388 Diary: 29 October 1954
389 Diary: 15 December 1954
390 Diary: 14 November 1975
391 Author interview with Edward Herrmann
392 Joseph Pearce: *Literary Converts: Spiritual Inspiration in an Age of Unbelief*, p. 218
393 Father Philip Caraman, S.J.
394 *The Diaries of Evelyn Waugh*, edited by Michael Davie, p. 735
395 *The Letters of Evelyn Waugh*, edited by Mark Amory, p. 451
396 *The Letters of Evelyn Waugh*, p. 451
397 Ford Madox Ford: *The Good Soldier*, p. 285
398 AG to Merula: 5 May 1944
399 Sheridan Morley: *John G.: the Authorised Biography of John Gielgud*, p. 84
400 *Blessings in Disguise*, p. 176
401 AG to Merula: 2 February 1950
402 Author interview with Quentin Stevenson
403 Diary: 19 September 1952
404 Diary: 20 October 1954
405 St Francis of Sales: op. cit., p. 251
406 AG to Chattie: 25 April 1944
407 Joseph Pearce, op. cit., p. 290
408 AG to Merula: 26 September 1955
409 Author interview with Michael Billington
410 Diary: 12 January 1983
411 AG to Merula: 24 August 1943
412 David Lean to Sam Spiegel: 10 August 1956. Quoted in Kevin Brownlow, op. cit., p. 363
413 AG: quoted in *Focus on Film*, Autumn 1972, p. 20
414 British Film Institute archive
415 AG to Merula: 11 November 1956
416 AG to Merula: 30 January 1957
417 Quoted in Kevin Brownlow, op. cit., p. 365
418 Quoted in Kevin Brownlow, op. cit., p. 366
419 Quoted in Kevin Brownlow, op. cit., p. 375
420 AG to Merula: 21 November 1956
421 AG to Merula: 3 December 1956
422 AG to David Lean: 9 September 1957
423 Diary: 26 December 1974
424 Diary: 19 May 1974
425 John Russell Taylor, op. cit., p. 102
426 Diary: 30 May 1945
427 Diary: 28 August 1954
428 Diary: 7 October 1954
429 Kenneth Tynan to Sir Michael Balcon: 24 October 1956. BFI archive

430 Michael Balcon to Laurence Evans: 12 December 1955. BFI archive

431 Michael Balcon to M.G. Muchnic: 13 December 1956. BFI archive

432 AG to Michael Balcon: 8 May 1957. BFI archive

433 Michael Balcon to M. Silverstein: 17 January 1958. BFI archive

434 Daphne du Maurier to Michael Balcon: 20 February 1958 BFI archive

435 Robert Hamer to Michael Balcon: 21 February 1958

436 Author interview with Annabel Bartlett

437 Diary: 8 October 1989

438 Michael Balcon to Sol Siegel: 6 March 1959

439 Daphne du Maurier to Michael Balcon: 10 September 1959. BFI archive.

440 AG to Merula: 5 January 1943

441 Author interview with Corin Redgrave

442 Diary: 7 June 1978

443 Author interview with Nicholas Blatchley

444 Diary: 13 November 1954

445 Diary: 18 January 1955

446 Diary: 16 April 1955

447 AG to Merula: 24 April 1961

448 AG to Merula: 13 May 1961

449 AG to Matthew: 26 February 1962

450 AG to Dame Felicitas: 2 May 1962

451 AG to Matthew: 27 May 1962

452 Merula to Dame Felicitas: 6 August 1962

453 Small Diary: 25 June 1962

454 Diary: 6 December 1952

455 AG to Merula: 29 April 1959

456 Diary: 19 January 1955

457 AG to Merula: 13 May 1961

458 Diary: 15 October 1966

459 AG to Matthew Guinness: 30 January 1956

460 AG to David Lean: 15 August 1958

461 *Blessings in Disguise*, p. 203

462 AG to Merula: 26 April 1959

463 quoted in Kenneth von Kunden: *Alec Guinness: The Films*, p. 128

464 Laurence Olivier to AG: 18 November 1960

465 Merula to AG: undated

466 Terence Rattigan: *Ross*, I, 2

467 Terrence Rattigan, op. cit., Act 2, Scene 1

468 Robert Tanitch, op. cit., p. 104

469 Sir Donald Wolfit to Ronald Harwood: quoted in Ronald Harwood: *Sir Donald Wolfit, CBE – His life and Work in the Unfashionable Theatre.*

470 Evelyn Waugh to Nancy Mitford: 18 May 1960.

471 *A Positively Final Appearance*, p. 123

472 Small Diaries: 1 June 1965

473 AG to Dame Felicitas: 23 July 1962

474 See Matt Ridley: *Nature Via Nurture*

475 Author interview with Matthew Guinness

476 Merula Guinness to Christopher Sinclair-Stevenson

477 AG to Dame Felicitas

478 Eileen Atkins to AG: undated

479 Merula to Anne Kaufman: undated

480 Author interview with Eileen Atkins

481 Small Diary: 22 June 1997

482 *Blessings in Disguise*, p. 44

483 AG to Merula: 12 June 1944
484 AG to Merula: 24 April 1961
485 AG to Merula: 29 May 1961
486 AG to Merula: 29 May 1961
487 AG to Merula: 24 April 1961
488 AG to Merula: 16 May 1961
489 AG to Merula: 9 May 1961
490 Kenneth von Gunden, op. cit., p. 151
491 AG to Merula: 29 July 1961
492 AG to Merula: 21 August 1961
493 AG to Matthew: 11 November 1961
494 AG to Dame Felicitas: 1 December 1962
495 Diary: 4 October 1954
496 AG to Matthew: 11 November 1961
497 AG to Merula: 5 March 1962
498 AG to Merula: 28 March 1962
499 AG to Merula: 1 March 1962
500 AG to Dame Felicitas: 25 March 1962
501 AG to Dame Felicitas: 11 June 1962
502 AG to Dame Felicitas: 18 May 1962
503 AG to Dame Felicitas: 11 June 1962
504 AG to Merula: 12 June 1962
505 AG to Dame Felicitas: 22 June 1962
506 Small Diaries: 1 July 1962
507 AG to Dame Felicitas: 23 July 1962
508 Author interview with Paul Channon (the Lord Kelvedon)
509 AG to Merula: 9 May 1961
510 AG to Dame Felicitas: 21 September 1962
511 Small Diaries: 8 October 1962
512 AG to Dame Felicitas: 15 October 1962
513 Small Diaries: 31 October 1962
514 AG to Dame Felicitas: 15 November 1964
515 AG to Dame Felicitas: 11 January 1963
516 AG to Merula: 19 January 1963
517 AG to Dame Felicitas: 11 January 1963
518 AG to Dame Felicitas: 10 February 1963
519 Small Diaries: 8 April 1963
520 Author interview with Eileen Atkins
521 Author interview with Eileen Atkins
522 AG to Dame Felicitas: 13 November 1961
523 AG to Merula: 19 July 1964
524 AG to Dame Felicitas: 12 August 1962
525 AG to Marriott Lefèvre: 21 June 1964
526 AG to Merula: 3 July 1964
527 AG to Merula: 13 July 1964
528 AG to Dame Felicitas: 31 January 1964
529 AG to Dame Felicitas: 22 March 1964
530 AG to Dame Felicitas: 6 January 1964
531 AG to Merula: 25 June 1964
532 AG to Marriott Lefèvre: 1 December 1964
533 Kenneth Tynan, op. cit., p. 94
534 Author interview with Tom Courtenay
535 Thomas Mann: Death in Venice, p. 18
536 Thomas Mann, op. cit., p. 61
537 Thomas Mann, op. cit., p. 54
538 AG to Merula: 2 November 1964
539 AG to Marriott Lefèvre: 22 December 1964
540 Merula to Dame Felicitas: undated

541 Merula to Dame Felicitas: 18 October 1965

542 AG to Dame Felicitas: 12 August 1965

543 See Kevin Brownlow, op. cit., p. 515

544 AG to Merula: 14 November 1964

545 Merula to AG: 17 November 1964

546 AG to Merula: 16 June 1967

547 Small Diary: 8 May 1965

548 Diary: 19 May 1973

549 AG to Merula: 28 April 1965

550 AG to Merula: 28 April 1965

551 Laurence Olivier to AG: 28 April 1969

552 Small Diaries: 11 January 1983

553 Diary: 3 November 1980

554 AG to Dame Felicitas: 24 August 1966

555 Author interview with Toby Salaman

556 Diary: 30 September 1984

557 Author interview with Alan Strachan

558 Merula to Dame Felicitas: 8 October 1966

559 AG to Dame Felicitas: 21 November 1966

560 Author interview with Matthew Guinness

561 Diary: 25 June 1985

562 Diary: 14 October 1985

563 Diary: 31 March 1986

564 AG to Edward Herrmann: 7 July 1992

565 AG to Anne Kaufman: 21 July 1988

566 Diary: 25 October 1980

567 Author interview with Jehane West

568 AG to Anne Kaufman: 20 January 1974

569 Author interview with Keith Baxter

570 Diary: 12 July 1974

571 AG to Anne Kaufman: 27 July 1974

572 AG to Dame Felicitas: 4 August 1974

573 Merula to Dame Felicitas: 20 October 1974

574 AG to Anne Kaufman: 29 September 1976

575 Diary: 4 June 1977

576 AG to Anne Kaufman: 9 October 1978

577 Diary: 4 September 1983

578 AG to Anne Kaufman: 11 August 1975

579 Diary: 15 January 1978

580 AG to Dame Felicitas: 17 June 1985

581 AG to Dame Felicitas: 7 October 1965

582 AG to Dame Felicitas: 8 March 1985

583 Diary: 3 February 1986

584 AG to Dame Felicitas: 13 February 1986

585 AG to Dame Felicitas: 29 May 1971

586 AG to Dame Felicitas: 8 May 1972

587 Merula to Dame Felicitas: 8 August 1972

588 Author interview with Mary Salaman

589 AG to Merula: 1962

590 AG to Eusty Salaman: 17 April 1964

591 Diary: 15 May 1984

592 Author interview with Toby Salaman

593 Merula to Dame Felicitas: 8 October 1962

594 AG to Dame Felicitas: 4 October 1936

595 AG to Dame Felicitas: 17 November 1962

596 AG to Dame Felicitas: 6 June 1963
597 Merula to AG: 29 June 1964
598 AG to Dame Felicitas: 16 December 1966
599 Author interview with Andrée Guinness
600 AG to Matthew: 22 February 1967
601 AG to Dame Felicitas: 23 April 1967
602 AG to Dame Felicitas: 12 June 1968
603 Small Diaries: 19 May 1974
604 Diary: 25 May 1974
605 Author interview with Matthew Guinness
606 Small Diaries: 2 April 1981
607 Diary: 1 January 1979
608 Marriott Lefèvre to AG: 18 January 1982
609 Marriott Lefèvre to AG: 27 January 1982
610 AG to Dame Felicitas: 2 May 1962
611 AG to Dame Felicitas: 25 December 1985
612 AG to Dame Felicitas: 29 July, 1989
613 AG to Jehane West: 23 April 1994
614 John Gielgud to AG: 16 March 1994
615 See *Blessings in Disguise*, p. 158
616 AG to Anne Kaufman: 9 October 1978
617 Diary: 14 July 1979
618 Diary: 12 February 1987
619 AG to Anne Kaufman: 2 April 1987
620 Diary: 1 January 1992
621 AG to Dame Felicitas: 13 July 1975
622 Diary: 5 May 1976
623 Diary: 24 June 1975
624 Merula to Anne Kaufman: 23 September 1975

625 Diary: 11 February 1974
626 Diary: 17 March 1976
627 Merula to Dame Felicitas: date unknown
628 Author interview with Eileen Atkins
629 AG to Merula: 5 December 1944
630 Merula to AG: 20 March 1984
631 Diary: 1 December 1985
632 Author interview with Eileen Atkins
633 Author interview with Alan Bennett
634 Author interview with Alan Bennett
635 Diary: 7 June 1978
636 Diary: 1 September 1980
637 Author interview with Anne Kaufman
638 Irene Worth to AG: 1 April 1992
639 Author interview with John Mortimer
640 Small Diaries: 2 April 1972
641 AG to David Lean: 20 September 1982. BFI archive.
642 AG to Dame Felicitas: 5 March 1965
643 Small Diary: 12 July 1968
644 AG to Anne Kaufman: 12 October 1980
645 *Blessings in Disguise*, p. 145
646 Author interview with Anne Kaufman
647 Diary: 1 June 1975
648 Anne Kaufman to AG: 5 July 1975
649 AG to Anne Kaufman: 18 October 1975
650 AG to Anne Kaufman: 15 March 1977
651 AG to Anne Kaufman: 17 February 1979
652 AG to Anne Kaufman: 13 May 1997

653   Diary: 14 November 1975

654   Diary: 25 July 1975

655   Diary: 21 November 1979

656   Diary: 24 August 1981

657   AG to Anne Kaufman: 30 January 1988

658   Diary: 22 October 1989

659   AG to Christopher Sinclair-Stevenson: 4 October 1998

660   See *Blessings in Disguise*, p. 225

661   AG to Anne Kaufman: 23 September 1975

662   Diary: 14 February 1982

663   AG to Dame Felicitas: 3 January 1975

664   AG to Anne Kaufman: 26 January 1975

665   Author interview with Alan Bennett

666   Diary: 7 April 1979

667   AG to Anne Kaufman: 12 April 1979

668   Author interview with Mary Salaman

669   Diary: 7 February 1990

670   Diary: 17 July 1987

671   AG to Dame Felicitas: 14 May 1988

672   AG to Anne Kaufman: 31 March 1993

673   Diary: 1 August 1994

674   AG to Eileen Atkins: 18 March 1999

675   AG to Quentin Stevenson: 9 September 1999

676   AG to Jehane West: 17 March 2000

677   Diary: 26 June 1975

678   AG to Anne Kaufman: 17 September 1975

679   Small Diaries: 20 November 1976–27 January 1978

680   Author interview with Sam Beazley

681   Robert Flemyng to AG: undated

682   Philip Caraman to AG: 23 September 1968

683   Small Diaries: 25 May 1962

684   Small Diaries: 18 June 1977

685   Small Diaries: 9 September 1977

686   Small Diaries: 1 August 1998

687   Author interview with Ronald Harwood

688   Diary: 24 December 1974

689   AG to Keith Baxter: 12 February 2000

690   AG to Anne Kaufman: 30 January 1988

691   Small Diaries: 23 May 1994

692   Small Diaries: 8 May 1987

693   Diary: 17 July 1987

694   Small Diaries: 21 May 1992

695   Small Diaries: 30 July 1992

696   Small Diaries: 28 April 1984

697   Small Diaries: 29 July 1994

698   Thomas à Kempis: *The Imitation of Christ*, Chapter 15

699   AG to Merula: 7 July 1967

700   AG to Matthew: 5 July 1967

701   AG to Merula: 7 July 1967

702   AG to Dame Felicitas: 4 February 1967

703   Graham Greene to AG: 17 June 1983

704   Author interview with Simon Gray

705   AG to Dame Felicitas: 26 August 1967

706   David Levine to AG: 12 October 1999

707   Merula to Dame Felicitas: 24 October 1967

708   *Blessings in Disguise*, p. 190

709   AG to Dame Felicitas: 18 May 1968

710   AG to Merula: 14 June 1969

711   AG to Anne Kaufman: 25 January 1980

712 AG to Merula: 5 June 1969
713 Small Diaries: 17 June 1969
714 Small Diaries: 6 August 1970
715 Merula to Dame Felicitas: 28 October 1969
716 Alec to Dame Felicitas: 2 December 1969
717 Diary: 26 October 1982
718 Merula to Dame Felicitas: 1 June 1960
719 Diary: 2 January 1982
720 Author interview with John Mortimer
721 AG to Dame Felicitas: 8 May 1972
722 AG to Dame Felicitas: 24 March 1973
723 Small Diaries: 25 August 1972
724 Julian Glover to AG: 28 October 1972
725 AG to Dame Felicitas: 1 October 1972
726 AG to Dame Felicitas: 24 March 1973
727 Diary: 3 December 1979
728 Small Diaries: 7 January 1973
729 AG to Dame Felicitas: 24 March 1973
730 AG to Anne Kaufman: 4 April 1973
731 Author interview with Alan Bennett
732 Diary: 11 February 1974
733 Alan Bennett to AG: 17 May 1973
734 Alan Bennett to AG: 8 August 1973
735 Diary: 11 February 1974
736 AG to Anne Kaufman: 14 June 1974
737 Diary: 23 July 1975
738 Author interview with Alan Strachan
739 Rachel Kempson to Michael Redgrave: 6 April 1974
740 AG to Anne Kaufman: 14 March 1975
741 AG to Dame Felicitas: 13 July 1975
742 AG to Merula: 22 November 1975
743 Author interview with John le Carré
744 Diary: 12 December 1975
745 AG to Anne Kaufman: 18 October 1975
746 AG to Dame Felicitas: 31 December 1975
747 AG to Dame Felicitas: 31 December 1975
748 AG to Anne Kaufman: 11 August 1975
749 AG to Ronald Harwood: 30 December 1975
750 AG to Ronald Harwood: 6 January 1976
751 AG to Anne Kaufman: 16 July 1976
752 AG to Anne Kaufman: 7 November 1976
753 AG to the Editor of the *Guardian*: draft letter dated 2 March 1977
754 Auberon Waugh to AG: 22 July 1977
755 Author interview with Alan Strachan
756 Diary: 4 December 1976
757 Diary: 20 December 1975
758 Diary: 17 March 1976
759 Diary: 27 March 1976
760 Diary: 16 April 1976
761 Diary: 20 June 1976
762 Diary: 12 June 1977
763 AG to Anne Kaufman: 25 July 1977
764 Diary: 13 May 1979
765 AG to Anne Kaufman: 30 June 1979
766 Diary: 18 August 1979
767 Diary: 25 August 1979
768 Diary: 2 July 1979
769 AG to Anne Kaufman: 14 February 1984

770   Small Diary: 18 January 1997
771   John Gielgud to AG: 19 October
      1980
772   AG to Dame Felicitas: 3 January
      1975
773   Diary: 2 June 1978
774   Diary: 5 June 1978
775   Author interview with
      John le Carré
776   Diary: 20 June 1978
777   Author interview with John le
      Carré
778   Diary: 30 July 1979
779   AG to Anne Kaufman: 1 January
      1981
780   Diary: 17 June 1981
781   Merula Guinness to Anne
      Kaufman: 14 July 1981
782   Diary: 4 August 1981
783   AG to Anne Kaufman:
      22 September 1982
784   AG to Anne Kaufman:
      28 February 1983
785   Small Diaries: 30 May 1984
786   AG to Dame Felicitas:
      17 February 1981
787   AG to Anne Kaufman:
      21 December 1981
788   AG to Dame Felicitas: 8 May 1982
789   AG to David Lean: 30 March 1983
      BFI Archive
790   AG to David Lean: 10 April 1983
      BFI Archive
791   Diary: 18 June 1983
792   Diary: 21 December 1983
793   Diary: 8 January 1984
794   AG to Merula: 6 February 1984
795   quoted in Kevin Brownlow: op.
      cit., p. 676
796   AG to David Lean: 22 May 1984.
      BFI Archive
797   Diary: 2 October 1984
798   AG to Anne Kaufman:
      10 November 1984
799   Small Diaries: 14 December 1984
800   Diary: 31 December 1984
801   Diary: 23 March 1985
802   Small Diaries: 2 April 1988
803   AG to Dame Felicitas: 6 October
      1982
804   Graham Greene to AG: 8 June
      1983
805   AG to Anne Kaufman: 8 April 1985
806   Diary: 15 June 1985
807   AG to Dame Felicitas: 17 June
      1985
808   AG to Anne Kaufman:
      14 December 1985
809   Diary: 10 November 1986
810   Cyril Cusack to AG: 19 August
      1992
811   Diary: 1 January 1992
812   Small Diaries: 3 February 1993
813   Small Diaries: 22 August 1982
814   Diary: 8 January 1984
815   Diary: 21 January 1984
816   Author interview with Patrick
      Garland
817   AG to Anne Kaufman: 18 July
      1984
818   Diary: 7 August 1984
819   Diary: 31 October 1984
820   Diary: 23 August 1986
821   23 September 1987
822   AG to Anne Kaufman: 22 June
      1988
823   AG to Anne Kaufman: 21 July
      1988
824   Author interview with Edward
      Herrmann
825   AG to Dame Felicitas:
      28 November 1988
826   Diary: 21 May 1989
827   AG to Edward Herrmann:
      11 June 2000
828   Tyrone Guthrie to AG:
      5 September 1944
829   Diary: 2 January 1982

830 Author interview with Jehane West
831 Diary: 14 January 1982
832 AG to Dame Felicitas: 13 July 1983
833 AG to Dame Felicitas:
22 December 1984
834 Diary: 31 December 1984
835 Small Diaries: 7 February 1985
836 AG to Anne Kaufman: 4 October
1985
837 AG to Dame Felicitas: 6 February
1986
838 Small Diaries: 22 June 1998
839 AG to Jane de Courcy Cato: 9
January 1998. This is the draft
letter from the Kettlebrook
archive. The final draft is lost.
840 Jane de Courcy Cato to AG:
undated. 'Received 28.1.98'
841 Small Diaries: 28 January 1998
842 Small Diaries: 13 May 1995
843 Diary: 8 October 1989
844 Small Diaries: 11 July 1993
845 AG to Edward Herrmann: 18 July
1997
846 Diary: 12 December 1985
847 AG to Dame Felicitas: 8 May 1989
848 Evening Standard: 11 November
2002
849 Author interview with Michael
Billington
850 A Positively Final Appearance, p. 220
851 AG to Merula: 27 April 1944
852 Author interview with Dame
Felicitas
853 Diary: 14 September 1985
854 Diary: 5 November 1986
855 Diary: 25 November 1986
856 Diary: 6 August 1987
857 Diary: 15 September 1989
858 Diary: 4 January 1987
859 Diary: 30 June 1981
860 Diary: 24 March 1990
861 A Positively Final Appearance,
p. 235–6

862 Evelyn Waugh to AG:
2 December 1964
863 The Diaries of Evelyn Waugh.
Edited by Michael Davie, p. 793
864 My Name Escapes Me, p. 135
865 AG to Dame Felicitas: 3 January
1965
866 AG to Dame Felicitas:
25 December 1965
867 AG to Dame Felicitas: 26 May 1967
868 AG to Dame Felicitas: 8 March
1970
869 AG to Dame Felicitas: 22 January
1981
870 AG to Dame Felicitas: 8 March
1985
871 Edward Herrmann to AG:
27 August 1992
872 Author interview with
Monsignor Murtagh
873 AG to Dame Felicitas: 22 March
1990
874 Author interview with Edward
Herrmann
875 Author interview with Anne
Kaufman
876 Author interview with Eileen
Atkins
877 Jean Marsh to AG: 26 October
1982
878 AG to Dame Felicitas:
22 February 1964
879 AG to Marriott Lefèvre: 17 July
1959
880 Diary: 15 December 1983
881 AG to Dame Felicitas: 15 July 1989
882 Author interview with Alan
Strachan
883 St Francis of Sales, op. cit., p. 168
884 Lyndall Gordon, op. cit., p. 273
885 AG to Dame Felicitas: 24 March
1973
886 Merula Guinness to Dame
Felicitas: 25 October 1982

887 Diary: 25 May 1984

888 AG to Dame Felicitas: 19 January 1988

889 AG to Anne Kaufman: 20 October 1989

890 Diary: 23 September 1989

891 AG to Dame Felicitas: 26 March 1990

892 Author interview with Eileen Atkins

893 Author interview with Marigold Kingston

894 Diary; 28 March 1992

895 Diary: 28 September 1985

896 Diary: 24 March 1989

897 AG to Edward Herrmann: 19 January 1998

898 Diary: 23 October 1989

899 Small Diaries: 1 June 2000

900 AG to Dame Felicitas: 8 April 1999

901 Author interview with Helen Spurdle

902 Author interview with Keith Baxter

903 Author interview with Jehane West

904 Small Diaries: 14 April 1999

905 AG to Dame Felicitas: 8 January 2000

906 AG to Jehane West: 14 March 2000

907 AG to Keith Baxter: 12 February 2000

908 AG to David Stewart: 11 April 2000

909 Dr Coggin to AG and Matthew Guinness: 23 May 2000

910 Author interview with Helen Spurdle

911 AG to Dame Felicitas: 8 October 1998

912 Author interview with Monsignor Murtagh

CHRONOLOGY

THEATRE

1934

April	*Libel* – Junior Counsel
August	*Queer Cargo* – coolie, pirate, sailor
November	*Hamlet* – Third player, Osric

1935

July	*Noah* – The Wolf
November	*Romeo and Juliet* – the Apothecary

1936

May	*The Seagull* – Workman, Yakov
September	*Love's Labour's Lost* – Boyet
November	*As You Like It* – Le Beau
	The Witch of Edmonton – Old Thorney

1937

January	*Hamlet* – Osric, Reynaldo
February	*Twelfth Night* – Sir Andrew Aguecheek
April	*Henry V* – Duke of Exeter
June	*Hamlet* – Player Queen, Reynaldo, Osric
July	*Richard II* – Aumerle, Groom
November	*School for Scandal* – Snake

1938

January	*Three Sisters* – Fedotik
April	*The Merchant of Venice* – Lorenzo
June	*The Doctor's Dilemma* – Louis Dubedat
September	*Trelawny of the Wells* – Arthur Gower
October	*Hamlet* – Hamlet
December	*The Rivals* – Bob Acres

1939

March–April	*Hamlet* – Hamlet
	Henry V – Chorus
	The Rivals – Bob Acres
	Libel! – Emile Flordon
June	*The Ascent of F.6.* – Michael Ransom
July	*Romeo and Juliet* – Romeo
December	*Great Expectations* – Herbert Pocket

1940

March	*Cousin Muriel* – Richard Meilhac
May	*The Tempest* – Ferdinand
September	*Thunder Rock* – Charleston

1942

December	*Flare Path* – Flight Lieut. Graham (New York)

1945
March   *Hearts of Oak* – Nelson

1946
June   *The Brothers Karamazov* – Mitya
July   *Vicious Circle* – Garon
September   *King Lear* – Fool
October   *An Inspector Calls* – Eric Birling
November   *Cyrano de Bergerac* – Comte de Guiche

1947
January   *The Alchemist* – Abel Drugger
April   *Richard II* – Richard II
December   *Saint Joan* – Dauphin

1948
February   *The Government Inspector* – Hlestakov
March   *Coriolanus* – Menenius Agrippa

1949
February   *The Human Touch* – Dr James Simpson
August   *The Cocktail Party* – Sir Henry Harcourt-Reilly

1950
January   *The Cocktail Party* – Sir Henry Harcourt-Reilly (New York)

1951
May   *Hamlet* – Hamlet

1952
May   *Under the Sycamore Tree* – The Ant Scientist

1953
July   *All's Well That Ends Well* – King of France (Stratford, Ontario)
                               Richard III – Richard III (Stratford, Ontario)

1954
March   *The Prisoner* – The Cardinal

1956
May   *Hotel Paradiso* – Boniface

1961
May   *Ross* – T.E. Lawrence

1963
September   *Exit the King* – King Berenger

1964
January   *Dylan* – Dylan Thomas (New York)

1966
January   *Incident at Vichy* – Von Berg
October   *Macbeth* – Macbeth

1967
October   *Wise Child* – Mrs Artminster

1968
June   *The Cocktail Party* – Sir Henry Harcourt-Reilly
November   *The Cocktail Party* – Sir Henry Harcourt-Reilly

1970
June   *Time Out of Mind* – John

1971
August   *A Voyage Round My Father* – Father

1973
May   *Habeas Corpus* – Dr Arthur Wicksteed

1975
April   *A Family and a Fortune* – Dudley Gaveston

1976
October   *Yahoo* – Dr Jonathan Swift

1977
September   *The Old Country* – Hilary

1984
September   *The Merchant of Venice* – Shylock

1988
November   *A Walk in the Woods* – Andrey Botvinnik

FILM

1934   *Evensong* – extra

1946   *Great Expectations* – Herbert Pocket

1948   *Oliver Twist* – Fagin

1949   *Kind Hearts and Coronets* – eight members of the d'Ascoyne family
A Run for Your Money – Whimple

1950   *The Last Holiday* – George Bird
            The Mudlark – Disraeli

1951   *The Lavender Hill Mob* – Holland
            The Man in the White Suit – Sidney Stratton

1952   *The Card* (US: *The Promoter*) – Denry Machin

1953   *The Malta Story* – Peter Ross
            The Square Mile – Narrator
            The Captain's Paradise – Captain Henry St James

1954   *Father Brown* (US: *The Detective*) – Father Brown
            Stratford Adventure – as himself

1955   *To Paris with Love* – Sir Edgar Fraser
            The Prisoner – the Cardinal
            The Ladykillers – the Professor

1956   *Rowlandson's England* – Narrator
            The Swan – Prince Albert

1957   *The Bridge on the River Kwai* – Colonel Nicholson
            Barnacle Bill (US: *All at Sea*) – William Horatio Ambrose

1958   *The Horse's Mouth* – Gully Jimson
            The Scapegoat – John Barratt and Compte Jacques de Gué

1959   *Our Man in Havana* – Jim Wormold

1960   *Tunes of Glory* – Major Jock Sinclair

1961   *A Majority of One* – Koichi Asano

1962   HMS *Defiant* (US: *Damn the Defiant*) – Captain Crawford
Lawrence of Arabia – Prince Feisal

1964   *The Fall of the Roman Empire* – Emperor Marcus Aurelius

1965   *Situation Hopeless – But Not Serious* – Herr Frick
Dr Zhivago – Yevgraf Zhivago

1966   *Hotel Paradiso* – Boniface
The Quiller Memorandum – Pol

1968   *The Comedians* – Major Jones

1970   *Cromwell* – King Charles I
Scrooge – Marley's Ghost

1972   *Brother Sun, Sister Moon* – Pope Innocent III

1973   *Hitler: The Last Ten Days* – Adolf Hitler

1975   *Murder By Death* – Bensonmum

1977   *Star Wars* – Ben (Obi-Wan) Kenobi

1980   *The Empire Strikes Back* – Ben (Obi-Wan) Kenobi
Raise the Titanic – John Bigalow
Little Lord Fauntleroy – Earl of Dorincourt

1983   *Lovesick* – Sigmund Freud
Return of the Jedi – Ben (Obi-Wan) Kenobi

1984   *A Passage to India* – Professor Godbole

1987   *Little Dorrit* – William Dorrit

1988 *A Handful of Dust* – Mr Todd

TELEVISION

1955 *Baker's Dozen* – The Major

1959 *The Wicked Scheme of Jebal Deeks* – Jebal Deeks

1969 *Conversation at Night* – the Executioner

1970 *Twelfth Night* – Malvolio

1974 *The Gift of Friendship* – Jocelyn Broome

1977 *Caesar and Cleopatra* – Julius Caesar

1979 *Tinker, Tailor, Soldier, Spy* – George Smiley

1982 *Smiley's People* – George Smiley

1984 *Edwin* – Sir Fennimore Truscott

1985 *Monsignor Quixote* – Monsignor Quixote

1991 *Kafka* – the Chief Clerk

1992 *Tales from Hollywood* – Heinrich Mann

1993 *A Foreign Field* – Amos

1995 *Mute Witness* – cameo role

1996 *Eskimo Day* – James Fleet

AWARDS

1950   National Board of Review Award for the Best Actor: *Kind Hearts and Coronets*
Picturegoer Gold Medal for the Most Popular Actor

1952   Best Actor Oscar nomination: *The Lavender Hill Mob*
Italian National Syndicate of Film Journalists' Silver Ribbon: *The Lavender Hill Mob*

1956   Award from the Office Catholique Internationale du Cinéma for role in *The Prisoner*
BAFTA Best British Actor Award: *The Prisoner*

1957   Best Actor Oscar: *The Bridge on the River Kwai*
New York Film Critics' Circle Award for Best Actor: *The Bridge on the River Kwai*
National Board of Review Award for Best Actor: *The Bridge on the River Kwai*
Golden Globe Award for Best Actor: *The Bridge on the River Kwai*

1958   Oscar nomination for Best Screenplay based on material from another medium: *The Horse's Mouth*
BAFTA Best British Actor Award: *The Bridge on the River Kwai*

1959   BAFTA nomination for Best Screenplay: *The Horse's Mouth*
Venice Film Festival Volpi Cup for Best Actor: *The Horse's Mouth*

1960   Evening Standard Drama Award for Best Actor: *Ross*
Emmy nomination for Outstanding Performance by an Actor: *The Wicked Scheme of Jebal Deeks*

1961   BAFTA Best Actor nomination: *Tunes of Glory*

1962   Berlin Film Festival. David O. Selznick Gold Laurel Award
              for adding to International Understanding

1963   Plays and Players Award for best theatrical performance:
              Exit the King

1964   Antoinette Perry Award ('Tony') for Best Actor: *Dylan*

1977   Best Supporting Actor Oscar nomination: *Star Wars*
              Saturn Award (USA) for Best Supporting Actor: *Star Wars*
              Variety Club of Great Britain Award for Best Actor: *The Old
              Country*

1978   Honorary Oscar 'for advancing the art of screen acting
              through a host of memorable and distinguished
              performances'
              Golden Globe nomination for Best Supporting Actor: *Star
              Wars*
              Evening Standard British Film Award for Best Actor: *Star
              Wars*

1980   BAFTA award for Best Actor: *Tinker, Tailor, Soldier, Spy*

1982   BAFTA award for Best Actor: *Smiley's People*

1983   Emmy nomination for lead actor in a limited TV series or
              special: *Smiley's People*

1985   Shakespeare Prize for services to English Literature

1987   Film Society of Lincoln Center: Gala Tribute

1988   Berlin Film Festival, Honorary Golden Bear award for
             services to the cinema

1989   The Society of West End Theatres Special Award
             Best Supporting Actor Oscar nomination: *Little Dorrit*
             Golden Globe nomination for Best Supporting Actor: *Little
             Dorrit*
             Los Angeles Film Critics' Association Best Supporting Actor
             Award: *Little Dorrit*

1990   London Film Critics' Circle: Special Achievement Award

1995   Evening Standard British Film Awards: Special Award

BIBLIOGRAPHY

Amory, Mark (Ed.) *The Letters of Evelyn Waugh*. London: Weidenfeld & Nicolson, 1980.

Blunt, Wilfrid. *Cockerell*. New York: Alfred A. Knopf, 1964.

Brownlow, Kevin. *David Lean*. London: Faber & Faber, 1996.

Bull, Peter. *To Sea in a Sieve*. London: Peter Davies, 1956.

Carter, Miranda. *Anthony Blunt: His Lives*. London: Macmillan, 2001.

Davie, Michael (Ed.) *The Diaries of Evelyn Waugh*. London: Weidenfeld & Nicolson, 1976.

Duff, Charles. *The Lost Summer: The Heyday of the West End Theatre*. London: Nick Hern Books, 1995.

Ford, Ford Madox. *The Good Soldier*. London: The Bodley Head, 1916.

Glendinning, Victoria. *Edith Sitwell, A Unicorn Among Lions*. London: Weidenfeld & Nicolson, 1971.

Gordon, Lyndall. *Eliot's New Life*. Oxford: Oxford University Press, 1988.

Grunberger, Richard. *A Social History of the Third Reich*. London: Weidenfeld & Nicolson, 1971.

Guinness, Alec. *Blessings in Disguise*. London: Hamish Hamilton, 1985.

Guinness, Alec. *My Name Escapes Me: The Diary of a Retiring Actor*. London: Hamish Hamilton, 1996.

Guinness, Alec. *A Positively Final Appearance: A Journal, 1996–1998*. London: Hamish Hamilton, 1999.

Guinness, Alec. *A Commonplace Book*. London: Hamish Hamilton, 2001.

Gunden, Kenneth von. *Alec Guinness: The Films*. Jefferson, North Carolina: McFarland Classics, 1987.

Guthrie, Tyrone. *In Various Directions: A View of the Theatre*. London: Michael Joseph, 1966.

Harwood, Ronald. *Sir Donald Wolfit, C.B.E. His Life and Work in the Unfashionable Theatre*. London: Secker & Warburg, 1971.

Hastings, Selina. *Evelyn Waugh. A Biography*. London: Sinclair-Stevenson, 1994.

Hobson, Harold. *Theatre*. London: Longmans, 1948.

Holroyd, Michael. *Augustus John, Vol 1, The Years of Innocence*. London: Chatto & Windus, 1996.

Kempis, Thomas à (trans. Leo Shirley-Price) *The Imitation of Christ*. London: Penguin Books, 1952.

Komisarjevsky, Theodore. *The Theatre*. London: Heinemann, 1929.

Lang-Sims, Lois. *A Time to be Born*. London: Andre Deutsch, 1971.

Lang-Sims, Lois. *Flowers in a Teacup*. London: Andre Deutsch, 1973.

Mann, Thomas (trans. H.T. Lowe-Porter). *Death in Venice*. London: Secker & Warburg, 1928.

Melly, George. *Rum, Bum and Concertina*. London: Weidenfeld & Nicolson, 1977.

Morley, Sheridan. *John G: The Authorised Biography of John Gielgud*. London: Hodder & Stoughton, 2001.

Neame, Ronald. *Straight from the Horse's Mouth: an Autobiography* (with Barbara Roisman Cooper). Lanham, Maryland, and Oxford: The Scarecrow Press, 2003.

O'Connor, Garry. *Alec Guinness. The Unknown*. London: Sidgwick & Jackson, 2002.

O'Connor, Garry. *The Secret Woman: A Life of Peggy Ashcroft*. London: Weidenfeld & Nicolson, 1997.

Pearce, Joseph. *Literary Converts: Spiritual Inspiration in an Age of Unbelief*. London: HarperCollins, 1999.

Quayle, Anthony. *A Time to Speak*. London: Barrie & Jenkins, 1990.

Redgrave, Corin. *Michael Redgrave: My Father*. London: Richard Cohen Books, 1995.

Ridley, Matt. *Nature Via Nurture*. London: Fourth Estate, 2003.

St Denis, Michel. *Training for the Theatre*. London: Heinemann, 1982.

Salaman, Merula. *Christopher's Book (Alphabet)*. London: The Cresset Press, 1942.

Salaman, Merula. *William and Cherry, Being a Record of the Adventures of William Matthew Walker and his Cow Cherry Brandy*. London: The Cresset Press, 1943.

Salaman, Merula. *Christopher's Rainy Day Book*. London: Pleiades Books, 1945.

Salaman, Merula. *Christopher's New House*. London: Pleiades, 1946.

Salaman, Merula. *The Kingdom of Heaven Is Like*. Introduction by Alan Bennett. London: The Herbert Press, 1992.

Sales, St Francis of (trans. Michael Day.) *Introduction to the Devout Life*. London: Everyman Library, 1961.

Socarides, M.D., Charles W. *The Preoedipal Original and Psychoanalytic Therapy of Sexual Perversions*. Madison, Connecticut: International Universities Press Inc., 1988.

Tanitch, Robert. *Guinness*. London: Applause, 1989.

Taylor, John Russell. *Alec Guinness: A Celebration*. Boston: Little, Brown and Company, 1984.

Tynan, Kenneth. *Alec Guinness*. London: Rockliff, 1953.

Tynan, Kenneth. *He That Plays the King: A View of the Theatre*. London: Longmans, 1959.

Various. *Alec. A Birthday Present for Alec Guinness*. London: Sinclair-Stevenson, 1994.

Extracts from the letters of Eileen Atkins are reprinted by kind permission of Eileen Aktins; from the letters of Michael Balcon by kind permission of Jonathan Balcon; from the letters of Daphne du Maurier by kind permission of The Chichester Partnership; from *Eliot's New Life* by Lyndall Gordon by kind permission of Sheil Land Associates; from the letters of Edward Herrmann by kind permission of Edward Herrmann; from *Death in Venice* by Thomas Mann published by Secker & Warburg by kind permission of The Random House Group Ltd; from *Rum, Bum and Concertina* by George Melly by kind permission of A M Heath on behalf of George Melly; from *Literary Converts* by Joseph Pearce by kind permission of HarperCollins Publishers Ltd.; from the letters of Edith Sitwell by kind permission of Francis Sitwell; from *Alec Guinness* by John Russell Taylor by kind permission of PFD on behalf of John Russell Taylor; from the letters of Kenneth Tynan by kind permission of Roxana Tynan; from *The Diaries of Evelyn Waugh* edited by Michael Davie and *The Letters of Evelyn Waugh* edited by Mark Amory by kind permission of PFD on behalf of the Estate of Laura Waugh and by kind permission of Weidenfeld & Nicolson.

The publishers have made every effort to contact all persons having any rights in the extracts reproduced in this work. Where it has not been possible the publishers will be happy to hear from anyone who recognises their material.

INDEX

AG stands for Alec Guinness

The post man came this morning with your letter.

and here
we are

> Do mind the top of [Snowdon] dear!

I promise you its true.

Love
Plee.

We are swimming back on Monday or Tuesday week. M goes to Aunt Louise's on Sunday — I to Bristol. Will write in a day or two,

4. Harrison Ford — ever heard of him?

Bright day has dawned. A letter for [Green] in the post. — A nightmarish night round and round in my head my [skin] with Andrés (a-in-law). But [asked] how difficult unpleasant thought to shake off. I had to sit up and for ½ hour at 2 a.m. to [receive] 4. — Gavin Kamin plague me about [Maugham's] best 'Yahoo,' if it [does] [anything] else, has enabled me to side-step one.

I went off to Audio and work [with] a dwarf (very sweet, — and he to wash in a bidet) and your [own] countrymen Mark Hamill and [Harrison] (that can't be right) Ford — [him] (? — no!?) — well, a [raw gay], [anguished] young man who is probably [intelligent] and amusing. But God, God, they make me feel [unsafe] — and treat me as if I was [6].

Love, Ann

The squinty Post Office girl is very contemptuous of anyone who asks anything and is [frenzied] at the [slightest] endless war. I shall [indulge] in a

Monday 1st August

Last Thursday, 28 July, I had audience with The Queen when she [invited] the C.H. I was alone with her for minutes. She was most affable and [asked] me to sit with her. When I saw [her] January, at The London Library she [twitchy] and distressed. It was [nice] her well recovered from her horrible [eyes] and smiling. Conversation [was] but wasn't startling. — She [enquired] many current films, the terrible [table] the [greenness] of speculation, the [election] so much of the countryside in. [There] is all sound clear-headed and gloomy, [wasn't]. An admirable lady.

A week ago we got back [from] holiday in the Dolomites. The [hotel] at Bressanone/Brixen was [awful] and I had one night at some thousand feet up. The changing Dolomites was mesmerising.

Its hours about [Nachmann's] but everyone is being brave and [best]

The [Mira] Salaman — La Belle and my love in the back of a car for 2 hrs chattering.

> I know everything!!